W9-CLB-071

Mt. Lebanon Public Library
16 Castle Shannon Boulevard
Pittsburgh, PA 15228-2252
412-531-1912
www.mtlebanonlibrary.org

Blood on the Stage, 1950–1975

Milestone Plays of Crime, Mystery, and Detection: An Annotated Repertoire

Amnon Kabatchnik

DISCARDED BY
MT. LEBANON PUBLIC LIBRARY

THE SCARECROW PRESS, INC.
Lanham • Toronto • Plymouth, UK
2011

Published by Scarecrow Press, Inc.
A wholly owned subsidiary of The Rowman & Littlefield Publishing Group, Inc.
4501 Forbes Boulevard, Suite 200, Lanham, Maryland 20706
http://www.scarecrowpress.com

Estover Road, Plymouth PL6 7PY, United Kingdom

Copyright © 2011 by Amnon Kabatchnik

All rights reserved. No part of this book may be reproduced in any form or by any electronic or mechanical means, including information storage and retrieval systems, without written permission from the publisher, except by a reviewer who may quote passages in a review.

British Library Cataloguing in Publication Information Available

Library of Congress Cataloging-in-Publication Data

Kabatchnik, Amnon, 1929–
  Blood on the stage, 1950–1975 : milestone plays of crime, mystery, and detection : an annotated repertoire / Amnon Kabatchnik.
    p. cm.
  Includes bibliographical references and index.
  ISBN 978-0-8108-7783-2 (cloth : alk. paper) — ISBN 978-0-8108-7784-9 (ebook)
  1. Detective and mystery plays—History and criticism. 2. Detective and mystery plays—Stories, plots, etc. I. Title.
  PN1952.K35 2011
  809.2'527—dc22
                                        2010047558

♾ ™ The paper used in this publication meets the minimum requirements of American National Standard for Information Sciences—Permanence of Paper for Printed Library Materials, ANSI/NISO Z39.48-1992.

Printed in the United States of America

MT. LEBANON PUBLIC LIBRARY
JUL 1 7 2012

For sweet Sutton and Sabrina

Contents

Acknowledgments

I would like to express my gratitude to the following friends and scholars who were extremely helpful in various ways and made this project possible.

Thanks to Marv Lachman, who, several decades ago, invited me to a series of literary parties at his Bronx apartment where he, Bob Aucott, Jon Breen, Lianne Carlin, Pat Erhardt, Allen J. Hubin, Francis Nevins Jr., Otto Penzler, Charles Shibuk, and Chris Steinbrunner suggested that I not only read and collect detective literature but also study its sources, history, and trends. These gifted ladies and gentlemen have since edited journals, penned books, and launched a wave of scholarship in the field. Their influence on the development of this resource book is highly appreciated.

I am greatly indebted to the late publisher Ted Dikty, who planted the seed of *Blood on the Stage* in my mind, and to Professor Robert Reginald of California State University at San Bernardino for encouraging me to develop an annotated checklist of suspense plays into a book-length endeavor.

A special note of thanks to Bryan Reddick, academic dean of Elmira College, and professors Jerome Whalen and Leonard Criminale, who offered valuable suggestions regarding classic criminous plays.

In my pursuit of old, out-of-print manuscripts and yesteryear's newspapers and magazines, I traveled to a number of near and far libraries. My gratitude goes in particular to the librarians of the Steele Memorial Library of Elmira, New York (notably Owen Frank); the Corning, New York, Public Library; the Olin and Uris libraries at Cornell University, Ithaca, New York; and the New York Public Library of the Performing Arts at Lincoln Center, Manhattan (especially Rod Bladel, Christopher Frith, Christine Karatnytsky, Jeremy McGraw, and the three little witches of the photocopy room). Thanks also to Howard Prouty, acquisition archivist at the Center for Motion Picture Study, Beverly Hills, California, and Shimon Lev-Ari, director of the Israeli Documentation Center for the Performing Arts in Tel Aviv, Israel.

My appreciation goes to past and present staffers of the national office of the Mystery Writers of America in New York City; Eleanor Bader of Brooklyn; Alexa Kelly, Brian Richardson, Andrew Charity, and Alvin and Myra Chanin of Manhattan; George Koch of Queens; Michele Slung of Woodstock, New York; Nancy McCaig of Corning, New York; Lindsay Bajo of San Diego, California; Helga Schier of Santa Monica, California; Lauren Holingsworth of Culver City, California; Diana James, publicist, of Pasadena, California; and Regina Miller of the Geffen Theatre, Westwood, California.

Finally, salutation to Peter E. Blau of Washington, D.C., and Andrew Joffe of New York City for their input on Sherlock Holmes and the collecting of Sherlockiana.

Introduction

The first play on record climaxed with a mass murder. In Aeschylus's *Prometheus Bound* (479 BC), the god Zeus dispatches a group of nymphs to Hades with a bolt of lightning, punishment for helping Prometheus steal fire from the heavens and sneak it down to earth. Aeschylus penned many popular tragedies of mayhem and violence, notably *The Danaid Tetralogy* (463 BC), in which the fifty daughters of Danaus plan to flee from Egypt to avoid marrying their cousins, the fifty sons of Aegyptus. When their escape is foiled, Danaus helps the women plot the murders of the bridegrooms on their wedding night. The daughters will thus preserve their virginity and avoid the fate of incestuous marriages.

The audiences of ancient Greece continued to shiver deliciously at the cesspool of intrigue in Aeschylus's *The Oresteia* (458 BC), a trilogy that begins with the murder of Agamemnon, king of Argos, at the hand of his wife, Clytemnestra. The queen, irate at her husband for returning from the Trojan War with the Princess Cassandra, throws a fishnet-like robe around Agamemnon, strikes him three times with an ax, and rejoices as his blood spurts. The feud passes from generation to generation, culminating in the revenge murder of Clytemnestra by her children, Orestes and Electra. In an early courtroom drama, the goddess Athena assembles a jury of twelve citizens in a trial of Orestes in Delphi. There is a tie vote, and Athena acquits Orestes.

Other ancient Greece tragedies of bloodletting include Euripides' *Medea* (431 BC), wherein the madly jealous title character sends a robe smeared with poison to Creusa, her rival, who dies engulfed in flames. Consumed with revenge, Medea murders her own children, places their bodies in a dragon-drawn chariot, and flies away, leaving her lover Jason in hopeless despair.

Sophocles, the third great tragedian of the time, wrote *Oedipus the King* (c. 430 BC), one of the first plays to introduce the motif of crime and punishment and relate the step-by-step investigation of a murder through the interrogation of witnesses. The play uses the ironic discovery that the detective is also the unwitting murderer.

Since then, villainies of all sorts have tainted the stages of the world. Awash with blood were the plays of the Roman Seneca; the Elizabethans William Shakespeare and Christopher Marlowe; the Jacobean John Webster, Thomas Kyd, Francis Beaumont, and John Fletcher; seventeenth-century Pedro Calderon of Spain and Jean Racine of France; and eighteenth-century Goethe and Schiller of Germany.

In the nineteenth century, sheer horror was exhibited in *Bertram, or, The Castle of St. Alobrand* (1816) by Charles R. Maturin; *Le Vampire* (1820) by Charles Nodier; and *Presumption, or, The Fate of Frankenstein* (1823) by Richard Brinsley Peake, adapted from the 1818 novel by Mary Shelley.

Sensational real-life crimes began to be captured on stage in such popular plays as *Maria Marten, or, The Murder in the Red Barn* (1828) by Montage Slater; *Vidocq, or, The French Police Spy* (1829) by Douglas Jerrold; and *The Murder at the Roadhouse, or, Jonathan Bradford* (1833) by Edward Fitzball. Dramatizations of suspenseful best sellers became the vogue with *Les Mysteres de Paris* (1844), from the novel by Eugene Sue; Alexandre Dumas's *Monte Cristo* (1848); Mrs. Henry Wood's *East Lynne*; and *The Woman in White* (1871) by Wilkie Collins. Crime investigation entered the scene in *Lady Audley's Secret* (1863) by William E. Suter, the first of many adaptations based on the 1862 novel by Mary Elizabeth Braddon; *The Ticket-of-Leave Man* (1863) by Tom Taylor, introducing the detective Hawkshaw; and *The Moonstone* (1877), dramatized by Wilkie Collins from his 1868 novel.

The latter part of the nineteenth century was flooded with varied fare: *Thérèse Raquin* (1873), a psychological thriller, adapted to the stage by Emile Zola from his 1867 novel; *An Enemy of the People* (1882), Henrik Ibsen's indictment of a community's insatiable greed; *Dr. Jekyll and Mr. Hyde* (1887), adapted by Thomas Russell Sullivan from the 1866 horror novella by Robert Louis Stevenson; Leo Tolstoy's *The Power of Darkness* (written, 1866; first performance, 1888), a harrowing drama about a child's murder; and the stage debut of the world's foremost consulting detective in *Sherlock Holmes* (1899) by William Gillette.

Blood-and-thunder melodramas were the rage at the dawn of the twentieth century. Stereotypes rampage on the stage—the moustached, sneering villain, often a lecherous landlord or a greedy ward; his cohort, an adventuress dressed in scarlet; the pretty, wide-eyed damsel-in-distress who is blessed with the singular talent to be in the wrong place at the wrong time and ends up gagged, bound, kidnapped, poisoned, stabbed, or placed on railroad tracks; the brawny, not very smart hero; and his sidekick, a courageous, spunky kid or a broad-comedy cowardly butler. All are enmeshed in wild plots, often appearing on the scene unexpectedly without motive, entangled in bizarre, life-or-death encounters, facing breathtaking cliff-hangers, and surrounded by special effects galore. The action is furious, the stage awash with blood—and justice triumphs.

Among the more successful melodramatists of the era were Theodore Kremer, James Halleck Reid, Owen Davis, Langdon McCormick, Lincoln J. Carter, Charles E. Blaney, Willard Mack, and Max Marcin—prolific authors who had a knack for whipping up sensational five-act plays within a week, year in and year out.

Eventually, as demonstrated in the first volume of this series, *Blood on the Stage, 1900–1925*, a more subtle approach emerged in the writings of Henry Bernstein, David Belasco, Bayard Veiller, and Elmer Rice. Mainstream playwrights became concerned with the motives of crime, and they probed the mind of the criminal. Over time, the overblown thrills of melodrama began to give way to a more realistic, true-to-life approach. August Strindberg, Maxim Gorky, and Eden Phillpotts provided psychological insight. Tragic overtones enveloped the works of Jacinto Benavente, John Masefield, and Eugene O'Neill. Social criticism crept into the dramas of Alexandre Bisson and John Galsworthy. Shady business manipulations and underhanded political machinations were exposed by Clyde Fitch, Charles Klein, and George Broadhurst. And the curtain rose on several lasting masterpieces: *The Lower Depths* by Maxim Gorky, *The Playboy of the Western World* by John Millington Synge, *The Tragedy of Nan* by John Masefield, *Justice* by John Galsworthy, *Desire under the Elms* by Eugene O'Neill, and *The Golem* by Halper Leivick.

As illustrated in the second book in the series, *Blood on the Stage, 1925–1950*, the old-fashioned melodrama was a dying breed, and only a few of the plays discussed in the book fall into this category: *Wooden Kimono* by John Floyd, *The Clutching Claw* by Ralph Tomas Kettering, *The Call of the Banshee* by W. D. Hepenstall and Ralph Cullinan, and *The Skull* by Bernard J. McOwen and Harry E. Humphrey. With the advent of detective literature's golden age, a period that began in the mid-1920s and lasted through the 1940s, stage fare, too, made a turn toward the whodunit-puzzle motif.

Englishman Edgar Wallace, author of hundreds of crime novels and short stories, was the first to make a specialty of detective drama. His *The Ringer, The Case of the Frightened Lady* (aka *Criminal at Large*) and *On the Spot* thrilled audiences on both sides of the Atlantic. Dorothy L. Sayers was not far behind; she brought her famous amateur sleuth, Lord Peter Wimsey, to the stage in *Busman's Holiday*. Agatha Christie, unhappy with several dramatizations of her early novels, jumped into the cauldron with a dozen or so plays of her own, beginning with *Ten Little Indians* (aka *And Then There Were None*). Christie's beloved Hercule Poirot and Jane Marple made the transformation from the printed page to the stage in a number of adaptations that became fixtures in summer stock and community theatres. Charlie Chan, Philo Vance, Ellery Queen, and Mr. and Mrs. North—heroes of novels, movies, radio, and television—also took to the stage, albeit rarely. And Sherlock Holmes continued to scratch on his Stradivarius and solve baffling cases in dramatizations of Arthur Conan Doyle's stories.

More mainstream playwrights entered the fold. Among the Broadway contributors who dabbled in theft, kidnapping, and murder were Sidney Howard, Guy Bolton, Paul Green, Elmer Rice, Philip Barry, George S. Kaufman, Robert E. Sherwood, Maxwell Anderson, Sidney Kingsley, Irwin Shaw, and Lillian Hellman—the Who's Who of the era's American theatre. In England, W. Somerset Maugham, A. A. Milne, Emlyn Williams, J. B. Priestley, Terence Rattigan, and Daphne du Maurier wrote plays of crime and detection. Betrayal and violence are key elements in the plays of the Hungarian Laszlo Fodor, the German Ernst Toller, the Spaniard Federico Garcia Lorca, the Italian Ugo Betti, and the Frenchman Jean Genet.

Famed novelists and poets Wilbur Daniel Steele, Robert Penn Warren, Aldous Huxley, and Herman Wouk also plunged into the world of grease paint and papier-mâché. Even Nobel Prize winners Eugene O'Neill, John Steinbeck, Ernest Hemingway, Albert Camus, and Jean-Paul Sartre smeared their pens with blood. Other names added to the unique roster are Mae West, Clare Boothe (Luce), Ayn Rand, and James M. Cain.

Dark psychological thrillers were in vogue, with *Jealousy*, *Rope*, *Gaslight* (aka *Angel Street*), *Payment Deferred*, *Night Must Fall*, *The Two Mrs. Carrolls*, *Blind Alley*, *Ladies in Retirement*, *Guest in the House*, *Black Chiffon*, and *The Man*.

This third volume of *Blood on the Stage* studies plays of crime, mystery, and detection mounted between 1950 and 1975, a quarter-century during which the genre moved in multiple directions. Covered here are entries varying greatly in content, format, and style. Evil versus good is the theme of allegorical stage adaptations of Herman Melville's *Billy Budd* and Oscar Wilde's *Lord Arthur Savile's Crime*. Political intrigue is covered in Gore Vidal's *The Best Man*; *The Gang's All Here* by Jerome Lawrence and Robert E. Lee; *Advise and Consent*, a dramatization by Loring Mandel from the novel by Allen Drury; *Darkness at Noon*, Sidney Kingsley's adaptation of Arthur Koestler's novel; *The Prisoner* by Bridget Boland; *Seven Days in May*, a stage version by Kristin Sergel based on the novel by Fletcher Knebel and Charles W. Bailey II; *The Hostage* by Brendan Behan; and *The White House Murder Case* by Jules Feiffer.

Communal greed, which at the turn of the twentieth century was the topic of Nikolai Gogol's *The Inspector General*, Henrik Ibsen's *An Enemy of the People*, and David Pinski's *The Treasure*, is rekindled to horrifying effect in *The Visit* by Friedrich Duerrenmatt. Bertolt Brecht's *The Resistible Rise of Arturo Ui* satirically equates the menace of the Nazi regime to the terror inflicted by a murderous gangster mob in Chicago. Ui (Hitler) sells "protection" to vegetable merchants and murders anyone who challenges him.

Domestic mayhem and homicidal husbands are introduced in *Dial "M" for Murder* by Frederick Knott, *Speaking of Murder* by Audrey and William Roos, *The Whole Truth* by Philip Mackie, *Gently Does It* (aka *Murder Mistaken*) by Janet Green, *Suddenly at Home* by Francis Durbridge, and *Murder among Friends* by Bob Barry.

Business shenanigans play a key role in *Calculated Risk* by Joseph Hayes and *Write Me a Murder* by Frederick Knott. Hayes also penned the excellent gangster play *The Desperate Hours*, and Knott penned *Wait until Dark*. Police corruption rears its ugly head in *Dead Pigeon*. Gambling takes its toll in *The Number* by Arthur P. Carter. The effect of hard drugs shocked audiences in Michael V. Gazzo's *A Hatful of Rain*. A quest for revenge was tested in *Someone Waiting* by Emlyn Williams and in Morris L. West's *Daughter of Silence*. Peter Shaffer came up with a dazzling psychological thriller, *Equus*, while his twin brother Anthony Shaffer played a cat-and-mouse game with the audience in *Sleuth* and *Murderer*.

Several gothic best sellers from the Victorian era were adapted to the stage: *East Lynne*, based on the novel by Mrs. Henry Wood; *Jane Eyre*, inspired by Charlotte Brontë's novel of the same name; and *Lady Audley's Secret*, from the story by Mary Elizabeth Braddon. Shivering horror is provided by a number of stage versions of Mary Shelley's classic *Frankenstein*, several dramatizations of Bram Stoker's brooding *Dracula*, and Robert Marasco's shadowy *Child's Play*. Very young murderers are exposed in Maxwell Anderson's *Bad Seed*, Mary Drayton's *The Playhouse*, and Shirley Jackson's *We Have Always Lived in the Castle*.

The pomp and ceremony of courtroom dramas—civil, military, and religious, some based on real-life events—is exhibited in Agatha Christie's *Witness for the Prosecution*; Barry England's *Conduct Unbecoming*; Jack Roffey's *Hostile Witness*; Saul Levitt's *The Andersonville Trial*; Henry Denker's *A Case of Libel* and *Time Limit!*; Meyer Levin's *Compulsion*; Herman Wouk's *The Caine Mutiny Court-Martial*; *Inherit the Wind* by Jerome Lawrence and Robert E. Lee; *Rashomon* by Fay and Michael Kanin; Philip Dunning's *Sequel to a Verdict*; Robert Shaw's *The Man in the Glass Booth*; and *The Ponder Heart*, a dramatization by Joseph Fields and Jerome Chodorov from a story by Eudora Welty.

The volatile 1960s—the aftermath of the McCarthy hearings, the Vietnam War, the demand for civil rights, the women's movement—impacted the theatre. A new format, the docudrama, exhibiting material from court transcripts, became popular with *In the Matter of J. Robert Oppenheimer* by Heinar Kipphardt, *Murder Story* by Ludovic Kennedy, *Inquest* by Donald

Freed, and *The Trial of the Catonsville Nine* by Daniel Berrigan. Racial animosities exploded in *Blues for Mr. Charlie* by James Baldwin, *Dutchman* by LeRoi Jones, and *The Blacks* by Jean Genet. Prison cells were designed for Brendan Behan's *The Quare Fellow*, Miguel Piñero's *Short Eyes*, and John Herbert's *Fortune and Men's Eyes*.

Amid the violence and bloodletting, comic relief and sly satire were furnished in plays such as *Remains to Be Seen* by Howard Lindsay and Russel Crouse; *My 3 Angels* by Sam and Bella Spewack; *Meet a Body* by Frank Launder; *A Shot in the Dark* by Marcel Achard; *Golden Fleecing* by Lorenzo Semple Jr.; *The Gazebo* by Alec Coppel; *Don't Drink the Water* by Woody Allen; and *The Real Inspector Hound* by Tom Stoppard. Musicals tinged with varied elements of crime included *Guys and Dolls*, *West Side Story*, *Baker Street*, *Redhead*, *Oliver!*, *Something's Afoot*, and *It's a Bird . . . It's a Plane . . . It's Superman*.

Like Edgar Wallace, Dorothy L. Sayers, and Agatha Christie before them, some established writers of suspense novels tried their hand at concocting stage mysteries—F. Tennyson Jesse, Ngaio Marsh, Helen MacInnes, Lucille Fletcher, Kelly Roos, Michael Gilbert, Henry Cecil, John Mortimer, Francis Durbridge, and James Yaffe among them. And enterprising adapters brought to the stage such famous literary sleuths as Perry Mason, Michael Shayne, and Lieutenant Columbo. The immortal Sherlock Holmes continued to baffle good Dr. Watson and the audience in various escapades unfolding behind the footlights.

During 1950–1975, a surprising array of award-winning authors contributed criminous plays to Broadway and the West End, among them William Faulkner, Arthur Miller, William Saroyan, Gore Vidal, Horton Foote, Herman Wouk, Jules Feiffer, John Osborne, Graham Greene, and Tom Stoppard. They were joined by two distinguished actors: Raymond Massey with his brooding crime play *Hanging Judge*, and Michael Redgrave with a drama of literary detection, *The Aspern Papers*, adapted from a novella by Henry James.

This work aims to provide an overview of milestone plays of crime, mystery, and detection that were produced in a rich era of stage mayhem. While I have chosen a wide parameter—each of the entries revolves around murder, theft, chicanery, kidnapping, political intrigue, or espionage—it was not my intention to embrace every crime-and-punishment play ever written. I have instead selected manuscripts of enduring importance, pioneering contributions, singular innovations, outstanding commercial or artistic successes, and representative works by prolific playwrights in the genre. And, as in the preceding volumes of *Blood on the Stage*, the slate includes some of my personal favorites.

This volume covers plays produced between 1950 and 1975 that were performed at least once in the English language. The entries are arranged in chronological order, and each consists of a plot synopsis, production data, a look at unique features, and the opinions of critics and scholars.

In order to gain a historical perspective, I have kept potentially offensive elements intact and did not edit out sexism, racial prejudices, anti-Semitic slurs, or other derogatory content. The plays must be seen in their historical context, each a work of art that is shaped by its era. The opinions set forth in the plays are not necessarily my own.

Please be advised that the entries will often reveal the solution or twist of a play, because each individual plot synopsis aims to be complete. I hope that the selections discussed in this work will ignite interest in neglected playwrights and forgotten plays.

Guys and Dolls (1950)

Book by Jo Swerling (United States, Russia-born, 1897–1964) and Abe Burrows (United States, 1910–1985), Music and Lyrics by Frank Loesser (United States, 1910–1969)

Damon Runyon was a journalist, a sports columnist, and the author of short stories chronicling the sleazy side of New York City. His colorful Broadway characters—described by reporter Jimmy Breslin as "petty mobsters, pickpockets, molls, grifters, touts, pool hustlers, and panhandlers"[1]—populate the short story collections *Guys and Dolls* (1932), *Take It Easy* (1938), *My Wife Ethel* (1940), *Runyon à la Carte* (1944), *In Our Town* (1946), and *Short Takes* (1946). The stage musical *Guys and Dolls* is based on two stories by Runyon, "The Idyll of Miss Sarah Brown" and "Blood Pressure," and it borrows characters from other Runyon tales.

The curtain rises on "Runyonland," a pantomime played to music, unfolding on a busy Manhattan street. Several shady characters are loitering on a corner, flipping coins. A policeman strolls by and gazes suspiciously at a pair of streetwalkers. Actors, chorus girls, and fans pleading for autographs mill about. An old woman is selling fruit and pretzels. A sidewalk photographer snaps pictures of a family of tourists, offers them an order form, is paid—and throws the form away as soon as the visitors walk away. A liquor vendor passes with a trick cabinet that quickly converts into a baby pram when the police are around. A heavyweight prizefighter skips rope across the stage. A sightseeing guide leads a group of out-of-towners, including an elderly married couple from Texas. A pickpocket approaches the male Texan, points to a tall building, and lifts the Texan's watch and chain. A streetwalker flirts with the pickpocket and deftly relieves him of watch and chain. The Texan realizes what happened and sets off in pursuit. Soon it seems that everybody is chasing somebody. When the dust settles, three small-time gamblers—Benny Southstreet, Rusty Charlie, and Nicely-Nicely Johnson—remain on stage, loitering near a newsstand. They buy a scratch sheet, sing "A Fugue for Tinhorns," and argue over which horse will win tomorrow's race: Paul Revere, Valentine, or Epitaph.

1

A Salvation Army band appears, led by Sergeant Sarah Brown, a pretty girl severely dressed, striking a tambourine. She stands on a box and pleads with a gathering crowd to quit the evils of drinking and gambling. She falters as her audience drifts away. The band, dispirited, moves on. "Poor Miss Sarah," says Nicely-Nicely. "I wonder why a refined doll like her is mixed up in the Mission dodge."

"Maybe she owns a piece of the Mission," muses Benny.

Harry the Horse, a rough character from Brooklyn, joins the three and asks whether Nathan Detroit has found a place for his crap game. Harry is itching to play. He has just acquired five thousand potatoes—the reward on his father.

Lieutenant Brannigan emerges from behind the newsstand. He is looking for Nathan Detroit, who has been running a floating crap game, moving it to a different spot every night.

Nathan Detroit enters—"a slim, nervous, alert man in sharp clothes." Brannigan warns him that he'll be breathing down his neck. When the police officer saunters away, Nathan tells the gamblers that he's under pressure because a convention of "high-rollers" is coming to town. But he is having a difficult time securing a place for the game. He might get the Biltmore Hotel's garage, only Joey Biltmore is demanding a $1,000 security deposit, which he does not have. He is so broke, sighs Nathan, that he can't even buy Adelaide a present for their anniversary. "We have been engaged for fourteen years," he explains.

Angie the Ox arrives with exciting news: Sky Masterson is in town—the highest player of them all. An idea strikes Nathan. Masterson likes crazy bets; why not bet him $1,000, a bet he can't lose? Enter Sky—young, handsome, charismatic—flush with fifty Gs that he won playing blackjack in Nevada. Nathan proposes a bet: Sky must take a doll of his choice to dinner—in Havana, Cuba. The Mission band appears, singing, and Nathan points to Sarah: "I name her!"

The second scene takes place in the interior of the Save-a-Soul Mission. Sky Masterson, dressed in a conservative dark suit, enters and inquires, "Do you take sinners here?" Sarah Brown and old Arvide Abernathy, the drummer in the Mission's band, greet him warmly. Sky sinks into a chair and confesses to having wasted a life by gambling. He soon asks Sarah for a dinner date but she coolly turns him down. However, she changes her mind when he proposes to save the Mission from closing by filling it with a dozen genuine sinners at the upcoming prayer meeting. He also tells her that his favorite restaurant is El Café Cubana in Havana. A plane will get them there in five hours and they'll return the same night.

Nathan, certain he'll win his bet, goes to the Hat Box nightclub and watches Adelaide and the Farmerettes perform "A Bushel and a Peck." After the show, Nathan and Adelaide sit at a table and she relates that she is getting a raise next week, suggesting that maybe, after having been engaged for fourteen years, it is time for them to get married. She is concerned about her mother, who lives in Rhode Island and believes that she and Nathan are married and the parents of five children. Nathan assures Adelaide that he'll never run a crap game again, but Mimi, one of the dancing girls, passes by their table and lashes out at Nathan: "I'm all dated up tomorrow with Society Max, and he breaks it on account of your dopey crap game!" Nathan leaves in a hurry and joins a gathering of crapshooters on a street off Broadway. All have red carnations in their lapels and are waiting to find out the location of the game. Nathan explains that he hasn't yet secured the funds for the Biltmore garage, but he'll soon get the advance money from Sky Masterson. The crowd becomes unruly. Big Jule from Chicago keeps growling, "I came here to shoot crap. Let's shoot crap." Harry the Horse warns Nathan that Big Jule does not like to be displeased.

Lt. Brannigan suddenly appears and wonders what the red carnations are for. Benny flounders, but he sees Adelaide approaching and says, "A bachelor party. Nathan's getting married." The gamblers begin to sing, "For he's a jolly good fellow," and Adelaide is thrilled. Extending congratulations, Brannigan moves on.

They hear the music of the Mission band. The band musicians march by and Nathan counts them. They are all there—except Sarah. Nathan collapses.

In Havana, prim-and-proper Sarah objects to dinner at a dance dive. She leads Sky on a lengthy tour of the sights, and they pause at a cheap café. She orders a milk shake and does not see Sky signaling the waiter to spike her drink. Sarah favors the taste, keeps ordering more, and, woozy, insists on returning to the dance dive. They dance intimately, until a Cuban man tries to butt in, and a Cuban girl flirts with Sky. A chair-breaking brawl ensues, at the end of which Sky picks Sarah up and carries her out. Intoxicated, Sarah croons, "If I Were a Bell I'd Be Ringing." She wants to stay in Havana for a few more days, but Sky lifts the struggling girl once more and heads for the airport. They arrive at the Mission at 4 a.m. Sky sings the sentimental "My Time of Day" and confides to Sarah that his real name is Obediah Masterson. A police siren is heard approaching. Suddenly the Mission's door opens and men scurry through it, putting on their coats, fleeing in all directions. Among them is Nathan, who, unable to secure the garage, had a brainstorm. Brannigan and two cops rush in—but too late. "I've seen a lot of things in my time," says the Lieutenant, "but this is the first time I ever seen a floating crap game going full blast in a Mission."

Sarah now believes that this is why Sky took her to Havana. He cannot convince her that he had nothing to do with the gamblers' invasion of the religious space. "It's no good, Sky," she says. And Adelaide, after her cabaret number "Take Back Your Mink," decides to part with Nathan.

The enterprising Nathan has moved his game to a sewer. The crap-shooters go through a rousing ballet. When the dance is over, Big Jule, a heavy loser, pats his shoulder holster and insists on continuing the game. He confronts Nathan, who won quite a bundle, and forces him to receive his marker, an "IOU $1,000," signed X. He now brings out his own dice, ones that are entirely blank, but, says Jule, he remembers where the spots formerly were. Big Jule cleans Nathan out of $6,000 and refuses Nathan's offer to play with his own marker. Sky comes down a ladder, lies to Nathan that he failed to take Sarah Brown to Havana, and announces to the men that he wants to talk to them about the local Mission. Jule faces Sky, warning him not to slow up the action. Sky offers him a bet: "Am I right-handed or left-handed?" Jule says he wouldn't know. "I'll give you a clue," says Sky, and knocks the big man with his right. Jule staggers and reaches for his gun, but Sky gets there first and tosses the weapon to Nathan, who gingerly passes it to Benny.

Sky tells the crowd that a midnight prayer meeting will be held in the Mission. He promised Sarah Brown a dozen sinners. He will play each man for a thousand cash against their markers. If a man wins, he gets a thousand; if he loses, he must show up at the meeting. Soon all the gamblers put up their markers. Sky sings "Luck, Be a Lady Tonight" and tosses the dice.

In the Save-A-Soul Mission, General Matilda B. Carstairs threatens to close the empty center immediately, but then the gamblers shuffle in. The general calls for the first volunteer to confess, and Nathan orders Benny to testify. "I ain't no stool pigeon," objects Benny. Under pressure he admits to being a gambler, but he ain't going to do it no more. Big Jule deposes: "Well, I used to be bad when I was a kid, but ever since then I have gone straight as I can prove by my record—thirty-three arrests and no convictions."

Officer Brannigan bursts in, ready for a major gambling pinch, but Nathan orders him to remove his hat and be silent. It is Nicely-Nicely's turn, and he confesses in the form of a rousing number, "Sit Down, Sit Down, You're Rocking the Boat!"

Nathan asks Brannigan if he would like to testify. The lieutenant announces that he will do it in court. He will accuse them of running a crap game the night before. "Miss Sarah," he says, "you saw them." Sarah looks at the men and after a suspenseful pause announces, "I never saw them before in my life." Big Jule exclaims, "There's a right broad!" and Brannigan leaves, defeated.

The last scene unfolds on the familiar Broadway street. We again meet the shady characters, the streetwalkers, the out-of-town tourists. Adelaide arrives in a wedding outfit, carrying a bouquet. The Hot Box dancers are her bridesmaids. We now realize that the man running the newsstand is Nathan. He sells the latest edition to Brannigan, pulls down a shade lettered "Nathan Detroit's News Stand," and emerges dressed in a cutaway, top hat, and cane. The Mission band marches in with the same personnel as always—except that old Arvide now has an assistant to carry and beat the drum for him. Wearing a Salvation Army uniform and singing lustily "Follow the Fold" is Sky Masterson.

* * *

Directed by George S. Kaufman, choreographed by Michael Kidd, and designed by Jo Mielziner, *Guys and Dolls* previewed in Philadelphia and opened at Broadway's Forty-sixth Street Theatre on November 24, 1950. The leading roles were played by Robert Alda (Sky Masterson), Sam Levene (Nathan Detroit), Isabel Bigley (Sarah Brown), and Vivian Blaine (Miss Adelaide).

The show garnered unanimous rave reviews. Brooks Atkinson liked "the fact that it has preserved the friendly spirit of the Runyon literature without patronizing and without any show-stop hokum."[2] Howard Barnes found that "the gags and situations are fresh and amusing" and that "the motley group of figures in the fable emerges with theatrical excitement and considerable conviction."[3] Richard Watts Jr. gushed, "The fabulous universe of Damon Runyon, the eminent sage and poet laureate of the Broadway underworld, is transformed to the stage with notable success in *Guys and Dolls*, the big, brash and bountiful musical comedy."[4] Robert Coleman wrote, "*Guys and Dolls* is a heart-warming and hilarious re-creation of Runyon's kaleidoscopic cosmos of mugs and dolls. We think Damon would have relished it as much as we did."[5]

The critics showered kudos on the artistic team. "*Guys and Dolls* is a show that deserves gold stars in many departments," opined William Hawkins. "To my mind the most startling contributions are the affectionately witty idea and musical vernacular of Frank Loesser's score, and Michael Kidd's sharply staged dances."[6] Jo Mielziner's "affable settings" and Alvin Colt's "noisy costumes" were also praised. Director George S. Kaufman "has done a singularly adept job of staging . . . as good a job of direction as seen in these parts for many a year."[7]

The actors were lauded, notably the "slick, handsome and persuasive" Robert Alda, the "delightful ingénue" Isabel Bigley, the "immense" Sam Levene, the "terrific" Vivian Blaine, and Stubby Kaye (Nicely-Nicely Johnson), Johnny Silver (Benny Southstreet), and B. S. Pully (Big Jule).

Guys and Dolls ran for 1,200 performances. A subsequent London production opened at the Coliseum on May 28, 1953, with some members of the Broadway cast reprising their roles, and ran for 554 showings.

New York's City Center revived the musical in 1955—for sixteen performances—featuring Helen Gallagher as Miss Adelaide and Walter Matthau as Nathan Detroit. Ten years later, in 1965, City Center presented *Guys and Dolls* again—for fifteen performances—with Jerry Orbach (Sky Masterson), Anita Gillette (Sarah Brown), Alan King (Nathan Detroit), and Sheila MacRae (Miss Adelaide). The following year, the New York City Center Light Opera Company produced a spring season of four Frank Loesser musical revivals, including *Guys and Dolls*, which had Hugh O'Brien as Sky and Vivian Blaine as Adelaide. It ran for twenty-three performances.

A 1976 revival of *Guys and Dolls* at the Broadway Theatre featured an all-black cast and ran for 239 performances. Jerry Zaks directed a 1992 reincarnation, starring Peter Gallagher, Nathan Lane, Faith Prince, and Josie de Guzman. It ran at the Martin Beck Theatre for 1,143 showings. In March 2009, a revival at the Nederlander Theatre marqueed Oliver Platt (Nathan), Craig Bierko (Sky), Kate Jennings Grant (Sarah), and Lauren Graham (Adelaide). The show opened to generally negative reviews. Ben Brantley of the *New York Times* peppered his assessment with such adjectives as "bland," "static," "rigid," "stiff," and "self-conscious."[8] It closed after 113 showings.

Later in 2009, *Guys and Dolls* was presented, in the format of concert staging, at the Hollywood Bowl in Hollywood, California, with Brian Stokes Mitchell assaying the role of Sky Masterson and Jessica Beal playing Sarah Brown. Beau Bridges portrayed the supporting role of Arvide Abernathy, the Mission's drummer. The theatre critic of the *Los Angeles Times*, Charles McNulty, complimented musical director Kevin Stites for "bringing out every cheeky nuance of [Frank] Loesser's irreplaceable score."[9]

In London, a 1982 revival played at the Royal National Theatre, directed by Richard Eyre, featuring Bob Hoskins (Nathan), Ian Charleson (Sky), Julie Covington (Sarah), and Julia McKenzie (Adelaide). The guys and dolls came back in 2005, to West End's Piccadilly Theatre, amusing audiences for almost two years. Helmed by director Michael Grandage, the principals were Ewan McGregor (Sky), Douglas Hodge (Nathan), Jenna Russell (Sarah), and Jane Krakowski (Adelaide). The well-known American actors Patrick Swayze and Don Johnson took over the role of Nathan Detroit in 2006 and 2007, respectively.

Distributed by MGM, *Guys and Dolls* was filmed in 1955, produced by Samuel Goldwyn, directed by Joseph L. Mankiewicz, starring Marlon Brando (Sky), Frank Sinatra (Nathan), and Jean Simmons (Sarah). Vivian Blaine (Adelaide), Stubby Kaye (Nicely-Nicely Johnson), and B. S. Pully (Big Jule) were recruited from the original cast. Budgeted at $5 million, the movie grossed in excess of $13 million, making it the number one moneymaking film of 1956. It went on to gross over $20 million globally.

* * *

Alfred Damon Runyan was born in 1880 to a family of journalists in Manhattan, Kansas, and grew up in Pueblo, Colorado, where he gained his initial writing experience at his father's newspaper. He soon worked as a reporter for various dailies in the Rocky Mountain area. He liked a typo that changed his name from Runyan to Runyon and adopted the new spelling of his name. When he was eighteen, Runyon enlisted in the U.S. Army to fight in the Spanish-American War. In 1910, he moved to New York City and for the next decade covered baseball and boxing for the *New York American*. A notorious gambler and heavy drinker, Runyon often painted his hard-boiled characters with similar vices. In his stories, he covered the underbelly of Manhattan with sympathy for the underdogs.

In collaboration with Howard Lindsay (1889–1968), Runyon wrote the play *A Slight Case of Murder*, the story of Remy Marko, a Prohibition beer racketeer from Brooklyn who goes legit, becoming a respectable brewer attempting to rise above his earthy, streetwise demeanor and fit into the aristocratic environment of Saratoga Springs during the racing season. Marko moves in with his socially minded wife, Nora. Members of his old gang attempt to adjust as cooks, butlers, and chauffeurs. Much of the humor of *A Slight Case of Murder* derives from a clash of cultures during a party, in which the gaudy guys and dolls of Brooklyn meet Saratoga Springs' elegant ladies and gents. Complications arise when the bullet-riddled corpses of four hoodlums are found in an upstairs room, sitting stiffly around a poker table. Somebody interrupted a card game and shot them. *A Slight Case of Murder* opened at the Forty-eighth Street Theatre in New York on September 11, 1935, for a modest run of sixty-nine performances; it made a smooth transition to the silver screen in 1938. Warner Brothers cast Edward G. Robinson, their number one gangster, in this humorous inversion of the genre and came up with a comic gem. Broderick Crawford played the beer baron in a 1952 remake titled *Stop, You're Killing Me*.

Many Damon Runyon stories were adapted to the cinema. Notable are *Lady for a Day* (1933) and its remake *Pocketful of Miracles* (1961), both based on the story "Madame La Gimp"; *Little Miss Marker* (1934), a Shirley Temple vehicle that spawned several remakes: *Sorrowful Jones* (1949), *Forty Pounds of Trouble* (1962), and *Little Miss Marker* (1980); *The Lemon Drop Kid* (1934, 1951); *Princess O'Hara* (1935); *The Big Street* (1942), inspired by the tale "Little Pinks"; *It Ain't Hay* (1943), adapted from "Princess O'Hara" for Bud Abbott and Lou Costello; and *Money from Home* (1953), starring Dean Martin and Jerry Lewis.

Damon Runyon Theatre dramatized fifty-two of Runyon's short stories for radio in 1949–1950. *Damon Runyon Theatre* aired on CBS TV during 1955–1956.

Runyon died in New York City from throat cancer in 1946. His body was cremated, and his ashes were scattered from an airplane over Broadway in Manhattan on December 18, 1946.

Jo Swerling was born in Bardichov, Russia. A refugee of the czarist regime, he grew up on New York's Lower East Side, where he sold newspapers to support his family. In the early 1920s he began as a reporter and feature writer for the *American Magazine*, the *Nation*, and the *New Yorker*. He launched his playwriting career with the musical revue *The New Yorkers* (1927) and the comedy *Kibitzer* (1929), which he cowrote with actor Edward G. Robinson.

Swerling moved to the West Coast and established a spectacular career in Hollywood in the 1930s and 1940s. He began by penning several Frank Capra movies—*Ladies of Leisure* (1930), *Dirigible* (1931), *The Miracle Woman* (1931), *Platinum Blonde* (1931), and *Forbidden* (1932). Among Swerling's notable credits are collaborations on the screenplays of *The Whole Town Is Talking* (1935), *Gone with the Wind* (1939), *The Westerner* (1940), *Blood and Sand* (1941), *The Pride of the Yankees* (1942), *Crash Dive* (1943), *Lifeboat* (1944), and *It's a Wonderful Life* (1946). His criminous movies include *The Squealer* (1930), *Behind the Mask* (1932), *Attorney for the Defense* (1932), *The Circus Queen Murder* (1933), *The Wrecker* (1933), *The Defense Rests* (1934), *I Am the Law* (1938), *Leave Her to Heaven* (1945), and *King of the Roaring Twenties* (1961).

Born Abram Solman Borowitz in New York City, Abe Burrows attended both City College and New York University. He worked as a Wall Street runner, an accountant, and a maple syrup salesman before plunging into a radio career, creating the successful series *Duffy's Tavern*, contributing material for a 1940s Danny Kaye program, and eventually hosting his own CBS radio program, *The Abe Burrows Show*, in 1948.

Burrows also worked as a scenarist for Paramount Pictures but shifted his focus to the theatre. He credits his success on Broadway to observing and learning from George S. Kaufman during the rehearsals of *Guys and Dolls*. His career as playwright and director mushroomed with the hit musicals *Can-Can* (1953), *Silk Stockings* (1955), *Happy Hunting* (1956), *Say, Darling* (1958), *How to Succeed in Business without Really Trying* (1961), and the comedies *Reclining Figure* (1954), *Golden Fleecing* (1959), *Cactus Flower* (1965), and *Forty Carats* (1968).

Burrows was in demand as a script doctor and served as the mentor of several comedy writers, including Larry Gelbart, Nat Hiken, Dick Martin, and Woody Allen. On television, he appeared as a panelist on various game shows, including *The Name's the Same*, *To Tell the Truth*, *The Match Game*, and *What's My Line?* His memoir, *Honest, Abe: Is There Really No Business like Show Business?*, was published in 1980. He died in New York City in 1985 after a battle with Alzheimer's disease.

Born in Manhattan to a musical family, Frank Henry Loesser never formally studied music. His father was a teacher of classical music and his older brother, Arthur, was a concert pianist. But as a teenager Frank's interest was in pop music, and he taught himself the harmonica and the piano. He dropped out of City College during the Depression and supported himself first as an errand boy and then as a publicist. He later became the city editor of a short-lived tabloid in New Rochelle. He soon began writing songs, sketches, and radio scripts.

In 1936, Loesser contributed five songs to a Broadway revue, *The Illustrator's Show*, which closed after five performances. He migrated to Hollywood and, under contract with Paramount, wrote his first hit song, "Moon of Manakoora," for the Dorothy Lamour–Jon Hall picture *Hurricane*. Sometimes uncredited, he went on to write lyrics for more than sixty films, including *Destry Rides Again* (1939), *North West Mounted Police* (1940), *Aloma of the South Seas* (1941), *Reap the Wild Wind* (1942), *Thank Your Lucky Stars* (1943), *My Favorite Brunette* (1947), *Neptune's Daughter* (1949), and *Hans Christian Anderson* (1952).

Loesser's lyrics helped set the mood of the crime-riddled *The Last Warning* (1938), *The Gracie Allen Murder Case* (1939), *Johnny Apollo* (1940), *This Gun for Hire* (1942), *The Glass Key* (1942), *Dark City* (1950), *A Place in the Sun* (1951), and posthumously, *The Godfather: Part II* (1974), *Bugsy* (1991), *The Hand That Rocks the Cradle* (1992), and *Devil in a Blue Dress* (1995).

Over the years, Loesser was a major contributor to the television specials of Frank Sinatra, Dinah Shore, Lawrence Welk, Jack Benny, Judy Garland, Jack Paar, Perry Como, Carol Channing, Pearl Bailey, Dean Martin, Marlene Dietrich, Barbra Streisand, and to several Academy Award ceremonies. Altogether, Loesser was the lyricist of more than seven hundred songs.

A workaholic who slept only a few hours a day, Loesser returned to New York in 1948 to create the score for a musical based on the Brandon Thomas classic comedy *Charley's Aunt*, called *Where's Charley?* and starring Ray Bolger. It was a smash hit, and Loesser followed it with a string of milestone musicals: the streetwise *Guys and Dolls* (1950), the operatic *The Most Happy Fella* (1956), the fable *Greenwillow* (1960), and the satirical *How to Succeed in Business without Really Trying* (1961), which ran for 1,417 performances.

Loesser died of cancer at the age of fifty-nine in New York City. His daughter, Susan Loesser, wrote her father's biography, *A Most Remarkable*

Fella: Frank Loesser and the Guys and Dolls in His Life, published in 1993. In 2006, PBS released the documentary *Heart and Soul: The Life and Music of Frank Loesser.*

Awards and Honors: *Guys and Dolls* won the 1951 Tony Award and the New York Drama Critics Circle Award as Best Musical, and it is a top-ten selection in *The Best Plays of 1950–1951*. A 1992 Broadway revival won the Tony Award and the Drama Desk Award for Outstanding Revival. London productions in 1982 and 2005 won the Laurence Olivier Award for Outstanding Musical.

Damon Runyon's short-story collection *Guys and Dolls* (1931) was included by Howard Haycraft and Ellery Queen in their Definitive Library of Detective-Crime-Mystery Fiction. In 2008, the Library of America selected Runyon's story "The Eternal Blonde" for inclusion in its two-century retrospective of American crime writing.

In 1967, Runyon was inducted into the writer's wing of the Baseball Hall of Fame. Named in his honor, the Damon Runyon Stakes is a thoroughbred horse race run every December at Aqueduct Race Track.

In Pueblo, Colorado, the Damon Runyon Repertory Theatre is named in his honor. One block of West Forty-fifth Street (between Eighth and Ninth avenues) in Manhattan's Hell Kitchen is named Runyon's Way. The house where Runyon was born in Manhattan, Kansas, is listed on the National Register of Historic Places.

The Damon Runyon Cancer Research Foundation, established in his honor, sponsors an annual five-kilometer run at Yankee Stadium. The Denver Press Club hands out the Damon Runyon Award to a notable journalist each year.

Jo Swerling received an Academy Award nomination for his screenplay of *The Pride of the Yankees* (1942).

Abe Burrows and Frank Loesser shared a Pulitzer Prize for *How to Succeed in Business without Really Trying* (1961). Loesser was awarded a Grammy Award that year for Best Original Album of the show.

Frank Loesser garnered the Academy Award for his song "Baby, It's Cold Outside" from the MGM picture *Neptune's Daughter* (1949). He was nominated four more times for Best Music, Original Song, including "Thumbelina" from the film *Hans Christian Anderson* (1952). In 1999, the U.S. Postal Service honored Loesser by issuing a stamp bearing his likeness.

NOTES

1. Jimmy Breslin, *Damon Runyon* (New York: Ticknor & Fields, 1991), 298.
2. *New York Times*, November 25, 1950.
3. *New York Herald Tribune*, November 25, 1950.

4. *New York Post*, November 26, 1950.

5. *Daily Mirror*, November 25, 1950.

6. *New York World-Telegram*, November 25, 1950.

7. George Simon Kaufman, renowned playwright and director, teamed with Marc Connelly, Edna Ferber, Ring Lardner, Morrie Ryskin, and Moss Hart, among others, to pen, produce, and stage some of America's most enduring comedies: *Merton of the Movies* (1922), *Beggar on Horseback* (1924), *The Royal Family* (1927), *June Moon* (1929), *Once in a Lifetime* (1930), *Dinner at Eight* (1932), *Stage Door* (1936), *You Can't Take It with You* (1936), and *The Man Who Came to Dinner* (1939)—all transferred to the silver screen. Kaufman also directed the milestone Broadway production of John Steinbeck's *Of Mice and Men* (1937). However, long-forgotten is Kaufman's collaboration with Alexander Woollcott on *The Dark Tower*, a 1933 murder melodrama that boasts an astonishing denouement (a plot synopsis and production data of *The Dark Tower* can be found in Amnon Kabatchnik's *Blood on the Stage, 1925–1950*, pp. 364–366, published by Scarecrow Press in 2010).

8. *New York Times*, March 2, 2009.

9. *Los Angeles Times*, August 3, 2009.

Anastasia (1951)

Marcelle Maurette (France, 1903–1972)

Is she Princess Anastasia, daughter of the czar and only surviving Romanov, or is she a con artist, groomed to lay claim to the ten million pounds of sterling deposited in foreign banks at the time of the Bolshevik revolution?

The play *Anastasia* is triggered by the historical fact that in 1918 Czar Nicholas II and ten members of the imperial family were shot in a cellar by the Reds. Legend has it that the youngest of the czar's four daughters, Anastasia, was found alive but amnesiac beneath the pile of bodies and was spirited out of Russia by Siberian muzhiks. Surviving in a number of asylums until 1926, one day, while in Berlin, she regained her memory and proved that she was the Grand Duchess.

The play focuses on a devious scheme by an exiled Russian prince, Bounine, now a Berlin taxi driver, and his associates—Chernov, Petrovin, Varya, and Sergei—to present a waif they found wandering on the bank of a canal as the resurrected princess.

The girl, Anna, is ideal for their conspiracy—she is fragile, dazed, her memory checkered. "Things seem to come and go—in the mists," she says. Bounine coaches her methodically in the habits of the czar's court. Various witnesses are brought in to test Anna's authenticity—a sleigh driver, a charwoman, a doctor—and she convinces them all. Yet the confrontation between Anna and the Old Ikon—Maria Fedorovna, the czar's mother—is a different matter entirely.

The Dowager Empress is skeptical. "To be a princess is to be an actress," she declares icily. "A rescue from the very edge of the grave. Years of lost memory in an asylum. Excellent material for melodrama."

Anna admits that Bounine and his associates have planned a ruse to get their hands on millions of pounds, but she insists that the men mean nothing to her and that she is willing to give the money away. The Empress dismisses Anna's notion, calls her "an imposter," and turns to leave. But when Anna recollects a necklace of emeralds that the Empress favored, reminds the Empress that she used to call her "Malenkaia," and speaks of an incident on board the royal yacht during a raging storm, the grand-mother is swayed and takes Anna in her arms.

The identity riddle of Anastasia is solved, but the play contains one more twist. Dr. Michael Serensky, a lover of Anna from Bucharest, arrives on the scene. The reborn Anastasia gives up "wealth, beautiful surround-ings, a sleek luxurious existence" and leaves with the idealistic, penniless doctor "to find life—her real life." Bounine laments: "There are ten mil-lion pounds at stake. Ten million!" The Dowager Empress responds: "The royal tradition has beaten you, Bounine. I had a feeling that it would."

* * *

Anastasia was first produced at the Theatre Antoine in Paris in 1951. Two years later, the play was presented on British television, adapted from the French by Guy Bolton, a prolific Anglo-American playwright. Bolton's version was subsequently optioned by Laurence Olivier, who produced the play at the Theatre Royal, Windsor, on May 4, 1953, before moving it to West End's St. James's Theatre on August 5. Featuring An-thony Ireland as Bounine, Mary Kerridge as Anna, and Helen Haye as the Dowager Empress, *Anastasia* was received with acclaim and ran for 117 performances.[1]

Anastasia opened at New York's Lyceum Theatre on December 29, 1954, directed by Alan Schneider, starring Joseph Anthony (Bounine), Viveca Lindfors (Anna), and Eugenie Leontovich (the Dowager Empress). The morning-after critics were unanimous about the high artistic level of the production's staging, acting, and design, but they were divided about the merit of the play itself. "Whatever the truth may be of the Anastasia mystery, the drama about it is superb," stated Brooks Atkinson. "*Anastasia* provides an absorbing evening in the theatre and a transcendent one when Eugenie Leontovich and Viveca Lindfors play their great scene together."[2]

John Chapman agreed: "Nothing could be more welcome. Here is Theatre with a capital T—not art, perhaps, but one grand show filled with heroes and heroines and the skullduggery of a most enchanting vil-lain."[3] Also enthusiastic was William Hawkins: "There is an enthralling, romantic melodrama at the Lyceum, *Anastasia* by name. It is filled with suspense, love, joy, fear, and chicanery."[4]

Robert Coleman gave the play a negative review: "*Anastasia* has a gor-geous outer glitter, but, beneath, it is paper mâché. It sparkles like imita-tion gems and is as hollow as the phony operatic prop."[5] Criticism also came from John McClain, who asserted, "This is an unsolved mystery, and the authors can't be blamed for not solving it, but in the meantime it seems they might have invested it with more surprise, and certainly more charm."[6]

Richard Watts Jr. had a mixed reaction: "I don't think it is possible to take *Anastasia* very seriously as a play. It has an operatic manner about it that makes you wonder when the first aria is going to be sung. . . . But its old-fashioned appeal has a curiously enthralling quality in its sheer frankness."[7] Walter F. Kerr thought that "the situation is a juicy one, florid enough for really lush theatre, plausible enough for honest psychological speculation," but the reviewer felt that Bounine and his fellow scoundrels were "as close to clowns as any figures in a sentimental swashbuckler dare be."[8]

Anastasia ran for 272 performances. Eugenie Leontovich joined a road company of the play in 1955, with Dolly Haas as Anna and John Emery as Bounine. The following year, another touring enterprise cast Signe Hasso, Gale Sondergaard, and Stiano Braggiotti. Also in 1956, Dolores Del Rio, Lili Darvas, and Stephen Elliott starred in a Westport Country Playhouse production.

Kleines Theater im Zoo of Frankfurt, Germany, presented *Anastasia* in 1955, and London's Cambridge Theatre in 1976.

A musical version of the play called *Anya*, with book by George Abbott and Guy Bolton, and music and lyrics by Robert Wright and George Forrest (based on themes by Rachmaninoff), premiered at New York's Ziegfeld Theatre on November 29, 1965. Abbott also directed, navigating Constance Towers in the title role and Lillian Gish as the Dowager Empress, but the endeavor garnered a lukewarm reception and closed after sixteen performances.

In 1967, the choreographer Kenneth MacMillan created a one-act ballet, *Anastasia*, for Berlin's Deutsche Oper Ballet, with the ballerina Lynn Seymour in the lead. Four years later, MacMillan expanded the work for Britain's Royal Ballet, which performed it in New York in 1972. Set to music by Tchaikovsky, the full-length *Anastasia* was restaged by the Royal in 1996 featuring its principal dancer Viviana Durante, who was coached for the part by Ms. Seymour. Durante also performed Anastasia in New York in 1999, presented by American Ballet Theatre at the Metropolitan Opera House. Because the role is complex, Durante said she never tires of dancing Anastasia. "The more you dance it, the more you search inside yourself to relate to the woman," she said. "Her story is a struggle toward the truth, and I think that's what we're all looking for—a truth in life."[9]

* * *

On January 23, 1955, Eugenie Leontovich and Viveca Lindfors appeared on Ed Sullivan's weekly television program in the recognition scene from *Anastasia*. A ninety-minute adaptation, directed by George Schaeffer and starring Julie Harris (Anastasia), Lynn Fontanne (the Dowager Empress), and Charles D. Gray (Bounine), was aired by NBC's Hallmark Hall of Fame on March 17, 1967.

Two motion pictures about Anastasia were made in 1956: a German version, based on historical data, with Lilli Palmer in the lead; and a memorable U.S. CinemaScope version, scripted by Arthur Laurents from the Marcelle Maurette play, directed by Anatole Litvak. Ingrid Bergman and Helen Hayes sparkled in the face-to-face sequence, Bergman winning her second Oscar as Best Actress (the first one was for *Gaslight* in 1944). Yul Brynner played the role of the rogue Bounine, who at the end fails in his fraudulent plot, but—in a departure from the original drama—wins the heart of Anastasia and they elope together. Thirty years later, in 1986, a movie-made-for-television, *Anastasia: The Mystery of Anna*, written by James Goldman, featured Amy Irving and Olivia de Havilland, supported by a stellar cast: Rex Harrison, Omar Sharif, Claire Bloom, Elke Sommer, and Edward Fox.

The legend of the only surviving child of the Russian royal family was the topic of Twentieth Century–Fox's first animated feature, *Anastasia*, released in 1997 with the tagline "Discover the adventure behind the greatest mystery of our time." Meg Ryan provided the voice for the elusive princess; other main characters were read by Angela Lansbury, John Cusack, Kelsey Grammer, Christopher Lloyd, Hank Azaria, Bernadette Peters, and Kirsten Dunst. The movie's original score was nominated for an Academy Award and two of its songs were nominated for Golden Globe Awards. The box office receipts topped $50 million.

* * *

Royce Ryton, an English playwright, took a different approach to Anastasia lore under the title *I Am Who I Am* at the Arts Theatre, Cambridge, on August 15, 1978. It was subsequently revived as *The Anastasia File* on February 5, 1986, at the Derby Playhouse.

The setting of *The Anastasia File* is but a couple of chairs, a table, and a coat tree. The bare stage represents a variety of places—a hospital, an office, several private drawing rooms. There are four thespians—the Inspector; Mrs. Manahan (Anastasia); and an Actor and an Actress playing numerous roles (doctors, nurses, patients, friends, secretaries). The coat tree holds the various coats, hats, and other props that they use to impersonate the various characters.

It is Ryton's theory that after Mrs. Manahan proves beyond a doubt that she is Anastasia, her family members turn against her to protect their interest in the late czar's assets. In order to put their hands on bank deposits worth twenty million rubles, they now insist that Manahan is an imposter. Even Aunt Olga, her most sympathetic supporter, relates to the authorities that she "couldn't swear an oath" whether or not Mrs.

Manahan was her niece, and that she "cannot do anything without the full approval of the family." The Inspector ruefully tells Manahan that money changes everything. Beforehand, he says, it was merely a question of recognition. Will the family recognize Mrs. Manahan or won't they? Now it is a legal problem. The bank won't surrender a halfpenny of that money until they are certain who she is. If she is not Anastasia, then the royal princess is dead and the family will get the money.

Years pass. The Inspector continues the Anastasia investigation. By the end of the play, he concludes that the massacre of the czar and his family in Ekaterinburg, Siberia, had not been proven; it is just hearsay. The tragic incident is known only through gossip passed around secondhand.

Exasperated, the Inspector turns to the only bona fide witness, Mrs. Manahan, and is shocked to find out from her that there was no massacre at Ekaterinburg.

> MRS. MANAHAN: Not at Ekaterinburg. I cannot tell you the rest.
> INSPECTOR: But then no one will ever know the truth.
> MRS. MANAHAN: That's not quite right. I know the truth. And if I told you, you would not believe me. No, you would not believe me. (Curtain)

The startling resolution of *The Anastasia File* appealed to the *Brighton Evening Argus*: "And the ending will not disappoint any mystery play enthusiasts. It is a twist worthy of any thriller." The play was called by *The Guardian* "dramatic, poignant, beautifully plotted." The *Sunday Times* stated: "Ryton has written a piece of first-rate escapist entertainment which yet pulls at your mind afterwards like a puzzling dream."

The Anastasia enigma acquired a bizarre deviation in a curious B movie, *Secrets of the French Police* (1933), based on serialized stories by H. Ashton-Woolfe and directed by Edward Sutherland. The far-fetched plot has former Russian general Mollof, played by Gregory Rattoff, hypnotizing a beautiful girl (Rochelle Hudson) into believing that she is Anastasia. As part of his dastardly plot, Mollof kills the girl's acquaintances, one by one, by various methods, which included the ingenious device of projecting onto a gigantic screen an oncoming truck, causing a car to veer and tumble into a canyon. Frank Morgan enacts the sûreté inspector who solicits the girl's boyfriend, safecracker Leon (Gwili Andre), to solve the case. Much of the action takes place in Mollof's chateau, equipped with a Frankenstein-like laboratory. The police enter the premises through an underground passage for a last-minute rescue.

* * *

Madame Marcelle Maurette was born in Toulouse, France, in 1903. She began writing at the age of seventeen and quickly received prizes in poetry. She wrote newspaper articles, short stories, and biographies, but ever since her first schoolgirl play, *La Légende de Blanche-Neige*, Maurette's main allegiance was to the theatre. In 1937 she became the Comtesse de Decdelievre.

In addition to *Anastasia*, Maurette had one more play produced on Broadway: *Madame Capet*, adapted from the French by George Middleton and starring Eva Le Gallienne as Marie Antoinette (Cort Theatre, October 25, 1938—seven performances). Maurette's *Laurette*, depicting the adventures of a lady crook, played in Paris during the 1966–1967 season with Danielle Darrieux in the title role.

For the movies, Maurette wrote the screenplay of *L'Etrange Madame X* (*The Strange Madame X*), a 1951 drama in which Michèle Morgan appeared as a housemaid who marries an aristocrat but is in love with a common laborer.

* * *

The play-writing career of Guy Reginald Bolton (1884–1979) spanned five decades, from the 1910s to the 1960s. For musical comedies, he often teamed with witticist P. G. Wodehouse and the elite composers of the era—Jerome Kern, Emmerich Kalman, Victor Herbert, George Gershwin, Bert Kalmar, Harry Ruby, Sigmund Romberg, Cole Porter, and Richard Rodgers.

Among Bolton's Broadway producers were George M. Cohan, David Belasco, Florenz Ziegfeld, and the Messrs. Shubert. Ziegfeld's sumptuous production of *Rio Rita* (1927), billed as a romantic musical comedy, with book by Bolton and Fred Thompson, boasts thirty song-and-dance numbers hinged on a Texas Ranger's pursuit of a notorious Mexican bandit, whose real identity is unmasked at the final curtain.

Bolton and his associates gingerly applied criminal touches in other happy musicals. A Monte Carlo female cat burglar is caught by one of her rich victims, falls head-over-heels for him, and reforms in *The Hotel Mouse* (1922); a seasoned thief and his youthful accomplice crack the safes of the wealthy in *Sitting Pretty* (1924); a spiritualist medium and his assistant, participating in the making of a movie in Mexico, track down the kidnappers of a beautiful star in *The Ramblers* (1926); an aristocratic Englishman, the Duke, becomes a bootlegger, turning his yacht into a rumrunner in *Oh, Kay!* (1926); Public Enemy No. 13 escapes aboard an Atlantic liner masquerading as the Reverend Dr. Moon, toting his "putt-putt-putt" machine gun in a clarinet case, in *Anything Goes* (1934); the Lone Rider of a radio serial, believed to be a daring cowboy, is enlisted, in spite of himself, to round up a dangerous Mexican desperado in *Hold On to Your Hats* (1940); a German spy is uncovered in *Follow the Girls* (1944).

Detours into crime also prevail in Bolton's comedy *Adam and Eva* (1919), cowritten with George Middleton, in which the staging of a faked jewel robbery is meant to stifle vulturous relatives and fortune-hunting suitors; *The Nightcap* (1921), teamed with Max Marcin, deals with a mistaken-identity murder; the play *Ladies Should Listen* (1933), adapted from the French of Alfred Savoir, depicts schemes by swindlers to gain possession of an option on a Chilean nitrate concession; the drama *Golden Wings* (1941), penned by Bolton and William Jay, introduces a philandering RAF flight lieutenant accused of shooting down the plane of his triangular rival.

In London, Bolton joined forces with Patricia Wallace on the libretto of *The Sun Never Sets* (1938), a musical version of Edgar Wallace's West African yarns about Commissioner Sanders and the native Bosambo. Bolton also teamed with Gerard Fairlie on the stage adaptation of Wallace's 1922 thriller *Number Six* (1938).

Bolton penned a number of screenplays, one of which, *The Murder Man* (1935), follows an ace reporter (Spencer Tracy) as he investigates the homicide of a crooked businessman and pinpoints a suspect in the case. The suspect is convicted and sentenced to death, but at the eleventh hour the reporter confesses that he committed the deed in revenge for a financial scheme that took his father's life savings.

More than fifty plays sans mystery and mayhem by Bolton—comedies, farces, musicals, and an occasional drama—were produced in New York and London. Among his frequent collaborators were George Middleton, Fred Thompson, and P. G. Wodehouse.

Acting Edition: *Anastasia*—Samuel French, Inc. *Recognition Scene from Anastasia*—Samuel French, Inc. *The Anastasia File*—Samuel French, Inc.

Awards and Honors: Mme. Marcelle Maurette received the Prix du Cercle de Paris in 1934 for *La Bague au Doigt*; the Cours de la Pièce en un Acte de Société des Auteurs et Compositeurs for her play *Printemps* in 1937; France's Prix National de Litterature in 1939; and, in 1964, was made an Officier de la Legion d'Honneur Titre Exceptionnel for playwriting.

NOTES

1. "Helen Haye had been fifty-five years on the stage, when at the age of seventy-nine she scored what was probably the biggest triumph of her career in *Anastasia*," said *Theatre World Annual*, London, 1953, p. 44. During her long and distinguished career, Haye appeared in many Shakespearean plays, including the roles of the Queen in *Hamlet* and Olivia in *Twelfth Night*, as well as in plays by Ibsen, Shaw, and Eliot.

2. *New York Times*, December 30, 1954.

3. *Daily News*, December 30, 1954.

4. *New York World-Telegram*, December 30, 1954.
5. *Daily Mirror*, December 30, 1954.
6. *New York Journal-American*, December 30, 1954.
7. *New York Post*, December 30, 1954.
8. *New York Herald Tribune*, December 30, 1954.
9. *New York Times*, May 30, 1999.

Darkness at Noon (1951)

Sidney Kingsley (United States, 1906–1995)

Generally acknowledged as Arthur Koestler's masterpiece, the 1940 novel *Darkness at Noon* is based on the Stalinist purges of the 1930s. Playwright Sidney Kingsley had optioned to dramatize the novel in the summer of 1949 and set to work on the play at once. According to Michael Scammell in his biography *Koestler*, the relationship between Koestler and Kingsley soured when Koestler "worried that the American wasn't capturing the nuances of the way communists talked to one another," and Kingsley allegedly completed the script without consultations. Writes Scammell: "Eventually Koestler wrote to Kingsley to say he wanted 'no share in the artistic responsibility of this play. Whether it is good or bad, it must be your burden.'" The conflict led to a suit by Koestler, but in 1952 a New York Arbitration Tribunal faulted him "for manifesting a 'strange apathy' toward the play in its formative stage by refusing to comment on the text when Kingsley was working on it."[1]

In his play adaptation, Sidney Kingsley confined much of the grim action to a Russian prison. One of the inmates, a Communist commissar named Rubashov, a former member of the Central Committee, demands to know the specific accusations against him. Ivanoff, the compound's warden and a former comrade of Rubashov, wants the prisoner to admit that he had been part of a plot to assassinate "the leader" but broke with the rebels when he perceived their aim. A confession would result in a few years of jail instead of a death sentence.

Rubashov refuses to admit to the trumped-up charges. For weeks, Ivanoff tries to break his spirit. Gletkin, a young interrogator, suggests that the warden turn Rubashov over to him, so that he may strong-arm a confession. "I know how to handle these old timers," he grins.

In a solitary cell, where the only communication with other prisoners is through tapping on the granite walls, Rubashov recalls the experiences that led to his arrest. Via flashbacks we learn that his beloved Luba and several close friends have been sacrificed to the will of the party with his complicity.

Rubashov concludes that no ends can justify these means, and he chooses to go to his death. It is "the tragedy of an idealist who saw his ideals grow sour, of a mighty dream that devoured its dreamers," deemed Richard Watts Jr. in the *New York Post*. [2] "What Rubashov failed to see," theorized Robert Coleman in the *Daily Mirror*, "was that Marxist revolution inevitably consumes its more sensitive, intelligent and visionary leaders; that the goons, the strong-arm boys, take over and perpetuate a reign of terror." [3]

* * *

Following a successful tryout in Philadelphia's Forrest Theatre, *Darkness at Noon* reached Manhattan's Alvin Theatre on January 13, 1951. The majority of the critics showered the play with praise. "A vital and compelling drama . . . a singular tour de force," declared Howard Barnes. [4] "Mr. Kingsley's work, both as dramatist and director, is clean, strong and brilliant," stated John Chapman. [5] "This is a stark and uncompromising exposition of life behind the Iron Curtain and one leaves the theatre with a prayer of thanks for the fact that it can't happen here," asserted John McClain. [6]

Brooks Atkinson was among the naysayers: "*Darkness at Noon* works as a pungent, spectacular melodrama of a popular theme. But it lacks the wild, evil music that made Mr. Koestler's novel so piercing and so memorable." [7] Hobe Morrison vehemently attacked the play, predicting "slight box office prospects," [8] but *Darkness at Noon* held audiences spellbound for 186 performances. Not surprisingly, the most vitriolic review by Bob Lauter was published in the *New York Daily Worker*, the official newspaper of the U.S. Communist Party: "A rather dull and pompous spectacle, but a dangerous one. . . . *Darkness at Noon* is an attempt to justify the sniveling cowardice, the colossal duplicity, and the utter moral bankruptcy of Koestler's heroes: Trotskyite criminals." [9]

Detouring from Hollywood to New York, Claude Rains, in the role of Rubashov, won applause ("superb," "sensitive," "memorable") and a Tony Award as Best Actor. [10] Also complimented were Alexander Scourby as Ivanoff, Walter J. (later Jack) Palance as Gletkin, Kim Hunter as Luba, and Phillip Coolidge as Prisoner 402.

In 1955, NBCTV's Producers Showcase presented *Darkness at Noon* in an adaptation by Robert Alan Arthur, directed by Delbert Mann, starring Lee J. Cobb.

* * *

Born in New York City in 1906, Sidney Kingsley studied at Cornell University in Ithaca, New York, where he wrote one-act plays for the drama

club. He began his professional career as an actor with the Group Theatre. In 1933, the company produced his play *Men in White*, which deals
with professional and personal dilemmas in the life of hospital doctors.
The first in a series of plays by Kingsley that are committed to social or
ideological causes, *Men in White* won the Pulitzer Prize and was filmed in
1934. *Dead End* (1935, filmed 1937) pictures the slums of downtown New
York as a breeding ground for juvenile crime. *Ten Million Ghosts* (1936),
a multimedia venture incorporating motion pictures, lambasts the manufacturing of munitions. *The World We Make* (1939) is about a mentally un-
balanced girl, an escapee from a sanatorium, who manages to heal herself
when she finds love and realizes that she is needed. *The Patriots* (1943),
a Drama Critics Circle Award recipient, pits Thomas Jefferson against
Alexander Hamilton in search of democracy during America's infancy.

In the late 1940s, many of the members of the Group Theatre were
investigated by the House Un-American Activities Committee. Kingsley,
who had penned scripts in Hollywood, was among those blacklisted. He
returned to New York to write for the theatre. *Detective Story* (1949, filmed
1951) has a fanatical crime-fighting police detective use third-degree
tactics, electing to be judge as well as sleuth, and destroying himself in
the process. *Lunatics and Lovers* (1954) is a frenzied farce zipping through
a Broadway hotel suite, populated with crooks, cops, and ladies of the
night. *Night Life* (1962) presents a microcosm of society's ills unfolding in
a Manhattan key club.

* * *

Arthur Koestler was born in Budapest, Hungary, in 1905, to a well-to-
do Jewish family. In 1922, he enrolled at the University of Vienna, where
he became a passionate Zionist and, forsaking his education, left for Palestine. He lived for a while in a kibbutz and kept moving, penniless, to
Tel Aviv, Haifa, and Jerusalem. Koestler proved to be a versatile journalist, and in 1929 he returned to Europe as a correspondent for a German
newspaper. Two years later he joined the Communist Party but left it
after the Spanish Civil War and the Moscow purges of the 1930s. During
World War II, Koestler was among the first to denounce the Nazi regime,
was detained by the French authorities for several months as a resident
alien, joined the Foreign Legion, and eventually escaped to England. He
served in the British army and became a British subject in 1945. A life
fraught with danger behind him, from then on he dedicated himself to
writing and lecturing, basing his works of fiction on his own experiences,
often interweaving psychology with politics. His topics were varied and
sometimes controversial, including mysticism, telepathy, the paranor-
mal, euthanasia, Darwinism, the drug culture, capital punishment, and
nuclear disarmament. He also wrote scathingly about the Soviet Union

and published a four-volume autobiography. His only play, a fantasy called *Twilight Bar*, was produced by Jean Vilar's theatre in Paris in 1946.

Fluent in many languages, Koestler wrote his novel *The Gladiators* (1939), on the revolt of Spartacus against Rome, in Hungarian; *Darkness at Noon* (1940) in German; and *Arrival and Departure* (1943), about a neurotic Communist intellectual, in English. He penned articles in English and French, and sketches in Hebrew for Tel Aviv's satirical cabaret Ha-Matateh (The Broom).

Known as a ladies' man, Koestler had three wives and a fleeting affair with Simone de Beauvoir. In 1983, suffering from Parkinson's disease and leukemia, he took his own life by swallowing an overdose of drugs. His third wife, Cynthia, died with him in a double suicide.

Acting Edition: Samuel French, Inc.

Awards and Honors: New York Drama Critics Circle Award: Best Play of 1950–1951. A top-ten selection in *The Best Plays of 1950–1951* ("A strong and striking drama.")[11] Other Sidney Kingsley top-ten selections in the Best Plays yearbook: *Men in White* (1933–1934), *Dead End* (1935–1936), *The World We Make* (1939–1940), *The Patriots* (1942–1943), and *Detective Story* (1948–1949). Kingsley served as president of the Dramatists Guild of America and was elected to the Theatre Hall of Fame in 1983.

Arthur Koestler received the Sonning Prize from the University of Copenhagen and an honorary doctorate from Queen's University, Ontario, in 1968. He was appointed CBE (Commander of the Order of the British Empire) in 1972.

NOTES

1. Michael Scammell, *Koestler* (New York: Random House, 2009), 375, 401.

2. *New York Post*, January 15, 1951.

3. *Daily Mirror*, January 15, 1951.

4. *New York Herald Tribune*, January 15, 1951.

5. *Daily News*, January 15, 1951.

6. *New York Journal-American*, January 15, 1951.

7. *New York Times*, January 15, 1951.

8. Nina Couch, ed., *Sidney Kingsley: Five Prizewinning Plays* (Columbus: Ohio State University Press, 1995), xxxii.

9. Couch, *Sidney Kingsley*, xxxiii.

10. London-born William Claude Rains (1889–1967) appeared in West End plays and was a teacher at the Royal Academy of Dramatic Arts (where his best-known students were Laurence Olivier and John Gielgud), before migrating to America and becoming a renowned character actor. His silky, polished voice was a major asset for his "criminal" career in the movies: mad scientist Jack Griffin in *The Invisible Man* (1933); jealous, murderous lawyer Lee Gentry in *Crime without*

Passion (1934); villainous uncle, John Jasper, in *The Mystery of Edwin Drood* (1935); Maximus, a phony music-hall mind reader in *The Clairvoyant* (1935); malicious Marquis Don Luis in *Anthony Adverse* (1936); power-hungry Earl of Hertford in *The Prince and the Pauper* (1937); Prince John in *The Adventures of Robin Hood* (1938); Don Jose Alvarez de Cordoba in *The Sea Hawk* (1940); corrupt senator Joseph Harrison Payne in *Mr. Smith Goes to Washington* (1939); the title role in *The Phantom of the Opera* (1943); Alexander Sebastian, member of a Nazi spy ring, in *Notorious* (1946); sadistic composer Alexander Hollenius in *Deception* (1946); Victor Grandison, a radio personality with blood on his hands, in *The Unsuspected* (1947); Arthur Martinage, the Machiavellian director of a South African mining company, in *Rope of Sand* (1949); Frederic Lannington, a sneering spouse who is done with, in *Where Danger Lives* (1950); Skalder, the captain of a Nazi supply ship in *Sealed Cargo* (1951); Kees Popinga, an embezzling clerk, in *The Paris Express*, aka *The Man Who Watched Trains Go By* (1953); an international thief, Aristedes Mavros, in *Lisbon* (1956). Rains was nominated four times for Best Supporting Actor Oscar, notably for the role of Inspector Louis Renault in *Casablanca* (1942), but won none. Detailed information about Claude Rains' career on stage and in the cinema can be found in *Claude Rains: An Actor's Voice* by David J. Skal (Lexington: University Press of Kentucky, 2008).

11. John Chapman, ed., *The Best Plays of 1950–1951* (New York: Dodd, Mead, 1951), 72.

Billy Budd (1951)

Louis O. Coxe (United States)
and Robert Chapman (United States)

Herman Melville began his novella *Billy Budd* in 1888 and completed it three years later. It was published posthumously in 1924. In 1947, two novice playwrights, fans of Melville since their student days at Princeton, embarked upon a dramatization of the incidents aboard HMS *Indomitable* in August 1798. "We saw in *Billy Budd* a morality play . . . a story of good, evil, and the way the world takes such absolutes," say the authors. "We will look far before we find another theme of equal interest or vitality."[1]

The entire action of the play is set aboard the British naval vessel *Indomitable* during the Napoleonic war. The master-at-arms, John Claggart, a malevolent sadist, insists that Enoch Jackson, an ailing sailor, climb up the ladder to the mainmast—"Just where does this sickness strike you? In the guts? . . . This ship needs all hands." Jackson falls to his doom. Claggart lies to the ship's captain, Edward Fairfax Vere, about ordering Jackson aloft. The next target of the master-at-arms is William Budd, a handsome, guileless, newly recruited foretop man, described fondly by the sailors as "half man, half child" and nicknamed "Baby."

"I want Billy on report," says the master-at-arms. But to Claggart's chagrin, Billy distinguishes himself during an encounter with a French frigate and is promoted to captain of the foretop. Jenkins, a bitter sailor, stalks Claggart with a knife, but Billy intervenes. A scuffle ensues, during which Billy wrestles the weapon from Jenkins. Saved by Billy, Claggart simmers even more and tells Captain Vere that "the sweet, vicious lad is dangerous . . . spreading unrest and rebellion in the crew."

Vere, doubtful of the accusation, orders an inquiry. The master-at-arms denounces Billy to his face for "acting against this ship, this Service, and the King," threatening the officers with murder, and bent on urging other men to mutiny.

Shocked, Billy tries to respond, but an impediment in his speech yields only incoherent sounds. After agonized dumb gesturing and stammering, Billy hits Claggart, who staggers, falls, then lies still, dead.

A court-martial convenes at Captain Vere's quarters. The officers vote to render a self-defense acquittal, but Vere reminds them that since this is a wartime cruise, according to the Admiralty code, they have no choice but to put to death a man who fatally struck his superior officer. They sentence Billy to be hanged.

At dawn the men are called. When they realize that Billy is to be executed, they rush the deck, but Billy shouts out fervently, with no trace of a stutter, "God bless Captain Vere!" He climbs quickly up the ropes and out of sight. Officers and mates, in deep breathless consternation, stare overhead as the curtain falls.

* * *

Louis O. Coxe and Robert Chapman presented *Uniform of Flesh* at AN-TA's Experimental Theatre on January 29, 1949, for seven performances and kept embellishing the text from a "strict poetic form, austere in tone and structure," to one with "dramatic incident, contrapuntal conflict, and realistic speech."[2] They reverted to Melville's original title, and *Billy Budd* opened at the Biltmore Theatre on February 10, 1951, under the direction of Norris Houghton.

It garnered split verdicts. Brooks Atkinson wrote, "Louis O. Coxe and Robert Chapman have made a horrifyingly candid drama" out of Melville's novel, and their play "has size and depth as well as color and excitement."[3] William Hawkins found *Billy Budd* "a striking parable about the existence of right and wrong in humans . . . unquestionably memorable theatre."[4] Richard Watts Jr. acclaimed it as "a remarkably sensitive and absorbing play that has the courage to raise an austere moral problem and face it on a high emotional and intellectual level."[5] Naysayers included John McClain, who stated that *Billy Budd* was "only casually convincing at best."[6] Bert McCord believed that "the argument is too diffused and the language too confused to create or even maintain any suspense."[7] Robert Coleman opined, "The action runs aground on metaphysical shoals."[8] John Chapman scoffed, "I should have been emotionally enthralled. Instead, I thought Billy was silly."[9]

The all-male cast of *Billy Budd*, headed by Dennis King as Captain Vere, Torin Thatcher as Claggart, and Charles Nolte in the title role, and with Jeff Morrow, James Daly, and Lee Marvin lending support, was applauded by the reviewers. Nevertheless, the grim drama would have closed soon after its opening had it not been for a good Samaritan, producer-director Herman Shumlin, who had no stake in the production but paid for a display advertisement in the *New York Times* expressing his admiration for the artistry of *Billy Budd*. The cast members volunteered to take wage cuts, and *Billy Budd* chugged along for 105 performances, coming within two votes of winning the 1950–1951 New York Drama Critics

Circle Award as the best play of the season (Sidney Kingsley's *Darkness at Noon* got the prize with ten votes; *Billy Budd* was close with eight).

Billy Budd was revived by the Masques at off-Broadway's Rooftop Theatre on May 3, 1955. Arthur Gelb declared the play "compelling and absorbing."[10] Still another resuscitation of *Billy Budd* took place at the DeWitt Clinton Adult Center, the Bronx, on February 27, 1959, before embarking on a borough tour. The Trinity Square Repertory Company in Providence, Rhode Island, adapted the Melville novel under Adrian Hall's direction, on March 3, 1969. A musical version, entitled *Billy*, with book by Stephen Glassman, music and lyrics by Ron Dante and Gene Allen, opened—and closed—at New York's Billy Rose Theater on March 22, 1969. Most of the critics savaged the effort: "A book that reduces the Herman Melville story to the level of pulp adventure" (Clive Barnes);[11] "It is the clumsiest and most childish grasp for Melville that I have yet seen" (Martin Gottifried);[12] "It is a noisy and physically energetic musical drama in which the sound and fury signify virtually nothing" (Richard Watts Jr.).[13]

Retitled *The Good Soldier*, the Coxe-Chapman play was presented at the Lyric Theatre, in the Hammersmith borough of London, on April 4, 1956, for twenty-one performances. Philip Bond portrayed Billy Budd, Leo McKern enacted Claggart, and Sean Connery appeared as one of the sailors.

Music lovers may be comforted by Benjamin Britten's 1951 masterful opera *Billy Budd* (libretto by E. M. Forster and Eric Crozier). A phonograph record is available with tenor Peter Pears, Britten's life companion, in the role of Captain Vere. The Dramatic Publishing Company, Chicago, published in 1969 a one-act condensation of the Melville novella by James M. Salem.

Billy Budd was transformed effectively to the screen in 1962, produced/directed/cowritten by Peter Ustinov, who also starred as Captain Vere. Terence Stamp made his film debut in the title role, for which he was nominated for an Academy Award. Robert Ryan played Claggart.

* * *

Herman Melville (1819–1891), an old sea dog, began his literary career with *Typee* (1846), loosely based on his adventures in the Marquesas Islands, followed by *Omoo* (1847), *Mardi* (1849), *Redburn* (1849), and *White Jacket* (1850), all involving ocean travel. In 1851, Melville published *Moby Dick*, the great whaling epic. *Moby Dick* was dramatized by Howard Rodman (1955), Orson Welles (1955), Philip Hanson (1961), and Christopher Martin (1970).

Other stories by Melville that have been converted to the stage include 1853's *Bartleby*—with a score by William Flanagan, libretto by James Hinton

Jr. and Edward Albee (1961)—and 1855's *Benito Cereno*, adapted by poet Robert Lowell (1964).

Melville's output may be found in *Romances of Herman Melville* (1928), *The Shorter Novels of Herman Melville* (1928), *Collected Poems of Herman Melville* (1947), *The Complete Stories of Herman Melville* (1949), *The Portable Melville* (1952), and in two all-encompassing volumes printed by The Library of America (1982, 1983). *The Letters of Herman Melville* was published by Yale University Press in 1960. The two standard biographies are *Herman Melville* by Leon Howard and *The Melville Log* by Jay Leyda, both appearing in 1951. *Melville, His World and Work*, by Andrew Delbanco, was published in 2005.

Adapter Louis O. Coxe wrestled with the problem of good versus evil again in *Witchfinders* (Provincetown Playhouse, May 10, 1956), setting the scene during the Salem, Massachusetts, witch hunt.

Acting Edition: Dramatists Play Service.

Awards and Honors: A top-ten selection in *The Best Plays of 1950–1951*.

NOTES

1. Louis O. Coxe and Robert Chapman, *Billy Budd* (New York: Hill & Wang, 1962), 88–90.
2. Coxe and Chapman, *Billy Budd*, 90.
3. *New York Times*, February 12, 1951.
4. *New York World-Telegram*, February 12, 1951.
5. *New York Post*, February 12, 1951.
6. *New York Journal-American*, February 12, 1951.
7. *New York Herald Tribune*, February 12, 1951.
8. *Daily Mirror*, February 12, 1951.
9. *Daily News*, February 12, 1951.
10. *New York Times*, May 4, 1955.
11. *New York Times*, March 24, 1969.
12. *Women's Wear Daily*, March 24, 1969.
13. *New York Post*, March 24, 1969.

A Pin to See the Peepshow (1951)

F. Tennyson Jesse (England, 1888–1958)
and H. M. Harwood (England, 1874–1959)

F. Tennyson Jesse and H. M. Harwood, a husband-and-wife team on several lighthearted thrillers, were in a grimmer mood when adapting to the stage the former's 1934 novel, *A Pin to See the Peepshow*, a fictional account of a real-life love triangle murder. Twenty-eight-year-old Edith Thompson had a successful London millinery store when in 1921 she attached herself to Frederick Bywaters, a shipping clerk eight years her junior, and together they began planning the elimination of Thompson's stodgy, bossy husband, Percy. On the evening of October 3, 1922, Percy Thompson was found stabbed to death on a side road. The relationship between Edith and Frederick was soon established, damning correspondence between them was unearthed, and bloodstains were discovered on young Bywaters' jacket. The lovers were found guilty and on January 9, 1923, they were hung.[1]

The play version of *A Pin to See the Peepshow* unfolds in two acts divided into thirteen scenes. Beginning in spring 1916, we follow Julia Almond, whose youthful ambition is "going into a shop, a dress shop." Julia's querulous mother disapproves, but the nineteen-year-old girl interviews for the position of apprentice at a fashionable dress shop and is hired.

By the winter of 1920, Julia has been promoted, and she regularly travels to Paris as a buyer. To get away from her drab home, she marries a middle-aged neighbor—Herbert Starling, a commissioned officer in His Majesty's Forces. Soon Julia realizes that they have nothing in common, and the fact that her salary is larger than Starling's is a constant source of irritation and bickering.

Julia soon meets a young sailor, Leonard Carr, and they fall in love. When Starling is found dead in a town square, his skull fractured, the relationship between Leonard and Julia is revealed. Letters written by Julia, found on Leo's ship, expressing the wish that her husband be "out of the way," are deemed incriminating enough to charge them with murder. Both are found guilty and condemned to hang.

The last few prison scenes are harrowing: Julia screams, tries to climb the green wall of her cell. She grabs at it with her nails, nearly mad. A doctor injects her with morphine. Two matrons converse quietly, one of them expressing the playwright's maxim that Julia is conceivably innocent: "I like her. I don't think she's bad . . . She got caught up in something like people being caught up in machinery, and it was stronger than she was." Julia is eventually led to the scaffold, supported by the female prison officers and accompanied by the Governor, Doctor, Hangman, and Chaplain. The cell remains empty. After a pause, the sound of the trap dropping is heard. Blackout.

* * *

A Pin to See the Peepshow was refused a license by the Lord Chamberlain. So the play was shown privately in a London theatre club—in May of 1951—under the direction of Peter Cotes (who had staged the initial production of Agatha Christie's *The Mousetrap*). Two years later, Cotes mounted *A Pin to See the Peepshow* at New York's Playhouse, casting his wife, Joan Miller, in the role of Julia Almond, and Roger Moore (later Agent 007 in several James Bond movies) as Leonard Carr.

The critics were unhappy. "A tepid play," frowned Brooks Atkinson. "In tedious details it chronicles the misadventures of a highly romantic lady."[2] Richard Watts Jr. complained of "a slow-starting and decidedly commonplace murder play."[3] Robert Coleman scoffed at "a sordid, awkward and dull drama,"[4] while John Chapman pouted, "It may be that truth is duller than fiction, after all."[5]

Most reviewers admired Miller's "arsenal of technical equipment," but some believed that it was "rather a mannered performance," needing "occasional restraint." The show opened, and closed, on September 17, 1953.

A Pin to See the Peepshow was adapted to British television in 1973, shown in four episodes, with Francesca Annis as Julia Almond and John Duttin as Leonard Carr.

* * *

Fryn Tennyson Jesse, the daughter of a clergyman and a great-niece of the poet laureate Alfred, Lord Tennyson, began her career as a painter and book illustrator but shifted to writing as a reporter and book reviewer for *The Times* of London. During World War I, she was a correspondent for the British Ministry of Information.

Jesse once wrote, "My chief passion is murder"—a zeal manifested in her nonfiction studies, short stories, novels, and plays. In *Murder and Its Motives* (1924, revised 1958), Jesse asserts, "Most criminals are great egoists and inordinately vain, but the two qualities are found in excess in murderers." Jesse edited several volumes in the *Notable British Trials* series, including the cases of Madeleine Smith, Timothy John Evans, and John Reginald Halliday Christie, all published in 1957. Jesse's collection, *The Solange Stories* (1931), featured a French girl, the daughter of a police scientist, who is "gifted by nature with an extra spiritual sense that warned her of evil."

In collaboration with her husband, playwright Harold Marsh Harwood (1874–1959), Jesse created several crime-oriented dramas. *The Black Mask*, a one-act play, is a three-character affair, unfolding in the kitchen of James Glasson's house in a small Cornish village. Years ago, a nearby mine had collapsed, leaving James with a scarred face and one eye. Since then he has been covering his warped features with a straight black mask. Even his wife Vashti—fierce-eyed and black-haired—does not have the nerve to look at his countenance.

When James pretends to go to the village for medicine, William Strick, Vashti's "'ansome lover" enters, and she is soon cuddled in his arms. James suddenly returns, Vashti escapes to the upstairs bedroom, and, after a fierce struggle, James plunges a knife into William's back. Vashti believes that it is her Willie climbing up the dark stairs. As James reaches the door, he pulls his mask off and enters the bedroom. There is a moment's silence, and then wild screams of terror, rising in intensity, as the curtain falls.

The Black Mask was presented by the Princess Players of New York as part of their seasonal repertoire, premiering September 27, 1913. The play opened at London's Garrick Theatre on August 9, 1915, for nine performances, and was revived on the West End in 1919, 1933, and 1936.

* * *

Jesse and Harwood's *How to be Healthy though Married* is jestly dedicated to "Each Other with a Pinch of $NaHCO_3$." But the chemical used by the play's main character, the French Madame Blanchard—"a brilliant, tempestuous creature of twenty-nine"—in an attempt to dispose of her elderly husband, Jacques, is the potent arsenic. Or so she thought. For weeks Claire Blanchard has been mixing Jacques's medicine with doses of white powder mailed to her clandestinely by her young lover, Leon Mercier. Upon Jacques's demise, the widow will inherit his vast estate and be free to unite openly with Leon.

Alas, Monsieur Deschanel, the Procureur de la Republique, discovers the scheme through a mix-up at the post office and summons the lovers to his office. When Deschanel warns them, "In France the *attempt* to murder is a crime punishable by death," Claire crumples, but Leon bursts out laughing. "Arsenic nothing!" he titters. "All I sent her was bicarbonate of soda. . . . All the time she imagines the poor man is fading away before her eyes, whereas, as a matter of fact, he never was so well in his life. It's cured his indigestion. He eats like a horse, and is fit as a fiddle."

An analysis of the powder verifies Leon's contention. He lightly explains that he has never intended "to put my head under the guillotine." Claire, her vanity wounded, is enraged. "Come, Madame," says Deschanel. "Be thankful you have been prevented from committing a terrible crime." But Claire is inconsolable: "Crime—crime? What crime was I committing, compared with what this man has done?—Killing my heart and soul! Making a mockery of me! He's a criminal! A miserable coward who hadn't the courage to kill like a man."

Deschanel will allow Claire to go back to her husband, but cautions: "This time there must be no more lovers." Claire, still hurt, assures the prosecutor, "After this I shall never *speak* to a man again. I *hate* them—*hate* them!" She returns home and when we next see her, eighteen months later, "she has lost her look of smoldering enmity towards the world, and indeed seems the most prosperous and content of women."

How to Be Healthy though Married opened at London's Strand Theatre on May 25, 1930, for a single performance.

Non-criminous plays by Jesse and Harwood include *Billeted* (1919), in which, during World War I, a fifty-year-old army colonel, James Preedy, and half-his-age Penelope Moon discover that age does not matter when the heart flutters; *Quarantine* (1924), a romantic comedy about an Englishman, Tony Blunt, who finds his true love during a week's quarantine in the Bahamas; and *The Pelican* (1926), a sentimental drama about an Englishwoman, Wanda Heriot, who sacrifices her happiness for the sake of her illegitimate son.

Harold Marsh Harwood was a prolific playwright and sought-after director. From 1919 to 1930 he leased the Ambassadors Theatre, a small playhouse in West Street, London. He teamed with Robert Gore-Browne, the author of several highly regarded detective novels, on the plays *Cynara* (1930), a drama of infidelity with tragic consequences, and *King, Queen, Knave* (1932), an adventure melodrama encompassing monarchy, revolution, patriotism, and betrayal in an imaginary European country, the Republic of Carmania. Harwood collaborated on the screenplay of *Queen Christina* (1933), a historical drama starring Greta Garbo as the Swedish queen who abdicated for love.

Awards and Honors: F. Tennyson Jesse's *The Solange Stories* (1931) was selected by Ellery Queen for inclusion in *Queen's Forum: A History of the Detective-Crime Story as Revealed in the 106 Most Important Books Published in the Field since 1845.*

NOTES

1. Francis Iles's *As for the Woman* (1939) is also a fictional account of the Thompson-Bywaters case. The plays *Spellbound* (1927) by Frank Vosper and *Leave Her to Heaven* (1940) by John Van Druten are based on the same real-life murder.
2. *New York Times*, September 18, 1953.
3. *New York Post*, September 18, 1953.
4. *Daily Mirror*, September 18, 1953.
5. *Daily News*, September 18, 1953.

Stalag 17 (1951)

Donald Bevan (United States, 1920–) and Edmund Trzcinski (United States, 1921–1996)

Based on their own World War II experiences as U.S. pilots, who after being shot down spent two years in a Nazi prison camp, novice playwrights Donald Bevan and Edmund Trzcinski penned an authentic comedy-melodrama that won accolades from the New York critics. It opened at Broadway's Forty-eighth Street Theatre on May 8, 1951, ran for 472 performances, and was promptly sold to the movies.

The barracks of Stalag 17, located somewhere in Germany, are populated by various American characters, who while away their imprisonment by horsing around, wisecracking, and exchanging latrine jokes. Under the lighthearted surface there is tension between captives and captors, constant plans for escape, and a struggle for survival amid harrowing living conditions.

Early in the proceedings it is evident that something is terribly wrong at Stalag 17. During a chilly December morning, the POWs are ordered outside. Two comrades have been shot while trying to bolt. A German guard, Corporal Shultz, enters stealthily and hides a note behind a loose brick under the stove.

The compound's leader, Herman Hoffman ("Hoffy"), and the security chief, Eddie Price, call a meeting. Hoffy believes that there is a German spy in the barracks. Every tunnel they have ever dug has been discovered; of the three radios in camp, the guards confiscated two; and now Johnson and Manfredi have fallen into a trap.

The suspicion falls on Sefton, a sullen, practical man who trades goods with the guards and whose chief goal has always been to endure in a dog-eat-dog world.

A new crop of prisoners arrives on the scene. Among them is James Schyler Dunbar, a blue-blood Bostonian who relates to the men that prior to his capture he burnt up a German freight train. Sefton mocks him as a "glamour boy" and "frigging pansy," prompting a fistfight. When the camp's commander orders the guards to take Dunbar out for interrogation, the men are certain that Sefton is the spy. At night, they converge on his bunk and badly beat him.

Ex-communicated as a "slimy creep" and a "crummy Kraut-lover," Sefton undertakes to unmask the mole. In the second act, he witnesses Shultz placing a note behind the loose brick, and it is the barracks' security chief, Price, who secretly retrieves the message, reads it, and throws it into the stove. (In the ensuing motion picture version, the identity of the spy is reserved to the end, which makes for a more suspenseful climax.)

The men of Stalag 17 plan to help Dunbar escape. Sefton proves his true mettle when he volunteers to lead Dunbar across the barbed wires. Prior to their departure, Sefton exposes Price. The men throw the informer out the door to be machine-gunned by the guards.

* * *

"One of the admirable things about *Stalag 17*, the play dealing with American war prisoners in a German prison camp," wrote critic Richard Watts Jr., "is that there is no pretense about it. Its authors, Donald Bevan and Edmund Trzcinski, who are writing from personal experience, haven't bothered with any deep or tragic psychological probing into the hearts and minds of men in war, but have confined themselves to telling a good, melodramatic story about an escape and a secret traitor in the camp, and a forthright, exciting melodrama they make of it too."[1]

Watts's colleagues echoed his sentiments: "*Stalag 17* is a stinging melodrama about something of crucial importance to the characters caught in it. Mr. Bevan and Mr. Trzcinski have made a turbulent and gusty play out of a haunting experience," stated Brooks Atkinson.[2] "Type—Comedy melodrama; Topic—Spies; I find it—Thrilling. . . . The play is beautifully staged by its producer Jose Ferrer, so that every ounce of its excitement and compelling bewilderment comes to the surface," gushed William Hawkins.[3] "*Stalag 17* is a boisterous thriller which keeps moving along its narrow course, and it is enjoyable as such," chirped Otis L. Guernsey Jr.[4] "The new arrival is a salty and authentic comedy-melodrama," lauded Robert Coleman.[5]

Only John Chapman of the *Daily News* had some reservations: "It's a well-made documentary, with a lot of rough humor and a certain amount of excitement, and it is well played for type by a company of young men. But I cannot say that it is a compelling piece of theatre. Interesting is the word for it—and 'interesting' is not a very interesting word."[6]

Featuring Martin Landau, *Stalag 17* had a successful national road tour in the United States, but failed to ignite London, where it opened at the Princess Theatre on April 4, 1953, and lasted only eleven performances. The play is rarely revived, as the large cast makes it cumbersome and expensive. The Lawton Community Theatre in Lawton, Oklahoma, presented *Stalag 17* during the 1955–1956 season, as did the Arena Players Repertory Theatre in East Farmingdale, New York, in 1990; Harvest Productions of Chicago, Illinois, in 1997; and the Mariemont Players in Cincinnati, Ohio, in 2009. Billy Wilder cowrote with Edwin Blum the 1953 movie version, and he directed it with an effective fusion of gritty drama and low-brow comedy. Robert Strauss and Harvey Lembeck were recruited from the Broadway show to repeat their clownish characterizations as two of the POWs; William Holden won a Best Actor Oscar as the cynical Sefton; Peter Graves enacted bad-guy Price. Otto Preminger and Sig Rumann played, to the hilt, the Nazi camp commander and Corporal Shultz.

Stalag 17 was the inspiration for CBS's long-running television sitcom *Hogan's Heroes* (1965–1971).

* * *

Edmund Trzcinski was born in the Bronx, New York, in 1921. His sole contribution to Broadway was *Stalag 17*. Donald Bevan wrote the episode *Deathline Korea* for television's Producers' Showcase in 1955, and he is perhaps best known for his celebrity caricatures, displayed on the walls of Sardi's Restaurant in the heart of the theatre district in Manhattan.

Acting Edition: Dramatists Play Service.

NOTES

1. *New York Post*, May 9, 1951.
2. *New York Times*, May 9, 1951.
3. *New York World-Telegram*, May 9, 1951.
4. *New York Herald Tribune*, May 9, 1951.
5. *Daily Mirror*, May 9, 1951.
6. *Daily News*, May 9, 1951.

The Hollow (1951)

Agatha Christie (England, 1890–1976)

"*The Hollow* was a book I always thought I had ruined by the introduction of Poirot," wrote Agatha Christie in her autobiography. "He was all wrong there. He did his stuff all right, but how much better, I kept thinking, would the book have been without him. So when I came to sketch the play, out went Poirot."[1]

The action of the play takes place in the garden room of Sir Henry Angkatell's country house, The Hollow, located on the outskirts of London. During a weekend party, a friend of the family, Dr. John Christow—a successful, pompous, womanizing surgeon—is found shot to death, with his wife Gerda—plain, timid, downtrodden—standing over the body, holding a French dueling pistol. She claims to have found her husband there, dead already.

Inspector Colquhoun's dogged investigation flushes out several foul-play candidates among the Angkatells: Henrietta, an attractive sculptress, mistress of the victim; Edward, tall, bookish, sensitive, in love with Henrietta; and Midge, the neatly dressed poor relation, enamored with Edward. They all play a role in a whirlwind of romance and jealousy.

And there is Veronica Craye, the famous, temperamental actress, a former lover of John Christow. Veronica rents a cottage across the way. She was heard threatening that if she can't have John, nobody can.

The denouement is tense: Gerda, the wife, is sitting on a sofa, crying softly. Henrietta moves behind her and puts her strong hands on Gerda's shoulders, near the neck, and pulls her back to an upright position. So, is Henrietta the villain of the piece, and is she contemplating another murder?

Henrietta says quietly: "There's just one thing, Gerda. What did you do with the holster?" And in an intake of breath we realize that the killer is Gerda, whom we mistakenly dismissed as a suspect when early in the proceedings a nincompoopish police sergeant said, "I think it's the wife."

Comic relief is provided by the beautifully etched character of the fidgety, feather-brained hostess, Lady Angkatell, who declares that "the worst of murder is it does upset the servants so."

* * *

Christie adapted *The Hollow* from her highly regarded 1946 novel. There were grave reservations about the validity of the dramatization, but novice producer Peter Saunders and first-time director Hubert Gregg undertook the assignment. Gregg recounts that upon his initial reading of the manuscript, he thought it "abysmal. The dialogue was unspeakable. . . . The characters were caricatures." In his book *Agatha Christie and All That Mousetrap*, Gregg tells of a love-hate relationship that developed between him and the author throughout the rehearsal process, and how step-by-step he managed to convince her of the necessary changes needed to make *The Hollow* stageworthy.[2]

The Hollow opened at London's Fortune Theatre on June 7, 1951, and subsequently transferred to the Ambassadors Theatre. Jeanne De Casalis as Lady Angkatell and Joan Newell as Gerda Christow were embraced by critics. The *Times* of London found act I's exposition dull, "but once the fatal shot has been fired and the police arrive to ask questions, there can be nothing but admiration for the impudent skill with which Mrs. Christie directs suspense first this way, then that, and yet contrives to let certainty arrive in due course with an effect of genuine surprise."[3]

The Hollow had a run of 376 performances and became a popular fixture at repertory, stock, and community theatres. In the United States, Pulse Ensemble Theatre of New York presented *The Hollow* during the 1995–1996 season.

* * *

Born in Torquay, Devon, Agatha Mary Clarissa Miller (1890–1976) was raised reading detective stories. Gaston Leroux's *The Mystery of the Yellow Room*, a sealed-room classic; Robert Barr's *The Triumphs of Eugene Valmont*, a pioneering volume of humorous sleuthing; and Marie Belloc Lowndes' creation of French investigator Hercules Popeau were among her treasured literary influences. During World War I, Agatha married Archibald Christie, a dashing colonel in the Royal Flying Corps. While working in the Volunteer Aid Detachment Hospital, she gained knowledge of drugs and poisons, information that came in handy later in her books.

Agatha had not planned to be a writer. In fact, Agatha's first novel was written as a response to a challenge by her sister, Madge. *The Mysterious Affair at Styles* (1920) introduced Hercule Poirot, the diminutive Belgian detective who was destined to rival the popularity of Sherlock Holmes.

In her second novel, *The Secret Adversary* (1922), Christie plotted an adventure tale in which the leading characters, Prudence Cowley, known to her friends as Tuppence, and Thomas Beresford, her beau, pursue an elusive man who plots to overthrow the British government.[4] Successive novels in the early 1920s introduced the recurring characters of Colonel Race and Superintendent Battle of Scotland Yard. In 1926 came the tour de force *The Murder of Roger Ackroyd*, which made Christie a household name.

Following the publication of *The Murder of Roger Ackroyd*, Agatha herself became a headline mystery. On December 3, 1926, the celebrated author did not return home. Her frost-covered car, a green Morris, was found alongside a dirt road with the lights still on. On the seat were a brown fur coat and a small dressing case that had burst open, scattering clothing and some papers, including an out-of-date driver's license in her name. Agatha's disappearance caused a sensation. Was she the victim of foul play? Did she commit suicide? Or was it merely an audacious publicity stunt? A nationwide search was launched immediately.

Author Gwyn Robyns, in *The Mystery of Agatha Christie* (1978), asserts that in order to understand the circumstances of the bizarre case it is important to learn that "it had been a traumatic year for Agatha Christie." Her mother had died after a severe illness, and her marriage had deteriorated.

Kathleen Tynan, in *Agatha* (1978), provides an imaginary scenario about the author's disappearance: preoccupied with the painful realization that she was losing her husband to a beautiful rival, the shy, sensitive author withdraws into herself—and drops out of sight. Tynan's speculative narrative attempts to penetrate the psyche of a woman betrayed. How will this accomplished mystery writer, plotter of intrigue and creator of suspenseful incidents, react? Will she remain passive, or will she direct her talents toward sinister revenge?[5]

Agatha returned home after eleven days, claiming temporary amnesia. Two years later the Christies were divorced. In 1930, Agatha Christie married Max Mallowan, an archaeologist. By accompanying him on digs to the Middle East, Agatha discovered exotic source material for such books as *Murder in Mesopotamia* (1936), *Death on the Nile* (1937), *Appointment with Death* (1938), *Death Comes as the End* (1945), and *They Came to Baghdad* (1951).

It is widely perceived that only the Bible and the plays of Shakespeare have sold more copies than Agatha Christie's murder mysteries. "In a career that spanned over half a century," writes popular-culture czar Peter Haining, "she published in all 78 crime novels, 19 plays (of which seven are adaptations of her books), six romantic novels under the pen-name Mary Westmacott, and four non-fiction titles. . . . It is true to say that Agatha Christie is the most widely published writer of any time and in any language, and the royalties deriving from her books alone now run in excess of two million pounds every year."[6] Haining calls attention to the energetic productivity and high achievements of Dame Christie in the world of entertainment—on stage, in films, and on radio and television: "This contribution amounts to at least 20 major theatrical productions on both sides of the Atlantic (not to mention a vast number of touring productions and repertory performances); two dozen films for the cinema; in excess of 50 radio programs; and an even larger number of individual stories and serials for both British and American television."[7]

Agatha Christie died peacefully at her home in Wallingford, Berkshire, on January 12, 1976, at age eighty-five.

Acting Edition: Samuel French, Inc. *The Hollow* is also included in *The Mousetrap and Other Plays* by Agatha Christie (New York: Dodd, Mead, 1978; Harper Paperbacks, 1993).

Awards and Honors: Agatha Christie became a Fellow, Royal Society of Literature, in 1950. She was awarded the C.B.E. (Commander, Order of the British Empire) in 1956, and was made a D.B.E. (Dame Commander, Order of the British Empire) in 1971. She was president of England's Detection Club (1954) and recipient of the Mystery Writers of America Grand Master Award (1955). DLitt, University of Exeter, 1961.

NOTES

1. Agatha Christie, *An Autobiography* (London: Collins, 1977), 473.

2. Following the modest beginning of *The Hollow*, Peter Saunders became producer of Agatha Christie's megahit *The Mousetrap* (1952). He continued with Christie's *Witness for the Prosecution* (1953), *Towards Zero* (1956), *Verdict* (1958), *The Unexpected Guest* (1958), *Go Back to Murder* (1960), and *Rule of Three* (1962)—the last three directed by Hubert Gregg. Saunders also produced two posthumous adaptations of Christie's novels, *A Murder Is Announced* (1977) and *Cards on the Table* (1981), both by Leslie Darbon.

3. *Times* of London, June 8, 1951.

4. Tuppence and Tommy will return in Christie's novels *Partners in Crime* (1929), *N or M?* (1941), *By the Pricking of My Thumbs* (1968), and *The Postern of Fate* (1973).

5. *Agatha* was filmed by director Michael Apted in 1979, featuring Vanessa Redgrave in the title role; Timothy Dalton as the fickle husband; and Dustin Hoffman as an American reporter, Wally Stanton, who tracks Agatha down to a seaside hotel.

6. Peter Haining, *Agatha Christie: Murder in Four Acts* (London: Virgin Books, 1990), 11.

7. Haining, *Agatha Christie*, 11–12.

Remains to Be Seen (1951)

Howard Lindsay (United States, 1889–1968) and Russel Crouse (United States, 1893–1966)

Howard Lindsay and Russel Crouse, producers and play-doctors of 1941's *Arsenic and Old Lace*, came back to the genre of macabre comedy ten years later as cowriters of *Remains to Be Seen*, to once again combine suspense elements with rollicking shenanigans.

The play is set in the living room of Travis Revercombe's 412 Park Avenue apartment. When the curtain rises, Revercombe is already dead, his body lying on the floor of an adjacent bedroom. A uniformed policeman, Edward Miller, is leisurely scrutinizing an oil painting of the deceased above the mantelpiece, the collection of African masks on the wall, and the pornography stacked in the tall bookcase. Bored with the art, he turns on TV to watch a boxing match in Madison Square Garden.

Revercombe's distinguished-looking attorney, Benjamin Goodman, and his physician, Dr. Charles Gresham, whose offices are in the same building, arrive on the scene. The doctor tells the lawyer that Revercombe was a diabetic and had a weak heart.

Waldo Walton, the young apartment house manager, lets himself in with a passkey and reports that he found Revercombe dead in the bedroom and called the police. The medical examiner, Dr. Chester Delapp, enters, showing more interest in the fight on television than in the corpse. Dr. Gresham says that he had warned Revercombe not to take more than twenty-five units of insulin a day. The medical examiner signs the death certificate—"natural causes"—and rushes out to watch the final rounds of the boxing match at Toots Shor's restaurant. Officer Miller, attracted to an illustrated pornographic novel in red binding, attempts to sneak it out but Benjamin Goodman sharply orders him to put the book back. A running gag has Miller using various methods to secure the book—including lassoing it with a string—only to be caught, again and again, by the sharp-eyed lawyer.

An undertaker arrives and goes into the bedroom to measure Revercombe's body. After a moment the undertaker comes rushing out, picks

41

up the telephone, dials a number, and yells into the phone that there's a carving knife sticking in the chest of the deceased!

The second scene introduces a team of bungling police detectives. They all show a keen interest in the erotic book collection and put a jazz record on the phonograph. The Japanese cook, Hideo Hayakawa, enters and raises hell about his missing kitchen carving knife. Summoned again, the medical examiner concludes that "this man was dead long before the knife was stuck into him." Detective Morris Rosenberg is relieved; he "can't work out a sweat" over someone stabbing a dead body.

Enter Jody Revere, Revercombe's niece. An attractive girl in her mid-twenties, Jody is a singer with Pee Wee Baker's band. Jody was summoned by Benjamin Goodman from Lawrence, Kansas, and is very disappointed to find out that the lawyer is not Benny Goodman, the bandleader. Goodman tells Jody that her uncle changed his will a week prior to his death and made her the sole beneficiary of his estate. Jody wants no part of the money. She hated her uncle for refusing to come to the aid of her ill father unless her mother would sleep with him.

When Jody is left alone in the apartment, she prepares to go to sleep. She does not see that behind her a section of the bookcase noiselessly swings open, disclosing a passageway. A handsome woman in a chiffon negligee appears, evidently surprised to see Jody. The woman makes a move toward Jody as if to spring at her, but at this second the doorbell rings. Jody puts on a nightgown and leaves for the front door. The woman draws back through the passageway, and the bookcase swings back into place.

As the drama continues, both Waldo Walton and Benjamin Goodman fall in love with Jody. Walton demonstrates to Jody his proficiency with the drums, and she promises to introduce him to Pee Wee Baker. Goodman manages to get her an appointment with Benny Goodman. Jody finds Walton's naïveté appealing, and he prevails.

It turns out that Hideo Hayakawa was the person who pierced the heart of dead man Revercombe. The Japanese cook was not satisfied with the heart-failure verdict and found a way to instigate an investigation of his employer's death.

The woman who appeared in the hidden passageway is discovered to be Valeska Chauvel, the executive secretary of the organization Unalingua—which advocates one universal language as the "hope of mankind for world peace"—and which upon Jody's refusal will inherit the estate. "What's the matter with English?" objects Jody. She decides to accept the money and donate it to the welfare fund of AGVA, the American Guild of Variety Artists. Valeska warns that she will contest Revercombe's will.

Late at night, Jody is awakened by a sound in the dark. She screams and turns on the light. It is policeman Miller, treading softly for the red-bound book. Jody's nerves are shattered, so Walton calls Dr. Gresham.

As if to help her, Gresham takes hold of the panels of Jody's kimono and knots them around her arms, tying her to the chair. He then admits to killing Jody's uncle with a double dose of insulin. The motive? He is in love with Valeska Chauvel, who got involved with Travis Revercombe and couldn't break away from him without giving up the means to keep her foundation alive. Getting rid of Revercombe meant eliminating a rival and saving Valeska's project. Now that Jody is in the way, she has to die too. Gresham pours hot water into a bottle of pills, shakes it, and fills a hypodermic syringe. Jody is saved by the timely arrival of Waldo, who knocks Dr. Gresham off balance and forces him to flee.

In the climactic sequence of the play, Dr. Gresham enters through the bookcase, a gun in hand. Valeska stands between him and Jody and pleads for him to lay off his weapon. Officer Miller reaches for his gun and Gresham shoots him. The bullet hits the red-bound book Miller hid under his coat. The doctor escapes through the foyer. A shot is heard off stage. Gresham has killed himself.

Jody decides to divide Revercombe's inheritance between Unalingua and AGVA. Walton resigns from his position as the building's manager. He and Jody plan to get married and join Pee Wee Baker's band.

* * *

Staged by Bretaign Windust, *Remains to Be Seen* opened at the Morosco Theatre, New York, on October 3, 1951. The cast included Janis Paige as Jody Revere, former child-star Jackie Cooper as Waldo Walton, playwright Howard Lindsay as Dr. Benjamin Goodman, and Warner Anderson as Dr. Charles Gresham. Most of the reviewers were supportive. William Hawkins wrote, "The play has all the traditional wonders of mysteries, the sliding panels, dimmed lights, screams and hair-breadth escapes, but it is always foremost a comedy, as laughter aquaplanes over shocks. . . . [It] is destined for a long, happy life at the Morosco."[1] Richard Watts Jr. welcomed "a shrewd and adroit show, attractively acted, expertly directed, and filled with all the pleasant tricks of the mystery melodrama, the music hall and the spoof of the old-time thriller."[2]

On the other hand, Bert McCord disparaged "a mystery angle" that "falls flat for the most part" and "long and tedious stretches of cross-examination by a squad of Mack Sennett cops."[3] John Chapman regretted that the authors "have found it necessary to squander many valuable minutes in setting up all the props for a farce—the characters, the motives and the plot mechanism—when a really first-class farce should tee off at the rise of the curtain."[4]

Remains to Be Seen ran for 199 performances. The play reached Her Majesty's Theatre in London on December 6, 1952, with Diana Dors as Jody Revere, but lasted only seven performances. A year later, MGM transferred

Remains to Be Seen to the screen starring June Allyson (Jody Revere) and Van Johnson (name changed to Waldo Williams), supported by Louis Calhern (Benjamin Goodman), Angela Lansbury (Valeska Chauvel), and John Beal (name changed to Dr. Glenson).

* * *

Born in Waterford, New York, Howard Lindsay attended Harvard University to prepare for the ministry but soon became more interested in the stage and left Harvard for the American Academy of Dramatic Arts in New York. He spent four years with road companies, played in vaudeville, worked as an extra in Hollywood, and joined Margaret Anglin's company as a background actor and assistant stage manager.

After World War I, in which Lindsay served as a corporal in the infantry, he appeared on Broadway and branched out into writing, directing, and producing. He directed Fred Astaire in *Gay Divorcee*, collaborated with Damon Runyon on the gangster comedy *A Slight Case of Murder*, and launched his partnership with Russel Crouse.

Russel Crouse hailed from Findlay, Ohio. He began his writing career as a reporter at Cincinnati, Kansas City, and New York newspapers, and he published several books and penned two musical comedies before teaming with Lindsay on a rewrite of the libretto of *Anything Goes* in 1934. The pair continued their immensely successful collaboration for three decades. Their work included the play *Life with Father* (1939), which starred Lindsay and his wife Dorothy Stickney and ran for seven years (a total of 3,224 performances), the longest-running nonmusical play on Broadway (filmed 1947); the political satire *State of the Union* (1945), which won the Pulitzer Prize and was filmed by Frank Capra two years later; and the hit college comedy *Tall Story* (1959, filmed 1960).

Lindsay and Crouse wrote the librettos for Cole Porter's *Red, Hot, and Blue* (1936); Irving Berlin's *Call Me Madam* (1950, filmed 1953); Rodgers and Hammerstein's *The Sound of Music* (1959, filmed 1965); and Berlin's *Mr. President* (1962). They incorporated suspense elements in their plays *The Prescott Proposals* (1953), in which the U.S. delegate to the UN solicits the help of British, French, Russian, and Pakistani representatives to clandestinely cart away the body of her lover, the Czech delegate, who died in her room of a heart attack, and *The Great Sebastians* (1956), the story of married vaudevillians who, upon performing in Prague, find themselves entangled in political intrigue.

Among the plays that Lindsay and Crouse produced on Broadway were Joseph Kesselring's *Arsenic and Old Lace* (1941), wherein two endearing elderly ladies offer elderberry wine spiked with poison to lonely old men and pray over their bodies in the basement of their Brooklyn home, and *Detective Story* (1949), Sidney Kingsley's photographic drama of an eventful day in a New York police precinct.

Russel Crouse named his daughter Lindsay Ann Crouse in tribute to his collaborator Howard Lindsay.[5]

Acting Edition: Dramatists Play Service (in manuscript form).

Awards and Honors: Howard Lindsay and Russel Crouse won a Pulitzer Prize for *State of the Union* (1946) and the Best Musical Tony Award for *The Sound of Music* (1960).

NOTES

1. *New York World-Telegram*, October 4, 1951.
2. *New York Post*, October 4, 1951.
3. *New York Herald Tribune*, October 4, 1951.
4. *Daily News*, October 4, 1951.
5. Actress Lindsay Crouse, the daughter of playwright Russel Crouse, married another playwright, David Mamet, in 1977, when he was on the threshold of his luminary career. Lindsay made her Broadway debut in *Much Ado about Nothing* (1972) and appeared in almost thirty movies since 1976, notably *Slap Shot* (1977), *Between the Lines* (1977), *The Verdict* (1982), *Daniel* (1983), *Iceman* (1984), *Places in the Heart* (1984, nominated for Best Supporting Actress Oscar), *House of Cards* (1987), *Communion* (1989), *Desperate Hours* (1990), *The Indian in the Cupboard* (1995), *The Arrival* (1996), *The Insider* (1999), and *Cherish* (2002). In recent years Crouse has returned to the stage, touring in a one-woman show, *The Belle of Amherst*, about the life of Emily Dickinson.

The Number (1951)

Arthur P. Carter (United States)

Recently divorced, Sylvia Berger takes the position of a "telephone girl" at the number and horse-betting office of Maury Slater, a racketeer. The telephone girls are supposed to take bets over the phone and are not allowed to engage socially with the clientele. But naive, simple-minded Sylvia falls for the sweet-talking, handsome bookie Dominic Spizzilini.

The good girl Sylvia and the bad boy Dominic are the main characters of Arthur Philip Carter's bittersweet melodrama, *The Number*. Its three-act action unfolds in various locales: Maury's office, where Sylvia, Dottie, and Alice are working at a table, handling incoming and outgoing calls; the Berger kitchen, where Bessie and Hyman Berger, middle-class and Jewish, cry over their "gangster" daughter and urge her to go back to Si, her stodgy husband; a corner of a restaurant located on a highway, a secretive meeting place for Sylvia and Dominic; and a tourist cabin just outside the city, where Sylvia and Dominic make love and hatch plans for the future. Dominic assures Sylvia that they'll get married as soon as he has "a big enough bundle to buy into a business."

The proceedings come to a head when Maury checks his books and discovers that Dominic has made some unusual wins. Maury ruthlessly interrogates his three clerks and learns that Dominic has slyly courted both Alice and Sylvia, promising each his hand in marriage when he is more financially secure. Thanks to his sweet talk, he has obtained number tips from both women.

Maury sends his goons after Dominic. The bookie escapes into the Berger home and pleads with Sylvia to hide him. He assures her that even though he began their relationship by using her, he has fallen deeply in love and there is nothing he wishes more than to start a new life with her. Sylvia wavers but is inclined to yield to Dominic's tearful pleas. However, when she discovers that Dominic has secretly stowed $25,000 in his briefcase for his getaway, the bitter truth sinks in: the dashing scoundrel has never loved her. She was a pawn, maneuvered to serve his ends.

But Maury's goons have the last word, killing Dominic when he tries to escape. Police sirens are heard as the curtain descends.

* * *

Following a three-week tryout in Philadelphia, *The Number* opened at the Biltmore Theatre in New York on October 30, 1951, staged by George Abbott, starring movie actors Martha Scott (Sylvia) and Dane Clark (Dominic). The morning-after critics were split in their verdicts. Richard Watts Jr. found *The Number* "shrewd, tense and well-acted . . . a conventional but agreeably suspenseful melodrama,"[1] and Robert Garland called it "a real good show, excellently produced."[2]

Walter F. Kerr, on the other hand, wrote that *The Number* "is not taut enough, or tough enough, for an engrossing evening on the rifle range,"[3] and William Hawkins concluded that "neither play nor the performance of it ever makes up its mind whether this is a rip-roaring melodrama or a satire on a soap opera."[4]

There were also opposite points of view about George Abbott's direction. "George Abbott, who likes racy yarns about uncouth malefactors," wrote Brooks Atkinson, "has staged *The Number* with a good deal of relish."[5] "The usually dependable George Abbott has failed to whip *The Number* into a winner," frowned Robert Coleman.[6]

There was general agreement among the reviewers that Murvyn Vye, in the role of big-shot racketeer Maury Slater, stole the show. "The play belongs to Menacing Murvyn," chirped John Chapman. "Everything about him—his looks, his voice, his dress, the bullseye timing of his lines—makes him worthy of the best melodrama anybody can write."[7]

The Number ran for eighty-seven performances. Arthur Carter's only other play, *High Fidelity*, in which a young producer's career and way of life are threatened by the star of his show, tried out at the Walnut Theatre in Philadelphia on September 14, 1961, ran for only four performances, and never reached New York.

Acting Edition: Dramatists Play Service.

NOTES

1. *New York Post*, October 31, 1951.
2. *New York Journal-American*, October 31, 1951.
3. *New York Herald Tribune*, October 31, 1951.
4. *New York World-Telegram*, October 31, 1951.
5. *New York Times*, October 31, 1951.
6. *Daily Mirror*, October 31, 1951.
7. *Daily News*, October 31, 1951. Murvyn Vye (1913–1976), Massachusetts-born and Yale-educated, specialized in playing underhanded and villainous characters

on stage, screen, and television. On Broadway he excelled in the roles of Jigger Craigin in *Carousel* and Jud Fry in *Oklahoma*, the two classic Rodgers and Hammerstein musicals. Vye's sinister, mean-looking countenance was utilized in the movies *Golden Earrings* (1947), *Whispering Smith* (1948), *Pickup on South Street* (1953), *Escape to Burma* (1954), *Voodoo Island* (1957), *The Boy and the Pirates* (1961), *King of the Roaring Twenties* (1961), and *The George Raft Story* (1961). Among the many television programs that featured Vye were *The Web* (1950), *Pulitzer Prize Playhouse* (1951), *City Detective* (1953), *Damon Runyon Theatre* (1955), *Climax!* (1956), *The Walter Winchell File* (1957), *M Squad* (1958), *Perry Mason* (1959), *Thriller* (1961), *The Untouchables* (1962), and *The Defenders* (1964).

Requiem for a Nun (1951)

William Faulkner (United States, 1897–1962)

Temple Drake is back. The depraved heroine of *Sanctuary*, William Faulkner's sensational novel, has returned, eight years older but not much wiser, in *Requiem for a Nun*.

Sanctuary (1931), which made Faulkner famous, is a Gothic thriller about a maiden-coed, Temple Drake, who is kidnapped and raped by the sadistic gangster Vitelli, nicknamed Popeye, who then sets her up in a Memphis whorehouse. Popeye arranges for a young thug, Alabama Red, to be Temple's lover so he can watch their lovemaking. Temple Drake becomes thoroughly perverted, joining an evil environment peopled with prostitutes, moonshiners, and mobsters. Interwoven within the lurid proceedings are a murder, a trial, and a mob lynching. Eventually, Temple is rescued by Gowan Stevens, a fellow student, who reappears with her in *Requiem for a Nun* as her husband and father of their two children.

Requiem for a Nun, the horror sequel, is part prose and part drama, peppered with long, didactic stage instructions. Nancy Mannigoe, a black woman with an even disposition, until recently a domestic servant, stands trial at a Mississippi courthouse for smothering an infant in its cradle. She is found guilty and sentenced to death by hanging.

The action shifts to Gowan and Temple Stevens' living room. It is their six-month-old baby girl who was suffocated by the nanny. The Stevens are planning to leave the next day on an extended trip to California and Hawaii. Gavin Stevens, their lawyer and Gowan's uncle, corners Temple, inquiring about a man who was there the night her daughter was killed.

But Temple avoids any explanation and leaves with Gowan and their son, Bucky. Four months later, a note from Gavin reminding her that there's only a week until the nanny will be hanged, brings the Stevens family back. Temple reluctantly agrees to approach the governor with a plea for clemency. Temple reveals to the governor that Alabama Red's younger brother, Pete, has been blackmailing her over sleazy letters she wrote during a dark past. The devil in Temple took over and she fell for Pete, "a hard and ruthless man, so impeccable in amorality."

Nancy Mannigoe, a former drug addict and prostitute, now the maid, nanny, and confidante, discovered that Temple had reneged on the plan to exchange money and jewels from her husband's strongbox for the incriminating letters.

A harrowing flashback takes us to Temple's private sitting room, where she and Pete contemplate eloping. When Pete goes to the car, Nancy confronts Temple, urging her to think of her two little children. Temple is not swayed; nothing will stop her, money or no money, children or no children.

Nancy crosses quietly toward the nursery, picking up a milk bottle from the table as she passes. She stops by the door, looks at Temple with a strange expression, and says, "I tried everything I knowed, you can see that," and exits.

Temple finishes her packing when Nancy emerges from the nursery, without the milk bottle, striding toward the kitchen.

Temple picks up a blanket and heads for the nursery. After a second or two, she screams, the lights fade, and the action returns to the governor's office.

The Governor does not grant a pardon but Temple realizes that Nancy, "the murderess, the nigger, the dope-fiend whore," sacrificed her life in order to save her, Temple, from abandoning her husband and child, running away with another man to a new chapter of hellish existence.

Temple and Gavin visit Nancy in jail a few hours before the scheduled execution. Calm and serene, ready to go to the gallows, Nancy asks Temple to trust in God: "Believe."

With a new sense of redemption, Temple walks steadily toward the exit. She goes out. The door closes with a clang.

* * *

The world premiere of a German version of *Requiem for a Nun* took place at the Grand Theatre of Zurich in 1951, directed by the Austrian Leopold Lindtberg. The show's success spawned *Requiem* productions in fourteen other countries on the Continent. Albert Camus translated and adapted the play for a Paris presentation in September 1956. The critics cheered. Jean Guignebat in *Liberation* wrote that "Mr. Faulkner's work could by its plot have been just another crime story but is a tragedy in the classic sense of the word in its intensity, nobility, simplicity of language and terseness of style."[1] Jean-Jacques Gautier in *Figaro* found the play "a mixture of Dostoyevsky and Tolstoy retouched by Protestantism plus a dash of psychoanalysis."[2] Guy Verdot of *Franc Tireur* saw Temple Drake as "an Antigone of evil, her husband being the antique chorus of Greek tragedy."[3]

Requiem for a Nun opened at London's Court Theatre on November 26, 1957, winning kudos for Ruth Ford's Temple Drake, Zachary Scott's Gavin Stevens, and Bertice Reading's Nancy Mannigoe, running for thirty performances. The three thespians crossed the Atlantic in a Tony Richardson production designed by Motley, anchoring at Broadway's John Golden Theatre on January 30, 1959. The reviewers were divided.

Walter Kerr recommended the play "for those who are willing to risk a calculated, somewhat over-written, but wholly valid experiment."[4] Frank Aston declared, "It proves how harsh, raw and stunning the mature theater can be."[5] Brooks Atkinson stated, "The slow, dark flow of dialogue is characteristic of Mr. Faulkner, who listens to a distant drum. As a man of feeling and insight, he is entitled to his own method."[6]

The naysayers included John Chapman, who wrote, "It is a murky and sordid affair which exhibits the famed Mississippi littérateur as a tyro at writing for the stage . . . much of what Faulkner wants to relate happens offstage, and much of what he relates should have happened offstage,"[7] and Robert Coleman, who claimed that *"Requiem* is long on talk and short on genuine action. Its people are difficult to accept. Even the script's resolution seems to have been tacked on."[8] A few aisle men had mixed emotions; Richard Watts Jr. praised "the dark and brooding moral intensity of the distinguished novelist's concern with sin and atonement" but regretted "Mr. Faulkner's lack of experience as a dramatist";[9] John McClain believed "it is a work of great power and nobility . . . but, sad to say, it fails as an entity to evoke the deep emotional reaction for which it strives."[10] *Requiem for a Nun* ran for forty-three performances.

Miriam Hopkins played the title role in the movie version of *Sanctuary, The Story of Temple Drake* (1933), directed by Stephen Roberts.[11] Lee Remick portrayed Temple in the remake of *Sanctuary* (1961), helmed by Tony Richardson. Ursula Lingen enacted Temple in *Requiem für eine Nonne*, presented on West Germany's television in 1965.

* * *

Born in 1897 in New Albany, Mississippi, William Cuthbert Falkner (later Faulkner) never graduated from high school and never received a college degree. He worked as an assistant bookkeeper at his grandfather's bank in Oxford, Mississippi, as an employee of the Winchester Repeating Arms Company in New Haven, Connecticut, and as a cadet in the Royal Air Force in Canada. When he tried to join the U.S. Army Air Force, he was turned down because he was only five feet six inches tall.

In 1919, Faulkner enrolled at the University of Mississippi at Oxford, where he contributed poems and short stories to the campus newspaper, *The Mississippian*, and helped found a dramatic club. At the university he wrote a one-act play, *The Marionettes*, a sensuous fable in which Pierrot, hero of French pantomime, is dreaming of seducing the beautiful Marietta.

In 1924, Faulkner published his first book of poetry, *The Marble Faun*. The following year he moved to New Orleans and wrote essays and sketches for the literary magazine *The Double Dealer*. In 1926, Faulkner's first novel was published, *Soldiers' Pay*, incorporating the experiences he encountered when in the RAF. With 1929's *The Sound and the Fury*, considered one of the most important novels of the twentieth century, he began his series about life in a fictional Mississippi county, Yoknapatawpha.

Faulkner was a voracious reader of suspense fiction and an admirer of Carr, Christie, Queen, Sayers, and Stout. He incorporated criminous elements not only in *Sanctuary* and *Requiem for a Nun* but also in other tales of the South. "Uncle" Gavin Stevens saves a black man framed for murder in *Intruder in the Dust* (1948, filmed 1949) and is the shrewd country lawyer of six detective stories in *Knight's Gambit* (1949), a volume also containing a 1930 mystery, "Smoke," and "An Error in Chemistry," which won second place in the *Ellery Queen Mystery Magazine* contest in 1946. Faulkner's novel *Light in August* (1933) hinges on a brutal murder motivated by a broken relationship and culminates with the lynching of the killer by a violent community mob. According to C. Hugh Holman in *Twentieth Century Crime and Mystery Writers*, Faulkner's *Absalom, Absalom!* (1936) utilizes "the double plot and time structure of the detective story to give form to a serious inquiry into the meaning of southern history and the reliability of history itself . . . *Absalom, Absalom!* has a past plot, dealing with the violent career of Thomas Sutpen, before, during, and after the Civil War."[12] The forward action of the novel is concerned with two characters, neither of whom had ever seen Sutpen, who are attempting to piece Sutpen's history together from the recollections of others, fragments of letters, and similar clues.

One of America's greatest novelists, Faulkner also penned *Mosquitoes* (1927), *Sartoris* (1929), *As I Lay Dying* (1930), *Pylon* (1935, filmed 1958 as *The Tarnished Angels*), *The Unvanquished* (1938), *The Wild Palms* (1939), *The Hamlet* (1940, filmed 1958 as *The Long, Hot Summer*), *Go Down, Moses* (1942), *A Fable* (1954), *The Town* (1957), *The Mansion* (1959), and *The Reivers* (1961, filmed 1969).

Faulkner's output also boasts fifteen collections of short stories, six books of verse, and a dozen volumes of nonfiction, letters, and interviews. An important anthology is *The Portable Faulkner* (1946), edited by Malcolm Crowley.

As a screenwriter, Faulkner contributed to the movie versions of Ernest Hemingway's *To Have and Have Not* (1944) and Raymond Chandler's *The Big Sleep* (1946), both directed by Howard Hawks, and starring Humphrey Bogart and Lauren Bacall. Faulkner collaborated on the screenplays of the war movies *Today We Live* (1933), *The Road to Glory* (1936), *Air Force* (1943), and *God Is My Co-Pilot* (1945), as well as the espionage thrillers *Background to Danger* and *Northern Pursuit* (both in 1943), and the suspense melodramas *Fog over London*, based on the play *The Amazing Dr. Clitterhouse* by Barré Lyndon, and *Escape in the Desert*, loosely based on the play *The Petrified Forest* by Robert E. Sherwood (both in 1944).

Though uncredited, highlights of Faulkner's Hollywood career include *Gunga Din* (1939), George Stevens' rollicking action-adventure; *Drums along the Mohawk* (1939), John Ford's Revolutionary War saga; *The Southerner* (1945), Jean Renoir's drama about the tribulations of a poor farming family; and *Mildred Pierce* (1945), adapted from James M. Cain's novel, directed by Michael Curtiz and starring Joan Crawford in her Oscar-winning role as an ambitious waitress who finds success in business but loses all when she shoots to death her fickle husband.

In his book *Faulkner and Film*, Bruce F. Kawin, a former professor of English and film at the University of Colorado at Boulder, analyzes an original screenplay by Faulkner, *Dreadful Hollow*, written in the late 1940s for director Howard Hawks but never produced. Kawin believes that *Dreadful Hollow* "is so genuinely frightening and so profoundly humanist that it demands comparison with the best of the genre: with *Vampyr*, *Nosferatu*, *Cat People*, *Isle of the Dead*, *The Wolf Man*, *The Black Cat*, and the like."[13] *Dreadful Hollow* is the story of an English girl, Jillian Dare, who has been engaged as a companion to the elderly Countess Czerner in a small town located 204 miles from London. The countess's niece, Vera, is a young, reckless, sensuous woman. Jillian learns to her horror that the countess is Vera, a vampire rejuvenated with the blood of little children.

Tomorrow, adapted by Horton Foote from a story by Faulkner for television's *Playhouse 90* in 1961, depicts a member of the jury casting a sole vote against the acquittal of a father accused of killing the wild young man who, while running off with his daughter, drew a gun. A lawyer discovers that the juror was the boy's adopted father who still believed in the boy he raised.

Acting Edition: Vintage Books.

Awards and Honors: A top-ten selection in *The Best Plays of 1958–1959*. William Faulkner was elected to the National Institute of Arts and Letters in 1939; awarded the Nobel Prize for Literature, 1949; Howells Medal, 1950; National Book Award, 1951, 1955; Pulitzer Prize, 1955, 1963; American Academy of Arts and Letters Gold Medal, 1962. The annual PEN/ Faulkner Award for Fiction is the largest peer-juried prize for fiction in the United States.

Faulkner's *Intruder in the Dust* (1948) is an entry in the Howard Haycraft–Ellery Queen Definitive Library of Detective-Crime-Mystery Fiction. *Knight's Gambit* (1949) is an entry in *Queen's Quorum: A History of*

MT. LEBANON PUBLIC LIBRARY

the *Detective-Crime Short Story as Revealed by the 106 Most Important Books Published in this Field Since 1845.*

NOTES

1. Quoted in the *New York Times*, September 24, 1956.
2. Quoted in the *New York Times*, September 24, 1956.
3. Quoted in the *New York Times*, September 24, 1956.
4. *New York Herald Tribune*, January 31, 1959.
5. *New York World-Telegram*, January 31, 1959.
6. *New York Times*, January 31, 1959.
7. *Daily News*, January 31, 1959.
8. *Daily Mirror*, January 31, 1959.
9. *New York Post*, February 1, 1959.
10. *New York Journal-American*, January 31, 1959.
11. The 1933 movie version of *Sanctuary: The Story of Temple Drake* caused an uproar and led to the strengthening of the rules of the Production Code. The film's audio was digitally restored in 2010.
12. John M. Reilly, ed., *Twentieth Century Crime and Mystery Writers*, 2nd ed. (New York: St. Martin's Press, 1985), 307.
13. Bruce F. Kawin, *Faulkner and Film* (New York: Frederick Unger, 1977), 137.

The Chase (1952)

Horton Foote (United States, 1916–2009)

The prolific, Pulitzer Prize–winning dramatist Horton Foote began his seven-decade playwriting career in the 1940s with several failed Broadway productions. Though compared by theatre connoisseurs to Chekhov and Faulkner, his name and works remained largely unknown to the general public. At long last, during the first decade of the twenty-first century, a succession of revivals of Foote's plays established his reputation as a foremost American playwright, master of sparse prose and creator of rich, down-to-earth characters. Born in Wharton, Texas, Foote often drew upon his formative memories and set the action in small, fictional Texas towns.

The Chase unfolds within twenty-four hours in two settings: the office of a jail in Richmond, a sleepy Texas town, and a cabin in the woods nearby. It is early evening when Sheriff Hawes, a kindly, thin, and wiry man, is sitting at his desk with his eyes closed, wearied with his job and its run of irritating problems, such as runaway boys and small robberies. Suddenly a teletype message arrives, informing him that Bubber Reeves, a killer he sent to prison several years ago, has escaped while being moved to the state penitentiary in Floriville.

Hawes instructs his deputies, Rip and Tarl, to be alert, for he has no doubt that Reeves will be bent on revenge and will be gunning for him. The sheriff's anxious wife, Ruby, believes that "this is the first place Bubber will head for."

The action shifts to Knub McDermont's cabin. McDermont, a tall and muscular farmer, shares his ramshackle dwelling with Bubber Reeves' wife, Anna, a thin, wistful girl in her twenties. Bubber's mother rushes in to ask if they've seen her son. Soon Bubber himself, a small, drawn, and intense man, slowly walks in.

"Anna's living with me now, Bubber," says Knub. After a tense silence, Bubber requests food, money, and the keys to Knub's car. He intends to drive to town and kill Sheriff Hawes. Mrs. Reeves pleads with her son but he stalks off.

Later that night, town citizens surround the sheriff's office to express their outrage and demand that Bubber Reeves be killed. Deputy Rip agrees, "I know if I catch the murdering bastard I'm gonna kill him." But Hawes vehemently objects; he plans to catch Bubber alive and send him back to prison.

Hawes promises Ruby that as soon as they can afford it, they'll leave Richmond and buy a farm elsewhere. Suddenly, from outside the jail, a revolver is fired. The window pane crashes. Ruby crouches on the floor and Hawes pulls down the shade. Deputy Tarl comes in and reports that the shot was fired from a passing car. Ruby rises and runs to Hawes. He takes her in his arms.

Escaping from the shooting scene, Bubber smashes the getaway car. The license plate on the car is traced to Knub McDermont. The sheriff and his deputies drive to Knub's cabin and ask him to tell Bubber that "the county is getting ugly" and soon he's "gonna have a lynching mob." The only chance Bubber has is to surrender to the sheriff peacefully.

When Knub delivers the sheriff's message to Bubber, the felon hits him with a metal pipe. The climactic face-to-face meeting between Hawes and Bubber takes place late at night in the cabin's courtyard. Mrs. Reeves pleads with Sheriff Hawes to spare her son's life. He assures her that he intends to take Bubber back to the penitentiary. While they converse, Bubber comes out of the cabin and starts toward the sheriff. Hawes whirls and sees Bubber rapidly approaching. Instinctively, he shoots and Bubber falls dead—killed, ironically, by the one man who wanted to keep him alive. Mrs. Reeves is sobbing as Deputy Rip searches the ground, but apparently Bubber was not carrying a gun.

At the police station, the deputies inform Hawes that the men have gone off the streets and "the town is quiet as the grave." Hawes embraces Ruby and sighs, "I failed; the chase is over and I've lost"; he tells her that he intends to resign. Ruby assures him that he did the best he could and insists that he cannot run away from his responsibilities. The phone rings and Hawes promises Dixie Graves that in the morning he will talk sense into her rebellious little boy.

He hangs up and tells Ruby, "I guess that's all a man can do is try. Just try and try and try."

* * *

In his biography *Horton Foote: America's Storyteller*, theatre maven Wilborn Hampton relates that Gary Cooper was interested in appearing on Broadway in *The Chase* as Sheriff Hawes, a character not unlike Marshal Will Kane, whom he portrayed in *High Noon*. However, Cooper "suffered terribly from stage fright" and "the thought of going onstage made him physically ill. In the end, Cooper did not do the play."[1] Instead of Cooper, producer-director Jose Ferrer cast movie star John Hodiak in his debut appearance on Broadway. The play, coined "a psychological Western," previewed in Philadelphia and opened at New York's Playhouse Theatre on April 15, 1952. The morning-after critics were decidedly split. Robert Coleman found *The Chase* "deeply moving and stimulating for much of its three acts."[2] Jim O'Connor exclaimed, "Here is drama; here is suspense; here is action; here is excitement; here is violence; here is sudden death . . . *The Chase* held me from beginning to end."[3] However, Richard Watts Jr. believed that *The Chase* "suffers from a tendency to repeat itself in the manner of an over-extended one-act play."[4] William Hawkins objected to "a moralizing melodrama told with a wealth of severe tension that ends up being more nervous than exciting."[5] Walter F. Kerr sniffed at "a sluggish, emotionally flat piece of writing. It is, in fact, for all the world like a watered down western with moral commercials."[6]

The performing ensemble garnered kudos. "The acting is excellent," wrote Brooks Atkinson. "John Hodiak plays with a loose, leisurely sincerity that is thoroughly agreeable . . . every performance has a flavor of its own. Nan McFarland's distraught mother of the killer; Kim Stanley's slow-witted wife; Murray Hamilton's wild man; and Lonny Chapman's moody accomplice."[7]

The Chase ran for thirty-one performances. In 1956, Foote turned the play into a novel, published by Rinehart. Ten years later *The Chase* was filmed, scripted by Lillian Hellman and directed by Arthur Penn, starring Marlon Brando as the sheriff (called Sheriff Calder in the movie), Robert Redford (Charlie "Bubber" Reeves), Jane Fonda (Anna Reeves), Angie Dickinson (Ruby Calder), and Miriam Hopkins (Mrs. Reeves).

* * *

Albert Horton Foote Jr. was born in 1916 in Wharton, Texas. At a young age he developed an affinity for both theatre and cinema. He saw every play mounted by a local drama company and enrolled in speech classes at Wharton High School. At the age of sixteen he convinced his parents to finance a two-year apprenticeship with the Pasadena Playhouse in Pasadena, California, where he rubbed shoulders with young Lee J. Cobb and Joseph Anthony, both destined to break through on Broadway as notable actor and director, respectively. Upon a trip to nearby Los Angeles, Foote was awed by Eva LeGallienne's appearances in Henrik Ibsen's *Hedda Gabler*, *A Doll's House*, and *The Master Builder*.

Foote moved to New York in the fall of 1935. He worked backstage at off-Broadway's Provincetown Theatre, took classes with famed acting guru Tamara Daykarhanova, made the rounds at Broadway production offices, appeared in an industrial film, got a job as an usher in a movie theatre, spent a summer with the Maverick Theatre in Woodstock, New York, was cast as a Spanish man falsely accused of being a spy in Ernest Hemingway's play *The Fifth Column* (a scene that was cut out before the Broadway opening)—and decided to change course from acting to playwriting.

Foote's first New York play, *Texas Town*, was produced by a fringe group, The American Actors Company, in a small, unnamed theatre on West 16th Street. The action unfolds on a single day in the drugstore of Richmond, Texas. A gallery of characters, young and old, congregate, each with a dilemma. Brooks Atkinson of the *New York Times* believed that "Mr. Foote's quiet play is an able evocation of a part of life in America."[8] Foote's biographer Wilborn Hampton writes: "Underneath the mundane concerns of daily life—foreclosures, jobs, affairs, and other human frailties—*Texas Town* explores issues that would occur throughout Foote's plays for the next seventy years: the inevitability of change and loss and the struggle to maintain one's dignity in the face of it."[9]

Only the Heart was first produced on the tiny Provincetown stage in 1942 to generally positive reviews. Reworked and recast, the drama came to Broadway's Bijou Theatre two years later. This time around, the story of Mamie Borden, a wealthy, domineering matriarch, played by June Walker, left the critics cold and the show closed after forty-seven performances.

The Chase and two Broadway follow-ups, *The Trip to Bountiful* and *The Traveling Lady*, were also box-office failures.

The Trip to Bountiful is a sentimental drama about a sweet, trapped old woman, Carrie Watts (played by Lillian Gish), who escapes from the home of her autocratic, persecuting daughter-in-law, Jessie Mae Watts (Jo Van Fleet), and returns to the small Texas town of her girlhood (Henry Miller Theatre, November 3, 1953—thirty-nine performances).

The protagonist of *The Traveling Lady* is Georgette Thomas, another gallant mother, albeit young (enacted by Kim Stanley), who takes a bus to meet her ex-husband, Henry Thomas (Lonny Chapman), just out of jail. Henry has been imprisoned for six years for stabbing a man to death during a drunken brawl. By the end, Georgette realizes that Henry is still a heel, swiping the belongings of a pair of elderly ladies, and is again headed to prison (The Playhouse Theatre, October 27, 1954—thirty performances).

While Foote's stage endeavors flopped, in the 1940s and 1950s he made a name for himself penning multiple television episodes for *The Philco Playhouse*, *Studio One*, *The United States Steel Hour*, and *Playhouse 90*. In the 1960s he wrote the screenplays of Harper Lee's *To Kill a Mockingbird* (1962), winning an Academy Award for Best Adapted Screenplay; *Baby, the Rain Must Fall*, from his play *The Traveling Lady* (1965); and William Faulkner's *Tomorrow* (1972). Foote garnered a second Oscar for his original screenplay of *Tender Mercies* (1983). In 1992, he adapted to the cinema John Steinbeck's *Of Mice and Men*.

A turnabout in Foote's theatrical career occurred when off-Broadway's Signature Theatre Company devoted its entire 1994–1995 season to his plays, presenting *Talking Pictures*, *Night Sessions*, *The Young Man from Atlanta*, and *Laura Dennis*. *The Young Man from Atlanta* won the Pulitzer Prize for drama and two years later was mounted again on Broadway. Set in 1950, it is the story of a middle-aged couple, Will and Lilly Kidder (Rip Torn and Shirley Knight), who attempt to cope with the death of their only son and face a crisis when Will is fired from a seemingly secure position with a wholesale grocery firm (Longacre Theatre, March 27, 1997—eighty-four performances).[10]

Playing off-Broadway at 59E59 Theatres before moving to Broadway, *Dividing the Estate* is a comedy about the quarrelsome, greedy Gordon family of Harrison, Texas, ruled with an iron fist by matriarch Stella (Elizabeth Ashley). "In outline this plot is familiar, bringing to mind an assortment of American dramas set in the South and steamy with avarice and mendacity, from Lillian Hellman's *Little Foxes* to Tennessee Williams's *Cat on a Hot Tin Roof*," wrote critic Ben Brantley in the *New York Times*. "What makes *Estate* so unmistakably a work of Horton Foote is the endearing ineffectuality of its schemers and the suggestion that the treasure chest everyone is after may be empty. Imagine Hellman's foxes declawed, an alteration that automatically turns melodrama into comedy"[11] (Booth Theatre, November 20, 2008—fifty performances).

In 2007, the artistic director of the Hartford (Connecticut) Stage Company, Michael Wilson, commissioned Foote to condense his collation of nine plays, *The Orphan's Home Cycle*, a mammoth, intricate family saga, into three parts of three plays each. Foote completed the task prior to his death on March 4, 2009, ten days short of his 93rd birthday and before the project went into performances, first at Hartford Stage (August 27 to October 17, 2009), then at off-Broadway's Signature Theatre (October 29, 2009, to April 11, 2010).[12]

In tribute to Foote, the night after his death, the lights on Broadway were dimmed for a minute before the evening's performance.

Acting Edition: Dramatists Play Service. *The Chase* is also included in *Horton Foote: Collected Plays*, Volume II (Smith and Krause, Inc., 1996).

Awards and Honors: Horton Foote was the recipient of two Academy Awards for his screenplays of *To Kill a Mockingbird* (1962) and *Tender Mercies* (1983); the William Inge Award for Lifetime Achievement in the American Theatre (1989); and a Pulitzer Prize for his play *The Young Man from Atlanta* (1995). In 1996 Foote was elected to the Theatre Hall of Fame.

In 1998 he was elected to membership in the American Academy of Arts and Letters, and that year received from the Academy the Gold Medal in Drama for the entire body of his work. In 1999 he garnered a Writer's Guild of America's Lifetime Achievement Award. A year later he received the PEN/Laura Pels Foundation Award for Drama, the New York State Governor's Arts Award, and the National Medal of Arts Award. In 2006 *The Trip to Bountiful* won the Lucille Lortel Award for Outstanding Revival, and he was given the Drama Desk Lifetime Achievement Award for his work. In 2010 *The Orphan's Home Cycle* picked up the New York Drama Critics' Circle Award as the best play of the year. Also in 2010, the Horton Foote Prize was established for promising new American playwrights. Each winner receives $15,000 and a picture of Foote.

NOTES

1. Wilborn Hampton, *Horton Foote: America's Storyteller* (New York: Free Press, 2009), 116.
2. *Daily Mirror*, April 16, 1952.
3. *New York Journal-American*, April 16, 1952.
4. *New York Post*, April 16, 1952.
5. *New York World-Telegram*, April 16, 1952.
6. *New York Herald Tribune*, April 16, 1952.
7. *New York Times*, April 16, 1952.
8. *New York Times*, April 30, 1941.
9. Wilborn Hampton, *Horton Foote: America's Storyteller*, 59.
10. Founded in 1991, off-Broadway's Signature Theatre Company devotes each season to the works of a single playwright. Among the playwrights presented by the Signature have been Arthur Miller, Sam Shepard, John Guare, Edward Albee, Romulus Linney, Tony Kushner, August Wilson, and Lanford Wilson.
11. *New York Times*, September 28, 2007.
12. Actress Hallie Foote, the playwright's daughter, appeared in several major roles in *The Orphan's Home Cycle* and is bent on pursuing high-caliber revivals of her father's works.

Dial "M" for Murder (1952)

Frederick Knott (China-born, England– United States, 1918–2002)

Playwright Frederick Knott was a former tennis champion and a member of the varsity team at Cambridge. Knott's lead character in *Dial "M" for Murder*, his first thriller, is Tony Wendice, an ex-Wimbledon victor, educated at Cambridge. Let us hope that the biographical resemblance ends here, for Wendice is one of the most despicable husbands ever to face a hissing audience.

While his wife, Margot (Sheila in the British production), is at the theatre with Max Halliday, an American writer of television mysteries, Tony invites to their London apartment an old acquaintance, Captain Lesgate, a shady gigolo who spent time in prison. Tony relates to Lesgate that he "always intended to marry for money." While he was in first-class tennis he met wealthy people all over the world, among them his wife, who had been a fan of his for some time.

Tony now wishes to get rid of Margot so he can take advantage of their new wills, which state that they leave everything to each other in case of accidents. Margot is worth just over ninety thousand pounds.

Tony divulges his perfect-alibi scheme: tomorrow evening, Halliday, Margot's former boyfriend, and he will go out to a stag party just down the road. She will stay at home. At exactly twenty-three minutes to eleven Lesgate will enter the house by the street door. He'll find the key to the apartment door under the stair carpet. He will go straight to the window and hide behind the curtains. At exactly twenty minutes to eleven, Tony will go to the telephone in the hotel to call his boss. He will dial a wrong number, his own. Margot will come down to answer the phone. When Lesgate finishes his task, he will pick up the phone, blow a soft whistle and hang up. Upon hearing the whistle, Tony will hang up and redial, the *correct* number this time. He will then speak to his boss as if nothing has happened and return to the party.

Lesgate agrees to strangle Margot for a fee of one thousand pounds, but the plan goes awry. In the scuffle, the wife turns the tables by stabbing her

61

attacker with a pair of scissors. The resourceful Tony now concocts a trap
through which Margot is accused of premeditated murder, found guilty,
and condemned to be hanged. The culprit is known to the audience from
the very beginning, but tension mounts as he manages to thwart any and
all evidence against him. It takes the combined efforts of Max Halliday
and Inspector Hubbard of Scotland Yard and the telltale hallway latchkey
to ensnare Tony and smash his "foolproof" plot.

* * *

Dial "M" for Murder was first presented as a live ninety-minute BBC television play before making it to the boards of the Westminster Theatre in
London on June 19, 1952. It was the first television offering to be adapted to
the stage in England. The production, directed by John Fernald and featuring Emrys Jones and Jane Baxter as the Wendices, became a smash hit, running for 425 performances, a feat repeated later that year when the thriller
was imported to New York's Plymouth Theatre on October 29.

The Broadway offering was staged by Reginald Denham, an old hand
in the ways of melodrama,[1] with Maurice Evans taking off his Richard II
doublets to play a modern villain. Gusti Huber enacted the role of Margot, supported by Richard Derr as Max, Anthony Dawson as Lesgate, and
John Williams as Inspector Hubbard in a highly praised performance.

The morning-after reviewers were ecstatic. "The answer to our prayers
is Frederick Knott's *Dial "M" for Murder*," crowed Richard Watts Jr. "It
is a kind of cool, cerebral game the author is playing . . . He manages it
so skillfully and fairly, and he is so thoroughly ingenious and intelligent
about it that the result is excellent fun for those of us who are fond of fictional homicide."[2] William Hawkins rejoiced: "Unlike most works of the
'mystery' category, this one has believable characters, convincing motives
and an entirely honest giveaway for its climax."[3] Robert Coleman gushed:
"*Dial "M" for Murder* is a constantly absorbing thriller. It holds your attention like a vise. It's a super-melodrama, done with urbanity."[4] Brooks Atkinson found it "original and remarkably good theatre—quiet in style but
tingling with excitement underneath. . . . Mr. Knott and Mr. Evans have
managed to squeeze a little youthful fun into our sophisticated theatre."[5]
Walter Kerr joined the cheering squad: "It's a holiday for the whodunit
fans, and, as such, it couldn't be more welcome."[6] John McClain urged his
readers, "Dial M and ask for the nearest ticket broker."[7]

The Broadway production ran for 552 performances, spawned a number of highly successful road companies, and became a stock favorite.[8]
The first professional revival of the play in New York City was undertaken by off-Broadway's Theatre by the Blind in 2004. The cast included a
number of sight-impaired actors, including George Ashiotis, who played
Tony Wendice.

Dial "M" for Murder has been translated into twenty-five languages and presented in more than thirty countries. In 1957, under the title *Telephone Call*, it was performed successfully in Soviet provincial theatres, Moscow's Pushkin Theatre, and the Leningrad Comedy Theatre, until *Pravda* put the chill on the suspense thriller by charging that it was a "base and vulgar boulevard drama profoundly alien to Soviet morals."[9] (A similar attack greeted Agatha Christie's *Witness for the Prosecution* when it premiered at Moscow's Central Transport Workers Theatre that same year.)

Stanley Richards included *Dial "M" for Murder* in *Best Mystery and Suspense Plays of the Modern Theatre*, praising it as "one of the theatre's most adroit and ingenious tales of blackmail, murder, and sleuthing."[10]

In 1954, Frederick Knott adapted *Dial "M" for Murder* for the screen, with Alfred Hitchcock at the helm. It was filmed in 3D, and John Williams and Anthony Dawson were recruited to repeat their stage roles of police inspector and would-be assassin, respectively. Ray Milland and Grace Kelly embodied the mismatched Wendices, joined by Robert Cummings as the loyal Max.

The play was adapted to television in West Germany (1959); Sweden (1960); England, with Laurence Harvey and Diane Cilento as the Wendices (1967); and the United States, starring Christopher Plummer and Angie Dickinson (1981).

Called *A Perfect Murder*, an updated, nastier, more sensuous 1998 film version departed significantly from its source. Written by Patrick Smith Kelly and directed by Andrew Davis, the cat-and-mouse games were transformed to New York City, where the husband, Steven Taylor, is a shady Wall Street bond trader in financial trouble. Taylor (played by Michael Douglas) hires his wife's lover, David Shaw, a struggling painter (Viggo Mortensen) to kill her. The cash offer is now scaled up to five hundred thousand dollars. Gwyneth Paltrow plays the rich wife, Emily, who has her own agenda.

* * *

Frederick Major Paull Knott was born in Hankow, China, on August 28, 1916. His parents, Quaker missionaries, sent him to England for his education. He graduated from Cambridge University in 1938. During World War II he served in the Royal Artillery.

Knott retreated to a cottage in Sussex and worked for eighteen months straight on *Dial "M" for Murder*. A succession of producers rejected the play and Knott, discouraged, almost tore up the script—when the BBC optioned it for a television presentation early in 1952. The rest is theatrical history.

Knott continued to contribute mightily to stage suspense with the thrillers *Write Me a Murder* (1961) and *Wait until Dark* (1966). A lesser-known black comedy, *Mr. Fox of Venice*, was produced in 1959 at West End's Piccadilly Theatre for twenty-one performances and since then has disappeared. The play was coupled with Ben Jonson's *Volpone* and the novel *The Evil of the Day* by Thomas Sterling as the basis for the 1967 motion picture *The Honey Pot*, in which Rex Harrison portrayed a wealthy man who pretends to be dying in order to test the love of his three former mistresses, played by Susan Hayward, Capucine, and Edie Adams. The hatched plan leads to an unexpected murder.

Knott's output was sparse. A *New York Times* obituary relates that he "received many offers of advances to write plays, turning them all down." His widow, Ann Hilary Knott, is quoted as saying, "He hated writing. . . . His drive was gone. He didn't want to live in Palm Beach."[11]

Acting Edition: Dramatists Play Service. *Dial "M" for Murder* is also included in *Best Mystery and Suspense Plays of the Modern Theatre*, edited by Stanley Richards (New York: Dodd, Mead, 1971).

Awards and Honors: A top-ten selection in *The Best Plays of 1952–1953* ("An English thriller that proffers murder without mystery. It was as urbane in tone as it was sound in workmanship: an excellent host, Mr. Knott—in terms of suspense—always refilled the audience's glass before it was empty").[12] *Dial "M" for Murder* won a special Edgar Allan Poe Award from the Mystery Writers of America in 1953.

NOTES

1. Among the thirty plays that Reginald Denham directed on Broadway were the criminous *Rope* (1929), *Suspense* (1930), *Ladies in Retirement* (1940), *Suspect* (1940), *Guest in the House* (1942), *The Two Mrs. Carrolls* (1945), *Portrait in Black* (1947), *Sherlock Holmes* (1953), *Bad Seed* (1954), and *Hostile Witness* (1966).

2. *New York Post*, October 30, 1952.

3. *New York World-Telegram*, October 30, 1952.

4. *Daily Mirror*, October 30, 1952.

5. *New York Times*, October 30, 1952.

6. *New York Herald Tribune*, October 30, 1952.

7. *New York Journal-American*, October 30, 1952.

8. During the summer of 1996, I staged *Dial "M" for Murder* for Vintage Theatre in the Glass Center, Corning, New York, and was gratified by the reaction of audiences glued to their seats, particularly throughout the climactic scenes.

9. Quoted in *New York Times*, January 9, 1957.

10. Stanley Richards, ed., *Best Mystery and Suspense Plays of the Modern Theatre* (New York: Dodd, Mead, 1971), 102.

11. *New York Times*, December 20, 2002.

12. Louis Kronenberger, ed., *The Best Plays of 1952–1953* (New York: Dodd, Mead, 1971), 17.

Lord Arthur Savile's Crime (1952)

Constance Cox (England, 1912–1998)

Based upon an 1891 short story by Oscar Wilde, Constance Cox's three-act *Lord Arthur Savile's Crime* preserves the original's witticisms but adds elements of farce and wrinkles of suspense.

The entire action of the play takes place in the plush drawing room of Lord Savile's house in Grosvenor Square, London, in the 1890s.

Lord Savile is described as "young and pleasant but not overburdened with brains." He confides to his stoic, middle-aged butler, Harold Baines, that he'll marry the "beautiful, sweet, gifted" Sybil Merton the next week, and Baines expresses his concern for his lordship, who'll be "treading that undiscovered bourne from which no traveler returns."

A knock at the front door announces Sybil, arriving with her dowager mother, Lady Julia, who has not yet given her consent to the marriage. Lady Julia insists that the cheiromantist Podgers, who is currently the rage of London, read Arthur's palm to ensure the purity of his past and future. Podgers, "a short little man with gold-rimmed spectacles," scrutinizes Arthur's palm, catches his breath, and takes out a handkerchief to mop his brow. He tells Lady Julia that Arthur is "a very charming young man" who led "a singularly uneventful life," and "will be married and have two children—a boy and a girl." Lady Julia is content, but later Arthur corners Podgers and is horrified to hear from the fortune-teller that at some time in the future he will commit a murder!

Arthur relates to his butler that he finds himself obliged to murder someone before the scheduled wedding ceremony next Thursday, for he feels that it would be unfair to his fiancée if he killed somebody *after* they were married. The faithful Baines suggests that they dispose of an insignificant relative, Lady Clementina, an aunt who always complains of pains, repeatedly telling them that she wouldn't mind to sleep forever. The aunt loves sweets—a disguised poisonous bonbon will do the trick.

A poisonous capsule is placed in the center of a *bonbonière* and a gallows humor scene ensues, when various visiting relatives and friends reach out for a piece of candy. Baines, unseen by the others, lifts the capsule from the box, drops it in a glass of port and takes it to Lady Clementina. There is a moment of apprehension—will the talkative aunt drink the poisonous port? Aunt Clementina hands it to Arthur, and he drains the glass of port to the dregs.

Arthur becomes gravely ill but recovers after an unpleasant treatment with a stomach pump. He asks Sybil to postpone the wedding and tells her about Podgers' prediction, emphasizing that he'd prefer to commit the murder before their nuptials, "so that no shadow of infamy or disgrace should fall across our married life." Sybil is touched by his "noble" gesture.

Searching for the next victim, Arthur and Baines decide upon an uncle, the Dean of Paddington. They consider and discard various lethal methods—a trapdoor to be contrived at the head of the stairs, a shooting accident, or an explosion of dynamite. They solicit the aid of an international anarchist, Herr Winkelkopf, who exhibits a small colored ball loaded with explosives, which Arthur carelessly tosses up and barely catches. Unexpectedly, the Dean arrives for a visit, and Winkelhopf loads his black umbrella with explosives to go off the moment it opens. However, by mistake the Dean leaves with the anarchist's identical umbrella. They wait for an explosion that never comes. Exasperated, Arthur opens and closes the Dean's umbrella several times and tosses it through the window. A tremendous explosion is heard, and Arthur faints.

As the Dean of Paddington is a passionate collector of timepieces, they decide to send him an antique clock filled with explosives. Word comes that the Dean is delighted with a clock that came by post and, upon the stroke of twelve, emits a little puff of smoke. The anarchist Winkelhopf offers additional lethal suggestions—cutting the Dean's throat, smothering him with a pillow, and stretching a dark thread across the stairs—but Arthur, by now exasperated, wishes to break off his engagement and go abroad. The clairvoyant Podgers' arrival contributes to Arthur's aggrieved state of mind. Podgers demands a thousand pounds for keeping silent about Arthur's attempts to commit capital crimes. He will wait for the lord at midnight to deliver the money on the Embarkment, by Cleopatra's Needle.

The next morning, Lady Julia and Sybil come by carriage with grave concerns about Arthur's strange behavior. Lady Julia opines that "Arthur has no brains and is therefore only fitted for the position to which his birth entitles him—the House of Lords." Furthermore, she states as she sweeps out, if Arthur does not arrive within ten minutes for the wedding rehearsal, the engagement is terminated.

Arthur enters and cheerfully presents Sybil with a large bouquet of flowers. He relates to Sybil and Baines that he could raise for Podgers only 150 pounds. When he arrived for their appointment, he saw the blackmailer leaning over the parapet, looking down into the water. He recalled that it was Podgers who has caused him so much misery, so if he had to murder somebody, why shouldn't it be Podgers? He seized his legs and with a mighty effort hurled him into the Thames. There was a cry—a splash—then all was silent. Nothing could be seen but Podgers' silk hat pirouetting on the water.

The original Oscar Wilde story concludes with a newspaper announcement about the tragic discovery of the body of Mr. Septimus R. Podgers, who is assumed to have committed suicide. Constance Cox, perhaps unwilling to present a sympathetic murderer, changed the ending in the play. Here Podgers does not drown but is found in the morning in his apartment shot through the head, an apparent suicide by a charlatan on the verge of being exposed as an utter fraud.

* * *

Directed by Jack Hulbert, *Lord Arthur Savile's Crime* previewed at the Theatre Royal in Aldershot on July 28, 1952, and came to London's Court Theatre on October 7, running for twenty-one performances. The principals were played by Claude Hulbert, the director's younger brother (Lord Arthur), Peter Haddon (butler Baines), John Garley (blackmailer Podgers), and Jean Lodge (Sybil Merton). Several months later, on October 23, another dramatization of the Oscar Wilde story, by Basil Dawson and St. John Clowes, directed by Alec Clunes, premiered at the Arts Theatre in London's West End and ran for thirty showings. Almost half a century later, in November of 2000, the Constance Cox adaptation was revived by the Boundary Players at the Newbury Theatre, UK.

Oscar Wilde's story was transferred to the screen in Hungary (1920) and Sweden (1922) as silent features, and most effectively as a segment in the three-part film of the supernatural, *Flesh and Fantasy* (1943), directed by Julien Duvivier, with Edward G. Robinson haunted by the murder prediction of psychic Thomas Mitchell. Anna Lee, Dame May Whitty, and C. Aubrey Smith provided solid support.

Lord Arthur was the comic hero of television adaptations in Norway (1955), the Netherlands (1957), the United States (1958), England (1960, with Terry-Thomas as the Lord, Robert Coote as Baines, Arthur Lowe as Podgers, and Ernest Thesiger as the Dean), in France (1968), Spain (1969), and Russia (1991).

* * *

Constance Shaw Cox was born in Sutton, Surrey, in 1912. She wrote her first play, a period drama, for the local Women's Institute, at the age of sixteen. Two years later she penned a three-act farce for the Brighton

Amateur Operatic Society. During World War II she worked as a post-mistress, lost her fighter pilot husband Norman Cox, and had a play produced in the West End—*The Romance of David Garrick*, with Donald Wolfit directing and starring as the celebrated eighteenth-century British actor (St. James's Theatre, December 29, 1942—thirty-five performances). Her subsequent West End plays include *The Boy from Belfast* (1944); *Remember Dick Sheridan* (1944); *Madame Bovary*, an adaptation of the novel by Gustave Flaubert (1945); *Vanity Fair*, from W. M. Thackeray's novel (1946), her biggest success (Comedy Theatre, October 29, 1946—seventy performances); *The Picture of Dorian Gray*, based on Oscar Wilde's novel (1947); and *Spring at Marino*, suggested by Ivan Turgenev's *Fathers and Sons* (1951).

Cox was a member of the Brighton Little Theatre from the early 1950s onward and directed many of her plays there, including adaptations of such classics as Alexandre Dumas's *The Count of Monte Cristo*; Charles Dickens's *A Christmas Carol* and *A Tale of Two Cities*; Wilkie Collins' *The Woman in White*; Charlotte Brontë's *Jane Eyre*; Emily Brontë's *Wuthering Heights*; Mary Elizabeth Braddon's *Lady Audley's Secret*; and Jane Austen's *Northanger Abbey*, *Pride and Prejudice*, and *Mansfield Park*.

Several of Cox's original plays were cloaked with crime and suspense: *Maria Marten, or Murder in the Red Barn* (1969), was based on a notorious 1827 real-life murder in Suffolk, England. A young woman, Maria Marten, was murdered by her lover, William Corder, in the Red Barn, a local landmark. Her body was found buried in the building. Corder was hanged after a sensational trial.[1]

In *Miss Letitia* (1969), Letitia Thompson, a companion to an elderly, invalid recluse, falls in love with a traveling salesman and steals precious china pieces from her employer for him—only to be betrayed by the man. She ultimately decides to become a recluse herself.

Brian Hamilton commissions an acquaintance, Gerry Stephens, to kill his wealthy wife and soon finds himself in the grip of a blackmailer in *The Murder Game* (1976). Stephens proves to be a psychopathic intruder who takes over all of Hamilton's possessions, moves in with him, and dictates Hamilton's way of life.[2]

Vampire, or the Bride of Death (1978) is the story of a young aristocrat, Sir Edward Clevedon, who proposes to the beautiful daughter of an English Lord but is revealed to be an undead creature.

The main characters of *A Time for Loving* (1985) are two youngsters who find shelter in an empty manor house—a pregnant girl running away from a tyrannical father and a fellow who drove the getaway car of a robbery gone wrong.

Cox found her stride as the adapter of classic books to television. In 1956, she converted Charlotte Brontë's *Jane Eyre* into a six-episode miniseries. She followed it with, among others, W. M. Thackeray's *Vanity Fair*; Louisa May Alcott's *Little Women*; H. G. Welles' *The History of Mr. Polly*; Charles Dickens's *Bleak House* (1959), *Oliver Twist*, *The Old Curiosity Shop*, *Martin Chuzzlewit*, and *A Tale of Two Cities*; Robert Louis Stevenson's *The Master of Ballantrae*; R. D. Blackmore's *Lorna Doone* (1963); and George Eliot's *Silas Marner* (1964). In 1967, Cox joined the team of writers of the immensely successful *The Forsyte Saga*, a thirty-six-part serial based on John Galsworthy's novels about a family of London merchants.

Cox also adapted classic works for radio serials, including Tolstoy's *War and Peace*, Trollope's *The Barchester Chronicles*, and Dickens's *Pickwick Papers*.

* * *

Oscar Fingal O'Flahertie Wills Wilde (1854–1900) was born in Dublin, Ireland, into an Anglo-Irish family. He studied classics at Dublin's Trinity College, was an outstanding student, and received a scholarship to Magdalen College, Oxford, where he continued his education from 1874 to 1878. Decorative arts were his main interest. While at college, his long hair, mode of dress, and general demeanor were considered that of an "effeminate dandy."

After graduating from Oxford, Wilde returned to Dublin. He courted Florence Balcombe, but she became engaged to Bram Stoker, author of *Dracula*. Wilde spent the next several years in Paris, went on a lecture tour in the United States, and settled in London, where he contributed articles and art reviews to the *Dramatic View* and *Pall Mall Gazette*. In 1885, he married Constance Lloyd, daughter of a wealthy Queen's counsel, and they had two sons. In the early 1890s, Wilde's novel *The Picture of Dorian Gray*, two collections of fairy tales, and the volume *Lord Arthur Savile's Crime and Other Stories* established his literary reputation. On stage, he had a series of popular comedies.

However, Wilde's widely known homosexual encounters, notably with the young Lord Alfred Douglas, led in 1895 to three successive *cause célèbre* trials, at the conclusion of which he was convicted of "gross indecency" and sentenced to two years' hard labor. Upon his release, Wilde spent his last three years, penniless, in Paris. He died of cerebral meningitis on November 30, 1900. His tomb in Pére Lachais was designed by the sculptor Sir Jacob Epstein.

Wilde's only novel, *The Picture of Dorian Gray* (1891), the haunting narrative of an artist who sells his soul to preserve his youth and indulge in debaucheries, has never been out of print and was adapted to the silent and talkie screen numerous times, in various countries, from 1910 to 2009. Famed Russian director Vsevolod Emilevich Meyerhold adapted and directed *Portret Doriana Greia* in 1915. The best-known version was made in

Hollywood in 1945, with Hurd Hatfield as Dorian. *The Picture of Dorian Gray* was also brought to television in 1953, 1961, 1973, 1976, and 1983. Stage adaptations of the novel were penned by G. Constant Lounsbery (1913), David Thorne (1928), Jeron Criswell (1936), Cecil Clarke (1936), Constance Cox (1947), Andy Milligan (1963), John Osborne (1973), Jack Sharkey and Dave Reiser (a musicalization, 1982), Joseph Bravaco (a musicalization, 1990), Allan Reiser and Don Price (a musicalization, 1996), and Joe O'Byrne (2001).

Among Wilde's short stories, perhaps the best known is *The Canterville Ghost* (1887), which was widely adapted for screen and television, notably MGM's 1944 version, directed by Jules Dassin, starring Charles Laughton in the title role. A musical version by Sheldon Harnick and Jerry Bock was presented on American television in 1966.

Wilde's comedies of manners, distinguished by biting satire, written between 1892 and 1895, were revived through the twentieth century, went through musical treatments, and were often adapted for the cinema and television: *Lady Windermere's Fan, A Woman of No Importance, An Ideal Husband*, and his masterpiece, *The Importance of Being Earnest*.

Wilde's early plays, all but forgotten, are laced with elements of crime, violence, and intrigue. *Vera, or The Nihilists* (1880) is an unblushing melodrama set in czarist Russia. Vera Sabouroff, a barmaid whose brother was sent to his doom in Siberia, vows revenge and becomes a top assassin for a band of revolutionaries. But Vera falls in love with the young czar and when she has the opportunity to pierce him with a poisonous sword, she stabs herself instead, saving him.

The Duchess of Padua (1891), a melodramatic tragedy, is the story of Guido Ferranti, a young man who is on a quest to avenge the death of his father by the autocratic Duke of Padua, Simone Gesso. Guido becomes enamored with the Duke's beautiful, gracious wife, Beatrice, and she reciprocates. When the Duchess learns that Guido intends to kill her husband, she herself stabs the Duke to death in order to save her lover. However, Guido is found next to the body with a dagger in his hand and is accused of the murder. A trial ensues, in which Guido takes the blame himself. Both Guido and Beatrice later commit suicide in the death cell.

A fragment of an incomplete play, *A Florentine Tragedy* (1893) is set at merchant Simone's house in Florence. When Simone returns from a business trip, he is greeted by his wife Bianca and a visitor, Prince Guido Bardi. The Prince purchases the merchant's goods while whispering sweet nothings in Bianca's ear. She is struck by the contrast between her mundane husband, who is only attuned to business, and the poetic, romantic aristocrat. Simone attempts to sell Guido a sword and invites him to cross rapiers. As they duel, Bianca quietly cheers for Guido, but it is Simone who overpowers Guido and throws him down over a table.

Simone grabs Guido by the throat, and we realize that he is aware of the clandestine undercurrent between the aristocrat and his wife. He tightens his pressure and Guido dies. In an ironic twist, Bianca goes toward her husband with outstretched arms. "Why did you not tell me you were so strong?" she says with admiration. They passionately kiss as the curtain falls.

First performed posthumously in 1906, *The Florentine Tragedy* was published in 1908, inspired a one-act opera by Austrian composer Alexander Zemlinsky in 1917, was revived in London in 1927, aired on Swedish television in 1965, and was resuscitated by New York's Food for Thought in 2004.

Oscar Wilde's *Salome* (1894) has a successful performance track. It is set in the palace of King Herod in ancient Judaea. The spoiled Princess Salome prances the dance of the seven veils and for her prize demands the head of Jokanaan, a young poet who infuriated her by refusing to succumb to her charms. A blood-drenched climax pictures a gigantic executioner beheading Jokanaan, Salome kissing the lips of the severed head, Herod ordering his men, "Kill that woman!" and soldiers rushing forward, crushing the princess beneath their shields.

First performed in Paris in 1896, *Salome* was transformed into an opera by Richard Strauss in 1905, and has been produced often in both categories. Arthur Wontner, destined to become a celebrated Sherlock Holmes, portrayed Jokannan in a 1911 London production.[3] Steven Berkoff directed and enacted King Herod in 1995 New York. Al Pacino played Herod in a production of *Salome* developed at the Actors Studio under the direction of Estelle Parsons and presented in Brooklyn (2002); in Poughkeepsie, New York (2003); on Broadway (2003); and in Los Angeles (2006). Since 1908, the play has been adapted to the screen many times, the latest version in 1988, called *Salome's Last Dance*, a British film directed by Ken Russell, wherein Oscar Wilde (played by Nickolas Grace) watches his play staged in a brothel.

Accounts of the real-life trials of Oscar Wilde were published by H. Montgomery Hyde in 1975, by Jonathan Goodman in 1995, and by Merlin Holland in 2003. Among others, biographies of Wilde include *The Life and Confessions of Oscar Wilde* (1914) by Frank Harris, *Oscar Wilde* (1987) by Richard Ellmann, and *The Stranger Wilde* (1994) by Gary Schmidgall. Peter Ackroyd penned *The Last Testament of Oscar Wilde* (1983), a fictional diary presumably written by Wilde when in exile in Paris after serving time in prison. In *The Wilde West* (1991), Walter Satterthwait uses Wilde's lecture tour in the United States as background for a tense mystery, in which the visiting author finds himself a suspect in the murder of prostitutes. The tour also serves Louis Edwards for a steamy adventure novel titled *Oscar Wilde Discovers America* (2003).

In a twist, Wilde becomes a clever sleuth in Gyles Brandreth's lively detective stories *Oscar Wilde and the Candlelight Murders* (2007), *Oscar Wilde and the Ring of Death* (2008, aka *Oscar Wilde and a Death of No Importance*), *Oscar Wilde and the Dead Man's Smile* (2009), and *Oscar Wilde and the Nest of Vipers* (2010). While a student at Oxford, Brandreth wrote and produced the play *The Trials of Oscar Wilde* (1974). Other plays about Wilde include *Oscar Wilde* (1936) by Leslie and Sewell Stokes, *The Importance of Being Oscar* (1961, arranged and acted by Michael MacLiammoir), *Dear Oscar* (1972, a musical with book and lyrics by Caryl Gabrielle Young), *Wildflowers* (1976) by Richard Howard, *Wilde West* (1988) by Charles Marowitz, *Stephen and Mr. Wilde* (1993) by Jim Bartley, *Gross Indecency* (1997) by Moises Kaufman, *The Judas Kiss* (1998) by David Hare, *Goodbye Oscar* (1999) by Romulus Linney, *Aspects of Oscar* (2001) by Barry Day, *A Man of No Importance* (2002) by Terrence McNally, and Brian Bedford's one-man show, *Ever Yours, Oscar* (2009), featuring Wilde's correspondence.

Two excellent motion pictures about Wilde's traumatic life in the straight-laced Victorian era were made in England in 1960: *Oscar Wilde*, with Robert Morley, and *The Trials of Oscar Wilde*, starring Peter Finch. A third biographical movie, *Wilde* (1998), featured Stephen Fry in the title role.

A naughty pastiche by Graham Greene, *The Return of A. J. Raffles* (1975), spotlights Oscar Wilde's lover, Lord Alfred Douglas, as he solicits the help of gentleman-burglar Raffles to penetrate the safe of his father—an act of revenge for stopping his allowance after the affair with Wilde became known.

An odd couple of the Victorian era, Sherlock Holmes and Oscar Wilde met on two occasions. In the play *The Incredible Murder of Cardinal Tosca* (1980), by Alden Nowlan and Walter Learning, good Dr. Watson learns from his roommate that his latest case revolves around a packet of compromising letters penned by Wilde. In Russell A. Brown's novel, *Sherlock Holmes and the Mysterious Friend of Oscar Wilde* (1988), Wilde, described as "a giant moth," arrives at 221B Baker Street to ask for the aid of the Great Detective in a case of blackmail in high society.

Acting Edition: Samuel French, Inc.

Awards and Honors: Constance Cox's BBC serial of Charlotte Brontë's *Jane Eyre* won the News Chronicle Award for Best Television Play in 1956. Her adaptation of Charles Dickens's *Martin Chuzzlewit* won the Television and Screenwriters Award in 1964. Cox's play *Maria Marten, or Murder in the Red Barn* was the recipient of the Advanced Cup and the Highest Marks in the 1969 Drama Festival of the Sussex Federation of Townswomen's Guilds.

In 2000–2001, the New York Public Library for the Performing Arts marked the centennial of the death of Oscar Wilde with a series of public programs that included lectures, readings of Wilde's works, and motion pictures based on his plays.

NOTES

1. The Red Barn murder elicited numerous newspaper articles, studies, ballads, and plays throughout the nineteenth and twentieth centuries.

2. Other plays about the invasion of a private household by a dangerous party include *Blind Alley* (1935), *Kind Lady* (1935), *Night Must Fall* (1935), *Ladies in Retirement* (1940), *Arsenic and Old Lace* (1941), *Guest in the House* (1942), and *The Man* (1950).

3. Arthur Wontner portrayed Sherlock Holmes in a series of motion pictures (1931–1937).

Hanging Judge (1952)

Raymond Massey
(United States, Canada-born, 1896–1983)

The tables have turned on the title character of Raymond Massey's *Hanging Judge*. Sir Francis Brittain, a ruthless High Court jurist, finds himself accused of fatally poisoning a blackmailer.

The action of the play takes place over a period of four months in England during the time between the First and Second World Wars.

The curtain rises on a small insert showing the judge's bench of a London criminal court. Sir Brittain, in scarlet robes and a wig, addresses an unseen jury: "Now, members of the jury, you must ask yourselves if it is reasonable to suppose that an innocent man could have acted in this manner . . . could have disposed of the girl's body in such a callous, brutish manner . . . by weighting it with stones and dropping it in the canal."

In a prison's death-row cell, three men are seated at a table playing poker. Two of them, Bill and Bert, are wardens, while the third, Harry Gosling, is a young man about twenty years old, due to be hanged this very night. Gosling is a card sharp. He shows the card players some tricks, dealing to the elder warden a full house, to the young one a flush, and to himself four aces. "I learned all that from my brother, when I was a kid," he relates.

John Teal, Gosling's older half-brother by a different father, has just arrived from America and is allowed by the Governor to visit the condemned man. Teal is shabbily dressed but is described as having "a touch of distinction about him." Gosling grasps his brother's hand and says, "Jack, I didn't do it. Before God, I didn't." Teal assures him that he does not doubt his innocence. Gosling confides that his pregnant girlfriend, Rose, became very agitated when he said he couldn't marry her because he had no money. Rose grabbed a knife which was on the table and stuck it in her heart three times before he could move. "She just dropped and she was dead," says Gosling. Panicky, he did the wrong thing and threw the body in the river. In court, the prosecutor got him twisted up, and the judge was worse, constantly stopping his lawyer and emphasizing to

74

the jury that Gosling is a "depraved" man, that there are no extenuating circumstances, and that they are not to be swayed by emotion.

The Governor of the prisons arrives with the bad news that the final appeal was rejected. Gosling's counsel, Sir Keith Nottingham, "a handsome, rugged man of middle age," enters and says, "We've done everything we possibly could, Harry, but we failed. . . . You've got to try to be brave." Gosling blubbers that he never hurt anybody, that the judge knew he wasn't guilty, that the judge is the real murderer, "killing me for his fun."

John Teal embraces his brother, telling him that he thought he would go first "for I can't last long." Before he too dies, declares Teal, he has "a job" to do.

The following evening, at the Adelphi Club, Gilbert West, an aggressive Member of Parliament, tells Sir Francis Brittain, a tight-lipped man in his sixties, that Harry Gosling stuck to his innocence to the end. Over whiskey and soda, Brittain scorns Counselor Nottingham: "He chose the wrong profession—the stage is his métier, Drury Lane melodrama. . . . The purpose of a penal code is to punish—to deter others from crime."

Several members of the club express their surprise that Gosling was not awarded a reprieve. In a corner, Sir George Sidney, a bluff, witty man of forty-eight, a product of Eton, converses with Colonel George Archer, a former chief of police in Singapore, now appointed Chief of the Norfolk Constabulary. Archer has recently returned from the Orient and is glad to meet Sir George, who was helpful to Archer in the capture of a drug-smuggling ring. Archer says that Sir George "is quite a detective." Sir Keith Nottingham joins them and Sidney introduces him to Archer, "a friend and a fellow sleuth; I the infallible Holmes and he the dogged Inspector Lestrade." The conversation turns to Judge Brittain. Nottingham says heatedly, "Brittain was trying me—not Gosling! He hates me!"

John Teal enters and asks to speak with Judge Brittain. Teal tells the judge that he knows all about his double-life existence. He is aware of the judge's alias as John Willoughby and of his farmhouse at Moxton in Norfolk. In hushed tones, Brittain suggests that they meet next Friday evening at the farmhouse.

The action shifts to Brittain's retreat in Norfolk. The area folk know him as John Willoughby. Mary Reddish, "a plump, pretty country woman in her thirties," enters and is greeted warmly by the judge. They kiss, and Mary complains that it has been eight weeks since he came home. She assures Brittain that she hasn't told her father, or anyone else, of their "little understanding."

He is sending her home early tonight, the judge says, because of a pending visit by a man whom he must see alone. After Mary's departure, he takes a folded paper from his pocket and pours the contents into a glass of brandy.

John Teal knocks on the door and walks in nervously. He reminds Brittain of his mother, Mabel Teal, who thirty years ago was the judge's lover, and declares, "I am your son, Brittain!" He exhibits to the judge a batch of letters to prove his claim, but Brittain calmly announces that he is well able to handle blackmailers and threatens to call the police. Teal becomes agitated and raves that he has only months to live, but he still has time to ruin Brittain and his "mess of dignity." He falls into a chair, trembling with a paroxysm of pain. The judge offers Teal a glass of brandy, and he gulps it down. He is seized with violent convulsions, crumples in agony, and falls to the floor, the glass rolling away.

Brittain stares at Teal in horror, then slowly crosses to the telephone, lifts the receiver, but rapidly replaces it. He goes to the body, realizes that Teal is dead, and removes the letters from a pocket. He throws them into the fireplace and lights a match as the curtain falls.

The second act unfolds at the Adelphi Club. Brittain relates to Sir Ronald Pond, "a dapper little man of fifty-five," that he was on a walking trip in Scotland, but had to curtail the venture because the mist became intolerable. Pond, an admirer of the John Thorndike detective stories,[1] tells the judge of the buzz generated by a body found in the well of a farmhouse at Moxton. Brittain teases him, and they exit for lunch.

Colonel Archer joins George Sidney and confides that he was assigned to the Norfolk case. It's pretty clear, says Archer, that a murder was committed; the prime suspect is the missing Willoughby, and nobody knows much about him. He seems to be in his sixties; he bought a converted farmhouse about two years ago and used it during holiday periods; he had announced that he was a schoolteacher from the Midlands; his presence at Moxton tallies with school vacations; none of the gentry knew him personally, and only a few by sight; he had a rather unsavory reputation: a former maid complained that he wanted amorous acquiescence in addition to culinary skills.

Archer tells Sidney that John Teal's body was found in the well in Willoughby's garden two days ago. A police surgeon reports that it definitely wasn't a case of drowning. The post mortem conclusions are due soon. Archer pulls an envelope from his pocket and produces several photostatic copies of letters. "They were found in a sort of secret pocket sewed up in Teal's coat under the left armpit," says Archer, adding that the papers were tucked in an oilskin wallet and are not badly spoiled. Among them was a birth certificate of thirty-five years ago, "November 30, 1899," with the names of the parents: "Frances Mabel Teal—John Willoughby." In the letters, "J. W." repudiates all responsibility of "your unfortunate condition."

A Moxton constable, Sergeant Scotton, arrives to provide a description of Willoughby as "a rather flabby, truculent chap in his middle sixties, who gives the impression that he was used to having authority." Willoughby was tracked to the Charing Cross Station, but no farther than that. Judge Brittain enters and peruses the Bradshaw timetable. Sidney introduces him to Colonel Archer. Sergeant Scotton gazes at Brittain, and the judge coolly explains that of course he is John Willoughby, a name he used to ensure privacy during his "leisure time." "Good God!" exclaims Sidney.

Archer asks Brittain to accompany him to Scotland Yard for questioning. Brittain requests to consult with his solicitor, Sir Reginald Pond, who is in the club's dining room. As Brittain departs, Sidney warns Archer that Pond "is about the most slippery lawyer in this country. . . . I'll lay you five to one that at this moment he is telephoning the Home Office to get this affair hushed up." And true enough, a phone call comes from the Commissioner of the Metropolitan Police with an instruction that "on no account is Judge Brittain to be taken to Scotland Yard." Archer gets another phone call and informs Sidney that the post mortem shows that Teal died of cyanide poisoning.

Sidney calls the *Evening Globe* and sets an immediate appointment with the editor, Lord Bradenham. Soon a stop-press edition of the paper arrives in the club, with a blazing headline: "The missing man Willoughby in the body-in-the-well case has been identified as Sir Francis Brittain, the High Court Judge."

The pace of the proceedings acclerates. At the Adelphi Club, members are astounded by the fact that a High Court Judge has been subjected to prosecution on a capital charge. Solicitor Pond urges Brittain to leave the country via a midnight plane, but the judge refuses; he intends to give himself up and trust the law of England to find him innocent.

In the jury room at the Norwich Hall of Assize, the jurors express opinions pro and con, mostly con. Juror No. 6 believes that the case against the defendant is "strong," Juror No. 2 opines that the "defense fellow is a trifle too smooth," and Juror No. 5 pronounces his disdain of the "old buzzard" on trial.

In a small room in the Norwich jail, Brittain, tense and haggard, theorizes to Solicitor Pond that Teal committed suicide. He saw Teal die while drinking a glass of brandy, with the powder in it. Long afterward, he dragged the body out to the well. Pond believes that this revelation will throw his defense "out the window," but Brittain insists that "the truth can never convict an innocent man—in this country, under the law of England!"

At the Adelphi Club, George Sidney, who intensely followed the trial, surprises all by suddenly exclaiming that Brittain is innocent. Yes, on account of him the judge is on the dock, but he has a change of heart. He does not believe that a guilty man would say, "I never saw him take any poison and I was watching all the time!" Like everyone else, Sidney refused to believe Brittain's statement that he put in the victim's brandy an innocent headache medicine; the police searched the judge's London house and found none. But last night, with doubts percolating in his mind, he looked up Henry Passmore, "a stupid ass" of a manservant, and solicited from him the information that in a routine cleanup he threw out "some old medicines"—a week before Brittain left for Moxton the last time.

Mr. Justice Parkinson, in scarlet robes and wig, addresses an unseen jury and points out that Passmore's testimony regarding medication in powdered form, stored at Judge Brittain's home, is an element to be considered in their discussions. In the jury room, Juror No. 6 asserts that the late John Teal, who couldn't have lived long anyway, may have committed suicide in a manner that would incriminate the judge. But the other jurors insist that an innocent man would not have thrown the body into the well and then disappear into his perfectly good hiding place—his real identity. Juror No. 6 bows under pressure, and the Foreman says with satisfaction, "That makes it complete. The verdict is 'guilty as charged.'"

The last scene takes place at the office of the Governor of Norwich Gaol. George Sidney reveals to the Governor, a retired army officer, that the Home Office received a letter written by John Teal, confessing that he was about to kill himself by swallowing cyanide at Brittain's country home, and describing how he would leave evidence proving that Brittain had poisoned him. Teal sent the letter to a friend in America to be forwarded back to England three months later. It came to light three days before the hanging! In the letter, Teal states, "I want Brittain to suffer, not to die. That's too easy."

The Governor tells Sidney that since the refusal of his appeal, Brittain has gone to pieces. He sends for the prisoner. Wardens bring in Brittain, dressed in prison denim clothes and looking very old. Sidney tells Brittain that his innocence has been established and that a Royal Pardon has been granted to him. But the former judge does not seem to comprehend, and keeps mumbling incoherently, with broken sentences, that both the jury and the Court of Criminal Appeal cannot be wrong . . . so he must have done it. He can't remember . . . he doesn't think so . . . but he has had judgment!

* * *

Hanging Judge was adapted to the stage by Raymond Massey from a 1948 novel, *Let Him Have Judgment* (U.S. title, *Hanging Judge*), by the British mystery writer Bruce Hamilton. The play opened at London's New Theatre on September 23, 1952, starring Godfrey Tearle as Sir Francis Brittain,[2] and ran for ninety-four performances. Famed filmmaker Michael Powell directed.

Born August 30, 1896, in Toronto, Canada, to affluent parents, Raymond Massey developed an interest in theatre when a student at Appleby College in Oakville, Ontario. He continued to enroll in acting classes at the University of Toronto and at Oxford University, England. During World War I he enlisted in the Canadian Field Artillery and while on duty appeared in an army minstrel show. Wounded in France, Massey returned home, but instead of joining the family business of making agricultural equipment, as expected of him, he decided to pursue a career in the theatre.

Massey's stage debut took place in a 1922 British production of Eugene O'Neill's *In the Zone*. During the 1920s, he established himself in London as a leading classical actor. In 1931, while playing Hamlet on Broadway, he was offered the role of Sherlock Holmes in a British film based on Arthur Conan Doyle's 1910 play version of *The Speckled Band*. He made his first Hollywood picture in 1932's classic *The Old Dark House* and returned to England, playing major roles for producer Alexander Korda (*The Scarlet Pimpernel*, 1935; *Things to Come*, 1936; *The Drum*, 1938) and director Michael Powell (*Forty-ninth Parallel*, 1941; *A Matter of Life and* Death, 1946; *The Queen's Guards*, 1961).

In 1938, Massey appeared on Broadway in his signature role: Abraham Lincoln, in Robert E. Sherwood's Pulitzer Prize–winning play, *Abe Lincoln in Illinois*, a part he repeated in the 1940 movie version. A wide variety of film characterizations followed, notably fierce abolitionist John Brown in Michael Curtiz's *Santa Fe Trail* (1940), murderous Jonathan Brewster in Frank Capra's *Arsenic and Old Lace* (1941), steely Nazi Major Otto Baumeister in Raoul Walsh's *Desperate Journey* (1943), victimized Brigadier General Ezra Mannon in Dudley Nichols's *Mourning Becomes Electra* (1947), powerful newspaper mogul Gail Wynand in King Vidor's *The Fountainhead* (1949), and the deeply religious Adam Trask in Elia Kazan's *East of Eden* (1955).

On television, Massey played Dr. Gillespie in the NBC series *Dr. Kildare* (1961–1966).

Massey became a naturalized citizen of the United States in 1944. In his witty autobiographies, *When I Was Young* (1976) and *A Hundred Lives* (1979), he tells the story of his three marriages and two children, Anna Massey and Daniel Massey, who followed him into acting.

Raymond Massey died of pneumonia in 1983 and is buried in Beaverdale Memorial Park in New Haven, Connecticut.

Englishman Bruce Hamilton (1900–1974) was educated at Westminster and University College, London. He spent much of his adult life as a teacher of history in Barbados, and he served as president of the Barbados Arts Council in 1958–1959. Hamilton was the author of ten well-regarded detective novels. The first, *Hue and Cry* (1931), is the story of a provincial footballer who kills the sadistic chairman of his club and escapes to London. The last, *Too Much of Water* (1958), depicts several murders on an ocean liner bound for Barbados.

Bruce was the older brother of Patrick Hamilton (1904–1962), author of the milestone stage thrillers *Rope* (1929) and *Gas Light* (1939, aka *Angel Street*). Bruce wrote a memoir of Patrick, *The Light Went Out*, in 1972.

Awards and Honors: Raymond Massey was an Academy Award nominee for Best Actor in *Abe Lincoln in Illinois* (1940).

NOTES

1. A forensic scientist and lawyer, Dr. John Evelyn Thorndyke is considered the premier medico-legal detective in the annals of the genre. Thorndyke was created by R. (Robert) Austin Freeman (1862–1943), an English physician and mystery writer, who in his short-story collection *The Singing Bone* (1912) introduced the "inverted" motif, wherein the reader is a witness to the crime, and the interest centers not on the identity of the culprit, but on how he will be apprehended. Thorndyke made his debut in the 1907 novel *The Red Thumb Mark*, and until 1942 was the scientific sleuth of twenty-two novels and six short-story collections.

2. American-born Godfrey Tearle (1884–1953) became a noted Shakespearean actor on the British stage, appearing in the title roles of *Macbeth*, *Othello*, and *Henry V*, among others. His memorable screen part was that of Professor Jordan, a respectable country squire whose missing finger unmasks him as an enemy agent, in Alfred Hitchcock's *The Thirty-Nine Steps* (1935).

Gently Does It (1952)

Janet Green (England, 1914–1993)

On the heels of *Dial "M" for Murder*, another successful English thriller about a greedy, homicidal husband was imported to New York, albeit with less spectacular results. Janet Green's *Murder Mistaken*, opening at the Playhouse on October 28, 1953, under the title *Gently Does It*, pictures the rise and fall of a Bluebeard scoundrel. Edward Bare resides with his motherly and wealthy wife Monica at the top of Sunrise Hill, just outside a small market town in Kent. When Edward discovers that Monica intends to change her will, he plies her with whiskey and turns on the gas. Ironically, Edward learns from the family's lawyer, Philip Mortimer, that his late wife intended to appoint him as her inheritor and that her premature death, ruled an accident, left Monica's riches in the hands of her Australian sister, Dora Mackintosh.

Undaunted, Edward turns on his boyish charms to court and marry another rich, older woman—brassy ex-barmaid Freda Jeffries. Planting the seeds for a rosy future, Edward already has set his sights on a third well-to-do victim—Charlotte Young, an attractive newcomer to the area. In a surprise twist, Charlotte is identified as sister Dora, who has arrived from Australia to confront Edward. "I wasn't satisfied with the results of the inquest. It was too slick," she tells him.

Edward meddles with Charlotte's car and confesses to Freda, who as his wife cannot testify against him. However, Charlotte/Dora does not drive the car and combines forces with attorney Mortimer to turn the tables on the lethal fortune hunter. Edward ends up committing suicide by driving the tampered car to his doom.

* * *

The morning-after critics analyzed *Gently Does It* in bits and pieces. William Hawkins felt, "This import has a neatly played, turbulent opening scene and a climax that is chock full of the stuff that fine thrillers are made of."[1] However, John McClain stated, "The British murder-meller

81

very nearly dies of that old complaint, third-act virus."[2] Walter F. Kerr found the second act "freshest,"[3] while Brooks Atkinson queried, "What's the purpose of all the cat-and-mouse loquacity in that second act?"[4] John Chapman was content: "This is an entertaining melodrama with some good scenes, some good acting and a fair chance of success,"[5] but Richard Watts Jr. lamented, "*Gently Does It* is very minor suicide."[6] The reviewers were unanimous in praising director Bretaigne Windust for breezy direction and designer George Jenkins for executing an evil reeking old house, and they lauded British thespians Anthony Oliver as the psychopathic Edward and Brenda Bruce as his shrewish second wife, Freda.

In 1952 in London, *Gently Does It* ran for 156 performances; the following year in New York it lasted for only thirty-seven.

Under its original title, *Murder Mistaken*, the play was novelized in 1953 by Janet Green and Leonard Gribble. Called *Cast a Dark Shadow*, it was filmed in England in 1955, featuring Dirk Bogarde as the dangerous Bluebeard. Four years later, Green created yet another nefarious husband in *Matilda Shouted Fire* (alternate title: *Murder, My Sweet Matilda*). But in this melodrama, the identity of a shadowy figure stalking Lesley Paul, a delicate, wide-eyed Londoner, remains concealed until the end.

Lesley is notorious as a compulsive hoaxer and is nicknamed "Matilda" after the nursery rhyme "Matilda told such dreadful lies, It made one gasp and stretch one's eyes." So for a while, no one believes her reports of anonymous calls threatening, in a high-pitched singsong voice, "I'm going to kill you before the month is out." Since some of the calls occur while Max, Lesley's husband, is at home, he is out of the loop of suspects. Doubts fall on Lesley's unsavory cousin, Malcolm; Johnson, a gigantic black bricklayer working across the street in a demolition site; Tom, a young, brash deliveryman; Eddy, the strong-arm collector of Max's booking agency; Fenton, the agency's manager; and Ash, a creepy stranger.

At the conclusion, Max drops his gentle, loving demeanor and assures his wife, "I'm just going to break your bloody little neck." Max's threats have been tape-recorded and heard through the telephone as it was being held against the speaker by his accomplice and lover, Peggy Thompson, Lesley's "friend" who lives downstairs. Lesley is saved in the nick of time by the unexpected arrival of the mysterious Ash, who turns out to be Peggy's estranged husband.

Matilda Shouted Fire was filmed by Universal International as *Midnight Lace* in 1960. Lusciously produced by Ross Hunter and smoothly directed by David Miller, the movie starred Rex Harrison as suave Max and Doris Day as petulant Lesley. A strong supporting cast included Myrna Loy, Herbert Marshall, John Gavin, Roddy McDowall, Natasha Parry, John

Williams, and Anthony Dawson. *Midnight Lace* was novelized by William Drummond in 1960, presented as *Murder, My Sweet Matilda* by off-off-Broadway's Manhattan Lambda Productions in 1977, and remade as a TV movie in 1980.

* * *

Born in Hertfordshire, Janet Green was a professional actress from childhood and wrote her first stage play in 1945. She entered the film industry as a writer in 1947 with the screenplay of her own story, *The Clouded Yellow*, in which a former secret agent, played by Trevor Howard, takes a job cataloguing butterflies and soon finds himself involved with the murder of a handyman.

Green contributed the stories or the screenplays of several taut criminous movies. In *Tears for Simon* (1957), the baby of an American embassy man in London is kidnapped. Two Scotland Yard inspectors (Jack Hawkins and John Stratton) investigate a string of safecrackings in *The Third Key* (1957). *Affair in Havana* (1957) focuses on a greedy wife who pushes her invalid husband in his wheelchair into the swimming pool for a $20 million inheritance. *The Gypsy and the Gentleman* (1958) stars Melina Mercouri as a tempestuous Gypsy whose band kidnaps an heiress for ransom. *Sapphire* (1959) follows two Scotland Yard detectives (Nigel Patrick and Michael Craig) as they investigate the murder of a young black woman who had been passing for white. *Victim* (1962) was controversial when released, as it tells the story of a lawyer (Kirk Bogarde) who undertakes to defend a former male lover (John McEnery) in a case that involves theft, blackmail, and murder. In *Walk in the Shadow* (1966), a father is accused of manslaughter when, because of religious convictions, he refuses a critical blood transfusion for his injured, dying daughter.

Janet Green is the pseudonym for Victoria McCormick. Her husband, producer/screenwriter John McCormick, collaborated on several of her movies. In 1971, Green wrote her sole novel, *My Turn Now*, a seriocomic supernatural fantasy in which two brothers—one a compassionate doctor, the other a wild painter—compete for the same body.

Acting Edition: *Gently Does It* (with a production note by the playwright, advocating a "straightforward" approach and emphasis on "character")—Dramatists Play Service. *Matilda Shouted Fire*—Dramatists Play Service.

Awards and Honors: As *Murder Mistaken*, a top-five selection in the British 1952–1953 *Plays of the Year*, chosen by J. C. Trewin. In 1960, Janet Green was awarded the Prix Femina du Cinema and the Edgar Award given by the Mystery Writers of America for Best Foreign Film *Sapphire*. The movie won the British Academy Award a year earlier.

NOTES

1. *New York World-Telegram*, October 29, 1953.
2. *New York Journal-American*, October 29, 1953.
3. *New York Herald Tribune*, October 29, 1953.
4. *New York Times*, October 29, 1953.
5. *Daily News*, October 29, 1953.
6. *New York Post*, October 29, 1953.

The Mousetrap (1952)

Agatha Christie (England, 1890–1976)

The Mousetrap, the longest-running play in theatre history, began in 1947 as the thirty-minute radio sketch *Three Blind Mice*, which Agatha Christie concocted for the BBC as homage to Queen Mary within a week.

Christie converted the playlet into a short story, followed by a full-length stage play retitled *The Mousetrap*, patterned after *Hamlet*'s play-within-a-play.

The curtain rises on a radio announcement accompanied by a shrill whistle of the tune *Three Blind Mice:* "According to Scotland Yard, the crime took place at 24 Culver Street, Paddington. The murdered woman was Mrs. Maureen Lyon. In connection with the murder, the police are anxious to interview a man seen in the vicinity, wearing a dark overcoat, light scarf, and a soft felt hat."

Three men and two women arrive separately at the newly renovated Monkswell Manor, a roadside inn, each wearing an outfit resembling the broadcast's description. They include Christopher Wren, "a rather wild-looking neurotic young man," sprightly, animated, perpetually in motion; Mrs. Boyle, "a large, imposing woman" who continuously displays a bad temper and negative vibes; Miss Casewell, "a young woman of a manly type," cynical and secretive; Major Metcalf, "a middle-aged square-shouldered man," militaristic in manner and bearing; and Mr. Paravicini, "foreign and dark and elderly," laughingly calling himself "the unexpected guest" and "the man of mystery."

The owners of Monkswell Manor are Giles and Mollie Ralston, a young married couple very much in love, awkwardly attempting to make a go at a new venture.

A heavy snowfall insulates Monkswell Manor, but Detective Sergeant Trotter, "a cheerful young man with a slight cockney accent," arrives on skis and notifies everyone that a notebook found at the scene of the Culver Street murder indicates a connection to the inn. With obvious relish, Trotter grills the proprietors and guests as to their roots, recent travels, and possible linkage to the murdered woman. Closet skeletons surface and alibis are destroyed while suspicion shifts from one person to another.

By the end of act I, an unknown party switches off the lights, whistles *Three Blind Mice*, and strangles Mrs. Boyle. Who? Wren? Paravicini? Metcalf? Casewell? Mollie? Giles? No. Sergeant Trotter himself is unmasked as the culprit, avenging the long-ago death of his sibling as a result of neglect and ill treatment. Casewell turns out to be Trotter's older sister, and she will now take him "somewhere where they will look after you, and see that you won't do any more harm."

Major Metcalf is revealed as the policeman assigned to the case. The surprise reversal of having the investigator exposed as the criminal, continues a tradition begun by Israel Zangwill in his 1892 novel, *The Big Bow Mystery*. The trend has been perpetuated by Gaston Leroux, Mary Roberts Rinehart, Edgar Wallace, Ellery Queen, and others.

* * *

The Mousetrap had its world premiere at the Theatre Royal in Nottingham on October 6, 1952, and played at five other provincial playhouses before opening at London's Ambassadors Theatre on November 25, 1952, under the management of Peter Saunders and the direction of Peter Cotes.[1]

"I must say that I had no feeling whatsoever that I had a great success on my hands or anything resembling it," wrote Christie in *An Autobiography*.[2] *The Mousetrap* strode triumphantly on, transferring to the St. Martin's Theatre twenty-two years later, and is still packing the house at the dawn of the twenty-first century. "Once the play was entrenched," wrote Sir Max Mallowan, Christie's second husband, "seeing *The Mousetrap* became a part of the American Tour, as important as a glimpse of Buckingham Palace and a visit to the Tower of London."[3]

When *The Mousetrap* hit the fifty-year mark in November 2002, celebrating its 20,807th performance with Queen Elizabeth II in the audience, Matt Wolf of the Associated Press asserted that "Christie's suspense drama long ago became a theatrical law unto itself."[4]

Richard Attenborough and his wife, Sheila Sim, appeared in the original cast as the young detective sergeant and the innkeeper of Monkswell Manor. The eight characters of the play, recast every ten months, have since been played by more than five hundred actors.

The first American production of *The Mousetrap* was presented at the Arena Stage, Washington, D.C., on May 17, 1955, under the direction of Zelda Fichandler. In New York, an off-Broadway mounting of *The Mousetrap* opened at the Maidman Playhouse on November 5, 1960, and ran for 192 performances. Barry Newman was featured as investigator Trotter.

Lewis Funke of the *New York Times* gave the play a lukewarm endorsement: "*The Mousetrap* will not exactly shake you up, but neither will it let you down."[5]

The Mousetrap has been performed in forty-five countries throughout the world, translated into twenty-four languages, and presented by numerous provincial groups and summer stock companies, including Dallas Theatre Center, Dallas, Texas (1962); off-off Broadway's National Arts Theatre, Manhattan (1975 and 1976); Playwrights Horizons' Queens Theatre, New York (1977); and Barter Theatre, Abingdon, Virginia (1982). During the summer of 1995, Vintage Theatre presented *The Mousetrap* at the Glass Center, Corning, New York, and in the fall of 2000 at the Strathmont Estate, Elmira, New York, a picturesque setting reminiscent of the English inn where the play's action unfolds.

* * *

Born in Torquay, Devon, Agatha Mary Clarissa Miller (1890–1976) was raised reading detective stories. Gaston Leroux's *The Mystery of the Yellow Room*, a sealed-room classic; Robert Barr's *The Triumphs of Eugene Valmont*, a pioneering volume of humorous sleuthing; and Marie Belloc Lowndes' creation of French investigator Hercules Popeau were among her treasured literary influences. During World War I, Agatha married Archibald Christie, a dashing colonel in the Royal Flying Corps. While working in the Volunteer Aid Detachment Hospital, she gained knowledge of drugs and poisons, information that came in handy later in her books. Agatha had not planned to be a writer. In fact, Agatha's first novel was written as a response to a challenge by her sister, Madge. *The Mysterious Affair at Styles* (1920) introduced Hercule Poirot, the diminutive Belgian detective who was destined to rival the popularity of Sherlock Holmes.

In her second novel, *The Secret Adversary* (1922), Christie plotted an adventure tale in which the leading characters, Prudence Cowley, known to her friends as Tuppence, and Thomas Beresford, her beau, pursue an elusive man who plots to overthrow the British government.[6] Successive novels in the early 1920s introduced the recurring characters of Colonel Race and Superintendent Battle of Scotland Yard. In 1926 came the tour de force *The Murder of Roger Ackroyd*, which made Christie a household name.

Following the publication of *The Murder of Roger Ackroyd*, Agatha herself became a headline mystery. On December 3, 1926, the celebrated author did not return home. Her frost-covered car, a green Morris, was found alongside a dirt road with the lights still on. On the seat were a brown fur coat and a small dressing case that had burst open, scattering clothing and some papers, including an out-of-date driver's license in her name. Agatha's disappearance caused a sensation. Was she the victim of foul play? Did she commit suicide? Or was it merely an audacious publicity stunt? A nationwide search was launched immediately.

Author Gwyn Robyns, in *The Mystery of Agatha Christie* (1978), asserts that in order to understand the circumstances of the bizarre case it is important to know that "it had been a traumatic year for Agatha Christie." Her mother had died after a severe illness, and her marriage had deteriorated.

Kathleen Tynan, in *Agatha* (1978), provides an imaginary scenario about the author's disappearance: preoccupied with the painful realization that she was losing her husband to a beautiful rival, the shy, sensitive author withdraws into herself—and drops out of sight. Tynan's speculative narrative attempts to penetrate the psyche of a woman betrayed. How will this accomplished mystery writer, plotter of intrigue and creator of suspenseful incidents, react? Will she remain passive, or will she direct her talents toward sinister revenge?[7]

Agatha returned home after eleven days—claiming temporary amnesia. Two years later the Christies were divorced. In 1930, Agatha Christie married Max Mallowan, an archaeologist. By accompanying him on digs to the Middle East, Agatha discovered exotic source material for such books as *Murder in Mesopotamia* (1936), *Death on the Nile* (1937), *Appointment with Death* (1938), *Death Comes as the End* (1945), and *They Came to Baghdad* (1951).

It is widely perceived that only the Bible and the plays of Shakespeare have sold more copies than Agatha Christie's murder mysteries. "In a career that spanned over half a century," writes popular-culture czar Peter Haining, "she published in all 78 crime novels, 19 plays (of which seven are adaptations of her books), six romantic novels under the pen-name Mary Westmacott, and four non-fiction titles. . . . It is true to say that Agatha Christie is the most widely published writer of any time and in any language, and the royalties deriving from her books alone now run in excess of two million pounds every year."[8] Haining calls attention to the energetic productivity and high achievements of Dame Christie in the world of entertainment—on stage, in films, and on radio and television: "This contribution amounts to at least 20 major theatrical productions on both sides of the Atlantic (not to mention a vast number of touring productions and repertory performances); two dozen films for the cinema; in excess of 50 radio programs; and an even larger number of individual stories and serials for both British and American television."[9]

Agatha Christie died peacefully at her home in Wallingford, Berkshire, on January 12, 1976, at age eighty-five.

Acting Edition: Samuel French, Inc. *The Mousetrap* is also included in the *The Mousetrap and Other Plays* by Agatha Christie (New York: Dodd, Mead, 1978; Harper, 1993).

Awards and Honors: Among the awards and honors that came Agatha Christie's way were Fellow, Royal Society of Literature, in 1950; the C.B.E. (Commander, Order of the British Empire) in 1956; and the D.B.E. (Dame Commander, Order of the British Empire) in 1971. She was president of England's Detection Club (1954) and recipient of the Mystery Writers of America Grand Master Award (1955) and DLitt, University of Exeter (1961).

NOTES

1. Peter Cotes (1912–1998), a British theatrical producer and director, was the older brother of John and Roy Boulting, the twin wonder kids of UK cinema. He was born in Maidenhead as Sydney Arthur Rembrandt Boulting but adopted the pseudonym Cotes from a childhood home called Northcotes to demonstrate independence from his siblings. Their parents, Arthur and Rose Boulting, were both variety actors, and Cotes continued their tradition, performing in revues and cabarets. After the Second World War, Cotes established a small private theatre in Notting Hill, London, where he staged plays by Ibsen and Strindberg, and works by modern American playwrights. In 1946, Cotes presented there a Broadway import, *Pick-up Girl* by Elsa Shelley, a courtroom drama about juvenile delinquency. The play has not been licensed for commercial production because of some risqué details, but Queen Mary came to see it and upon her approval *Pick-up Girl* was transferred to the West End.

Cotes worked periodically in television, wrote two autobiographies, expressed his disdain for the star system in the book *No Star Nonsense* (1949), and collaborated on *The Little Fellow*, a biography of Charlie Chaplin (1951). He often worked with his second wife, the actress Joan Miller (who died in 1988). In 1953 Cotes brought to New York *A Pin to See the Peepshow*, F. Tennyson Jesse's interpretation of the 1922 Thompson-Bywaters murder case. The production was lambasted by the critics and closed after one performance, in direct contrast to *The Mousetrap*, for which Cotes was paid a 1.5 percent share of the proceeds, an income that amounted to well over $25 million over the years.

2. Agatha Christie, *An Autobiography* (London: Collins, 1977), 512.

3. Dennis Sanders and Len Lovallo, *The Agatha Christie Companion* (New York: Delacorte Press, 1984), 413.

4. *San Francisco Chronicle*, November 28, 2002.

5. *New York Times*, November 7, 1960.

6. Tuppence and Tommy would return in Christie's novels *Partners in Crime* (1929), *N or M?* (1941), *By the Pricking of My Thumbs* (1968), and *The Postern of Fate* (1973).

7. *Agatha* was filmed by Director Michael Apted in 1979, featuring Vanessa Redgrave in the title role, Timothy Dalton as the fickle husband, and Dustin

Hoffman as the American reporter Wally Stanton, who tracks Agatha down to a seaside hotel.

8. Peter Haining, *Agatha Christie—Murder in Four Acts* (London: Virgin Books, 1990), 11.

9. Peter Haining, *Agatha Christie*, 11–12.

The Crucible (1953)

Arthur Miller (United States, 1915–2005)

During the Cold War, when America and Russia were involved in a mighty clash, there arose fear in the United States that Communism was threatening the American way of life. In the late 1940s and into the 1950s, Senator Joseph McCarthy of Wisconsin headed the House Un-American Activities Committee. HUAC held hearings and conducted wide-ranging investigations of suspected Communists. Author Arthur Miller, who in his plays championed the cause of the common man, was called to appear before the HUAC on May 21, 1956. He denied that he was a Communist, freely admitted that he attended certain meetings, and refused to name others who had been present. By a vote of 373–9, the House of Representatives found Miller in contempt of Congress, and he was blacklisted by Hollywood. The ruling was reversed by the courts in 1958. There is little doubt that the drama *The Crucible*, about the 1692 Salem witch trials, is a parable about McCarthyism.

The curtain rises on Reverend Samuel Parris's house in Salem, Massachusetts, in the spring of 1692. It is a stark interior with a black backdrop and sparse wooden furniture: "the mood must be one of high mystery, impending revelation." The minister is kneeling at the bedside of his ten-year-old daughter, Betty, who is strangely ill. Word comes from the town's doctor that he cannot discover an appropriate medicine in his books. Dr. Griggs believes that the cause of Betty's malady is "unnatural."

Abigail Williams, the Reverend's strikingly beautiful seventeen-year-old niece, is an orphan who was brought up in his home. She tells her uncle that she, Betty, and several of their girlfriends danced in the forest, but she insists that it was "only sport" and no witchcraft was involved.

Enter Mrs. Ann Putnam, "a twisted soul of forty-five, a death-driven woman, haunted by dreams." She has buried seven babies and wants to know about Betty's illness so as to compare it to her daughter Ruth's symptoms. She believes that "there are hurtful, vengeful spirits layin' hands on these children." Ann's husband, Thomas Putnam, arrives and declares that no doubt there is a murdering witch among the townsfolk.

Upstairs, by Betty's bed, several girls meet and compare notes on how much Reverend Parris knows about their dancing naked in the woods. The timid Mary Warren is scared to death that they will be named as witches and hung. The presumably sick Betty sits up and accuses Abigail of drinking blood as a charm to kill farmer John Proctor's wife. Abigail slaps Betty's face and warns the girls to keep mum about their frolicking.

John Proctor and Abigail meet and we learn that they have had a romantic liaison. Abigail tells Proctor that she has been waiting for him every night, but he insists that he never committed himself to an ongoing relationship. Abigail now speaks angrily, calling Proctor's wife Elizabeth "a cold sniveling woman."

Reverend John Hale, a ruddy, bright young man from the town of Beverly, arrives carrying half a dozen heavy books "weighted with authority." He tells a gathering of community people that "in these books the Devil stands stripped of all his brute disguises. Here are all your familiar spirits—your witches that go by land, or air, or by sea; your wizards of the night and the day."

Hale attempts to communicate with the ill Betty, but she fails to respond. When Hale asks Abigail what happened in the forest, she accuses the household slave, Tituba, of making Betty drink blood. The shocked slave, realizing that she may be hung as a witch, opts to "confess" and distributes the blame by suggesting that the Devil has many surrogate witches. Betty rises and soon she, Tituba, and Abigail cry out names of townspeople they saw "with the Devil." The curtain of the first scene descends on their hysterical, frenzied name calling.

The second scene takes place at John Proctor's farmhouse. As Proctor and his wife converse, we learn that four judges were sent to Salem from Boston, headed by a deputy-governor, and that there are fourteen women in jail awaiting trial. A band of girls led by Abigail Williams, seemingly possessed, howl and fall to the floor; the person they mention is clapped in jail for bewitching them.

Mary Warren, the young servant who works for the Proctors, enters and informs them that there are now thirty-nine prisoners to be tried. Goody Osburn confessed that she made a compact with Lucifer and has been sentenced to hang by the deputy-governor. Mary says that she is an official of the court and as such she's expected to be there every day. Proctor is on the verge of whipping the girl, when Mary points at Elizabeth and declares that she saved her life today. She cannot reveal who accused Elizabeth, for she's sworn to secrecy. Pompously, Mary strides off to bed. "Abigail wants me dead," says Elizabeth. "She thinks to take my place."

There is a knock on the door. It is Reverend Hale, who seems different now, drawn. There is a sense of guilt about him as he relates to the Proctors that he has just come from Rebecca Nurse's home. Elizabeth dismisses the notion that a pious seventy-year-old woman like Rebecca has trafficked with the Devil. The Proctors are shocked to hear that Rebecca is charged with the murder of Ann Putnam's seven babies.

The rumble of an upcoming wagon is heard. From it comes the clerk of the court, Ezekiel Cheever, with a warrant from the deputy-governor for Elizabeth's arrest. Proctor rips the warrant, picks his gun up, and points it at Cheever. Elizabeth presses the rifle down and says that she must go as ordered. She is chained and taken away. Hale attempts to calm Proctor: "The court is just." The farmer cries: "Little crazy children are jangling the keys of the kingdom, and common vengeance writes the law!" Hale is shaken and greatly disturbed.

The second act begins at night in the woods, where John Proctor, holding a lantern, meets Abigail and warns her that if she does not withdraw her accusation against Elizabeth, he will confess in open court that they have committed adultery, a deadly sin in this strict religious community. But to his terror, Abigail calmly promises to save him from himself.

In the forbidding, high-beamed anteroom of the General Court, one can hear the examination taking place in an adjacent courtroom. Salem Judge Hathorne and Deputy-Governor Danforth are mercilessly cross-examining Martha Corey. They are clearly suspicious of her hobby of reading fortunes. Martha's husband, Giles, one of the oldest men in the community, attempts to intercede, only to be pushed out by the guard and left to wait in the vestry. Deputy-Governor Danforth, a grave man in his sixties, follows. Giles Corey, Francis Nurse, and John Proctor ask Danforth to receive their depositions on behalf of their respective wives, but Danforth will not allow anyone to tamper with his authority. He does not accept depositions and has no doubt that the voice of Heaven is speaking through the accusing children. He has sent nearly four hundred sinners to jails from Marblehead to Lynn, and upon his signature, seventy-two have been condemned to hang. He knows where his duty lies.

Proctor submits to Danforth a paper signed by more than ninety friends and neighbors, declaring their good opinion of Elizabeth, Rebecca Nurse, and Martha Corey. Danforth hands the paper to Cheever and orders him to issue a warrant for every person who signed the petition. Reverend Hale tries to counsel moderation and casts doubt at the accusations claimed by the girls. Danforth asks Cheever to go into court and bring the children.

Proctor introduces Danforth to his frail witness, Mary Warren, who weakly states that the girls' finger-pointing was nothing but pretense. Mary is then confronted by Abigail, Mercy Lewis, Susanna Walcott, and

Betty Parris. Abigail cunningly becomes marvelously indignant as she listens to Mary's confession and with the support of Judge Hathorne, Reverend Parris, and the officious Cheever, becomes haughty and threatening, then suddenly goes into a frightened, trance-like state. The girls join her, shivering and moaning; Mary falters, reduced to whimpery hysteria. Proctor cannot take more of this and ruins himself by accusing Abigail of lechery: "She thinks to dance with me on my wife's grave." He and Giles Corey are taken off to jail.

The last scene unfolds three months later in a cell in a Salem jail. The window is barred, and by a light effect, a bar-like image is produced on the floor and faces of the actors. Danforth, Hathorne, and Cheever enter, the latter carrying a dispatch case and a flat wooden box containing writing materials. They talk of Reverend Hale's return to Salem, praying with Rebecca Nurse and Martha Corey. They wonder if Hale preaches in Andover, where the court was overthrown, and there is outright rebellion.

Parris walks in—gaunt, sweating, frightened. He reveals that his niece and her young friends are gone, and are now aboard ship. He is concerned, for news of Andover has broken here, and there may be a riot. As a matter of fact, upon opening his door to leave the house, a dagger clattered to the ground, a warning for him. He suggests the postponing of hanging for a time. But Danforth will not budge. He will hang whoever dared to rise against the law.

Hale enters, exhausted and sorrowful. He, too, begs Danforth for more time—no one has yet confessed. Danforth decides that the court's best chance of obtaining a confession lies with John Proctor; his pregnant wife might soften his resistance.

The jailer, Hopkins, ushers in Elizabeth and removes her chains. She is now heavy with child, gaunt and pale, but still shows amazing strength of character. Hale pleads with her to prevail upon her husband to confess— let him lie, but live, as life is God's most precious gift. Elizabeth responds quietly, "I think that be the Devil's argument." Proctor is brought in from his three months' incarceration in a dungeon—filthy, bearded, his eyes misty. He halts inside the doorway and catches sight of Elizabeth. The emotion flowing between them prevents anyone from speaking for an instant. Hale begs the judges to leave the Proctors alone. Danforth sweeps out, his retinue following.

The Proctors clasp hands. Elizabeth tells John that their boys are being well taken care of by friends. None of their group has confessed to witchery. Giles Corey died under cruel torture. John tells his wife that he is thinking of making a confession. She weeps, "I cannot judge you, I cannot." The judges return and Proctor says that he will have his life. Danforth, elated, asks him to sign a confession; it will be posted upon the church door. Under protest, Proctor signs, but when asked if he has seen other prisoners in the company of the Devil, he says that he'll not sell out his friends and tears his confession. He embraces his wife and is led out. Hale asks Elizabeth to plead with John to change his mind, but she says firmly, "He have his goodness now. God forbid I take it from him."

A drum roll is heard. It heightens in intensity as the curtain falls.

* * *

Staged by Jed Harris and designed by Boris Aronson, *The Crucible* premiered at New York's Martin Beck Theatre on January 22, 1953. The leading roles were played by Arthur Kennedy (John Proctor), Beatrice Straight (Elizabeth Proctor), Madeleine Sherwood (Abigail Williams), Jenny Egan (Mary Warren), Walter Hampden (Deputy-Governor Danforth), and E. G. Marshall (Reverend John Hale). It is reported that a mesmerized opening-night audience greeted *The Crucible* with nineteen curtain calls. However, the morning-after reviews ran the gamut of opinions. John Chapman applauded "a strong production, splendidly acted and strongly written."[1] Robert Coleman cheered "a rip-roaring melodrama about the historic witch trials in Salem, Mass. . . . It should spellbind those who relish real drama, conflict and impassioned action."[2] William Hawkins found the play "big and bold and very theatrical."[3] Richard Watts Jr. appreciated "a drama of emotional power and impact . . . a hard-biting and effective play . . . written with feeling and indignation."[4]

The naysayers included Walter F. Kerr, who appreciated the playwright's "shrewd theatrical gifts" but believed that the drama was a "mechanical parable," catering to the "intellect, not the heart."[5] Brooks Atkinson felt that "it may be that Mr. Miller has tried to pack too much inside his drama, and that he has permitted himself to be concerned more with the technique of the witch hunt than its humanity."[6] John McClain sighed, "I was not greatly moved by anything that had happened. . . . I never felt myself part of the proceedings."[7]

There was general consensus that Jed Harris has directed the play "with great force and precision," and that Boris Aronson "succeeded in creating some dour New England settings." Kudos were handed to Arthur Kennedy, "at his rare best as the farmer who must live or die for honor," and Walter Hampden, "as the stern and unrelenting magistrate who sends the blameless to the gallows."

The Crucible ran for 197 performances. Translated into Hebrew by Aharon Amir, it was presented by the Habimah Theatre of Israel in 1954.[8] Adapted by Marcel Aymé under the title *Les Sorcières de Salem* (*Witches of Salem*), the play reached Paris in February 1955 to great fanfare by the *Figaro* critic and his colleagues. The theatre reviewers of London also warmly welcomed *The Crucible* when it opened on April 9, 1956, at the Royal Court Theatre, directed by George Devine, who also appeared as

Deputy-Governor Danforth, featuring Michael Gwynn (John Proctor) and Kenneth Haigh (Reverend John Hale), and introducing future stars Mary Ure (Abigail Williams), Joan Plowright (Mary Warren), and Alan Bates (jailer Hopkins). *Theatre World Annual* stated, "Mr. Miller portrays with uncanny insight the rising tide of mass hysteria inaugurated by a group of adolescent girls hitherto repressed by a stern, joyless puritanism, and said now to have consorted with the Devil in the woods nearby."[9] The play, however, ran for only thirty-two performances.

The Crucible was revived at off-Broadway's Martinique Theatre on March 11, 1958, directed by Word Baker, with Michael Higgins (John Proctor), Barbara Harris (Elizabeth Proctor), Ford Rainey (Deputy-Governor Danforth), and Ann Wedgeworth (Abigail Williams). The long-running production, amassing 571 performances, was called by Lewis Funke of the *New York Times* "provocative, stimulating, and, most of all, an inspiring creation."[10] Simultaneously, the drama was presented with great success by the Horseshoe Stage Theatre of Hollywood, California, with Dwight Frye, star of Universal's horror films, as Reverend Samuel Parris.[11]

In 1964, a somewhat revised version of *The Crucible* was presented by Eva Le Gallienne's National Repertory Theatre at Broadway's Belasco Theatre. Critic John Chapman of the *Daily News* felt that the passage of time had not been kind to the play and it "now seems a rather juvenile and stereotyped exercise in dramatics."[12] But other reviewers were awed. "A brilliant revival," wrote Judith Crist. "*The Crucible* now glows as it never has before."[13] Howard Taubman asserted that "Arthur Miller's play retains the fury of its intensity and its pride in the inviolability of man's dignity and honor."[14] Norman Nadel pointed out the play's "timelessness" and complimented director Jack Sydow for his "earnest and urgent" staging.[15] John McClain singled out set designer Peter Larkin for employing "some bleached beams and other bits of crude driftwood to suggest the environs of early New England, with extremely good effect."[16] The entire cadre of critics applauded actors Farley Granger and Anne Meacham as the Proctors and Thayer David in the role of Deputy-Governor Danforth. The revival was shown for sixteen performances during the month of April, in repertory with Anton Chekhov's *The Seagull*. A year later, in 1965, The Long Wharf Theatre in New Haven, Connecticut, was founded and as its inaugural production presented *The Crucible*.

Across the Atlantic, England's National Theatre mounted *The Crucible* at the Old Vic on January 20, 1965, under the direction of Laurence Olivier. "A stunning production," said reviewer B. A. Young in a dispatch to the *New York Times*, adding special kudos to actors Colin Blakely (John Proctor), Robert Lang (Reverend John Hale), Joyce Redman (Elizabeth Proctor), and Pearl Prescod (the slave Tituba).[17] Scholar Martin Esslin, in

Plays and Players, called the production "a gripping and moving experience" and hailed its "triumphant demonstration of genuine ensemble acting."[18] The National Youth Theatre of Great Britain revived *The Crucible* on September 16, 1982, for a week's run.

New Yorkers had several more opportunities to see *The Crucible*. In 1972, the play was presented by the Repertory Theatre of Lincoln Center, directed by John Barry, designed by Jo Mielziner, featuring Robert Foxworth (John Proctor), Martha Henry (Elizabeth Proctor), Pamela Payton-Wright (Abigail Williams), and Aline MacMahon (Rebecca Nurse). In 1991, Tony Randall's National Actors Theatre produced *The Crucible* at Broadway's Belasco Theatre, garnering mixed reviews. *USA Today* called the show "a searing success"[19] and *New York Newsday* found it "ablaze with first-rate actors making powerful theatre,"[20] but the major critics had strong reservations, throwing darts at director Yossi Yzraely for failing "to mold the actors into a solid ensemble"[21] and instructing them "to perform at an emotional, hand-wringing level that takes the play straight toward melodrama."[22] Frank Rich scoffed at "actors who tend to saw the air with their hands, thump their chests and declaim to the Belasco's two balconies." He was particularly unhappy with two stars: Martin Sheen in the role of John Proctor, "looking more like Daniel Boone than a New England farmer . . . in a vocally constricted performance of sloppy emotions and knee-jerk righteous indignation"; and Michael York as Reverend John Hale, who "is allotted but a single (and weepy) note . . . and looks here as if he stepped off a Dutch Masters cigar box." The critic was also irked by the drama's villains who, "with the exception of Fritz Weaver's majestically malevolent Deputy-Governor Danforth, are routinely presented as snarling, physically unattractive screamers."[23]

The Crucible ran for thirty-one performances. The following year, 1992, the play was revived at Broadway's Virginia Theatre, directed by Richard Eyre. "Playing husband and wife under moral siege during the Salem witch trials, Liam Neeson and Laura Linney bring a transfixing heat to Richard Eyre's otherwise merely sweaty revival," said the *New York Times*. "Mr. Eyre is far less confident in overseeing the rest of his large and exasperatingly uneven cast, or in making a worthy old war horse of a play gallop like a young stallion."[24] The production ran for 103 showings.

The most revived play in the Arthur Miller canon, *The Crucible* was produced in May 2009 by Actors Co-op of Hollywood, California, directed by Marianne Savell, who, according to the *Los Angeles Times*, after a rocky first act, "hits her stride in the more intimate second act encounter between flawed hero John Proctor and his steadfast wife Elizabeth."[25] In January 2010, the drama was mounted by off-off-Broadway's Manhattan Theatre Source, staged by Jessica Solce, and in March, by off-off-Broadway's The Old Stone House, helmed by Claire Beckman.

The world premiere of an opera based on the play, with libretto by Bernard Stambler and music by Robert Ward (who won a Pulitzer Prize for his composition), took place at the New York City Center on October 26, 1961. A radio adaptation, featuring Donald Houston as John Proctor and Donald Wolfit as Deputy-Governor Danforth, was aired by London's Radio Four in May 1970. A 1956 French motion picture, adapted by Jean-Paul Sartre and directed by Raymond Rouleau, starred Yves Montand and Simone Signoret as the Proctors, while a 1996 movie, scripted by Arthur Miller and directed by Nicholas Hytner, featured Daniel Day-Lewis (John Proctor), Joan Allen (Elizabeth Proctor), Winona Ryder (Abigail Williams), and Paul Scofield (Deputy-Governor Danforth) and was nominated for several Academy and Golden Globe Awards.

The Crucible was televised in 1959 by UK's ITV Play of the Week with Sean Connery in the role of John Proctor and Susannah York as Abigail Williams. In 1965, it was seen on Spain's Estudio 1 with Francisco Piquer and Gemma Cuervo in those roles, and on Norway's television with Tom Stokke and Liv Ullmann as the Proctors. Don Taylor directed in England a 1980 television replica.

* * *

Arthur Miller was born in New York City in 1915. His father, Isadore Miller, was a successful ladies-wear manufacturer who lost his fortune during the Great Depression. The family's struggle to make ends meet left its mark on young Arthur and later influenced his writings. After graduating from high school in 1932, Miller worked for two years in an auto parts warehouse to earn money for college, and in 1934 he enrolled at the University of Michigan, where he twice won the Avery Hopwood award for playwriting.[26] He received his BA degree in 1938 and returned to New York, joining the Federal Theatre Project and writing radio scripts for such programs as "The Cavalcade of America" and "The Columbia Workshop." For "Theatre Guild on the Air," he adapted Ferenc Molnar's *The Guardsman* and John Cecil Holm's *Three Men on a Horse*.

In 1944, a Hollywood studio hired Miller to tour Army camps and gather material for the war movie *The Story of GI Joe*. That same year he had his first play produced at Broadway's Forrest Theatre, *The Man Who Had All the Luck*, about a small-town prosperous businessman who becomes obsessed with the idea that some disaster awaits him. It lasted for only four performances. His next effort was far more successful: *All My Sons*, a domestic drama about an upper-middle-class family whose existence turns into a nightmare when it is discovered that the much-loved father, Joe Keller, supplied defective equipment to the Army Air Force, causing the death of twenty-one pilots (Coronet Theatre, January 29, 1947, with Ed Begley as Keller—328 performances; London, Lyric Theatre,

May 11, 1948, with Joseph Calleia—148 performances; filmed 1948 with Edward G. Robinson). Miller followed *All My Sons* with his masterpiece, *Death of a Salesman*, a cornerstone of modern American drama. It is the story, revealed in flashbacks, of an aging traveling salesman, Willy Loman, who is peremptorily fired, and in an act of devotion to his family, commits suicide so that, with his insurance money, they can rid themselves of debt and make a new start (Morosco Theatre, February 10, 1949, with Lee J. Cobb as Loman—742 performances; Phoenix Theatre, London, July 28, 1949, with Paul Muni—204 performances).

Miller took a stand against the corruption of authority in his adaptation of Henrik Ibsen's drama *An Enemy of the People* (Broadhurst Theatre, December 28, 1950, with Fredric March and Florence Eldridge—thirty-six performances) and in 1953's *The Crucible*. Then came *A View from the Bridge*, in which a married Brooklyn dockworker, Eddie Carbone, falls in love with his adopted eighteen-year-old niece, Catherine. When Catherine plans to marry the young and handsome Rodolpho, an illegal Sicilian immigrant, Eddie's jealousy drives him first to accuse Rodolpho of being a homosexual, and then to betray him and a cousin, Marco, to the immigrant authorities. Marco avenges the exposure by confronting Eddie on the waterfront and stabbing him to death (Coronet Theatre, September 29, 1955, with Van Heflin as Eddie—149 performances; Comedy Theatre, London, October 11, 1956, with Anthony Quayle—219 performances; off-Broadway, Sheridan Square Playhouse, January 28, 1965, with Robert Duvall—780 performances).

In 1964, the newly formed Lincoln Center Repertory presented two plays by Miller at the ANTA–Washington Square Theatre: *After the Fall* is a stream-of-consciousness drama in which Quentin, a successful lawyer, strives to determine the extent of his guilt in relation to people who shaped his life, particularly the three women to whom he committed himself. The play brought Miller a storm of criticism, for critics noted the resemblance between his recently deceased second wife, the actress Marilyn Monroe, and Maggie, the blond-wigged, drug-addicted protagonist in the play, and accused him of defiling Monroe's image (January 23, 1964, with Jason Robards Jr. as Quentin, Barbara Loden as Maggie—208 performances). *Incident at Vichy* is the story of a group of several men and a boy of fifteen, all suspected of being Jews, who wait in a barren room to be interrogated in Vichy, France, in 1942 (December 3, 1964—thirty-two performances).

Miller's last significant play was *The Price*, wherein two brothers, Victor and Walter Franz, meet after their father's death to dispose of the family's furniture and clash with mutual accusations (Morosco Theatre, February 7, 1968, with Pat Hingle and Arthur Kennedy—429 performances). Miller's later plays—among them, *The Creation of the World and Other Business* (1972), a comedy based on the Old Testament, featuring Adam, Eve, Cain, and Abel; *The Archbishop's Ceiling* (1977), a drama set behind the Iron Curtain; *The American Clock* (1980), an episodic play unfolding during the Great Depression; *Danger! Memory!* (1987), about the danger of remembering and the danger of forgetting; and *Broken Glass* (1994), the story of a Jewish married couple living in Brooklyn in 1938, and the effect upon them of the Kristallnacht (Night of Broken Glass) in Nazi Germany—were not well received, and he took to denounce Broadway as obsessed with commerce and greed.[27]

Miller also wrote essays, novels, short stories, and a 1987 autobiography, *Timebends: A Life*.[28] He was married three times: in 1940 he married his college sweetheart, Mary Grace Slattery, from whom he was divorced in 1955; the following year he married Marilyn Monroe, and they were divorced in 1960; two years later, he married Swedish photographer Ingeborg Morath, who died in 2002. When Marilyn Monroe was his spouse, he wrote for her the screenplay of *The Misfits* (1961), a brooding story about over-the-hill cowboys in the Nevada desert, in which she costarred with Clark Gable and Montgomery Clift under John Huston's direction. Miller's sister is the actress Joan Copeland, and his daughter is the filmmaker Rebecca Miller, who is married to the actor Daniel Day-Lewis. Miller died at his home in Roxbury, Connecticut, of congestive heart failure, on February 11, 2005, at the age of 89. Broadway theatres dimmed their marquee lights at curtain time in his memory.

Acting Edition: Dramatists Play Service.

Awards and Honors: Winner of the 1953 Tony Award as Best Play, and a top-ten selection in *The Best Plays of 1952–1953*.

Miller's *All My Sons* was a top-ten selection in 1947, won two Tony Awards, and took the New York Drama Critics' Circle Award.

Miller's *Death of a Salesman* (1949) won the triple crown of the Pulitzer Prize, the New York Drama Critics Circle Award, and the Tony. The fiftieth anniversary production of the play received the Tony and Drama Desk Awards for Best Revival of a Play, as did the Roundabout Theatre's production of *A View from the Bridge*. Miller was the recipient of a 1999 Tony for Lifetime Achievement. Off-Broadway's Signature Theatre Company dedicated its 1997–1998 season to his plays.

Miller garnered the National Association of Independent Schools Award in 1954, an American Academy of Arts and Letters Gold Medal in 1959, the National Medal of Arts in 1993, the National Book Foundation 2001 Medal for Distinguished Contribution to American Letters, Japan's 2001 Praemium Imperiale for lifetime achievement in arts, Spain's Principe de Asturias Prize for Literature as "the undisputed master of modern drama" in 2002, and the Jerusalem Prize in 2003.

Miller was international president of PEN, London and New York, 1965–1969, and a member of the American Academy of Arts and Letters since 1971. He held honorary doctorate degrees from the University of Michigan, Harvard University, and Oxford University, and he received the Creative Arts Award from Brandeis University.

A 1998 survey by Britain's Royal National Theatre of more than eight hundred playwrights, directors, actors, and critics chose Arthur Miller as the best playwright of the twentieth century. Although Samuel Becket's *Waiting for Godot* was selected as the century's best play, Miller wound up with two plays in the top ten, *Death of a Salesman* at number two and *The Crucible* at number six.

NOTES

1. *Daily News*, January 23, 1953.
2. *Daily Mirror*, January 23, 1953.
3. *New York World-Telegram*, January 23, 1953.
4. *New York Post*, January 23, 1953.
5. *New York Herald Tribune*, January 23, 1953.
6. *New York Times*, January 23, 1953.
7. *New York Journal-American*, January 23, 1953.
8. In addition to its 1954 Habimah Theatre production, *The Crucible* was mounted two more times in Israel—by the Haifa Municipal Theatre in 1970, a highly theatrical interpretation of the play with an emphasis on pictorial tableaus, and by the Be'er Sheva Municipal Theatre in 1991.
9. *Theatre World Annual*, 1956.
10. *New York Times*, March 12, 1958.
11. Dwight Frye (1899–1943) etched notable movie characterizations as Fritz, the hunchbacked, sadistic tormentor of the Monster in *Frankenstein,* and mad, fly-eating Renfield in *Dracula*, both films released in 1931. On Broadway in 1933, he played the sympathetic Chinese murderer Ah Sing, who is unmasked by Honolulu police sergeant Charlie Chan in Earl Derr Biggers' *Keeper of the Keys*. That same year he enacted at the Alcazar Theatre of San Francisco the role of the double-faced Lord Lebanon in Edgar Wallace's *The Case of the Frightened Lady* (aka *Criminal at Large*). In the late 1930s, Frye portrayed Dan, the baby-faced killer, in a Los Angeles production of Emlyn Williams' *Night Must Fall*.
12. *Daily News*, April 7, 1964.
13. *New York Herald Tribune*, April 7, 1964.
14. *New York Times*, April 7, 1964.
15. *New York World-Telegram*, April 7, 1964.
16. *New York Journal-American*, April 7, 1964.
17. *New York Times*, January 20, 1965.
18. *Plays and Players*, March 1965.
19. *USA Today*, December 12, 1991.
20. *New York Newsday*, December 6, 1991.
21. Howard Kissel, *Daily News*, December 11, 1991.
22. Edwin Wilson, *Wall Street Journal*, December 20, 1991.

23. *New York Times*, December 11, 1991.

24. *New York Times*, May 31, 2002.

25. *Los Angeles Times*, May 8, 2009.

26. Avery Hopwood (1884–1928) was a prolific and popular author of many Broadway comedies, farces, and musicals during the first quarter of the twentieth century. His most memorable achievement was the 1920 classic melodrama *The Bat*, on which he collaborated with Mary Roberts Rinehart, an adaptation from her 1908 novel, *The Circular Staircase*.

27. Though it received mixed reviews in New York, *Broken Glass* won the 1995 Olivier Award for best play in London.

28. *The Theatre Essays of Arthur Miller*, edited by Robert A. Martin and published by Viking Press in 1978, collects articles, prefaces, and interviews published in books, newspapers, and magazines over a thirty-year period. Edited by Christopher Bigsby with an introduction by Harold Clurman, Viking also published in 1971 *The Portable Arthur Miller*, a comprehensive overview of Miller's contributions to the stage, and in 2001, a slim volume by Miller, *On Politics and the Art of Acting*, analyzing the thespian skills of Ronald Reagan, Bill Clinton, JFK, and FDR.

My 3 Angels (1953)

Sam Spewack
(Ukraine-born American, 1899–1971)
and Bella Spewack
(Romania-born American, 1899–1990)

Murder is made amusing, even palatable, in a Christmas fable about a trio of angelic rogues—an embezzler and two assassins—who have been banished to a penal colony in Cayenne, French Guiana. The convicts Joseph, Jules, and Alfred are the heroes of *My 3 Angels*, adapted by Sam and Bella Spewack from the 1952 French comedy *La Cuisine des Anges* by Albert Husson.

On Christmas Eve 1910, Joseph, Jules, and Alfred are assigned to repair the roof of Felix Ducotel's general store. They find the Ducotel family in a sorry state—the impractical father, Felix, is on the verge of losing his business to an unscrupulous landlord, Henri Trochard. Felix's naive daughter, Marie Louise, is victimized by her lover, Paul, Trochard's nephew, who, like his uncle, is a mean opportunist.

The convicts descend from the roof and gradually solve the Ducotels' problems. They steal a chicken and a tree from the governor's yard for Christmas dinner; increase the sales of the store; forge a will that benefits the poor shopkeeper; prevent Marie Louise from committing suicide, and, playing Cupid, guide her to a suitable romantic attachment; and finally—with help from their pet snake Adolphe—dispatch Henri and Paul to their Maker. Content with their Christmas adventure, the chivalrous benefactors decide, "Let's do it again next year."

* * *

When *My 3 Angels* premiered at New York's Morosco Theatre on March 11, 1953, most critics greeted it warmly. "The Spewacks have typed their script with persuasive wit and unorthodox wisdom," smiled Robert Coleman. "They set themselves an almost impossible task and accomplished it brilliantly. They have blended humor, drama, and suspense into a solid click."[1] John Chapman concurred: "*My 3 Angels* is a good spring tonic; it's easy to take and will make you feel better."[2] John McClain called the play "a sure-pop hit. . . . The elements of humor are endless and both the director (Jose Ferrer) and the authors have exploited them wonderfully well."[3]

The macabre sense of humor of *My 3 Angels* also appealed to William Hawkins: "*My 3 Angels* turns out to be an entirely enchanting evening at the Morosco. . . . The play is unpretentious and casual. If you dissect its plot you find a remarkable parallel to some children's fairy tale, where right in disguise triumphs over pompous, self-righteous wrong. The comedy is marked by a delightful comic manner, practical and honest so that its purity of outlook constantly surprises you."[4]

Some reviewers dissented. Richard Watts Jr. found the first act of *My 3 Angels* "so freshly engaging that it sets up the highest hopes for an evening of continuous delights. After that happy beginning, unfortunately, the interest and invention run almost steadily down-hill."[5] Brooks Atkinson shared Watts's disappointment: "All this begins very wittily. For the adapters have written the first act with the wicked insouciance of expert comedians. . . . But then the homely honesty of our American traditions begins to intrude on *My 3 Angels,* and things become a good deal duller."[6] Walter F. Kerr, too, had mixed feelings: "A good bit of the evening has a gleefully wicked gleam in its eye. . . . The casual irony and mocking impudence of *My 3 Angels* are altogether fetching. It must be admitted, though, that the fun is almost entirely lodged in the play's basic idea and that the Spewacks, once they have made that idea plain to us, have not been especially inventive in elaborating on it. Devices are repeated from act to act, the characterizations become a bit paler as time goes on, and there are disturbing lulls as the antic materials make way for some sober last-act sentimentality."[7]

The entire cadre of critics saluted Walter Slezak, Jerome Cowan, and Darren McGavin in the title roles, and Boris Aronson's design of "a mat-and-bamboo house that invites pleasant insanity."

La Cuisine des Anges, the source of *My 3 Angels,* was Albert Husson's first play. It won the Tristan Bernard Prize when produced in Paris in 1952. On Broadway, *My 3 Angels* ran for 344 performances. A subsequent production in 1955, at London's Lyric Theatre, garnered 228 showings. That same year, a motion picture version called *We're No Angels,* directed by Michael Curtiz, starred Humphrey Bogart, Aldo Ray, and Peter Ustinov as the Devil Island convicts, supported by Joan Bennett and Leo G. Carroll as the victimized shopkeepers, and Basil Rathbone in the role of their scrooge-like relative. In 1959, the Spewacks adapted the play into a ninety-minute television special, with Walter Slezak reprising his role as Joseph.[8] Several decades later, in 1985, Canadian composer David Warrack turned the play into a musical, but its reception at St. Lawrence Center in Toronto was lukewarm. In 1989, David Mamet adapted and Neil Jordan directed a new film version of

My 3 Angels loosely based on Husson's original, starring Robert De Niro and Sean Penn as the convicts, but the movie was a major box office flop. Still, upon perusing the Spewacks' text today, the comedy has preserved a high degree of whimsical freshness, sly eeriness, romantic glow, and allegorical wisdom.

* * *

Born in the Ukraine in 1899, Samuel Spewack was brought up on the East Side in New York, educated at Stuyvesant High School and Columbia University. When working as a reporter for the *New York World*, he met Romanian immigrant Bella Cohen, also a journalist, and the couple married in 1922. Over the years, Sam and Bella Spewack teamed on a number of Broadway comedies, the most popular of which was *Boy Meets Girl*, a Hollywood satire inspired by the couple's own experiences (Cort Theatre, November 27, 1935—669 performances). The Spewacks are perhaps best known as the collaborators, with Cole Porter, on the musical *Kiss Me, Kate*, about husband and wife actors whose feuds mirror the plot of a show they are performing, Shakespeare's *The Taming of the Shrew* (Century/Shubert Theatres, December 30, 1948—1,077 performances).

During the 1930s, the Spewacks penned the scenarios of several B-movies tinged with criminous elements: *Clear All Wires!*, *The Solitaire Man*, *The Gay Bride*, and *Rendezvous*. In the 1940s they scripted the exuberant romantic comedies *My Favorite Wife* (starring Irene Dunne, Cary Grant, and Randolph Scott) and *Weekend at the Waldorf* (with Ginger Rogers, Lana Turner, Walter Pidgeon, and Van Johnson).

On his own, Sam wrote for the New York stage the successful *Two Blind Mice*, a caustic farce about Washington bureaucracy (Cort Theatre, March 2, 1949—157 performances) and the failed *Once There Was a Russian* (aka *The Prince and Mr. Jones*), a historical charade involving John Paul Jones, Prince Potemkin, and Catherine the Great of Russia (Music Box Theatre, February 18, 1961—one performance). He also tried his hand at writing two suspense novels—*Skyscraper Murder* (1928) and *Murder in the Gilded Cage* (1929; filmed as *The Secret Witness* in 1931).

Bella Spewack broke the story on Anna Anderson, who claimed to be Anastasia, the long-lost Grand Duchess of Russia. In 1922, at age twenty-three, she wrote her autobiography, *Streets: A Memoir of the Lower East Side*, which was published posthumously in 1995 by Feminist Press. In 1946, Bella broadcast on the ABC radio network a series of reports covering her journeys through Eastern Europe as a representative of the United Nations. She also made a name for herself as the publicist for the Camp Fire Girls and the Girl Scouts of America.

The Samuel and Bella Spewack papers and play scripts are housed at the Rare Book and Manuscript Library of Columbia University in Manhattan.

Acting Edition: Dramatists Play Service.

Awards and Honors: *My 3 Angels* was a top-ten selection in *The Best Plays of 1952–1953*, though editor Louis Kronenberger had some reservations: "*My 3 Angels* gained greatly on Broadway from Walter Slezak's performance as angel-in-chief; he gave it what it needed in English—something not only funny but foreign. For from the Spewacks' American version of this impudent and escapist morality play, something Gallic had itself escaped. No doubt, too, the story is a little thin, and, in making merry with murder, skates, here and there, on thin ice. But beyond what is piquant in the theme, enough remains in the telling for an enjoyable evening. Treating of three friendly scoundrels possessed of every criminal art and penal grace, it makes a nice practical French *Christmas Carol* in which it seems simpler to bump Scrooge than to convert him."[9]

Samuel Spewack's comedy *Two Blind Mice* was a top-ten selection in *The Best Plays of 1948–1949*.

Sam and Bella Spewack were nominated for an Academy Award for Best Original Story for *My Favorite Wife* (1940) and won a 1949 Tony Award for their book of the musical *Kiss Me, Kate*.

NOTES

1. *Daily Mirror*, March 12, 1953.
2. *Daily News*, March 12, 1953.
3. *New York Journal-American*, March 12, 1953.
4. *New York World-Telegram*, March 12, 1953.
5. *New York Post*, March 12, 1953.
6. *New York Times*, March 12, 1953.
7. *New York Herald Tribune*, March 12, 1953.
8. Walter Slezak plays a noble villain in *My 3 Angels*, but his movie career is splattered with darker characters. Slezak won the hisses of audiences as the club-footed, brutal torturer Dr. Skaas in *The Fallen Sparrow* (1943); the Nazi U-boat captain Willi, in Alfred Hitchcock's *Lifeboat* (1944); the corrupt governor Don Alvarado in *The Spanish Main* (1945); an oily middle-man, Melchior Incza, in *Cornered* (1945); Albert Arnett, a shady private detective, in *Born to Kill* (1947); Eric Molinar, the leader of a gang of homicidal thugs, in *Riff Raff* (1947); the notorious Caribbean pirate "Mack the Black" in *The Pirate* (1948); an avaricious gold hunter in *White Witch Doctor* (1953); and the blackguard "the Baron" in *Emil and the Detectives* (1964). Bad-guy Slezak clashed, to his downfall, with comedians Bob Hope (*The Princess and the Pirate*, 1944), Danny Kaye (*The Inspector General*, 1949), Red Skelton (*The Yellow Cab Man*, 1950), and Abbott and Costello (*Abbott and Costello*

in the Foreign Legion, 1950). Austrian-born Slezak (1902–1983) appeared in over 100 films. He also acted on the stage for many years. In 1955, he won the Tony Award as Best Actor for his role of Panisse, an old man who marries a young pregnant woman, in the musical *Fanny*.

9. Louis Kronenberger, ed., *The Best Plays of 1952–1953* (New York: Dodd, Mead, 1953), 8.

Sherlock Holmes (1953)

Ouida Rathbone
(United States, Spain-born, 1885–1974)

Basil Rathbone, the quintessential Sherlock Holmes of the movies, returned to 221B Baker Street in a disastrous stage play penned by his wife.

Ouida Rathbone's *Sherlock Holmes* is based on Conan Doyle's *The Adventure of the Bruce-Partington Plans* and *The Adventure of the Second Stain*, with cuttings from *A Scandal in Bohemia*, *The Final Problem*, *The Empty House*, and *His Last Bow*. A cast of twenty-three populates a series of elaborate sets that are scattered along three acts; each act is divided into three scenes.

A scrim curtain dissolves and we find ourselves in the Baker Street study. Holmes is seated beside the fireplace, playing his Stradivarius. Watson, who has been jotting notes at a table, becomes irritated: "I say, Holmes, do you have to play that same tune all day?" A mild verbal duel ensues, during which the detective scoffs at Watson's "woefully neglected" musical education. His chronicler retorts, claiming that Holmes is the most ignorant man in the world about everything that doesn't affect his work.

Holmes's brother, Mycroft, enters and introduces a companion, the Right Honorable Trelawney Hope, Secretary of the Navy.[1] The visitors state that they are there about a matter of pressing importance: one of the most jealously guarded naval secrets has been stolen; its loss might easily lead to European complication of the gravest kind. Hope adds, "If the plans are not recovered, I am a ruined man."

Designs for the Bruce-Partington submarine, enclosed in a large blue envelope, were secretly kept in a safe in a confidential office protected by burglar-proof doors and windows. Exact copies were made and brought to London for an important cabinet meeting.[2] Hope never let the copies out of his sight and took them each evening to his house in Whitehall Terrace, where they were locked in a second-floor bedroom safe. The only people who knew of this arrangement were Hope's private secretary,

Arthur Cadogan West, and the head of the Submarine Department, Sir James Walker.

The theft of the plans had been discovered earlier that morning. Hope and his wife are light sleepers and are prepared to swear that no one entered the bedroom during the night. When Hope first arrived home and placed the papers in the safe, he left his keys on a table and exited the room to bathe and change. Hope believes that the theft must have taken place during that time. He states that he believes a burglar must have concealed himself in the bedroom, arriving earlier.

After the visitors' departure, Holmes lights his "old oily clay pipe" and begins pacing. He pooh-poohs the theory that some agent managed to plant himself in Hope's bedroom and startles Watson by declaring, "There is in every man a spot where you may touch him and find a hidden weakness lingering there. Sir James Walker—Cadogan West—even Trelawney Hope himself."

Holmes believes that Professor Moriarty is "playing a major role in such a bold game." The detective has already tried to penetrate the veil that has shrouded Moriarty's syndicate of espionage, and he is aware of three people to investigate: Eduardo Lucas, a bachelor of uncertain nationality, "well known and liked in society, a cunning philanderer and a tremendous gambler"; the count Louis de Rothiere, born Louis Barton, alias Basil Younopolos, "one of those French Intellectuals that I would love to cross swords with in more ways than one"; and Hugo Oberstein, who "rarely visits this country—but when he does 'watch out.'"[3]

They find the first "link," Eduardo Lucas, lying dead in his study. He was stabbed through the heart, no doubt by the dagger found at his side. As Holmes and Watson search the room, the doorbell rings. They hide behind curtains and see Lady Trelawney Hope—"very beautiful, about thirty, handsomely gowned"[4]—enter cautiously, kneel on the floor, pull back a rug and press on one of the squares of the hardwood floor. A panel opens. She extracts a blue envelope, closes the opening, notices blood on her hand, turns, sees the dead body, and stares at it for a moment as she stifles a scream. Holmes and Watson come out.

Lady Hope sobs and tells them that she knew Eduardo Lucas in Italy before her marriage to Trelawney, and that he recently came back into her life, threatening to expose her love letters to him unless she delivered a certain blue envelope with a red seal on it. She was afraid to lose her husband's love and respect—"our marriage would end in divorce"—so when she saw him leave the keys on the table, she opened the safe and took the envelope. She put it in her muff when going to the opera, complained of a headache, took a cab to Eduardo's apartment, gave him the envelope, and received her letters. The doorbell rang and Eduardo became agitated. He hurriedly lifted the rug and put the envelope into the compartment under the floor. Then he showed her the way out through the garden. Later that night, when she realized the serious consequences of what she had done, she decided to come back and beg Eduardo to return the envelope.

Lady Hope hands the envelope to Holmes. He breaks the seal—and finds blank pages. Who could have done it? Watson wonders. "The person who murdered Eduardo Lucas," says Holmes grimly.

The action shifts to the dressing room of Lydia Dorovna at Drury Lane Theatre. Flowers are everywhere. Count de Rothiere opens the drawers of the dressing table, one by one, as if searching for something. There is a knock on the door. Holmes and Watson enter. The Count tells Holmes that he is a great admirer—"your fame has even reached France." The detective responds by asking whether de Rothiere knows Eduardo Lucas, who was murdered near the Count's residence in Godolphin Square.

The Count departs with a smile, "Good night, gentleman," eliciting a comment from Holmes, "Cool as ice . . . and as poisonous as a cobra. . . . If Lucas had the plans and de Rothiere knew it, he might have paid him a little visit."

Lydia Dorovna sashays in. "She is a very beautiful Russian ballerina." Dorovna does not ruffle at Holmes's rapid cross-examination and keeps insisting that her fiancé, Arthur Cadogan West, Trelawney Hope's secretary, "is the most patriotic man on earth." When the detectives leave, de Rothiere walks in from an adjacent dressing room, slaps Dorovna, and says harshly that her blundering affair with Cadogan West has made it impossible for him to remain in this country. He will leave tonight for the Continent—and she is coming with him. She's much too dangerous to leave behind.

At 221B Baker Street, Mycroft Holmes bursts in to inform his brother that Cadogan West was found murdered beside the tracks of the underground. On his body were discovered seven of the ten Bruce-Partington plans. The most important three are still missing. Holmes has no doubt that the same person who earlier killed Lucas has now dispensed with West. "Watson, in all our joint researches, we have never had a case with more wheels within wheels," says Holmes as he paces the floor restlessly.

The trail leads Holmes and Watson to the third "link"—Hugo Oberstein, a foreign operative. They follow Oberstein to Switzerland and the proceedings shift to Professor Moriarty's Swiss chalet, perched on the Reichenbach Falls. De Rothiere relates to the Professor's secretary, Miss Dunbar, that the dancer Dorovna, upon hearing that West had been murdered, committed suicide by throwing herself overboard as they crossed the channel. "She was faithless, stupid, disloyal and ungrateful," says de Rothiere coldly. "She got what she deserved."

A valet enters with an announcement that there's a gentleman downstairs—a Mr. Sherlock Holmes. Astonished, Miss Dunbar speaks into a house phone, replaces it, and tells the valet to show the visitor up. Holmes is ushered in, followed by Moriarty. The play's description reads: "As nearly as possible, he should look like the late William Randolph Hearst. A big man, taller and larger than Holmes. Small eyes set in a hawk-like face, with a high forehead, which domes out in a wide curve. . . . He is clean-shaven, pale and aesthetic looking, retaining something of the professor in his features. His shoulders are rounded from much studying, and his face protrudes forward and is forever slowly oscillating from side to side in a curiously reptilian fashion."

The face-to-face meeting between the two antagonists begins pleasantly. Holmes compliments Moriarty for the display of El Greco paintings along the walls. Moriarty chuckles, "You would have made an admirable criminal, Mr. Holmes . . . and I—the greatest of detectives."

Holmes brings up the subject of the Bruce-Partington plans. He is authorized by the British government to exceed any figure that Moriarty may have been offered, for the return of the papers. Moriarty laughs and says that he does not like Mr. Gladstone, a "good dull man," and he would never raise a finger to help the prime minister under any circumstances.[5]

Moriarty's demeanor changes and he becomes more and more agitated, recounting how Holmes crossed his path on several occasions, an intolerable situation that requires extreme measures.

Moriarty moves to the windows and opens them. He tells Holmes that it will be presumed that on the path below he stopped to view the falls and fell to his death. A search party will find his hat and cape on a bench. The rail will be broken. Later his body will be washed ashore by the raging torrent.

Like a flash of lightning, Holmes leaps at Moriarty. Both men lose their balance and fall into the canyon. We hear the roar of the waterfall as the curtain slowly descends.

Two months pass. The "late" Sherlock Holmes shocks Dr. Watson and Mrs. Hudson by appearing at the doorstep of 221B Baker Street, a soft hat drawn down over his eyes, a scarf covering the lower part of his face and his arm in a sling.

Holmes reveals that as he and Moriarty were hurtling into the abyss, he fell on a narrow ledge of snow, while the Napoleon of Crime tumbled down. Holmes came out of the descent with a broken arm and soon learned that Moriarty, too, was still alive.

Following the dictates of *The Empty House,* a wax dummy resembling Holmes is placed by the window seated in a chair. A lamp is tilted so that it makes a silhouette of the figure on a window blind. Colonel Sebastian Moran, chief of staff to Professor Moriarty, shoots at the dummy from across the street and is apprehended by Inspector Lestrade of Scotland Yard.

Two constables take the colonel to headquarters, but just as it seems that the affair is winding up, a new set of circumstances—and characters—is introduced. Irene Adler, the one and only woman who softened the misogynist Holmes, is recruited from *A Scandal in Bohemia* to join Professor Moriarty at his Swiss abode. "Radiantly beautiful and magnificently dressed in the height of Paris fashion," Adler, a former opera diva, entertains the professor and his guests at the piano.

Moriarty, seated in a wheelchair, confides to his secretary, Miss Dunbar, that he shall remain crippled for life and that his last great adventure will be to bring the Bruce-Partington submarine business to a successful conclusion.

Among Moriarty's guests are Baron Von Bork and Captain Von Herling from Berlin.[6] The professor introduces them to Mr. Altamont, a man with red hair and beard, a broad nose, a florid complexion, and an Irish accent. Altamont, brash and impudent, shocks them all by gulping down, without pause, a glass of Tokay from the private cellar of the Emperor Franz Josef.

Moriarty thanks Adler for acquainting him with Altamont, thus making it possible "to conclude our most ambitious undertaking." Altamont rips the sole of his shoe and pulls out the submarine plans. Von Herling examines the designs with a magnifying glass, exchanges words in German with Von Bork and seems satisfied. Von Bork fetches his red leather wallet and counts bills for Moriarty—500,000 marks. Altamont insists that half the money belongs to him, snatches the plans and calls out, "Lestrade . . . Gregson . . . Monsieur Villard."[7] The lawmen enter and arrest Von Bork, Von Herling, and de Rothiere.[8] When Moriarty is wheeled out, he says, "Good night, Mr. Holmes. I dare say we shall meet again." Holmes smiles, "Yes, Professor, at Old Bailey."

Holmes picks up the bottle of Tokay and pours a glass for Miss Adler. She says that it has been a great privilege to have been associated with him on this case. Holmes sighs, "I shall never understand women, Miss Adler. Your sex will ever remain an enigma to me." She nonetheless invites him to Covent Garden in July, as her guest, to hear her sing.

A final scene, back at Baker Street, depicts Watson returning happily from the Old Bailey, telling Mrs. Hudson that Holmes had been in the witness box for two hours—calm, incisive, triumphant; that the Great Detective was invited to meet with the prime minister in Downing Street; that there is no doubt he will be offered a title of some kind, "which, of course, he will refuse." But when Holmes returns home, he stands at the door, erect and very pale. He wearily asks for brandy and announces that he is about to ring down the curtain. He will retire to his little bee farm at Heathfield in Sussex, where perhaps he shall write a book; a wise man always retires at the height of his career.

Both are silent for a moment, and Holmes goes through a slightly revised recitation from *His Last Bow*: "There's an East wind coming, Watson. . . . If not now, it will come later. The storm clouds are gathering. There will be such a wind as never blew over England. It will be cold and bitter and the living will wither before its blast. But 'tis God's own wind none the less, and a cleaner, better, stronger land will lie in the sunshine when the storm has cleared."

They are both now standing before Queen Victoria's picture over the mantel. Holmes raises his glass: "To her Majesty, the Queen." Watson responds: "The Queen."

They drink. Curtain.

* * *

In his 1962 autobiography *In and Out of Character*, Basil Rathbone wrote, "The Sherlock Holmes stories are dated and their pattern and style, generally speaking, unacceptable to an age where science has proven that science fiction is another outdated joke. . . . The only possible medium still available to an acceptable present-day presentation of Sir Arthur Conan Doyle's stories would be a full length Disney cartoon."[9]

Rathbone said that working on his first Holmes picture, *The Hound of the Baskervilles*, was "the stimulating experience of creating, within my own limited framework, a character that has intrigued me as much as any I have ever played." But, he complains, "the continuous repetition of story after story after story left me virtually repeating myself each time in a character I had already conceived and developed. The stories varied but I was always the same character merely repeating myself in different situations."[10]

In due course, writes Rathbone, the endless repetitions forced him into a critical analysis of the detective and he came to the conclusion that "there was nothing lovable about Holmes."[11] If he could, he would have done what Arthur Conan Doyle did, and send the detective down the Reichenbach Falls. "But I could not kill Mr. Holmes," laments Rathbone, "so I decided to run away from him."[12] In 1946, to the chagrin of his wife Ouida, his longtime friend Nigel Bruce, and his agents at the Music Corporation of America, Rathbone decided to pack and leave Hollywood for New York.

Five years later, in 1951, Rathbone had a change of heart and suggested to his wife that she write a Sherlock Holmes play for him. "Ouida read all the *Adventures* very carefully," reports Rathbone, "making copious notes. After some months she came up with what seemed a masterly construction, using material from five of the Conan Doyle stories.[13] It was a workmanlike job, and most faithful to the traditions that made these stories classics."[14]

With the blessings of the Conan Doyle estate, *Sherlock Holmes* was sent to several New York producers but was continually rejected until early 1953, when Bill Doll, a well-known press agent going into management, "read the play and fell for it 'hook, line and sinker.'"[15] Reginald Denham, an expert in murder melodrama, was engaged as director.[16] The role of Moriarty was assigned to Hollywood heavy Thomas Gomez,[17] while Watson went to the Australian Jack Raine, who had recently gained acclaim in the London production of *Dear Murderer*.[18]

A pre-Broadway tryout was scheduled, for three weeks, in Boston. Rathbone describes a "catastrophic" dress rehearsal where "everything went wrong, including the stage manager who fainted at his desk from a mild heart attack. . . . Tempers were frayed and everyone was 'passing the buck.' It was the most incompetent stage crew I have ever worked with . . . tired actors, including myself, started to muff their lines. . . . The ugly spectre of failure lurked in dark corners."[19]

Sherlock Holmes opened at Boston's Majestic Theatre on October 10, 1953. Aware that the local engagement was meant to doctor the play and shape its production, the reviewers were cautiously optimistic. "When the mechanics of the staging have smoothed down . . . *Sherlock Holmes* should become a welcome perennial for Broadway and the road," wrote Alta Maloney.[20] "A few more performances will iron out the difficulties. . . . This is a highly diverting item of make-believe," chirped Cyrus Durgin.[21] "Generally well acted and really enjoyable" was the verdict of Elinor Hughes.[22] Peggy Doyle rejoiced at Basil Rathbone's "lean, self-contained materialization of Arthur Conan Doyle's master detective," Jack Raine's "perfect foil" Watson, and Thomas Gomez's "admirable acting achievement" as Moriarty.[23]

But the dean of Boston's critics, Elliot Norton, was caustic: "There is altogether too much talk and too little progressive coherent action in this new *Sherlock Holmes* at the moment."[24] Norton sent a dire telegram to Sam Zolotow of the *New York Times*: "Afraid *Sherlock Holmes* can't make the grade. Too much talk, too little action. Needs drastic rewriting to survive."

Sherlock Holmes moved to Manhattan's New Century Theatre on October 30, 1953. The critics were not amused. "Last night on the stage at the Century, the great detective talked himself into exhaustion and the audience into lethargy," pouted William Hawkins.[25] "The truth is that, if you went to the trouble of following the plot line of *Sherlock Holmes*, you would probably find yourself in deep trouble merely trying to keep up with it," frowned Richard Watts Jr.[26] "Mrs. Rathbone's salute to the celebrated detective is cumbersome and uneven," scowled Brooks Atkinson.[27] Walter Kerr believed that "the acting, for the most part, hasn't half enough relish in it" and Reginald Denham's direction "is oddly unsettled."[28]

Sherlock Holmes closed its doors after three performances.

* * *

Ouida Bergere Rathbone (1885–1974) was born on a train enroute to Madrid, Spain. As a child she lived in Madrid, Paris, and London. At the age of eleven she came to the United States, dwelling in Connecticut, Virginia, Louisiana, Arkansas, and Kentucky.

Ouida's initial goal was to become an actress; she joined the Shubert Stock Company in Brooklyn, New York, played in vaudeville, and at the age of twenty-six was cast in the Broadway production of *The Stranger*, a melodrama by Charles T. Dazey. During World War I, Ouida headed her own talent agency, representing such well-known actors as Nazimova, Richard Barthelmes, Adolphe Menjou, and Lionel Atwill.

Ouida found her true calling when writing scenarios for silent motion pictures, many directed by her first husband, George Fitzmaurice. Beginning in 1915 and throughout the next decade, Ouida wrote the stories for more than forty films. Among them were many five-reelers based on plays and novels tinged with criminous elements: *Via Wireless* (1915), *At Bay* (1915), *Big Jim Garrity* (1916), *Arms and the Woman* (1916), *Kick In* (1917 and 1922), *A Japanese Nightingale* (1918), *The Hillcrest Mystery* (1918), *The Cry of the Weak* (1919), *The Profiteers* (1919), *Counterfeit* (1919), *The Witness for the Defense* (1919), *On with the Dance* (1920), and *Three Live Ghosts* (1922).

In 1922, Ouida saw Basil Rathbone perform on Broadway in *The Czarina*. She reportedly turned to her escort and said, "One day I'm going to marry that man." They met at a party and Basil was immediately taken by the "young and petite" Paramount screenwriter, "with the most beautiful natural red hair I have ever seen . . . eyes that danced with the joy of living, and a skin texture like alabaster."[29] Ouida and Basil were married on April 18, 1926.

Samuel Goldwyn threw a fit when Ouida asked to be released from all pending contracts and tied her fate to an actor who had not yet "arrived." Ouida became Basil's business manager, and when they bought a home in Bel Air, she won the admiration of the movie colony by hosting many lavish social functions.

* * *

Philip St. John Basil Rathbone was born in Johannesburg, South Africa, in 1892. Four years later, his father was accused by the Boers of being a British spy, and the family escaped to England. While attending Repton School from 1906 to 1910, Rathbone developed an interest in theatre. He joined a Shakespearean troupe managed by his cousin, Frank Benson; went on tour all over England, Scotland, and Ireland; and soon advanced from playing bit parts to juvenile leads.

In 1914 Rathbone made his debut on the London stage, supporting H. B. Irving in *The Sin of David* by Stephen Phillips. A pair of Shakespearean roles followed: Louis in *Henry V* (1914) and Lysander in *A Midsummer Night's Dream* (1915).

During World War I, Rathbone worked in intelligence, and received England's Military Cross for bravery.

In 1920, Rathbone returned to the London stage in the title role of *Peter Ibbetson*, a drama founded on George du Maurier's novel, and as the poet Alfred de Musset in *Madame Sand* by Philip Moeller. This was followed, in rapid succession, by feature and leading roles in Somerset Maugham's *The Unknown*, Victorien Sardou's *Fedora*, William Shakespeare's *Henry IV* and *Othello*, Maugham's *East of Suez*, and Karel Čapek's *R.U.R.*

Rathbone first appeared on Broadway in *The Czarina* (1922), a period drama adapted by Edward Sheldon from the Hungarian. Rathbone played a dashing count who comes to the aid of Catherine II of Russia during a period of turmoil.

Among the more challenging roles Rathbone played in New York were Dr. Nicholas Agi, the shy tutor who falls in love with a princess, in Ference Molnar's romantic comedy *The Swan* (1923); Jacques Virieu, a Parisian tormented by a failed marriage, in Arthur Hornblow Jr.'s *The Captive*, an early play about lesbianism (1926);[30] Cassius, a leading conspirator, in William Shakespeare's *Julius Caesar* (1927); Romeo, the adolescent lover, in Shakespeare's *Romeo and Juliet* (1934); Maurice, a newlywed insanely jealous of his wife's guardian, in Louis Verneuil's *Obsession,* staged by Reginald Denham (1946); strict, conservative Dr. Austin Sloper, who forbids his daughter to establish a romantic liaison with a handsome courtier, in *The Heiress*, a Ruth and Augustus Goetz adaptation of the Henry James novel *Washington Square* (1947);[31] and Henry Hutton, accused of poisoning his invalid wife in order to marry a much younger woman, in Aldous Huxley's *The Gioconda Smile* (1950).

Rathbone's appearances in New York following the debacle of *Sherlock Holmes* were limited to the 1957 thriller *Hide and Seek* by Stanley Mann and Roger Macdougall, in which he portrayed Sir Roger Johnson, a British nuclear scientist, another outing with director Reginald Denham; and the 1958 Pulitzer Prize–winning allegory *J.B.* by Archibald MacLeish, taking over the role of Mr. Zuss when Raymond Massey departed, and the part of Nickles upon Christopher Plummer's exit.

Basil Rathbone began his movie career in 1921, appearing in *Innocent*, adapted from a novel by Marie Corelli. Rathbone portrayed a big-city artist who woos a naive farm girl, causing her to get caught in a storm and die—thus immediately establishing himself as a cad, signposting a gallery of movie villains. In *The School for Scandal* (1923), a film version of Richard Brinsley Sheridan's play, Rathbone played Joseph Surface, a fortune hunter. *The Masked Bride* (1925) featured Rathbone as a Parisian apache who forces his lover to steal a precious diamond necklace from a visiting American millionaire. Next came the role of a German secret agent in *The Great Deception* (1926).

Rathbone was cast as the romantic lead, Lord Arthur Dilling, in *The Last of Mrs. Cheyney* (1929), based on the play by Frederick Lonsdale, winning the heart of cat burglar Norma Shearer; as amateur sleuth Philo Vance in *The Bishop Murder Case* (1930); and as Ferdinand de Levis, a wealthy Jew who yearns to be accepted by London's upper classes but faces a whiff of anti-Semitism when complaining to the police about a 1,000-pound theft during a weekend party—in *Loyalties* (1933), from the play by John Galsworthy.

In 1935, Metro-Goldwyn-Mayer brought Rathbone back to his unsympathetic roles. In the star-studded *David Copperfield*, inspired by the Dickens novel, he plays the brutal Mr. Murdstone who torments his wife's young son (Freddie Bartholomew); in Tolstoy's *Anna Karenina* he is the cruel husband, Vronsky, who causes the suicide of his wife (Greta Garbo); in Dickens's *A Tale of Two Cities*, Rathbone is the Marquis St. Evremonde, an arrogant French aristocrat;[32] in *Kind Lady*, based on the play by Edward Chodorov, Rathbone appears as Henry Abbott, the menacing leader of a gang that imprisons an elderly woman in her home.

Rathbone continued to exhibit a dark side in *The Last Days of Pompeii* (1935), portraying the despotic ruler Pontius Pilate; in *Private Number* (1936), enacting an evil butler; in *Confession* (1937), as a wicked Polish composer who is shot to death by a wronged woman; and in *Love from a Stranger* (1937), adapted from a story by Agatha Christie and a play by Frank Vosper, impersonating a serial killer.

Bad-guy Rathbone lost sword duels to Errol Flynn in *Captain Blood* (1935) and *The Adventures of Robin Hood* (1938); to Leslie Howard in *Romeo and Juliet* (1936);[33] to Tyrone Power in *The Mark of Zorro* (1940); and to Danny Kaye in *The Court Jester* (1956). Rathbone also came to a sorry end in a climactic fight with Gary Cooper when playing Ahmed, the treacherous emperor's adviser, in *The Adventures of Marco Polo* (1938).

On a lighter note, Rathbone appeared as a Soviet commissar in the comedy *Tovarich* (1937) and as Louis XI in the historical *If I Were King* (1938), for which he was nominated for a Best Supporting Actor Oscar. He lost to Walter Brennan (in *Kentucky*).

In 1939, Rathbone and Nigel Bruce were cast in *The Hound of the Baskervilles*, the first of fourteen Holmes-Watson pictures, endowing the silver screen with characterizations considered the flagship embodiment of the Great Detective and his Boswell.[34]

Also in 1939, Rathbone made his first horror flick, playing Baron Wolf von Frankenstein in *Son of Frankenstein*, accompanied by Bela Lugosi as Ygor, the demented aide, and Boris Karloff as the Monster. Rathbone cemented his identification with the genre in *Tower of London* (1939), portraying Richard, Duke of Gloucester, the King's brother, who is determined to usurp the throne. *The Mad Doctor* (1941) has Rathbone in the title role, Dr. George Sebastian, who marries wealthy women for their money and disposes of them. In *The Black Cat* (1941), Rathbone is a menaced inheritor who spends a restless night in a dark old house. Cesar Ferrari (Rathbone) uses hypnotism to mesmerize an ax murderer into a series of grisly killings in *Fingers at the Window* (1942).

Rathbone made a comeback to first-class pictures, though still delivering unsympathetic roles, in *Paris Calling* (1941), as a World War II traitor; in *Crossroads* (1942), as a suave blackmailer; in *Above Suspicion* (1943), as a Gestapo officer; in *Frenchman's Creek* (1944), as a lecherous lord; and in *We're No Angels* (1955), as a despicable cousin. He also played heinous characters in *The Court Jester* (1956) and *The Last Hurrah* (1958).

In 1950, Rathbone made a television pilot—aired live on *NBC Showcase*—of *Sherlock Holmes*, but it was not optioned. Throughout the fifties he continued to appear on television in Robert Louis Stevenson's *Dr. Jekyll and Mr. Hyde*, Edwin Justus Mayer's *The Firebrand*, James Thurber's *The Thirteen Chairs*, Charles Dickens's *A Christmas Carol*, George du Maurier's *Trilby*, Herman Melville's *Billy Budd*, and Jean Anouilh's *The Lark*.

In the 1960s Rathbone returned to the horror genre in "B" pictures of dubious quality: *The Magic Sword* (1962), *Tales of Terror* (1962), *The Comedy of Terrors* (1963), *Queen of Blood* (1966), *Ghost in the Invisible Bikini* (1966), and *Voyage to a Prehistoric Planet* (1967)—a sad epitaph to the greatest Sherlock Holmes of them all.[35]

Basil Rathbone passed away of a heart attack, on July 21, 1967.

NOTES

1. In the canon, Trelawney Hope is the Secretary for European Affairs, "the most rising statesman in the country." He comes to seek Holmes's aid in *The Adventure of the Second Stain*. Mycroft Holmes, "heavily built and massive," arrives on his own in *The Adventure of the Bruce-Partington Plans*.

2. A long, thin, blue-colored envelope sealed with red wax stamped with a crouching lion, is the Macguffin of *The Second Stain*, while the stolen submarine designs are the source of concern in *The Bruce-Partington Plans*. Ouida Rathbone combined the two.

3. Lucas, de Rothiere, and Oberstein are international agents under suspicion in *The Second Stain*. De Rothiere and Oberstein also appear in *The Bruce-Partington Plans*.

4. Not specified in this play, the lady's full name in *The Second Stain* is Hilda Trelawney Hope.

5. William Ewart Gladstone was prime minister of England four times between 1868 and 1894.

6. Von Bork is the Kaiser's top spymaster and Von Herling is the chief secretary of the German legation in London in *His Last Bow*.

7. Holmes masquerades as Altamont to penetrate Von Bork's spy ring in *His Last Bow*.

8. G. Lestrade and Tobias Gregson are Scotland Yard inspectors involved in various Holmes cases. Francois Le Villard is a French detective appearing in *The Sign of Four*. Ouida Rathbone had done her homework in identifying and gathering the three lawmen for the climactic arrest (though it is unclear why the Swiss authorities are left out, allowing the foreigners to take charge).

9. Basil Rathbone, *In and Out of Character* (New York: Doubleday, 1962), 180.

10. Rathbone, *In and Out of Character*, 181. Basil Rathbone portrayed Sherlock Holmes in fifteen pictures and 200 weekly radio broadcasts between 1939 and 1946.

11. Rathbone, *In and Out of Character*, 182.

12. Rathbone, *In and Out of Character*, 183.

13. Actually, Ouida Rathbone borrowed ingredients from *six* Conan Doyle stories.

14. Rathbone, *In and Out of Character*, 207–208.

15. Rathbone, *In and Out of Character*, 209.

16. Reginald Denham directed the Broadway thrillers *Rope*, *Ladies in Retirement* (of which he was coauthor), *The Two Mrs. Carrolls*, *Guest in the House*, and *Dial "M" for Murder*. During World War I, Denham portrayed Sherlock Holmes in an army production of *The Speckled Band*.

17. Thomas Gomez served a seven-year stint with the acting company of the Lunts on Broadway and spent seven years in Hollywood. He received an Academy Award nomination for the film noir *Ride the Pink Horse* (1947).

18. Nigel Bruce, who, as Dr. Watson, partnered with Basil Rathbone in their motion picture series, had first call for the role, but was recuperating from a heart attack at the time.

19. Rathbone, *In and Out of Character*, 210.

20. *Boston Traveler*, October 12, 1953.

21. *Boston Globe*, October 12, 1953.

22. *Boston Herald*, October 12, 1953.

23. *Boston American*, October 12, 1953.

24. *Boston Post*, October 12, 1953.

25. *New York World-Telegram*, October 31, 1953.

26. *New York Post*, November 1, 1953.

27. *New York Times*, October 31, 1953.

28. *New York Herald Tribune*, October 31, 1953.

29. Rathbone, *In and Out of Character*, 54.

30. One night, after a seventeen-week run, plainclothes policemen showed up backstage and escorted the cast to night court, where they met Mae West and her company, who were playing in *Sex*. *The Captive* was forced to close, and a trial ensued. The actors, charged with offending a moral code, pleaded guilty "under protest." That was the end of the matter. Arthur Wontner, another future Sherlock Holmes of the cinema (he wore the deerstalker cap in five British features from 1931 to 1937), was a cast member of *The Captive*, booked by the police.

31. Rathbone won a Tony Award for his portrayal of Dr. Sloper, alongside Henry Fonda in *Mister Roberts* and Paul Kelly in *Command Decision*.

32. The casts of *Anna Karenina* and *A Tale of Two Cities* included three inter-
preters of Sherlock Holmes. In addition to Basil Rathbone, Robert Warwick and
Reginald Owen enacted the Great Detective—Warwick on Broadway (in William
Gillette's *Sherlock Holmes*, 1928), Owen on the screen (*A Study in Scarlet*, 1933).

33. As Tybalt, nephew to Lady Capulet, Rathbone was nominated for an Oscar
in the category of Best Supporting Actor, but he lost to Walter Brennan (in *Come
and Get It*).

34. Basil Rathbone and Nigel Bruce also participated, as Holmes and Watson,
in *Crazy House* (1943), an Olsen and Johnson madcap comedy.

35. A sketchy description of all of Rathbone's movies can be found in *Basil Rathbone: His Life and His Films* by Michael B. Druxman (Cranbury, NJ: A. S. Barnes,
1975).

The Caine Mutiny
Court-Martial (1953)
Herman Wouk (United States, 1915–)

Herman Wouk took a portion of his sprawling 1951 Pulitzer Prize–winning novel, *The Caine Mutiny*, and turned it into a pulsating courtroom drama.

The time is February 1945. The scene is the General Court-Martial Room of the Twelfth Naval District, San Francisco. Lt. Stephen Maryk is accused of mutiny in wartime, for "willfully, without proper authority, and without justifiable cause" relieving from duty Lieutenant Commander Philip Francis Queeg, the captain of the SS *Caine*.

Lt. Maryk's contention is that during a raging typhoon in the Pacific, he believed that Captain Queeg lost his faculties and became numb with panic. In order to save the ship, he relieved the skipper of duty and seized control.

During the first act, prosecutor John Challee summons to the witness stand Navy officers and experts, building up a strong case against Maryk.

In the second act, Maryk's defense attorney, Barney Greenwald, turns the tables. In a grueling cross-examination, he proves that the captain of the SS *Caine* was a petty tyrant and paranoid coward. Throughout a rambling account of stolen strawberries, a missing icebox key, and incomplete officers' logs, the outwardly self-assured captain gradually disintegrates and ends up trembling and sobbing, a broken man.

Lt. Maryk is exonerated, but playwright Wouk has one more arrow in his shaft. During an acquittal party, a drunk, tormented Barney Greenwald hails the Queegs of the Navy for staving off the Nazis while the nation was preparing for war. He lashes out at Maryk's friend, Lt. Thomas Keefer, as "the guy who started the whole idea that Queeg was a dangerous paranoiac," and instead of helping the sick captain, inflamed a mutiny that yanked out of action the SS *Caine*, a minesweeper, when it was most needed in the hottest part of the war.

* * *

The Caine Mutiny Court-Martial was first presented at the Granada Theatre in Santa Barbara, California, on October 12, 1953. After sailing around the country for more than three months, the play, under the direction of Charles Laughton, anchored in New York's Plymouth Theatre on January 20, 1954, docking there for 415 performances. It won unanimous raves from the critics: "Mr. Wouk's drama has some of the unforced inevitability for a tragedy," stated Brooks Atkinson. "It is remarkably well-planned and it is written neatly."[1] Walter Kerr pointed out that the play "builds to a second-act climax of such hair-raising intensity that you are sure nothing, and no one, can ever top it. Some one then proceeds to top it. . . . *The Caine Mutiny Court-Martial* is a thrilling achievement."[2]

Richard Watts Jr. expressed similar sentiments, "*The Caine Mutiny Court-Martial* is provocative and arresting."[3] John Chapman added, "It is enormously compelling and exciting."[4] William Hawkins agreed: "A brilliantly exciting drama about heroes under stress. . . . The drama's full impact hits like dynamite,"[5] and Robert Coleman urged his readers to "rush to the Plymouth Theatre box-office immediately. . . . An arresting, absorbing and completely fascinating evening of theatre."[6]

The all-male cast, headed by Henry Fonda as Greenwald, John Hodiak as Maryk, and Lloyd Nolan as Queeg, was saluted enthusiastically.

The courtroom drama opened at London's Hippodrome on June 13, 1956, with Lloyd Nolan directing and repeating the role of Captain Queeg. It ran for 132 performances.

Almost thirty years later, a revival of *The Caine Mutiny Court-Martial* was mounted at the Hartman Theatre in Stamford, Connecticut, on May 5, 1983, on its way to Broadway's Circle in the Square Uptown. "Holds its own admirably," wrote John Beaufort.[7] "Wouk's words have lost none of their power," echoed Joel Segal.[8] "Strong stuff," agreed Clive Barnes.[9] The play, staged by Arthur Sherman, featured Jay O. Sanders (Maryk), Michael Moriarty (Queeg), and John Rubinstein (Greenwald). It ran for 213 performances.

Charlton Heston directed and starred as Queeg in a highly acclaimed London production in 1984. Heston later brought the show to the Kennedy Center's Eisenhower Theatre in Washington, D.C.

The Caine Mutiny Court-Martial was revived at Broadway's Gerald Schoenfeld Theatre on May 7, 2006, in a disappointing production that ran for only seventeen performances. Charles Isherwood of the *New York Times* called it "torpid" and "plodding," performed by a "blandly efficient cast" and directed "with metronome in hand by Jerry Zaks."[10]

A top-notch 1954 movie version of *The Caine Mutiny*, scripted by Stanley Roberts and directed by Edward Dmytryk, starred Humphrey Bogart as Captain Queeg, Van Johnson as Lieutenant Maryk, Fred MacMurray as Thomas Keefer, and Jose Ferrer as Defense Attorney Greenwald.

In 1988, Robert Altman directed an effective made-for-television version of *The Caine Mutiny Court-Martial* for CBS, with Eric Bogosian as Greenwald and Brad Davis as Queeg.

* * *

Herman Wouk was born in the Bronx in 1915, the son of Russian-Jewish immigrants. In 1934, he received his Bachelor of Arts degree at Columbia University, where he majored in comparative literature and philosophy. In college, Wouk edited the humorous *Columbia Jester* and wrote several varsity shows.

Between 1935 and 1941, Wouk worked as a radio writer and producer. In 1942, he enlisted in the Navy and served for three years as a deck officer on the destroyer USS *Zane* and as an executive officer on the USS *Southard*. While on duty in the Pacific, Wouk began to write his first novel, *Aurora Dawn*, a satire about radio advertising.

Wouk's play *The Traitor* was produced on Broadway in 1949. It is a Cold War story of a young nuclear scientist who believes that the only way to stop catastrophe is to let the Russians in on the secret of the atomic bomb.

Among Wouk's best-selling novels are *Marjorie Morningstar* (1955), the chronicle of a Jewish girl who, to the chagrin of her traditional family, wishes to become an actress, and *Youngblood Hawke* (1962), a critique of the publishing world, based on the life of Thomas Wolfe. The epic *The Winds of War* (1971) and *War of Remembrance* (1978) focus on a family of naval heroes before and after the Japanese attack on Pearl Harbor. Judaism is the main factor in *Inside, Outside* (1985), while *The Hope* (1993) and *The Glory* (1994) tell the story of the land of Israel. In 2010, at the age of ninety-five, Wouk published the brief *The Language God Talks*, described by Louisa Thomas of *Newsweek* magazine as "an unusual work—partly a quick trip through developments in cosmology, partly an episodic memoir, partly an essay on faith and science."[11]

Acting Edition: Samuel French, Inc.

Awards and Honors: A top-ten selection in *The Best Plays of 1953–1954*. *The Caine Mutiny Court-Martial* was the Drama Critics Circle runner-up in the category of Best Play (the winner was *Teahouse of the August Moon* by John Patrick).

Herman Wouk received the Pulitzer Prize for his novel *The Caine Mutiny* (1952); the Columbia University Medal of Excellence (1952); the American Academy of Achievement Golden Plate Award (1986); the U.S. Navy Memorial Foundation Award (1987); the Guardian of Zion Award (1998); and the Library of Congress Award for Lifetime Achievement (2008).

NOTES

1. *New York Times*, January 21, 1954.
2. *New York Herald Tribune*, January 21, 1954.
3. *New York Post*, January 21, 1954.
4. *Daily News*, January 21, 1954.
5. *New York World-Telegram*, January 21, 1954.
6. *Daily Mirror*, January 21, 1954.
7. *Christian Science Monitor*, May 11, 1983.
8. *WABC TV 7*, New York, May 5, 1983.
9. *New York Post*, May 6, 1983.
10. *New York Times*, May 8, 2006.
11. *Newsweek*, April 9, 2010.

Witness for the Prosecution (1953)

Agatha Christie (England, 1890–1976)

Agatha Christie's masterpiece is arguably *Witness for the Prosecution*, a three-act play she expanded from a short story included in the collection *The Hound of Death* (1933). Her research embraced the perusal of the *Famous Trials* series and the study of the British judicial system.

In her autobiography, Christie cheerfully states, "One night at the theatre stands out in my memory especially: the first night of *Witness for the Prosecution*. I can safely say that that was the only first night I have enjoyed."[1] The Queen of Crime recounts how she had to fight, tooth-and-nail, for the triple-twist ending: "Nobody liked it, nobody wanted it, everyone said it would spoil the whole thing. . . . I don't often stick out for things, I don't always have sufficient conviction, but I had here. I wanted that end. I wanted it so much that I wouldn't agree to have the play put on without it."[2] In the original short story, the resolution allows the murderer to get away with the crime, while in the play he escapes legal justice but does not go unpunished.

The action begins at the Temple Chambers of Sir Wilfrid Robarts, Q.C. Mr. Mayhew, a middle-aged solicitor, escorts a likeable, friendly young man, Leonard Vole. Leonard, looking slightly worried, informs Sir Wilfrid that he may be arrested for murder any minute. It's the case of Miss Emily French, he explains, which has been widely reported in the press—a middle-aged lady living alone but for an elderly housekeeper, in a house in Hampstead, found hit on the back of the head, killed.

Leonard relates that he met French a few months before. She dropped her parcels in the middle of Oxford Street, and he managed to get her to the curb safely when "a bus was almost on top of her." A grateful Miss French invited Leonard to visit her, and they struck up a warm friendship.

Leonard admits airily that he is broke. The murdered woman was well off, and she left all her assets to Leonard. Therefore Leonard's wife,

Romaine, warned that the authorities might suspect him of the foul deed and suggested that he hire a lawyer.

On the fateful evening of October 14, Leonard had a cup of coffee and played cards with Miss French until 9:00 p.m. At 9:30, the housekeeper, Janet Mackenzie, returned to the house and heard somebody talking with Miss French. "It wasn't me," claims Leonard, confident that Romaine, a devoted wife, will confirm his story.

A Scotland Yard inspector enters with a warrant, and Leonard is taken away. Sir Wilfrid and Mayhew are impressed favorably by the young suspect, who does not seem to realize the danger of his position. Romaine Vole arrives and confides that Leonard is not really her husband. They went through "a form of marriage" in Berlin so that Leonard could get her out of the Russian zone and bring her to England. To the chagrin of the attorneys, Romaine, "cool as a cucumber," is not very reassuring about Leonard's alibi.

The proceedings now shift to the Central Criminal Court, London—better known as the Old Bailey. Before the bewigged, stern Mr. Justice Wainwright, the jurors are sworn in and the Clerk intones the indictment. Prosecutor Myers, Q.C., describes the circumstances of the case and calls to the stand Detective Inspector Robert Hearne, who negates the theory of a robbery in conjunction with the murder and emphasizes that bloodstains were found on Vole's jacket sleeves. Dr. Wyatt, a police surgeon, takes the stand and affirms that Emily French was coshed to death between the hours of 9:30 and 10 p.m. Finally, Janet Mackenzie, a dour Scotswoman, the housekeeper of the victim, testifies that she heard Mr. Vole conversing with Miss French on the eve of October 14. She also relates that later that night she found her mistress dead, and that neither she nor Miss French were aware that the prisoner was married.

Sir Wilfrid shakes Mackenzie's testimony when he cross-examines her in a low voice, proving that she is in need of a hearing apparatus and could not be relied upon to distinguish Leonard's voice from behind closed doors. Sir Wilfrid also produces a sharp-edged French vegetable knife, explaining that the stains on Vole's sleeve were caused by a nasty cut obtained when the accused was carving a loaf of ham.

Tension vibrates in court when the prosecutor calls "Romaine Heilger." Romaine asserts that her marriage to the accused is not valid and that she is willing to testify against him. She relates that her husband was not with her as stated but didn't return until after 10 p.m., with blood on his sleeve, telling her that he killed Miss French. "When it is murder," says Romaine, "I cannot come into Court and lie and say that he was there with me at the time it was done. I cannot do it."

In rebuttal, Sir Wilfrid calls the accused to the witness box. Leonard insists that he reached home at "twenty-five minutes past nine," that his clothes were not smudged with blood, and that he had no knowledge of the terms of Miss French's last will. "I didn't kill her. I've never killed anybody. Oh God! It's a nightmare. It's some awful, evil dream."

Back at chambers, Sir Wilfrid and solicitor Mayhew are discussing the status of the case when "a rather common young woman, violently and crudely made-up, her blonde hair falling over one side of her face, flamboyantly but cheaply dressed," is ushered in. In a shrill cockney accent the woman offers to sell them letters, written by that wicked Jezebel who gave evidence at court—letters "that might do the prisoner a bit of good." The woman haggles for fifty pounds, gets twenty, takes out a packet of letters from her shabby handbag and throws them on the desk. "What have you got against Romaine Vole?" asks Sir Wilfrid. The woman dramatically swings the desk lamp so that it glows on her face and pushes back her hair to reveal a slashed, scarred cheek. Bitterly she explains that Romaine stole her chap, and when she found them together, her ex-lover cut her up with a razor.

The woman thrusts her disfigured face toward Sir Wilfrid: "Want to kiss me?" He shrinks back. As the men turn to examine the letters, she quietly slips out of the room.

At the Old Bailey, the next morning, Sir Wilfrid offers in evidence letters from Romaine Heilger and calls her to the stand. "Do you know a certain man whose name is Max?" he asks. Romaine starts violently, hesitates, and then answers: "Certainly not." Sir Wilfrid picks up a letter and quotes: "My beloved Max . . . An extraordinary thing has happened. I believe all our difficulties may be ended."

Romaine interrupts, denying that she wrote the letters, but Sir Wilfrid continues: "The old lady I told you about has been murdered and I think Leonard is suspected. . . . His alibi depends on me. Supposing I say he came home much later. . . . If Leonard is convicted of murder, I could come to you safely and we could be together for always. . . . Your adoring Romaine."

Stonily, Romaine admits to writing the letter. The jury finds Leonard Vole not guilty.

A policeman suggests that Romaine wait in the courthouse for a while to avoid the crowd riled up against her. Mayhew congratulates Leonard on being free—and rich. Sir Wilfrid warns Romaine that proceedings for perjury will be launched shortly. Measuring her balefully, the barrister tells Romaine that since their first meeting he made up his mind to beat her at her "little game. And, by God, I've done it. I've got him off—in spite of you."

In the ensuing conversation, it turns out that Romaine and the woman selling the letters are one and the same. Romaine wanted the jury to dislike and mistrust her, to believe that she was lying when she was testifying against Vole. In a Cockney accent, Romaine says, "So now you know the whole story, Mister—like to kiss me?"

Sir Wilfrid is thunderstruck: "Couldn't you just trust me? We believe, you know, that our British system of justice upholds the truth. We'd have got him off." Romaine utters slowly: "I couldn't risk it. You see, you *thought* he was innocent . . . " Sir Wilfrid interrupts with quick appreciation: "And you *knew* he was innocent. I understand." Romaine responds: "But you do not understand at all. I *knew* he was *guilty.*"

The Duchess of Crime still has another trick up her sleeve. A young, strawberry blonde girl rushes in, embracing Leonard. Romaine is puzzled.

Leonard flings off all disguise of manner and says with coarse brutality: "She's fifteen years younger than you are." He laughs and moves toward Romaine menacingly: "I've got the money. I've been acquitted, and I can't be tried again, so don't be shooting off your mouth, or you'll just get *yourself* hanged as an accessory after the fact."

Leonard turns to the girl and kisses her as Romaine picks up a knife from the exhibit table. She says calmly, "I shall not be tried as an accessory after the fact. I shall not be tried for perjury. I shall be tried for murder— the murder of the only man I ever loved." She stabs Leonard in the back.

* * *

Produced by Peter Saunders and directed by Wallace Douglas, *Witness for the Prosecution* previewed at the Theatre Royal, Nottingham, on September 28, 1953, and opened at London's Winter Garden Theatre a month later, for a run of 458 performances. David Horne portrayed Sir Wilfrid Robarts, with Derek Blomfield as Leonard Vole and Patricia Jessel as Romaine. In New York, the play raised its curtain at Henry Miller's Theatre on December 16, 1954, and enjoyed a run of 645 performances. The Broadway replica was staged by Robert Lewis and featured Francis L. Sullivan (Sir Wilfrid), Gene Lyons (Vole), and Patricia Jessel, recruited from the London production for the role of Romaine.

Critic Robert Coleman found Miss Jessel "electrifying as the wife, as menacing as a cobra one moment and as frantic as a lioness at bay the next."[3] The reviewers unanimously showered superlatives on the play, such as "a decisive knockout," "a platinum-plated whodunit," and "theatrical skullduggery at its peak," while gingerly skipping around the punchy denouement.

Equity Library Theatre of Manhattan revived *Witness for the Prosecution* in March, 1966, and off-off-Broadway's Wonderhorse Theatre did the same in August 1975. The straining requirement of thirty cast members did not deter the Oakland University Professional Theatre Program, Rochester, Michigan, from presenting *Witness* in 1975, nor the Old Globe Theatre of San Diego, California, in 1980; Studio Arena

Theatre, Buffalo, New York, 1982; and Players State Theatre, Coconut Grove, Florida, 1983.

A splendid motion picture version, directed by Billy Wilder, was made in 1957, with the stellar cast of Charles Laughton (Sir Wilfrid), Tyrone Power (Leonard), and Marlene Dietrich (Christine instead of Romaine). A facsimile of the Old Bailey courthouse was built in Hollywood on the Samuel Goldwyn lot, where much of the action was shot. The publicity department drummed up the surprise ending and a great deal was made of a huge poster hung outside the studio requesting everyone entering to sign a pledge "not to reveal any of the secrets relating to the film's electrifying climax." *Witness of the Prosecution* received six Academy Award nominations: Best Picture, Best Director (Wilder), Best Actor (Laughton), Best Supporting Actress (Elsa Lanchester), Best Sound, and Best Film Editing—but won none.

Acting Edition: Samuel French, Inc. *Witness for the Prosecution* is also included in *Best Mystery and Suspense Plays of the Modern Theatre*, edited by Stanley Richards (New York: Dodd, Mead, 1971) and in *The Mousetrap and Other Plays* by Agatha Christie (New York: Dodd, Mead, 1978; Harper Paperbacks, 1993).

Awards and Honors: *Witness for the Prosecution* won the New York Drama Critics Award for best foreign play of the 1954–1955 season, and is a top-ten selection in *The Best Plays of 1954–1955*.

NOTES

1. Agatha Christie, *An Autobiography* (London: Collins, 1977), 514.
2. Christie, *An Autobiography*, 514.
3. *Daily Mirror*, December 17, 1954.

Someone Waiting (1953)

Emlyn Williams (Wales, 1905–1987)

Emlyn Williams based his revenge play *Someone Waiting* on an actual 1931 murder in the South of England. The police were certain that the victim, Julia Wallace, was killed by her husband, yet evidence was insufficient for a conviction. On his deathbed, the husband confessed, boasting that he had planned every detail of the "perfect crime" by moves on a chessboard.

The lead character of *Someone Waiting*, Walter Fenn, a tutor of jurisprudence, had been working in Australia, when his son, Paul, an Oxford student, was arrested and convicted for the strangulation of a Swedish woman during a Christmas party.

Now Fenn is back in London. Described as "an insignificant-looking boyish man in his early forties," Fenn visits Paul in his cell on the eve of his execution and believes the young man when he claims, "Daddy, I didn't do it."

Following Paul's hanging, Fenn secures a position at the Mill Court flat in the Regent's Park District, home of John and Vera Nedlow, where the murder was committed. Fenn is determined to find the real killer and prove his dead son's innocence.

John Nedlow is a distinguished-looking man of fifty, who prides himself "on his looks, charm, vitality and virility." Nedlow Motors is a successful enterprise, and John is renowned for generous charitable contributions. His wife Vera, smart and pretty, is also a pillar of their community. The Nedlows seem to have an estranged relationship with their stepson Martin, a sulky boy of twenty, a law student at Oxford, who was friends with Paul. Both Vera and John keep complaining about Martin's past friendship with a killer.

Fenn is engaged to tutor Martin. He soon learns that there is an undercurrent of tension between John and Vera, and that a wall of hostility separates them from Martin. Fenn also notices that the elder Nedlow flirts unabashedly with the maid, Hilda, and his secretary, Beryl.

Fenn confides in Martin and learns that he too suspects that his father, John Nedlow, terrified of scandal and blackmail, killed his Swedish lover. They rummage through the drawers of Nedlow's desk, find a loaded gun and a suicide note, and conclude that after strangling the girl, John Nedlow convinced his wife that he intended to take his own life. They believe that Vera, horrified, agreed to keep mum. "I'm going to kill him," says Fenn.

While playing chess in the flat's drawing-room, Fenn weaves step-by-step revenge maneuvers. He explains to Martin that a pawn has to be sacrificed before a major move. Accordingly, says Fenn, either the maid, Hilda, or secretary, Beryl, must be killed first, as a preliminary step, in order to entrap the major target, John Nedlow.

Fenn believes that the fulfillment of the quest for revenge will redeem him from a meaningless existence. Martin doubts that Fenn has it in him to kill. When the critical moment arrives and the distraught avenger faces Hilda, his first potential victim, he begins to tighten a tie around her neck, but her pleading eyes affect him and his hands drop. Nor can Fenn master the gumption to shoot Nedlow with the loaded gun he found in the tycoon's desk drawer.

Despondent and delirious, Fenn's thirst for vengeance culminates with his nestling the handle of the revolver in Nedlow's palm to register his fingerprints, then pointing the barrel carefully at his own heart, calling loudly "Help—help!" and squeezing the trigger.

* * *

Someone Waiting premiered in Liverpool, the scene of the Julia Wallace murder some twenty years before. The show moved to Cardiff, then to London, where it opened at the Globe Theatre on November 25, 1953, running for 156 performances. *Theatre World Annual* stated that even though the "psychological murder thriller" lacked "the compelling simplicity of the earlier *Night Must Fall* (1935), nevertheless, in spite of a plot of considerable complexity, Mr. Williams in *Someone Waiting* achieved a thriller of unusual intensity. . . . As the somewhat seedy examination coach, Mr. Fenn, Emlyn Williams himself gave a performance of great subtlety. . . . Noel Willman's direction was swift from clue to clue."[1]

Someone Waiting came to New York's John Golden Theatre on February 14, 1956. The director, Allan Davis, was imported from England. The set was designed by American Ben Edwards. Leo G. Carroll, who won high praise as Inspector Rough in *Angel Street* and had been a Hitchcock movie fixture, portrayed Walter Fenn. Critic John Chapman greeted *Someone Waiting* with a rave: "As a playwright, Mr. Williams has an admirably tidy mind—and a tricky one. He obeys all the rules of good manners and logic, but is a slippery devil all the same. His new play is a drama of murder and revenge which stretches suspense from the first moments of the first act to the final line of the third act."[2]

The rest of the reviewers were unanimously negative. "The whole thing is enormously complex, and the time comes when you cease to care," frowned John McClain.[3] "We can't get worked up over a thriller that doesn't thrill, or care what happens to people who are about as genuine as a stack of three-dollar bills," complained Robert Coleman.[4] "Between its garrulousness, its lack of sympathetic characters, its indecisiveness and its odd sluggishness, the result is that even the play's potentially effective ironic ending isn't very entertaining," deemed Richard Watts Jr.[5]

Someone Waiting lasted fifteen performances.

In England, the revenge thriller was revived by the Colchester Repertory Theatre on August 30, 1965, for two weeks. In the United States, it was presented by the University of Southern Mississippi in July of 2002, and by Theatre Forty of Los Angeles a month later.

In 1957, *Someone Waiting* was adapted effectively to the screen, retitled *Time without Pity*, scripted by Ben Barzman and directed by Joseph Losey. The motion picture version varies from the play by having the father, portrayed by Michael Redgrave, save his condemned son in the eleventh hour by instigating the murderer, enacted by Leo McKern, to shoot him during a struggle.

Richard Findlater, in *Emlyn Williams: An Illustrated Study of His Work*, maintains that even though Williams, the actor, "added, with his performance of Fenn, another striking portrait to his gallery of killers and misfits," he has "never written a play in which so many characters are so unilaterally unlikable."[6]

* * *

George Emlyn Williams, the son of a grocer in a Welsh mining town, was fortunate to be noticed by an exceptional teacher, Sara Grace Cooke, who sensed his potential, helped him to perfect his English, and helped him win a scholarship to Oxford. There he became involved in amateur theatrics, and his first plays—*Virgil*, a one-act allegory tinged with black magic, and *Full Moon*, a full-length drama about a young man torn between a possessive father and a loving maiden—were produced by the Oxford University Dramatic Society. At Oxford, he also appeared in plays by Sophocles, Shakespeare, Ibsen, and Pirandello.

Upon graduation, Williams moved to London, where he launched a two-pronged career as an actor and playwright. While touring in the popular thrillers *The Ringer, Interference*, and *The Trial of Mary Dugan*, Williams penned *Glamour*, a play about a pair of innocents who travel to London for their pot of gold. *Glamour* opened at London's Court Theatre on December 31, 1928, and ran for twenty-four performances. Williams's breakthrough as an author came with *A Murder Has Been Announced* (1930), a supernatural thriller that ran for seventy-seven showings at the St. James.

Williams established himself as an actor of the first rank in two Edgar Wallace potboilers: *On the Spot* (1930), in which he portrayed the sinister henchman of a Chicago racketeer, played by Charles Laughton; and *The Case of the Frightened Lady* (1931), enacting the role of fey Lord Lebanon, who at first seems to be the victim of a possessive mother but at the end turns out to be a homicidal maniac. Williams reprised this part both on Broadway, where the play was called *Criminal at Large,* and on the screen.

Through the years, Williams appeared in many demanding roles, including Sir Robert Norton in Terence Rattigan's *The Winslow Boy*, Pope Pius XII in Rolf Hochhuth's *The Deputy*, Thomas More in Robert Bolt's *The Man for All Seasons*, the inquisitor Izquierdo in Lillian Hellman's *Montserrat*,[7] Hjalmar Ekdal in Henrick Ibsen's *The Wild Duck*, Iago in William Shakespeare's *Othello*, Shylock in *The Merchant of Venice*, and the title role in *Richard III*. In 1951, Williams donned a Dickensian beard for a one-man show presenting selections from Charles Dickens works. He continued to offer "Emlyn Williams as Charles Dickens" on both sides of the Atlantic for many years, adding to his repertoire solo performances devised from the works of Dylan Thomas and "Saki" (H. H. Munro).

Among the twenty plays written by Emlyn Williams, several are tinged with criminous elements. *Port Said* (1931) is set in the underbelly of this notorious city at the Suez Canal. Williams himself portrayed a native drifter who is knifed to death by a shady young Englishman, played by Jack Hawkins. Art forgery plays a pivotal role in *The Late Christopher Bean* (1933), which Williams adapted from a comedy by Sidney Howard, who in turn molded it from Rene Fauchois's Parisian success. *Night Must Fall* (1935) focuses on a likeable, baby-faced bellhop who turns out to be a serial killer of elderly women. *He Was Born Gay* (1937) unfolds during the summer of 1815, when Napoleon was defeated at Waterloo. The play is seething with danger and intrigue, as pretenders to the throne keep popping up. Williams not only created the drama, but also codirected it with John Gielgud, and both appeared in key roles: Williams as a police secret agent unmasks Gielgud's "music master" as the real Dauphin.

A disturbed, vicious sixteen-year-old girl attempts to destroy an idyllic family in *Guest in the House* (1946), adapted by Williams from the play by Hagar Wilde and Dale Eunson. A spiritualist medium is exposed as a charlatan during a tense séance sequence in *Trespass: A Ghost Story in Six Scenes* (1947). Blackmail rears its ugly head in *Accolade* (1950), a grim drama about a famous author who leads a secret double life, has bedded an underage girl, and is threatened with exposure.

Williams's outstanding noncrime play is *The Corn Is Green* (1930), a semi-autobiographical play about a teacher, Miss Moffat, and her prize pupil, Morgan Evans, in a remote Wales mining town. Williams himself directed *The Corn Is Green* and costarred with Sybil Thorndike. Among the distinguished actresses who have portrayed Miss Moffat—on stage, on screen, and on television—are Ethel Barrymore, Bette Davis, Eva Le Gallienne, Blanche Yurka, Katharine Hepburn, and Cicely Tyson.

Successive West End box-office hits included an adaptation by Williams of Turgenev's *A Month in the Country* (1943), a pastoral drama that he also directed; and *The Druid's Nest* (1944), a whimsical account of Williams's Welsh childhood, memorably providing Richard Burton with his first professional stage role.

For the cinema, Williams wrote the dialogue of the gloomy melodrama *Friday the Thirteenth* (1934), in which a London bus crashes in a storm, leaving several people dead. The clock is turned back twenty-four hours and a flashback reveals the passengers' stories. "Additional Dialogue" was contributed by Williams to Alfred Hitchcock's 1935 version of *The Man Who Knew Too Much*, and to *The Citadel* (1938) from the book by A. J. Cronin about a struggling young doctor in a Welsh mining town, played by Robert Donat.

Williams penned the screenplays of such varied fare as *Evergreen* (1934), a musical based on a play by Benn W. Levy, wherein a daughter masquerades as her mother, causing romantic complications; *Broken Blossoms* (1936), a drama of doomed love, flickering and extinguished in London's dreary Limehouse district; and *This England*, aka *Our Heritage* (1941), a patriotic wartime epic depicting England's fight for freedom throughout the ages. Williams wrote, directed, and starred in *The Last Days of Dolwyn* (1949), a socially conscious drama unfolding in a Welsh village at the turn of the twentieth century. The village is flooded by greedy city slickers. Williams, the snarling villain of the piece, comes to a sorry end, his body floating in the gushing sea.

Williams appeared in thirty-seven motion pictures, notably as a vicious blackmailer in *Friday the Thirteenth* (1934); a Chinese lad in a 1936 remake of D. W. Griffith's *Broken Blossoms*; an effeminate, sadistic Caligula in *I Claudius*, a 1937 Alexander Korda film that was never finished or distributed; a Jekyll-and-Hyde headmaster of a boys' school who doubles as a homicidal financial counselor in *Dead Men Tell No Tales*; an ex-convict wrongfully accused of murder in *They Drive by Night*; a sinister wrecker in Alfred Hitchcock's pirate adventure *Jamaica Inn*—all in 1939; a bookmaker who betrays the hero and steals his fiancée in Carol Reed's *The Stars Look Down* (1940); a dastardly murderer who ensnares an innocent nurse as a prime suspect by piling up a web of circumstantial evidence against her in *Girl in the News* (1941); a Yorkshire veterinarian who administers a deadly horse serum to a double female murderer in *Another Man's Poison* and a dangerous killer in *The Scarf*—both in 1951.

In 1957, Williams played Emile Zola, the French novelist who crusaded on behalf of Captain Dreyfus, in *I Accuse*. Ten years later, he appeared as the ill, mournful patriarch of a French vineyard family engaged in sacrificial rites in *Eye of the Devil*.

Obsessed with real-life trials, Williams was gripped by the 1966 Yorkshire Moors murders. Brady and Myra Hindley were found guilty of killing a seventeen-year-old boy and a ten-year-old girl, making recordings of their victims' piteous pleas before striking them down. The Hindleys were sentenced to life imprisonment. Williams inspected the scene of the crimes, interviewed witnesses and police officers, and collated the material into a book: *Beyond Belief: A Chronicle of Murder and Its Detection* (1967). Another sensational murder trial was researched by Williams and published under the title *Dr. Crippen's Diary* in *Great Cases of Scotland Yard* (1978).

Williams penned *George: An Early Autobiography* in 1961 and *Emlyn: An Early Autobiography, 1927–1935* (1973), but he never completed *From Stage to Stage: An Adventure*. Two illuminating books about the life and art of the playwright-actor are *Emlyn Williams* by Richard Findlater (1956) and *Emlyn Williams: A Life* by James Harding (1993).

Acting Edition: Dramatists Play Service.

Awards and Honors: In 1949, Emlyn Williams was awarded an honorary LLD by the Duke of Edinburgh (with Prime Minister Atlee and Princess Elizabeth participating). In 1962, Williams was made Commander of the British Empire (CBE).

Williams's *The Corn Is Green* won the New York Drama Circle Award in 1941 as Best Foreign Play, and was a top-ten choice in the yearbook *The Best Plays of 1940–1941*.

NOTES

1. *Theatre World Annual*, 1954.
2. *Daily News*, February 15, 1956.
3. *New York Journal-American*, February 15, 1956.
4. *Daily Mirror*, February 15, 1956.
5. *New York Post*, February 15, 1956.
6. Richard Findlater, *Emlyn Williams: An Illustrated Study of His Work* (London: Rockliff, 1956), 96–97.
7. Lillian Hellman directed her own adaptation of Emmanuel Robles's *Montserrat*. She cast Emlyn Williams, who had staged Hellman's *The Little Foxes* and *Watch on the Rhine* in London, in the pivotal role of a sadistic inquisitor. A cold, even hostile relationship developed between Hellman and Williams during rehearsals, as aptly described by Carl Rollyson in *Lillian Hellman: Her Legend and Her Legacy* (New York: St. Martin's Press, 1988), 280–293. *Montserrat* opened at Broadway's Fulton Theatre on October 29, 1949, and ran for sixty-five performances.

Dead Pigeon (1953)

Lenard Kantor (United States, 1925–1984)

The three acts of the melodrama *Dead Pigeon* unfold within twenty-four hours at the seaside Hotel Atlantic, in the suburb of a large metropolitan city. A mob doll, blonde Sherry Parker, has been secretly whisked from the state penitentiary, where she is doing eleven years on a false homicide charge, to a suite in the hotel. Sherry is a material witness in a gangland murder and is being protected by the police during the weekend prior to the trial of a syndicate boss.

Sherry is guarded by Ernest Brady, a rookie cop, and veteran Lieutenant Monahan. Unbeknownst to her—and for a while unbeknownst to the audience as well—is the fact that the two police officers are being paid by the underworld to make sure that she never leaves the hotel alive.

Isolated within four walls, Ernest, a diamond in the rough, and the attractive, brassy Sherry share a bottle of scotch, dance to radio music, go to sleep together—and fall in love. Not yet hardened by corruption, Ernie decides to take a stand and save Sherry.

In a tense climax, Lieutenant Monahan signals with a pocket mirror to a gunman who lurks outside, and soon an oblong of sunlight reflects from a mirror outside and dances around the walls. Ernie thrusts Sherry onto the bed and faces Monahan, who retreats toward the window. A barrage of shots ring out and the lieutenant slumps forward and drops to the floor, dead.

Ernie promises Sherry that he will reactivate an investigation of her case and calls headquarters.

* * *

Dead Pigeon premiered at New York's Vanderbilt Theatre on December 23, 1953. The critics were by and large unhappy. Robert Coleman declared that the play was "essentially a one-act thriller, padded into three."[1] Walter F. Kerr complained, "In general, the author has dawdled over everything we'd willingly take for granted, and skimped on the three-way tug-of-war that might have been exciting."[2] Brooks Atkinson scoffed at "a verbose, monotonous script."[3] William Hawkins concluded, "The trouble is that neither the story nor the people are ever really arresting. The conflict never comes to life."[4]

Isolated positive reviews came from John McClain, who found *Dead Pigeon* "a diverting and entirely authentic little melodrama,"[5] and John Chapman, who believed that "Kantor has spilled his story most adroitly" and that "*Dead Pigeon* is an excellent piece of theatrical fiction."[6]

The players received unanimous positive comments—Joan Lorring (Sherry Parker), Lloyd Bridges (Detective Ernest Brady), and James Gregory (Lieutenant Monahan). Richard Watts Jr. wrote: "Miss Lorring is both sympathetic and humorous as the girl. . . . Mr. Bridges[7] brings a quiet, rugged charm and simplicity to the part of the detective. . . . Mr. Gregory plays with admirable credibility and incisiveness."[8]

Dead Pigeon ran for twenty-one performances. In 1955, the play was adapted to the screen by Columbia Pictures under the title *Tight Spot*. The cast was enlarged to fifteen speaking roles, but the action remained primarily confined to the hotel suite. Ginger Rogers appears in the role of convict Sherry, Edward G. Robinson portrays a U.S. attorney who offers Sherry her freedom if she agrees to testify in the trial of a notorious crime kingpin (Lorne Greene), and Brian Keith plays the corrupt police detective who changes his mind and saves Sherry at the cost of his life. The cinematic treatment added some scenes, including a poignant reunion between Sherry and her sister, and the murder of a sympathetic prison matron escort.

* * *

Dead Pigeon was Lenard Kantor's sole contribution to Broadway. During the 1950s, 1960s, and 1970s, Kantor wrote numerous television episodes for ABC's *The Untouchables*, *The Fugitive*, and *Most Wanted*; NBC's *The Doctors*; and CBS's *Cannon*. For the silver screen, Kantor cowrote the screenplay of *Jamboree* (1957), a rock-and-roll musical featuring Kay Medford and Frankie Avalon.

Acting Edition: Samuel French, Inc. (in manuscript form).

NOTES

1. *Daily Mirror*, December 24, 1953.
2. *New York Herald Tribune*, December 24, 1953.
3. *New York Times*, December 24, 1953.
4. *New York World-Telegram*, December 24, 1953.
5. *New York Journal-American*, December 24, 1953.

6. *Daily News*, December 24, 1953.

7. Lloyd Bridges (1913–1998) was born in San Leandro, California. He grew up in various northern California towns and graduated from Petaluma High School in 1931. While studying law at the University of California at Los Angeles, he became interested in acting. He soon appeared on the Broadway stage, founded an off-Broadway theatre, directed plays for a Catskills company, and in 1936 made his film debut. Bridges performed in many crime films, including *The Lone Wolf Takes a Chance* (1941), *Alias Boston Blackie* (1942), *Crime Doctor's Strangest Case* (1943), *Secret Agent X-9* (1945), *Moonrise* (1948), *Hideout* (1949), *The Limping Man* (1953), *Third Party Risk* (1954), and *Wetbacks* (1956). Among his westerns are *The Royal Mounted Patrol* (1941), *West of Tombstone* (1942), *Riding West* (1944), *Abilene Town* (1946), and the important Cecil B. DeMille's *Unconquered* (1947) and Fred Zinnemann's *High Noon* (1952). In the latter he played a deputy marshal who goes through a savage fistfight with Gary Cooper among the hoofs of startled horses. Lloyd Bridges proved his versatility in the war sagas *Sahara* (1943) and *A Walk in the Sun* (1945); the dramas *Home of the Brave* (1949) and *The Rainmaker* (1956); the adventurous *Daring Game* (1968) and *Bear Island* (1979); and the 1980s parodies *Airplane!*, *Hot Shots!*, and *Jane Austen's Mafia!*, his last film. Beginning in the early 1950s and for the next three decades, Bridges appeared on television in a variety of genres. His crime-ridden episodes were shown on the *Westinghouse Summer Theatre*, *Climax!*, *Playhouse 90*, *Kraft Suspense Theatre*, *Mission Impossible*, and *Police Story*. Perhaps his most renowned TV role is as scuba diver Mike Nelson in the adventure series *Sea Hunt* (1958–1961). In 1962–1963 he had his own *The Lloyd Bridges Show*. Lloyd died in 1998, but his sons Beau and Jeff Bridges have been treading successfully in their father's footsteps.

8. *New York Post*, December 24, 1953.

The Quare Fellow (1954)

Brendan Behan (Ireland, 1923–1964)

A native of Dublin, Ireland, Brendan Behan followed in his father's footsteps and joined the Irish Republican Army in his teens. At the age of sixteen he was imprisoned for attempting to blow up a British battleship in Liverpool harbor.

Behan spent most of the years 1939–1946 in English and Irish penal institutions. During his incarceration in a borstal in Suffolk, he frequented its library and, inspired by Oscar Wilde, Sean O'Casey, and André Gide, he began to write. His experiences in jail supplied him material for his first play, *The Quare Fellow*, an Irish idiom for "a man who is about to be hanged."

The Quare Fellow unfolds in the wing of an Irish prison during the twenty-four hours preceding an execution. The condemned man, who has butchered and dismembered his brother, does not have a name and is never seen. The prison population—inmates and wardens—react with both pity and cynicism to the upcoming dawn hanging.

Playwright Behan labeled *The Quare Fellow* a comedy-drama. The bleak environment and the unfortunate fate of the characters are counterpointed with satirical darts and gallows humor, which, for example, has the official hangman get drunk in a pub and lose the box containing the rope.

The proceedings take place on a bare platform. The background consists of metal cell doors. On a side wall there is a window, from which may be seen the laundry yard of the women's prison. On another wall is printed in large block Victorian lettering the word "SILENCE." Despite the warning, a noisy sound track keeps offering melodic songs, presumably crooned by off-stage prisoners, triangle trills to indicate passing hours, and the pounding of spades when a grave is being dug.

The somewhat formless first act introduces several inmates, including Dunlavin, a talkative old man, who has spent most of his life in jail but is still sprightly and alert; Prisoner B, thirty-six years old, gentle, and easygoing; Neighbor, elderly, quarrelsome, hobbling on a stick; and two adolescents, Shaybo and Scholara, who were recruited from the Juvenile Wing for cleaning chores but pass their time peering through the window at "the mots" hanging out laundry. One of the wardens, veteran Regan, is affected by the horror of hanging.

The curtain rises on three prisoners sharing gory details about the act of execution. Warden Regan escorts in a newcomer, a middle-aged man condemned to a life sentence for murder. "How do you live through it?" he asks. "A minute at a time," says Prisoner A, a cynic described as "a Hard Case."

Dunlavin and Neighbor reminisce about the women in their lives: Lottie, who was nabbed for pushing a soldier into Spencer Dock; and May, arrested for breaking a curfew and found to be carrying two concealed Thompson submachine guns, three Mills bombs, and a stick of dynamite.

When Warden Regan brings in a second newcomer, Dunlavin and Neighbor learn from the card on his cell's door that he is "a bloody sex mechanic."

Regan begins to rub the feet of Dunlavin and Neighbor with "methylated spirit." While bending down he does not notice that the two rascals take swallows from the medicine bottle. Typical of the play as a whole, this lighthearted moment is followed by a grim one, when the lifer newcomer is found hanging in his cell. They lay him down, unconscious, in the passage and attempt to resuscitate him. Two stretcher-bearers rush in, and the curtain falls.

The second act unfolds in the prison yard, where the convicts wander about. Some are standing by a half-dug grave, debating the prospect of a last-minute reprieve. Prisoner E, a bookie, takes bets on whether tomorrow's execution will take place. Neighbor declares that the Quare Fellow "hasn't got a chance" and bets his Sunday bacon with Dunlavin, who feels "in his bones" that a reprieve will come through before morning. Young Shaybo and Scholara dive into the grave for a forbidden smoke but are driven away by Warden Donelly. An English prisoner, from a window above, sends down a pound in a bucket, asking Mickser, who is soon going free, to contact his friend in Dublin. Mickser promises to do so but as soon as the money is in his possession, he sends back a note, "Get a bucket and bail yourself out." Mickser, perhaps the least sympathetic character of the lot, seizes Neighbor and with a yell of delight, throws him into the grave. The men gather around, kicking dirt on the old man. Soon their attention turns toward an inmate wearing a white apron who comes through the hospital gate carrying a covered tray. They immediately surround him, venting guesses at the contents of the Quare Fellow's last meal: Rushers and eggs? Fish and chips? Sausage and bacon? Steak and onions?

The Hangman comes slowly down the steps. He asks Warden Regan about the Quare Fellow's weight and the thickness of his neck in order to measure the hanging drop.

The third act transpires later that night. The Governor arrives in evening dress and hears from the Chief Warden that the Hangman went to a succession of bars on a drinking spree and left behind the black box that contains his rope, his washers, and other odds and ends. Squad cars were sent out, and the box was found in a tavern down the North Wall.

The hour strikes. A faint echo is heard as the prisoners tap messages from one cell to another. The wardens cross themselves. We do not see the execution, which takes place at dawn. Later in the morning, Prisoners A, B, and C enter carrying shovels, hammers, and chisels, and begin to carve "E.777" on a stone. Neighbor reminds Dunlavin that he won his bet—the Quare Fellow did not receive a reprieve; Dunlavin owes him a Sunday's bacon.

The playwright throws a last dart of cynicism prior to the final curtain, as the prisoners divide among themselves a batch of letters that belonged to the hung man. "They're worth money to one of the Sunday's papers," says Prisoner A.

* * *

The Quare Fellow premiered at the tiny Pike Theatre Club, Dublin, Ireland, in 1954. Two years later, on May 24, 1956, Joan Littlewood's Theatre Workshop presented the play at Theatre Royal, Stratford, East London, running for twenty-nine performances, with playwright Brendan Behan portraying one of the prisoners.[1] In July, *The Quare Fellow* was moved to West End's Comedy Theatre, where it ran for seventy-nine showings. A dispatch to the *New York Times* reported that "the audience roundly cheered Brendan Behan's *The Quare Fellow*."[2] Critic Cecil Wilson of the *Daily Mail* said that the author, "who has spent five years in prison, has packed these years into a play with all the humors and horrors, the boredom, the brutality and the desperate comradeship of prison life."[3] The *Daily Telegraph*'s Patrick Gibbs opined that "it may well be hailed a masterpiece by those in favor of the abolition of capital punishment but for ideological rather than artistic reasons."[4] Kenneth Tynan wrote in the *Observer*, "Joan Littlewood's production of this unforgettable play was a model of restraint and disciplined naturalism."[5] *Theatre World Annual* lauded Behan's "Irish gift for words" and stated that "the prison documentary is not so grim as it sounds. . . . Though obviously a plea for the abolition of capital punishment, there is considerable humor, albeit sardonic."[6]

The Quare Fellow crossed the Atlantic and on November 27, 1958, was presented by off-Broadway's Circle in the Square, staged by Jose Quintero and designed by David Hayes. Critic Brooks Atkinson believed that "a loose, sprawling, loquacious play is redeemed of the grimness of its subject by the intimacy of the author's knowledge of the strange, dark manners of prison life and by the rude exuberance of the dialogue . . . original, boisterous and perceptive."[7] *The Quare Fellow* ran for sixteen weeks.

The play was filmed in 1962. Screenwriter-director Arthur Dreifuss focused on a new warden, Thomas Crimmins (played by Patrick McGoohan), who arrives on the scene naive and idealistic only to face the stark reality of prison life. In an added subplot, Crimmins becomes involved with the wife of one of the condemned men, Kathleen (Sylvia Syms).

* * *

Brendan Behan's literary output includes several lighthearted radio playlets that were converted to the stage: *Moving Out* and *A Garden Party* (broadcast 1952; produced 1958) and *The Big House* (broadcast 1957; produced 1958). The three-act *The Hostage* (1958) is a tragicomedy unfolding in a Dublin brothel, where the Irish Republican Army imprisons an English soldier. He is to forfeit his life unless the British authorities cancel the planned execution of an Irish patriot in Belfast. *Richard's Cork Leg*, set largely in a cemetery, is nevertheless considered "a joyous celebration of life." Behan began the play in the early 1960s, scribbled several drafts, but had not finished it by the time he succumbed to diabetes and alcoholism in 1964. Alan Simpson, the artistic director of Dublin's Abbey Theatre, edited and enlarged a rambling manuscript for production in 1972. The journal *Plays and Players* reported that "it has all the familiar Behan obsessions—death with a corpse that won't lie down; work as the curse of the unemployed; sex without overdue concern about gender; patriotism as the best excuse for coming home late and staying in bed in the morning; alcohol as the great leveller, literally and metaphorically."[8]

An autobiography by Behan, *Borstal Boy* (1958), was adapted to the stage by Frank McMahon and presented at the Abbey in 1967. The play was shown with great success in Paris in 1969 and exported to New York, where it opened at the Lyceum Theatre on March 31, 1970, ran for 143 performances, and won the Tony Award and the Drama Critics Award for best play of 1969–1970. A 2000 motion picture version of *Borstal Boy*, filmed in Dublin and directed by Peter Sheridan, had Shawn Hatosy in the role of Brendan Behan as an idealistic youth who goes through three years in a reform school and learns to soften his radical stance. One of the highlights is an inmates' production of Oscar Wilde's *The Importance of Being Earnest*.

Brendan Behan: A Biography by Ulick O'Connor was published by Hamish Hamilton, London, in 1970. A one-man show, *Shay Duffin as Brendan Behan*, was presented at Manhattan's Irish Arts Center in 2006. Critic

Anita Gates wrote that when imitating the playwright, "Mr. Duffin slurs his words, gasps for breath, grasps his left arm and takes long pauses while searching for words. . . . He is more than believable as Behan, who in later life (his 40s) was said to make public appearances while passing-out drunk. The re-creation is painful to watch."[9]

Acting Edition: *The Quare Fellow* is included in *The Complete Plays of Brendan Behan*—Samuel French, Inc., and in *Brendan Behan: The Complete Plays*—Grove Press.

Awards and Honors: Brendan Behan was the recipient of an Obie Award, 1958; Paris Festival Award, 1958; French Critics Award, 1962.

NOTES

1. Joan Maud Littlewood was born to a sixteen-year-old unmarried housemaid in 1914. She established her highly innovative Theatre Workshop after World War II in the London area known as Stratford East. For years her troupe of actors slept in hammocks in the auditorium and shared box-office income. In 1956, Littlewood became Brendan Behan's mentor, helped him rewrite the manuscripts of *The Quare Fellow* and *The Hostage*, and staged both plays to international acclaim. Even though she thoroughly took control of Behan's career, she was unable to stem his drinking bouts that were instrumental in his death in 1964 at the age of forty-one. In 1958, Littlewood's company presented Sheila Delaney's *A Taste of Honey*, a drama about a white Lancashire girl who becomes pregnant after an affair with a black sailor. Five years later came the improvised *Oh, What a Lovely War!*, a music hall revue intended, she said, to "mock the absurdity, the vulgarity of war." In 1994, Littlewood penned her autobiography, *Joan's Book*, which she described as "plain, moody, and often amusing sometime." A recluse in old age, Littlewood died in London at the age of eighty-seven. The *New York Times* obituary of September 24, 2002, called her "one of the most important and original figures responsible for the regeneration of the British theatre in the 1950's and 60's."

2. *New York Times*, July 10, 1956.

3. Quoted in the *New York Times*, July 25, 1956.

4. Quoted in the *New York Times*, July 25, 1956.

5. Louis Kronenberger, ed., *The Best Plays of 1955–1956* (New York: Dodd, Mead, 1956), 32.

6. *Theatre World Annual* (London, 1956), 46.

7. *New York Times*, November 28, 1958.

8. *Plays and Players*, November 1972.

9. *New York Times*, October 19, 2006. Born in Dublin, Ireland, Shay Duffin (1931–2010) won a 1975 Los Angeles Drama Critics Circle Award for his performance in the one-man show about Brendan Behan, which he also wrote. Duffin took the play to other cities and presented it thousands of times. He also appeared in about thirty-five movies (including *The Departed* and *Titanic*) and television shows (he was a regular on *City*, 1990). Duffin died on April 23, 2010, of complications from heart surgery at UCLA Medical Center.

The Prisoner (1954)

Bridget Boland (England, 1913–1988)

Bridget Boland's psychological drama *The Prisoner* is inspired by the plight of Catholic Cardinal József Mindszenty (1892–1975), an opponent of fascism and communism. On September 16, 1945, Pope Pius XII appointed Mindszenty as Cardinal of Hungary. The Communist regime maintained that church schools were anti-democratic and in 1948 proposed the nationalization of all Catholic schools. Cardinal Mindszenty crusaded against the plan and was arrested. He was charged with treason and was sentenced to life imprisonment. Following the 1956 revolution, Mindszenty was freed.

The Prisoner unfolds on a gloomy set divided into an interrogation room and the prisoner's cell, both furnished only with essentials—a desk, two chairs, a file cabinet in the interrogation room; a chair, table and a bench covered with a blanket in the cell. There are high, barred windows in both rooms. An overhead light is always on.

The curtain rises on a Warden, a stocky man who sporadically sniffs loudly and unpleasantly, ushering in the Prisoner, a man of middle age and "considerable pride of bearing," dressed in the cassock of a Roman Catholic cardinal.

Enter the Interrogator, who represents the totalitarian government. He too is middle-aged, exhibiting "a genuinely pleasant manner." He is followed by the Secretary, a bustling, self-important man who puts some papers on the desk. At first, the give-and-take between Interrogator and Prisoner is amicable. The Prisoner remembers the Interrogator as a young, brilliant barrister, expert at cross-examination. He appreciates the Interrogator's background—a lawyer and a doctor, a gentleman from a noble family. The Interrogator asks His Eminence to relax and stop treating him like a police inspector. He has deep personal respect for the priest as a World War II Resistance hero.

The Prisoner warns the Interrogator that he has already gone through a similar experience with the Gestapo and that he is difficult to trap and impossible to persuade. He is also inured to most physical pain. The Interrogator assures him that no "racks and thumbscrews" will be used, as a confession from a broken body "seldom looks really spontaneous."

He offers the Prisoner water, but the cardinal rejects it for fear it is contaminated with a "truth drug." The Interrogator declares that neither drugs nor torture will be used. Theirs is a mental duel. He is intent on finding the Prisoner's "human weakness, the chink in the plate of armour" that will destroy his record as a national hero. He is seeking a conversion, an open confession made in public.

The Interrogator pooh-poohs the previous attempts by the newly formed government to trap the cardinal by planting photographs of a secret arsenal in his cathedral crypt, and microphones under the rim of his desk. This will be a chess game, between two worthy opponents.

Deprived of sleep, the Prisoner holds on. A coffin is brought to his cell. He is ordered to lift the lid and to his horror sees his mother. It turns out that she is still alive, but she is sick with cancer. It was a shock tactic, but it does not break the spirit of the cardinal.

It is the Interrogator who begins to show the strain of the encounter. But eventually, after the relentless and calculated pressure of questioning, he discovers his antagonist's one vulnerable spot: the cardinal's deep sense of personal guilt for a life built on pride. Playing on that, the Interrogator twists and confuses the Prisoner into a confession, charging that he does not love his fellow men and never had any love for God; that he has become a priest for his own glory; that he betrayed his country during the war; that he led a life of lies.

In the final scene the Prisoner is given an elaborate breakfast, which he believes is his last meal before being hung. The Interrogator arrives with the news that his sentence has been commuted. The government does not want him to become a martyr. "I had counted on execution, this is the heavier sentence," laments the Prisoner. The Interrogator produces a revolver from an inner pocket. He offers to shoot the Prisoner with the excuse of fending off an attack. But the Prisoner rejects this form of escape; he has accepted a future of being branded "like Cain."

The Interrogator relates that he is resigning his post at the Ministry of Justice. His encounter with the Prisoner has destroyed his belief in what he has been doing; he realizes that he has ruined something more noble than his own cause.

* * *

Staged by Peter Glenville, *The Prisoner* premiered at the Lyceum Theatre in Edinburgh, Scotland, on March 1, 1954, and moved to London's Globe Theatre six weeks later. Alec Guinness and Noel Willman portrayed the Prisoner and the Interrogator, respectively. Wilfrid Lawson and Richard Easton played the chief wardens. *Theatre World Annual* wrote: "There are snatches of grim humour in Bridget Boland's play, but one is left with a feeling of almost unbearable intensity."[1] The drama ran for sixty performances.

The following year, Boland adapted her play to the screen, with Glenville making his debut as a film director and Guinness reprising his role as the Prisoner. Jack Hawkins played the Interrogator and Wilfrid Lawson portrayed the Warden. Deemed too controversial, *The Prisoner* was banned from the Cannes and Venice Film Festivals.[2]

In 1963, *The Prisoner* was presented on British television, featuring Alan Badel as the Cardinal and Patrick McGoohan as the Interrogator.

* * *

London-born Bridget Boland was educated at Oxford University, where she received her BA, with honors, in 1935. During World War II she became senior commander in the Auxiliary Territorial Force. In addition to *The Prisoner*, Boland penned several plays for the West End during the 1940s and 1950s, notably *Cockpit* (1948), a drama about displaced persons in postwar Europe that utilized several Continental languages and was staged in an unconventional manner at the time, breaking through the Fourth Wall and spilling into the auditorium to involve the audience.

Boland made an important contribution to suspense cinema when in 1940 she coscripted, with A. R. Rawlinson, the movie version of Patrick Hamilton's play *Gaslight*, starring Anton Walbrook as Mr. Manningham, a dastardly husband who attempts to drive his wife Bella, portrayed by Diana Wynyard, out of her mind.

Boland collaborated on the screenplays of *This England* (1941); *War and Peace* (1956), from the novel by Leo Tolstoy; *Damon and Pythias* (1962); and *Anne of the Thousand Days* (1969), from the play by Maxwell Anderson. Boland was also the author of the radio play *Sheba* (1954) and the teleplay *Beautiful Forever* (1965).

Acting Edition: Dramatists Play Service.

Awards and Honors: Bridget Boland was conominee, in 1969, for an award from the Writers Guild and for an Academy Award for best screenplay for *Anne of the Thousand Days*.

NOTES

1. *Theatre World Annual*, 1954.
2. An earlier motion picture, *Guilty of Treason* (1950), is based on the tumultuous life of Cardinal József Mindszenty. The movie was scripted by Emmet Lavery, directed by Felix Feist, and featured Charles Bickford as the cardinal.

Meet a Body (1954)

Frank Launder (England, 1906–1997) and Sidney Gilliat (England, 1908–1994)

Subtitled "An Improbable Adventure in Three Acts," *Meet a Body* is a rollicking comedy thriller riddled with unexpected twists. Much of the action unfolds during one evening in the lounges of two small, adjacent houses in St. John's Wood, London.

William Blake, a vacuum-cleaner salesman, arrives by appointment for a demonstration at the villa Windyridge. To his astonishment, the house seems to be unoccupied and the furniture is draped with sheets. Ann Vincent, a young, good-looking woman, enters and declares that she is the fiancée of Reginald Willoughby-Pratt, a well-known BBC announcer, and that this is to be their home. Soon Reginald makes an appearance and proves to be pompous and authoritative. A mutual dislike develops between him and the debonair salesman.

Mrs. Bostock, the owner of Windyridge, who made the appointment with William, seems to have disappeared. Bloodstains on the carpet cause concern. At the end of act I, William plays a one-finger melody on the piano, when suddenly the instrument emits a clicking sound. William lifts the lid, and a woman's arm flops inertly over the downstage side of the piano.

Next door, at the villa Appleby, the benign Harry Hawkins is playing a game of chess with Sergeant Basset of the local police, when a terrified William bursts in with the news that he found a dead woman in the piano at Windyridge. Upon returning to the scene of the crime, the men are startled to discover that the body has disappeared.

William realizes that the nameplates of the adjacent villas, Windyridge and Appleby, have been swapped, and he concludes that the kindly Mr. Hawkins is involved.

It turns out that the woman-in-the-piano is not dead, only dazed. Incoherently, she tells William and Ann that she is Winifred, secretary of Sir Gregory Upshott, a government envoy to the Middle East. Winifred mutters, "Ten forty-eight—it's going to go off at ten forty-eight—hurry— they're going to kill him," and faints. To the chagrin of her fiancé, Ann

147

joins William as they travel to The Green Man hotel in Newcliffe, hoping to save Sir Gregory's life.

The Green Man is a small eighteenth-century hotel standing on the cliffs of the Sussex coast. Sir Gregory Upshott arrives with his very young, highly nervous secretary, Joan Wood, who is already regretting this clandestine excursion. William and Ann conduct a frantic search for the time bomb they are convinced will blow up at 10:48. They uncover the explosive device in the lounge radio and hurl it out down a cliff just in time. Sir Gregory thanks the heroic couple for saving his life and makes a hasty exit back to London, to the relief of his squeamish secretary.

Meanwhile, Reginald Willoughby-Pratt finds out that Ann is spending the night with the vacuum-cleaner salesman at a far-off hotel and makes some frantic telephone calls. Ann and William, who together went through one evening of adventure, decide to share "the fun" for the rest of their lives.

* * *

An early version of *Meet a Body* was performed in Streatham Hill, England, on July 29, 1940. An updated version, directed by Henry Kendall and designed by Hal Henshaw, opened fourteen years later at London's Duke of York's Theatre on July 21, 1954. *Theatre World Annual* praised "an admirable cast headed by Brian Reece (William) and Joy Shelton (Ann)" that "kept the action moving to the accompaniment of much laughter and the sub-plot of foreign agents, time bombs, etc."[1] *Meet a Body* ran for fifty-three performances, was revived the following year by the Wolverhampton Repertory Theatre, and in 1956 was converted to the screen by its two playwrights under the title *The Green Man*. In adapting the play to the cinema, Frank Launder and Sidney Gilliat enlarged the role of Harry Hawkins (played by Alistair Sim), a mild watchmaker who in his spare time is a professional assassin. Equipped with a bomb, Hawkins is after the pretentious cabinet minister, Sir Gregory Upshott (Raymond Huntley). The bumbling vacuum-cleaner salesman, William Blake (George Cole), inadvertently foils Hawkins's dastardly scheme.

* * *

Meet a Body was the only play written by Launder and Gilliat. The duo collaborated most successfully on the scripting of a number of British motion pictures, notably the railroad thrillers *Rome Express* (1932), directed by Walter Forde; *Seven Sinners* (1936), directed by Albert de Courville; Alfred Hitchcock's *The Lady Vanishes* (1938); and Carol Reed's *Night Train to Munich* (1940). Together or individually, Launder and Gilliat penned several suspense screenplays for director Forde: *The Ghost Train* (1931), which they adapted from the play by Arnold Ridley; *Bulldog Jack* aka

Alias Bulldog Drummond (1935), from Sapper's novels about the rugged adventurer; and *The Gaunt Stranger* aka *The Phantom Strikes* (1938), from Edgar Wallace's hit play *The Ringer*. They also teamed as writer-producer-directors on the social comedy *The Rake's Progress* (1945), the spy yarn *I See a Dark Stranger* (1946), the lyrical romance *The Blue Lagoon* (1949), the action drama *State Secret* aka *The Great Manhunt* (1950), the biographical *The Great Gilbert and Sullivan* (1953), the romp *Wee Geordie* (1956), the farcical St. Trinian's series (1954–1966), and Agatha Christie's whodunit *Endless Night* (1972).

In addition to their fruitful contributions to the cinema, Launder and Gilliat wrote the radio serials *Crooks Tour* (1941) and *Secret Mission 609* (1942).

Launder was a civil servant, an actor, and a studio assistant prior to his first collaboration with Gilliat in the early 1930s. Educated at London University, Gilliat began his career as a film critic for the *London Evening Standard* and wrote movie titles during the silent era. He became scenario chief at British International Pictures in 1928, was elected president of the Screen Writers Association in 1936, and was nominated chairman of Shepperton Studios in 1961.

Acting Edition: Samuel French Ltd., London.

NOTE

1. *Theatre World Annual*, 1954–1955 (London: Rockliff Publishing Corporation, 1955), 43.

Murder Story (1954)

Ludovic Kennedy (Scotland, 1919–2009)

A real-life case, known as the Croydon Rooftop Murder, inspired Ludovic Kennedy's drama *Murder Story*, a protest against capital punishment. Nineteen-year-old Derek Bentley and sixteen-year-old Christopher Craig exchanged bullets with the police on the premises of a Croydon factory. Craig shot and killed a policeman while trying to escape over a rooftop. The two boys were tried and convicted of murder. Craig, being under age, was sentenced to prison; Bentley was sentenced to death.

Kennedy was deeply affected by the fact that the jury's recommendation for mercy was rejected, and by the notion that the murderer should survive while his accomplice, who didn't even carry a gun that fatal night, would be executed.

Murder Story raises its curtain on the living room of Arthur and Elsie's house in Paddington, a working-class district in London. Their modest abode includes a tiled brick fireplace, a moth-eaten chaise longue, a television and radio set, and bric-a-brac. On the wall hangs a color photograph of the Queen and the Duke of Edinburgh.

The Tanners' daughter, Daisy Richards, twenty-two and pregnant, arrives with a suitcase. Her husband Fred, a sailor, is in the Far East. Daisy is planning to stay with her parents for the Christmas holiday. As they set the table for dinner, Mrs. Tanner tells Daisy that her brother, Jim, has lost five jobs during the last three months. "A boy of nineteen fooling about with toy soldiers like a kid," sighs Mrs. Tanner. Daisy also learns that her father, Arthur, had a mild heart attack several weeks ago and was ordered by his doctor to get a less stressful job. "But what kind of a sit-down job can I do?" says Tanner. "I been used to working with me hands all me life."

The door opens and Jim Tanner comes in. Jim is a stocky youth with a vacant expression. His movements and reactions are noticeably slow and his speech toneless, almost monotonous. Jim tells his anxious family that

150

he "got the sack." When new tobacco jars arrived in the store, he informed the tobacconist, Johnson, that he couldn't read the labels. Johnson started to laugh, says Jim, so he "let fly at him" and called the boss "a lot of names and things."

Later in the day Jim has a visitor. Ted Clift, described as "a pale, weedy-looking, spiv-like young man of about twenty-six," tells Jim about a "little job" at tobacconist Johnson's store. This is a chance to pay him back, says Clift. And there is good money in it—"fifty smackers apiece." They'll pick up a few cigar boxes, take them out through the back door, and load them into a waiting car. The whole thing won't take more than ten minutes. Reluctantly, Jim agrees to partake in the robbery. Clift produces a gun from his pocket and proudly shows it to Jim, but promises not to use it.

The second scene unfolds an hour later. Daisy is sitting by the fire, knitting; Tanner is having a beer; and Mrs. Tanner is cooking in the kitchen when Jim enters hurriedly, out of breath, and runs upstairs to his room. Daisy and her parents settle in front of the television set to watch "Who Am I?," a show in which a quiz team guesses the identity of celebrities in disguise.

There is soon a loud knock on the front door. A plainclothes police inspector comes in, followed by a policeman in uniform. They request to see Jim, "in connection with the murder of police-constable Albert Tomkins." The Tanners hear Jim describe to the lawmen how he and Ted Clift entered the tobacco shop, were accosted by a "copper," and during the ensuing scuffle a shot rang out and the policeman fell down. Both Ted and he fled the scene.

The Inspector ushers Jim out to go to the station. Daisy and her parents are frozen in shock when the lights fade out.

Act II takes place in "the condemned cell of one of Her Majesty's prisons." It is a bleak room with high, bare walls. The only furniture is a bed in one corner and a table and chairs in the middle. Above the table hangs a naked bulb. High up is a barred window, looking out on to the prison yard. In one of the side walls is a door leading to a lavatory. A locked, bigger door in the opposite wall leads directly to the execution shed.

A pair of prison guards, Graves and Bartholomew, Chief Officer Briggs, the Chaplain, and the Governor of the prison are all sympathetic to Jim and hope that the jury's recommendation for mercy will prevail and negate the pending execution. The officers teach Jim to spell and read. The Chaplain calms Jim's fears and influences him to pray. Jim, the former simpleton, gains self-esteem and grows in stature.

But the Governor arrives with the message that the Court of Criminal Appeal has refused clemency. Officer Graves bemoans that while the law doesn't allow anyone under twenty-one to get married or sit on a jury, it allows them to be hung.

Tanner, Jim's father, circulates a petition on behalf of his son. Even Mrs. Tomkins, the widow of the dead policeman, asks the authorities for a reprieve, arguing that an additional death will not help matters. But all the efforts are in vain.

The last scene reverts back to the Tanner home. The Chaplain brings a note from Jim to his parents: "Cheerio and keep your chins up." Tanner says quietly, "Well, I'm not complaining. The law's the law, and there it is." Mrs. Tanner begins sobbing but controls herself admirably. Tanner takes his wife's hand in his as the lights fade out slowly.[1]

* * *

Murder Story previewed at the Hippodrome Arts in Aldershot, England, on June 14, 1954, and, as reported by *Theatre World Annual,* was transferred to West End's Cambridge Theatre five weeks later, "giving London the opportunity of applauding Donald Bradley in the role of Jim Tanner, the feeble-minded boy who was sentenced to death as an accessory with a companion who shot a policeman. . . . The prison scenes are excellent and the dialogue convincing."[2] *Theatre World Annual* added that "Ludovic Kennedy's dramatic first play, based on the Bentley-Craig murder case, aroused deep feelings in all who saw it, though the author, in his sincere desire to protest against capital punishment, overstated his case, presenting in Jim Tanner, the mentally retarded 'murderer,' a victim of circumstances which must have brought his reprieve under the law."[3] John McKelvey directed, and the realistic sets were designed by Ann Tabor.

Murder Story ran for sixty performances. In 1958, the play was adapted for television as a one-hour presentation on UK's Armchair Theatre.

* * *

The son of a Royal Navy captain, Ludovic Henry Coverley Kennedy was born in Edinburgh, Scotland, in 1919. He attended Eton College and followed his father into the Navy. He served as an officer on the HMS *Tartar,* which pursued the battleship *Bismark,* and he later wrote about it in his book *Pursuit* (1974).

After the war Kennedy began a career as an investigative reporter, writing for a number of publications, including *Newsweek.* In the 1950s, he edited the First Reader series on BBC's Third Programme, presented BBC's current affairs *Panorama,* and became a newsreader on Independent Television News.

Kennedy penned several books that attacked what he believed were miscarriages of justice. His *10 Rillington Place* (1961) examines the conviction of Timothy Evans, who was executed for the murder of his baby daughter.[4] In *The Airman and the Carpenter* (1985), Kennedy argued that Bruno Richard Hauptman did not kidnap and kill Charles Lindbergh's baby, but had been railroaded by the police as a scapegoat to pacify an angry public.[5] *Thirty-six Murders and Two Immoral Earnings* (2003) analyzes a number of notable cases, including the Birmingham Six, the Guildford Four, and the Maguire Seven, groups of men who spent years in prison for fatal pub bombings against England attributed to Irish terrorists. All the convictions were eventually overturned.

In 1989, Kennedy published his autobiography, *On My Way to the Club*. Two years later came *Truth to Tell: Collected Writings of Ludovic Kennedy*. Kennedy championed liberal causes but failed in his attempt to be elected to Parliament as a Liberal candidate. His efforts, however, contributed to the abolition of the death penalty in Britain in 1965.[6]

In 1950, Kennedy married Moira Shearer, the ballerina of the classic 1948 film *The Red Shoes*. Their fifty-six-year marriage ended with Shearer's death in 2006 at the age of eighty. Three years later Ludovic died of pneumonia at a nursing home in Salisbury, Wiltshire, England. He was eighty-nine.

Acting Edition: Victor Gollancz LTD, London.

Awards and Honors: Ludovic Kennedy was knighted by Queen Elizabeth II in 1994 for contributions to journalism. He received honorary degrees from the Universities of Edinburgh, Stirling, and Strathclyde.

NOTES

1. The real-life story of Derek Bentley and Christopher Craig is related in the 1991 movie *Let Him Hang It*, directed by Peter Medak, featuring Christopher Eccleston as Bentley and Paul Reynolds as Craig.

2. *Theatre World Annual* (London: Rockliff Publishing Corporation, 1953–1954), 8.

3. *Theatre World Annual*, 46.

4. *10 Rillington Place* was filmed in 1971 under the direction of Richard Fleischer, starring John Hurt as Timothy Evans and Richard Attenborough as serial killer John Christie.

5. *The Airman and the Carpenter* was made into a 1996 HBO film, *Crime of the Century*, with Stephen Rae and Isabella Rossellini.

6. The published edition of *Murder Story* (1956) includes an "Epilogue on Legal Killing," in which Ludovic Kennedy contends that "there is no reason at all for supposing that legal killing is a better deterrent against murder than a long term imprisonment." He further argues that capital punishment "is the only penalty still existing in English law which, if a miscarriage of justice be discovered afterwards, cannot be made good." Furthermore, writes Kennedy, "For the

condemned man, yes, there is an ending, but for those who love him none. The memory of his death, and the manner of it, will remain with them for the rest of their lives. The family are one group of people on whom legal killing inflicts widespread and sometimes lasting misery." Kennedy maintains that "legal killing is a form of human sacrifice no less revolting and unnecessary than those practiced by primitive tribes to placate moody gods." Ludovic Kennedy, *Murder Story* (London: Victor Gollancz LTD, 1956), 141–160.

Bad Seed (1954)

Maxwell Anderson
(United States, 1888–1959)

Rhoda Penmark, a neat, quaint, and pretty little girl of eight, lives with her doting parents in a Southern suburb. "You're just too good to be true," says Rhoda's father, Colonel Kenneth Penmark, upon departing for duty at the Pentagon in Washington, D.C. "Now, what will you give me if I give you a basket of kisses?"

Rhoda responds with an angelic smile "I'll give you a basket of hugs" and jumps into her father's arms.

There seems to be no cloud over this family idyll, except Rhoda's complaint that she should have won the class penmanship medal, instead of nerdy Claude Daigle. Rhoda's mother, Christine, a lovely, gentle, and gracious woman, attempts to calm the girl but is rebuffed.

During a school picnic, Claude Daigle is found drowned in the bay; it is assumed that the bruises found on Claude's forehead and hands were caused by his body being wedged amid the pilings. Miss Fern, the school principal, informs Christine that the penmanship medal was not found on Claude and that Rhoda was the last one to see the poor boy alive. Shocked, Christine discovers the medal in her daughter's treasure box.

At first Rhoda claims not to know how the medal got there, but when Christine persists, Rhoda admits to having followed Claude up the beach and getting the medal from him for fifty cents. Christine's misgivings and doubts are dissipated.

A family friend and writer of detective fiction, Reginald Tasker, is an expert in the history of crime. He tells Christine that just as there are child geniuses among mathematicians and musicians, there are also child geniuses among criminals. Tasker theorizes that heredity overtakes environment, and that even the best families cannot teach a blind child to see, or a bad child to acquire moral scruples.

Christine, concerned now, prods her father about her heritage. To her shock, Richard Bravo reveals that he is not her blood father and that Bessie

Denker, a serial murderess, was her mother. When Bessie vanished, the Bravos adopted Christine, "an astonishingly sweet and beautiful little thing."

Christine catches her daughter sneaking out to burn a pair of shoes in the basement incinerator. Rhoda confesses that she hit Claude with the shoes. Christine realizes that her daughter murdered the boy for the medal. Rhoda shows no remorse, but insists that it was Claude's fault for not giving her the medal and threatening to tell on her.

To her horror, little by little, Christine learns that Rhoda has pushed a former landlady off icy steps to her doom and has set a feeble-minded handyman afire in a pyre of excelsior. Concluding that her daughter, by heritage, is a habitual murderess, Christine gives Rhoda an overdose of sleeping pills and shoots herself in an off-stage den.

A shocking final scene pictures little Rhoda alive and well, having been saved by neighbors who rushed in when they heard the fatal shot. "I love you, Daddy," says Rhoda sweetly. "What will you give me for a basket of kisses?"

Kenneth Penmark answers, "I'll give you a basket of hugs!" Rhoda runs into her father's arms, smiling impishly over his shoulder toward the audience as the curtain falls.

* * *

Adapted by Maxwell Anderson from the 1954 novel by William March (1894–1954), *Bad Seed* premiered at the Forty-sixth Street Theatre in New York on December 8, 1954. The morning-after reviewers greeted the play and its production values with unanimous acclaim: "An extraordinary literate horror story and a superior bit of theatre," said Brooks Atkinson.[1] "A tense, macabre, frightening study in infantile infamy," wrote Robert Coleman.[2] "A horrifying and literary play. . . . There hasn't been a more fiendish small girl around since *The Innocents*," opined John Chapman.[3] "As showmanship, it is a genuine fourteen-carat, fifteen-below chiller," added Walter Kerr.[4]

Director Reginald Denham, an old hand at suspense plays, and his cast were showered with kudos: Nancy Kelly as the doomed Christine; Patty McCormack as the evil moppet; Henry Jones as Leroy, the simpleton janitor; Eileen Heckart as the distraught Mrs. Daigle; and Evelyn Varden as a motherly neighbor.

Bad Seed ran for 332 performances and repeated its success in London, where it opened at the Aldwych Theatre on April 14, 1955, for 195 showings, with Diana Wynyard and Carol Wolveridge playing mother and daughter. Kelly, McCormack, Jones, Heckart, and Varden re-created their stage roles in a 1956 motion picture version, directed by Mervyn Leroy, in which the glum ending was reversed—Christine recovers from her attempted suicide while Rhoda goes to the bay on a stormy night to retrieve the pendant as lightning strikes the wooden pier. A playful curtain call introduces the actors in the form of a tableau, with McCormack sprawled across Kelly's knees, being zestfully spanked. Flashed on the screen is an appeal to refrain from revealing "the unusual climax."[5]

Bad Seed was included by Stanley Richards in his *Best Mystery and Suspense Plays of the Modern Theatre.* "When Maxwell Anderson's adaptation of William March's novel *The Bad Seed* opened on Broadway in 1954, it came to some as a shocker, both on stage and off stage," writes Richards, "for as far as could be determined, the author had not attempted a pure 'thriller' before. To those more familiar with the Anderson prolificacy, however, it was still further proof of his varied range as a dramatist."[6]

More than a half-century later, in 2007, *Bad Seed* was no less of a shocker when produced by Buzzworks Theatre Company at The Lounge Theatre in Hollywood, California, with the homicidal little girl, Rhoda Penmark, played in drag by Danny Schmidt, who also directed. Reviewer Charles McNulty of the *Los Angeles Times* believed that "Schmidt's lampoon magnifies to our delight the ordinary freakishness surrounding Rhoda's creepily extraordinary kind."[7]

* * *

James Maxwell Anderson's distinguished career is strewn with plays incorporating criminous elements, in both contemporary and historical settings: *White Desert* (1923), his first produced venture, is the tragic story of a lonely woman in the North Dakota prairies who is shot to death by a jealous husband. *Outside Looking In* (1925), based on Jim Tully's autobiographical *Beggars of Life*, is a picaresque comedy populated with rowdy hobos and tramps who live by their own code of the road, highlighted by the story of Edna, who killed her abusive stepfather, and Little Ned, the vagrant who helps her escape. *Buccaneer* (1925), written with Laurence Stallings, shows how Henry Morgan of the British Navy turns pirate but is later pardoned and knighted by King Charles II.

Gods of the Lightning (1928) is based on the controversial real-life indictment, trial, and execution of Nicola Sacco and Bartolomeo Vanzetti for the 1920 robbery and murder of a paymaster and his guard in Braintree, Massachusetts. *Winterset* (1935) depicts an imaginary aftermath, when a son of one of the executed men crusades to clear his father's name.

Webs of palace intrigue are the core of the Tudor trilogy *Elizabeth the Queen* (1930), *Mary of Scotland* (1933), and *Anne of the Thousand Days* (1948), as well as the period drama *Richard and Anne* (1955), inspired by Josephine Tey's 1951 novel of historical detection, *The Daughter of Time,* which attempts to clear the reputation of hunchbacked, demonized Richard III.

Both Your Houses (1933) is a study of intrigue, graft, and corruption in congressional committees. *High Tor* (1937) is a comic fantasy about a nature-loving youth who refuses to sell his inherited rocky mountain and gets entangled with city slickers, crooked rogues, and bank robbers. *Key Largo* (1939) depicts a Loyalist Spain crusader, who left his comrades behind, redeeming himself clashing with ruthless gangsters in a Florida Keys hotel. *Lost in the Stars* (1949), based on Alan Paton's novel *Cry, the Beloved Country* with a score by Kurt Weill, is the epic saga of a black parson whose son murders a British planter's son, unfolding against the background of racial animosities in South Africa. In *Barefoot in Athens* (1951), Socrates goes on trial for his life, charged by zealots for corrupting the minds of youth. *The Day the Money Stopped* (1958), cowritten with Brendan Gill, based on his novel, is about the black sheep of a respectable Connecticut family who resorts to blackmail when left out of his father's will.

Between 1924 and 1958, Anderson also penned a potpourri of noncrime plays—tragedies, dramas, comedies, fantasies, and musicals—some in verse, others in prose; some historical, others contemporary; some hitting theatrical jackpot, others fizzling fast—all dedicated by him "to the exaltation of the spirit of man."

The artists who mounted Maxwell Anderson's plays throughout thirty-five years of productivity represent the Who's Who of Broadway—directors Arthur Hopkins, Guthrie McClintic, George Cukor, Lee Strasberg, Worthington Miner, John Houseman, Joshua Logan, Harold Clurman, Margo Jones, H. C. Potter, and Reginald Denham; designers Jo Mielziner, Lee Simonson, Robert Edmond Jones, Howard Bay, Boris Aronson, and George Jenkins; actors James Cagney, Ruth Gordon, Humphrey Bogart, Luther and Stella Adler, Franchot Tone, Paul Muni, Jose Ferrer, Uta Hagen, Alfred Lunt, Lynn Fontanne, Helen Hayes, Katharine Cornell, Burgess Meredith, Peggy Aschcroft, Hume Cronyn, Lillian Gish, Edmund O'Brien, Walter Huston, Karl Malden, Lotte Lenya, Marlon Brando, Ingrid Bergman, Rex Harrison, Nancy Kelly, Richard Basehart, and Viveca Lindfors.

Several of Anderson's plays were adapted to the screen: *Winterset* (1936); *Elizabeth the Queen*, filmed as *The Private Lives of Elizabeth and Essex* (1939); *Knickerbocker Holiday* (1944); *Joan of Lorraine*, retitled *Joan of Arc* (1948); *Key Largo* (1948); *Anne of the Thousand Days* (1969); and *Lost in the Stars* (1974).

Anderson scripted a television version of *A Christmas Carol* (1954) from the story by Charles Dickens; a few radio plays between 1937 and 1944; and, with others, the motion pictures *All Quiet on the Western Front* (1930), *We Live Again* (1934), *So Red the Rose* (1935), *Joan of Arc* (1948), and *The Wrong Man* (1957).

The prolific author also wrote the verse volumes *You Who Have Dreams* (1925) and *Notes on a Dream* (1971), as well as the nonfiction *The Essence of*

Tragedy (1939); *The Bases of Artistic Creation*, with Rhys Carpenter and Roy Harris (1942); and *Off Broadway* (1947). In 1938, he joined S. N. Behrman, Sidney Howard, Elmer Rice, Robert Sherwood, and John Wharton to form the Playwrights' Company.

The *New York Times* obituary of March 1, 1959, noted that Anderson "looked upon the theatre as the central artistic symbol of the struggle of good and evil within men. Set a man on the stage, he once said, and you know instantly where he stands morally with the race. The theatre to Mr. Anderson . . . was an affirmation also that men have within themselves the beasts from which they descend and the God towards which they climb."[8]

Acting Edition: Dramatists Play Service. *Bad Seed* is also included in *Best Mystery and Suspense Plays of the Modern Theatre*, edited by Stanley Richards (New York: Dodd, Mead, 1971).

Awards and Honors: A top-ten selection in *The Best Plays of 1954–1955*: "In its catalogue and crescendo of horrors, *Bad Seed* has a number of gripping scenes and chilling moments. The horror grows, moreover, through the play's quasi-realistic tone, its reassuringly middle-class atmosphere. As a literate shocker, *Bad Seed* is successful; while even as a problem play, with the mother confronting the pathology of her child, no Ibsen could have raised a graver issue."[9]

Maxwell Anderson was the recipient of the Pulitzer Prize—*Both Your Houses* (1933) and the New York Drama Critics Circle Award—*Winterset* (1935–1936) and *High Tor* (1936–1937). Top-ten selections in the Best Plays yearbook were *What Price Glory?* (1924–1925), *Saturday's Children* (1926–1927), *Gypsy* (1928–1929), *Elizabeth the Queen* (1930–1931), *Both Your Houses* (1932–1933), *Mary of Scotland* (1933–1934), *Valley Forge* (1934–1935), *Winterset* (1935–1936), *High Tor* (1936–1937), *The Star-Wagon* (1937–1938), *Key Largo* (1939–1940), *Candle in the Wind* (1941–1942), *The Eve of St. Mark* (1942–1943), *Storm Operation* (1943–1944), *Joan of Lorraine* (1946–1947), *Anne of the Thousand Days* (1948–1949), *Lost in the Stars* (1949–1950), *Barefoot in Athens* (1951–1952), and *Bad Seed* (1954–1955). Nineteen Best Play entries put Anderson ahead of George S. Kaufman, who has had fifteen, and Eugene O'Neill, who has had eight. Anderson received the American Academy of Arts and Letters Gold Medal in 1954.

NOTES

1. *New York Times*, December 9, 1954.
2. *Daily Mirror*, December 9, 1954.
3. *Daily News*, December 9, 1954.
4. *New York Herald Tribune*, December 9, 1954.

5. The original resolution was retained in my production of *Bad Seed* at Elmira College, Elmira, New York, 1984, still evoking gasps from the audience. A 1992 camp revival in Minneapolis had actor-director Danny Schmidt comb his hair in pigtails and don a girl's smock to play Rhoda Penmark. The mocking production, peppered with gay innuendos, wandered to Hollywood's Tamarind Theatre in 1996 and to the same area's Lounge Theatre in 2007.

6. Stanley Richards, ed., *Best Mystery and Suspense Plays of the Modern Theatre* (New York: Dodd, Mead, 1971), 590.

7. *Los Angeles Times*, July 27, 2007.

8. *New York Times*, March 1, 1959.

9. Louis Kronenberger, ed., *The Best Plays of 1954–1955* (New York: Dodd, Mead, 1955), 7.

Spider's Web (1954)

Agatha Christie (England, 1890–1976)

With *The Mousetrap* and *Witness for the Prosecution* still packing houses in London, Agatha Christie came up with a third smash hit—the comedy-thriller *Spider's Web*, written especially for English star Margaret Lockwood.[1]

Lockwood portrayed the role of Clarissa Hailsham-Brown, the ditzy wife of a government official who discovers a dead body in her drawing room and goes through manifold efforts to dispose of it.

Clarissa and her husband Henry have leased Cobblestone Court in Kent, the home of an antique dealer. The old house comes complete with a hidden panel, behind which there is a recess leading into the library. A handsome period writing desk is prominent among musty furniture pieces. Pippa, Henry's autistic daughter from a first marriage, has discovered in the desk a secret compartment filled with autographed papers. Pippa's mother, Miranda, a drug addict, had left home and married sleazy Oliver Costello who, one evening in March, suddenly shows up and informs Clarissa that he intends to take custody of Pippa.

Oliver plans to blackmail Clarissa, but she summons the gardener, Mildred Peake, who carries a large hedge shears, to show the intruder out. Pippa has witnessed the encounter and breaks into a fit of hysterics, threatening to kill Oliver if he takes her away.

That night Oliver enters stealthily through the French windows, switches on a lamp, and searches the desk. The wall panel slowly opens. Someone unseen hits Oliver on the head and he collapses behind a sofa. Clarissa finds him there, dead; she is horrified, and certain that Pippa is the culprit.

Determined to shield the child, Clarissa solicits the help of three family friends—the distinguished Sir Rowland Delahaye, the irascible Hugo Birch, and the elegant Jeremy Warrender. Someone has called the police (who?), and Inspector Lord unexpectedly rings the doorbell. Clarissa cajoles her cohorts to hastily hide Oliver's body in the secret chamber and proceeds to bamboozle the poor inspector with a succession of fabricated stories.

Complications pile up, and merrily the corpse keeps disappearing and reemerging. Deeper and deeper, Clarissa's spins get her into a tangled web of danger, climaxed by a life-or-death confrontation with Warrender, who is revealed as the man who used his golf club to eliminate a competitor in search of a priceless stamp concealed in the Victorian desk.

* * *

Spider's Web tried out at the Theatre Royal in Nottingham, on September 27, 1954, underwent rewriting on tour, opened at London's Savoy Theatre on December 14, enjoyed support from the press, and ran for 774 performances. Director Wallace Douglas surrounded Margaret Lockwood with a solid cast that included Felix Aylmer as Sir Rowland and Desmond Llewelyn, later "Q" in the James Bond movies, as a bumbling police constable.

In the United States, *Spider's Web* was presented off-off-Broadway at Manhattan's Lolly's Theatre Club in 1974 and at the Hudson Guild Theatre in 1978. The play was also seen in Washington, D.C.'s Olney Theatre in 1976, at Louisville's Actors' Theatre in 1981, and at Palos Verdes Players Theatre in Los Angeles in 2002.

Charles Osborne, who had done the same for Christie's *Black Coffee* and *The Unexpected Guest*, novelized *Spider's Web* in 2000.

A 1960 low-budget British-made film version of *Spider's Web* was directed by Godfrey Grayson, who cast Glynis Johns in the role of Clarissa.

Acting Edition: Samuel French, Inc.

NOTE

1. Trained at the Royal Academy of Dramatic Arts in London, Margaret Lockwood (1916–1990) became Britain's most popular leading lady in the 1940s. Among the cinematic thrillers she graced—as heroine or villainess—were *Doctor Syn* (1937), *The Lady Vanishes* (1938), *Night Train to Munich* (1940), *Alibi* (1942), *The Man in Grey* (1943), *The Wicked Lady* (1945), *Bedelia* (1946), *Highly Dangerous* (1950), *Trent's Last Case* (1952), and *Cast a Dark Shadow* (1955).

Inherit the Wind (1955)

Jerome Lawrence (United States, 1915–2004) and Robert E. Lee (United States, 1918–1994)

The historic "monkey trial" of Tennessee high school teacher John T. Scopes, accused of teaching Charles Darwin's theory of evolution in defiance of state law, was dramatized by Jerome Lawrence and Robert E. Lee in a rousing fashion. *Inherit the Wind* was first presented at the Dallas Theatre on January 10, 1955. Later that year, on April 21, it opened to great fanfare in New York's National Theatre for a whopping run of 803 performances.

"The authors of *Inherit the Wind* have followed the outline of the trial very closely and have not neglected its humorous aspects," wrote critic John Chapman in the *Daily News*, "but they have done much more than manufacture a documentary. They have made a play which, in addition to abundantly satisfying the desires of a theatergoer, stirs the mind."[1]

The events that took place in Dayton, Tennessee, during the scorching July of 1925 are the genesis of the play. The playwrights fictionalized the place and the characters but remained faithful to the titanic clash between defense attorney Clarence Darrow (in the play, Henry Drummond) and prosecutor William Jennings Bryan (Matthew Harrison Brady) over a person's right to think.

The drama unfolds in the makeshift courthouse of Hillsboro. Matthew Harrison Brady basks in the adulation of the fundamentalist townspeople. Henry Drummond's defense is steamrolled by a strict judge. No specialists or scientists are allowed to submit evidence. Drummond changes tactics and receives permission to summon a witness who is a Scripture expert, none other than Matthew Harrison Brady. Brady is delighted to take the stand, consumed with righteousness and confident of himself as the champion of the people. There are loud "Amens" and much applause from the spectators.

The courtroom duel between Drummond and Brady is the high point of *Inherit the Wind*. Drummond picks up a copy of Darwin's *Origin of Species*, but the judge decrees that he will confine his questions to the Bible.

163

Drummond tosses Darwin's volume on the counsel table and gets a copy of the Bible. He solicits from Brady his belief that "everything in the Bible should be accepted, exactly as it is given there." Drummond queries Brady about the story of the whale swallowing Jonah, about Joshua making the sun stand still, and Brady insists, "I have faith in the Bible."

Drummond and Brady continue to parry about various biblical segments, drawing heated reactions from the Hillsboro audience. At last the judge resorts to his gavel: "Colonel Drummond, the court must be satisfied that this line of questioning has some bearing in the case." Brady says calmly that he is willing to endure "Mr. Drummond's sneering, disrespect, and contempt for all that is holy." Heated, Drummond insists that he finds the individual human mind holy, that an idea is a greater monument than a cathedral. When Brady insists that people should not abandon faith, for faith is the most important thing, Drummond counters with "Then why did God plague us with the power to think?" and points out that the power to reason is the one faculty that lifts human beings above other earthly creatures.

Gradually, the crowd slips away from Brady and aligns itself more and more with Drummond.

Drummond points at teacher Cates and roars, "This man wishes to think!" He then displays a rock about the size of a tennis ball and asks Brady how old he thinks the rock is. Brady lamely jokes that he is more interested in "the Rock of Ages than in the Age of Rocks." Drummond relates that according to experts the rock is at least ten million years old. Brady dismisses the notion, asserting that the rock could not be more than six thousand years old; he argues that a careful computation of the ages of the prophets as set down in the Old Testament proves that "the Lord began the Creation on the 23rd of October in the year 4,004 B.C. at 9 a.m."

Drummond pounces sarcastically, demanding to know if that was Eastern Standard, Rocky Mountain, or perhaps Daylight Saving Time. Brady loses his equanimity, becomes confused, and begins to stutter. Relentlessly, Drummond continues to lunge at a deflated Brady until he breaks him completely. The astonished crowd shifts its support to the defendant.

The teacher, Bertram Cates, is found guilty, but his light sentence—a fine of $100—punctures the mighty Evolution Law. Bending history but achieving a touchy climax, the playwrights picture Brady attempting in vain to address his once-faithful flock. Alas, all focus is drawn away from him, and, quivering, Brady falls, dying.

A cynical Baltimore reporter, E. K. Hornbeck (H. L. Menkin), eulogizes Brady as "a Barnum-bunkum Bible-beating bastard." Drummond's reaction is surprising. He admonishes Hornbeck for forgetting that Brady was once "a giant" who got lost because he was looking for God too high up and too far away.

Left alone, Drummond intends to put Darwin's *Origin of Species* in his briefcase when he notices the Bible on a desk. He picks it up and weighs the two books, one in each hand. Smiling, he slaps the books together, inserts them both in the briefcase, and ambles off into the sunset.

* * *

Most of the critics greeted *Inherit the Wind* with hosannas. "An effectively provocative chronicle drama," wrote Richard Watts Jr.[2] "The town has a hit that is distinguished and challenging," stated William Hawkins.[3] "The new arrival is at its tense best during the trial episodes," asserted Robert Coleman. "These hold the interest in a vise-like grip. It is something like that memorable one in *The Caine Mutiny Court-Martial*. It has drive, suspense and color. Technically, it is exciting theatre."[4]

Paul Muni's portrayal of Henry Drummond won plaudits from the entire cadre of reviewers. "There's a whale of an old-fashioned, free-swinging, suspender-snapping fight going on at the National, and Paul Muni wins it," declared Walter F. Kerr. "In the rich, raucous, rough-and-tumble second act in the courthouse, he gets hold of the role like a starved hound of magnificent ancestry and shakes it till the feathers fill the room."[5] John McClain gushed, "Hold up your count, Mr. Auditor, we've got a whole flock of new votes for the best performance of the year. Paul Muni, returning to the stage after a long and unauthorized absence, has just brought in a large plurality for his superb delineation of Clarence Darrow."[6] Even Lewis Funke, who dissented from his brethren and found *Inherit the Wind* "lacking in suspense" and "only intermittently compelling," credited Mr. Muni with "a magnificent performance."[7]

Kudos were also showered on Ed Begley as Brady, Tony Randall as Hornbeck, Karl Light as Cates, Bethel Leslie as Rachel, and Staats Cotsworth as Rachel's fundamentalist father, Reverend Jeremiah Brown. Paul Muni won the 1956 Tony Award for Best Actor, Ed Begley won the Tony as Best Featured Actor, and Peter Larkin got the nod for his scene design. Director Herman Shumlin was nominated.[8]

Inherit the Wind did not replicate its New York success when it came to London's St. Martin's Theatre in 1960, running for sixty-nine performances.

The play was revived on Broadway in 1996, directed by John Tillinger, featuring George C. Scott as Drummond and Charles Durning as Brady (forty-five performances), and in 2007, staged by Doug Hughes, with Christopher Plummer as Drummond and Brian Dennehy as Brady (100 performances).

Stanley Kramer directed an engrossing movie version of the play in 1960, starring Spencer Tracy (Drummond), Fredric March (Brady), and

Gene Kelly (E. K. Hornbeck). A radio rendering was aired in 1965. Television adaptations were broadcast in 1965, with Melvyn Douglas and Ed Begley winning Emmy Awards for their performances as Drummond and Brady; in 1988, with Jason Robards and Kirk Douglas; in 1999, with Jack Lemmon and George C. Scott, the latter now switching roles, playing Brady.

* * *

Both Jerome Lawrence and Robert Edwin Lee were born in Ohio—Lawrence in Cleveland in 1915, Lee in Elyria in 1918. Both inherited an interest in writing from their mothers—a poet and a teacher, respectively. Both excelled at top learning institutions; Lawrence graduated from Ohio State University and the University of California at Los Angeles, Lee from Northwestern University in Illinois and Ohio Wesleyan. Both served as consultants to the secretary of war during World War II, and it was there that they met and cofounded Armed Forces Radio.

The first play that Lawrence and Lee wrote together was the book for the 1948 musical *Look, Ma, I'm Dancing!*, directed by George Abbott and choreographed by Jerome Robbins, cheerfully spotlighting the behind-the-scene escapades of a traveling ballet company. Their next Broadway venture was *Inherit the Wind*. They continued their collaboration on ten additional dramas, comedies, and musicals produced in New York, including the book and lyrics for *Shangri-La* (1956), based on the novel *Lost Horizon* by James Hilton, about a group of strangers stumbling into a utopian Tibetan land; *Auntie Mame* (1956, London 1958, filmed 1958; revived 2004), based on the autobiographical novel by Patrick Dennis, in which young Patrick is indoctrinated by his flamboyant aunt to become as free-spirited as she is; and *The Gang's All Here* (1959), depicting the corrupt administration of President Warren Harding.

The protagonist of *Only in America* (1959), based on a book by Harry Golden, is a Lower East Side New Yorker who moves to North Carolina and publishes his first book. *A Call on Kuprin* (1961), aka *Checkmate*, based on a novel by Maurice Edelman, is a suspense melodrama in which an American tourist in Russia helps a friend escape from the police state. *Diamond Orchid* (1965), aka *Sparks Fly Upward*, pictures the rise and fall of an obscure radio actress who becomes the First Lady of a Latin American country but is not accepted by the social and intellectual elite of the nation.

Lawrence and Lee wrote the book and lyrics of *Mame* (1966), an enormously successful musical comedy (1508 performances; filmed 1974; revived 1983), based on their play *Auntie Mame*. They also wrote the book of *Dear World* (1969), a musical inspired by Jean Giraudoux's play, *The Madwoman of Chaillot*, a fable about an old woman who saves Paris from the scheme of greedy prospectors who plan to tear up the city in order to unearth an oil field. *The Incomparable Max* (1971), drawn from two stories by Max Beerbohm, is about a poet who makes a pact with the devil, and a young man who can see into the future. *First Monday in October* (1978; filmed 1981), is a pre–Sandra Day O'Connor comedy-drama about the first woman appointed to the Supreme Court of the United States and her clash with the chauvinistic all-male body.

Plays penned by Lawrence and Lee that were performed outside of New York include the early 1970s *The Crocodile Smile*, in which a beautiful French woman is in love with two inspired comedians and agrees to marry the "better actor," instigating a rivalry between them to prove their superiority; *Jabberwock*, subtitled "Improbabilities Lived and Imagined by James Thurber in the Fictional City of Columbus, Ohio"; and *The Night Thoreau Spent in Jail*, a dramatization of biographical incidents in the life of author-poet-naturalist Henry David Thoreau.

Lawrence and Lee's last collaboration, seen at the Missouri Repertory in Kansas City in 1994, was *Whisper in the Mind*, recounting an imaginary meeting between Benjamin Franklin and the eighteenth-century hypnotist Frank Anton Mesmer.

In addition to their important contribution as playwrights, Lawrence and Lee left an indelible mark as cofounders of the American Playwrights Theatre and as committed educators who taught and lectured extensively in the field. Lee served as an adjunct professor of playwriting at UCLA for twenty years. Lawrence was a visiting professor at Ohio State, New York, and Baylor universities. Ohio State University houses the Jerome Lawrence and Robert E. Lee Theatre Research Institute.

Acting Edition: Dramatists Play Service.

Awards and Honors: A top-ten selection in *The Best Plays of 1954–1955*. Winner of the Donaldson Award, the Outer Critics Circle Award, and the Variety Critics Poll Award both in New York (1955) and London (1960).

Jerome Lawrence and Robert E. Lee earned two George Foster Peabody Awards for distinguished achievement in broadcasting (1949, 1952). They received the Lifetime Achievement Award from the American Theatre Association (1979), the Ohioana Award, keys to the City of Cleveland, an Ohio State Centennial Medal, the Ohio Governor's Award, a Cleveland Play House Plaque, a Pegasus Award, the Moss Hart Memorial Award for plays of the Free World, and a U.S. State Department Medal. In 1984, Lawrence and Lee received the Writers Guild of America Valentine Davies Award for contributions to the entertainment industry. In 1990, they were inducted into the Theatre Hall of Fame and named Fellows of the American Theatre. Among other recognitions, Lawrence and Lee were the recipients of honorary doctorates from the College of Wooster and Ohio State University.

MT. LEBANON PUBLIC LIBRARY

NOTES

1. *Daily News*, April 22, 1955.
2. *New York Post*, April 22, 1955.
3. *New York World-Telegram*, April 22, 1955.
4. *Daily Mirror*, April 22, 1955.
5. *New York Herald Tribune*, April 22, 1955.
6. *New York Journal-American*, April 22, 1955.
7. *New York Times*, April 22, 1955.
8. Paul Muni (1895–1967) was born Meshilem Meier Weisenfreund in Lvov, Poland (now Lviv, Ukraine). His parents, Jewish actors, took the boy to America in 1902 and joined New York's Yiddish theatre. Muni made his stage debut at the age of twelve, joined the Yiddish Art Theatre, and in 1926 made his first appearance on Broadway in *We Americans*, portraying an elderly Jewish man. Hollywood beckoned. In 1932, Muni appeared in two milestone crime films: as the mobster Antonio Camonte, in Howard Hawks' *Scarface*; and as James Allen, an innocent man victimized by the justice system, in Mervyn LeRoy's *I Am a Fugitive from a Chain Gang*. Muni's wide variety of screen roles included the lawyer Johnny Ramirez in *Bordertown* (1935); coal miner Joe Radek in *Black Fury* (1935); the famous French scientist in *The Story of Louis Pasteur* (1936); farmer Wang in *The Good Earth* (1936); the title role in *The Life of Emile Zola* (1937); the Mexican leader Benito Juarez in *Juarez* (1939); Pierre Esprit Radisson, the founder of a fur-trading company, in *Hudson's Bay* (1941); Erik Torensen, a Norwegian fighting the Nazis, in *Commandos Strike at Dawn* (1942); Professor Joseph Elsner, mentor of Chopin, in *A Song to Remember* (1945); Eddie Kagle, a murdered convict who is sent back to earth by the Devil as a respected judge, in *Angel on My Shoulder* (1946); and Dr. Sam Ableman, a kind Brooklyn family doctor, in *The Last Angry Man* (1959). Muni was nominated for an Academy Award five times, winning once for *The Story of Louis Pasteur*.

Prior to *Inherit the Wind*, Muni added to his laurels highly regarded Broadway appearances as ex-convict Benny Horowitz in George Abbott's *Four Walls* (1927); the lawyer George Simon in Elmer Rice's *Counsellor-at-Law* (1931); King McCloud, who confronts a gang of gamblers in Maxwell Anderson's *Key Largo* (1939); Tevya, a concentration camp survivor, in Ben Hecht's *A Flag is Born* (1946); and Tony, a Napa Valley winegrower, in Sidney Howard's *They Knew What They Wanted* (1949, revival).

The Desperate Hours (1955)

Joseph Hayes (United States, 1918–2006)

The invasion of a peaceful household by a variety of marauders tingled the nerve of audiences in *The Petrified Forest* (1934), *Blind Alley* (1935), *Kind Lady* (1935), *Night Must Fall* (1935), *Key Largo* (1939), *Ladies in Retirement* (1940), *Arsenic and Old Lace* (1941), *Guest in the House* (1942), and *The Man* (1950).

Joseph Hayes adopted the motif—with a vengeance—in his best-selling 1954 novel *The Desperate Hours*, which he then converted into a slam-bang play. In a *New York Times* article, Hayes wrote that *The Desperate Hours* was inspired by several true events that occurred around the country: "Frightened and dangerous men entered houses, held families captive in their own homes; these were headline stories, soon forgotten. Some ended tragically, others did not. . . . I found myself left with a curious and a very strong emotion—a sense of personal identification with the victims."[1]

Dan Hilliard is an Indianapolis businessman with a nice family—an attractive wife, a spunky teenage daughter, a likable small boy. When three escaped convicts take possession of their suburban home and hold them hostage, psychological warfare develops between the Hilliards and the homicidal intruders. In spite of unequal odds, the play "manages to be a cheering and credible little tribute to the potential courage of decent average people when pushed too far," stated Richard Watts Jr. in the *New York Post*.[2]

One of the unusual aspects of *The Desperate Hours* lies in the criminals' gambit of allowing Dan Hilliard and his daughter Cindy to go to work while Mrs. Eleanor Hilliard and ten-year-old Ralphie remain imprisoned in the house. The senseless murder of a garbage collector, Mr. Patterson, punctuates the brutality of the jailbirds and the helplessness of the Hilliards. Suspense mounts as the police force closes in. Deputy Sheriff Jess Bard is torn between his personal vendetta against one of the escapees and his concern for the besieged family.

The three bad guys, who intend to stay at the Hilliards' home until their confederates deliver their escape money, are vividly etched: the leader,

Glenn Griffin, takes his hatred of his own father out on the world, eventually wilting under pressure; his younger brother Hank, always under Glenn's thumb, finally rebels—but too late; Robish, the third partner in crime, is a primitive, brutish, trigger-happy mobster.

"Let's not pretend that *The Desperate Hours* is a work of art like Dostoevsky," wrote critic Brooks Atkinson upon the opening of the play at the Ethel Barrymore Theatre on February 10, 1955. "But it does show more interest in the characters than most thrillers do. The Hilliards are people of courage and pride. Their home represents to them an ideal of living. Apart from the terror of being threatened with guns, they feel that the privacy of their home has been violated. . . . Like a genuine writer, Mr. Hayes is interested in the inner life of his people."[3]

Reviewers formed a cheering squad. John McClain wrote, "It seems a regrettably long time between good, action-packed melodramas on Broadway these days. . . . That's why it's a joy to welcome *The Desperate Hours*: this is the best-seller thriller at its best, lots of actors shoot each other, and everybody winds up satisfied."[4] William Hawkins said, "*The Desperate Hours* is a melodrama that frankly sets out to pulverize your nerves. Before it is over, it does just that."[5] Wrote Robert Coleman: "*The Desperate Hours* is a terrific psychological thriller . . . the most absorbing chiller-diller of its kind to hit Broadway since *Blind Alley*. . . . Seldom have we seen an audience so spellbound in recent semesters as was that in the Ethel Barrymore Thursday evening. The first-nighters were rolling with the punches, rooting for the heroes and almost leaping on stage to clutch the throats of the villains."[6] John Chapman said, "I cannot remember any melodrama which has been as steadily and intensely exciting as is *The Desperate Hours*—or one which has been better acted or better staged. This is the topmost thriller of many seasons."[7] And from Walter F. Kerr came: "*The Desperate Hours* is a beaut. . . . I think you'll find the life-and-death chase loaded with theatrical tension."[8]

Basking in glorious superlatives were director Robert Montgomery; actors Karl Malden and Nancy Coleman as the beleaguered Hilliards; Paul Newman, George Grizzard and George Matthews as the three hoods; James Gregory as Sheriff Bard; and set designer Howard Bay for his detailed multilevel reproduction of the Hilliard house.

The Desperate Hours ran for 212 performances. A subsequent 1955 London production, featuring Bernard Lee as Dan Hilliard, played at the Hippodrome for 167 showings.

Scripted by Hayes, a motion picture version was made later that year under William Wyler's direction, and another impressive cast was recruited: Fredric March and Martha Scott as the victimized parents; Humphrey Bogart, Dewey Martin, and Robert Middleton as the deadly invaders; Arthur Kennedy as the understanding deputy sheriff.

A 1990 remake, directed by Michael Cimino, with Anthony Hopkins, Mimi Rogers, and Mickey Rourke, was snubbed by Leonard Maltin as "ludicrous."[9]

* * *

Joseph Arnold Hayes was born in Indianapolis, Indiana, in 1918, the son of a furniture factory worker. He briefly planned to join the priesthood, but upon graduating from Indiana University in 1941 left for New York, where he wrote for radio and television and became a full-time professional playwright and novelist. His first Broadway play, the romantic drama *Leaf and Bough* (1949), lasted three performances. Following the success of *The Desperate Hours*, Hayes codirected and coproduced with Howard Erskine the hit comedy *The Happiest Millionaire* (1956), starring Walter Pidgeon. It ran for 271 performances.

Hayes's next contribution to Broadway nail biting was *Calculated Risk* in 1962, an industrial espionage caper behind the scenes of a New England corporation. His other plays, penned mostly in collaboration with his wife Marrijane, were lightweight comedies. In 1962 they wrote *Bon Voyage!*, a Disney movie starring Fred MacMurray. Mrs. Hayes died in 1991.

Hayes's novels of suspense include *The Hours after Midnight* (1958), *Don't Go Away Mad* (1962), *The Third Day* (1964), *The Deep End* (1967), *Like Any Other Fugitive* (1971), *The Long Dark Night* (1974), *Missing . . . and Presumed Dead* (1976), *No Escape* (1982), and *The Ways of Darkness* (1986).

In 2006, Hayes died of complications from Alzheimer's disease at a nursing home in St. Augustine, Florida.

Acting Edition: Samuel French, Inc. *The Desperate Hours* is also included in *Ten Classic Mystery and Suspense Plays of the Modern Theatre*, compiled by Stanley Richards (New York: Dodd, Mead, 1973).

Awards and Honors: *The Desperate Hours* won the Tony Award as Best Play of 1954–1955. It was a top-ten selection in the annual *The Best Plays of 1954–1955*.

Joseph Hayes received the Charles H. Sergel Drama Prize awarded by the University of Michigan in 1948. He won the Indiana authors Day Award in fiction for the novel *The Desperate Hours*, 1955. The next year, his screenplay for the movie version won an Edgar Allan Poe Award from the Mystery Writers of America.

NOTES

1. *New York Times*, January 30, 1955.
2. *New York Post*, February 11, 1955.
3. *New York Times*, February 11, 1955.

4. *New York Journal-American*, February 11, 1955.

5. *New York World-Telegram*, February 11, 1955.

6. *Daily Mirror*, February 11, 1955.

7. *Daily News*, February 11, 1955.

8. *New York Herald Tribune*, February 11, 1955.

9. *Leonard Maltin's 2009 Movie Guide* (New York: Penguin, 2008), 345.

The Whole Truth (1955)

Philip Mackie (England, 1918–1985)

It was R. (Richard) Austin Freeman who revolutionized detective fiction, in his short story collection *The Singing Bone* (1912), by introducing the "inverted" motif, wherein the reader is a witness to the crime, and the interest centers not on the identity of the culprit, but on how he or she will be apprehended.

And it was A. A. (Alan Alexander) Milne, immortalized by his *Winnie the Pooh* children's stories, who first brought the "inverted" form to the stage—in 1928's *The Fourth Wall*, aka *The Perfect Alibi*. Instead of holding the solution in abeyance until 11 p.m., the audience is witness to a murder committed in act I by two malefactors, who claim a touch of genius by clearing all evidence behind them. For the balance of the play the investigative process sifts the truth by pinpointing the killers' mistakes. This structure is commonplace today (note television's *Columbo* and most other cops-and-robbers flicks on both tube and screen). But in the 1920s, the golden age of the chess-like whodunit (popularized by Agatha Christie in England and S. S. Van Dine in the United States), Milne's approach was a novelty.

Philip Mackie's twisty *The Whole Truth* follows the "inverted" pattern. The curtain rises on the living room of Lewis and Brenda Paulton's house in Hampstead, a borough of London. It is a big room, furnished in good, modern taste, with no sparing of expense. A bay window looks onto the front garden and driveway. A swinging door leads to the kitchen. Next to it is a dining area with a table and four chairs. It is half-past seven in the evening. Deenie, a Dutch maid, prim and humorless, is setting the table for four. She is perplexed by the correct arrangement of the silverware and mutters under her breath.

Brenda Paulton, good-looking, intelligent, comes down the stairs. She is followed by two somewhat similar-looking girlfriends, Jill and Vera. As the women chat, we learn that the Paultons are expecting guests for dinner, and that Lewis Paulton is a well-known movie producer. Jill and

Vera leave, and soon Lewis comes in through the front door. He is in his late twenties—personable, charming, something of a spoiled child. Just now he is worried and preoccupied, but he tries to conceal this under a jaunty manner. He carries a film script, which he puts on the desk, and he crosses to a cabinet to mix himself a drink.

Brenda greets her husband with a kiss, tells him that the studio has been trying to reach him all afternoon, and informs him that their friend Tony Hart and the actress Marion Gray will be joining them for dinner. Lewis is not happy that the invitation includes Marion, saying, "I'm scared of actresses who want to be stars," but Brenda insists: "It was high time we invited her."

Lewis goes to his room to change his shirt when the front doorbell chimes. Deenie opens the door to a pleasant-looking young man who introduces himself as "Hugh Carliss." Deenie exits to the kitchen and Brenda climbs the stairs to change for dinner. Momentarily alone, Carliss looks around. He sees a letter opener on the desk, takes out a handkerchief, wraps the knife, and puts it into his inside breast pocket. Lewis comes down struggling with a cuff link, not yet fixed into his shirt. He breaks the cuff link and tosses it on the sideboard.

Carliss tells Lewis that he is a detective-sergeant from District Headquarters. He is there to see Lewis in connection with an acquaintance of his, Marion Gray, who was found dead, stabbed with a knife, in her apartment. The porter of her building identified Lewis Paulton as the gentleman who came to see Marion that afternoon. Lewis, staggered by the news, says that he visited Marion "about twenty to four" and left about "a quarter past." He says that he has known Marion for a year or so and reports that she was in one of his films, *The Flying Trapeze*.

Carliss states that the medical examiner concluded that Marion was killed about four o'clock. Lewis says that Marion was expecting someone, so got rid of him in a hurry. Carliss looks at the dinner table set for four, and suggests that Lewis call to cancel the invitation. When Lewis picks up the phone to talk to Tony, Carliss slips the broken cuff link into his pocket.

Carliss departs. Brenda comes down and Lewis relates to her that the man she saw, Carliss, is a policeman who came with the shocking information that Marion Gray is dead—"Murdered. Stabbed. At her flat." Lewis now confesses that he had an affair with Marion, "a first-class devil" who wouldn't let go. It was half seduction, half blackmail, confesses Lewis. He wrote her "some stupid letters" and she kept them. He admits that he called on her earlier in the afternoon and came within an inch of killing her.

The front doorbell rings. Lewis opens the door and Marion sails in. The Paultons stare at her. When they recover, they tell Marion that they were informed that she was dead; the man who lied to them pretended to be a policeman. Lewis mentions the name Hugh Carliss and Marion is startled, but she tries to hide her surprise from the others. Lewis accuses Marion of sending Carliss to cause a breach between him and Brenda. Marion denies it, says she'll skip the dinner, and asks Lewis to see her to her car.

They go out. Brenda and Deenie start to remove two sets of dishes from the dining table. Lewis returns, looking grim. He asks Brenda if she wants him to leave, perhaps divorce him, but Brenda declares that she intends to stay married.

Brenda opens a window and her gaze travels slowly along the driveway. "She hasn't gone," says Brenda. "Her car's still here." Lewis joins Brenda at the window. They look out and see Marion sitting in the car, motionless. Lewis goes out through the front door and Brenda, impulsively, closes the window's curtain. Lewis returns, shocked and half-dazed. "She's dead," he whispers. "Somebody killed her. . . . There must have been someone hiding, watching us. . . . Someone must have killed her the moment I returned to the house."

For a terrible moment Lewis and Brenda consider driving Marion's car away and hiding the body, but they immediately discard the idea. Lewis has no doubt that the police will find his letters at Marion's apartment and will consider him a prime suspect, but he believes that they must tell the authorities "the whole truth." He picks up the telephone and asks the operator to connect him to the police as the curtain descends.

The second act takes place an hour or so later. A uniformed police-constable, Briggs, stands just inside the front door. Lewis prowls about, restless and nervous. Brenda peers out the window and reports on the activity outside—photographs, fingerprints. Inspector Brett and Sergeant Petty enter, both in plain clothes. The inspector announces that at this early stage he is simply trying to put the pieces together. He acknowledges the fact that there was a man who came to see Lewis—the wife and the maid confirm it. He notes that Lewis had a quarrel with the victim when walking her to the car. Marion Gray was found inside the car; she had been stabbed in the back while fumbling with her keys. It seems that she grabbed at the murderer's right hand. A broken cuff link was found on the floor of the car. One cuff link is missing on the sleeve of Lewis's shirt. Lewis contends that the phony policeman must have purloined it during his visit, and no doubt placed it in Marion's car to incriminate him.

Inspector Brett exhibits the murder weapon—a paper knife that has been identified by the maid Deenie. Lewis and Brenda theorize that Hugh Carliss came to make trouble, making sure that there would be a major quarrel between Lewis and Marion in front of witnesses, a maid, for instance; Carliss purloined the cuff link and paper knife on the spur of the moment; he waited behind the bushes in the yard for Marion to exit, certain that she would not stay for dinner after a confrontation; he killed Marion, planted the incriminating evidence against Lewis—and then disappeared into the blue. His name is obviously not Hugh Carliss, and finding him will be worse than finding a needle in a haystack.

There is a knock on the door. Officer Petty hands Briggs a note. Briggs whispers to Inspector Brett, who signals to Petty. Hugh Carliss is ushered in. Inspector Brett explains to the Paultons that he simply found Carliss in the telephone directory under the C's, and asked him to come. Upon Brett's cross-examination, Carliss, the son of millionaire Sir Andrew Carliss, asserts that he saw Marion that afternoon, that she told him that Lewis Paulton had just been there, and that she broke off her relationship with him. Carliss adds that then and there he proposed to Marion, and she accepted. He knew that Marion was coming to dinner at the Paulton's home. On the way to Bond Street to buy a ring, he decided to pay a visit to Lewis Paulton and break the news to him first—it would make it easier for all concerned. No, he never stole a cuff link or a knife. That evening he was home reading a book and made one phone call to his father, telling him about his engagement. This can easily be verified.

Lewis insists that "the whole thing is mad, like an enormous jigsaw puzzle" in which the pieces don't fit. He has no doubt that Carliss planned and executed his scheme down to the last detail. But Inspector Brett concludes that the place of death, the opportunity, the motive, the weapon, and the clues found at the scene of the crime all point in one direction—and he places Lewis under arrest for the murder of Marion Gray.

The first scene of act III unfolds at Inspector Brett's small office. Brenda insists that her husband is innocent and signs her statement. The inspector declares that this is "an open-and-shut case." She rejects his offer to send her home in a car and irately insists, "I'll walk."

After a while, Officer Petty brings Lewis in. Inspector Brett informs him that tomorrow he'll appear before a magistrate. When Lewis hears that Brenda is on her way home by foot, he is overcome by a premonition of danger and asks the inspector to send someone after her. Brett pooh-poohs the notion. Lewis appeals: "Look, inspector, in a few minutes my wife will get back to the house. Carliss may be there already. There must be something he still has to do. He's a cold-blooded murderer. Ring my house."

Brett gives in, sighs, and reaches for the telephone. He then changes his mind, withdraws his hand, and says, "Oh, what's the good of it?"

At the Paulton's home, a knock on the door brings Deenie down the stairs in her dressing gown. She switches on a light. It is Carliss, apologizing for the late hour and asking to come in for a moment to find the cigarette case he left behind. He goes to the sofa, takes a cigarette box from his pocket and slips it behind a cushion. He pretends to find it and lights a cigarette. He converses with Deenie and draws from her the information that she noticed that Mr. Paulton had no cuff link in his right sleeve. She intends to mention it to the inspector in the morning, a bit of news that seals her fate. Carliss pulls a stocking from his pocket and twists it around Deenie's neck, strangling her. He lets the body fall behind the sofa.

Carliss is crossing to the front door when he hears the sound of a key in the lock. He dodges into a dark corner as Brenda, tired, comes in, flings her bag, and intends to fall into the armchair when she sees Carliss's hat. She turns her head and sees Carliss himself. A tense scene ensues, during which Brenda asks point blank whether Carliss killed Marion. He denies it. He is circling around her when suddenly the telephone rings. Carliss quickly picks it up and answers in a disguised voice: "Hullo? . . . Hmmm . . . Who? . . . No, this is Belsize three-five-three-seven." He hangs up as Brenda notices Deenie's body. The telephone rings again and Brenda dashes to it. Carliss catches her, they struggle, and the phone stops ringing.

Carliss now admits to Brenda that he killed Marion, for she knew some scandalous events from his past and tried to blackmail him. Brenda makes several attempts to run for the telephone, but Carliss keeps pushing her into the armchair. At last he locks his arms around her neck.

There is a furious hammering on the front door. A key is thrust in the lock and Inspector Brett bursts in, followed by Petty and Lewis. Before they enter, Carliss has already released Brenda, who breaks away and falls gasping into the sofa. Carliss exclaims that Brenda killed her maid and regrettably he was too late to save her. Brett snaps his fingers at Petty, who immediately grabs Carliss and holds his arms behind his back. Brett tells Carliss that he told one lie too many. If he had simply said "wrong number" when Brett called from the police station, he would have been all right. However, Brett checked and there's no such number as Belsize three-five-three-seven.

* * *

Philip Mackie first wrote *The Whole Truth* for television. It was shown by BBC's Sunday Night Theatre on July 17, 1955. Mackie adapted his teleplay to the stage and *The Whole Truth* opened at London's Aldwych Theatre on October 11, 1955. Three cast members of the TV show were recruited to reprise their roles: Sarah Lawson (Brenda Paulton), Ellen Blueth (Deenie), and Arnold Bell (Inspector Brett). The other lead actors were Ernest Clark (Lewis Paulton), Leslie Phillips (Hugh Carliss), and Faith Brook (Marion Gray). Leslie Linder directed. Michael Eve designed the sets.

Theatre World Annual found *The Whole Truth* "a well-written murder thriller. . . . The dialogue is natural and convincing, and the characterization interesting. The company at the Aldwych gave a good account of themselves."[1] The play ran for 145 performances.

In 1958, *The Whole Truth* made a third turn and became a feature film. Scripted by Jonathan Latimer and directed by John Guilerman, the movie starred Stewart Granger and Donna Reed as the Paultons, and George Sanders as Carliss. The action was shifted to the French Riviera. German television broadcast *Die volle Warheit*, filmed in Munich, on January 27, 1963.

* * *

Philip Mackie was born in Salford, Lancashire, England, in 1918. He graduated in 1939 from University College, London; served in the military during World War II; and joined the Ministry of Information Films Division in 1946. In 1954, Mackie began writing for the BBC, and four years later he joined Granada TV as their first head of drama. His major writing assignments included *The Edgar Wallace Mystery Theatre*, an eight-part adaptation from Wallace's novels, notably *The Sinister Man* (1961), *The Clue of the Silver Key* (1961), and *Number Six* (1962); *Saki* (1962), eight episodes based on short stories by H. H. Munro ("Saki" was his pseudonym); *Mauppassant* (1963), thirteen episodes adapted from the work of the French author; *The Victorians* (1963), an anthology of eight plays produced during the nineteenth century, among them Tom Taylor's detective thriller *The Ticket-of-Leave Man* of exactly a hundred years previous; *Paris 1900* (1964), a series consisting of six farces by Georges Feydeau; and *The Caesars* (1968), a six-part, large-scale production depicting the Roman emperors.

In the 1970s, Mackie wrote and produced the period detective episodes of *The Rivals of Sherlock Holmes* (1971–1973); a political drama *The Organization* (1972); a series about a young and romantic Napoleon in *Napoleon and Love* (1974); *The Naked Civil Servant* (1975), a controversial telecast based on the autobiography of homosexual Quentin Crisp; *Raffles* (1975–1977), in twelve parts, about the colorful escapades of E. W. Hornung's gentleman-burglar; and *Malice Aforethought* (1979), four episodes based on Francis Iles's classic 1931 murder novel of the same name.

In the early 1980s, Mackie adapted to television Émile Zola's novel of passion, adultery, and murder, *Thérèse Racquin* (1980); *Preying Mantis* (1982), a milestone novel about obsession, blackmail, and homicide by French author Hubert Monteilhet; an eight-part serial *The Cleopatras* (1983), a horror history account about the ancient Egyptian dynasty; and two episodes for *Jemima Shore Investigates* (1983), featuring novelist Antonia Fraser's snooping reporter.

For the stage, Mackie followed *The Whole Truth* with *Open House*, a wild farce of mistaken identities and the battle of the sexes, first produced at the Leas Pavilion, Folkestone, England, on April 20, 1957, and three effective thrillers. *The Key of the Door* begins with the discovery of a dead woman in the locked bedroom of a country cottage. The door key is missing. An accident and suicide are soon overruled. Who among the five inhabitants of the cottage was the murderer? How was the foul deed committed? And why? The solution is reached during a series of flashbacks showing the victim, Stella, arriving on the scene for the weekend and clashing with her hosts and other guests. A perfect butler looms in the background. *The Key of the Door* premiered at the Lyric Theatre, Hammersmith, London, on May 27, 1958, featuring Signe Hasso as Stella.

Mackie's *The Big Killing* is reminiscent of Frederick Knott's *Dial "M" for Murder*, in which a former tennis champion, Tony Wendice, blames his wife for a murder he himself commissioned. The protagonist of *The Big Killing*, Peter Ashbury, a former race car driver, creates a web of circumstantial evidence to trap his wife into becoming the prime suspect in a homicide he committed. In both *Dial "M" for Murder* and *The Big Killing*, a plodding, efficient police inspector solves the case prior to the final curtain. *The Big Killing* opened at London's Princess Theatre on February 1, 1962, with Leslie Phillips as the dastardly husband.

Maigret and the Lady is an adaptation by Mackie from a novel by famed Belgian-born, French detective story writer Georges Simenon.[2] Simenon's sleuth, Jules Maigret, a pipe-smoking family man with a knack for deciphering human nature, utilizes the bar of the Hotel des Anglais in the town of Etretat as his headquarters, with villagers and relatives making contact to tell him their version of how Rose Trochu, the plump maid of Madame Valentine Besson, was poisoned. *Maigret and the Lady* previewed in Manchester, England, in 1965 before coming to London's Strand Theatre later that year. Frank Cox, reviewer of *Plays and Players*, enjoyed "a satisfying evening" and lauded Rupert Davies in the role of Maigret as "the most relaxed performer in the production."[3]

The Chairman satirizes behind-the-scene manipulations and backstabbing in a large, important public relations firm, where employees sell their souls for career advancement. The title character is never seen; he pulls the strings from a distance through his surrogates. *The Chairman* was initially produced at the Thorndike Theatre, Leatherhead, England, and subsequently moved to London's Globe Theatre on May 10, 1976. Gareth Davies directed.

Mackie's last play, *Marriage*, also premiered at the Thorndike Theatre, in 1977, but did not make it to the West End. It is a comedy with serious overtones about the breakup of a marriage.

Philip Mackie died on December 23, 1985.

Acting Edition: The Dramatic Publishing Company.

NOTES

1. *Theatre World Annual*, 1956.
2. Georges Simenon, author of several hundred books of which seventy-five feature Inspector Jules Maigret, in 1966 received the Mystery Writers of America's highest honor, the Grand Master Award.
3. *Plays and Players*, January 1966.

The Chalk Garden (1955)

Enid Bagnold (England, 1889–1981)

Enid Bagnold's comedy-drama, *The Chalk Garden*, unfolds in a manor located in a Sussex village by the sea, where the soil is lime and chalk. The garden surrounding the house becomes a metaphor for the barren existence of the inhabitants.

The curtain rises on three applicants for the position of a governess to take charge of an odd, precocious girl of sixteen, Laurel. Laurel is living with her grandmother, Mrs. St. Maugham, an old, somewhat ditzy, once beautiful ex-hostess of London society.

The only serious candidate for the job seems to be the quiet, straightforward Miss Madrigal. The butler, Maitland, tells Madrigal that he was given his position several months ago, when the old-time family servant, Pinkbell, had a stroke; since then, he has been lying upstairs under the care of a nurse.

Young Laurel enters and confides to Madrigal that her father shot himself when she was twelve. Her mother has married again.

Mrs. St. Maugham appears from the garden and interviews Miss Madrigal. Madrigal states that she's the daughter of a hussar in the Indian Army, she has private means, and she has not taken such a post before. That's why she has no references.

Madrigal learns from Mrs. St. Maugham that the girl Laurel has lied to her. Laurel's father died of a liver ailment when the girl was three years old. Laurel's mother, Olivia, is coming by ship from Arabia to claim her daughter. However, says Mrs. St. Maugham, the girl hates her mother and will refuse to go. Four years ago, when Laurel realized that she could not stop her mother's wedding, she ran away from her hotel room at night and was violated in Hyde Park, at the age of twelve. "It has upset her nerves," states Mrs. St. Maugham, who then hastens to assure Miss Madrigal that Laurel's fixations are minimal and that she is "a charming, intelligent girl."

Mrs. St. Maugham also reveals that the new butler, Maitland, has been in prison for five years as a conscientious objector.

Laurel tells Madrigal that she and Maitland share a crime library. Bit by bit they have been collecting the Notable Trial Series. And, says Laurel, they like to act the parts—Lizzie Borden, Dr. Crippen.

While Laurel guides Madrigal to the garden, Olivia arrives and confronts her mother. Olivia contends that she is not the fragile girl that her mother remembers, the inept, dropping-the-china girl. She can take care of Laurel. Mrs. St. Maugham vehemently objects.

Madrigal enters from the garden and admonishes Mrs. St. Maugham for planting rhododendrons, lilies, and roses in chalk soil without proper care. Mrs. St. Maugham, nonplussed, stammers that she followed Pinkbell's orders—and continuously sprayed the flowers. Madrigal tells her that she has been badly advised. If Mrs. St. Maugham will accept her, she'll take the position.

Madrigal soon learns that butler Pinkbell has ruled the household with an iron fist and is still sending down instructions from his sickbed. The unseen Pinkbell hovers on the play's proceedings like a dark shadow. The main thrust of the play, however, lies not in the glib Mrs. St. Maugham, the troubled Laurel, or the checkered Maitland, but in unmasking the enigmatic governess, who seems to have come from nowhere, knows everything about gardening, and feeds her new employer a pack of lies about her past.

A month or two have passed. A visitor is expected, a friend of Mrs. St. Maugham, a judge she calls "Puppy." Miss Madrigal is jarred at the news. Laurel, fond of playing amateur detective, notices the initials CDW on Madrigal's paint box. When she asks the governess, "Who is CDW?," Madrigal is taken aback momentarily, then says, "My married sister, Clarrisa Dalrymple Westerham." Laurel draws Madrigal into a question-and-answer game, during which she attempts to gather information about her governess's past. Laurel conveys to Maitland her "deduction" that Miss Madrigal, who never gets mail and is pretending to have a sister, must have gone through some intense, perhaps dreadful experience.

The Judge arrives. When, over lunch, he takes off his sunglasses, Madrigal drops a wine cup. Laurel pesters the Judge with queries, and he chats about the "remarkable" trial of Connie Dolly Wallis, who was tried for the murder of her stepsister. Wallis was reprieved, says the Judge, as some doubts crept into the case.

In a twosome scene between the Judge and Madrigal it becomes clear that she is Connie Dolly Wallis. She asks whether the Judge will reveal her true identity and emphasizes that the child, Laurel, needs her. Their conversation is interrupted by the successive entrances of Olivia, Laurel, and Mrs. St. Maugham. Olivia pleads that Laurel join her and her husband, an army officer. They are to leave tonight for the Suez Canal. Mrs. St. Maugham is unyielding, but Madrigal suddenly throws her weight on the mother's side: "Laurel must go, Mrs. St. Maugham, go with her mother. . . . This is a house where nothing good can be made of her . . . why, even the garden is demented."

While Olivia and Laurel go upstairs to pack the girl's clothes, Madrigal confesses to Mrs. St. Maugham that she was once sentenced to death by the Judge. The Judge adds mildly that Madrigal came to this house directly from prison.

Mrs. St. Maugham explodes with rage and orders Madrigal to gather her things immediately and leave. The nurse descends the steps and announces, "Mr. Pinkbell is dead." Olivia and Laurel say good-bye to Mrs. St. Maugham, nod to Madrigal, and go out.

In a quiet coda, Mrs. St. Maugham sighs, "Am I to die unloved?" She slowly turns to Madrigal and asks her to stay, suggesting that together they will grow windbreakers, Dierama, Wand Flower. Madrigal disagrees: "When will you learn you live on chalk?" Still, she says, if they work together, with potash and a little granular peat, they can make it work.

Mrs. St. Maugham hesitatingly asks whether Madrigal had committed the murder. Unperturbed and calm the governess deflects the question— leaving it nebulous not only for Mrs. St. Maugham but for the audience as well. The two women are beginning to peruse a horticultural catalogue when the curtain descends.

* * *

Staged by Albert Marre, *The Chalk Garden* tried out in New Haven and Boston before opening at New York's Ethel Barrymore Theatre on October 26, 1955. Its stellar cast included Siobhan McKenna (Miss Madrigal), Gladys Cooper (Mrs. St. Maugham), Betsy von Furstenberg (Laurel), Fritz Weaver (Maitland), Marian Seldes (Olivia), and Percy Waram (the Judge). Cecil Beaton designed the sets and costumes.

Critic Brooks Atkinson called *The Chalk Garden* "a drama of quality . . . an odd, unyielding comedy by a witty writer with a highly personal style." Atkinson complimented "a gifted company," embraced Gladys Cooper's "extraordinarily vivacious performance," welcomed the "richly talented young Irish actress Siobhan McKenna," and applauded "a wonderful comic performance of the butler by Fritz Weaver."[1] John Chapman called *The Chalk Garden* "a tantalizing, fascinating and stimulating piece of theatre."[2] Walter Kerr wrote, "Out of all that is circuitous and eccentric and delightfully left-field, something very real is communicated."[3]

The Chalk Garden was nominated for a Tony Award and ran for 182 performances. The drama opened at London's Haymarket Theatre on April 11, 1956, directed by John Gielgud, with Peggy Ashcroft (Miss Madrigal),

Edith Evans (Mrs. St. Maugham), Judith Stott (Laurel), Rachel Gurney (Olivia), George Rose (Maitland), and Felix Aylmer (the Judge). *Theatre World Annual* wrote: "Enid Bagnold's delightful play comes as a breath of fresh air into the stultified atmosphere of an abortive season, providing a new experience with its light-hearted symbolism and rich-sounding dialogue. Laughs are plentiful and yet the theme has an inherent seriousness, finishing on a note both pertinent and moving."[4] Critic Kenneth Tynan gushed in *The Observer*: "On Wednesday night a wonder happened: The West End Theatre justified its existence. . . . The occasion of its triumph was Enid Bagnold's *The Chalk Garden* (Haymarket) which may well be the finest artificial comedy to have flowed from an English (as opposed to an Irish) pen since the death of Congreve. . . . We eaves-drop on a group of thoroughbred minds, expressing themselves in speech of an exquisite candour, building ornamental bridges of metaphor, tiptoeing across frail causeways of simile, and vaulting over gorges impassable to the rational soul."[5] The play had a whopping run of 658 performances.

Edith Evans returned to her role of Mrs. St. Maugham in a 1968 radio broadcast.

The Chalk Garden was reincarnated by off-Broadway's Roundabout Theatre Company in March 1982, featuring Irene Worth as Miss Madrigal and Constance Cummings as Mrs. St. Maugham. Frank Rich of the *New York Times* found the play "extraordinarily modern for a high comedy set in the drawing room of a stuffy Sussex manor house; its plot and structure are elliptical; its witty lines aren't brittle but instead redolent with what the author calls 'the shape and shadow of life.'" The critic admired both Worth and Cummings but complained of "stodgy staging" by John Stix, "weak casting of other principal roles," and the "cheesy fixtures of the set."[6] The play ran for ninety-six performances. Later that year, in November, the American Conservatory Theatre of San Francisco presented *The Chalk Garden*, for thirty-three showings, with Annette Bening in the role of Olivia.

The Berkshire Theatre Festival revived *The Chalk Garden* in 1988. Off-Broadway's Actors Company Theatre mounted the play in 2004. Four years later, *The Chalk Garden* was produced by London's Donmar Warehouse in "a must-see production," according to Ben Brantley of the *New York Times*.[7]

The Chalk Garden was adapted to the screen in 1964, scripted by John Michael Hayes and directed by Ronald Neame, starring Deborah Kerr (Miss Madrigal), Edith Evans (Mrs. St. Maugham), Hayley Mills (Laurel), John Mills (Maitland), Elizabeth Sellars (Olivia), and Felix Aylmer, reprising his stage role of the Judge.

* * *

Born in Rochester, Kent, England, in 1889, Enid Bagnold was the daughter of an officer in the Royal Engineers and spent her childhood on a coffee plantation in Jamaica. She was educated in England at the Huxley School, which was run by Aldous Huxley's mother, and in finishing schools in Germany and Switzerland.

In 1920, at the age of thirty-one, Bagnold married Sir Roderick Jones, owner of Reuters News Agency. As Lady Roderick Jones, she and her husband lived in a sumptuous estate in Rottingdean, Sussex. Bagnold studied painting but following the publication of her *Diary without Dates*, a chronicle of her experiences as a driver with the French Army during World War I, she decided to dedicate herself to full-time writing.

In 1924 Bagnold published the best seller *Serena Blandish*, which was adapted in 1929 into a play by S. N. Behrman. In 1935 she scored another success with the horse-racing novel *National Velvet*, which in 1944 starred Elizabeth Taylor and Mickey Rooney in an excellent MGM movie version. Bagnold adapted her novel to a play in 1961.

Despite high-power casts, Bagnold's other plays were unsuccessful: *Poor Judas* (1951), *The Last Joke* (1960), *The Chinese Prime Minister* (New York, 1964; London, 1965), and *Call Me Jacky* (1967), produced in New York in 1976 as *A Matter of Gravity*, starring Katharine Hepburn.

Bagnold died in 1981 at the age of ninety-one.

Acting Edition: Samuel French, Inc. *The Chalk Garden* is also included in *Four Plays by Enid Bagnold* (Boston: Little, Brown, 1970).

Awards and Honors: A top-ten selection in *The Best Plays of 1955–1956*. Enid Bagnold was the recipient of the Arts Theatre Prize, 1951; American Academy of Arts and Letters Award of Merit, 1956; CBE (Commander, Order of the British Empire), 1976.

NOTES

1. *New York Times*, October 27, 1955.
2. *Daily News*, October 27, 1955.
3. *New York Herald Tribune*, October 27, 1955.
4. *Theatre World Annual*, 1957, 130.
5. Quoted in Enid Bagnold's *Autobiography* (Boston: Little, Brown, 1969), 308.
6. *New York Times*, April 30, 1982.
7. *New York Times*, July 27, 2008.

A Hatful of Rain (1955)

Michael V. Gazzo (United States, 1923–1995)

Created through improvisations at the Actors Studio—with in-house director Frank Corsaro and thespians Ben Gazzara, Shelley Winters, and Anthony Franciosa—Michael V. Gazzo's *A Hatful of Rain* is a pioneering, candid drama about drug addiction and illicit drug dealing.

Set on New York's Lower East Side, *A Hatful of Rain* depicts the plight of Johnny Pope, a war veteran who went through a traumatic overseas ordeal. Hidden in a cave for thirteen days and tortured as a POW, Pope became hooked on drugs while in a military hospital. Johnny's pregnant wife, Celia, and his visiting father, John Pope Sr., cannot understand why he failed to sustain a machinist job and keeps disappearing from home at night. Celia suspects that there is another woman. Johnny's sympathetic brother, Polo, a bouncer in "a cat house," supplies him with funds to purchase morphine from a gang of pushers.

The drug traffickers are a colorful, brutal trio: Mother, a reptilian wearing a trench coat and a pair of dark glasses; Apples, a knife-happy simpleton; and Chuch, a sadistic giggler. Mother, Apples, and Chuch sweep in to collect the $700 Johnny owes them. When he pleads that he can't get that kind of money, they hand him a pistol as a ready means to cold cash, and beat him up as a warning of things to come. But Johnny is an honest man and despite several tries, he cannot bring himself to use the gun. "They'll be coming for me," he tells Polo.

Johnny's domestic crisis deepens when the unhappy Celia complains that she spends more time with his brother and almost succumbed to him. She tells Johnny point blank that she's leaving him. Johnny confesses that he is a junkie and promises to drop the habit.

Celia decides to stay with Johnny, provided she notifies the police and he agrees to enter a rehabilitation program. Johnny gasps through a spasm attack and asks her to call. As Celia picks up the phone and says,

"Give me the police—I'd like to report a drug addict, my husband," the curtain slowly falls.

* * *

A Hatful of Rain opened at the Lyceum Theatre in New York on November 9, 1955, to mixed reviews. Walter F. Kerr called the play an "electrifying new social study" that "spits fire on the Lyceum stage."[1] William Hawkins found it "the unforgettable first work of an extremely talented playwright."[2] Brooks Atkinson believed *A Hatful of Rain* to be "a forthright statement of things that are horrifying and true."[3]

Among the naysayers were John McClain, Robert Coleman, and Richard Watts Jr.: "This tortured examination of dope addiction does not sustain itself as an evening in the theatre";[4] "Neither the action nor the dialogue flows as smoothly or effectively as it should";[5] "Despite its deadly earnest intentions, it is not possible to express much admiration for *A Hatful of Rain*, even as a frank melodrama."[6] John Chapman predicted that the play's "life on Broadway may not be long,"[7] but *A Hatful of Rain* ran for 398 performances. Unanimous kudos were bestowed upon Ben Gazzara as the addicted Johnny, Shelley Winters as his shattered wife, Anthony Franciosa as the brother who loves them both, Frank Silvera as the obtuse father, and Henry Silva, Paul Richards, and Harry Guardino as the chilling hoodlums.

A 1957 movie version, coscripted by Gazzo from his play and directed by Fred Zinnemann in CinemaScope, recruited Franciosa and Silva to repeat their stage roles, with Don Murray and Eva Marie Saint as Johnny and Celia Pope.

Londoners saw *A Hatful of Rain* at the Princess Theatre beginning on March 7, 1957, for ninety-one performances. Sam Wanamaker, who directed, also enacted the role of Polo, with George Coulouris as John Pope Sr. and Bonar Colleano and Sally Ann Howes portraying the troubled couple.

A Hatful of Rain was adapted to television in 1968, featuring Sandy Dennis, Michael Parks, and Peter Falk in the principal roles. Two years later it was revived in Manhattan by the Equity Library Theatre (in a partially rewritten version) for twelve performances.

* * *

Michael Gazzo's next contribution to Broadway was *The Night Circus* at the Golden Theatre on December 2, 1958, for seven performances. It was also staged by Frank Corsaro, with Ben Gazzara playing a hardboiled sailor who meets a pampered rich girl (Janice Rule) in a sleazy bar and begins a tempestuous, ill-fated relationship. Critic Brooks Atkinson admonished playwright Gazzo for immersing himself "up to the ears in psychic, spiritual and literary problems."[8] Gazzo's *What Do You Really Know about Your Husband?*, a comedy about a writer in desperate financial straits, tried out at the Shubert Theatre in New Haven on March 9, 1967; it never made it to New York.

Born in Hillside, New Jersey, Michael Vincente Gazzo was trained at Erwin Piscator's Dramatic Workshop and at the Actors' Studio. He appeared in the Broadway productions of *Yes Is for a Very Young Man* (1949), *Night Music* (1951), and *Camino Real* (1953), surrounded by many Actors' Studio alumni. For the movies, Gazzo wrote the script for the Elvis Presley vehicle *King Creole* (1958) and, due to his craggy appearance and raspish voice, was often cast as a Mafioso. His portrayal of mobster Frankie Pentangeli in *The Godfather, Part II* (1974) earned him an Academy Award nomination as Best Supporting Actor, which he lost to Robert De Niro for the same film.

Beginning in 1953 and through a span of four decades, Gazzo appeared in many crime-oriented television programs, including *The Defenders*, *Kojak*, *Ellery Queen*, *Serpico*, *Starsky and Hutch*, *Baretta*, *Columbo*, *Magnum P.I.*, *Partners in Crime*, and *L.A. Law*.

Acting Edition: Samuel French, Inc.

NOTES

1. *New York Herald Tribune*, November 10, 1955.
2. *New York World-Telegram*, November 10, 1955.
3. *New York Times*, November 10, 1955.
4. *New York Journal-American*, November 10, 1955.
5. *Daily Mirror*, November 10, 1955.
6. *New York Post*, November 10, 1955.
7. *Daily News*, November 10, 1955.
8. *New York Times*, December 3, 1958.

The Visit (1956)

Friedrich Duerrenmatt
(Switzerland, 1921–1990)

Not since Henrik Ibsen's *An Enemy of the People* has there been such a devastating drama about human corruptibility as *The Visit*. Friedrich Duerrenmatt's macabre exercise, unfolding like a surrealist hallucination, scolds an entire town for its avarice.

Called *Der Besuch der alten Dame* (*The Visit by the Old Woman*), the play was first performed on January 19, 1956, at the Schauspielhaus, Zurich, Switzerland. Adapted by Maurice Valency as *The Visit*, directed by Peter Brook, designed by Teo Otto, and starring Alfred Lunt and Lynn Fontanne, the play toured Great Britain and Ireland, with the intention of bringing it to London's West End. Instead, it was taken to New York as the opening production of a new theatre carrying the Lunts' name on May 5, 1958.

Lynne Fontanne appeared as Madame Claire Zachanassian, the richest woman in the world, who returns to the provincial, impoverished Central European hamlet of her youth, Güllen, to exact vengeance on the man who seduced her when she was seventeen, got her pregnant, then jilted her and drove her out of town in disgrace. The child died. After languishing in a Hamburg brothel, Claire managed to marry seven or eight wealthy husbands, accumulating vast riches. Secretly she bought the industries of Güllen and stifled its commerce until the place went bankrupt.

Claire steps off the train with an entourage comprised of an obedient fiancé, two blind eunuchs, two American gangsters serving as bodyguards, and a black panther. Her luggage includes an empty coffin, and the townspeople soon learn that Claire does not intend to keep it empty for long.

Hoisted on a quilted-satin sedan chair and puffing a cigar, Claire addresses the awe-stricken local inhabitants with a proposal: she will donate one billion marks to the district on one condition: "I want the life of Anton Schill." The villagers must kill her deceiver.

Schill (played by Alfred Lunt) is the town's manager of the general store, a pillar of the community. At first, the people are indignant, even angry, at Claire's bid. The Burgomaster declares that the citizens of Güllen may be poor but are not heathens, and in the name of humanity they will never accept such an offer. All applaud wildly.

Gradually the villagers yield to the bribe. They begin to spend the promised blood money on food, clothing, household utensils, office equipment. Even Schill's wife dons a new fur coat, his son purchases a shiny Opel, and his daughter enrolls in a class of French literature.

The townsfolk, represented by a kaleidoscope of society—mayor, teacher, doctor, pastor, postmaster, policeman, painter, journalist—make a last effort to plead with the lady. The Teacher says that at first he thought of her as an avenging fury, a Medea, a Clytemnestra, but he now realizes that she is a warmhearted woman who has suffered a terrible injustice and has returned to teach them an unforgettable lesson. He begs for her mercy.

Claire retorts, "When I have had justice." The Teacher points out that Madame is asking for one injustice to cure another, that horror will succeed horror, and it will settle nothing. But Claire insists: "The world made me into a whore; now I make the world into a brothel. Those who wish to go down, may go down. Those who wish to dance with me, may dance with me."

The villagers then begin to look at their planned murder as "justice." They bemoan the ill treatment that Madame Zachanassian received in her youth. They talk of reestablishing justice among them, of ridding the community of a burden of guilt. In a town meeting they vow to return to the principles for which their forefathers lived and fought, the principles that form the soul of their Western culture. They'll take action not out of love for worldly gains, but out of love for what is right.

Under the guidance of the Burgomaster, the villagers unanimously vote to accept Madame Zachanassian's gift as conditioned. Schill, mastering his fright and giving in to the inevitable with unexpected dignity, looks at the hard faces of those who surround him. He sinks slowly to his knees. The men close in and lean over. When the knot of men pulls back, Schill is dead. Only the doctor is left, kneeling by the corpse. "Heart failure," announces the doctor.

At the end, Claire scornfully drops the check at the Burgomaster's feet. The sound of an approaching train grows louder. The train stops. Church bells start pealing. The American bodyguards carry the coffin across the stage. Claire and her retinue board the train.

STATION MASTER: Güllen-Rome Express. All aboard, please!

The train starts; it moves off sluggishly, picking up speed. The crowd turns, gazing after the departing train in complete silence. Slow curtain.

* * *

The New York critics greeted *The Visit* with morbid fascination. Richard Watts Jr. called it "a strikingly sardonic drama . . . one of the most savage dramatic studies of greed since Ben Jonson's *Volpone*. . . . It employs color, movement, fantasy, humor, off-stage music, and occasional symbolism to capture an impressive dramatic pattern of mingled bitterness, scorn and pity. For all of its contemptuous irony, it is, in the end, remarkably moving."[1]

"The play and players state with a theatrical blend of brute force and exquisite grace the case for futility most contemporary writers find too big for them," wrote Frank Aston. "Here in three fiercely pounding acts is heard the cry of those who believe man is guided more often by hypocrisy than by mercy."[2]

"A devastating drama," declared Brooks Atkinson. "Herr Duerrenmatt is a sufficiently powerful dramatist to make an unpalatable theme acceptable. He writes with wit and humor when he is setting his snares. But he writes with cold fury when he gets to the core of his theme. The slow disintegration of character, the hypocritical turning on Anton Schill by his neighbors, the community malevolence of the town meeting when the awful vote is taken—are written with a calculated cruelty that proves Herr Duerrenmatt's cruel theme."[3]

As often is the case, another morning-after reviewer, Robert Coleman, had an opposite reaction: "It is difficult to understand how the Producers Theatre persuaded the wonderful Lunts to dull their sparkle in such dreary, unrelievedly sardonic fare. But it has, and more's the pity."[4] And John McClain summed up his mixed notice with, "*The Visit* will be many things to many people. To me it was a most compelling yet oddly unfulfilled evening; a little item called the soul seemed to be missing."[5]

The Visit ran for 189 performances. The Lunts accompanied the play to London, where it opened at the Royalty Theatre on June 23, 1960.

Duerrenmatt's nightmarish allegory was produced by the Seattle Repertory Theatre, Seattle, Washington (1967, thirty performances) and the Asolo State Theatre, Sarasota, Florida (1968, twenty-two performances)—both regional theatres. It was also revived twice in New York City. A November 25, 1973, production by the New Phoenix Repertory Theatre, under the direction of Harold Prince, featured Rachel Roberts as the vengeful madame and John McMartin as her doomed target. *The Visit* was called "a powerful drama" by Richard Watts in the *New York Post*,[6] "a modern classic" by Edwin Wilson in the *Wall Street Journal*,[7] and "a diabolical masterpiece" by Geoffrey Holder on NBC4 TV.[8] It ran for thirty-two performances.

Off-Broadway's The Roundabout Theatre presented *The Visit* on January 23, 1992, with Jane Alexander as a crippled Claire ("a limp that would have done Richard III proud," critic Clive Barnes wrote)[9] and Harris Yulin as a befuddled Anton Schill. Director Edwin Sherin's expressionistic conceit put every actor except the two leads in fiendish masks. "*The Visit* remains a classic," asserted Doug Watt;[10] "A darkly riveting work," opined John Beaufort;[11] "Friedrich Duerrenmatt's morality play *The Visit* seemed shockingly cynical when the Lunts brought it to Broadway in the '50s," stated William A. Henry III. "In a sad measure of the disillusioning years since, it now triumphs as a comedy."[12] The revival had a limited run of twenty-six previews and forty-five regular performances.

Productions of *The Visit* kept popping up all over the globe. Israel's Habimah Theatre produced the drama in 1959, with Hanna Rovina, the country's supreme actress, in the lead. In 1994, Israel's two prominent repertory theatres, the Habimah and the Cameri, joined forces to present a highly successful Hebrew version of the play in Tel Aviv. Leah Koenig, a notable local actress whom this writer had the pleasure of directing in her first Israeli stage endeavor (*Genesis*, at the Habimah), received kudos as Claire Zachanassian.

A German-French-Italian motion picture version, filmed in 1964, featured Ingrid Bergman and Anthony Quinn as the lead antagonists, with a stellar international cast in supporting roles. Bernhard Wicki directed. "Intriguing but uneven film parable of greed and evil," asserts film critic Leonard Maltin in his annual *Movie and Video Guide*.[13] Though generally faithful to the play, the celluloid ending allots Anton Schill a different kind of retribution: Madame Zachanassian instructs the townspeople to let him live—as a pariah in the community.

The play was adapted to television in West Germany (1959), France (1971), Yugoslavia (1976), Switzerland (1982, starring Maria Schell), the Soviet Union (1989), Senegal (1992), Portugal (1994), Estonia (2006), and Germany (2008).

A musical version of *The Visit* was created by Terrence McNally (book), John Kander (music), and Fred Ebb (lyrics), first produced in 2001 at Chicago's Goodman Theatre, starring Chita Rivera and John McMartin. A planned New York engagement for the fall of 2003 was scrapped after two main investors withdrew from the production. In 2008, a revised version played at the Signature Theatre in Arlington, Virginia, with Rivera and George Hearn. Critic Charles Isherwood found the production, staged by Frank Galati, "creepy and chilling," but believed that "this softer-edged adaptation, too full of lively or elegiac musical divertissements to carve its way deeply into the psyche, is more likely to inspire mild clucks of philosophical regret."[14]

The Visit of the Old Lady was made into an opera by Gottfried von Einem to a German libretto by Duerrenmatt. It premiered at the Vienna State Opera on May 23, 1971. The first American production took place at the San Francisco Opera, translated into English by Norman Tucker and directed by Francis Ford Coppola. The New York City Opera first presented *The Visit of the Old Lady* in 1997, under the direction of JoAnne Akalaitis.

* * *

Friedrich Duerrenmatt was born in Konolfingen, Canton Bern, Switzerland, in 1921, the son of a Protestant pastor. He went through the rigorous discipline of the village school, but was enamored with the fanciful works of Karl May and Jules Verne. His imagination was also fired by his father's stories of the heroes of Greek mythology.

In 1935, the Duerrenmatts moved to Bern. At a private prep school, Friedrich was unhappy with the curriculum and spent his time reading novels and painting pictures. At the University of Bern he studied German literature. In 1942, he took up residency in Zurich, enrolled at the local university, and became part of the city's bohemian life. Ten years later he published his first book, *Die Stadt* (*The City*), a collection of short stories.

In 1946, Duerrenmatt married the actress Lotti Geissler, whom he had met while a student. The couple lived in Basel, where Lotti was performing at the city theatre while Duerrenmatt wrote his first plays, *Es steht geschrieben* (*It Is Written*, 1947), a historical drama set in sixteenth-century Germany, and *Der Blinde* (*The Blind Man*, 1948), a parable depicting the clash between a blind duke and a manipulative governor.

Billed as "an unhistorical historical comedy," *Romulus der Grosse* (*Romulus the Great*) was written in 1949. Set in the year AD 476, it tells of the last emperor of Rome, who atones for the sins of the empire by offering no resistance to the attacking Goths. The play's first performance took place at the Stadttheater, Basel, in 1958. Called *Romulus*, it was adapted by Gore Vidal and performed at New York's Music Box Theatre in 1962, with Cyril Richard in the title role, running for sixty-nine performances. Television versions of *Romulus* were produced in West Germany (1965), Denmark (1969), and France (1971).

Duerrenmatt's first success as a dramatist came with *Die Ehe des Herrn Mississippi*, a satire in which a public prosecutor kills his wife, marries a woman who murdered her husband, and the two dedicate themselves to "absolute justice," presiding over the state's executions. At the end, the prosecutor suspects his wife of infidelity and poisons her coffee. Simultaneously, he dies after drinking poisoned coffee intended for the wife's lover. The play premiered at the Kammerspiel, Munich, in 1952, was translated as *The Marriage of Mr. Mississippi*, and ran for twenty-three performances at London's Art Theatre in 1959, directed by Clifford Williams and starring Douglas Wilmer in the title role. It was filmed in Berlin two years later.

Ein Engel kommt nach Babylon (*An Angel Comes to Babylon*, 1953) is a comedy about a virtuous young girl who is sent to earth to bestow her love on the poorest Babylonian beggar. Complications arise when King Nebuchadnezzar disguises himself in rags and joins a beggars' contest. The play was presented at the University of California, Berkeley, in 1962.

Following *The Visit*, Duerrenmatt's *Die Physiker* (*The Physicists*), a metaphysical thriller taking place in an insane asylum, has also gained universal acclaim. Three murders and Cold War espionage serve as a facade for the playwright's warning of world catastrophe in an era of unleashed technological discoveries. The play first performed at Zurich's Schauspielhaus in 1962 and was adapted to television in West Germany (1964), Belgium (1970), Argentina (1972), and Norway (1988).

Der Meteor (*The Meteor*) is the story of a Nobel Prize–winning author who is declared clinically dead but is resurrected. The author wishes to die like everyone else, but to his horror he realizes that his quest for death will go on and on forever. The play premiered at the Schauspielhaus, Zurich, in 1966. A Swiss–West German motion picture of *The Meteor* was made in 1968. Yugoslavia televised it the following year.

Other plays by Duerrenmatt include *Play Strindberg* (1968), based on Strindberg's *Dance of Death*; *König Johann* (*King John*, 1968) and *Titus Andronicus* (1970), inspired by Shakespeare's tragedies; and *Urfaust* (1970), from the play by Goethe. Among Duerrenmatt's eight radio scripts, notable are *Nächtliches Gespräch mit einem verachteten Menschen* (*Conversation at Night with a Despised Man*, 1952), in which a well-known writer, now an undesirable citizen, confronts an executioner sent by the state (John Gielgud and Alec Guinness played the roles in a BBC2 airing in 1970), and *Abendstunde im Spätherbst* (translated as *One Autumn Evening* and *Incident at Twilight*, 1959), wherein a private detective proves that the best-selling author of twenty-two mystery novels based his plots on actual murders that he has committed.

Esoteric novellas of suspense by Duerrenmatt, wherein thrills are intertwined with truths, include *Der Richter und sein Henker* (*The Judge and His Hangman*), serialized during 1950–1951 in a semimonthly periodical, and a 1953 sequel, *Der Verdacht* (*The Quarry*). The lead character of both stories is Hans Bärlach, an aging Bern police commissioner who is dying of stomach cancer. In *The Judge and His Hangman*, Bärlach pursues a serial murderer who has cleverly eluded the police for forty years. The villain of *The Quarry* is a Nazi concentration camp doctor who continues his sadistic murder of patients in a clinic in Zurich.

The Judge and His Hangman was made into a 1975 English-language movie, titled *End of the Game*, by a German/Italian production company. Maximilian Schell directed. Martin Ritt portrayed investigator Bärlach, supported by Jon Voight, Jacqueline Bisset, and Robert Shaw. The novel was also adapted to television in the United States (1956), West Germany

(1957), England (1961), and France (1974). *The Quarry* was filmed in the Soviet Union in 1972.

The story *Die Panne* (1956), which translates as "breakdown," begins with the engine failure of a traveling salesman's Studebaker. Stranded, Alfredo Traps finds refuge at the isolated home of three retired judges who jocularly convince him to play a mock trial game. Traps does not realize that the end result carries a death sentence. Translated into English as *Traps*, the story was adapted to the stage and renamed *The Deadly Game* by James Yaffe in 1960. A sardonic play about sin and punishment, *The Deadly Game* is a variation on both the courtroom drama and the dark old house motifs.

The Broadway presentation of *The Deadly Game*, on February 2, 1960, was preceded by a 1957 episode on television's *Suspicion*, with Alfred Hitchcock serving as executive producer, Boris Karloff appearing as the chief judge, and Gary Merrill portraying the unsuspecting salesman. A 1982 television remake cast George Segal as a stranded American tourist confronted by Trevor Howard, Robert Morley, and Emlyn Williams. A motion picture based on *Die Panne* was made in India in 1971, called *Silence! The Court Is in Session*. The following year, a French-Italian film boasted the stellar cast of Alberto Sordi, Michel Simon, Charles Vanel, Claude Dauphin, and Pierre Brasseur.

Duerrenmatt continued to blend the conventions of the detective story with philosophical implications in the novella *Der Auftrag* (*The Assignment*, 1986), wherein a Swiss psychiatrist engages a female filmmaker to solve and document the murder of his wife, and in the novel *Justiz*, translated as *The Execution of Justice* (1989), which begins with literally a bang when a distinguished Zurich councilman, Dr. Isaac Kohler, walks into a restaurant during the dinner hour and shoots a university professor in open view. *Justice* was transferred to the screen in 1993 by a German-Swiss producing company, featuring Maximilian Schell as Dr. Kohler.

Duerrenmatt's sole original screenplay was *Es geschah am hellichten Tag* (*It Happened in Broad Daylight*, 1958), a moody thriller in which a retiring Swiss police inspector, played by Heinz Rühmann, takes it upon himself to investigate the brutal rape and murder of a little girl. Duerrenmatt novelized the script under the title *Das Versprechen* (*The Pledge*) in 1959. It spawned several remakes: a UK/Netherlands/Germany production in 1996; a German made-for-television the following year; and an Americanized feature directed by Sean Penn and starring Jack Nicholson in 2001.

"Inspired notably by Brecht, Kafka and Wilder," writes H. M. Klein in *St. James Guide to Crime and Mystery Writers*, "but with an intellectual punch and theatrical drive altogether his own, Duerrenmatt hit the post-war German-speaking stage like a meteor and has left an indelible mark on the whole of contemporary drama. Particularly *Fools Are Passing Through* (*The Marriage of Mr. Mississippi*), *The Visit* and *The Physicists* include crimes dear to detectives. . . . His novels, already classics, show an amazing but probably—for him—inevitable sweep through the genre."[15]

Acting Edition: An acting edition of Maurice Valency's adaptation was published by Samuel French, Inc. A more complete English translation, from the German *Der Besuch der alten Dame*, by Patrick Bowles, was copyrighted in 1962 and published, in soft cover, as an Evergreen original, by Grove Press, New York.

Awards and Honors: "A theatre piece of fascinatingly acrid power," commented Louis Kronenberger when he chose the play as one of the top ten of 1957–1958, "*The Visit* begins misleadingly with light colors and a farce-comedy look, suddenly to darken the face of its canvas, to blacken the hearts of its characters. A grisly fable of a woman's revengeful hate, it shows a whole community succumbing to greed."[16]

The Visit was chosen Best Foreign Play by the New York Drama Critics Circle in 1959; it won the Molière Prize in Paris that same year.

One of the most significant European dramatists of the twentieth century, Duerrenmatt received the Schiller Prize of the City of Mannheim in 1959, the Grand Prize of the Swiss Writers Foundation in 1960, the Grillparzer Prize of the Austrian Academy of Sciences in 1968, the Buber-Rosenzweig Medal for Christian-Jewish cooperation in 1977, the Grand Prize for Literature of the City of Bern in 1979, and the Büchner Prize in 1986. A vocal supporter of the land of Israel, in 1974 Duerrenmatt was elected a fellow of Ben-Gurion University. He was given honorary doctorates by Temple University in 1969, the Hebrew University in Jerusalem and the University of Nice in 1977, and the University of Neuchâtel in 1979.

NOTES

1. *New York Post*, May 6, 1958.
2. *New York World-Telegram*, May 6, 1958.
3. *New York Times*, May 6, 1958.
4. *Daily Mirror*, May 6, 1958.
5. *New York Journal-American*, May 6, 1958.
6. *New York Post*, November 26, 1973.
7. *Wall Street Journal*, December 10, 1973.
8. NBC4 TV.
9. *New York Post*, January 24, 1992.
10. *Daily News*, January 31, 1992.

11. *Christian Science Monitor*, January 31, 1992.

12. *Time Magazine*, February 3, 1992.

13. *Leonard Maltin's 2009 Movie Guide* (New York: Penguin, 2008), 1497.

14. *New York Times*, May 31, 2008.

15. Jay P. Pederson, ed., *St. James Guide to Crime and Mystery Writers*, 4th ed. (Detroit, MI: St. James Press, 1996), 328.

16. Louis Kronenberger, ed., *The Best Plays of 1957–1958* (New York: Dodd, Mead, 1958), 24.

Time Limit! (1956)

Henry Denker (United States, 1912–)

Major Harry Cargill is about to be court-martialed for treason. He is accused of betraying his fellow Americans in a North Korean prison camp by cooperating with the enemy, making propaganda broadcasts, and confessing falsely that the United States unleashed germ warfare.

The major admits that he is guilty and offers no defense. But a zealous judge advocate in charge of the case, Lt. Col. William Edwards, is not satisfied and insists on digging deeper. *Time Limit!* centers on Edwards's investigation as he interrogates a few former POWs. Their accounts are related via flashbacks.

Edwards's superior, Major General Joseph Connors, whose son died in a Korean stockade, declares that it is an open-and-shut case of betrayal. But Edwards persists. Following an interview with Cargill's wife, Mary, Edwards remarks to his secretary, WAC Corporal Jean Evans, that Cargill seems to be two men—and the man his wife described would not have committed treason.

The breakthrough in the case occurs when Edwards and Evans notice that various witnesses used identical phrases when presenting the Korean events; they all said "it happened suddenly" and described a disease as "an acute case of dysentery," "bacillary dysentery," and "dehydration." None said "a bad case" or "a violent case," muses Edwards, always "an acute case."

By the end of the second act, in a harrowing flashback, we learn that it was General Connor's son who cracked under pressure and informed on his fellow prisoners. The American captives cast lots in choosing an executioner, and against Cargill's protestations ("This is a cold-blooded murder"), young Connors is strangled while the group sings a rousing chorus of "Caissons" to drown out his screams.

In a shattering scene that elevates *Time Limit!* from a mere thriller to the realm of provocative ideas, General Connors learns the bitter truth about his son. At first the general refuses to believe it, but he later insists that he cannot forgive cowardice, not even in his own son. Edwards attempts to convince him that everyone has his limit and that there is no crime in being human.

Major Cargill then reveals his motive in collaborating with the enemy. Upon the killing of young Connors, the commander of the camp, furious, addressed Cargill as the ranking officer and threatened that unless he cooperated, all eighteen men would be tried for murder and executed. To him, says Cargill, eighteen men—their wives, their families—seemed important. He just gave the Koreans everything they wanted, everything.

Edwards appreciates the fact that Cargill initially didn't defend himself, reluctant to involve the men. However, General Connors believes that no matter the circumstances, anyone who gives aid or comfort to the enemy is a traitor. He feels sorry for Cargill, for everything that happened to him, for having been through the horrors of a prison camp, but no man is exempt, not his son, not anyone. The fact remains: he helped the enemy. That is the code of conduct. Their job is to obey rules, not remake them.

Edwards tells the general that if Cargill is tried, he will volunteer to defend him.

* * *

The passage of time has eroded some of the impact generated by *Time Limit!* when it premiered at the Booth Theatre on January 24, 1956. The New York critics were enthusiastic. "Out of a sample case of prison camp treason, the authors of *Time Limit!* have written a stunning drama," stated Brooks Atkinson. "They have taken a look at a horrifying wartime situation that cannot be resisted, and they have asked some searching questions about it that cannot be dismissed."[1]

John Chapman found the play "a crisp, tightly fashioned, suspenseful thriller about a brain-washing job in Korea and what happens afterward."[2] William Hawkins called *Time Limit!* "a bombshell of human endurance."[3] John McClain assured his readers, "It seems fairly safe to say there's a new hit in town. . . . My wife said she enjoyed it immensely—and I think you'll agree with her."[4] Richard Watts Jr. peppered his review with superlatives: "*Time Limit!* is a taut and striking topical melodrama with disturbingly thoughtful overtones. . . . an extremely moving and unsettling play . . . movingly and excitingly depicted. . . . Another excellent drama has come to town."[5] Robert Coleman declared, "*Time Limit!* is a gripping drama about what makes men break under pressure. . . . An absorbing and exciting experience in the theatre. It is an intelligent and thoughtful appraisal of some of the issues which our Army, and nation, must face. We think you will find an evening at the Booth rewarding."[6]

The sole dissenter was Walter F. Kerr: "Why, then, does *Time Limit!* seem to thin out along the way, to approach its roaring climax with a kind of waning sense of responsibility? . . . I suspect that author Denker has, finally, built his plea around too extraordinary a case for the purposes of general illumination. . . . *Time Limit!* has taken a robust whack at the barbed-wire that tangles men's minds. But when it cuts through, it does not cut quite clean."[7]

In his introduction to *Best Plays of 1955–1956*, Louis Kronenberger suggests that an "uneasy blend of truth and theatre reduced the value and blurred the integrity of *Time Limit!* . . . The debate asks at what point cracking up might be forgivable, and how far a moment of capitulation must cancel out a lifetime of loyalty. It asks finally whether Communist brainwashing tactics may not call for revised standards of judgment— and justice. In asking such questions, *Time Limit!* offered, beyond scenes that proved vibrant and tense, a nice new twist from a thriller. What cost its distinction was its commonplace writing; what reduced its importance was its letting a serious theme too often defer to a lurid plot; what blurred its point was having Cargill, even when he turned traitor, act from such worthy motives. This last maneuver meant salvaging the play's hero at the cost of jettisoning its problem."[8]

Guided by director Windsor Lewis, the acting ensemble of *Time Limit!* was unanimously hailed. Atkinson: "As the inquiring Judge Advocate, Arthur Kennedy gives another one of those performances that are simple in outline but that represent concentrated emotion."[9] Kerr: "Richard Kiley, as the suspect man who is willing to take any punishment meted out to him, shapes the rising tension with shrewd skill."[10] McClain: "In the uniformly superb cast . . . Thomas Carlin, a most promising neophyte, who plays the unhappy Lt. George Miller; Allyn McLerie, most decoratively filling the uniform of a WAC corporal and Harvey Stephens lending dignity in the role of the major general."[11]

McClain also compliments designer Ralph Alswang, who "has contrived a set which can switch from an office in an Army post to a Korean prison compound by the flick of a switch."[12]

Time Limit! ran for 127 performances.

Scripted by Henry Denker, an effective movie version of *Time Limit!* was directed by Karl Malden in 1957, featuring Richard Widmark (Lt. Col. William Edwards), Richard Basehart (Major Harry Cargill), Carl Benton Reid (Maj. General Joseph Connors), Dolores Michaels (WAC Corporal Jean Evans), and June Lockhart (Mary Cargill).

* * *

Born in New York City in 1912, Henry Denker received his Law Qualifying Certificate from New York University in 1931 and his doctorate in

1934. A member of the New York State Bar Association, Denker penned another stirring courtroom drama: *A Case of Libel* (1963), based on the book *My Life in Court* by Louis Nizer. The action, unfolding mostly in New York County's Supreme Court, is rooted in the once-famous Quentin Reynolds–Westbrook Pegler lawsuit. Denker also probed legal system machinations in a number of best-selling novels, notably *My Son, the Lawyer* (1950), *Error of Judgment* (1979), *Judge Spencer Dissents* (1986), *Labyrinth* (1990), *Doctor on Trial* (1992), *This Child Is Mine* (1995), and *Cla$$ Action* (2005).

Denker's best play is arguably *A Far Country* (1961), a poignant depiction of Sigmund Freud's first critical psychoanalysis case, that of young Viennese Elizabeth von Ritter, who had lost the use of her legs after the death of her father.[13] The playwright's contributions to the stage include a number of comedies whose topics range from the generation gap (*What Did We Do Wrong?*) to the love affair between two senior citizens (*The Second Time Around*) to the cementing of a stormy relationship between a Jewish widower in a wheelchair and his African-American therapist (*Horowitz and Mrs. Washington*).

For radio, Denker wrote *Radio Reader's Digest* (CBS, 1943–1946) and was writer, director, and producer of *The Greatest Story Ever Told* (ABC, 1947–1957). For television, he originated the series *False Witness* (NBC, 1939); wrote *Give Us Barabbas* (Hallmark Hall of Fame, NBC, 1961); produced *The Man Who Wanted to Live Forever*, aka *The Only Way Out Is Death* (1970), the supernatural tale of an isolated medical research center catering to eternal youth; and penned *A Time for Miracles* (1980), a chronicle of the life story of America's Elizabeth Bayley Seton who, as Mother Seton, was canonized in 1975.

For the cinema, Denker immersed himself in crime: he penned the screenplays for *The Hook* (1962), about a psychopathic serial killer who has a hook in place of one of his hands; *Twilight of Honor* (1963), in which a young lawyer defends a black-jacket rebel accused of murder; *Judgment: The Court Martial of Lt. William Calley* (1975), spotlighting the man responsible for the My Lai massacre during the Vietnam War; and *Outrage!* (1986), still another trial case, the tale of an idealistic attorney who defends a client accused of killing the man who allegedly raped and murdered his daughter.

Acting Edition: Samuel French, Inc.

Awards and Honors: Henry Denker's *A Far Country* was a top-ten selection in *The Best Plays of 1960–1961*. As author-director of the religious radio series *The Greatest Story Ever Told*, Denker received the Peabody Award, the Christopher Award, the *Variety* Showmanship Award, and the Brotherhood Award from the National Conference of Christians and Jews.

NOTES

1. *New York Times*, January 25, 1956.
2. *Daily News*, January 25, 1956.
3. *New York World-Telegram*, January 25, 1956.
4. *New York Journal-American*, January 25, 1956.
5. *New York Post*, January 25, 1956.
6. *Daily Mirror*, January 25, 1956.
7. *New York Herald Tribune*, January 25, 1956.
8. *The Best Plays of 1955–1956* (New York: Dodd, Mead, 1956), 15, 16.
9. *New York Times*, January 25, 1956.
10. *New York Herald Tribune*, January 25, 1956.
11. *New York Journal-American*, January 25, 1956.
12. *New York Journal-American*, January 25, 1956.
13. Years later, *A Far Country* still proved to be both suspenseful and thought provoking when it was presented, under my direction, at Stanford University and, in a Hebrew translation, at the Zavit (Angle) Theatre in Tel Aviv, Israel.

The Ponder Heart (1956)

Joseph Fields (United States, 1895–1966) and Jerome Chodorov (United States, 1911–2004)

Uncle Daniel Ponder has a heart as big as the sky. He doesn't meet a person without giving him something. Uncle Daniel inherited a fortune from his father, which he keeps distributing among the villagers of Clay, a small Southern town, and to newcomers who cross his path. His niece, Edna Earle, cannot stop him from dispensing with his suits of clothes, calves, pigeons, a goat, a Shetland pony, a cow pasture, a cypress cistern, a field of Dutch clover, even his own cemetery plot. But now the man with "the sweetest disposition in the world" is being tried for the murder of his wife.

Joseph Fields and Jerome Chodorov based *The Ponder Heart* on a story by Eudora Welty (1909–2001) that was published in 1953 in *The New Yorker* and reprinted the following year by Harcourt Brace. The Fields-Chodorov adaptation focuses on a claim by the backwoods family of Bonnie Dee Peacock, goaded by an ambitious district attorney, that Uncle Daniel killed his child bride during a thunderstorm. In the whimsical spirit of *Alice in Wonderland,* Uncle Daniel escorts his accusers to the trial so that they "get good seats in the front row"; congratulates his nemesis, Prosecutor Dorris R. Gladney, for "one of the most movin' and beautiful pleas I ever heard to a jury"; insists on taking the stand against advice by counsel; and invites Gladney to grill him.

In a flashback, we meet his late wife Bonnie Dee, a seventeen-year-old simple-minded waif whom he encountered at a candy store. She marries her suitor so she can stay in bed as late as she pleases at the Ponder Hill House, lick pistachio ice-cream cones, and admire the shiny dishwashing machine.

Uncle Daniel claims proudly, "I just married the sweetest little doll on two feet," while the bride is described by Edna Earle as someone who "could sit all day and try to figure out how the tail of the C got through the L in the Coca-Cola sign."

Back at the County Courthouse, Mr. Gladney equates the case to *Othello,* and casts Uncle Daniel as Dr. Jekyll and Mr. Hyde. The local boys retort by squirting the prosecutor with water pistols. Judge Waite, chomping on a cigar, his feet on the desk, permits the accused to leave the premises to stretch his legs.

On the witness stand, Uncle Daniel gives away all his assets: a trust fund in Edna Earle's name; his big house up on the hill to the Peacocks; the Studebaker to his dear friend, Miss Teacake Magee; and to Judge Waite, the pickup truck. All his possessions, says Uncle Daniel, give him only trouble.

Uncle Daniel describes how during a severe thunderstorm, Bonnie Dee was literally frightened to death. He pulled the girl from under the sofa, held her in his arms, and could feel her heart beatin' like a frightened rabbit. She took her last breath in his arms, "an' blew off like one of those little dandelion puffballs like we used to tell time by." That's exactly what happened, declares Uncle Daniel, the whole truth and nothin' but the truth. As expected, by the Clay townsfolk and by the New York audience, Uncle Daniel is found not guilty.

* * *

The Ponder Heart opened at New York's Music Box on February 16, 1956. The morning-after reviewers admired David Wayne as Uncle Daniel, Sarah Marshall as Bonnie Dee, Una Merkel as Edna Earle, Will Geer as District Attorney Gladney, and John McGovern as Judge Waite, but they were split on the merits of the play. The yessers included Walter F. Kerr, who lauded "a bubbling spirit beneath its lazy graces";[1] Brooks Atkinson, who found the play "original, charming and funny";[2] and Richard Watts Jr., who considered it "one of the funniest and most engaging of the season's comedies."[3]

The naysayers were Robert William Hawkins, who believed that *"The Ponder Heart,* for all its attractions, is not about anything much";[4] John McClain, who objected to "a plot that wears thin. We see what's coming down the pike, and we don't much care";[5] and Robert Coleman, who called it "a frail vehicle."[6] *The Ponder Heart* beat for 149 performances.

The Ponder Heart was not converted to the silver screen, but in 1964, West Germany's television adapted the play to television under the title *Angeklagter: Onkel Daniel,* with Rudolf Platte playing the title role.

* * *

In 1955, Eudora Welty's *The Ponder Heart* was awarded The Howells Medal of the American Academy of Arts and Letters. Welty was a notable novelist and short story writer, whose output includes *A Curtain of Green* (1941), *The Robber Bridegroom* (1942), *The Wide Net* (1943), *Delta Wedding*

(1946), *Golden Apples* (1949), *The Bride of Innisfallen* (1955), *The Shoe Bird* (1964), *Losing Battles* (1970), *The Optimist's Daughter* (1972), *The Eye of the Story: Selected Essays and Reviews* (1977), and *The Collected Stories of Eudora Welty* (1980).

Native New Yorkers Joseph Fields and Jerome Chodorov found each other in Hollywood, where they began their collaboration on crime-riddled *The Gentleman from Louisiana* (1936), a yarn about horse-race fixing, and *Reported Missing* (1937), in which planes are sabotaged by a gang of robbers. Among Fields-Chodorov's notable movies are *Two Girls on Broadway* (1940), with Lana Turner and Joan Blondell; *Dulcy* (1940), a comedy based on the Broadway hit by George S. Kaufman and Marc Connelly; *Louisiana Purchase* (1941), a Bob Hope vehicle; and *Man from Texas* (1948), a Western adventure founded on the play *Missouri Legend* by Elizabeth B. Ginty.

Fields and Chodorov's first Broadway play, *Schoolhouse on the Lot* (1938), spoofed filmland intrigue. A succession of generally successful productions included *My Sister Eileen* (1940), a dramatization of Ruth McKenney's stories about the misadventures of two Ohio sisters in Greenwich Village; *Junior Miss* (1941), an adolescent comedy extracted from the *New Yorker* sketches by Sally Benson; *The French Touch* (1945), depicting the patriotic zeal of Parisian actors during the Nazi occupation; *Wonderful Town* (1953), the musicalization of *My Sister Eileen*; *The Girl in Pink Tights* (1954), a musical taking place following the Civil War in the theatrical district of New York; and *Anniversary Waltz* (1954), a domestic comedy of marital discord.

On his own, Jerome Chodorov contributed material to the review *Alive and Kicking* (1950); wrote the book for the Coney Island musical *I Had a Ball* (1964); penned the comedy *Three Bags Full* (1966), about a womanizing sports goods tycoon; drafted the book for the Los Angeles tryout of *Dumas and Son* about the great French writer (1967); revamped the Viennese operetta *The Great Waltz* (1970); tinkered on the road with a Claudette Colbert vehicle, *A Community of Two*, during the 1973–1974 season; and, with Mark Bramble, adapted the John O'Hara–Richard Rodgers musical *Pal Joey* (1978).

Chodorov's sentiment for suspense was expressed in his film adaptation of Earle Stanley Gardner's *The Case of the Lucky Legs* (1935), his Broadway direction of Alec Coppel's mystery-comedy *The Gazebo* (1958), and his penning, with Norman Panama, of *A Talent for Murder* (1982), starring Claudette Colbert and Jean-Pierre Aumont.[7]

Joseph Fields's solo work encompasses *The Doughgirls* (1942), a comedy unfolding in wartime, overcrowded Washington; and *I Gotta Get Out* (1947), about a gang of bookies setting up shop in the kitchen of a trusting Long Island matron. With Anita Loos, Fields wrote the book for the successful musical *Gentlemen Prefer Blondes* (1949), going back in time to the flapper days of the 1920s; with Peter De Vries, he penned *The Tunnel of Love* (1957), poking fun at expecting wives and unwed mothers; with Oscar Hammerstein II, he adapted the novel by C. Y. Lee for the musical *Flower Drum Song* (1958), a romance set in San Francisco's Chinatown.

Fields staged on Broadway Arthur Miller's *The Man Who Had All the Luck* (1944) and William Marchant's *The Desk Set* (1955).

For the cinema, Fields wrote the screenplays of many B-movies during the 1930s and 1940s. He incorporated crime elements into *Lightning Strikes Twice* (1934), *Waterfront Lady* (1935), *The Walking Dead* (1936, with Boris Karloff on a revenge quest), *Grand Jury* (1936), *Reported Missing* (1937), *The Girl and the Gambler* (1939, based on the play *The Dove* by Willard Mack), *The Spellbinder* (1939), *Two Thoroughbreds* (1939), and *Phantom Raiders* (1940, featuring Walter Pidgeon as sleuth Nick Carter).

Other motion pictures scripted by Fields include *Annie Oakley* (1935), starring Barbara Stanwyck as the legendary sharpshooter; *A Night in Casablanca* (1946), with the Marx Brothers confronting a ring of Nazi spies; and *The Farmer Takes a Wife* (1953), a period musical romance enlivened by Betty Grable.[8]

Acting Edition: Samuel French, Inc. (in manuscript form).

Awards and Honors: A top-ten selection in *The Best Plays of 1955–1956*: "Beguiling entertainment . . . a nice light pastel daffiness about it, a way of making things look delightfully woozy through wrong-prescription rose-colored glasses."[9] Jerome Chodorov and Joseph Fields wrote the book of *Wonderful Town*, the 1953 Tony Award winner for Best Musical.

NOTES

1. *New York Herald Tribune*, February 17, 1956.
2. *New York Times*, February 17, 1956.
3. *New York Post*, February 17, 1956.
4. *New York World-Telegram*, February 17, 1956.
5. *New York Journal-American*, February 17, 1956.
6. *Daily Mirror*, February 17, 1956.
7. Jerome Chodorov's older brother, Edward Chodorov, was also a playwright, author of the nerve-wracking *Kind Lady* (1935).
8. Joseph Albert Fields was the son of vaudevillian Lew Fields and the brother of writers/lyricists Herbert and Dorothy, who collaborated on musicals composed by Richard Rodgers, Cole Porter, George Gershwin, and Irving Berlin and penned the libretto and lyrics of *Redhead* (1959), a Broadway musical murder mystery set in a waxworks museum in 1880s London.
9. Louis Kronenberger, ed., *The Best Plays of 1955–1956* (New York: Dodd, Mead, 1956), 8.

Towards Zero (1956)
Agatha Christie (England, 1890–1976)

Agatha Christie's gambit in *Towards Zero,* which she adapted—in collaboration with Gerald Verner—from her 1944 novel, is to pile a mountain of damning facts against the murder suspect, young Nevile Strange, "first-class tennis player and all-round sportsman." His fingerprints are stamped on the blunt instrument of death, a golf club; the cuffs and sleeves of his dinner jacket are stained with the victim's blood; he had a flaming fight with Lady Camilla Tessilian prior to her sudden passing; and he is the adopted son who will inherit 100,000 pounds upon her demise.

Superintendent Battle of Scotland Yard (a Christie series character) scoffs that there is "too much evidence against him" and concludes that Nevile has been framed by a nefarious culprit. Of course, any seasoned follower of whodunits will concur with the superintendent and shift the finger of guilt toward other members of the Cornwall abode—each with a motive to dispense with the autocratic dowager—only to make a complete circle at the denouement wherein, surprisingly, Nevile is unmasked as the clever murderer.[1]

Following a tryout engagement at the Theatre Royal in Nottingham, *Towards Zero* opened at the St. James's Theatre on September 4, 1956, under the direction of Murray Macdonald. The reviews were favorable and the play ran 205 performances.

Charles Osborne, in *The Life and Crimes of Agatha Christie,* relates that the "painfully shy and ill at ease" author has "toughened up as the rehearsals progressed." When actress Mary Law, who played the role of Kay Strange, the killer's wife, asked, "Do you mind if I alter this difficult line?" Christie replied from the stalls, "Yes, I do mind. I want you to say, 'I hate her, I hate her, I hate her.'"[2]

In the United States, *Towards Zero,* directed by Leo Brady, was presented at the Olney Theatre, Washington, D.C., in 1977, and by the Pulse Ensemble Theatre in New York City, staged by Alexa Kelly, in 2001.[3]

Acting Edition: Dramatists Play Service.

NOTES

1. A similar conceit of misdirection was utilized by Ayn Rand in her little-known play, *Think Twice* (1939).

2. Charles Osborne, *The Life and Crimes of Agatha Christie* (London: Collins, 1982), 132.

3. Gerald Verner, who teamed with Agatha Christie on the dramatization of *Towards Zero*, had previously adapted to the stage two novels by Peter Cheyney—1938's *The Urgent Hangman*, under the title *Meet Mr. Callaghan* (Garrick Theatre, London, May 27, 1952—340 performances), and 1939's *Dangerous Curves* (Garrick Theatre, April 14, 1953—fifty-three performances), both featuring Terence De Marney as the hard-boiled Slim Callaghan, hero of a dozen Cheyney novels and short story collections (Terence's brother, Derrick De Marney, who directed the plays, portrayed Callaghan in a 1954 motion picture version of *Meet Mr. Callaghan*).Verner is the prolific author of approximately one hundred novels of suspense, written from 1927 to 1967.

Speaking of Murder (1956)

Audrey Roos (United States, 1912–1982) and William Roos (United States, 1911–1987)

Edgar Allan Poe (1809–1849) depicted with relish the entombing of live victims in airless catacombs. Some twentieth-century disciples of Poe concocted their own fiendish buried-alive plots.

The title character of Owen Davis's *Edna, the Pretty Typewriter* (1907) is locked in an airless safe by a dastardly villain.

In 1910, Paul Armstrong's *Alias Jimmy Valentine* features a breathtaking scene in which a blindfolded retired cracksman unscrambles the combination of a formidable vault to save an entrapped child.

The heroine is imprisoned in a time-locked vault and is rescued from certain suffocation by the Secret Service in Hal Reid's *Time Lock Number 776* (1915).

Elizabeth McFadden, in *Double Door* (1933), created an autocratic, ruthless dowager who lures her daughter-in-law to a secret, hermetically sealed vault.

An elusive murderer locks a newly married couple in an airless, soundproof film vault in *The Four of Hearts Mystery* (1949), dramatized by Audrey and Wiliam Roos from Ellery Queen's Hollywood mystery.

Seven years later, in 1956, the Rooses, prolific writers of detective fiction under the pseudonym Kelley Roos, focused the action of their play *Speaking of Murder* around a soundproof, fireproof, dustproof, airproof vault. Originally built for a rare book collection, the vault, now used to store fur coats, is centrally located in the library of the Ashton home on the east bank of the Hudson River, north of Tarrytown.

Charles Ashton, a wealthy architect, has just married his second wife, Connie, a celebrated movie actress. Foolishly, he has kept on the governess of his two children, the wicked Annabelle Logan, who pushed his first wife off a balcony to her death in the hopes of snaring Charles for herself. Annabelle is being blackmailed by an alcoholic neighbor, Ethel Walworth. When Annabelle relates to her that "the movie actress won't be here for long," Mrs. Walworth's response is, "Of course, my dear, I shall have to raise my rates. Double at least, I should think. That would be eighty dollars a week."

Annabelle rehearses her murder method by locking the family dog in the vault. Then, while Charles and daughter Janie are away at a carnival, she tricks Connie into the slow-suffocating trap, arranging the scene to blame nine-year-old Ricky for the eventual demise of his stepmother.

The dastardly scheme would have succeeded except for two coincidences: little Jane eats too much at the carnival, resulting in a stomachache, so she and her father return home early, and Mrs. Walworth, drunk, is fatally hit by a car, shattering Annabelle's alibi. During a nerve-wracking third act, Charles and Detective Lieutenant Mitchell search frantically for Connie—will they find her in time? At the end, Connie is saved, the unmasked Annabelle escapes into the vault, and Charles, who must have read Poe, says, "I'll have it sealed tomorrow." Curtain.

* * *

Staged by Delbert Mann, *Speaking of Murder* opened on December 19, 1956, at Manhattan's Royale Theatre. The reaction of the critics was mixed. Richard Watts Jr. declared the play "deficient as a thriller."[1] Tom Donnelly found the chiller "as taut as a string of a 10-cent violin" and ridiculed Annabelle's "doing all manner of dreadful things with a grin that would seem excessive on a Cheshire cat full of canaries."[2] Robert Coleman concluded sarcastically, "*Speaking of Murder* proves once again that 'Crime doesn't pay.'"[3]

Conversely, Walter Kerr endorsed *Speaking of Murder* as "splendid fun";[4] John Chapman found it "entertaining and attractively acted";[5] and John McClain, a self-admitted "solid sucker for almost any theatrical murder-melodrama," proclaimed that "for those who like that sort of thing it is a delightfully sinister evening in the theatre."[6]

Speaking of Murder closed after thirty-seven performances. However, the play was received warmly in London, where, under the direction of Hubert Gregg, it opened at the St. Martin's Theatre on June 4, 1958, and ran for 173 performances.

* * *

Born in Pittsburgh, Pennsylvania, William Roos met Audrey Kelley of New Jersey at Carnegie Tech, where they both majored in acting. They fell in love, got married, and moved to New York to pursue their careers. William decided that his future lay in playwriting and had several productions mounted on Broadway, but eventually he and Audrey combined forces and became more prolific and better known as "Kelley Roos," a joint pseudonym for more than twenty mystery novels they wrote between 1940 and 1971. Nine feature the investigative duo Jeff and

Haila Troy and a few unfold in theatrical settings, most notably *Made Up to Kill* (1940) and *What Did Hattie See?* (1970). "In all cases Roos provided a substantial plot, good characters, and relief from the anxieties of a commonplace world," writes Fred Dueren in *Twentieth-Century Crime and Mystery Writers.*[7]

In 1949, the Rooses dramatized Ellery Queen's *The Four of Hearts,* a baffling murder mystery set in Hollywood. Ten years later, they novelized the movie *Scent of Mystery,* the only cinematic endeavor released in Glorious Smell-a-Vision.

On his own, William wrote a few nongenre comedies: *Triple Play* (1937); *The Life of Reilly* (1942); *January Thaw* (1946); *As the Girls Go* (1948); *Peep Show* (1950); *Boy Wanted* (1947); the book for the musical *Courtin' Time,* based on Eden Phillpotts's *The Farmer's Wife* (1951); and *Belles on Their Toes* (1952).

Acting Edition: Samuel French, Inc.

Awards and Honors: In 1961, Audrey and William Roos received an Edgar Allan Poe Award from the Mystery Writers of America for their television adaptation of John Dickson Carr's novel *The Burning Court.*

NOTES

1. *New York Post,* December 20, 1956.
2. *New York World-Telegram,* December 20, 1956.
3. *Daily Mirror,* December 20, 1956.
4. *New York World-Tribune,* December 20, 1956.
5. *Daily News,* December 20, 1956.
6. *New York Journal-American,* December 20, 1956.
7. John M. Reilly, ed., *Twentieth-Century Crime and Mystery Writers* (New York: St. Martin's Press, 1980), 1281.

The Hidden River (1957)

Ruth Goetz (United States, 1908–2001) and Augustus Goetz (United States, 1901–1957)

The husband-wife collaborators of *The Heiress* came up with another adaptation from a novel—Storm Jameson's 1953 *The Hidden River*. Here, too, the melodramatic proceedings are tinged with human dilemmas, and large issues are at stake.

The action takes place in a manor house, owned by a family of vintners, on the bank of the Loire River, France. World War II has left its scars on the Monnerie tribe. Young Robert, a Resistance leader who helped spirit downed Allied pilots out of the country, was exposed and captured in 1944, and tortured to death by the Nazis. The head of the family, Uncle Daniel, has been imprisoned for befriending a German general during wartime and is now set free to go home. Robert's embittered mother, Marie, suspects that Daniel was the one who informed on her son, but his cousins, Jean and Francis, who run the estate, welcome him back.

A British intelligence officer, Adam Hartley, returns to visit the family that sheltered him during the war. His quest to solve the identity of Robert's betrayer makes for a mystery melodrama, but it soon becomes clear that Daniel was only sheltering the adolescent Francis, who was the one who turned Robert in to save the family's vineyards. Francis justifies his act to his shocked brother Jean by contending that it was the only way to salvage the vines from "being pulled up by the roots and burned." If it wasn't for him, maintains Francis, they would have become paupers "standing on a heap of rubble waving their little flags."

At the end, Francis's fiancée Elizabeth deserts him, his brother Jean leaves home to search for "a place where a man won't sell his friend," and Francis is left to cope with the acrid, unforgiving Marie.

* * *

Directed by Robert Lewis, *The Hidden River* opened at The Playhouse in New York on January 23, 1957, to mostly appreciative reviews. "As the story progresses, as steadily as the River Loire itself," stated John Chap-

212

man, "one comes to hear much of the pointlessness of war, much about the reason why men kill to protect whatever country happens to be theirs. One follows the inevitable unmasking of the traitor with quickening interest, and the finale of the drama is a thrilling one."[1]

"There is suspicion and suspense galore at The Playhouse, where *The Hidden River* inundated the premises last night," wrote John McClain. "It is skillfully mounted and wonderfully well executed."[2] Richard Watts Jr. pointed out that the play "combines suspense melodrama with contemplation of moral issues. . . . Its concern with a painful subject is inescapably stimulating."[3] Tom Donnelly ascertained that "as it goes thundering along with the involved parties confronting one another with storm and blast, *The Hidden River* shapes up as a sufficiently bountiful display of emotional fireworks."[4]

Paul V. Beckley praised the actors: "Lili Darvas gives one of the finer performances of the season as the bitter mother of the slain man. . . . Dennis King is magnificently urbane as the imprisoned uncle. . . . Robert Preston (as Jean Monnerie) makes very real the struggle between honesty and mercy. . . . Peter Brandon gives a remarkable performance as the simpering, cowering, retreating, swerving Francis."[5] Brooks Atkinson summed up his glowing review, "The writing is skillful and the performance is superb."[6]

The sole dissenter was Robert Coleman: "*The Hidden River* doesn't hide its secret long enough. Early in the second act, we began to be reasonably sure of the identity of the traitor in the Monnerie household. We kept wondering why it took those on stage such a lengthy span to ferret him out. . . . We regret to say that the Goetzes' venture is on the shallow side."[7]

The play ran for sixty-one performances.

The Hidden River opened at London's Cambridge Theatre on April 13, 1959, under John Dexter's direction, running for sixteen performances.

The passage of time has eroded the impact of *The Hidden River*. Today it seems weighed down by a preachy treatment of issues such as patriotism, loyalty, and betrayal under the duress of war. There are too few surprises along the way to sustain interest, and the characters lack the depth and nuances that distinguish the Goetzes' *The Heiress*.

* * *

Ruth Goetz, the daughter of a notable Broadway producer, Philip Goodman, was brought up in show business, worked as a costume and scenic designer, and read scripts for Samuel Goldwyn. Augustus Goetz, whose father was in insurance, found Wall Street boring and aspired to become a writer. During a trip to Europe, he met and married Ruth Goodman. They lived for several years in Paris and Vienna, then returned to the United States, establishing their home in Bucks County, Pennsylvania.

In 1940, the Goetzes collaborated on *Franklin Street*, a comedy based on Philip Goodman's memoirs. It closed before reaching New York. Five years later, they wrote *One-Man Show*, a drama about the relationship between a domineering father and a painfully yielding daughter. Another play dealing with the breach between father and daughter is *The Heiress*, which in 1947 the Goetzes adapted from Henry James's 1880 novel, *Washington Square*. In 1954, they adapted *The Immoralist* from a novel by André Gide, a controversial play at the time. In it, James Dean portrayed a homosexual Arab youth.

In Hollywood, Ruth and Augustus teamed on the screenplays of *Carrie* (1952), based on the novel by Theodore Dreiser; *Rhapsody* (1954), from the novel by Henry Handel Richardson; and *Stage Struck* (1958), based on a play by Zoe Akins.

Acting Edition: Dramatists Play Service.

NOTES

1. *Daily News*, January 24, 1957.
2. *New York Journal-American*, January 24, 1957.
3. *New York Post*, January 24, 1957.
4. *New York World-Telegram*, January 24, 1957.
5. *New York Herald Tribune*, January 24, 1957.
6. *New York Times*, January 24, 1957.
7. *Daily Mirror*, January 24, 1957.

The Potting Shed (1957)

Graham Greene (England, 1904–1991)

Henry C. Callifer is dying. Family members gather. However, one of H. C.'s sons, James, and H. C.'s brother, William, are not invited. Why has their kin shunned them all these years? Why is James afflicted with a childhood memory block? What is the "something awful" that happened in Wild Grove's potting shed long ago, causing him to grow up lost and haunted, incapable of emotion?

James's niece, Anne, a precocious thirteen-year-old, functions as the deus ex machina of *The Potting Shed*. "I'm curious by nature. I'd make a good detective," declares Anne and sets out to rattle closet skeletons. She telegrams James about his father's condition, thus instigating his arrival and confrontation with his former wife Sara and the matriarchal Mary Callifer.

James's mother wants to let sleeping dogs lie, but Anne relentlessly concocts a meeting between James and Mrs. Potter, the widow of the old gardener; a visit with James's uncle, Pastor William Callifer; and a family reunion during Christmas.

Piece by piece the events that occurred when James was fourteen years old surface. James, hounded by a taskmaster father, hanged himself in the potting shed. "You'd used a cord from the play room," recalls the gardener's wife. "Potter cut you down. . . . There wasn't any life in you, sir. . . . Your heart stopped."

Uncle William, the pastor, arrived and prayed to God: "Take my faith, but let him live."

Miraculously, James was restored to life.

Pastor William lost his religious beliefs and became a shell of a man— an alcoholic "whose breath smells in the confessional," a clergyman who cynically calls his tasks "useless" and "slave labor."

Now that the occurrence at the symbolic tool house is squarely faced, the Callifers will embark on a clear future—James will go back to his wife Sara; Mother goes to the potting shed and is not frightened anymore;

William reunites with his faith; and Anne receives from her uncle James "suitable presents for a detective"—a toy gun and a magnifying glass.

* * *

An intellectual psychological thriller, *The Potting Shed* is tinged with autobiographical elements of the playwright's bleak outlook on Catholicism, his manic-depressive bouts, and his suicidal tendencies.

Director Carmen Capalbo and his associate Stanley Chase, flush with the success of *The Threepenny Opera*, flew to London and convinced Graham Greene to let them present *The Potting Shed*'s world premiere in New York. The play opened at the Bijou Theatre on January 29, 1957, running for 143 performances. The critics, who in 1954 scoffed at Greene's *The Living Room* (disagreeing with their London colleagues, who hailed it as "the best first play of a generation"), unanimously embraced *The Potting Shed*. "An enormously provocative drama," wrote Richard Watts Jr. "A distinguished event in our theatrical season."[1] Tom Donnelly agreed, "*The Potting Shed* is a brilliantly wrought entertainment, fascinating from first to last. It has bite, it has drive, it has wit."[2] Brooks Atkinson believed *The Potting Shed* to be "an original drama that probes deep into the spirit and casts a spell. . . . As usual, Mr. Greene is blundering down the tortuous labyrinth of life, meeting people who have a scar on their souls."[3] Walter Kerr opined, "The unrelenting eye of the author is steady here, the tone quietly honest and crackling literate, the psychological detective-story processes firm enough to overcome the play's technical awkwardness."[4] John McClain found "the first two stanzas skilled and captivating" but "a last act which is repetitious and uneventful."[5] Richard Coleman, however, observed that "by the evening's end, the first-nighters were brought to the edges of their seats."[6] High praise was bestowed on director Carmen Capalbo and actors Robert Flemyng (James), Sybil Thorndike (Mrs. Callifer), Leueen MacGrath (Sara), Frank Conroy (Father William), and Carol Lynley (young Anne).

In a successive London production presented at the Globe Theatre on February 5, 1958, John Gielgud enacted the role of James, supported by Gwen Frangcon-Davies, Irene Worth, Redmond Phillips, and Sarah Long. Graham Greene attended the opening night and later wrote: "The audience was very sticky, the performance A–, reception good. The notices have been mixed . . . but the 3rd programme [BBC] last night, a superb 'rave' notice comparing me to Montaigne."[7] *The Potting Shed* ran for 101 performances.

The passage of time has not been kind to *The Potting Shed*. Today, the play seems bogged down with unreal, high-flown dialogue. "I couldn't love you any more than you can love a tree, a glass of wine, a cat," says James to Sara.

Michael Shelden, in *Graham Greene: The Enemy Within*, states that "*The Potting Shed* is important for its autobiographical insights, but as a piece of drama it develops with agonizing slowness and overwhelms the audience with too much background information."[8]

Other plays by Graham Greene are similarly occupied by the element of good versus evil. There is the metaphoric *Carving a Statue* (London, 1964; New York, 1968), in which the protagonist is a sculptor who has been working obsessively, for fifteen years, on a massive rendition of God the Father. Isolating himself from the real world, the sculptor despairs of ever molding God and turns his creative juices toward the demon Lucifer. The pastiche *The Return of A. J. Raffles* (London, 1975) is a rollicking resurrection of Greene's boyhood hero, E. W. Hornung's Amateur Cracksman. The farce *For Whom the Bell Chimes* (Leicester, 1980) swirls around the body of a murdered woman hidden in a bed enclaved behind the wall of a compact studio.

Greene's masterpiece *The Power and the Glory* (1940), a multilayered novel about a hunted and haunted alcoholic priest, was dramatized by Dennis Cannan and Pierre Bost, and, starring Paul Scofield, "was given a powerful production by Peter Brook"[9] at London's Phoenix Theatre in 1956. Two years later, the adaptation was produced by New York's Phoenix Theatre, staged by Stuart Vaughan and featuring Fritz Weaver, running seventy-one performances. "It is wonderful acting in a wonderful play that fills the Phoenix with power and glory," wrote Brooks Atkinson in the *New York Times*.[10] *Travels with My Aunt* (1969), Greene's exhilarating narrative, encompassing drug trafficking, stolen art, Interpol, and murder, was adapted to the stage by Giles Havergal in 1989.

Noncrime plays by Greene include *The Living Room* (London, 1953; New York, 1954), *The Complaisant Lover* (London, 1959; New York, 1961), and the one-act *Yes and No* (Leicester, 1980). In 2000, a recently discovered play, *A House of Reputation*, disowned by Greene, was given its world premiere at Berkhamsted, England, Greene's birthplace. It is set in a brothel, reflecting the playwright's long-life fondness for prostitutes and frequent visits to seedy houses of ill repute.

Greene scripted, with director Carol Reed, the film noir masterpiece *The Third Man* in 1949 and novelized it the following year. Altogether, Greene wrote or cowrote ten screenplays, including several based on his works: *Brighton Rock* (1947), *The Fallen Idol* (1948), *Our Man in Havana* (1960), and *The Comedians* (1967).[11]

Crime plays a dominant role in the bulk of Graham Greene's fiction, most notably in the novels he considered "entertainments": *Stamboul Train* (1932, U.S. title *Orient Express*), *A Gun for Sale* (1936, U.S. title *This Gun for Hire*), *Brighton Rock* (1938), *The Confidential Agent* (1939), and *The Ministry of Fear* (1943). All were transferred to the screen. In 1943, *Brighton*

Rock was dramatized by Frank Harvey and ran for 100 performances at West End's Garrick Theatre, featuring Richard Attenborough as Pinkie Brown, a psychotic teenage gangster. In 2004, film composer John Barry and lyricist Don Black collaborated on a musical version of *Brighton Rock*; it was lambasted by the critics and ran for less than a month at London's Almeida Theatre.

On July 15, 2009, the *New York Times* reported the discovery of an unfinished murder mystery novel by Greene, called *The Empty Chair*. Greene began writing the novel in 1926 and apparently abandoned it. He was twenty-two at the time, apprenticing with the *Times* of London. The manuscript, written in longhand, was discovered in 2008 in the Greene archive at the Ransom Center of the University of Texas. It is a country-house whodunit with a protagonist who is "a sly, Columbo-like detective-inspector," said the *New York Times*.[12]

British TV presented adaptations of the short stories by Greene under the banner *Shades of Greene* in the fall of 1975.

The prolific author penned *The Little Steam Roller: A Story of Mystery and Detection* (1953) for the young readers market and, with Dorothy Glover, the catalogue *Victorian Detective Fiction* (1966). Among others, Greene edited *British Dramatists* (1942), *The Best of Saki* (1950), and, with Hugh Greene, *The Spy Bedside Book* (1957). Various short pieces were collated in Greene's *The Lost Childhood and Other Essays* (1951) and *Collected Essays* (1969), while his numerous film criticisms were assembled in *Graham Greene on Film*, edited by John Russell Taylor (1972). Greene's autobiography, *A Sort of Life*, was published in 1971, and his memoir *Ways of Escape* in 1980. Other real-life accounts were delineated in *Revenge* (1963), *Getting to Know the General* (1984), *Reflections* (1990), and *A World of My Own*, published posthumously in 1992.

Norman Sherry's 1989 *The Life of Graham Greene, Volume I: 1904–1939*, won the Edgar Allan Poe Award from the Mystery Writers of America for best critical/biographical work. *Volume II: 1939–1955* (which details Greene's participation in British Intelligence during the Second World War) was released in 1995, *Volume III: 1955–1991* in 2004.

"The depth of Greene's work comes from the inexhaustible themes of guilt and redemption, of evil's influence on the innocent and vice versa," writes William L. DeAndrea.[13] George Woodcock concludes: "The criminal rather than the crime, the sinner rather than the sin, are Greene's ultimate concerns."[14]

Acting Edition: Samuel French, Inc.

Awards and Honors: A top-ten selection in *The Best Plays of 1956–1957*: "*The Potting Shed* is the most truly dramatic of detective stories, a what-done-it, a shadowy trek backward from an effect to cause. . . . It has an emotional force born of its characters' harassed bafflement and needs."[15]

Among other honors, Graham Greene was the recipient of the Hawthorn Prize (1941), Black Memorial Prize (1949), Chevalier of the Legion of Honor (1967), Shakespeare Prize, Hamburg (1968), Thomas More Medal (1973), Mystery Writers of America's Grand Master Edgar (1976), the Jerusalem Prize (1981), and the Order of Merit (1986).

NOTES

1. *New York Post*, January 30, 1957.
2. *New York World-Telegram*, January 30, 1957.
3. *New York Times*, January 30, 1957.
4. *New York Herald Tribune*, January 30, 1957.
5. *New York Journal-American*, January 30, 1957.
6. *Daily Mirror*, January 30, 1957.
7. Norman Sherry, *The Life of Graham Greene*, vol. 3 (New York: Viking, 2004), 98.
8. Michael Sheldon, *Graham Greene: The Enemy Within* (New York: Random House, 1994), 142.
9. *Theatre World Annual*, 1957.
10. *New York Times*, December 12, 1958.
11. An analysis of Graham Greene's motion pictures is provided in *Graham Greene: The Films of His Fiction* by Gene D. Phillips (New York: Teachers College Press, Columbia University, 1974).
12. *New York Times*, July 15, 2009.
13. William DeAndrea, *Encyclopedia Mysteriosa* (New York: Prentice Hall, 1994), 142.
14. John M. Reilly, ed., *Twentieth-Century Crime and Mystery Writers* (New York: St. Martin's Press, 1980), 701.
15. Louis Kronenberger, ed., *The Best Plays of 1956–1957* (New York: Dodd, Mead, 1957), 12.

West Side Story (1957)

Book by Arthur Laurents (United States, 1918–), Music by Leonard Bernstein (United States, 1918–1990), Lyrics by Stephen Sondheim (United States, 1930–)

Three hundred and sixty-three years following the composition of *Romeo and Juliet*, the play about two star-crossed young lovers inspired a modernized musical version.

Shakespeare's tragedy now unfolds on New York's West Side. The feuding houses of Montague and Capulet are now two rival street gangs claiming the same turf—the native Jets and the Puerto Rican Sharks. Adolescent lovers Tony and Maria belong to opposite sides, but their feelings—ignited on fire-escape balconies—transcend youthful rancor and social prejudice.

Norris Houghton, in an introduction to the Laurel-Leaf Library edition of *Romeo and Juliet/West Side Story*, expounds on the parallelism between the two plays: "By introducing us into this feuding world through younger and lesser members of the gangs, Laurents follows Shakespeare, Sampson and Gregory becoming A-Rab and Baby John. Prince Escalus and his Veronese officers who break up the first street fight find their counterparts in Officers Krupke and Schrank. In both plays the atmosphere of violence and hate, uneasily held in check by authority, is quickly established. So, too, is the youthfulness and impetuosity of the world of both. It may be helpful to try to think of Benvolio and Tybalt, Mercutio and Romeo as scarcely older than Bernardo and Chino, Riff and Tony."[1]

Tony and Maria meet at a settlement-house dance and fall in love at first sight. During a rumble, Bernardo, leader of the Sharks, knifes Riff, the Jets' strongman, and is subsequently stabbed by Tony—following the pattern of the killing of Mercutio by Tybalt, and of Tybalt by Romeo. Switchblades take the place of swords.

From here on the plot of *West Side Story* deviates from Shakespeare. Tony, a fugitive hiding in a neighborhood drugstore run by Doc, Friar Laurence's counterpart in the modern version, plans to escape with Maria. Anita, mourning for her lover Bernardo, delivers a false message to Tony, claiming that Chino, Bernardo's friend, has found out about the clandestine love affair and has shot Maria. Crazed with grief, Tony roams the dark alleyways of the neighborhood at midnight, shouting, "Hey, Chino! Come get me, damn you! . . . Chino, I'm calling for you, Chino! . . ." Suddenly, a figure steps out of the shadows. Tony utters an unbelieving whisper, "Maria . . . Maria?" With arms outstretched they run toward each other as Chino appears. A gun blasts. Tony stumbles and falls. Maria cradles him in her arms.

The two rival gangs rush in. Maria gently rests Tony on the pavement. "We all killed him," she tells the shocked youngsters. Together the Jets and the Sharks lift Tony's body and carry him away. Touched by the tragedy of young love snuffed out, the teenage warriors, like the Capulets and Montagues, will now make peace.

* * *

Arthur Laurents relates in his autobiographical *Original Story By* that in the late 1940s, "Jerry [Jerome Robbins] had approached Lenny [Leonard Bernstein] and me about writing a musical based on a contemporary version of *Romeo and Juliet*. Romeo and the Montagues would be Catholic, Juliet and the Capulets Jewish; the action would occur on the Lower East Side during Easter-Passover."[2] Laurents, Robbins, and Bernstein could not develop the idea and let the project linger. The recent phenomenon of juvenile delinquent gangs made them change course. "We began with an outline," writes Laurents. "I divided the play into two acts, detailing in each scene the characters, action, and musical elements. The story line followed Shakespeare's fairly closely, although I eliminated and changed to suit contemporary time and place, and to allow song and/or dance tell us much of the story as one or other or both could."[3]

Among the changes made by Laurents was the elimination of the parents of both lovers "because the play no longer centered on a family feud but on a tribal feud: ethnic warfare between juvenile gangs. The impartial, civilized Duke who ruled the territory became the police who ruled the streets. . . . No potion for Maria (Juliet) to fake death with, and no suicide for her, either; the girl was too strong to kill herself for love."[4]

Laurents tells that initially the manuscript of *West Side Story* was turned down by every producer in New York "as too depressing, too operatic, too uncommercial."[5] Eventually, Roger L. Stevens, who had earlier helmed Laurents's *The Time of the Cuckoo*, took it upon himself to take charge of the show's finances.

After tryouts in Washington, D.C., and Philadelphia beginning in August 1957, *West Side Story* opened at New York's Winter Garden Theatre on September 26. The critics unanimously raved. "*West Side Story* adds to the dramatic power of the American musical theatre," wrote Richard Watts Jr.[6] "A provocative and artful blend of music, dance and plot," stated John Chapman.[7] "An incandescent piece of work that finds odd bits of beauty amid the rubbish of the streets," cheered Brooks Atkinson.[8] "A chiller, a thriller, as up-to-the-minute as tomorrow's headlines," opined Robert Coleman.[9] "What an eye-popping, ear-soothing, conscience-busting combination it was," declared Frank Aston.[10] "Director, choreographer and idea-man Jerome Robbins has put together, and then blasted apart, the most savage, restless, electrifying dance patterns we've been exposed to in a dozen seasons," applauded Walter Kerr.[11]

West Side Story ran for 732 performances and subsequently was a hit in London, running for 1039 performances at Her Majesty's Theatre. The musical was revived in 1960 at Manhattan's Winter Garden for 253 showings, with Larry Kert and Carol Lawrence repeating the roles of Tony and Maria. New Yorkers again saw *West Side Story* at City Center in 1964 (thirty-one performances), at Lincoln Center in 1968 (eighty-nine performances), and at the Minskoff Theatre in 1980 (333 performances).

London brought back the musical for the seasons of 1973–1974, 1974–1975, 1998–1999, and 2008–2009.

In 1961, an American production of *West Side Story* traveled to Israel, Africa, and the Near East. The following year, a British show went on a five-month tour to the Scandinavian countries. Several American regional opera companies presented *West Side Story* during the 1980s: San Diego Civic Light Opera (1983), Civic Light Opera of Pittsburgh (1984), Banff Musical Theatre (1984), and Michigan Opera Theatre (1985). U.S. national tours were mounted in 1987 and 2002. A Hong Kong production, incorporating Cantonese lyrics, was produced outdoors in 2000. Three years later, the Austrian Bregenz Festival presented *West Side Story* in a German translation. In 2008, a French language adaptation played in Montreal, Quebec, and a Spanish translation was seen in Lisbon, Portugal.

In 2007, the Fulton Opera House in Lancaster, Pennsylvania, and Fifth Avenue Theatre in Seattle, Washington, were granted the production rights to *West Side Story* on the fiftieth anniversary of its Broadway premiere. At the age of 90, librettist Arthur Laurents directed a revival that was mounted at the National Theatre in Washington, D.C., in December 2008 and came to New York's Palace Theatre in February 2009. It was a bilingual production, interweaving dialogue and songs in Spanish. Critic Ben Brantley found the revival "startlingly sweet. . . . What prevails is a tenderhearted awareness of the naked vulnerability of being young and trapped in an urban jungle. . . . This *West Side Story* is most enthralling when Tony and Maria cross the ethnic divide to pursue the pipe dream of happiness together."[12] Charles McNulty, however, commented that "Laurents is smart to up the vicious criminal ante,"[13] and Adam Feldman felt that "Laurents has piloted the Jets out of lovable-ruffian territory and into a darker zone, where (despite likable flashes of humor and believable camaraderie) they often exude a sense of reckless menace."[14] The show closed in January 2011 after a run of 748 performances that recouped its $14 million investment.

A top-notch movie version of *West Side Story*, arguably the best celluloid adaptation of any Broadway musical, was made in 1961, scripted by Ernest Lehman and codirected by Robert Wise and Jerome Robbins. Natalie Wood and Richard Beymer played the doomed lovers, with Oscar-winning support by George Chakiris as Bernardo and Rita Moreno as Anita. Photographed in Super Panavision 70, *West Side Story* was the winner of ten Academy Awards, including Best Picture, Direction, Editing, and Scoring.

Also in 1961, *West Side Story* was novelized by Irving Shulman (1913–1995) and published as an original paperback by Pocket Books.

* * *

Born in Brooklyn, New York, in 1918, to a father who was a lawyer and a mother who was a schoolteacher, Arthur Laurents was brought up in a traditional Jewish home, but following his bar mitzvah he gradually became an atheist. He went to Cornell University and began his professional career writing scripts for various radio shows, among them *Lux Radio Theatre*.

During World War II, Laurents wrote training films and episodes for *Armed Service Force Presents*, a radio show that emphasized contributions made by all branches of the armed forces.

In 1945, Laurents had his first play, *Home of the Brave*, a psychological drama about anti-Semitism in the military, produced on Broadway, running for sixty-nine performances.[15] Five years later, his second play, *The Bird Cage*, a drama unfolding in a metropolitan nightclub, ran for only twenty-one performance. However, in 1952, *The Time of the Cuckoo*, starring Shirley Booth as an elderly secretary vacationing in Venice and falling in love with a married man, ran for 263 performances.[16] Later in the 1950s came Laurents's major successes, the musicals *West Side Story* and *Gypsy*, the latter based on the memoirs of Gypsy Rose Lee.

Laurents's career on Broadway continued to have its ups and downs. *Anyone Can Whistle* (1964), the tale of a bankrupt town, for which he wrote the book and Stephen Sondheim the music, flopped, but *Hallelujah, Baby!* (1967), featuring Leslie Uggams, was a hit, running 293 performances. *Nick and Nora* (1991), spotlighting Dashiell Hammett's sophisticated sleuths, closed after nine showings.

Laurents's notable directing assignments include *I Can Get It for You Wholesale* (1962), which introduced Barbra Streisand; *La Cage aux Folles* (1983), which ran for 1,761 performances; and revivals of *Gypsy* (1974, 1989, 2003) and *West Side Story* (2009).

In Hollywood, Laurents penned the screenplay of Alfred Hitchcock's *Rope* (1948), based on Patrick Hamilton's play, which in turn was inspired by the Richard Loeb–Nathan Leopold thrill-murder case of 1924. Laurents continued to dabble in nefarious plots in *Caught* (1949), about a woman who marries a millionaire for his money only to discover that he is sadistic and dangerous; in *Anna Lucasta* (1949), which he adapted to the screen from Philip Yordan's play, the story of a prostitute and her scheming brother-in-law; and in *Anastasia* (1956), from Marcelle Maurette's play, spotlighting of a band of con men who attempt to pass off an impostor as a Russian grand duchess.

Other movies of note written by Laurents are *The Snake Pit* (1948, uncredited); *Bonjour Tristesse*, from Francoise Sagan's novel (1958); *The Way We Were* (1973); and *The Turning Point* (1977).

In 2000, Laurents published *Original Story By*, a memoir of Broadway and Hollywood, and in 2009, *Mainly on Directing*, detailing the experiences he had reviving both *Gypsy* and *West Side Story* on Broadway. Writes Laurents: "Many say *West Side Story* forever changed the American musical. . . . What it really changed, what its real contribution to American musical theatre was, was that it showed that any subject—murder, attempted rape, bigotry—could be the subject of a popular musical."[17]

In 2010, Laurents established a generous annual playwriting award, providing $50,000 to an emerging writer and an additional $100,000 toward the production costs for mounting the recipient's play.

* * *

Leonard Bernstein was born in Lawrence, Massachusetts, in 1918 to a Polish-Jewish family from the Ukraine. He was captivated by music at a tender age and to the chagrin of his father, a businessman, he attended Harvard University with a concentration on music and became involved with the Harvard Glee Club in 1934. Bernstein continued his musical education at the Curtis Institute of Music in Philadelphia and came to New York. In 1943, he made his conducting debut with the New York Philharmonic on last-minute notification, after Bruno Walter came down with the flu. That was the beginning of a distinguished career as conductor, composer, and educator.

In 1946, Bernstein conducted his first opera, the American premiere of Benjamin Britten's *Peter Grimes*. Although Bernstein is mostly associated with the New York Philharmonic, through the years he also conducted the Boston Symphony, the Israel Philharmonic Orchestra, the Vienna Philharmonic Orchestra, the Berlin Philharmonic Orchestra, and the London Symphony Orchestra. In 1982, he founded the Los Angeles Philharmonic Institute.

Prior to *West Side Story*, Bernstein composed the highly regarded Broadway musicals *On the Town* (1944), *Wonderful Town* (1953), and *Candide* (1956). For the movies, he wrote the score of the masterful *On the Waterfront* (1954).

In order to deflect rumors about his homosexuality, in 1951 Bernstein got married to the Chilean actress Felicia Montealegre. They had three children. Eventually, Bernstein left home to live with his lover, Tom Cothran. A heavy smoker, he died of pneumonia and a pleural tumor in 1990. It is reported that on the day of his funeral procession through the streets of Manhattan, construction workers removed their hats and yelled, "Good-bye, Lenny!"

* * *

Born in New York City in 1930, Stephen Sondheim was educated at Williams College, where he won the Hutchinson Prize for musical composition. He began his professional career writing scripts for TV's *Topper* series. For his first Broadway credit, Sondheim composed the theme song of N. Richard Nash's 1956 drama *Girls of Summer*. Following *West Side Story*, he continued to provide the scores of many Broadway hits, becoming one of the giants of the modern American musical.

Among his early successes were *Gypsy* (1959) and *A Funny Thing Happened on the Way to the Forum* (1962). In the 1970s he peaked with *Company* (1970), *Follies* (1971), *A Little Night Music* (1973), *Pacific Overtures* (1976), and *Sweeney Todd, the Demon Barber of Fleet Street* (1979). Along the way he provided additional lyrics to a revival of *Candide* (1973), wrote the music and lyrics for Aristophanes' *The Frogs* (1974), provided the lyrics for the musical cabaret *By Bernstein* (1975), and spawned a show dedicated to his body of work: *Side by Side by Sondheim* (1977).

The indefatigable composer-lyricist continued to score mightily during the 1980s: *Sunday in the Park with George* (1984), *Into the Woods* (1987), and *Jerome Robbins' Broadway* (1989), which included Sondheim's "You Gotta Have a Gimmick" from *Gypsy* and "Comedy Tonight" from *A Funny Thing Happened on the Way to the Forum*. Less spectacular were *Merrily We Roll Along* (1981) and *A Little Like Magic* (1986), a puppet show that included "Send In the Clowns." Sondheim also contributed to various revues: *Marry Me a Little* (1980), *You're Gonna Love Tomorrow* (1983), *Barbara Cook: A Concert for the Theatre* (1987), *Lillian Montevecchi on the Boulevard* (1988), *Together Again for the First Time* (1989), and *Putting It Together* (1993).

In 1991, Sondheim composed *Assassins*, an experimental musical which probes the minds of the men who had attempted to assassinate United States presidents. Three years later he collaborated with James Lapine on *Passion*, the tale of a triangular love affair in 1863 Milan.

Several of Sondheim's major shows were revived in London and New York during the 1980s, 1990s, and the first decade of the twenty-first century. In 1996, he teamed with playwright George Furth on a whodunit, *Getting Away with Murder*, which was savaged by the critics and ran at Broadway's Broadhurst Theatre for only seventeen performances.

In 1953, Sondheim wrote ten episodes for the television comedy series *Topper*. For the silver screen, Sondheim coauthored with Anthony Perkins the mystery *The Last of Sheila* (1973), composed the music for the epic *Reds* (1981), and contributed five songs to *Dick Tracy* (1990).

Acting Edition: Laurel-Leaf Library, Dell Publishing Company.

Awards and Honors: *West Side Story* was nominated for a Tony Award for Best Musical but lost to *The Music Man* (book, lyrics, and music by Meredith Wilson). It did, however, receive the New York Drama Critics Award for Best Musical. In London, *West Side Story* won the 1958 *Evening Standard* Award for the best musical of the year.

Arthur Laurents's *Hallelujah, Baby!* won the Tony Award for Best Musical (1968). Laurents garnered a Drama Desk Award as Outstanding Director of a Musical for *Gypsy* (1975) and a Tony Award for Best Direction of a Musical for *La Cage aux Folles* (1984).

Leonard Bernstein won a Tony Award for Best Original Score for *Wonderful Town* (1953) and nine Grammy Awards, including a Lifetime Achievement Award. He received the Kennedy Center Honors award in 1980.

Stephen Sondheim received seven Tony Awards, more than any other composer, for Best Score for *Company* (1971), *Follies* (1972), *A Little Night Music* (1973), *Sweeney Todd, the Demon Barber of Fleet Street* (1979), *Into the Woods* (1988), *Passion* (1994), and for Lifetime Achievement in the Theatre (2008). He also won the Pulitzer Prize for *Sunday in the Park with George* (1985), and an Oscar for Original Song, "Sooner or Later," in *Dick Tracy* (1990).

With coauthor Anthony Perkins, Sondheim received the Mystery Writers of America 1974 Edgar Allan Poe Award for Best Motion Picture Screenplay for *The Last of Sheila*.

Sondheim served as president of the Dramatists Guild, the professional association of playwrights, composers, lyricists, and librettists, from 1973 to 1981. He was an honoree at the 1993 Kennedy Center Celebration of the Performing Arts. In 2010, Sondheim's eightieth birthday was celebrated by a gala performance of *Sondheim: The Birthday Party*, starring Elaine Stritch, at Lincoln Center's Avery Fisher Hall, and by a multimedia revue, *Sondheim on Sondheim*, featuring Barbara Cook, at Manhattan's Studio 54. Also on that occasion, New York's Roundabout Theatre Company renamed Henry Miller's Theatre on West Forty-third Street the Stephen Sondheim Theatre.

NOTES

1. *Romeo and Juliet/West Side Story* (New York: Laurel-Leaf Library, Dell, 1965), 8.

2. Arthur Laurents, *Original Story By* (New York: Knopf, 2000), 329.

3. Laurents, *Original Story By*, 348.

4. Laurents, *Original Story By*, 349.

5. Laurents, *Original Story By*, 328.

6. *New York Post*, September 27, 1957.

7. *Daily News*, September 27, 1957.

8. *New York Times*, September 27, 1957.

9. *Daily Mirror*, September 27, 1957.

10. *New York World-Telegram*, September 27, 1957.

11. *New York Herald Tribune*, September 27, 1957.

12. *New York Times*, March 20, 2009.

13. *Los Angeles Times*, March 20, 2009.

14. *TimeOut New York*, March 26–April 1, 2009.

15. A 1949 movie version of *Home of the Brave*, scripted by Carl Foreman and directed by Mark Robson, changed the anti-Semitic aspect of the play into a racial dilemma. It is not a Jewish soldier, but a black private who is abused by fellow GIs while on a Pacific island mission.

16. In 1955, *The Time of the Cuckoo* was filmed by David Lean, starring Katharine Hepburn, under the title *Summertime*. Ten years later, it was converted into a musical by Richard Rodgers, *Do I Hear a Waltz?*

17. Arthur Laurents, *Mainly on Directing* (New York: Knopf, 2009), 145.

Monique (1957)

Dorothy Blankfort (United States) and Michael Blankfort (United States, 1907–1982)

Pierre Boileau and Thomas Narcejac's fiendishly clever 1952 novel, *Celle qui n'était plus*, translated into English as *The Woman Who Was No More*, served as the basis for the spellbinding French movie *Diabolique* (1955), about an oppressive schoolmaster (played by Paul Meurise) who is drowned in a bathtub by his long-suffering wife (Vera Clouzot) and wily mistress (Simone Signoret). The two women dump the body into the school's pool but find themselves stalked and haunted by the presumably dead man. The nerve-wracking motion picture, brilliantly directed by Henri-Georges Clouzot,[1] was both damned and hailed by critics around the world. Its twist ending is still terrifying.

In the play version, Dorothy and Michael Blankfort changed the pattern of the relationships. The deadly triangle consists of a shrewish wife, a weak husband, and a domineering mistress. Fernand Ravinel, a traveling salesman of sporting goods, lives with his wife Lucienne in a country house an hour and a half from Paris. The marriage is on the rocks, but Lucienne does not want a divorce. Monique, an attractive, icy doctor, manipulates the tormented man and convinces him that, instead of letting Lucienne "suck his life's blood," they should get rid of her once and for all. Whenever Fernand wavers, Monique tightens the psychological screws to get him back in line.

On the designated evening, Fernand offers Lucienne a glass of water mixed with a sedative. He and Monique carry the drowsy wife and lower her into the bathtub. Ill at ease, Fernand lets Monique finish the violent act. They transport the body to the garden and dump it in a brook. "That's all," says Monique. "She fainted. She fell in the water. She drowned."

Fernand returns to the brook to collect the soiled towels they left behind. He forces himself to look at his wife's face—just for a second. It is white and, strangely, he tells Monique, "she seemed at peace."

The next part of the plan goes awry. Fernand is to leave for a few days on his sales route, then return to find the dead wife. However, the body has vanished. Did the maid, Henriette, hide it with the intention of blackmail? Did the sixteen-year-old neighbor, Lisette, who is enamored with Fernand, have designs of her own? Or is Lucienne still alive?

Suspense mounts. A telegram arrives: Lucienne notifies Fernand that she will return home "at nine tonight." The phone rings. It is Lucienne's voice, warning Fernand, "Don't try to run away. . . . There's no place to run."

No wonder Fernand asks a friend of the family, retired Police Inspector Merlin, "Do you believe in life after death?"

Merlin adds to Fernand's anxiety by stating that there is an energy in some people that transcends the moment of death, a passion to live so strong that it overcomes the weakness of flesh.

On the stroke of nine, the overwrought Fernand hears the gate opening, notes approaching footsteps, and there is a knock on the door. Terrified, he draws a pistol. When the shadow at the door speaks in Lucienne's voice, he shoots himself in the heart and falls dead into the armchair near the fireplace.

For a moment the shadow at the door remains immobile. Then it moves into the room and crosses to the telephone. It is Monique. She dials, and asks an attendant at Mercy Hospital to send an ambulance to 21 Canal Street and notify the police.

A final twist reveals that Fernand's suicide was the culmination of a conspiracy between lesbian lovers Monique and Lucienne. How did they fool Fernand with the pretense of Lucienne's death? They were certain that Fernand wouldn't have the courage to look at Lucienne long enough to see that she was holding her breath. When they put her in the bath, he ran out of the room.

The motive for the elaborate charade becomes clear when Lucienne expresses some pangs of regret; she could have given Fernand a divorce. Monique rebukes her, pointing out that their bank book now contains the insurance money—all ten million francs of it.

The two women get away with their lethal scheme, but the play ends on an ominous note when Monique declares that she will be making all future decisions, and Lucienne, holding the bank book, realizes to her horror that her own life may now be in jeopardy.

* * *

Monique opened at the John Golden Theatre on October 22, 1957. The critics were decidedly divided. "As a devoted thriller-chiller fan it pains me to report that *Monique* does not succeed in its eerie mission," sighed John McClain. "There is a surprise ending, to be sure, but the play follows a tedious and rambling path to the conclusion and, once there, trails off in several unresolved directions."[2]

John Chapman stated categorically, "Here is a play about murder which dies before the victim does. . . . It isn't a whodunit but a whydoit."[3] Robert Coleman theorized, "The trouble with *Monique* is that you follow it with all the feeling that you'd bring to the solution of a crossword puzzle. You seek to unwind the strands along with authors Dorothy and Michael Blankfort without caring about the people caught in them."[4]

In the other camp, Brooks Atkinson believed that "the first half of the evening is invitingly gruesome. . . . Although *Monique* is not the best thriller ever written, it will do until a neater one comes along. Any man contemplating the murder of his wife would do well to see it before he makes his final preparations."[5]

Richard Watts Jr. concurred: "*Monique* is certainly not, to my mind, in the very top rank of its school, which would have been high praise, indeed. But it has an arresting murder situation to consider, its passions are dark and sinister, its characters are enigmatic and deceptive, its atmosphere is menacing, its detective is intelligent if not infallible, and its motives are devious. Finally, it has a solution that is steeped in treachery and evil and is quite likely to surprise you."[6]

Patricia Jessel, portraying Monique, was unanimously praised by the reviewers, who were still reeling over her electric performance in Agatha Christie's *Witness for the Prosecution* in 1954.

Monique ran for sixty-three performances.

While not in the same league with the masterful Clouzot film or with the fine 1974 television remake, titled *Reflections of Murder*, *Monique* is nevertheless an effective melodrama of treachery and evil whose depraved characters are possessed by the base passions of lust, greed, and power.

An Americanized motion picture remake of *Diabolique* (1996) is a perverse simulation of the Clouzot original. An illogical, happier ending was imposed on the material. Isabelle Adjani portrays the wife, Sharon Stone plays the mistress, Chazz Palminteri is the sadistic schoolmaster, and Kathy Bates enacts a snooping sleuth, the counterpart of an elderly, retired male detective in the French film, played by Charles Vanel.

* * *

Monique is Dorothy Blankfort's sole credit on Broadway. However, her husband, Michael, began contributing to the New York theatrical scene in the 1930s. In 1933, he left his position as a psychologist at the state prison in New Jersey and began writing, directing, and producing Broadway and off-Broadway plays. He joined the new social drama movement by serving as assistant director on George Sklar's plays of protest, *Peace on Earth* and *Stevedore*, both in 1934. He contributed sketches and lyrics to the musical revue *Parade* in 1935, and in the following year he penned the drama *Crime*, about a labor strike, and the one-act *The Brave and the Blind*, about the Spanish civil war, in 1937.

Blankfort migrated to Hollywood and wrote many screenplays between 1939 and 1978. He adapted to the screen James Warwick's play *Blind Alley*, about a group of dangerous hoodlums who hide out in the home of a psychologist. He scripted a remake of *Blind Alley*, titled *The Dark Past*, in 1948.

Also in 1948, Blankfort wrote *The Act of Murder*, the story of a judge who decides to kill his terminally ill wife. He continued to write screenplays in a variety of genres, notably the war drama *Halls of Montezuma* (1950), an adaptation of Herman Wouk's *The Caine Mutiny* (1954), the South African adventure *Untamed* (1955), the Western *Tribute to a Bad Man* (1956), and the criminous *The Other Man* (1970).

* * *

Frenchmen Pierre Boileau (1906–1989) and Thomas Narcejac, aka Pierre Ayraud (1908–1998), collaborated on forty-three novels of suspense, of which eleven were translated into English, including *D'entre les morts* (1954), translated as *The Living and the Dead*, on which Alfred Hitchcock based his masterpiece *Vertigo* in 1958.

Scholar H. M. Klein writes in the *St. James Guide to Crime and Mystery Writers* that the bulk of the Boileau-Narcejac work is "centered on the victim (as opposed to the offender or the investigator), . . . sophisticated novels of suspense (rather than action), of internal, claustrophobic pressure, of subtle but overpowering terror as it grows in the individual consciousness, often in such a way as to merge with the existential *angst* of modern man fumbling about in a bleak hostile world, manipulated by forces beyond his control."[7] Klein asserts that "the females in Boileau-Narcejac are the harder, stronger-willed personalities."[8] Monique and Lucienne prove his theory.

Acting Edition: Samuel French, Inc. (in manuscript form).

Awards and Honors: Michael Blankfort served as president of the Writers Guild of America, West (1967–1969) and as governor of the Academy of Motion Picture Arts and Sciences (1969–1971).

Pierre Boileau won the prestigious Prix du Roman d'Adventures, awarded annually to the best detective novel, for *Le repos de Bacchus* (*The Sleeping Bacchus*) in 1938; Thomas Narcejac won it for *La mort est du voyage* (*Death on the Trip*) in 1948. Boileau and Narcejac's *Et mon tout est homme* (translated as *Choice Cuts*) won the Humor Noir prize in 1965.

NOTES

1. Often compared to Alfred Hitchcock, the French film director Henri-Georges Clouzot (1907–1977) specialized in movies of suspense. His credits include the crime-oriented *L'assassin habite au 21* (*The Murderer Lives at Number 21*, 1942), *Le Corbeau* (*The Raven*, 1943), *Le salaire de la peur* (*The Wages of Fear*, 1953), *Les diaboliques* (*Diabolique*, 1954), *Les espions* (*The Spies*, 1957), *La vérité* (*The Truth*, 1960), and *La prisonnière* (*Woman in Chains*, 1968). Clouzot's unfinished film *L'enfer* (*Inferno*, 1964), the story of mad, uncontrolled jealousy, was reconstructed, and its making is told in a 2009 documentary, released in the United States a year later.

2. *New York Journal-American*, October 23, 1957.

3. *Daily News*, October 23, 1957.

4. *Daily Mirror*, October 23, 1957.

5. *New York Times*, October 23, 1957.

6. *New York Post*, October 23, 1957.

7. Jay P. Pederson, ed., *St. James Guide to Crime and Mystery Writers*, 4th ed. (Detroit, MI: St. James Press, 1996), 89.

8. Jay P. Pederson, *St. James Guide to Crime and Mystery Writers*, 89.

Compulsion (1957)

Meyer Levin (United States, 1905–1981)

Nathan Leopold, age nineteen, and Richard Loeb, age eighteen, spoiled sons of Chicago millionaires, conspired to kill a fourteen-year-old boy, Bobby Franks, for the thrill of it. Intellectually brilliant, the two collegiates set out to commit the perfect crime. When caught and brought to trial, the counsel for the defense, Clarence Darrow, convinced the judge that the heinous act was rooted in a pathologically compulsive, uncontrollable urge, so instead of the chair, Leopold and Loeb were condemned to life imprisonment.

Author Meyer Levin based his 1956 novel, *Compulsion*, on the 1924 Leopold-Loeb *cause célèbre* trial, following the facts of the case closely while changing names. A year later he reenacted the event in a sprawling dramatization of twenty explicit scenes with fifty-one intense characters.

During the tryout preparations for the opening of *Compulsion* on Broadway, a feud ensued between author Levin and producer Michael Myerberg. According to behind-the-scenes mavens, it was Robert Thom who inked the final rendition of the play (billed in the program as the "Producer's Version"). Whoever wrote it, *Compulsion* captures what Brooks Atkinson of the *New York Times* calls the "morbid, horrible, degenerate, odious" elements of the case.[1]

The action zigzags through various locales. A prologue takes place in a prison cell, where Sid Silver, a middle-aged journalist, interviews Judd Steiner (Loeb), who after being incarcerated for thirty years is now eligible for parole; his partner Artie Straus (Leopold) died in jail. "We believed we could be gods," says Judd. "Gods! With power over life and death!"

A flashback transfers us to a river embankment where a murder has just been committed. Judd and Artie hide the body in a concrete sewer cistern—"It's as good as Edgar Allan Poe," chuckles Artie.

In order to sidetrack the police, the cocky young murderers send a ransom note to the victim's family and go out to celebrate in a speakeasy.

Artie and Judd keep reassuring one another that "our minds are superior; we must win," but two mistakes cause their downfall. A pair of spectacles found in the vicinity of the corpse was too big to fit the murdered boy, so it is concluded that they must have been dropped by the culprit; eventually the glasses are tracked to Judd. And an analysis of the ransom note leads the police to Judd's portable typewriter, where an identical "p" is out of line. The discovery of the instrument of death, a chisel with a taped blade, clinches the case against the killers.

Compulsion ruminates upon Judd's idolization of Artie and their homosexual relationship. Judd confesses to Dr. McNarry, director of the Washington Hospital for the Mentally Diseased, that he completely identified himself with Artie, would even watch with envy the food Artie ate and the drink going down his throat.

Defense Attorney Jonathan Wilk (Darrow) decides to have the pair plead guilty before a judge alone and present the accuseds' mental condition as a mitigating circumstance. The trial of Illinois State versus Judah Steiner Jr. and Arthur Straus, charged with the willful kidnapping and murder of Paulie Kessler (Franks), pits prosecution and defense psychiatrists against each other. Questions of juvenile delinquency and capital punishment are also subjects of the courtroom battle.

The judge's verdict, chiefly in consideration of the defendants' age, was life imprisonment instead of death.

* * *

Compulsion premiered at the Ambassador Theatre on October 24, 1957, to a mixed critical reception. John Chapman called the play "overpowering for a good stretch of the way—a story of crime to make the blood run cold."[2] Robert Coleman found the script "rough, raw and gripping. . . . It is melodramatic meat for those with strong stomachs. . . . It is as fascinating to watch as a cobra, head puffed up with venom, ready to strike. It is like sinking into a jazzed-up replica of *Dante's Inferno*."[3] John McClain greeted *Compulsion* as "the most ambitious production of the new season, generally a bounteous and brilliant exploration of the facts in the case, legal and psychological."[4]

Walter Kerr was less enthusiastic: "*Compulsion* lacks the dramatic shape to sustain, and pull together, its many virtues. . . . The materials are interesting, if coldly clinical; the incidental excitements are often real; the end result is a mammoth labyrinth from which no identifiable play emerges."[5] Frank Aston concluded, "Among the shortcomings are its great length and lack of suspense. You can't sit on the edge of your seat wondering how it will come out when everyone has known the answer these last 33 years—not for three hours you can't."[6] Richard Watts Jr. believed that *"Compulsion* talks itself into ineffectuality."[7]

Brooks Atkinson praised Peter Larkin's "stunning unit set in which a monstrous bridge presses down on the drama with a weight that is remorseless and sinister," and hailed the performances: "Roddy McDowall and Dean Stockwell play the two boys brilliantly—Mr. McDowall gay, antic and arrogant; Mr. Stockwell crushed, weak, gloomy."[8] In a follow-up article Atkinson bemoaned that the play "lasts more than three hours, which is a long time to be steeped in crime, perversion and morbidity. . . . If *Compulsion* were a serious work of theatre art, these actors could endow it with wisdom and beauty. They are less mechanical than the play in which they are appearing."[9]

Compulsion ran for 140 performances on Broadway. It was adapted to the screen in 1959, under Richard Fleischer's direction, with Dean Stockwell repeating the role of Judd, Bradford Dillman as Artie, and Orson Welles as attorney Wilk.

Other plays inspired by the Leopold-Loeb case include Patrick Hamilton's *Rope* (1929), filmed by Alfred Hitchcock in 1948, featuring John Dall and Farley Granger as the youthful murderers;[10] John Logan's *Never the Sinner*, which premiered in Chicago in 1985, played in Adelaide, Australia, in 1994, opened in London in 1990, and ran successfully off-Broadway in 1997; George Singer's *Leopold and Loeb*, produced by off-Broadway's Emerging Artists Theatre Company in 1997; *Thrill Me* (2003), with book, lyrics, and music by Stephen Dolginoff, whose conceit is that Nathan Leopold left behind the incriminating glasses purposely, counting on a verdict of life imprisonment and thus having the fickle Richard Loeb all to himself forever; and *Dickie and Babe* (2008), written and directed in Hollywood, California, by Daniel Henning after three years of immersing himself in court transcripts, medial reports, and other documents related to the case.

* * *

Born in 1905, Meyer Levin emerged from one of the crime-riddled sections of Chicago to become a reporter for the *Chicago Daily News* and a contributor to the literary magazine *The Menorah Journal* at the age of eighteen. When twenty-four, he drew on his experiences and published his first novel, *The Reporter*. In 1931, Levin wrote the novel *Yehuda*, about the tribulations of farmers on a kibbutz in Palestine. Six years later he examined assimilation among Chicago's second-generation Jews in *The Old Bunch*, regarded by some as his best novel.

In the 1930s, when ten steel mill strikers were shot down, Levin campaigned against Chicago police brutality and covered the event in *Citizens*, a 1940 novel admired by Ernest Hemingway.

During World War II, Levin made documentary films for the U.S. Office of War Information and became a war correspondent for the Jewish Telegraphic Agency. After the war he went to Palestine, joined the Haganah underground, and in 1947, a year before the creation of the state of Israel, he made two films in Hebrew: the drama *Bayit Avi* (*My Father's House*), about a boy's search for his parents, who disappeared after being held in a concentration camp; and the documentary *Lo Tafhidenu* (*The Unafraid*), also known as *The Illegals*, an account of a ship that smuggled Jewish escapees from war-torn Europe.[11]

Levin's *Compulsion* (1956), the chronicle of the Leopold and Loeb case, was the first "documentary novel," a style later used in Truman Capote's *In Cold Blood* and Norman Mailer's *The Executioner's Song*. Mailer referred to Levin as "one of the best American writers working in the realistic tradition."

Levin penned a powerful trilogy dealing with the Holocaust: *Eva* (1959), *The Fanatic* (1963), and *The Stronghold* (1965). His historical novels *The Settlers* (1972) and *The Harvest* (1978) are concerned with early pioneering life in pre-Israel Palestine.

In 1951, Levin became aware of "The Diary of Anne Frank" and conceived it as a play and movie. His dramatization was accepted for production but suddenly the producers decided that it was "unstageworthy" and mounted on Broadway an adaptation of the diary by Frances Goodrich and Albert Hackett. It became a big hit and spawned a major motion picture. Levin launched a twenty-year legal battle to have his rejected version performed, and he told the agonizing story in *The Obsession* (1974).[12]

Levin also wrote a series of nonfiction books about Judaism and its philosophy, and he composed an illustrated Haggadah for the Passover ceremony.

Acting Edition: Dramatists Play Service (in manuscript form).

Awards and Honors: The novel *Compulsion* was given a Special Edgar Allan Poe Award by the Mystery Writers of America in 1957.

NOTES

1. *New York Times*, October 25, 1957.
2. *Daily News*, October 25, 1957.
3. *Daily Mirror*, October 25, 1957.
4. *New York Journal-American*, October 25, 1957.
5. *New York Herald Tribune*, October 25, 1957.
6. *New York World-Telegram*, October 25, 1957.
7. *New York Post*, October 25, 1957.
8. *New York Times*, October 25, 1957.

9. *New York Times*, November 3, 1957.

10. In addition to the movie versions of *Rope* (1948) and *Compulsion* (1959), the low-budget, black-and-white *Swoon* (1992) was also inspired by the Leopold-Loeb story.

11. In 1978, Meyer Levin described what became of the passengers of the *Unafraid* in a thirty-eight-minute short made in the United States.

12. The saga of Mayer Levin's painstaking lobbying for his version of *The Diary of Anne Frank* is accounted in the play *Compulsion* by Rinne Groff, presented February 1 to March 13, 2011, at off Broadway's Public Theatre. Mandy Patinkin played a fictionalized version of Levin.

Murder Is My Business (1958)

James Reach (United States, 1909–1970)

Created by Brett Halliday (1904–1977), Michael Shayne is one of the most famous fictional private eyes—the two-fisted hero of more than sixty novels, countless short stories, his own magazine, and radio-television-film series. In 1958, the prolific American playwright James Reach adapted to the stage *Murder Is My Business*, a 1945 Halliday novel in which Shayne untangles a complicated case of blackmail and murder.

Murder Is My Business features not just one attractive blonde, but three, each deadlier than the other. The original novel deliberately tries to bamboozle the detective—and the reader—with mistaken identities among the three blondes. However, this device doesn't quite work in a medium where live actresses, by their respective appearances, make it clear who's who. The show's playbill alone, listing the names of the characters and the actors portraying them, eliminates some of the identity riddles that give the Halliday novel its who-done-it core (in a few rare instances—*Sleuth, Accomplice, Solitary Confinement*—enterprising playwrights have used the playbill to advantage by tricking the audience).

The stage version of *Murder Is My Business* is less a detective play than an action yarn. The audience is privy to the first murder, which takes place in Room 420 of Miami's Hibiscus Hotel. Here a cold-blooded blackmailer, Lanny Ford, stabs young Charles Barnes to death.

The victim's blonde sister, Mary, hysterical with fear, solicits the help of Michael Shayne. Mary relates to him that she has discovered her brother's corpse lying on the floor of their hotel room, but now the body has vanished. Worse, there isn't even a trace of blood to back up her story.

Shayne's investigation leads him to a confrontation with a scar-faced stranger, an encounter with Miami's police chief Will Gentry (a regular in the novels), and an entanglement with a dead man floating in Biscayne Bay.

Since plays rely mostly on dialogue and less on physical action, the majority of stage adaptations of whodunit novels are of the cozy type.

However, Reach managed to incorporate active moments such as plunging a knife into a victim's stomach; Shayne grabbing an intruder's wrist and twisting it to subdue him; the detective under the threatening muzzle of a gun, aimed at him by a man who declares, "I came up here for only one reason, Shayne—to kill you"; Shayne turning his desk over onto an adversary, whose pistol shot goes wild; Shayne ducking under a knife arc that barely misses his shoulder, then savagely punching the attacker; and, when a dangerous blonde throws herself at him, scratching and clawing, trying to get at his eyes with her fingernails, the tough PI says, "I never did this to a woman before, but—" and smacks her jaw with a short uppercut.

The action of *Murder Is My Business* begins at nine o'clock on an autumn evening and is over before midnight. The unit set consists of three hotel rooms in Miami, Florida: a bedroom in the Hibiscus Hotel; the living room of Lucy Hamilton's hotel suite; and the office in Michael Shayne's hotel apartment. Set change is accomplished by stage lights shifting from one area to another.

In the early phase of the Shayne saga, which began in 1939 with *Dividend on Death*, the detective was in love with beautiful Phyllis Brighton. By the third book, *The Uncomplaining Corpse* (1940), they were happily married. According to William L. DeAndrea in *Encyclopedia Mysteriosa*, "This, however, did not sit well with the movie studio that had bought the film rights to Shayne. Instead of adapting Halliday's books about the married detective, the studio ignored the wife and instead adapted stories from other writers, including Raymond Chandler. Economics, therefore, dictated the death of Phyllis Shayne between the eighth and ninth book. This paved the way for the introduction, in *Michael Shayne's Long Chance* (1944), of Lucy Hamilton, another beautiful young woman who loves Shayne, but doesn't get him to the altar. Instead, she follows him from the New Orleans setting of the novel back to Florida and settles in for a long stretch as Shayne's secretary."[1]

Playwright Reach took liberties with the employer-employee relationship between Mike Shayne and Lucy Hamilton by injecting a strong mutual romantic attachment. At the end, in the nick of time, Shayne rescues the rope-bound Lucy from the disturbed, gun-brandishing Nellie Paulson. The rugged detective now states, "That'll close it out for Will Gentry. And he ought to be along any minute now. So hurry up and kiss me before he walks in—"

LUCY: Kiss you?
MICHAEL: Yeah—I believe it's customary when two people become engaged.
LUCY: Why—Michael! (Closes her eyes and puckers up for him as he bends down to kiss her.)

The entire community of the hard-boiled detective story must have been reeling over that sentimental curtain.

* * *

Alongside Dashiell Hammett's Sam Spade and Raymond Chandler's Philip Marlowe, Mike Shayne is a resilient six-foot-one-inch redhead who has come to epitomize the hard-knuckled private eye in detective fiction. Like them, he is a lone wolf without a family; like them, he utilizes quick wit and mighty fists to escape scrapes; and like them, he is doggedly loyal to his clients.

Actor Wally Maher was heard as Shayne on radio from 1944 to 1946. Jeff Chandler was featured in a brief weekly radio series, "Michael Shayne, Private Detective," during the early 1950s. Richard Deming starred as Shayne in thirty-two NBC television programs in 1960–1961. Lloyd Nolan portrayed the private eye in a series of films for Twentieth Century–Fox, released during 1941 and 1942, not based on Brett Halliday works but rather on novels by such prominent mystery writers as Frederick Nebel, Clayton Rawson, and Raymond Chandler.

Murder Is My Business was filmed in 1946 by PRC with Hugh Beaumont as Shayne; it was a tepid sixty-four-minute program. Beaumont continued to portray the hard-nosed private eye in four additional B-movies.

"Historically, the Shayne series is significant," states Leonard Maltin in his *Movie and Video Guide*, "because it presented a self-assured (and down-to-earth) private investigator on the screen *before* the vogue for Sam Spade/ Philip Marlowe–type hard-boiled detectives flourished in the 1940s."[2]

* * *

Brett Halliday, pseudonym for Davis Dresser, was born in Chicago, Illinois, in 1904 and raised in Texas, where at the age of fourteen he ran away from home and joined the U.S. Army Cavalry. Dresser was educated at Tri-State College, Angola, Indiana, and spent his youth working in the rugged construction camps and oil fields of the Southwest and Mexico.

Certified in civil engineering, Dresser began writing in 1927, contributing short stories—crime, adventure, and western—to pulp magazines under varied pen names. As "Asa Baker," he published his first novel, *Mum's the Word for Murder*, in 1938. The following year came the first Michael Shayne novel, *Dividend on Death*. William L. DeAndrea, in *Encyclopedia Mysteriosa*, quotes Brett Halliday's account that he based the detective on "a huge, red-haired American with craggy features and bleak gray eyes" whom he had met while working in Mexico on an oil tanker.[3]

Halliday was a founding member of the Mystery Writers of America. In addition to his writing, he edited several important anthologies, including *Twenty Great Tales of Murder* (1951), *Dangerous Dames* (1955), *Big Time*

Mysteries (1958), *Murder in Miami* (1959), and two annuals: *Best Detective Stories of the Year* (1961, 1962). Halliday also edited the *Mike Shayne Mystery Magazine*, and with his first wife, mystery writer Helen McCloy, established the publishing firm Torquil & Company. Halliday's second and third wives, Kathleen Rollins and Mary Savage, were also authors.

Jacques Barzun and Wendell Hertig Taylor, in *A Catalogue of Crime*, noted that Halliday's plots were "complicated but often adroitly worked out, action is swift and rough, liquor flows like water (for Shayne nearly always brandy), and sex is somewhat surprisingly underplayed."[4]

Dennis Lynde, in *Twentieth-Century Crime and Mystery Writers*, maintains that Brett Halliday's fame "is probably secure, but the reputation has sometimes been tarnished by critics. It is true that Halliday was not a literary stylist, a penetrating psychologist, or a keen analyzer of current society. But he was a writer who knew a good story when he found one, and who knew how to tell that story. . . . Above all he knew something more important than everything else—he knew that his audience did not want literary style, or unique plot, or dazzling psychology—they wanted to see their hero in action."[5]

Michael Shayne's long career spanned from 1939 to 1976 in sixty-eight hardcover volumes and original paperbacks. Brett Halliday retired from writing in 1958; the rest of the books were ghostwritten, mostly by Robert Terrall, under the Halliday byline.

* * *

James Reach is among the prolific American dramatists whose plays have not been performed on Broadway but are constantly mounted by little theatre groups across the land. Other playwrights who share the same fate include Tim Kelly, Wilbur Braun, Jack Sharkey, Jules Tasca, Don Nigro, Fred Carmichael, Wall Spence, and F. Andrew Leslie.

No doubt influenced by Earl Derr Biggers' Charlie Chan, Reach began his four-decade playwriting career by introducing a proverb-quoting Oriental valet, Wing, in *One Mad Night* (1935) and *Lunatics at Large* (1936), two farcical melodramas in the tradition of *The Bat* and *The Cat and the Canary*.[6] Wing becomes a detective with the New York police in *The Case of the Squealing Cat* (1937), the yarn of a tyrannical old millionaire who is murdered before he can alter his will, and in *The Case of the Laughing Dwarf* (1938), wherein a munitions maker is found dead in his hotel room awash with his own blood, but with no apparent wound on his body!

In *The Green Ghost* (1935), a mysterious apparition roams the mansion of elderly Caroline Van West when she assembles all her living relatives to help draft her will. Soon the legendary Van West pearls are stolen! Similarly, the eccentric old millionaire Benjamin Garth summons his heirs to his isolated mountain mansion in *The Night Was Dark* (1940). Ghosts, vanishing guests, talking portraits, screams in the night—all these contribute to the bewilderment of hapless family members.

Danger—Girls Working! (1938) unfolds in a New York girls' boarding house, where a package of perfect uncut diamonds disappears from the safe. A ruthless and fiercely ambitious movie star is murdered in *Storm over Hollywood* (1946). The heroines of *The Clock Struck Twelve* (1949) are three young, struggling singers who find shelter in a lonely mansion during a savage storm, only to encounter a group of strange and sinister characters. Another isolated estate is the scene of devious action in *Dark Doings* (1951).

Once upon a Midnight (1948) is the story of Dusty Rhodes, an unemployed radio comic, and his gag writer, Rufus Nichols, whose car breaks down on a country road during a stormy night. They seek shelter at the Lame Duck Inn. The hotel has been deserted for several years, ever since a series of murders were committed there. On this wild night, a gaggle of oddly assorted characters converge on the Inn—including a hobo, a professional medium, a girl in a hypnotic trance, and the guardian of a young heiress whose kidnapping has become a national sensation—for a blend of chills, thrills, and comedy scenes. Playwright Reach returned twice more to the plot device of a radio comic and his sidekick (albeit with different names) stranded on the road during a storm. In *Murder, She Says!* (1952) the duo escape into Good Luck Lodge, an isolated retreat near the Canadian border, only to get entangled with another assemblage of bizarre people and a double murder. In *Black Oaks* (1953), at a country estate "situated several miles from the nearest community," they encounter an escaped murderer, solve a past homicide, and find romance.

With three more thrillers, 1953 proved to be a banner year for Reach. A happy couple plan to spend their two-week honeymoon in a far-removed country house that is supposed to be unoccupied, and they find themselves *Afraid of the Dark* as they get enmeshed in a dastardly spy plot. A novice policewoman is assigned to her first case, the brutal murder of a nurse, in *Women in White*. *The Girl in the Rain* is found lying unconscious on the road and seems to be suffering from amnesia—but is her malady a sham? Could she be the notorious killer sought by the police for the poisoning of several wealthy husbands?

Dragnet (1956) is an adaptation of the popular NBC radio-television series, depicting hard-boiled Sergeant Joe Friday of the LAPD and his sidekick Officer Frank Smith on the case of a locked-room murder—the victim is found shot in a study with the door bolted on the inside and the windows shuttered.[7]

Bear Witness (1970) explores a dilemma: should a law-abiding citizen cooperate with the police when he sees a crime committed? In the middle-class neighborhood of a large city, a widow and her children witness a brutal gangland murder and determine to get involved and identify the killer. The decision results in a harrowing ordeal for the family.

Reach had an affinity for courtroom dramas. *The Missing Witness* (1936) pictures three successive days in the trial of an attractive musical star for the murder of a district attorney. *You, the Jury* (1958) invites the audience to act as jurors and vote on whether young Barbara Scott, on trial for the first-degree murder of her gambler-employer, is innocent or guilty. *We're All Guilty* (1962) takes place in a juvenile court, where a compassionate judge conducts a hearing concerning a seventeen-year-old, the son of well-to-do parents, who is under indictment for deliberately sideswiping a car, causing it to overturn and injuring its occupants—two girls—one of them seriously.

Reach also adapted to the stage the motion pictures *Patterns*, a tense drama dealing with the corrosive pressures of the world of giant corporations, and the more delicate *David and Lisa*, the story of two mentally disturbed adolescents. From television, Reach borrowed the comedies *My Friend Irma*, about the big-city misadventures of a ditzy stenographer from Minnesota, and *Dear Phoebe*, covering the hectic events that take place in the editorial offices of a metropolitan tabloid.

Acting Edition: Samuel French, Inc.

NOTES

1. William L. DeAndrea, *Encyclopedia Mysteriosa* (New York: Prentice Hall, 1994), 325.

2. *Leonard Maltin's 2002 Movie and Video Guide* (New York: Signet, 2001), 895.

3. William L. DeAndrea, *Encyclopedia Mysteriosa* (New York: Prentice Hall, 1994), 325.

4. Jacques Barzun and Wendell Hertig Taylor, *A Catalogue of Crime* (New York: Harper & Row, 1971), 221.

5. John M. Reilly, ed., *Twentieth-Century Crime and Mystery Writers* (New York: St. Martin's Press, 1980), 718.

6. The madcap antics of the classic melodramas *The Bat* (1920) and *The Cat and the Canary* (1922) are described in Amnon Kabatchnik, *Blood on the Stage*, 1900–1925 (Lanham, MD: Scarecrow Press, 2008), 276–280, 303–307.

7. The "impossible" situation in a crime scene was invented by the father of the detective story, Edgar Allan Poe, in *The Murders in the Rue Morgue* (1841; throttled bodies found in the chimney of a locked room). The technique was utilized by Israel Zangwill in *The Big Bow Mystery* (1892; a victim with a cut throat is discovered in a shuttered bedroom), by Arthur Conan Doyle in *The Story of The Lost Special* (1898; the disappearance of a train from a railroad line guarded at both ends), and by Gaston Leroux in *The Mystery of the Yellow Room* (1912; a woman found mortally wounded in a sealed room surrounded by witnesses who claim that no one has entered or left it).

Among the better known, and fiendishly ingenious, practitioners of the hermetically sealed puzzles were English authors Edgar Wallace, Margery Allingham, E. C. Bentley, Anthony Berkeley, G. K. Chesterton, and Agatha Christie. American writers who concocted impossible predicaments include Melville Davisson Post, Ellery Queen, S. S. Van Dine, and John Dickson Carr/Carter Dickson, the foremost exponent of the "locked room" mystery.

On stage, locked-room murders were depicted in *In the Next Room* (1923), dramatized by Eleanor Robson and Harriet Ford from Burton E. Stevenson's 1912 novel, *The Mystery of the Boule Cabinet*; *The Canary Murder Case* (1928), adapted by Walton Butterfield and Lee Morrison from S. S. Van Dine's 1927 novel of the same name; *Alibi*, aka *The Fatal Alibi* (1932) by Michael Morton, based on Agatha Christie's 1926 novel, *The Murder of Roger Ackroyd*; *The Locked Room* (1933) by Herbert Ashton Jr.; and *Busman's Honeymoon* (1936) by Dorothy L. Sayers and Muriel St. Clare Byrne.

Jane Eyre (1958)

Huntington Hartford
(United States, 1911–2008)

The pseudonymous publication of *Jane Eyre* in 1847 by "Currer Bell" proved a sensational success, selling out within three months. The public clamored for any information on the identity of the mysterious author, and speculation was rampant. Charlotte Brontë was identified only after the gothic novel had gone through several editions. By that time, it was already clear that she had written a classic of English literature.[1]

Through the years, *Jane Eyre* has been dramatized by various hands. A 1958 version by Huntington Hartford confines the sprawling proceedings to one Tudor room in Thornfield Hall, the manor house of Edward Fairfax Rochester, on the moors near the village of Millcote, England. The home's gloomy atmosphere registers immediately when the audience sees a twisted, leafless tree standing outside the window.

There's a massive fireplace in the left wall. A circular staircase leads to the upstairs bedrooms. At right a door opens to the kitchen and servants' quarters. The wind is howling across the moors.

The adaptation skips the early part of the Brontë novel in which the child Jane Eyre, an orphan, endures the brutal treatment of her aunt, Sarah Reed, and the constant bullying of her cousins. At the age of ten, Jane is sent to Lowood School, a charity institution run by Mr. Brocklehurst, a stingy, insensitive minister. There she thrives on academic success and, after completing her studies, serves two years as a teacher. When she decides to move on to another position, she advertises in the *Herald*. There is one reply—from Mrs. Alice Fairfax of Thornfield Hall. Jane decides to interview for the job of governess for the master's ward, ten-year-old Adèle Varens, who speaks French sprinkled with newly learned bits of English. The master of Thornfield, Edward Rochester, often travels, while Fairfax runs the house.

In the first scene, Jane, described as "a plain, direct girl of about nineteen, not pretty, but attractive in a disarming way," meets the household servants—the maid Leah, the coachman Gregory, and Grace Poole, whose duties are unclear. Jane establishes an immediate rapport with the middle-aged Mrs. Fairfax and the precocious Adèle. Fairfax explains that the master, Mr. Rochester, "out of the goodness of his heart, has taken in the poor little waif." Adèle's mother, a French dancer, abandoned her, and "there are some who say that he and the mother. . . ."

Jane relates that on her way to Thornfield, when she was crossing the footbridge, a man on horseback almost knocked her down, his horse slipped, and he was flung from the saddle. As they converse, a scream echoes from the upper stories. Little Adèle says that it must be Grace Poole, who is known to drink heavily.

The sound of horse's hooves is heard, dogs bark furiously, and Edward Rochester enters—"a tall, well-built man of about forty." He walks with a slight limp and growls that "some wretched little sprite of a girl" bewitched his horse, and he had to ride all the way to Dr. Courcey "to get this damned leg attended to." Despite their unfortunate first encounter, the brusque Mr. Rochester seems to like Jane's honest, direct demeanor and hires her as governess.

Months pass. A newcomer makes an appearance—Richard Mason, "dark and swarthy with flashing eyes and a continental charm that covers his strange behavior." Mason meets Grace Poole at the bottom of the staircase, hands her money, and she gives him a key. He runs upstairs.

Several guests arrive for a dinner party—Lord Theodore Ingram, his dowager wife, and their daughter Blanche, a local beauty. As the Ingrams chitchat, it becomes clear that they have hatched a plan for Blanche to marry their host. A society fortune hunter, Blanche pretends to be in love with Rochester but is interested only in his money.

After the Ingrams depart, Mason comes down the stairs, his shoulder bleeding. Rochester sends Jane for a sponge and some bandages. He grabs Mason by the throat and barks, "One word in front of the girl and you will bear the consequences." Mason groans in pain and whispers, "She got hold of a knife, Edward. It was terrifying. . . . She sprang at me like a tiger. She bit me." Rochester tells Mason that this must be his last visit to Thornfield Hall; he has to return to Jamaica. He, Rochester, will take care of the woman upstairs. He has done it for fifteen years, and will continue to do so, he says.

The governess, Jane, and the master, Rochester, fall in love. To her astonishment, he proposes marriage. She dismisses Mrs. Fairfax's concern about the question of social position and the great difference in their ages, and accepts. But Jane has a premonition that something is wrong. She may have dreamed it, but during the night she felt that someone entered her room. Worse, Jane thinks she saw the reflection of a "discolored, savage face" in the wall mirror.

Things come to a head during the wedding ceremony. Clergyman Wood is conducting the ritual when a London solicitor, Briggs, bursts in and declares, "This marriage must not take place." Jane is shocked to learn that Rochester already has a wife, Bertha (Richard Mason's sister), who is mad and resides in the attic (the original novel suggests that Bertha, a Creole woman from Spanish Town, Jamaica, inherited her affliction from her mother). In order to protect Bertha from the horrors of an asylum, where she would be chained and whipped, Rochester locked her in the third story of Thornfield, with Grace Poole as her keeper. Jane learns that Bertha occasionally escaped her confinement, perpetrating violence when she got loose.

Stunned by the new turn of events, Jane flees from the manor and takes the morning coach. She is not there when the deranged wife sets the place on fire and dies in the pyre.

The last scene transpires a year later. Jane returns and realizes that the Hall has been damaged by fire. Mrs. Fairfax tells her that "the poor demented creature" kindled Jane's bed and the fire spread. Mr. Rochester carried Adèle to safety and returned to the burning wing in a hopeless attempt to save Bertha.

Soon Jane learns that in the fire, Rochester suffered a mangled hand and was blinded. She reveals her presence, kneels by him, declares, "I love you; I'll always love you," and asks, "Edward, will you marry me?" Rochester orders Mrs. Fairfax to prepare a feast of wild fowl, brandied peaches, and delicate herbs, and embraces Jane tightly as the curtain descends.

* * *

Jane Eyre opened at New York's Belasco Theatre on May 1, 1958. The next-morning critics expressed divided opinions. John McClain felt that "*Jane Eyre* is still a solid and appealing love story" and found in the play "many moments of valid pathos."[2] John Chapman wrote, "The company of *Jane Eyre* is admirable. Eric Portman puts dramatic urgency in his portrayal of the brooding, mysterious Rochester. Blanche Yurka is in a role cut to fit as the firm-handed housekeeper. And a newcomer from London, Jan Brooks, is a genuine find for the part of Jane Eyre."[3] Robert Coleman admired Ben Edwards's design of a manor house "that is at once aristocratic and sufficiently atmospheric for eerie and horrendous events."[4]

The naysayers were Richard Watts Jr. ("The play isn't a botch, but it hasn't steady interest, either"[5]), Frank Ashton ("As a play it's far more ridiculous than it is as a novel"[6]), and Brooks Atkinson ("The play is a scrap-pile of old-fashioned stage machinery—the wind machine, hoof-beats, the fireplace bellows blowing up a fraudulent blaze, lugubrious light, arch acting, mincing steps up and down the endless flight of steps"[7]).

Jane Eyre ran for fifty-two performances, losing the entire investment of close to $500,000, the costliest nonmusical to reach Broadway until that date.

* * *

Born in New York City in 1911 and educated at Harvard University, George Huntington Hartford II was an heir to the A&P supermarket, which at one point was the largest retail empire in the world. He headed a number of other business enterprises and was a renowned philanthropist.

Hartford coproduced the 1969 Broadway production of *Does a Tiger Wear a Necktie?* by Don Peterson. A racially charged drama about teen drug addiction, it ran at the Belasco Theatre for nine previews and thirty-nine performances, and launched the career of Al Pacino. Huntington Hartford Productions made several films, including 1949's *Africa Screams*, in which comedians Bud Abbott and Lou Costello go on safari.

Married three times, Hartford lived in Lyford Cay, the Bahamas, with his daughter, Juliet, where he died in 2008, at the age of 97.

* * *

An early stage version of *Jane Eyre*, by John Brougham (1814–1880), a pioneering, prolific Irish-American actor-playwright, was presented by New York's Laura Keene's Varieties in 1856, with Laura Keene in the title role and George Jordan as Edward Fairfax Rochester. Faithful to the Brontë novel, the five acts take place in various locales, beginning at the Lonwood Academy, where the windows are barred "prison like," and orphan Jane Eyre is maltreated by the mean, miserly minister, Mr. Brocklehurst. Eight years pass, and Jane advertises in the *Herald* for a position. On her way to a job interview, she causes a rider to sharply rein his horse, fall to the ground, and hurt his foot (this scene is skipped in most adaptations of the novel). The man, gruff and cursing, turns out to be Jane's prospective employer, Edward Rochester, who is looking for a governess for his six-year-old ward, Adèle.

The action shifts to the interior of Rochester's manor, where a group of pompous aristocrats are waiting for him. All are after Rochester's money, and together they concoct a plan to have the host marry the beautiful, haughty Blanche Ingram. Brougham's version, more than others, throws satirical, savage darts at the Ingram family and their society friends.

From the very first production, many dramatizations of *Jane Eyre* were flawed. The drama critic of the *New York Times* said in 1870 that to try "to copy" the classic novel on the stage "is something like painting the color of the dying dolphin or clutching a fallen star. We may praise the daring of the attempt, but not often the results." While rejecting an adaptation by Charlotte Birch-Pfeiffer, the reviewer found Mme. Seebach's Jane Eyre "a bold and stirring piece of art. The changes of age and idiosyncracy between the acts are admirably denoted, and many passages are worked up with an energy and a pathos that win plaudits from the coldest of judges."[8]

Four years later, the *New York Times* welcomed another "reproduction" of *Jane Eyre*, an "excellent dramatization of Charlotte Brontë's famous novel" by an anonymous writer, mounted at the Union Square Theatre with "elegance and completeness. . . . Miss Charlotte Thompson gave her usual portraiture of the heroine."[9] In 1876, Thompson reprised the role at the Brooklyn Theatre "and proved that she had lost none of the fervor with which she formerly delineated the personage of the orphan girl."[10]

The next actress to triumph in the role of Jane Eyre was Maggie Mitchell, who, according to the *New York Times*, demonstrated "power over an audience" in an adaptation by Clifton W. Tayleure, which played at New York's Grand Opera House in 1885. "Miss Mitchell is well supported by Mr. Charles Abbott, who invests the character of Rochester with interest and sympathy. The supporting company is better than is usually found in a star combination, and the scenery is good."[11]

An adaptation of *Jane Eyre*, written and directed by Phyllis Birkett, opened at the Theatre Royal in Huddersfield, England, on September 12, 1929, and two years later made it to London's Kingsway Theatre, running twenty performances. A more notable dramatization of the Brontë novel was penned by Helen Jerome in 1936. Jerome had made a name for herself a year earlier with a stage version of Jane Austen's *Pride and Prejudice*, which debuted at New York's Plymouth Theatre on November 5, 1935, to critical acclaim, ran for 219 showings, and leaped across the Atlantic to London, where it opened at the St. James Theatre for a lengthy engagement.[12] Jerome's *Jane Eyre* premiered at the Queen's Theatre, London, on October 13, 1936, with Curigwen Lewis (Jane) and Reginald Tate (Rochester). It ran for 299 performances. The play's success prompted the Theatre Guild to option it for a Broadway production. Katharine Hepburn (1907–2003), reeling from several motion-picture box-office duds, was cast in the lead with an assurance of a long tryout tour to ready the show for New York. *Jane Eyre* played to full houses and smashed all road-show records by pulling in $340,000 by the end of its run. In December 1937, following a performance at Boston's Colonial Theatre, the *New York Times* praised Helen Jerome for deriving "from the 89-year-old novel, a play with pleasantly Victorian atmosphere, considerable quaint humor, a large measure of charm, and a mingling of sentiment and melodrama."[13]

The provincial reviewers showered Hepburn with personal accolades. However, perhaps not confident enough to risk the darts and arrows of the New York critics, Hepburn left the show and went to Hollywood; this caused the production to close its doors.[14] In 1938, Hepburn felt obliged to return to the Guild in *The Philadelphia Story*, as socialite Tracy Lord, and rejuvenated her then-tottering career.

A dramatization of *Jane Eyre* by Marjorie Carleton[15] confines the action to a single box-set depicting a reception room in the country home of Edward Rochester. A short flight of stairs leads to a door centered upstage, and arches up right and up left serve as exits to the rest of the house.

Candles on the mantelpiece supply the illumination for night scenes. This version begins with Jane arriving for an interview for the position of governess in which the child does not appear. The Carleton adaptation was published by the Walter H. Baker Company in 1936. That same year, the Northwestern Press published *Jane Eyre: A Romantic Play in Three Acts* by Wall Spence.[16] Here too the entire action unfolds in one setting—a spacious drawing room at Thornfield Hall. This adaptation is more melodramatic than most, punctuating the action with frequent appearances by mad Bertha, who laughs maniacally and threatens Jane, "You will never marry him—never, never!" She also attacks her brother Mason and sets the place on fire. A unique character is that of an old, wrinkled gypsy woman, Zita, who in a cracked voice predicts that Blanche Ingram's plan to marry Rochester will go "poof" while Jane Eyre's "clouds" will give way to "a rainbow" of happiness.

Mesmerized playwrights kept adapting *Jane Eyre* to the stage throughout the twentieth century, generally faithful to the Brontë original novel but inserting nuances and wrinkles of their own. Notable dramatizations were by Pauline Phelps (published by Wetmore Declamation Bureau, 1941); Jane Kendall (first produced by The Canterbury Players, Chicago, Illinois, on April 26 and 29, 1945, and published that year by the Dramatic Publishing Company); Constance Cox (adapted from a highly successful television serial broadcast by the BBC during February and March 1956 and first produced on stage on July 9, 1956, at Her Majesty's Theatre in Carlisle, England, and published by J. Garnet Miller, Ltd., 1959); Peter Coe (who directed his version for the Chichester Festival Theatre, July 23–September 26, 1986); Fay Weldon (produced by the Birmingham Repertory, September 30–October 29, 1986); Willis Hall (presented at the Crucible Theatre, Sheffield, England, November 5–28, 1992, and published by Samuel French, Ltd., 1994); Charles Vance (first presented at the Forum Theatre, Billingham, England, on February 20, 1996, and published by Samuel French, Ltd., later that year); Robert Johanson (first produced at the Paper Mill Playhouse, Millburn, New Jersey, in February 1997 and published by Dramatic Publishing, 1998); and Polly Teale (first performed by Shared Experience Theatre Company at the Wolsey Theatre, Ipswich, England, on September 4, 1997, and published by Nick Hern Books, 1998, arriving at the Brooklyn Academy of Music in February 2000).

A two-act ballet based on *Jane Eyre* was created by the London Children's Ballet in 1994, and a ballet named *Jane* premiered at the Civic Auditorium, Kalamazoo, Michigan, in 2007. An opera inspired by Brontë's novel was composed by John Joubert between 1987 and 1997, with libretto by Kenneth Birkin. Another opera, created by English composer Michael Berkeley with a libretto by David Malouf, was first presented by Music Theatre Wales at the Cheltenham Festival in 2000.

A musical version of *Jane Eyre*, with book by John Caird, music and lyrics by Paul Gordon, bounced around the regional circuit for several years before opening at Broadway's Brooks Atkinson Theatre on December 3, 2000. Marla Schaffel and James Barbour played Jane and Rochester. The *New York Times* critic, Bruce Weber, paid tribute to the original novel, "a magnificent melodrama, a horrid Gothic romance set in dark chambers," but found the musical "gloomy and mundane," capturing only "few of the richly available nuances." Weber appreciated the "very handsome, if very dark" physical aspects of the show, notably "a techno-sleek beauty" provided by British scene designer John Napier, but scoffed at "a tepid score" and "a fitful and hurried pace . . . an overall gallop through Brontë's significant plot that has the teasing quality of a movie trailer. . . . It's a failing that the directors have used the Brontë story for mere stage directions. The result is that a great adult fable has been attenuated to the thinness of a children's story."[17] The $7.3 million musical ran for 209 performances. It emerged in 2003 at the Mountain View Center for the Performing Arts in Mountain View, California. Another musical version, with book by Jana Smith and Wayne R. Scott, score by Jana Smith and Brad Roseborough, premiered in 2008 at the Lifehouse Theatre, Redlands, California. A Jane Eyre–inspired symphony by Michel Bose premiered in Bandol, France, on October 11, 2009.

Jane Eyre has been transferred to the screen many times. Silent film versions were made in 1910, 1914, 1915 (two films, one released as *The Castle of Thornfield*), 1918 (called *Woman and Wife*), 1921, and 1926 (German, *Orphan of Lowood*). *Jane Eyre* talkies include a 1934 version featuring Colin Clive and Virginia Bruce; 1943's *I Walked with a Zombie*, a classic horror film loosely based on Brontë's novel; 1944's much admired rendition, scripted by John Houseman and Aldous Huxley, starring Orson Welles and Joan Fontaine; a 1956 version made in Hong Kong; and a 1963 version shot in Mexico, called *The Secret*. George C. Scott and Susannah York played Rochester and Jane in a 1970 made-for-TV movie that was released theatrically in Europe, while William Hurt and Charlotte Gainsborough undertook the roles in a 1996 Franco Zeffirelli film. A new motion picture version of *Jane Eyre*, featuring Mia Wasikowska in the title role, Michael Fassbender as Edward Rochester, and Judi Dench as housekeeper Mrs. Fairfax, was released in March 2011.

A live television broadcast of *Jane Eyre* was produced by Westinghouse Studio One in 1952. Additional TV adaptations, on British and American television, took place in 1956 and 1961. BBC aired dramatizations of *Jane Eyre* in 1963, 1973, 1982, 1983, and 2006.

* * *

The Brontë sisters—Charlotte, Emily, and Anne—are the heroines of *The Brontës* by Alfred Sangster, a popular venture that premiered at the Repertory Theatre in Sheffield, England, in May 1932 and moved to London's Royalty Theatre a year later, running 238 performances. The three sisters and their brother Branwell are spotlighted in *Wild Dreamers* by Clemence Dane, a biographical drama that opened at West End's Apollo Theatre on May 26, 1933, with Diana Wynyard as Charlotte and Emlyn Williams as Branwell.[18] In 1934, the Birmingham Repertory Theatre produced John Davison's *The Brontës of Haworth Parsonage*, which focuses on the decline and fall of Branwell Brontë and the rise and triumph of Charlotte Brontë. *Branwell*, a play by Martyn Richards about the sisters' lesser-known brother, was published by Longmans Ltd. in 1948. Margaret Webster arranged, adapted, and performed excerpts from works by and about Charlotte, Emily, and Anne Brontë, under the title *The Brontës*, shown at off-Broadway's Theatre de Lys in October 1963 (two performances) and at the Phoenix Theatre two months later (twenty performances). The one-woman show traveled to London's New Arts Theatre in January 1964 for a limited run. *Wide Sargasso Sea*, a 1966 novel by Jean Rhys, a prequel to *Jane Eyre* set in Jamaica and focusing on Rochester's deranged Creole wife, was filmed in 1993, made into an opera in 1997, and adapted by BBC Wales for television in 2006.

William Luce wrote *Currer Bell, Esq.* (Charlotte Brontë's nom de plume) as a radio play for the actress Julie Harris to perform on WGBH's *Masterpiece Radio Theatre*. It was subsequently filmed with Harris under the direction of Delbert Mann. Luce then turned the work into a stage play, retitled *Brontë: A Solo Portrait of Charlotte Brontë*, which Harris performed at benefits, colleges, and universities. With Charles Nelson Reilly as director, *Brontë* formally opened at the Marines Memorial Theatre in San Francisco on January 20, 1988. Similarly, actress Jill Alexander toured with a one-woman show about Charlotte Brontë in 2003.

Warner Brothers filmed a strong drama about the lives, loves, and literary triumphs of the Brontë family, *Devotion* (1946), with Olivia de Havilland (Charlotte), Ida Lupino (Emily), Nancy Coleman (Anne), and Arthur Kennedy (Branwell).

An imagined tale about the Brontë sisters, *Becoming Jane Eyre*, was penned by Sheila Kohler in 2009. At its center are Charlotte and the writing of *Jane Eyre*. Laura Joh Rowland launched a Victorian-era mystery series with *The Secret Adventures of Charlotte Brontë* (2008), in which Charlotte travels to London to clear her name of the false accusation of plagiarism, unintentionally witnesses a murder, and finds herself embroiled in a dangerous chain of events. A 2010 sequel, *Bedlam: The Further Secret Adventures of Charlotte Brontë*, begins with a tour that Charlotte takes of the most sinister institution in London, the Bedlam Insane Asylum, and continues with a dangerous quest to unravel a secret that high-powered conspirators will kill to protect.[19]

NOTES

1. In September 2010, Bauman Rare Books in New York City offered a first edition of *Jane Eyre*, three volumes bound in calf-gilt, for $36,000.

2. *New York Journal-American*, May 2, 1958.

3. *Daily News*, May 2, 1958.

4. *Daily Mirror*, May 2, 1958.

5. *New York Post*, May 2, 1958.

6. *New York World-Telegram*, May 2, 1958.

7. *New York Times*, May 2, 1958.

8. *New York Times*, October 6, 1870.

9. *New York Times*, November 17, 1874.

10. *New York Times*, February 8, 1876.

11. *New York Times*, November 17, 1885.

12. Helen Jerome's adaptation of *Pride and Prejudice* served as the basis for MGM's celebrated 1940 picture, starring Greer Garson and Laurence Olivier, and for the 1959 Broadway musical *First Impressions*, with book by Abe Burrows, featuring Polly Bergen, Hermione Gingold, and Farley Granger (Alvin Theatre, March 19, 1959—eighty-four performances). Jerome's third costume drama, *Maria Walewska*, was adapted to the screen under the title *Conquest* (1937), with Greta Garbo as the Polish countess who had a passionate but doomed affair with Napoleon Bonaparte (played by Charles Boyer).

13. *New York Times*, January 3, 1937.

14. Katharine Hepburn's costar in the tryout run of *Jane Eyre*, playing Edward Rochester, was British actor Dennis Hoey (1893–1960), best known for the role of Inspector Lestrade in Universal's Sherlock Holmes films. Hoey adapted to the stage Anthony Gilbert's whodunit *Something Nasty in the Woodshed* (aka *Mystery in the Woodshed*), under the title *The Haven*, and starred in the play as series sleuth Arthur Crook. *The Haven* opened at Broadway's Playhouse Theatre on November 13, 1946, was lambasted by the critics, and closed after five performances.

15. Marjorie Carleton (1897–1964) was the American author of half a dozen suspense novels published between 1947 and 1963. Detective literature scholars Jacques Barzun and Wendell Hertig Taylor, in *A Catalogue of Crime*, find exceptional merit in Carleton's novels *A Bride Regrets* (1950) and *Vanished* (1955).

16. Inspired, no doubt, by old-dark-house classics like *Seven Keys to Baldpate*, *The Bat*, and *The Cat and the Canary*, Wall Spence specialized in wild melodramas unleashed in isolated gothic manors, situated over steep cliffs, complete with shadowy nooks, secret panels, and underground passages. The proceedings unravel continuously during a thunder-and-lightning storm or on the night of the full moon. The telephone line is cut, the lights flicker and go out at critical moments, heavy footsteps emanate from above, ghastly faces peer through windows, long arms reach out from corners, bodies fall out of closets, and eerie voices seem

to issue from nowhere. Often, the plot hinges on a will read at midnight or a treasure chest hidden in a fireplace compartment. Villains nicknamed "The Phoenix" (*Whispering Walls*, 1935) or "The Owl" (*Mystery in Blue*, 1942) stalk beautiful women. Suspicious characters turn out to be masquerading detectives. Denouements reveal the identity of blackguards with little surprise. There is generally a lame attempt to logically explain the extraordinary happenings. Broad comedy is provided by frightened maids, scatterbrained spinsters, and buffoonish sheriffs. A spunky female reporter outwits a gang of rum-runners in *Ghostly Fingers* (1932). A philosophical Chinese houseboy, emulating Charlie Chan, solves the murder of an atomic scientist in *The Face on the Stairs* (1948). A medium attempting to communicate with the dead provides a pivotal clue in *How Betsy Butted In* (1954). While Spence's plays were generally produced by community theatres and summer-stock companies, one burlesque-mystery, *The House of Fear*, made it to Broadway's Republic Theatre on October 7, 1929. It is the tale of a psychic, Mme. Zita, who conducts a séance to frighten a murderer into a confession of the crime for which her son has been imprisoned in Sing Sing. The play ran for forty-eight performances, during which Wall Spence appeared across the street in the whodunit *Subway Express* as one of the suspects in a baffling murder case.

17. *New York Times*, December 11, 2000.

18. Clemens Dane (1888–1965), a pseudonym of Winifred Ashton, an English dramatist and novelist, began her career in the theatre as an actress. The success of her first play, *A Bill of Divorcement* (1921), which deals sympathetically with the problem of divorce on the grounds of insanity, led her to give up acting and concentrate on writing. Her better-known plays include *Will Shakespeare* (1921), *Naboth's Vineyard* (1925), *Granite* (1926), *Mariners* (1927), *Gooseberry Fool* (1929), *Moonlight Is Silver*, aka *Here Lies Truth* (1934), *Come of Age* (1934), *Cousin Muriel* (1940), *The Saviours* (1942), and *Eighty in the Shade* (1959). She also adapted to the stage *L'Aiglon* (1934, from the French play by Edmond Rostand), *The Happy Hypocrite* (1936, from a short story by Max Beerbohm), and *Herod and Mariamne* (1938, from the German of Friedrich Hebbel). For radio, Dane dramatized Schiller's *Don Carlos* and *Mary Stuart*. For the movies, she collaborated on the screenplays of *Anna Karenina* (1935), *The Amateur Gentleman* (1936), *Fire over England* (1937), *Sidewalks of London* (1938), *Perfect Strangers* (1945, winning an Academy Award for Best Story), *Bride of Vengeance*, aka *Mask for Lucretia* (1949), and *The Angel with the Trumpet* (1950). Dane collaborated with Helen Simpson on the superior detective novels *Enter Sir John* (1928), *Author Unknown* (1930), and *Re-Enter Sir John* (1932). Alfred Hitchcock filmed the first one as *Murder!* (1930), featuring Herbert Marshall as amateur sleuth Sir John Menier.

19. Novels inspired by *Jane Eyre* include *Rebecca* (1938) by Daphne du Maurier; *The Ivy Tree* (1961) by Mary Stewart; and *Jenna Starborn* (2002), a science-fiction saga by Sharon Shinn. Jasper Fforde's *The Eyre Affair*, a fantasy set in England in 1985, is the story of a female detective who pursues an archvillain who has kidnapped Jane Eyre from the pages of the Charlotte Brontë novel.

Verdict (1958)

Agatha Christie (England, 1890–1976)

Agatha Christie considered *Verdict* the best play she had ever written, with the possible exception of *Witness for the Prosecution*. Yet *Verdict* was also her greatest debacle. "Perhaps the most startling event in the London theatre recently was the booing of a new play by Agatha Christie at the opening performance," blazed a Reuters dispatch.[1]

"It failed, I think, because it was *not* a detective story or a thriller," responded Christie in her autobiography. "It was a play that concerned murder, but its real background and point was that an idealist is always dangerous, a possible destroyer of those who love him—and poses the question of how far you can sacrifice, not yourself, but those you love, to what you believe in, even though they do not."[2]

The idealist in *Verdict* is Professor Karl Hendryk, a political refugee from Eastern Europe, now residing in a flat in Bloomsbury. Hendryk is a scholar, a teacher, and a humanitarian. He is taking care of his wheel-chair-bound wife, Anya, with the help of a longtime secretary, Lisa Koletzky. Karl and Lisa are in love but they do not confess it to one another, for both are devoted to Anya.

Into their world swoops Helen Rollander, a beautiful, self-assured, amoral woman of twenty-three. A pupil of Karl, Helen is infatuated with her professor. Described by her wealthy, proud father as "the kind of girl who doesn't take no for an answer," Helen declares her love for Karl, pooh-poohs his claim that his wife is dearer to him than anyone else, and empties a bottle of strong medicine into Anya's glass of water.

Helen watches as Anya's head drops sideways onto the pillow. Hesitant, she takes the old woman's wrist to check the pulse. After a moment, she picks up the glass, wipes it with her handkerchief, leans over and puts it carefully into Anya's left hand. She gently presses Anya's right hand round the medicine bottle and places it on a side table.

Helen looks around, crosses quickly to the sofa for her bag and gloves, flings open the door and exits.

A few days later, Helen confides to Karl that she killed his wife. "I'm not ashamed of it," she states. "People who are sick and worn out and useless should be removed so as to leave room for the ones who matter." Aghast, Karl seizes Helen by the throat, flings her away, and orders her to leave.

Karl tells Lisa of Helen's confession. The secretary suggests that they call the police but he objects. He feels responsible, considering Helen did it out of love for him.

Detective Inspector Ogden, who has a pleasant manner and a poker face, notifies Karl that the fingerprints found on the fatal medicine bottle and glass were without a doubt planted. "It means," says Ogden, "an ugly word—murder."

Mrs. Roper, the Hendryk's shifty and unpleasant housekeeper, testifies that she suspects a clandestine relationship between the professor and his secretary, and soon Lisa is arrested.

Karl reveals to the inspector that his student, Helen Rollander, admitted to him that she gave Anya an overdose of heart medicine, but Ogden draws a newspaper clipping from his pocket and points to a story recounting the accidental death of Helen in a traffic accident. The Inspector suspects that Hendryk is using the dead girl as a ready culprit to protect his mistress.

After a two-month trial, Lisa is found innocent. She plans to leave England and start a new life without Karl. "You put ideas first, not people," says Lisa bitterly. "Ideas of loyalty and friendship and pity. And because of that the people who are near, suffer. . . . Because of your mercy and compassion for the girl who killed your wife, you sacrificed *me*. I was the one who paid for your compassion. But I'm not ready to do that any more."

Carrying a suitcase, Lisa leaves. Karl puts on a record and sinks into an armchair, his head down. The door opens slowly, Lisa enters, moves in slowly, puts her hands gently on Karl's shoulders and tells him that she has come back, because "I am a fool."

* * *

When *Verdict* premiered at London's Strand Theatre on May 22, 1958, the stage manager mistakenly cued the final curtain to descend prior to the return of Lisa, which changed the upbeat ending to that of despair.

The reviews were caustic. "*Verdict* is a dislocation of the Christie formula, trying to do an Ibsen on us and achieving lesser Pinero," intoned the critic of the *Observer*.[3] "Mrs. Christie, in trying to create flesh-and-blood characters, succeeded only is giving us dull dummies," scowled R. B. M. of *The Stage*.[4] "A play by Agatha Christie without any 'guess-who' is brandy and soda without the brandy," pouted H. G. M. in *Theatre World*.[5] "It is an embarrassingly sickening tale of emotions which are as unlikely as they are regrettable," hammered Lisa Gordon Smith in *Plays and Players*.[6]

Notwithstanding a game cast of players that included Gerard Heinz as Professor Hendryk, Patricia Jessel as Lisa Koletzky, and Moira Redmond as Helen Rollander, *Verdict* bowed to the sentence of the critics and faded out after thirty-six performances.

In New York, *Verdict* was presented by off-Broadway's Meat and Potato Company on May 20, 1980, for several performances, and at St. Bart's Playhouse, running January 31 through February 10, 1985.

The Valley Theatre Company of Poughkeepsie, New York, produced *Verdict* in February of 1982, eliciting a vitriolic drubbing by Rachel Cassidy in the *Poughkeepsie Journal*: "The entire play is cliché-ridden . . . a dragged out, turgid, stultifyingly dull play."[7] However, when Berkeley's Shotgun Players, California, resuscitated *Verdict* in December 1988, reviewer Chad Jones of the *Oakland Tribune* praised a production that has "taken Christie's troubled, rather dusty play" and infused it with "youthful energy" and "a wry sense of humor. . . . This one's a winner."[8]

Acting Edition: Samuel French, Inc. *Verdict* is also included in *The Mousetrap and Other Plays* by Agatha Christie (New York: Dodd, Mead, 1978; Harper Paperbacks, 1993).

NOTES

1. W. Macqueen Pope, *Morning Telegraph*, New York, June 3, 1958.
2. Agatha Christie, *An Autobiography* (London: Collins, 1977), 520.
3. *Observer*, London, May 25, 1958.
4. *The Stage*, May 29, 1958.
5. *Theatre World*, July 1958.
6. *Plays and Players*, July 1958.
7. *Poughkeepsie Journal*, February 23, 1982.
8. *Oakland Tribune*, December 1998.

The Unexpected Guest (1958)

Agatha Christie (England, 1890–1976)

Agatha Christie quickly rose from the ashes of her disastrous 1958 failure, the thriller *Verdict*. Within weeks she submitted to producer Peter Saunders another original play, *The Unexpected Guest*.

During a foggy night, a stranger, the "unexpected guest" of the title, runs his car into a ditch of a twisty lane off the coast of South Wales. Seeking shelter, he comes upon a lonely house, where he finds a dead body perched in a wheelchair, a bullet hole parting its mop of gray hair, and an attractive blonde woman hovering nearby with a revolver in hand.

The woman says her name is Laura Warwick and admits killing her husband, Richard. She suggests that the newcomer call the police. Instead, he introduces himself as Michael Starkwedder, an engineer who works for Anglo-Iranian, just home from the Persian Gulf, and insists that Laura tell him the circumstances that led to the shooting of her husband.

It seems that Richard Warwick, a well-known big-game hunter, was accidentally mangled by a lion. A cripple, he became vindictive and cruel, and he made life impossible for everyone in the household—his mother, Mrs. Warwick; his housekeeper-secretary, Miss Bennett; and a nurse attendant, Angell. To top it all off, Richard kept threatening that he would send his sweet and retarded half-brother, Jan, to an institution.

Richard's idiosyncrasies also included, says Laura, sitting by an open window, watching for stray cats or rabbits and shooting them. He routinely held a gun by his side.

Michael decides to help Laura. Together they concoct a story that will get her off the hook. In addition to the family members, there are others who might have had a grudge against Richard. There is an abused, sacked gardener. And the father of a little boy killed two years earlier by Richard's drunken driving.

While Laura is offstage in her bedroom, establishing an alibi, Michael fires a pistol and rushes out. Soon Bennett enters, followed by Jan, Mrs. Warwick, and Angell.

They approach the wheelchair and realize that Richard is dead. Stark-wedder comes in through the window, explains that his car ran into a ditch and that while approaching the house to get some help, he heard a shot and someone scurried out, collided with him, and dropped a gun. "Don't touch anything," says Starkwedder. "You'd better get in touch with the police."

The sarcastic Inspector Thomas and poetry aficionado Sergeant Cad-wallader painstakingly check all fingerprints found in the study and cross-examine all. Toward the end of act I, the investigators surmise that Laura has not killed her husband but is shielding someone—the tortured Jan? The troubled mother-in-law who has not long to live? Or perhaps her lover, Julian Farrar, a candidate for Parliament?

It is young, unstable Jan Warwick who confesses to the killing of Richard: "I showed him. I showed him! He won't send me away now!" But in a typical Christie sleight-of-hand there awaits a surprise in the play's last lines: the unexpected guest, Michael Starkwedder, reveals to Laura that he is the father of the child killed by Warwick's careless driving, that he changed his name and built a new identity for himself in another country as part of his burning desire for revenge. Laura is incredulous as Starkwedder goes out by the French window and disappears into the mist.

* * *

The Unexpected Guest previewed for a week at the Hippodrome in Bristol, then moved to London's Duchess Theatre, where it opened on August 12, 1958. Hubert Gregg directed a cast headed by Renee Asherson (Laura Warwick) and Nigel Stock (Michael Starkwedder). The reviews were unanimously enthusiastic, suggesting that the burial of Agatha Christie's reputation due to the failure of *Verdict* was premature.

The Unexpected Guest raised its curtain for 614 performances. Though one of Christie's tightest and most effective efforts, the play did not make it to Broadway. It was performed at the Coconut Grove Playhouse, Miami, Florida (1965); Cohoes Music Hall, Cohoes, New York (1978); Hartman Theatre, Stamford, Connecticut (1980); Alley Theatre, Houston, Texas (1982); Oakland University's Meadow Brook Theatre (1983); and Thirtieth Street Theatre, New York City (2000).

Paris saw *The Unexpected Guest,* adapted by another fiendishly clever writer, Robert Thomas, during the 1968–1969 season.[1]

In 1990, *The Unexpected Guest* was novelized by Charles Osborne, who had done the same to two other original plays by Christie—*Black Coffee* (1997) and *Spider's Web* (2000).

Acting Edition: Samuel French, Inc.

NOTE

1. Robert Thomas's *Piège pour un homme seul*, shown at London's Savoy Theatre in 1963 (under the title *Trap for a Lonely Man*) and at New York's Morosco Theatre in 1965 (as *Catch Me If You Can*), boasts one of the most surprising denouements in the annals of suspense drama.

The Resistible Rise of Arturo Ui (1958)

Bertolt Brecht (Germany, 1898–1956)

Underappreciated and less-known than such Bertolt Brecht plays as *Mother Courage, The Threepenny Opera,* and *The Caucasian Chalk Circle, The Resistible Rise of Arturo Ui* is a satiric parable comparing Adolf Hitler and the National Socialist Party's rise to power to organized crime in Chicago. Brecht wrote the play in 1940, after he had escaped Nazi Germany and was en route to refuge in the United States.[1] But it wasn't produced until eighteen years later, in Stuttgart, West Germany, where it opened on November 10, 1958, at the Württembergisches Staatstheater. By then Brecht was dead, and he never saw a production of *Arturo Ui.*

The main characters of the play are Arturo Ui (Adolf Hitler), Old Dogsborough (President Paul von Hindenburg), Emanuele Giri (Hermann Goering), Giuseppe Givola (Joseph Goebbels), and Ernesto Roma (Ernst Roehm). Chicago represents Germany, Cicero stands for Austria. The Cauliflower Trust is a counterpart to German industrialists.

In keeping with Brecht's presentational style, *The Resistible Rise of Arturo Ui* begins with an Announcer breaking through the fourth wall, addressing the audience directly, and introducing the personage of this "great historical gangster play." The Announcer asks the audience to pay particular attention to "a notorious warehouse fire," "gang warfare," and several murders instigated by Arturo Ui, "public enemy number one." The Announcer also points at signs that appear in the background, illustrating parallel events that took place in Germany during the 1930s.

Background music swells and mingles with the sound of machine-gun bursts as the lights come up on Chicago's financial district. Five businessmen, the directors of the Cauliflower Trust, are in a nervous huddle, expressing their concern about the recent bankrupties, liquidations, and auctioning off of local companies. They are aware that a man named Arturo Ui has been offering protection to various shopkeepers, and they bitterly laugh at "a new concept of salesmanship—bombs and machine-guns."

Arturo Ui, his lieutenant Ernesto Roma, and a bodyguard saunter by. In passing, Roma stares menacingly at the businessmen.

The scene shifts to a bookmaker's office, where Ui whisks through a batch of newspapers, disappointed with the lack of attention he's received. "Two months without a murder and a man's forgotten," he complains. Roma suggests that instead of "idly brooding," they should smash windows, wreck furniture, and pour kerosene on some establishments, starting on Eleventh Street. Ted Ragg, a reporter at the *Star*, approaches them. He is slightly drunk and jokingly mentions a rumor that one of their gang, Giuseppe Givola, had been to see Al Capone about a job. He then pokes fun at Ui, calling him "yesterday's hero who has been long forgotten." Ui bellows, "Shut him up!" and several bodyguards approach Ragg, who bows out, now very much afraid.

Ui begins his ascendance by confronting Old Dogsborough, the influential boss of the waterfront and a major shareholder in the Cauliflower Trust. Ui suggests that a payment will ensure their protection by "thirty men armed to the teeth." At first, Dogsborough declines "to change the Trust's typewriters for tommy-guns," but upon the murder of shipyard owner Sheet, Dogsborough relents. Ui now spreads his protection racket across Chicago.

Aspiring to break into high society, Ui moves to the flashy Hotel Mammoth. Born in the Bronx, one of seven siblings, to a penniless family, Ui realizes that his manners are not up to par. To gain respectability, he engages an actor to coach him in matters of speech and gesture. In a humorous scene, a ragged has-been thespian of the old school, Mahonney, demonstrates to Ui how to walk in "the grand style" of "Julius Caesar, Hamlet, Romeo—that's Shakespeare." To the chagrin of his bodyguards, Ui imitates Mahonney's gait. He follows instructions, and in front of a mirror, throws his head back, touches the floor toe first, and puts his arms in front of his genitals. The actor then coaches Ui on how to sit—"hands on thighs, to abdomen, elbows away from the body"—and, drawing a little book from his pocket, intones Mark Anthony's famous speech from *Julius Caesar*. Ui speaks the lines after him, in the main keeping his rough staccato delivery. A background sign appears to relate that Hitler "quickly transformed himself into a statesman. He is believed to have taken lessons in declamation and bearing from one Basil, a provincial actor."

At the office of the Cauliflower Trust, Ui and his lieutenants, Ernesto Roma, Giuseppe Givola, and Emanuele Giri, are addressing a group of vegetable sellers. Old Dogsborough, pale and ill, is sitting with them on the platform. Ui foxily complains about the wave of "murder, extortion, highway robbery" that has engulfed the city, "murders in broad daylight of people going about their business." The town leaders are not doing a thing to remedy the situation, says Ui, and "chaos is rampant." He offers a solution: protection. Hook, a vegetable wholesaler, rises in objection. Roma, Giri, and Givola move to a corner for a hurried, whispered consultation. Then Giri motions to his men and they saunter out. They reemerge behind the crowd, carrying large gasoline cans, making their way to the exit.

One of the bodyguards steps forward and croons a sentimental song. The meager applause at the end is interrupted by howling police and fire sirens. A red glow is seen through a large window in the background. A goon enters and tells the dealer, Hook, that his warehouse is on fire. Ui declares with faked shock: "First murder and now arson!" A sign appears: "February 1933, the Reichstag fire. Hitler accuses his enemies of instigating the fire and gives the signal for the Night of the Long Knives."

The warehouse fire is investigated. An unemployed man named Charles Fish is accused and brought to trial. He sits in court in utter apathy. The stage is populated with a Judge, a Prosecutor, a Defense Counsel, bodyguards, and vegetable dealers. Giri testifies that he saw Fish "slinking down the street clutching a gasoline can to his chest." The Defense Counsel cross-examines Hook, who states that on the day of the fire he attended a meeting at the office of the Cauliflower Trust and saw Giri and four men carrying gasoline cans passing through the room. A commotion rises on the press bench while the bodyguards boo. The Judge adjourns the session.

When the lights go on, Hook is sitting in the witness chair in a state of collapse, with a cane beside him and bandages over his head and eyes. In answer to the Prosecutor's question, Hook mumbles that no, he's not prepared to say that he ever saw Giri before.

Several henchmen take the stand next, testifying under oath that they recognize the defendant as a seasoned mobster who once sprayed City Hall with a Webster submachine gun. The Judge finds Charles Fish guilty of arson and sentences him to fifteen years' hard labor. A sign appears: "The Supreme Court in Leipzig condemns an unemployed worker to death for causing the fire. The real incendiaries get off scot-free."

Dogsborough writes a will and a confession, in which he admits to acquiescing in the machinations of "that bloody gang" and tolerating the series of murders committed by Arturo Ui and his mob. At the Hotel Mammoth it becomes evident that Ui's lieutenants are engaged in a power struggle. Givola tells Ui that Giri is spending "a little too much time" with Dogsborough and should not be trusted. Roma pulls out a gun and orders Giri and Givola to raise their hands; he is convinced that the two men are selling Ui out to competing gangs. Roma quietly asks Ui to allow him to deliver them to the morgue. Ui shakes his head and suggests that he shoot Giri and Givola at night in the garage.

It is a rainy evening. Ernesto Roma and his gunmen are waiting in the garage. Roma tells the young gunsel, Inna, that he has known Ui for eighteen years and that they have established a warm relationship. They hear a noise outside, cock their machine guns, and raise the bulletproof shutter. Ui and Givola enter briskly, followed by bodyguards. Ui goes to Roma, holding out his hand. Roma grasps it. At this moment, when Roma cannot reach for his gun, Givola shoots him from the hip. Roma falls and his men stand, bewildered. In an image borrowed from the notorious St. Valentine's Massacre, they are ordered to line up against a wall and are mowed down by machine-gun fire. "You stinking Rats! You traitors!" cries Inna before falling dead. Ui tells Givola to finish the wounded Roma off and stalks out.

A sign appears: "On the night of June 30, 1934, Hitler overpowers his friend Roehm at an inn where Roehm has been waiting for him. Up to the last moment Roehm thinks that Hitler is coming to arrange for a joint strike against Hindenburg and Goering."

Now in control of Chicago's commerce, Ui plans to widen his protection net across America. His next target is Chicago's neighboring city, Cicero, and he begins by sending his gunmen to ambush and kill the crusading local newspaper editor, Ignatius Dullfeet. In a scene reminiscent of Richard wooing Lady Anne over her husband's corpse in Shakespeare's *Richard III*, when Dullfeet's coffin is being carried into the Cicero funeral home, Ui flirts with his attractive widow, Betty. Betty calls Ui "a serpent . . . a monster." He offers her his hand. Cringing with horror, she runs out.

At the Hotel Mammoth, Ui tosses in his bed, plagued by a nightmare. His bodyguards sit next to the door, their revolvers on their laps. The wall behind Ui becomes transparent. The ghost of Ernesto Roma appears, a bullet hole in the forehead, and tells Ui that his murderous deeds are all in vain, that those he betrayed and killed will rise and take arms against him. Ui jumps up with a start and orders his men to shoot the intruder. They fire at the spot on the wall indicated by Ui. Roma's ghost fades away.

In the financial district, Chicago vegetable dealers greet the vegetable dealers of Cicero. All are shaken by a series of extortions and murders. They feel helpless against the show of brute force and are concerned that "this plague will sweep the country."

Enter Ui, Giri, and Givola, flanked by bodyguards. The entourage includes Betty Dullfeet, who has become Ui's paramour. Ui addresses the group as "friends, countrymen, Chicagoans and Ciceronians!" He relates that a year ago, Old Dogsborough, "God rest his honest soul," appealed to him to protect Chicago's green-goods trade, and he responded to his wish. More recently, says Ui, another civic leader, Ignatius Dullfeet, approached him with the same request, this time concerning Cicero. He has consented to put the city under his protection, and will continue to service both Chicago and Cicero if the dealers, freely, want him to.

Giri calls, "All those in favor of Arturo Ui, raise your hands." A Ciceronian goes out in a huff. Two bodyguards follow him. A shot is heard. Giri says, "All right, friends, let's have your decision." All raise both hands. Ui thanks the crowd for helping a humble son of the Bronx realize his dream, and promises that after Chicago and Cicero he'll go to other cities clamoring for protection—Washington, Milwaukee, Detroit, Toledo, Pittsburgh, Cincinnati, Philadelphia, Columbus, Charleston, and New York!

A sign appears: "On March 11, 1938, Hitler marched into Austria. An election under the Nazi terror resulted in a 98% vote for Hitler." Amid drums and fanfare the curtain falls.

* * *

Peter Palitzsch, who directed the 1958 world premiere of *Der aufhaltsame Aufstieg des Arturo Ui* in West Germany's Stuttgart, also staged a much-admired production of the play for East Germany's Berliner Ensemble, opening on March 23, 1959, with Ekkehard Schall as Ui, an acrobatic performance described as being "Chaplinesque."

Jean Villar directed *Arturo Ui* and played the title role in a production that opened at the Palais de Chaillot, Paris, on November 15, 1960. It was an epic endeavor, utilizing thirty-eight actors, countless set changes, and brash background music. Critic Jean-Pierre Lenoir dispatched a rave review to the *New York Times*, hailing Villar's performance as "an extraordinary tour de force."[2]

Adapted by George Tabori, directed by Tony Richardson and designed by Rouben Ter-Arutunian, *Arturo Ui* came to Broadway's Lunt-Fontanne Theatre on November 11, 1963. Ui was played by Christopher Plummer. His henchmen were portrayed by veteran motion picture heavies Lionel Stander, Elisha Cook, and Mervyn Vye. Madeleine Sherwood enacted Betty Dullfeet. Critic Howard Taubman of the *New York Times* found "troubles everywhere—in George Tabori's adaptation, in the vacillating styles that make a confusion of the scenes, in the wild mixture of individual acting styles, and in the hopped-up scenic effects." Taubman compared the show unfavorably to recent productions of the play that he had seen at East Berlin's Berliner Ensemble and at Warsaw's Erwin Axer's theatre.[3] In a follow-up piece, Taubman elaborated on his negative assessment of Tony Richardson's "maltreatment" of *Arturo Ui* and scowled at a production that "stressed the hopped-up showiness of a carnival. . . . The essence of *Arturo Ui*, despite the surface clownishness of its gangsters and capitalists in the early scenes, is the evil that saturates its people and world. The thugs meant to represent Hitler, Goering and Goebbels are not comic mobsters out of Damon Runyon and there should not be an instant when they make you think of *Guys and Dolls*."[4]

The play ran for only eight performances. New Yorkers had another chance to see *The Resistible Rise of Arturo Ui* when the Minnesota Theatre Company brought its production to Broadway's Billy Rose Theatre on December 22, 1968. Reviewer Dan Sullivan declared, "I loved it. . . . Brecht asks us to see Hitler as nothing more than a second-rate thug whose rise— a 'resistible' rise, in George Tabori's apt translation—depended more on other people's weaknesses than on his own strength." Sullivan praised Edward Payson Call's "bold" staging and found Robin Gammell's Ui "possibly the most nervous person ever seen on the legitimate stage. . . . The image is that of a puppet being manipulated by an invisible puppeteer with a bad case of the jerks. . . . Even more admirable, I think, is his refusal to play the role, even for the tiniest instant, for sympathy. Funny as his little rat is, it remains a rat."[5]

However, most other critics treated the show with disdain. John Chapman was "not particularly stirred by the notion that Hitler was a housepainting punk from Brooklyn who muscled into the cauliflower business."[6] Richard Watts Jr. found the production "surprisingly flat."[7] Martin Gottfried asserted that "*Arturo Ui* is one of Brecht's clumsiest and silliest plays," and that he suffered through "an awfully unexciting evening."[8]

Nonetheless, the Minnesota Theatre Company's production moved to Los Angeles's Mark Taper Forum on January 17, 1969, for forty-five performances.

Michael Blakemore directed George Tabori's adaptation of *The Resistible Rise of Arturo Ui* for a production that premiered in September 1967 at the Citizens' Theatre in Glasgow, Scotland; was performed in August 1968 at the Lyceum, Edinburgh, Scotland; and was re-created by England's Nottingham Repertory Theatre in April 1969 before moving to London's Saville Theatre in July 1969. *New York Times* critic Clive Barnes wrote, "Brecht's cartoon picture of Hitler, rising from a Chaplinesque nonentity into a world monster, is chillingly provocative. . . . It is the great virtue of Michael Blakemore's staging that the humor is never underplayed, even though the political machinations and motivations are unraveled with uncommon skill." Barnes lauded Leonard Rossiter's "outstanding tragicomic portrayal of Ui. Mr. Rossiter is perfect—a trampled paranoid, comically mean-minded, with the timing of a comedian and, stealthily developing, the arrogance of a madman."[9]

While Leonard Rossiter rocketed to stardom in London, that same year, 1968–1969, Robert Hirsch's characterization of Ui was considered one of the season's highlights in Paris.

A new adaptation by Ralph Manheim served as the basis for a highly acclaimed film produced by UK's BBC TV in 1972, starring Nicol Williamson in the role of Ui.

Notable stage productions of the play were mounted in England by East London's Half Moon Theatre Company, with Simon Callow as Ui (1978); at the Bench Theatre in Havant, directed by Jacquie Penrose (1982); by the National Theatre in London, featuring Antony Sher (1991); at Hampton Hill Playhouse, staged by Christopher Ivey (1999); and by London's fringe Bridewell Theatre, helmed by Phil Willmott (2002). The Berliner Ensemble in Berlin featured Martin Wuttke as Ui in 1995.

Al Pacino played Arturo Ui in a 2002 production offered by Tony Randall's National Actors Theatre at Pace University in New York. Pacino led a star-studded cast that included Steve Buscemi (Givola), John Goodman (Giri), Chazz Palminteri (Roma), Charles Durling (Dogsborough), Paul Giamatti (Prosecutor), Billy Crudup (Defense Counsel), and Tony Randall (the Actor). The production garnered both rave reviews and sighs of disappointment. Critic Peter Marks complimented guest director Simon McBurney, of London's Theatre de la Complicite, for his "bravura physical style," for creating a "stimulating visual language, a sophisticated brand of imagemaking," and for staging "Arturo's ruthless ascent with a loving nod to American gangster films."[10] Michael Kuchwara found Al Pacino "mesmerizing in the title role"; lauded the "mighty contributions" of Charles Durning, John Goodman, Chazz Palminteri, and Steve Buscemi; and pointed out that Tony Randall's drunken actor sequence was "one of the play's most inspiring moments."[11] However, Donald Lyon opined that Al Pacino's portrayal of a gangster in *Godfather* and *Scarface* were "more clever and ominous than this *Arturo Ui.*" On the whole, wrote Lyon, "This *Arturo Ui* has spurts of energy and impudence—but only spurts."[12]

Despite the fact that the entire cast, including Pacino, worked for "scale," the minimum pay required by the Actors Equity union, tickets for the show cost $115, the highest price in off-Broadway history. The play ran at Pace University's 750-seat theatre from October 3, 2002, through November 10.

During the first decade of the twenty-first century, *Arturo Ui* found its stride in a number of worldwide productions. Tom Kerr staged the play at the Jericho Arts Center, Vancouver, Canada, March 7–17, 2002; an adaptation by Jennifer Wise, directed by Brian Richmond, was presented at the University of Victoria, Canada, November 14–30, 2002; in 2003, director Steph Kirton used projections to link the two histories of the play at The Garage Theatre of Edinburgh, Scotland; Erin Thomas helmed a production conceived in response to the invasion of Iraq under the leadership of President George W. Bush at the Pact Theatre, Sidney, Australia, in 2004; the Carlton Dramatic Society of Wimbledon, England, played *Arturo Ui* to sold-out houses in 2006; the fringe company Outer London offered *Arturo Ui* at the Lyric Theatre, Hammersmith, in 2008, transporting the proceedings to an African country ruled by a despot such as Idi Amin or Robert Mugabe and casting a Zimbabwean actor, Lucian Msamati, as Ui. Also in 2008, the experimental theatre Countdown to Zero presented the play in Denver, Colorado; the Abbey Theatre of Dublin, Ireland, revived *Arturo Ui* in both 2008 and 2010; California State University at Fresno mounted the play in 2009, and West Texas A&M University a year later. Also in 2010, *Arturo Ui* was included in the repertoires of the TC's troupe of Birmingham City, England, and the Bruiser Theatre Company of Belfast, Northern Ireland, the latter show utilizing six actors/musicians for more than fifty characters.

* * *

Bertolt Brecht (Eugen Berthold Friedrich Brecht) was born on February 10, 1898, in Augsburg, Germany, the son of a paper manufacturer. He studied medicine and science at the Ludwig Maximilian University in Munich. In 1918 he was drafted as a medical orderly. Seeing so much carnage in the medical wards made him a lifelong pacifist. After World War I, Brecht began his association with revolutionary communists and penned controversial poems. It is reported that during the early 1920s he could often be seen in Munich's literary cafés, playing the banjo and singing ballads.

Brecht's first play, *Drums in the Night* (1922), is the cynical study of a soldier returning from war and discovering that his sweetheart has become engaged to a profiteer. In *Baal* (1923), the title character is a drinking, brawling, womanizing minstrel who kills his only friend when they compete over a waitress. *In the Jungle of Cities* (1923) pictures a relentless feud in Chicago between a timber merchant and a librarian. The merchant employs every means to possess the librarian's soul but meets with stubborn resistance. *Edward II* (1924), after Christopher Marlowe, has the king alienate his wife, his lords, and his church for the love of a man.

"Brecht's early plays," asserts the *McGraw-Hill Encyclopedia of World Drama*, "bear the imprint of German expressionism. Violence, squalor, and depravity of all kinds invest these plays with a contemporary exoticism."[13]

In the autumn of 1924, Brecht moved to Berlin, where he became a dramatic consultant to famed director Max Reinhardt. During the late 1920s Brecht began his association with composer Kurt Weill and also worked closely with theatre director Erwin Piscator, a founder of epic theatre. In 1927, Brecht married his second wife, the actress Helene Weigel, who later gave brilliant stage interpretations to his female characters.

The *McGraw-Hill Encyclopedia of World Drama* states: "Appalled by the economic and political crises wracking Germany after World War I,

Brecht had undertaken an intensive and sympathetic study of Marxist philosophy and economics, and concluded that the only solution to the problems besetting both his country and the world was Communism."[14]

Brecht now wrote his plays to sharpen the class consciousness of his audience. In his stagecraft he challenged Stanislavsky's realism by an approach that he called *Verfremdungseffekt*, "alienation effect," reminding the audience that they were in a theatre, discouraging them from going through an emotional catharsis, inducing them to regard the events with critical detachment. Abandoning Aristotelian dramatic unities and the constraints of the "well-made" play, Brecht often covered decades in a series of small scenes and frequent changes of locale.

Brecht contributed to the stage some forty plays and several essays that clarify his political theories on the function of theatre. His masterpieces include *The Threepenny Opera* (*Die Dreigroschenoper*, 1928), a collaboration with composer Kurt Weill based on John Gay's *The Beggar's Opera* (1728), a witty and colorful exposé of corrupt society; *Saint Joan of the Stockyards* (*Die heilige Johanna der Schlachthöfe*, 1932), a prose and blank-verse play in which Joan Dark, a Salvation Army volunteer, attempts to help the poor of Chicago; *The Exception and the Rule* (*Die Ausnahme und die Regel*, written 1930, produced 1947), wherein a merchant, traveling across a desert, wrongly assumes that his guide is dangerous and shoots him to death; *The Mother* (*Die Mutter*, 1932), an adaptation of Maxim Gorky's novel about a Russian woman who joins her son's revolutionary group after he is shot in Siberia.

The Private Life of the Master Race (*Furcht und Elend des dritten Reiches*, 1938) contains twenty-eight scenes depicting the reign of terror during the Nazi domination in Germany. *Galileo* (*Leben des Galilei*, written 1938–1939, produced 1943) is loosely based on the astronomer's life, focusing on the Church's opposition to his theory that the earth is only one of many planets and not the center of the universe. *Mother Courage and Her Children* (*Mutter Courage and ihre Kinder*, 1941) chronicles the Thirty Years' War during which old Anna Fierling, a canteen manager, doggedly refuses to give up her wagon and saves her goods despite enemy fire.

The Good Woman of Setzuan (*Der gute Mensch von Sezuan*, 1943) is a parable about a penniless Chinese prostitute who is rewarded by the gods for her good deeds. *Mr. Puntila and His Hired Man, Matti* (*Herr Puntila und sein Knecht Matti*, written 1940–1941, produced 1948) spotlights a wealthy farmer, Puntila, who is kind and generous when drunk, mean and brutal when sober. *Schweyk in the Second World War* (*Schweyk im zweiten Weltkrieg*, written 1941–1942, produced 1957), a comedy inspired by Jaroslav Hašek's novel *The Good Soldier Schweik*, has the title character emerge in German-occupied Prague and become involved with patriots, informers, the SS, and the Gestapo. *The Caucasian Chalk Circle* (*Der kaukasische Kre-idekreis*, 1948), based on the Chinese drama *The Circle of Chalk*, reaches its high point in court, where two women claim to be the mother of the same baby.

Brecht's immense theatrical output also includes plays borrowed from Sophocles, Shakespeare, Molière, and Gorky, among others. Many of his plays were adapted to the screen and to television. *Baal, Galileo, Herr Puntila and His Servant Matti, Mother Courage and Her Children,* and *The Caucasian Chalk Circle* were filmed more than once in Germany, Russia, England, and the United States. The German movie *The Farewell* (2002) chronicles a day in the life of Brecht, emphasizing his appetite for women and cigars.

With the rise of Nazism, Brecht sought asylum in Denmark, Sweden, and Finland. In 1941 he settled in the United States, where he lived in California as part of the Hollywood refugee community. There he wrote the original screenplay for Fritz Lang's *Hangmen Also Die!* (1943), depicting the assassination of the brutal Nazi "protector" Reinhard Heydrich by the Czech resistance fighters. In 1947, Brecht was summoned before the House Un-American Activities Committee; he left the country rather than testify, returning to East Germany where he received an offer from the government to establish his own theatre in East Berlin, the Berliner Ensemble.

Established in January 1949, the Berliner Ensemble theatre company made Helene Weigel, Brecht's wife, a director and key player, and garnered world recognition. Brecht became a seminal figure in the exploration of drama as a forum for political ideas. In due time his plays were recognized for moving a story beyond the unities of time and place, regularly imbued with larger human and social meaning. A Brechtian vogue swept Europe and the United States.[15] Theatre scholar Martin Esslin called Brecht "one of the most significant writers of the twentieth century." Critic Kenneth Tynan declared Brecht "the most ambiguous and perpetually fascinating figure of the twentieth-century European theatre."

Brecht died in 1956 of a coronary thrombosis. He was fifty-eight.[16]

Acting Edition: Samuel French, Inc. (translation by George Tabori). Samuel French, London (translation by Ranjit Bolt). Eyre Methuen (translation by Ralph Manheim).

Awards and Honors: Bertolt Brecht was the recipient of the East German State Prize on October 7, 1951, and the Stalin Peace Prize on May 25, 1955. Brecht won several posthumous awards, including the 1970 Drama Desk Award Outstanding Lyrics for *Rise and Fall of the City of Mahagonny*. He was nominated for a Best Play Tony Award in 1963 for *Mother Courage and Her Children* and for a Best Original Score Tony in 1977 for *Happy End*.

NOTES

1. Also in 1940, Charlie Chaplin made his first talkie, *The Great Dictator*, a devastating satire, combining slapstick and social commentary, about Adolf Hitler.

2. *New York Times*, November 16, 1960.

3. *New York Times*, November 12, 1963.

4. *New York Times*, November 24, 1963.

5. *New York Times*, December 23, 1968.

6. *Daily News*, December 23, 1968.

7. *New York Post*, December 23, 1968.

8. *Women's Wear Daily*, December 23, 1968.

9. *New York Times*, August 18, 1969.

10. *Washington Post*, October 22, 2002.

11. Associated Press, October 23, 2002.

12. *New York Post*, October 21, 2002.

13. Stanley Hochman, ed., *McGraw-Hill Encyclopedia of World Drama* (New York: McGraw-Hill, 1984), 394.

14. Stanley Hochman, ed., *McGraw-Hill Encyclopedia of World* Drama, 389.

15. Brecht's works were frequently produced on American stages, thanks to translations and promotion efforts by Eric Bentley, Martin Esslin, John Willett, George Tabori, and Ralph Manheim.

16. France's leading literary award, the Prix Goncourt, touched off a controversy when in 2003 it was bestowed on Jacques-Pierre Amette for *La maîtresse de Brecht* (*Brecht's Mistress*). The novel recounts the return of the playwright to post–World War II East Berlin and his affair with an actress.

The Hostage (1958)

Brendan Behan (Ireland, 1923–1964)

Brendan Behan's bawdy, wild comedy-drama *The Hostage* unfolds in a sleazy Dublin brothel. The building is owned by a deranged Englishman, known as Monsewer, who is still convinced that he is a great soldier and keeps popping in dressed in a kilt and playing his bagpipes. The caretakers of the establishment are the loquacious Pat, who loves to tell embellished tales about a heroic past, and his gruff, sharp-tongued "almost wife," Meg. Milling around are harlots Colette and Bobo; transvestites Rio Rita and Princess Grace; Teresa, a gentle, convent-bred maid; Eustace Mulleady, a meek, clerkish-looking man who admits to having been incarcerated for absconding with church funds; and Evangeline Gilchrist, a bespectacled social worker who occasionally stops the action of the play to croon hymns.

Amid songs, dances, vaudeville gags, and winking asides to the audience, a skeletal plot emerges: a young member of the Irish Republican Army, accused of shooting a British policeman, is to be hanged in a Belfast jail the next morning. Armed officers of the IRA sneak into the brothel a nineteen-year-old English soldier, Leslie Alan Williams, whom they have captured as a hostage against the threatened Belfast execution.

Williams, a London Cockney, turns out to be naive, friendly, and down-to-earth. The inhabitants of the brothel become fond of him, and he is given beer, tea, and cigarettes. The maid Teresa falls in love with him. But in the morning, the Belfast execution takes place, Mulleady turns out to be a member of the English Secret Police, the brothel is surrounded, and young Williams is accidently cut down by a volley of machine-gun bullets. Teresa, crying, kneels by his body and vows, "I will never forget you, Leslie. Never, till the end of time."

Before the final curtain, Behan wishes to emphasize that it is all just playacting, only a theatrical game, by having the "dead" Williams jump to his feet and sing lustily, warning the audience that "the bells of hell go ting-a-ling-a-ling" not for him but for them.

* * *

The Hostage was first presented by Joan Littlewood's Theatre Workshop at the Theatre Royal, Stratford, London, on October 14, 1958. The play ran initially for sixty-two performances but reopened at Wyndham Theatre in the West End on May 14, 1959, for a whopping run of 452 showings. *Theatre World Annual* wrote: "This is a slice of Dublin life in which Behan emerges as a kind of Irish Dylan Thomas. He cocks a snook with brilliant verbiage at the whole of life (though often political, naturally, where Thomas was not) and with fine irony takes in his stride the fortuitous demise of a young Cockney soldier hostage in Dublin; a stranger indeed in a wild foreign land!"[1]

The Hostage traveled to New York's Cort Theatre on September 20, 1960, featuring many members of the original British cast. The reviews were split. Richard Watts Jr. called Brendan Behan "a man of extraordinary talent," and found the play "brimming with magnificent exuberance, wild, unruly, scornful, satirical and mocking, filled with comic gusto and streaked through with an oddly embarrassed compassion."[2] Frank Ashton believed *The Hostage* to be "priceless" and admired the play's "topsy-turvy dialogue."[3] Walter Kerr applauded a play that "makes for a wild night and a welcome one."[4]

Conversely, John McClain scowled at "a series of soiled vignettes, with atrocious language and no plausible point."[5] John Chapman objected to "a ramshackle affair which wore itself and me out before the end of its first performance."[6]

The Hostage ran for 127 performances. A subsequent touring company landed the following year at the O'Keefe Centre in Toronto, Canada, and at the Geary Theatre in San Francisco, California. An off-Broadway revival at One Sheridan Square opened on December 12, 1961, was hailed by Louis Calta of the *New York Times* as "irreverent, mad and mirth-provoking,"[7] and ran for 545 performances.

During the 1961–1962 season, one of the most popular productions in Paris was the Madeleine Renaud–Jean-Louis Barrault Company's production of *The Hostage*, with Pierre Blanchar as Monsewer, Aletty as Meg, and Mme. Renaud as Evangeline Gilchrist. Translated into Hebrew by T. Carmi, *The Hostage* was produced by the Haifa Municipal Theatre, Israel, in 1963, with Haim Topol, famed for *Fiddler on the Roof*, in the role of caretaker Pat. In the late 1960s, the play was presented by Manhattan's Actors' Equity Theatre; Arena House Theatre, Harrisburg, Pennsylvania; Actors Theatre, Louisville, Kentucky; Hartford Stage Company, Hartford, Connecticut; Seattle Repertory Theatre, Seattle, Washington; Cleveland

Playhouse, Cleveland, Ohio; Syracuse Repertory Theatre, Syracuse, New York; and by Theatre of the Living Arts, Philadelphia, Pennsylvania. Seldom revived since then, *The Hostage* was resuscitated in the twenty-first century by off-Broadway's Irish Repertory Theatre (2000), Adelphi University (2003), and Theatre Banshee in Burbank, California (2009).

Acting Edition: *The Hostage* is included in *The Complete Plays of Brendan Behan*—Samuel French, Inc., and in *Brendan Behan: The Complete Plays*—Grove Press.

Awards and Honors: Brendan Behan was the recipient of an Obie Award, 1958; Paris Festival Award, 1958; and French Critics Award, 1962.

NOTES

1. *Theatre World Annual*, 1959, 34.
2. *New York Post*, September 21, 1960.
3. *New York World-Telegram*, September 21, 1960.
4. *New York Herald Tribune*, September 21, 1960.
5. *New York Journal-American*, September 21, 1960.
6. *Daily News*, September 21, 1960.
7. *New York Times*, December 13, 1961.

Cue for Passion (1958)
Elmer Rice (United States, 1892–1967)

Elmer Rice's *Cue for Passion* offers a twentieth-century twist on *Hamlet*, moving the action to Southern California, incorporating events that resemble the Shakespearean tragedy.

Young Tony Burgess has dropped out of the University of California at Berkeley and traveled to the Far East. He returns home bitter and suspicious over what has transpired during his absence—his father has been killed, presumably in an earthquake, and his mother Grace has remarried an old beau, the lawyer Carl Nicholson.

Nicholson tells Tony that he was playing chess with his father by the fireplace when there was an earthquake tremor. It knocked some pieces off the board. They both stooped to pick them up. There was a second tremor, severe enough to dislodge the bronze bust of Tony from the mantle and strike his father "full force on the head, fracturing his skull. . . . He died almost instantly."

Hugh Gessler, a neighbor and family doctor, the Polonius of the piece, informs Tony that an autopsy had not been done as the cause of death was evident. Gessler's daughter, Lucy, the Ophelia of Southern California, dissolves into tears when she realizes that her beloved Tony is tormented by suppositions of treachery and murder.

Tony's friend Lloyd Hilton, the modern Horatio, a psychologist-criminologist at Alcatraz Prison, is summoned by the Nicholsons to help calm the distraught Tony.

Tony's suspicions of foul play are rekindled when he hears that his late father was cremated. He goes to the mantel, picks up the bust, puts it back, scatters a few chess pieces on the hearth, and tells the elderly housekeeper, Mattie Haines, to climb up and push the head off. Mattie refuses and on her way out suggests that Tony sober up "before it's too late."

The wind blows the terrace door open. An intoxicated Tony, his eyes dilated, follows the progress of a ghostly figure from the door to the chess board. He believes that the apparition of his father is telling him that he was murdered. Tony picks up a poker from beside the fireplace and brandishes it; this, he assumes, was more likely the instrument of death.

Echoing *Hamlet*, Tony confronts his mother and reveals his Oedipal complex when he suddenly seizes and kisses her passionately. Then, as she tears herself away from him, he notices the silhouette of a man behind the terrace door and shoots at it with a revolver. It is Dr. Gessler. But while Polonius dies behind the curtain from Hamlet's sword, here the good doctor is only wounded.

Realizing that he, himself, wished to kill his father, Tony leaves home, determined never to return. As the final curtain descends, Grace is left with a gnawing doubt: did Carl murder her former husband?

* * *

Cue for Passion opened at the Henry Miller Theatre in New York on November 25, 1958, to mixed reviews. "It is a steadily absorbing play," wrote Richard Watts Jr.[1] "A piercing drama," stated Frank Ashton.[2] "The author has spun a thoughtful and constantly-mounting story of suspense and volcanic emotions," asserted John McClain.[3]

The naysayers included Robert Coleman, who claimed that "*Cue for Passion* is a high-falutin' windy re-working of the Shakespeare masterpiece."[4] John Chapman criticized it as "a citrus belt version of *Hamlet* with a twist of *Oedipus Rex*."[5] Likewise, Walter Kerr believed that "the play, which is surely intended as a serious comment, does sit uneasily at the fulcrum of a teeter-totter—Shakespeare going down while Freud goes up, and vice versa."[6]

Cue for Passion garnered kudos for John Kerr (Tony Burgess) and Diana Wynyard (Grace Nicholson), but lasted only thirty-nine performances. West German television presented *Cue for Passion* in 1961 with Hartmut Reck and Gisela Uhlen in the leads.

* * *

In 1913, just as Elmer L. Reizenstein was admitted to the New York State bar, he resigned his post as managing clerk at the law offices of House, Grossman, and Vorhans and began to write a play. He completed *On Trial* in the spring of 1914 and, ignorant of conventional procedure, left copies of the manuscript with the receptionists of two producers—Arthur Hopkins and Edgar Selwyn (the latter had mounted the successful Bayard Veiller courtroom melodrama *Within the Law* a year earlier). Hopkins responded first and, within a week, twenty-one-year-old Reizenstein found himself on the threshold of Broadway—he signed a contract and received an advance fee of $500.

On Trial was considered revolutionary because it introduced a cinematic flashback as a tool to tell the story. The main setting is that of a courtroom, and the action covers two days in a murder trial. During the testimony of several key witnesses, the lights dim, and with the utilization of two joined platforms that pivot on- and off-stage, the action shifts to other locales, informing viewers of events that preceded the trial.

On Trial previewed in Stamford, Connecticut, on August 14, 1914, and opened at New York's Candler Theatre five days later. The *New York Times* stated that "Mr. Reizenstein has done his work well. . . . His first work has the manner and fascination of a good detective story. . . . He has reproduced with singular success the very manner of our courtrooms."[7]

Other critics applauded "a triumph of dramatic construction." Burns Mantle believed *On Trial* to be "one of the noted dramas of the American theatre" and selected it as one of the ten best plays of the decade.[8]

On Trial ran for 365 performances, went on tour, and crossed the Atlantic, opening at London's Lyric Theatre on April 29, 1915. It raised its curtain for 174 showings. The *London Post* reported that the play "had as enthusiastic a reception as any play this season."[9] The *London Times* was also complimentary.

On Trial was filmed in 1917, 1928, and 1939 and earned novice playwright Reizenstein well over $100,000 in royalties.

Over the next half-century, Reizenstein wrote thirty-five plays under the name Elmer Rice, establishing himself as a foremost American dramatist. His crime-tinged works include *For the Defense* (1919), *It Is the Law* (1922), *The Adding Machine* (1923), *The Mongrel* (1924), *Cock Robin*, with Philip Barry (1928), *Street Scene* (1929), *See Naples and Die* (1929), *We, the People* (1933), *Judgment Day* (1934), *Flight to the West* (1940), *The Grand Tour* (1951), and *Cue for Passion* (1958).

Rice leaned on his legal background when penning *Find the Woman* (*For the Defense*), a courtroom drama about a young district attorney forced to prosecute the woman he loves for murder. Flashbacks were used again in *It Is the Law*, Rice's dramatized version of Hayden Talbot's novel. The action revolves around a fiendish plan hatched by a spurned suitor to implicate his rival in a murder he had committed.

The Adding Machine is an expressionistic drama about a small-time clerk who kills his boss after being fired from his job despite twenty-five years of service. The protagonist of *The Mongrel*, adapted from the German of Herman Bahr, is a forester who kills the dog of an old neighbor and finds himself the target of deadly revenge. *Cock Robin*, cowritten with Philip Barry, pictures a murder committed in full view of the audience attending a community theatre's performance. *Street Scene* is a Pulitzer Prize–winning drama unfolding in a squalid New York neighborhood where a boorish, jealous husband fatally shoots his wife and her lover. In *See Naples and Die*, a deposed Russian prince is assassinated by East European agents. In *We, the People*, a radical student is accused of shooting a police officer during a rally. Though innocent of the crime, he is found guilty and sentenced "to be hanged by the neck until dead." *Judgment Day* is an anti-Nazi courtroom drama that unfolds at the Palace of Justice in a capital of southeastern Europe.

The entire action of *Flight to the West* takes place aboard a transatlantic clipper on two successive days in July 1940. A dozen passengers have taken the trip from Lisbon to New York, and, in *Grand Hotel* style, the focus shifts from character to character as people are flung together within confined quarters. One of the passengers is a Russian spy who is exposed by a snoopy American newspaperwoman.

The protagonist of *The Grand Tour* is a lonely Connecticut schoolteacher who, upon her father's death, inherits $60,000 and decides to travel first-class to the continent. On the deck of an ocean liner she meets and falls in love with a banker from Minnesota but soon finds out that he has embezzled a large amount of money from his bank to maintain a standard of living beyond his means.

Successful plays without criminal motifs by Elmer Rice include *The Left Bank* (1931), focusing on two bohemian, mismatched American couples living in Paris; *Counsellor-at-Law* (1931), depicting the personal and professional tribulations of a rags-to-riches Manhattan lawyer; and *Dream Girl* (1945), in which the romantic manager of a bookstore flees from reality into a fantasy world, imagining herself as a prostitute on the city's streets, a murderess on the dock, and a Broadway star.

Rice came full circle in his last play, *Court of Last Resort* (1965), returning to the matters of law and jurisprudence that launched his career in 1914's *On Trial*.

Acting Edition: Dramatists Play Service (in manuscript form).

NOTES

1. *New York Post*, November 26, 1958.
2. *New York World-Telegram*, November 26, 1958.
3. *New York Journal-American*, November 26, 1958.
4. *Daily Mirror*, November 26, 1958.
5. *Daily News*, November 26, 1958.
6. *New York Herald Tribune*, November 26, 1958.
7. *New York Times*, August 20, 1914.
8. Burns Mantle, ed., *The Best Plays of 1909–1919* (New York: Dodd, Mead, 1943), 202.
9. Quoted in the *New York Times*, May 16, 1915.

The Gazebo (1958)

Alec Coppel (England, 1909–1972)

In 1937, playwright Alec Coppel wrote a baffling whodunit, *I Killed the Count*, in which four people, one after another, claim to have shot a dastardly aristocrat. The problem? There is only one bullet in his carcass. In a foretaste of *Rashomon*, each of the suspects reenacts the crime for befuddled Scotland Yard investigators, and their statements unfold in the form of a flashback. The play premiered at London's Whitehall Theatre on December 10, 1937, to morning-after raves: "The best detective play I have seen for years" (*Evening News*), "Very funny . . . really ingenious . . . ranks high among thrillers" (*Daily Mail*), "Top marks for originality, surprise, thrills, laughter" (*Referee*). It ran for 185 performances.

Five years later, *I Killed the Count* crossed the Atlantic and opened at Broadway's Cort Theatre on August 31, 1942. Unlike their London counterparts, the New York reviewers greeted *I Killed the Count* with battering rams, complaining of "heavy dialogue . . . obvious intricacies" (*New York Sun*) and concluding that "the whole evening was on the dreary and the feeble side" (*New York World-Telegram*). The play folded after twenty-nine showings.

It took ten years after the opening of *I Killed the Count* for Coppel to publish his first suspense novel—*A Man about a Dog* (United States title: *Over the Line*, 1947). After that and until his death in 1972 the author's output included four more novels and one play—*The Gazebo*.

This time around, Coppel took fewer chances and concocted a lightly amusing crime escapade about a writer of television whodunits, Elliott Nash. When his wife Nell, a famous soap opera actress, becomes the target of blackmail, Nash decides to silence the blackmailer with his six-shooter and conceal the body in the fresh concrete foundation of a new garden gazebo. The next morning, Nash is horrified when the corpse turns up on the floor of his Long Island living room. In desperation, he calls Alfred Hitchcock for advice, asking how to get rid of a dead body that keeps coming back. Soon the house is crawling with detectives and

Nash is the prime suspect. Just as the writer believes that all is lost, a plot deviation reveals that the blackmailer actually died of a heart attack. This is a mild surprise and exceedingly unbelievable, for wouldn't Nash, whose bullet missed its target, notice the lack of blood when burying the cadaver?

Directed by Jerome Chodorov and designed by Jo Mielziner, *The Gazebo* opened at New York's Lyceum Theatre on December 12, 1958. In contrast to their devastation of *I Killed the Count*, the critics were kind to *The Gazebo*. Brooks Atkinson found it "as real as a TV crime play and a thousand times more diverting."[1] Walter Kerr described the play as a "very cheerful little artifice."[2] John Chapman praised it as "a jolly little melodramatic farce."[3] John McClain believed "it was suspenseful and funny and should succeed."[4]

Richard Watts Jr. was less complimentary: "It suffers seriously from the fact that its plot's rather complex blackmailing conspiracy is handled with surprising ineffectuality and lack of persuasiveness, giving its comic aspects small support in the way of actual suspense."[5] Robert Coleman stated bluntly: "It's a frail suspense-chuckler. . . . There were times when a good gust of wind might have blown *The Gazebo* right off the Lyceum's stage."[6]

The critics were unanimous in praising "moon-faced, rotund" Walter Slezak and "the very handsome" Jayne Meadows as Mr. and Mrs. Nash. The play ran for 218 performances. A subsequent production opened at London's Savoy Theatre on March 29, 1960, starring Ian Carmichael and Moira Lister, and was even more successful, running for 479 showings.

The Gazebo was filmed in CinemaScope in 1959, with Glenn Ford and Debbie Reynolds taking over the lead roles. The play was twice adapted to the screen in France—in 1971 under the title *Jo*, starring Louis de Funes and Claude Gensac, and in 1995, for television, as *Une femme dans les bras, un cadavres sur le dos*. Alec Coppel had a real-life relationship with Alfred Hitchcock. With Samuel Taylor, Coppel coauthored the director's masterpiece, *Vertigo*, in 1958.

During the 1940s and the 1950s, Coppel penned a succession of screenplays for British cinema, most tinged with crime elements. *Obsession*, aka *The Hidden Room* (1949), based on his novel *A Man about a Dog*, depicts the revenge of a henpecked man against his wife's latest lover, while *Mr. Denning Drives Home* (1951), adapted from his novel of the same title, tells of a father killing his daughter's loathsome boyfriend. In *The Smart Aleck* (1951), a would-be inheritor of a considerable fortune hatches a foolproof plan to dispatch his uncle. Two deadly rivals find themselves stranded on an ice floe in *Hell below Zero* (1954).

Among Coppel's noncriminous screenplays were *The Captain's Paradise* (1953), a comedy about a bigamist who shuttles back and forth between wives in Gibraltar and Morocco, and *The Black Knight* (1954), a swash-buckling adventure.

In the late 1950s and early 1960s, Coppel contributed nerve-wracking episodes to such TV programs as *Alfred Hitchcock Presents*, *Schlitz Playhouse of Stars*, *General Electric Theatre*, and *Kraft Suspense Theatre*.

Acting Edition: *The Gazebo*—Dramatists Play Service. *I Killed the Count*—Samuel French, Inc. (in manuscript form).

Awards and Honors: Alec Coppel was nominated for a 1954 Academy Award for his screenplay of *The Captain's Paradise*.

NOTES

1. *New York Times*, December 13, 1958.
2. *New York Herald Tribune*, December 30, 1958.
3. *Daily News*, January 2, 1959.
4. *New York Journal-American*, December 29, 1958.
5. *New York Post*, December 29, 1958.
6. *Daily Mirror*, December 30, 1958.

Rashomon (1959)

Fay Kanin (United States, 1917–) and Michael Kanin (United States, 1910–1993)

About a thousand years ago, at the edge of the Rashomon Gate in Kyoto, the ancient capital of Japan, a Buddhist priest, tired and defeated, sits on the stone floor, near a meager bonfire. "The gate," says a production note, "fell into bad repair and became a decayed relic with an unsavory reputation, a hideout for thieves and a dump for unclaimed corpses." It is raining hard on this "crumbling and deserted edifice."

A woodcutter, his handmade ax stuck in his belt, comes running through the rain and asks the Priest if the rumor of his going away is true. The Priest acknowledges that the "savagery of men toward one another" is beyond his understanding. A wigmaker enters, with hair stolen from cadavers, and asks about the recent sensational murder. The woodcutter relates that he was the one who found a man's body in the woods, behind a clump of bamboo shoots, next to a woman's sedge hat, with a veil on it, dangling from a brush. He tore his legs and arms running to the police.

The cynical wigmaker, eager for details, learns from the woodcutter that the victim was a samurai warrior who had been run through with a sword, his frightened wife was found lost in the woods, and the culprit—accused of rape and murder—was arrested. "It's Tajomaru," says the woodcutter, "the most dangerous bandit in this part of the country." The Priest, haltingly, joins the conversation and relates that he was present when Tajomaru was questioned.

Tajomaru's account at the police court is visualized in the form of a flashback. The husband, Takehiko, is seen leading a small white horse, on which his wife Kinume is riding, through a winding path in the forest. A breeze flutters among the leaves, blowing the woman's veil. Tajomaru, who was lounging about, is fascinated by her exquisite face. "In that first moment," says the bandit, "I made up my mind to take her. Even if I had to kill the man."

After a struggle, Tajomaru binds the husband to a bamboo stump, then accosts the wife. Kinume struggles wildly, but gradually succumbs,

282

her hand moving along Tajomaru's back to clasp him in a reciprocating embrace.

Later, Kinume pleads with Tajomaru, "At least, give my husband a chance to avenge my honor—and his own." Tajomaru unties Takehiko's bonds. A fierce sword fight ensues, at the end of which the husband stumbles and the bandit plunges his weapon downward to its fatal conclusion. During the contest, the wife runs away. No, says Tajomaru, he didn't look for her. She was just a woman, after all.

Three contradictory versions of the event are related by the wife, by the spirit of the dead husband via a medium, and by the woodcutter.

Kinume describes how following the rape she released her husband's bonds, but he kept looking at her with cold, silent disdain. Desperate and angry, she must have fainted. When she came to, she found her husband dead, the sword in his breast. It was then that she realized that she had killed him. She ran into the woods, deeper and deeper, tried to drown the sight of herself in the river. But even the river scorned her.

Takehiko, speaking from the dead, accuses Kinume of submitting to Tajomaru willingly, and requesting the bandit to slay her husband—"As long as he lives I'll always be his wife. I can never be completely yours. Kill him. Kill him! Kill him!" Tajomaru, disgusted, cuts the husband's rope, and the wife flees. Takehiko is left alone, his eyes filled with tears—a man whose hopes are shattered, his pride gone. He draws the sword, raises it above his breast, and thrusts it into himself. "I sank down, down into the blackness of space," says Takehiko through the medium.

The woodcutter claims to have watched the event from behind a bush and insists that "none of their stories are true. They lied—all of them." His tale unfolds in broadly comic strokes. As both men decide to leave the woman behind, she lashes at her husband for being a coward and at the bandit for being a small, cheap imitation of himself with exaggerated reputation.

The two men are now impelled to prove their mettle. The wife smiles with triumphant satisfaction as they assume en garde positions. A sword duel follows—a spineless, bloodless pantomime filled with slapstick pratfalls. After a while, the husband stumbles and is impaled by his own weapon.

Rashomon winds up on an optimistic note. A baby is left crying by the gate. The woodcutter says that even though he has six children at home who are sometimes hungry and cold, he will take the baby with him; there is little enough, but how much can such a small mouth eat? This glimmer of man's goodness revitalizes the downcast Priest. His face is now at peace. The rain has stopped, and he finds the air clean and sweet. "The Rashomon," says the Priest. "Somehow, it's no longer so fearsome—

with all its crows, and corpses and jackals. Even out of its crumbling ruins can come—life."

* * *

Piercing through the play's melodramatic aspects is the issue "What is truth?" When *Rashomon* opened on January 27, 1959, at New York's Music Box, critic Richard Watts Jr. pointed out its theme: "How much do motives of fear, pride and self-interest cause one to see what one wants to see?"[1]

Brooks Atkinson asked, "What is the truth? Is the bandit a brute or a romantic figure? Is the wife a woman of modesty or a strumpet? Is the husband a man of honor or a coward? Truth has many sides according to the witness, for the witness sees what he wants to see and tells what he wants the world to believe." Atkinson praised the authors of the play, saying that "Mr. and Mrs. Kanin preserved the integrity of the theme; the writing is reserved and passionless"; the director, Peter Glenville, who "has transmuted the material into a perfectly imagined microcosm of sound, color and movement"; the thespians who "act their suitable parts with subtlety, conciseness and unfailing skill"; and the entire enterprise: "pure art of the theatre. Out of a legend it conjures a mood. No one need despair of a commercial theatre that can deal in exclusive materials with so much delicacy, expertness, and charm."[2]

John McClain saluted the all-star cast: "Rod Steiger, the brawny and bellowing bandit, gives a performance of enormous strength and persuasion in contrast to Claire Bloom's fragile and fluttering efforts as an ex-domestic who has wed the aristocrat. But it is Oscar Homolka, playing a cynical and disreputable wigmaker (his product comes straight from the grave) who has been assigned most of the best lines and he has a merry time for himself. Akim Tamiroff is convincing as the woodcutter-witness and Noel William is a suitably proud and disdainful Samurai."[3]

The sole dissenter among the morning-after reviewers was John Chapman of the *Daily News*: "*Rashomon* is a pretentious bore—overwritten, overset, overacted and overdirected. Now and then it gets so far over in one department or another that it is ridiculous, and in these brief moments it is fun—which is not what the authors intended."[4]

Rashomon ran for 159 performances.

Many community theatres and university drama clubs found this philosophical excursion to the ancient Far East a worthwhile endeavor. *Rashomon* does not require the sumptuous sets and costumes of the original Broadway production to create a magical and thought-provoking ambience. But it has taken almost three decades for the play to be revived in New York. Off-Broadway's Roundabout Theatre presented *Rashomon* with an all-Asian cast in 1988.

Theatre Works of Silicon Valley, California, included *Rashomon* in the company's 1990–1991 season. The Shaw Festival of Niagara-on-the-Lake, Ontario, Canada, presented *Rashomon* in 1996. The play triggered a hub of activity at the turn of the twenty-first century with productions mounted by the Rude Guerilla Theatre Company in Santa Ana, California (1999); Pan Asian Rep in uptown Manhattan, New York (2001); and the Blunt Theatre Company in downtown Manhattan (2004). The Golden West College Theatre, Huntington Beach, California, offered *Rashomon* in 2009.

Rashomon was adapted by the Kanins from two stories by Ryunosuke Akutagawa (1892–1927), "Father of the Japanese short story." The same stories served as the basis for Akira Kurosawa's 1950 masterful motion picture, Oscar winner as Best Foreign Film. The movie catapulted Toshiro Mifune, in the role of the notorious bandit, and Machiko Kyo, as his raped victim, to international fame. "The film's very title has become part of our language," states Leonard Maltin in his annual *Movie and Video Guide*.[5]

A lackluster U.S. remake, *The Outrage* (1964), directed by Martin Ritt, had Paul Newman as a Mexican bandit who allegedly rapes Claire Bloom while her husband Laurence Harvey helplessly stands by.

Rashomon was transferred to television by America's Play of the Week in 1960, featuring Ricardo Montalban as the bandit and Carol Lawrence as the wife, and by British BBC the following year, with Lee Montague and Yoko Tani.[6]

* * *

Fay Mitchell Kanin was born in New York City and raised in Elmira, New York, where she attended the private Elmira College. She wrote items for the *Elmira Star-Gazette* and edited the college yearbook. When visiting her grandmother, who lived in the Bronx, Kanin saw a matinée of Robert E. Sherwood's *Idiot's Delight*, starring Alfred Lunt and Lynn Fontanne, and decided to devote herself to the theatre.

Kanin spent her senior year at the University of Southern California and after graduation was hired by RKO Pictures as a story editor at $75 a week. It is there that she met Michael Kanin, a writer in the B unit, and soon they got married. Their first team effort was *Sunday Punch* (1942), a bittersweet comedy about the misadventures of a group of fledgling boxers living in a boardinghouse. Many other collaborative projects followed, with Michael, who was trained as an artist, providing a visual sense, and Fay concentrating on character and dialogue.

Among the Kanins' films were *My Pal Gus* (1952), a domestic comedy starring Richard Widmark; *Rhapsody* (1954), with Elizabeth Taylor torn between two musicians; *The Opposite Sex* (1956), a comedy-with-music inspired by Clare Boothe Luce's *The Women*; *Teacher's Pet* (1958), about a hard-knuckled newspaper editor, played by Clark Gable, who pretends to be a student in a class conducted by journalism teacher Doris Day; *The Right Approach* (1961), in which a group of young bachelors living together in the Hollywood Hills find their peaceful existence shattered upon the arrival of an ambitious, ruthless newcomer (Frankie Vaughan) who will stop at nothing on his way to fame as a singing star.

The Kanins detoured to Italy for *Swordsman of Siena* (1962), a swashbuckling adventure, and to West Germany for the comedy *Mein oder Dein* (*Mine or Yours*, 1964).

For the Broadway stage, Fay Kanin wrote the comedy *Goodbye, My Fancy*, and her husband produced it at the Morosco Theatre in 1948. The protagonist is a liberal congresswoman who returns to her alma mater as an honorary visitor and clashes with the rigid trustees. *Goodbye, My Fancy* ran for 446 performances at the Morosco Theatre and was filmed in 1951 with Joan Crawford. *His and Hers*, by both Fay and Michael Kanin, is the story of a husband and wife playwriting team who after a succession of failures dissolve their marriage and they each start writing a new play. When the plays end up rather similar, the two find themselves in court suing each other for plagiarism. The 1954 comedy ran at the Forty-sixth Street Theatre for seventy-six performances.

Suggested by Arthur Schnitzler's *The Affairs of Anatol*, the Kanins wrote the book for the *The Gay Life* (aka *The High Life*), with music by Arthur Schwartz, lyrics by Howard Dietz, highlighting the romantic escapades of a notorious ladies' man in turn-of-the-century Vienna. The musical premiered at the Shubert Theatre in 1961 and ran for 113 performances.

On her own, Fay Kanin wrote the book for the 1985 musical *Grind*, picturing a burlesque theatre including both black and white performers, in Chicago of 1933. Though directed by master Hal Prince and featuring the powerhouse cast of song-and-dance man Ben Vereen and slapstick comic Stubby Kaye, the reviews were mixed and the show closed after seventy-one performances, losing its entire $4.75 million investment.

In the early 1970s, Fay Kanin began to focus on made-for-television movies. Her efforts include *Heat of Anger* (1972), about the relationship between an older woman and a younger man, both lawyers; *Tell Me Where It Hurts* (1974), centered on a group of women who get together to exchange ideas; *Hustling* (1975), the story of a prostitute who recounts her past to a reporter; *Friendly Fire* (1979), the Emmy-winning drama of a mother who discovers that her son was killed by friendly fire in Vietnam; *Fun and Games* (1980), covering sexual harassment in the workplace; and *Heartsounds* (1984), dealing with a married couple coping with heart disease.

Fay Kanin was elected president of the Academy of Motion Picture Arts and Sciences in 1979, and held the position for four terms until 1983. She also served as president of the Screen Branch of the Writers Guild of

America and as a member of the board of directors of the American Film Institute. Since 1999, she has been a member of the board of governors of the Academy of Motion Picture Arts and Sciences.

* * *

Michael Kanin, the older brother of writer/director/producer Garson Kanin, was born in Rochester, New York. He began his show business career writing and acting in Catskill resort shows, and he worked as a commercial artist. In 1939 he was signed to a screenwriting contract by RKO Pictures. A year later he married RKO colleague Fay Mitchell.

Several B-movies penned by Michael Kanin were tinged with elements of crime. *Panama Lady* (1939) featured Lucille Ball as a saloon dance-hall girl who gets entangled with a gun smuggler and ends up facing lethal danger in the jungles of Ecuador. In *They Made Her a Spy* (1939), a patriotic Secret Service girl infiltrates a ring of saboteurs.

Classier efforts by Kanin included *Anne of Windy Poplars* (1940), a sequel to *Anne of Green Gables*, in which a schoolteacher in a small Canadian town becomes prey to the local gossips. *Woman of the Year* (1942), directed by George Stevens, about rival reporters, was the first of the Spencer Tracy–Katharine Hepburn comedies.[7] *The Cross of Lorraine* (1943) centered on a group of French soldiers who were prisoners of war during World War II.

Kanin served as producer of *A Double Life* (1947), in which Ronald Colman enacted an obsessed thespian who loses himself when playing Othello and strangles Desdemona on stage. Colman won the Oscar for his portrayal, as did Miklos Rosza for Original Score.

Kanin's sole directing assignment was the modest *When I Grow Up* (1951), in which Bobby Driscoll played a young boy who feels neglected and intends to run away from home, but leafing through his grandfather's diary he gains a new understanding of his elders and changes his mind. Kanin's last movie script, in collaboration with Ben Starr, was *How to Commit Marriage* (1969), a Bob Hope–Jackie Gleason–Jane Wyman comedy that rotates around an adopted baby.

Acting Edition: Samuel French, Inc.

Awards and Honors: Michael Kanin and Ring Lardner Jr. shared an Academy Award for the screenplay of *Woman of the Year* (1942). Fay and Michael Kanin were nominated for an Academy Award and a Writers Guild of America Award for their screenplay of *Teacher's Pet* (1959). Fay Kanin won the American Bar Association Gavel Award for *Heat of Anger* (1972) and a Writer of the Year Emmy for *Tell Me Where It Hurts* (1974). Fay's *Hustling* was nominated for an Edgar for Best Television Feature and for an Emmy for Outstanding Original Teleplay (1976). Fay's *Friendly Fire* won an Emmy for Outstanding Drama/Comedy Special (1978). Her

Heartsounds was nominated for an Emmy, and *Grind* was nominated for a Tony (both in 1985).

NOTES

1. *New York Post*, January 28, 1959.
2. *New York Times*, January 28, 1959.
3. *New York Journal-American*, January 28, 1959.
4. *Daily News*, January 28, 1959.
5. *Leonard Maltin's 2008 Movie Guide* (New York: Signet, 2007), 1122.
6. In 2005, playwright-composer Michael John LaChiusa based his musical *See What I Wanna See* on the same short stories by Ryunosuke Akutagawa, moving the proceedings from ancient Japan to modern New York. On a stroll through Central Park, a married couple is accosted by a brash thief who rapes the wife and murders the husband. Or does he? The conflicting accounts of what happened raise doubts.
7. Four decades after the making of the film *Woman of the Year*, a Broadway musical version, with book by Peter Stone, music by John Kander, and lyrics by Fred Ebb, based on the screenplay by Michael Kanin and Ring Lardner Jr., was presented at the Palace Theatre, starring Lauren Bacall and Harry Guardino, running 770 performances.

Redhead (1959)

Book by Herbert Fields and Dorothy Fields (United States, 1897–1958 and 1905–1974), Lyrics by Dorothy Fields, Music by Albert Hague (United States, Germany-born, 1920–2001)

At rise, the stage is dark except for the face of a beautiful girl seated before a dressing-table mirror. From the makeup she applies, it is obvious that she is in the theatrical profession. She is whistling gaily as she beautifies herself.

Silently, on the other side of the stage, a door opens and the silhouette of a man is seen slipping inside and closing the door noiselessly. By the use of a special effect, a purple scarf becomes gradually visible as it is cautiously pulled from the man's pocket.

The girl is oblivious to the scarf moving toward her; it seems to float with its own inner life, and it comes up behind her with slow, terrifying precision. Then, suddenly, it is hooked around her throat and pulled tight.

The girl screams shrilly until she is strangled. As she sinks into the surrounding blackness, a light replaces her face with that of her killer. His bright red hair and red beard make him easily identifiable. The light on his face slowly fades out.

This homicide-in-the-dark is not the start of an Edgar Wallace thriller or a Stephen King horror play, but the unusual prologue of the Broadway musical *Redhead*. The action of *Redhead* unfolds in turn-of-the-century London. The main character is Essie Whimple, a timid twenty-nine-year-old girl who sculpts replicas of historical murderers for her aunts' wax museum. An opening number, "The Simpson Sisters' Waxworks," sung by the entire company, describes a museum filled with "cadavers by the score," "shrunken heads," and "smelling salts galore."

Essie runs in and apologizes to her aunts, Maude and Sarah Simpson, for being late. She had one of those recurring visions about the same man. Left by herself, Essie sings "The Right Finger of My Left Hand," in which she expresses yearning for "a small, gold band."

Soon people arrive and Essie draws open a curtain, unveiling her latest "blood-curdling exhibit"—the tableau of the Strangler and his Victim. It is an exact replica of the murder committed in the prologue. The girl is being strangled, her beautiful face grotesquely contorted, her eyes bulging, the purple scarf twisted around her throat. The face of the murderer is a blank expanse of wax.

At the sight of the sculpture, the spectators gasp. Some turn away. Two men carry a woman out. The general reaction is one of horrified fascination.

Enter Tom Baxter, a tall, handsome American who is appearing at the nearby Odeon Theatre in a strong man act, and his friend George Poppett, a lithe singer-comedian. Baxter offers to buy the sculpture, explaining that the murdered girl, Ruth La Rue, was "like a kid sister" to him. He brought her from America to England to appear in a show, and he resents "making a money-making spectacle out of her murder." Essie is taken by the big American but Aunt Maude tells him crisply that the exhibit is not for sale. Tom, angry, strides to the sculpture and pulls down the curtains. Aunt Maude is not intimidated. She crosses to the exhibit, draws the curtains open, and is astounded: "Oh, the purple scarf. It's gone!" Someone shouts, "The killer's here!" and, panicky, people start to run every which way.

In Essie's workroom, where the statuary for the museum is created and repaired, a few samples of human limbs are strewn about carelessly, endowing the place with the aura of a surrealist nightmare. Inspector White of Scotland Yard and several of his officers search the place and notice an exit to an outside alley. The inspector concludes that the Strangler slipped away through the alley, and exits with his men. Essie, enamored with Tom Baxter from first sight, stops Tom and George from leaving by telling them tall tales about her late parents' show business prowls, their leaving her at her aunts' doorstep, and being beaten and tortured by the cruel aunts. Tom and George are sympathetic to her plight and croon "Just for Once!" assuring Essie that she's "beautiful," "passionate," "seductive," and smart enough to "do something foolish."

Essie confides to her aunt Sarah that she's in love with "the strongest man in the whole world." Aunt Sarah squelches Essie's enthusiasm by insisting that "the only one Baxter wants to see is the girl's killer. He's one of those one-track-mind types." But Essie is not deterred and she hatches a plan, using herself as "bait" for the killer.

At the Odeon Theatre, producer-director-choreographer Howard Cavanaugh is staging George and the chorus in the splashy "Uncle Sam Rag." Following the number, Tom steps on stage to rehearse his act. He strains lifting a load of 200 pounds above his head when he hears the stage doorman, Alfy, attempting to stop someone. Essie pushes her way in, followed by her aunts. She breathlessly tells Tom that the Strangler tried to kill her and she can make a wax head of his image. Tom insists that they leave the buffoonish Inspector White out of it; he'll only gum up the works; from now on he, Tom, is taking over.

In order to keep a protective eye on Essie, Tom asks Howard Cavanaugh to give her a chorus part in the finale. Tom also suggests that Essie and her aunts move to his place; he'll move in with his friend, Sir Charles Willingham. When Aunt Maude objects, Tom rebukes the "old witch" for treating "poor Essie with sticks" and "working her to death." Maude sits down stunned.

George leads Essie to a dressing-room for makeup. When left by herself, she switches off the light, closes her eyes, and attempts to conjure a "vision" of Ruth La Rue's killer. The door opens. In the eerie light that filters in from the hallway a man with red hair and a red beard appears. Essie opens her eyes, turns, and has time for only a fleeting glance before the man retreats and disappears.

On the stage of the Odeon, the show has reached the finale. Essie, in the chorus, becomes completely lost and fouls up the formations. There comes a point where she seems to be doing fine, working in unison with the other dancers. But then something in one of the theatre boxes catches her attention. A man with red hair and a red beard is seated there.

Petrified, Essie cannot concentrate and by the time the curtain falls she has turned the finale into utter chaos. She makes a dash for the wing and tells Tom that she believes she saw the man who appeared in her vision, the man with red hair and a red beard, in Box A. Tom laughs and tells her that the man is his good friend, Sir Charles Willingham.

Dejected and forlorn, Essie remains behind on a darkened stage. As she picks up a wall telephone and asks the operator to connect her with Scotland Yard, she sees a shadow cast against the theatre background. Sir Charles removes his hat and says, "Miss Whimple? I understand you know who murdered Ruth." She drops the receiver, and he advances as the curtain falls.

The second act begins at Tom's apartment, later that night. Tom tells George that Essie has accused Sir Charles of killing Ruth. George does not pooh-pooh the possibility and instead expresses concern for Essie's life. Tom attempts to convince his friend that as far as he is concerned "there is no more Essie Whimple" and sings "I'm Back in Circulation."

Essie escapes from Sir Charles into the Green Dragon Pub where she instigates a general brawl, attacks a police captain, and is hustled to jail. She feels secure in the cell she's sharing with a gaggle of prostitutes. Aunts Sarah and Maude arrive for a visit and sneak a nail file in. George comes and convinces Essie that the only way for her to get Tom back is to prove that Sir Charles is the killer. She then lures a guard into a sexy dance, "The Pickpocket Tango," with the women in the cell beating out the rhythm. She manages to steal the key, leads the guard to the cell, and locks him in. Then she and the women rhythmically dance their way out of prison.

Tom and Essie meet in the waxworks museum and confess their love for one another. In a surprising twist, the lovers discover that the killer is not Sir Charles but their friend George Poppett, who has disguised himself as the aristocrat with a red wig and beard. Tom and George meet face-to-face on stage and exchange blows until Essie gets a mace, mounts a stage weight, and swings at George. The police later pick up George and take him out as Essie, Tom, and the chorus reprise the "Uncle Sam Rag."

* * *

Redhead opened at New York's Forty-sixth Street Theatre on February 5, 1959, staged and choreographed by Bob Fosse, designed by Rouben Ter-Arutunian, starring Gwen Verdon as Essie Whimple and Richard Kiley as Tom Baxter.

Most of the morning-after reviews were ecstatic. "Toss a whodunit, a romance and plenty of hoke into the musical comedy hopper, and you may come up with a walloping hit," cheered Robert Coleman.[1] "The music is chirpy, the lines are both droll and adult," wrote Frank Aston. "It is funny, fast, opulent, refreshing. Its numerous and talented performers even have a good story to work on—a whodunit told in respectable tunes, slick lines and exceedingly bright dance numbers from the brow of Bob Fosse."[2] Walter Kerr smiled, "*Redhead* is a sort of pink-champagne-and-black-tights murder mystery. . . . Herbert and Dorothy Fields, working with Sidney Sheldon and David Shaw, have provided at least as many surprise twists as are needed."[3]

"*Redhead* is a combination of musical comedy, murder mystery and Gwen Verdon, and the greatest of those is Gwen Verdon," declared Richard Watts Jr. "She is incomparable. You would have to go back to memories of Gertrude Lawrence to find a kinship in charm, skill and authentic glamour."[4] John McClain applauded Bob Fosse's "brilliant and original dance conceptions" as well as the sets and costumes designed by Rouben Ter-Arutunian, which "give a genuine flavor of the London of the turn of the century. The interior of a wax-works is particularly spooky, and the Green Dragon Pub will be remembered as the seediest trap of the season."[5]

A negative assessment came from Brooks Atkinson of the *New York Times*. He found Gwen Verdon "enchanting as usual" and Richard Kiley "an excellent leading man," but felt that "the promise is not fulfilled. *Redhead* drifts off at random into anything that may work for the moment."[6] In a follow-up piece, Atkinson touted Gwen Verdon's "effortless grace" and "unique gifts," but he lamented "an adroit performer picking her way through the labored jocosities of the book. . . . The performance as a whole is a routine job based on a flat libretto."[7]

Louis Kronenberger, in *The Best Plays of 1958–1959*, also hailed Gwen Verdon's contribution to *Redhead*, but asserted that "there was little musical comedy excitement. . . . by the time she had found her feet, the audience had all but lost interest in the show."[8]

Redhead ran for 452 performances. The Costa Mesa Playhouse in Costa Mesa, California, a troupe that specializes in the mounting of lesser-known musicals, had a successful run of *Redhead* in June of 1981. San Francisco's Forty-second Street Moon presented a staged concert of *Redhead* in September 1998.

* * *

The son of Lew Fields, a Jewish immigrant from Poland who found fame as half of the Weber and Fields vaudeville act, Herbert Fields (1897–1958) was born in New York City, where he began his theatrical career as an actor, detoured to direction and choreography, and eventually turned to playwriting. He penned the book for most of the Rodgers and Hart musicals of the 1930s, scored big with Cole Porter's *DuBarry Was a Lady* (1939; filmed 1943) and *Panama Hattie* (1940; filmed 1942), and collaborated with his younger sister Dorothy on the books for Porter's *Let's Face It!* (1941), *Something for the Boys* (1943), and *Mexican Hayride* (1944). The brother and sister teamed with composer Sigmund Romberg on the hit Broadway operetta *Up in Central Park* (1945), and with Irving Berlin on their biggest success, *Annie Get Your Gun*, a musical inspired by Annie Oakley (1946; filmed 1950). For the movies, Fields scripted several B movies in the 1930s. He also worked on *The Wizard of Oz* but was not credited.

Dorothy Fields (1905–1974) was born in Allenhurst, New Jersey, and grew up in Manhattan. She began her career as a lyricist on Broadway's *Blackbirds of 1928*, for which she wrote the enormous hit "I Can't Give You Anything but Love, Baby." In the mid-1930s she started to write lyrics for motion pictures, notably collaborating with composer Jerome Kern on the films *Roberta* (1935) and *Swing Time* (1936), two Fred Astaire–Ginger Rogers vehicles.[9]

Among the renowned composers Dorothy Fields worked with were Harold Arlen (the movie *Mr. Imperium*, 1951), Arthur Schwartz (the play *A Tree Grows in Brooklyn*, also 1951), Cy Coleman (the musicals *Sweet Charity*, 1966, and *Seesaw*, 1973).

One of the first successful female Tin Pan Alley and Hollywood songwriters, Dorothy Fields wrote more than four hundred songs for Broadway musicals and motion pictures.[10]

Composer and songwriter Albert Hague (1920–2001) was born to a Jewish family in Berlin, Germany. His father, a psychiatrist, and his mother, a chess champion, considered their Jewish heritage a liability and raised Hague as a Lutheran.

Hague came to America in 1939 on a scholarship to the University of Cincinnati in Ohio. After graduating in 1942, he served in the U.S. Air Force during World War II. In addition to *Redhead*, Hague's Broadway musicals include *Plain and Fancy* (1955) and *The Fig Leaves Are Falling* (1969). Famous songs he wrote include "Young and Foolish," "Look Who's in Love," and "Did I Ever Really Live?" In 2000, he composed the sound track for the TV musical cartoon, *How the Grinch Stole Christmas*.

Hague also was an actor, notably on the television series *Fame*, where he played Mr. Shorofsky, the white-bearded, bespectacled music teacher, and in the movie *Space Jam* as the psychiatrist who helped professional basketball players regain their skill.

Hague died in 2001, at the age of 81, from cancer at a hospital in Marina del Rey, California, where he lived.

Acting Edition: Music Theatre, Inc.

Awards and Honors: *Redhead* (1959) won five Tony Awards: Best Musical, Best Actor in a Musical (Richard Kiley), Best Actress in a Musical (Gwen Verdon), Best Choreography (Bob Fosse), and Best Production Design–Costume Design (Rouben Ter-Artunian).

NOTES

1. *Daily Mirror*, February 6, 1959.
2. *New York World-Telegram*, February 6, 1959.
3. *New York Herald Tribune*, February 6, 1959.
4. *New York Post*, February 6, 1959.
5. *New York Journal-American*, February 6, 1959.
6. *New York Times*, February 6, 1959.
7. *New York Times*, February 15, 1959.
8. Louis Kronenberger, ed., *The Best Plays of 1958–1959* (New York: Dodd, Mead, 1959), 35.
9. A Dorothy Fields lyric was utilized by Barack Obama in his inauguration speech as the forty-fourth president of the United States on January 20, 2009, when he said, "Starting today, we must pick ourselves up, dust ourselves off, and begin again the work of remaking America." This alludes to the song "Pick Yourself Up" from the 1936 film *Swing Time*, in which Ginger Rogers and Fred Astaire sang Fields's words, "Pick yourself up; dust yourself off; start all over again."
10. A show business family, Herbert and Dorothy Fields had an older brother, Joseph Fields (1895–1966), who was a notable playwright, stage director, screen-

writer, and film producer. Joseph Fields made his Broadway debut in 1938 with the play *Schoolhouse on the Lot*, cowritten with Jerome Chodorov. The pair went on to write *My Sister Eileen* (1940), *Junior Miss* (1941), *The French Touch* (1945), *Wonderful Town* (1953) for which they won the Tony Award for Best Musical, *The Girl in Pink Tights* (1954), *Anniversary Waltz* (1954), and *The Ponder Heart* (1956). With Anita Loos, Fields wrote the book for the Jule Styne musical *Gentlemen Prefer Blondes* (1949), and he teamed with Oscar Hammerstein II on the book for *Flower Drum Song* (1958).

Frankenstein: The Gift of Fire (1959)

David Campton (England, 1924–2006)

On the night of June 19, 1816, four friends were trapped by a storm at a lodge in the Swiss Alps. Trying to pass the time, they decided to concoct ghost stories. Lord Byron hosted this impromptu party, and his guests included Byron's physician, Dr. John Polidori, the poet Percy Bysshe Shelley, and Shelley's then lover (later wife), young Mary Wollstonecraft Godwin, daughter of the author William Godwin.[1]

That night two important works were born. Polidori would embellish his ghost story and come up with the novella *The Vampyre*, introducing the enigmatic, suave vampire Lord Ruthven; and Mary would build on her story and write the gothic novel *Frankenstein; or, The Modern Prometheus*. Shelley edited Mary's manuscript and *Frankenstein* was first published, in three hardcover volumes, on January 1, 1818.

Five years later, Richard Brinsley Peake adapted the novel to the stage under the title *Presumption; or, The Fate of Frankenstein*. James Wallack enacted Dr. Frankenstein, and Thomas Potter Cooke, a renowned stage villain, portrayed the monster.[2] The play scored a huge success. Within three years, fourteen other dramatizations of *Frankenstein* were mounted on English and French stages, of which the important ones are *The Monster and the Magician* by John Kerr and *The Man and the Monster* by Henry M. Milner, both produced in London in 1826. These were the torchbearers of over a hundred plays to date utilizing the Frankenstein theme.[3]

In the twentieth century, the first play to present a Frankenstein motif was *The Last Laugh* (1915) by the American playwrights Charles W. Goddard (1879–1951) and Paul Dickey (1885–1933). *The Last Laugh* lampoons the Frankenstein saga by having its wild action swirl around a wooden crate containing a body wrapped in bandages—the centerpiece in the private laboratory of a doctor intent on creating a human life. [4]

In 1927 came Peggy Webling's *Frankenstein: An Adventure in the Macabre*. Actor-manager Hamilton Deane, basking in the success of his dramatization of Bram Stoker's *Dracula*, added Webling's *Frankenstein* to his company's repertoire, and *Dracula* and *Frankenstein* ran alternatively in the English provinces, with Deane himself portraying the two monsters. *Dracula* was then produced in London with considerable success, running for 391 performances,[5] and the American publisher-producer Horace Liveright optioned it for New York. With some rewrites by John L. Balderston and featuring Bela Lugosi in the title role, *Dracula* ran on Broadway for 261 performances and then took to the road for several years.

Deane brought *Frankenstein* to London's Little Theatre on February 10, 1930. The reviews were caustic. *The Graphic* of February 22, 1930, said, "It would be idle to pretend that *Frankenstein* is a very noteworthy play. . . . There are times when we wish that the authoress would cut the cackle and come to the monster." However, the reviewer complimented Deane's portrayal of the monster: "The elemental pain that streaks across his eyes, the inarticulate twistings of his great red mouth, would be a credit to Mr. Charles Laughton or Sir Henry Irving. This is a fine piece of acting in which the ugliness is far more than skin-deep."[6] *Frankenstein* ran for seventy-two performances. Producer Liveright planned to export the play to New York in 1931 and engaged Balderston to doctor it. But Liveright was wiped out by the stock market crash, could not mount a stage production, and sold his option to Universal Studios. The Webling-Balderston play served as the basis for Universal's two classic horror films—*Frankenstein* (1931) and *Bride of Frankenstein* (1935), both directed by James Whale, both starring Boris Karloff as the monster and Colin Clive as his creator.[7]

It has taken more than seven decades for the Webling-Balderston version of *Frankenstein* to reach the stage of a legitimate theatre. Announced as a world premiere, *Frankenstein* was presented at Chandler Hall in Newtown, Pennsylvania, from October 31 to November 3, 2002. It was a Halloween event by special permission given by Jack Balderston, the author's son and heir. The cast included Blaise Guld as Henry Frankenstein, Antonio Mastrantonio as Dr. Waldman, and Brian Albert as The Creature. Eric Stedman directed.

"For a production mounted on a miniscule budget," wrote Frankenstein maven David J. Skal, "the stage effects were frequently impressive, ranging from creation paraphernalia inspired by the 1910 Edison version's magician's cabinet, the Hammer mad labs of the fifties and sixties, and even *Re-Animator* (1985). The creature's demise in an electrical crucifixion was Stedman's original contribution, but perfectly in keeping with the script."[8]

Many other dramatizations of Mary Shelley's story were written and produced throughout the twentieth century. Gladys Hastings-Walton's version was seen in Glasgow in 1936. Donald F. Glut reports that the adaptation remained faithful to the original novel, and adds, "Miss Hastings-Walton tried to show the very real horror of man's being replaced by the machines that he created."[9]

During the early 1940s, the drama department at Fairmont High School in Marion, Indiana, presented a spoof, *Goon with the Wind*, in which a young student who would later rise to fame—James Dean—portrayed the Frankenstein monster.

* * *

The stage is divided into three parts in David Campton's 1959 *Frankenstein: The Gift of Fire* (also subtitled *A Gothic Thriller in Two Acts*): Victor Frankenstein's laboratory, Henri Clerval's house, and a blank, neutral space. "This arrangement," states a production note, "made it possible for the scenes to flow into each other almost cinematically."[10] In the first scene we learn that Victor has often secluded himself in a hidden laboratory. He tells his friend Henri, "In centuries to come my name will be whispered with awe." At Clerval's home, during supper, there is talk of a recent grave robbery—a body has been snatched a few hours after the funeral. Elizabeth expresses to Henri her concern about her fiancé, Victor, who keeps disappearing, and "each time he returns haggard, wild-eyed, and farther from me than ever."

During a thunder-and-lightning storm, in a tense scene, a gigantic creature with "patchwork features" emerges from a covered sheet. Henri pleads with Victor to kill the giant. Victor attempts to prove that the creature possesses human emotions by giving it a doll. The creature cradles the doll in his arms, then, with one jerk, detaches the head from the body. Convinced that the creature must be destroyed, Victor offers him a poisoned flask, but relents, knocks the flask from the creature's hand, and urges, "Leave this place. Hide. Go to the mountains."

The plot takes a turn and becomes a murder mystery. Master William, Victor's young brother, is discovered dead in his bed amid splattered blood. The maid Justine, who was found in the child's room, is accused of his murder. The argument against her is that the snow beneath the window was unmarked. Despite Victor's protestations that Justine has not committed the crime, she is found guilty. Before Henri Clerval can corroborate Victor's testimony, he is found dead on the town's old roadside, his spine broken.

At the climax, the Monster enters Clerval's house through a window and confronts Elizabeth. In a departure from the original novel and from all other stage adaptations, as the creature advances menacingly toward

Elizabeth, she shoots him point blank with a pistol. The creature staggers and falls. Victor pleads with Elizabeth to forgive him. He has learned his lesson. Everything will be different—next time.

David Campton's adaptation was first presented at the Library Theatre in Scarborough, England, on July 16, 1959. Campton himself played Mr. Clerval, Henri's father. Alan Ayckbourn, soon to become an important dramatist, portrayed Henri. Stephen Joseph enacted The Creature and directed.

* * *

In the mid-1950s, the avant-garde Living Theatre Company, founded by Julian Beck and his wife Judith Malina and known for its off-beat productions of *The Connection* and *The Brig*, began to rehearse their interpretation of *Frankenstein* while on a European tour. It was a sharp departure from the original novel. Pierre Biner, in his book *The Living Theatre*, cites that for Beck and Malina "the play's philosophical foundation is embedded in the idea that the world must be changed, that a new man must evolve, and all human suffering must be eliminated. The motives of Dr. Frankenstein are to be found in that idea."[11]

Running six hours (an abridged version ran three and a half hours), the play evolved from a skeletal script developed by actors' improvisations during rehearsals. The curtain rose on the tossing of a girl into a coffin. "From that point," relates Donald F. Glut, "the stage erupted into a series of murders and executions in numerous brutal ways, with the long-haired members of the cast screaming and howling and running through the audience. Dr. Frankenstein (played by Beck) entered the scenes of violence and began to dismember the various corpses so that the dead could be given new life. While Dr. Frankenstein labored on his monster, Jewish cabbalists imitate him by building a female Golem. Sigmund Freud assisted in the creation of the Frankenstein Monster. Blood was pumped into the corpse creation of Frankenstein."[12]

In a turnabout, the Living Theatre's *Frankenstein* ends with the characters engaging in acts of love. The world premiere took place at the Teatro La Perla in Venice on September 26, 1965. In October the production moved to Berlin, where it was filmed. The play eventually came to the United States. Upon its opening at the Brooklyn Academy of Music, in repertoire with three other Living Theatre productions, critic Clive Barnes wrote, "The evening is at times repetitious, at times banal, here and there (and only here and there) a little boring. But the overwhelming impression is of a new physical style of theatre, raw, gutsy and vital."[13] The production won an Obie Award.

Written by Sheldon Altman and Bob Pickett, *I'm Sorry, the Bridge Is Out, You'll Have to Spend the Night*, is a musical spoof on horror movies of the

1930s and 1940s. The show opened at Hollywood's Coronet Theatre on April 28, 1970. The zany plot centers around Dr. Frankenstein's quest to obtain a suitable brain for his monster. A storm brings down the bridge and forces John David Walgood and his pretty fiancée Mary Ellen Harriman to take refuge in the castle. The couple, innocent and naive, are oblivious to danger when surrounded by the Mummy, the Wolf Man, Igor, and other creatures that go bump in the night.

* * *

More stage adaptations of Shelley's novel followed. *Frankenstein's Monster* by Sally Netzel was presented at the Dallas Theatre Center in the summer of 1972. Wolfgang Deichsel's *Frankenstein* played in Paris during the 1972–1973 season. In 1974, the prolific Tim Kelly penned a two-act *Frankenstein* (aka *The Rage of Frankenstein*) that unfolds entirely in a chateau on the shores of Lake Geneva, Switzerland. Five years later, *The Frankenstein Affair* by Ken Eulo was produced at off-Broadway's Courtyard Playhouse, rotating the action between Mary Shelley's bedroom and Dr. Frankenstein's laboratory in an attempt to illustrate a parallel between the author's tribulations in her marriage with those of the Monster.

On January 4, 1981, the Monster made it to Broadway. *Frankenstein* by Victor Gialanella premiered at the Palace Theatre under the direction of Tom Moore, featuring David Dukes (Victor Frankenstein), Keith Jochim (The Creature), Dianne Wiest (Elizabeth Lavenza), and John Carradine (blind hermit DeLacey). The critics unanimously savaged the effort, calling it "clumsy," "inept," "plodding," "unpleasant," and "a mumble-jumbled Victorian melodrama." The play closed after one performance.

In Brighton, England, an adaptation of *Frankenstein* by Geoff Parker opened at the Gardner Centre on November 29, 1984, and elicited this comment by the *London Theatre Record*: "Geoff Parker has unwisely spread his net wide, following the Mary Shelley novel from childhood to death. The result is a broad unfocussed evening that could do with a fair degree of pruning."[14]

Back in the United States, Manhattan's City Stage Company produced an adaptation of *Frankenstein* by Laurence Maslon on November 3, 1985, for twenty-three performances. Here the Monster is a sympathetic creation, more sinned against than sinning. The following year, on October 29, 1986, Second Avenue Theatre came up with the musical *Have I Got a Girl for You!*, book by Joel Greenhouse and Penny Rockwell, music and lyrics by Dick Gallagher. This "wildly campy spoof of *Bride of Frankenstein*"[15] improbably takes place at a Bavarian forest just east of Hollywood and is populated with a mixed chorus of peasants and movie stars. *Have I Got a Girl for You!* ran for seventy-eight performances.

In the late 1980s the Monster was given life on the stages of Cincinnati's Playhouse in the Park (by David Richmond and Bob Hall) and the Tyrone Guthrie Theatre in Minneapolis (by Barbara Field). George Abbott wrote the book, Joseph Turrin the music, and Gloria Nissenson the lyrics for *Frankie*, a 1989 musical comedy produced off-Broadway by the York Theatre Company. The venture was called "a woeful modernization of Frankenstein" in *The Best Plays of 1989–1990*.[16]

The Monster continued to chill audiences on both sides of the Atlantic during the 1990s. An adaptation written and directed by Julia Bardsley played at the Haymarket Studio, Leicester, England, in 1992. "It's a dazzling demonstration of the use of imagistic theatre techniques to grab the audience by its imagination," applauded the *Royal Exchange*, Manchester.[17] A year later, New York's off-Broadway Triangle Theatre Company offered Barbara Field's *Playing with Fire (After Frankenstein)*, in which the final confrontation between Dr. Frankenstein and his creation is set in the barren wastes of the North Pole. Back in England, in 1999, the Sandbach Players of Cheshire mounted *The House of Frankenstein* by Martin Downing, featuring a gaggle of monsters—Frankenstein, vampire, werewolf, zombie, and phantom—converging under a full moon in a cobwebbed castle. The following year, the creatures gathered again at off-Broadway's Triad Theatre in *Miami Beach Monsters*, billed as "a vaudeville with a bite."[18]

Mary Shelley's creature continued his rampage in the twenty-first century. In 2000, off-Broadway's La Mama presented *Frankenstein: The Rock Musical*, with book, music, and lyrics by William Electric Black. Tim Kelly's 1974 *Frankenstein* was directed by Stewart F. Lane at the Powerhouse Performing Arts Center for Halloween of 2001. Howard Brenton's 1984 drama *Blood Poetry*, set in a Lake Geneva lodge in 1816 with Mary Shelley, Percy Bysshe Shelley, Lord Byron, and Dr. Polidori collaborating on ghost stories and sly mischief, was revived in 2001 at the Connelly Theatre.

The year 2002 proved to be a banner year for Frankenstein productions. In January, Manhattan's Classic Stage Company mounted *Monster*, an unorthodox adaptation of Shelley's novel by Neil Bell. Directed by Michael Greif, the Monster flounders about naked, Frankenstein's fiancée exposes herself, and the doctor kisses a male friend. Critic Donald Lyons called it "a preposterous and unintentionally funny vulgarization of the tale."[19] In February, the Scottish Opera of Glasgow presented *Monster* by Sally Beamish. Her libretto focuses on the 1816 house party celebrated by Mary Wollstonecraft, Lord Byron, and Percy Bysshe Shelley. In October, H. K. Gruber's whimsical one-man oratorio *Frankenstein!* was performed by the Cleveland Orchestra. Bernard Holland wrote in the *New York Times*, "The wild-eyed Mr. Gruber recites, rants, mugs, sings and plays toy instruments."[20]

Mid-October, off-Broadway's Looking Glass Theatre presented *The Tragedy of Frankenstein*, an adaptation written and directed by William Gilmore, who utilized a grotesquely dressed chorus to mingle with the audience and comment on the proceedings.

Later in October, the McGinn/Gazale Theatre presented Scott Blumenthal's *So Frightful an Event Is Single in the History of Man*. Flashbacks take us to Dr. Frankenstein's abode where we meet his parents (both die during the proceedings with a broken heart), his beloved Elizabeth, and his friend Henry (both are killed by a vengeful Creature). At the end, the Creature escapes to an unknown destination by running through the auditorium's aisle.

Robert George Asseltine is the composer, librettist, and lyricist of *Frankenstein . . . Do you Dream?* The show, advertised as an "epic musical experience, a faithful telling of Mary Shelley's original story," was seen in Toronto, Canada, in 2003, and migrated the following year to New York City's fringe Belt Theatre.

Following several out-of-town stage readings, Catherine Bush's *The Frankenstein Summer*, a fictional treatment of the real-life famous gathering of Percy Bysshe Shelley, Mary Shelley, Lord Byron, and Dr. Polidori, came to Manhattan's Theatre at the Clements in October 2004. The emphasis is on personal relationships of love, lust, and friendship.

The Flying Machine, a young company trained in French mime, brought its *Frankenstein* to off-Broadway's Soho Theatre later in 2004. The show combined music and movement, and its setting was a geometrical maze. "All of mankind appears monstrous in this production," said reviewer Jason Zinoman. "Every actor wears pointy ears and fake protruding teeth, making them look vaguely animalistic, an effect emphasized by the cast's bustling, sweaty energy."[21]

Frankenstein, the Musical, by Robert Mitchell, was presented at off-Broadway's Wing Theatre in 2006. The show had forty musical numbers—none memorable—and very little spoken dialogue. The production reached some momentum during the last few scenes, when Victor Frankenstein confronts his monstrous creation. Andrea Stevens of the *New York Times* admonished director John Henry Davis for "mistaking melodrama for drama by increasing the violence."[22] The *New York Post*'s Frank Scheck found the "new creature more cheesy than scary."[23]

In 2007, New Yorkers were offered still two more musicals based on the Frankenstein lore. *Frankenstein*, with music by Mark Baron, book and lyrics by Jeffrey Jackson, was announced as "extraordinarily faithful to Mary Shelley's original novel while offering a bold, new experience for modern theatre audiences." The show, presented at off-Broadway's Thirty-seven Arts, was called by Raven Snook in *Time Out New York* "this monster dud is DOA. . . . The staging is stiff, the songs sound like *Sweeney*

Todd meets Jim Steinman, and the storytelling—which relies heavily on melodramatic monologues and an overused projection screen—is rarely engaging."[24] The *New York Times'* Charles Isherwood ended his negative review with a description of the Creature roaming the stage "in something between a swagger and a stagger" as if he "was fighting through a fearsome case of constipation."[25]

Simultaneously opening at Broadway's Hilton Theatre on November 8, 2007, was the highly budgeted musical *Young Frankenstein*, directed by Susan Stroman, for which Mel Brooks wrote the music and lyrics and cowrote the book (with Thomas Meehan). Ben Brantley of the *New York Times* compared the show unfavorably to Brooks's 1974 movie on which it was based, claiming it "never stops screeching at you and it leaves you with a monstrous headache."[26]

Frankenstein (Mortal Toys), a puppet show written by Eric Ehn, premiered at the Velaslavasay Panorama of Los Angeles in December 2007, won kudos from the *Los Angeles Times*, and travelled East to New York's HERE Arts Center, where it opened in January 2008. The *New York Times'* Rachel Saltz lauded directors-designers Janie Geiser and Susan Simpson: "They have deftly recreated the atmosphere of Shelley's novel in poetic, visual terms. . . . We are treated to the spectacle of artists, fully engaged, transforming and illuminating material they obviously love."[27]

Man-Made, written and directed by Susan Mosakowsky, has undergone two workshops over a seven-year development program and at last was presented by the Creation Production Company at off-Broadway's Ohio Theatre from February 29 to March 22, 2008. Among the characters are the fathers of the evolution theory, Charles Darwin and Alfred Russell Wallace. Mary Shelley appeals to them to find for her Creature an appropriate mate. Andrea Stevens of the *New York Times* wrote that the "play of ideas reads better than it is performed."[28]

At the end of Mary Shelley's novel and by the final curtain of its many stage adaptations, the Monster dies. But, not unlike such immortal literary creations as Dracula and Sherlock Holmes, he keeps coming back. In May 2008, the Chicago-based ensemble 500 Clown brought its circus comedy *Frankenstein* to the Orange County Performing Arts Center in Costa Mesa, California. No doubt, more faithful and unfaithful stage adaptations of the Mary Shelley classic novel are on their way to a nearby theatre.

* * *

The Frankenstein lore first appeared on the screen in a 1910 one-reel produced by Thomas Alva Edison, adapted and directed by J. Searle Dawley.[29] *Life without Soul* (1915), directed by Joseph W. Smiley, is about a doctor who creates a soulless man. It turns out that a young man has dreamed the horrific events when he fell asleep reading Mary Shelley's

Frankenstein. In Germany, Paul Wegener's silent film *Der Golem* (1920) was based on the legend of the medieval giant created by a rabbi out of clay, a forerunner of the Frankenstein monster.[30]

The enormous success of Universal's 1931 talkie *Frankenstein* spawned the masterful *Bride of Frankenstein* (1935) and the fine sequels *Son of Frankenstein* (1939), *The Ghost of Frankenstein* (1942), *Frankenstein Meets the Wolf Man* (1943), and *House of Frankenstein* (1944). *Abbott and Costello Meet Frankenstein* (1948) is the best in the comedians' series of horror spoofs. *I Was a Teenage Frankenstein* (1957) was a campy failure, but England's Hammer Studios injected distinction in *The Curse of Frankenstein* (1957) and *The Revenge of Frankenstein* (1958), both with Peter Cushing as the possessed scientist.

Low-budget embarrassments include *Frankenstein Conquers the World* (1965), *Frankenstein Meets the Space Monsters* (1965), *Jesse James Meets Frankenstein's Daughter* (1966), *Dracula vs. Frankenstein* (1971), and *Frankenstein and the Monster from Hell* (1972). Better quality is exhibited in Victor Erice's *The Spirit of the Beehive* (Spain, 1973), the story of a morose Castilian girl, who watches a dubbed print of *Frankenstein* in the town square and makes Karloff's monster a father figure. Severed heads and hands are the main attraction in the X-rated 3-D version of *Andy Warhol's Frankenstein* (1974), written and directed by Warhol's collaborator, Paul Morrissey. *Young Frankenstein* (1974), Mel Brooks's highly regarded parody, had Gene Wilder in the title role, Peter Boyle as the monster, and Marty Feldman as a hunchbacked assistant, all in top form.

In *Frankenstein Island* (1981), the monster appears only at the very end. *The Bride* (1985) is a pale remake of *Bride of Frankenstein*. In *Gothic* (1986), British director Ken Russell attempts to capture the events of the 1816 night when Mary Shelley was inspired to write her gothic classic. The relationship among Mary Wollstonecraft, Percy Bysshe Shelley, and Lord Byron is explored in Gonzalo Suarez's *Rowing with the Wind* (1987) and Ivan Passer's *Haunted Summer* (1988). Roger Corman's *Frankenstein Unbound* (1990) is a take-off on the novel by Brian W. Aldiss. Robert De Niro portrays the creature and Kenneth Branagh plays Victor Frankenstein in *Mary Shelley's Frankenstein* (1994). *Rock and Roll Frankenstein* came to the silver screen in 1998.

Frankenstein made many appearances on television, notably in ABC's 1952 *Tales of Tomorrow*, with Lon Chaney Jr. as the Monster; NBC's 1957 *Matinee Theatre*, featuring Primo Carnero; 1958's *Screen Gems*, adapted and directed by Curt Siodmak; CBS's 1964–1966 series *The Munsters*, with Fred Gwynne playing the head of the family, Herman Munster, in Karloff-Monster makeup; 1968's *Thames Television*, with Ian Holm as Dr. Frankenstein; 1973's *ABC Special*, starring Robert Foxworth as Dr. Frankenstein, Susan Strasberg as Elizabeth, and Bo Svenson as the Monster;

NBC's *Frankenstein: The True Story*, 1973, with Michael Sarrazin as the Creature, surrounded by a stellar supporting cast that included James Mason, Michael Wilding, Ralph Richardson, John Gielgud, David McCallum, Jane Seymour, Margaret Leighton, and Agnes Moorehead; 1993's direct-to-cable *Frankenstein*, filmed in Eastern Europe with Patrick Bergen as the medical genius, Randy Quaid as the rebellious humanoid, and John Mills as the blind hermit who befriends the Monster; *Yahoo!*'s 1997 *House of Frankenstein*; and *Hallmark*'s 2004 remake.

Engrossing TV documentaries about the creation of the monster are *It's Alive: The True Story of Frankenstein* (1994), hosted by Roger Moore and narrated by Eli Wallach, and *Decoding the Past: In Search of the Real Frankenstein* (2006), shown on the History Channel.

* * *

Born in Leicester, England, in 1924, David Campton was educated at Wyggeston Grammar School for Boys. During World War II he served in the Royal Air Force. In the mid-1950s Campton gave up a secure job with the East Midlands Gas Board in order to write for a living. He occasionally diverted into acting and directing with the Scarborough Theatre and the Phoenix Theatre in Leicester.

Over a thirty-five-year span Campton penned more than a hundred one-act and twenty full-length plays—dramas, comedies, and allegories. His crime-tinged plays include *The Laboratory* (1954), in which an apothecary in Renaissance Italy is visited by a court official, his wife, and his mistress, each asking for poison to dispose of the others; and *Memento Mori* (1957), wherein a young man wishes to purchase an old house so that he can bury his recently murdered wife under the floorboards. The estate agent refuses the request because his wife is already there. In *Dead and Alive* (1964), a family feud ends with four simultaneous corpses. *Usher* (1962) is based on the horror story by Edgar Allan Poe, while *Carmilla* (1972) is derived from Sheridan Le Fanu's vampire tale. A gossipy old woman attempts to control her nieces by blackmail in *A Point of View* (1967). *Provisions* (1971) is the story of a stranger who stops at an isolated shack for a drink of water, unaware that the owners of the shack live by eating strangers. In *The Do-It-Yourself Frankenstein* (1975), a demonstrator and his assistant exhibit the latest in the firm's selection of robots. The question arises, Who is the robot—the demonstrator, the assistant, the audience?

With his affinity for the bizarre, Campton contributed episodes to the 1960s British television programs *Late Night Horror, Out of the Unknown*, and *Journey to the Unknown*.

Acting Edition: J. Garnet Miller Ltd. *Frankenstein* is also included in David Campton's *Three Gothic Plays* (London: J. Garnet Miller Ltd., 1973).

Awards and Honors: David Campton won first prize in a competition sponsored by the Tavistock Repertory Company. In 1958 he received a British Arts Council bursary for playwriting. He was the recipient of British Theatre Association prizes in 1975, 1978, 1985.

NOTES

1. William Godwin (1756–1863) wrote *Things As They Are; or, The Adventures of Caleb Williams* (1794), the very first novel about detecting a murder.

2. According to scholar Donald F. Glut, T. P. Cooke played the Frankenstein Monster 365 times, and, like Boris Karloff more than a century later, became identified with the role. Donald F. Glut, *The Frankenstein Legend* (Lanham, MD: Scarecrow Press, 1973), 29.

3. *Hideous Progenies* by Steven Earl Forry recounts the plots and production data of *Frankenstein* dramatizations from the nineteenth century to the present (Philadelphia: University of Pennsylvania Press, 1990).

4. In addition to *The Last Laugh,* Charles W. Goddard and Paul Dickey collaborated on *The Ghost Breaker* (1913), a farcical thriller that ran for seventy-two performances on Broadway and spawned three movie adaptations in 1922, 1940, and 1953; *The Misleading Lady* (1913), depicting the abduction of a budding actress by a hard-boiled adventurer to an Adirondack bungalow; and *The Broken Wig* (1920), relating the antics of a wealthy American rancher and a smiling but dangerous Mexican bandit. Suspense plays written by Dickey are described in Amnon Kabatchnik, *Blood on the Stage, 1900–1925* (Lanham, MD: Scarecrow Press, 2008), 191.

In Hollywood, Dickey wrote the screenplay of *Fog Bound* (1923), a tangled melodrama sketching the murder of a federal revenue agent during a raid on a Florida gambling resort, the escape of an innocent suspect into the Everglades, and the unmasking of a deputy as the killer.

Charles William Goddard penned the original story of *The Perils of Pauline* (1914), a torch-blazing serial that had Pearl White menaced by the dastardly Koerner—and his cohorts, bloodthirsty Indians, Orientals, Gypsies, and pirates—through twenty cliff-hanging episodes, on land, in the air, and underwater.

5. In the London production of *Dracula*, Hamilton Deane played Professor Van Helsing, and Raymond Huntley portrayed the vampire.

6. Quoted in Donald F. Glut, *The Frankenstein Legend* (Metuchen, NJ: Scarecrow Press, 1973), 44.

7. James Whale (1889–1957), British born, was a cobbler before demonstrating talent for signwriting and enrolling at the Dudley School of Arts and Crafts. During World War I he was taken prisoner, and it is reported that while incarcerated, he continued to embellish his talent of drawing and sketching. After the armistice, Whale embarked on a stage career. His breakthrough came when directing a fringe production of R. C. Sherriff's *Journey's End*, starring a young, unknown Laurence Olivier. The play was transferred to the West End, with Colin Clive taking over the lead role; it ran for 593 performances. Whale also directed the ensuing

Broadway production of *Journey's End* (485 performances) and its film version. In Hollywood, Whale left an indelible mark with his horror masterpieces *Frankenstein* (1931), *The Old Dark House* (1932), *The Invisible Man* (1933), and *Bride of Frankenstein* (1935). Among his major movies are the original *Waterloo Bridge* (1931) and *Show Boat* (1936), *The Great Garrick* (1937), and *The Man in the Iron Mask* (1939). After a debilitating stroke, Whale, openly gay, became lonely and depressed. In 1957, at the age of fifty-seven, he committed suicide by drowning himself in his swimming pool. The film *Gods and Monsters* (1998), starring Ian McKellen, is a fictionalized character study of Whale.

London-born Boris Karloff (1887–1969), whose real name was William Henry Pratt, travelled to Canada, where he appeared in small-town repertory theatres, and then to Hollywood, where he made more than fifty silent films, including the serials *The Lightning Raider* and *The Masked Rider*, both in 1918; *The Hope Diamond Mystery* (1920); and, in the late 1920s, *The Vanishing Rider*, *Vultures of the Sea*, *The Fatal Warning*, and *The King of the Kongo*. Karloff became a star as the monster in *Frankenstein*, a role rejected by Bela Lugosi. Karloff and Lugosi teamed on some memorable horror films, including *The Black Cat* (1934), *The Raven* (1935), *Black Friday* (1939), and *The Body Snatcher* (1944). Karloff worked with some of Hollywood's top directors: Howard Hawks (*The Criminal Code*, 1930; *Scarface*, 1931); Mervyn LeRoy (*Five Star Final*, 1931); Raoul Walsh (*The Yellow Ticket*, 1931); Karl Freund (*The Mummy*, 1932); John Ford (*The Lost Patrol*, 1933), Michael Curtiz (*The Walking Dead*, 1935); Edward Dmytryk (*The Devil Commands*, 1941); Mark Robson (*Isle of the Dead*, 1945); Cecil B. DeMille (*Unconquered*, 1947); Roger Corman (*The Terror*, 1963); Jacques Tourneur (*The Comedy of Terrors*, 1964); Peter Bogdanovich (*Targets*, 1967). Karloff will also be remembered as the Oriental archvillain in *The Mask of Fu Manchu* (1932) and the Oriental sleuth, Mr. Wong, in a series of movies made in the late 1930s and early 1940s. He also served as foil to the comic antics of Danny Kaye (*The Secret Life of Walter Mitty*, 1946) and Abbott and Costello (*Abbott and Costello Meet the Killer, Boris Karloff*, 1949, and *Abbott and Costello Meet Dr. Jekyll and Mr. Hyde*, 1953). On Broadway, Karloff appeared as Jonathan Brewster, the black sheep of the family who becomes homicidal when compared to Boris Karloff, in the immensely popular macabre comedy *Arsenic and Old Lace* (1941). He also played Descious Heiss, an underworld fence in *The Shop at Sly Corner* (1949), Captain Hook in *Peter Pan* (1951), and Bishop Cauchon in *The Lark* (1955), for which he was named for a Tony Award as Best Actor.

Englishman Colin Clive (1900–1937) attended the Royal Military Academy Sandhurst, but an injured knee disqualified him from military service. He turned to acting, appeared in the London production of *Show Boat* alongside Paul Robeson, and was cast by James Whale in *Journey's End*. Clive moved to Hollywood, and during the 1930s was a leading man for major stars Katharine Hepburn, Bette Davis, Joan Bennett, and Jean Arthur. In *Mad Love* (1935), adapted from the German classic *The Hands of Orlac*, Clive played the pianist who unwittingly becomes a murderer when, following an accident, his injured hands are replaced by surgeon Peter Lorre. A chronic alcoholic, Clive died of pneumonia in 1937 at the age of thirty-seven.

8. *Scarlet Street* magazine 47 (2002).

9. Donald F. Glut, *The Frankenstein Legend* (Metuchen, NJ: Scarecrow Press, 1973), 45.

10. David Campton, *Frankenstein* (London: J. Garnet Miller, 1973), 6.

11. Pierre Biner, *The Living Theatre* (New York: Horizon Press, 1972), 111.

12. Donald F. Glut, *The Frankenstein Legend*, 49.

13. *New York Times*, October 3, 1968.

14. *London Theatre Record*, December 11–15, 1984.

15. *New York Times*, November 2, 1986.

16. Otis L. Guernsey Jr. and Jeffrey Sweet, eds., *The Best Plays of 1989–1990* (New York: Applause, 1990), 473.

17. *Royal Exchange*, Manchester, December 17, 1992.

18. Other twentieth-century adaptations of Mary Shelley's novel include *Frankenstein: A Melo-Drama*—book, music, and lyrics by Gene Wright (1973); *Dr. Frankenstein and Friends*, a one-act play by Val R. Cheatham (1975); *Frankenstein Follies: A Musical in Two Acts* by Peter Walker and Katherine Jean Leslie (1977); *The Mary Shelley Play* by Mary Humphrey Baldridge (1978); *Frankenstein* by John Gardner (1979); *Ms. Frankenstein's Monster: A Comedy in Three Acts* by Albert Green (1979); *Frankenstein: The Monster Play* by Christopher O'Neal (1980); *Frankenstein*, a one-act play by John Mattera and Stephen Barrows (1981); *Frankenstein* by Alden Nowlan and Walter Learning (1981); *Frankenstein's Centerfold: A Two-Act Comedy* by Eddie Cope (1984); *The Frankenstein Monster Show*—book by John Crocker and Tim Hampton, music by Ken Bolam, lyrics by Les Scott (1984); *The Curse of Frankenstein* by Robert S. Mulligan (1985); *Frankenstein* by Austin Tichenor (1990); *Frankenstein* by Philip Pullman (1990); *Frankenstein, the Modern Prometheus*, music and libretto by Libby Larsen (1990); *The Bride of Frankenstein* by David Yeakle (1992); *Genesis and Other Plays* (includes a monologue, *Frankenstein*) by Don Nigro (1992); *Frankenstein: A Dramatic Adaptation* by Arnold Ryan Bigler (1995); *Frankenstein Unbound: Another Monster Musical* by Sheldon Allman and Bob Pickett (1995); *Frankenstein 1930* by Fred Carmichael (1996); *Frankenstein's Guests: A Comedy* by Martin Downing (1998).

19. *New York Post*, February 11, 2002.

20. *New York Times*, October 8, 2002.

21. *New York Times*, December 15, 2004.

22. *New York Times*, July 18, 2006.

23. *New York Post*, July 21, 2006.

24. *Time Out New York*, November 8–14, 2007.

25. *New York Times*, November 2, 2007.

26. *New York Times*, November 9, 2007.

27. *New York Times*, January 14, 2008.

28. *New York Times*, March 7, 2008.

29. J. Searle Dawley (1877–1949) was arguably the first U.S. film director. In the spring of 1907, he was engaged by the Thomas A. Edison Company to shoot hundreds of one-reelers, including the classic *Rescued from an Eagle's Nest*, in which he cast D. W. Griffith as a woodsman struggling with an eagle who carried off his child. Among Dawley's silent shorts were renditions of *The Prince and the Pauper* (1909), *A Christmas Carol* (1910), *Aida* (1911), *The Three Musketeers* (1911), *The Corsican Brothers* (1912), *Treasure Island* (1912), *Martin Chuzzlewit* (1912), *The Charge of*

the Light Brigade (1912), *Tess of the d'Urbervilles* (1913), *Four Feathers* (1915), *Snow White* (1916), *Uncle Tom's Cabin* (1918), and twelve episodes of the screen's first serial, *What Happened to Mary?* (1912–1913).

30. The saga of *The Golem*, as seen on stage and screen, is recounted in Amnon Kabatchnik, *Blood on the Stage, 1900–1925* (Lanham, MD: Scarecrow Press, 2008), 369–374.

The Aspern Papers (1959)

Michael Redgrave (England, 1908–1985)

Not unlike Morris Townsend of Henry James's *Washington Square*, the nameless narrator of James's novella *The Aspern Papers* is an 1890s gentleman of physical and intellectual vitality who cunningly pierces his way into a peaceful, aristocratic household, then utilizes his charms to take advantage of a vulnerable spinster.

Renowned actor Michael Redgrave adapted *The Aspern Papers* (1888) to the stage in 1959. In the play version, Henry Jarvis (H.J.), a critic, historian, and publisher obsessed with the works of Jeffrey Aspern, an early, unappreciated American poet, manages to hoodwink Aspern's reclusive one-hundred-year-old former mistress, Juliana Bordereau, into renting him rooms at her peeling Venetian Villa. Juliana was Aspern's Dark Lady of the Sonnets, and H.J., contemplating a centenary edition of Aspern's work, is determined to locate her diaries, letters, and memorabilia.

Calling himself Henry Jessamine (shades of Henry James), H.J. flirts with Juliana's withered niece, Tina, shakes her sensibilities, and solicits from her the promise to get him the Aspern papers.

Gradually falling in love, Tina blossoms. Ignoring her overtures, H.J. insists that they immediately secure the papers, locked in an old green box, in order to prevent the proud Juliana from destroying them before she dies.

H.J.'s foxy manservant, Pasquale, removes the trunk from Juliana's bedroom and hides it beneath a pile of wood by the stove. H.J. feverishly pulls at the worn straps binding the trunk when Juliana hobbles in and realizes what is happening. The old lady gasps, hisses "You publishing scoundrel," and falls to the floor, unconscious. After a few days she dies.

Tina, brokenhearted and fearful, approaches H.J. with a proposal of marriage but is flatly refused. Mrs. Prest, a local dignitary, relates to Tina that at times Henry is the best of friends, the most charming companion a woman ever had, and at other times he is, quite simply, a monster.

Dejected, Tina keeps her chin up, informs H.J. that she burnt the Aspern papers, and requests that he leave. In a final poignant moment, Tina kneels by the stove, fishes out from the trunk a packet of ribboned papers, strikes a match, and lights the first document. As she picks up another letter, the bells of a nearby church are chiming, and the curtain falls.

* * *

Michael Redgrave not only dramatized *The Aspern Papers*, but also coproduced and directed the play and played Henry Jarvis. With Flora Robson playing Tina and Beatrix Lehmann as Juliana, *The Aspern Papers* premiered on August 12, 1959, in the West End at the Queen's Theatre. It ran for 370 performances. The *London Times* complimented Sir Michael's "theatrical skill, which James himself surely would have admired and perhaps envied a little."[1]

The Aspern Papers opened in New York's Playhouse Theatre on February 7, 1962, under the direction of Margaret Webster, with Maurice Evans as H.J., Wendy Hiller as Tina, and Françoise Rosay as Juliana.

"A mystery with a heart," declared critic Howard Taubman, "a suspense story—a riddle of belles-lettres. . . . It shades gradually from a hunt for the missing papers in the literary mystery until it encompasses a warm and touching revelation of character."[2] Richard Watts Jr. believed *The Aspern Papers* to be "thoughtful, subtle, quietly but deeply ironical and thoroughly interesting."[3] John Chapman found it "a bewitching play . . . one of the most exciting stage pieces of the season."[4]

Other critics dissented: "It strikes us as being a minor tempest in a picturesque Venetian teapot. It is a bit too elusive and remote for our taste," said Robert Coleman.[5] "I was only mildly caught by the situation," claimed John McClain.[6] "An extremely curious dramatic miscalculation," frowned Walter Kerr.[7]

The Aspern Papers were searched for and ultimately burnt for ninety-three performances. The play had a rare eleven-performance revival at the Alley Theatre, Houston, Texas, on May 20, 1964. Twenty years later it was resuscitated in London, featuring Redgrave's daughter, Vanessa Redgrave, accompanied by Christopher Reeve and Wendy Hiller, this time in the role of Juliana Bordereau.

The 1947 film *The Lost Moment* is based on *The Aspern Papers*. Robert Cummings played the narrator, Susan Hayward portrayed Tina, and Agnes Moorehead enacted Juliana.

In 1998, the Dallas Opera presented the world premiere of Dominick Argento's opera *The Aspern Papers*.

* * *

Born in Bristol, England, and educated at Magdalene College, Cambridge, Michael Scudamore Redgrave began his distinguished acting career with the Liverpool Playhouse troupe in 1934, moved to London two years later, and continued to play a wide variety of parts at the Old Vic, the Queen's Theatre, the Shakespeare Memorial Company, the first Chichester Festival, and the National Theatre. Among Redgrave's most memorable roles were Mr. Horner in Wycherley's *The Country Wife,* Surface in Sheridan's *The School for Scandal,* Macheath in Gay's *The Beggar's Opera,* the title role in Chekhov's *Uncle Vanya* and Baron Tusenbach in *Three Sisters,* Rakitin in Turgenev's *A Month in the Country,* Solness in Ibsen's *The Master Builder,* and the Captain in Strindberg's *The Father.*

Shakespearean challenges included Orlando in *As You Like It,* Ferdinand and Berowne in *Love's Labour Lost,* Laertes to Laurence Olivier's Hamlet and Claudius to Peter O'Toole's Hamlet, Sir Andrew Aguecheek in *Twelfth Night,* Prospero in *The Tempest,* Benedict in *Much Ado about Nothing,* Shylock in *The Merchant of Venice,* Anthony in *Anthony and Cleopatra,* and the name parts of *Macbeth, Hamlet, Richard II,* and *King Lear.*

Redgrave's repertoire in the modern theatre encompassed Detective Anderson in Mary Roberts Rinehart's *The Bat,* Lord Harry in T. S. Eliot's *The Family Reunion,* Colonel Stjerbinsky in Franz Werfel's *Jacobowsky and the Colonel,* Charleston in Robert Ardrey's *Thunder Rock,* Hector in Jean Giraudoux's *Tiger at the Gates,* Dean in Robert Bolt's *The Tiger and the Horse,* Rhodes in Graham Greene's *The Complaisant Lover,* Crocker-Harris in Terence Rattigan's *The Browning Version* and the Regent in Rattigan's *The Sleeping Prince,* Hobson in Harold Brighthouse's *Hobson's Choice,* the Duke in Patrick Hamilton's *The Duke in Darkness,* the title role in Thomas Job's *Uncle Harry,* the alcoholic actor in Clifford Odet's *The Country Girl,* and the Father in John Mortimer's *A Voyage round My Father.*

Redgrave made his silver screen debut as Gilbert, the romantic lead in Alfred Hitchcock's spy thriller *The Lady Vanishes* (1938). Among the scores of movie characters he portrayed were Fenwick in *The Stars Look Down* (1939); the role of *Kipps* (1941); Flight Lt. Archdale, *The Way to the Stars* (1945); the ventriloquist Frère, *Dead of Night* (1945); Orin, *Mourning Becomes Electra* (1947); Crocker-Harris, *The Browning Version* (1951); Worthing, *The Importance of Being Earnest* (1952); Graham, *Time without Pity* (1957); Fowler, *The Quiet American* (1958); Nyland, *The Wreck of the Mary Deare* (1959); The Uncle, *The Innocents* (1961); Governor, *The Loneliness of the Long-Distance Runner* (1962); W. B. Yeats, *Young Cassidy* (1965); the Medical Officer, *The Hill* (1965); the Headmaster, *Goodbye, Mr. Chips* (1969); Peggotty, *David Copperfield* (1970, TV); Leo as adult, *The Go-Between* (1971); Grand Duke Sazonov, *Nicholas and Alexandra* (1972); Danvers, *Dr. Jekyll and Mr. Hyde* (1973, TV).

Redgrave formed his own repertory company in 1957 and directed many productions. He is the author of two stagecraft books, *The Actor's Way and Means* (1955, revised 1979) and *Mask or Face* (1958), as well as the novel *The Mountebank's Tale* (1958). His autobiography, *In My Mind's Eye*, was published in 1983. *Michael Redgrave, Actor* (1956), penned by Richard Findlater, summarizes an illustrious career.

Though bisexual, Redgrave was married to the actress Rachel Kempson for fifty years until his death. Their children, Vanessa, Corin, and Lynn, have also carved notable theatre and film careers, as did their granddaughter Natasha Richardson (1963–2009).

* * *

Henry James (1843–1916) sought a career in the theatre—with disastrous results. His stage adaptation of the 1877 novel *The American* was given a trial performance in London on January 3, 1891, followed by a formal opening night on September 26. It was a misfire: "a mass of bald melodrama has been pitchforked into it, with a painfully incongruous effect," lamented the *New York Times* correspondent.[8] James's *Guy Domville* was hissed, hooted, and booed at its London bow on January 5, 1895. *The High Bid* (1909), *Disengaged* (1909), and *The Saloon* (1911) fared somewhat better but fell short of expectations. It is ironic that posthumous adaptations of James's stories have triumphed on stage and screen. There are *Berkeley Square* (1926) by John L. Balderstone and J. C. Squire, based on James's unfinished 1917 novel *The Sense of the Past*; *The Comic Artist* (1928), a conversion by Hubert Griffith of 1890's *The Tragic Muse*; *The Heiress* (1947), the Ruth and Augustus Goetz dramatization of 1881's *Washington Square*; William Archibald's *The Innocents* (1950), from Henry James's 1898 horror novella, *The Turn of the Screw*; *Letters from Paris* (1952), an adaptation by Dodie Smith of 1888's *The Reverberator*; *Child of Fortune* (1956), which Guy Bolton transformed from 1920's *The Wings of the Dove*; *Eugenia* (1957) by Randolph Carter, based on 1878's *The Europeans*; an operatic version of *The Wings of the Dove*, with libretto by Ethan Ayer, music by Douglas Moore (1961); *The Summer of Daisy Miller* (1963), a play by Bertram Greene based on 1879's *Daisy Miller*; *The Wings of the Dove* (1963), still another stage adaptation of James's longest, most complex novel, by Christopher Taylor; and Ronald Gow's *A Boston Story* (1968), suggested by the 1871 novella, *Watch the Ward*.

A 1990's tidal wave of renewed interest in James triggered a lavish New York revival of *The Heiress* (1995) and a major biography, *Henry James, the Young Master*, by Sheldon M. Novick (Random House, 1996). Novick came up with a sequel, *Henry James, the Mature Master*, eleven years later (Random House, 2007). The University of Nebraska Press plans to publish all twelve thousand of James's surviving letters. The filming of *The Aspern*

Papers, Portrait of a Lady, Washington Square, The Wings of the Dove, and *The Golden Bowl,* as well as a Masterpiece Theatre–PBS television production of *The American,* indicate that Henry James, a failed playwright, has returned—with a vengeance.

Acting Edition: Samuel French, Inc.

Awards and Honors: Michael Redgrave received the New York Critics Award for his performance as Hector in *Tiger at the Gates* (1955). He was an Academy Award nominee for his portrayal of Orin Mannon in *Mourning Becomes Electra* (1947), and recipient of Best Actor prize at the Cannes Festival for *The Browning Version* (1951). He twice won Best Actor trophies in the *Evening Standard Awards* (1958, 1963) and twice received the Actor of the Year Award from the Variety Club of Great Britain (also in 1958, 1963). Redgrave was appointed Commander of the Order of the British Empire (CBE) in 1952, and knighted in 1959. The repertory theatre in Farnham, Surrey (1974–1998) was named in his honor.

NOTES

1. Quoted in the *New York Times,* August 13, 1959.
2. *New York Times,* February 8, 1962.
3. *New York Post,* February 8, 1962.
4. *Daily News,* February 8, 1962.
5. *New York Mirror,* February 8, 1962.
6. *New York Journal-American,* February 8, 1962.
7. *New York Herald Tribune,* February 8, 1962.
8. *New York Times,* September 27, 1891.

The Gang's All Here (1959)

Jerome Lawrence (United States, 1915–2004) and Robert E. Lee (United States, 1918–1994)

One of the darkest episodes in our federal history, the case of President Warren Gamaliel Harding and his corrupt regime, was dramatized by the duo, who in 1955 had written the stirring account of the Bryan-Darrow "monkey trial," *Inherit the Wind.*

"Our play is not about *a* President, or *the* President, but about the Presidency itself: the father image, the godhead we send to Washington," announced Jerome Lawrence and Robert E. Lee prior to the Broadway premiere of *The Gang's All Here.*[1] Their treatment captures—in a thinly disguised fashion—the characters and rampaging skullduggery of the Harding administration. The President, here named Griffith P. Hastings, is presented as a small-town Ohio editor rocketed into the White House by opportunistic politicians. "The party wants you, the party needs you," declares Walter Rafferty, a backroom kingmaker. Hastings, nudged by his ambitious wife, Frances, succumbs to the temptation.

Aware of his shortcomings as a leader, Hastings escapes the rigors of the office by going to see old cronies who call him "Griff," and share naughty jokes, a bottle of booze, and high-stakes poker, while craftily soliciting key government appointments. The gullible president trusts his friends and believes that he has nothing to worry about.

When a Senate investigating committee closes in, Hastings discovers to his horror that he has been betrayed by hucksters bent on plundering the country—the unscrupulous attorney general, the crooked secretary of the interior, and the money-hungry director of the Veteran's Bureau. Faced with exposure, Hastings reveals the dastardly schemes to the press, takes a vial of poison from his doctor's medical satchel, and commits suicide in an attempt to save the dignity of the high office he never wanted.

* * *

"The Gang's All Here is effective drama with a conscience," wrote Brooks Atkinson upon the opening of the play at the Ambassador Theatre

on October 1, 1959. "It provides a provocative and absorbing theatrical experience."[2] Walter Kerr found in the drama "a trim, generally taut, often tub-thumping morality lesson . . . lively, interesting, colorful show-manship . . . and I suggest you join the gang."[3] Frank Aston agreed: "*The Gang's All Here* is a shock, a thrill, a stimulus."[4]

Other critics dissented: "The new play is not another *Inherit the Wind*," lamented John Chapman. "It is written mostly in the bold terms of old-style melodrama and its characters are written on the surface."[5] "A few years in the life of a bumbling President is neither very exciting history nor theatre," opined John McClain.[6] "Its characters tend to be stereotypes. Their actions and their speech are seldom such as to arouse your anger or your pity," asserted Robert Coleman.[7]

The entire cadre of reviewers complimented George Roy Hill's "illuminating" direction, Jo Mielziner's "stunning" sets, and Melvyn Douglas's "superb" interpretation of President Hastings. *The Gang's All Here* played its political chicaneries for 132 performances.

Acting Edition: Samuel French, Inc.

NOTES

1. *New York Herald Tribune*, September 27, 1959.
2. *New York Times*, October 2, 1959.
3. *New York Herald Tribune*, October 2, 1959.
4. *New York World-Telegram*, October 2, 1959.
5. *Daily News*, October 2, 1959.
6. *New York Journal-American*, October 2, 1959.
7. *Daily Mirror*, October 2, 1959.

Golden Fleecing (1959)

Lorenzo Semple Jr. (United States, 1923–)

The farcical premise of Lorenzo Semple Jr.'s *Golden Fleecing* sends three American naval personnel to Venice, Italy, where they concoct a scheme to hit the jackpot at the local gambling casino. Lieutenant Ferguson Howard, ensign Beauregard Gilliam, and engineer Jackson Eldridge, masquerading as civilians, flash signals from their plush suite at the Gritti Palace Hotel to the anchored SS *Elmira*, where an accomplice, signalman Taylor, is operating a hush-hush computer capable of deciphering winning roulette numbers.

Pete DiLucca, a local thug planted at the Lido Casino, warns the roguish sailors, "There's only one sure way to beat a roulette wheel and that is to don't play it."

However, Lt. Howard, mastermind of the project, assures DiLucca that "this is like no system you've ever dreamt of! It's pure witchcraft." The mechanical aspects of the caper come through smoothly and effectively, but complications arise when two lovely girls appear on the scene.

Howard falls head-over-heels for Julie Fitch, the admiral's spunky daughter, while Eldridge rekindles his romance with old flame Ann Knutsen, now betrothed to a stuffed-shirt State Department official. Soon the blinker-method is spotted, triggering an intense manhunt for enemy spies with radar, sonar, and telescopes.

Howard's cohorts believe in Murphy's Law (If something can go wrong, it will), but the lieutenant, who claims, "I seem to function better when there's a risk afoot," manages to enlist not only the aid of the dubious Julie, but also that of her father, "Old Barracuda" himself, by donating the winning loot to the Navy Relief Fund.

* * *

Golden Fleecing opened at Henry Miller's Theatre in New York on October 15, 1959. The reviewers saluted Abe Burrows's "broad style of direction," Frederick Fox's "rich and authentic design," and "a good cast,

MT. LEBANON PUBLIC LIBRARY

headed by the skillful Tom Poston," supported by "humorous, romantically appealing Suzanne Pleshette and Constance Ford."

The play itself got mixed notices. John Chapman cheered "this most enjoyable form of innocent entertainment,"[1] but Richard Watts Jr. sadly concluded that "it is apparently much harder to manufacture a good, amusing, thoroughly satisfactory comedy than it is to break the bank at the Lido."[2] Brooks Atkinson found the buffoonery "original, innocent, good natured and enjoyable in all the right places,"[3] while Walter Kerr scoffed at "the lazy gagging and the lulls that ensue."[4] John McClain believed that *Golden Fleecing* provided "an evening which has more than the usual helpings of madness and hilarity."[5] In contrast, Robert Coleman contended that the farce "had to gallop to have a chance at the money; that it will break the tape a winner is doubtful."[6]

Golden Fleecing ran for eighty-four performances.

Retitled *The Honeymoon Machine*, the comedy was transformed to the screen in 1961, with Steve McQueen (Howard), Jim Hutton (Eldridge), Jack Mullaney (Gilliam), Dean Jagger (Admiral Fitch), Brigid Bazlen (Julie), and Paula Prentiss (Ann). George Wells scripted and Richard Thorpe directed an MGM CinemaScope production that opened up the action to the SS *Elmira* and Venice's canals. A drawn-out sequence, in which signalman Taylor (Jack Weston) wobbles on a high ledge of the hotel, a climactic brawl among the casino gamblers as they engage in a free-for-all, and the addition of suspicious Russian spies diffuse the proceedings and diminish the charm of the original play.

* * *

A native of New York City, and a recipient of a Bronze Star during World War II, Lorenzo Semple Jr.'s writing career began in 1951, when he contributed short stories to the magazines *Collier's Weekly* and *The Saturday Evening Post*. Semple's only other venture on Broadway was *Tonight in Samarkand*, which he embellished from the French of Jacques Deval (Morosco Theatre, February 16, 1955—twenty-nine performances). *Tonight in Samarkand* is a melodramatic fantasy about a traveling circus magician (played by Louis Jourdan) and his beloved tiger tamer (Jan Farrand), who cannot escape their predestined, ill-fated kismet.

During the 1960s, Semple proved that his forte was writing for television: he penned episodes for *Target, Pursuit, Kraft Suspense Theatre, The Rogues, Burke's Law, The Rat Patrol, The Green Hornet*, and notably, sixteen episodes for the series *Batman* (1966–1967). He also wrote for the cinema, sometimes in collaboration: the subsequent feature of *Batman*; the tongue-in-cheek spy caper *Fathom* (1967); odd, suspenseful *Pretty Poison* (1968), and *Daddy's Gone a-Hunting* (1969); the escape-from-Devil's-Island adventure *Papillon* (1973); the drug-market busting *The Super Cops* (1974);

political thrillers *The Parallex View* (1974) and *Three Days of the Condor* (1975); the mystery *The Drowning Pool* (1975); and James Bond's *Never Say Never Again* (1983).

Some of Semple's movies bombed, such as the gory *The Sporting Club* (1971); campy remakes of *King Kong* (1976) and *Flash Gordon* (1980); and the jungle frolic *Sheena* (1984). This triggered the scorn of Wheeler Winston Dixon in *The International Dictionary of Films and Filmmakers*: "It may be that at some future date Semple's work will be seen, in retrospect, as being prescient, subtle, or possessed of a sardonic, original comic vision. But for the moment, it seems as if Semple is simply an assembly-line screenwriter with an unfortunate penchant for laden parody."[7]

In his eighties at the time of this printing, Semple provides brief, terse, and forceful critiques of recent movies on YouTube.

Acting Edition: Samuel French, Inc.

Awards and Honors: Lorenzo Semple Jr. received the New York Film Critics Circle Award in 1968 for *Pretty Poison*. In 1975, *The Parallax View*, written by Semple and David Giler, was nominated by the Screen Writers Guild of America for Best Drama Adapted from Another Medium, and by the Mystery Writers of America for an Edgar Allan Poe Award for Best Motion Picture. The following year, Semple's and David Rayfiel's *Three Days of the Condor* won the Best Motion Picture Edgar. In 2008, Semple was saluted by the Writers Guild of America as a Living Legend.

NOTES

1. *Daily News*, October 16, 1959.
2. *New York Post*, October 16, 1959.
3. *New York Times*, October 16, 1959.
4. *New York Herald Tribune*, October 16, 1959.
5. *New York Journal-American*, October 16, 1959.
6. *Daily Mirror*, October 16, 1959.
7. James Vinson, ed., *The International Dictionary of Films and Filmmakers*, vol. 4, *Writers and Production Artists* (Chicago: St. James Press, 1987), 394.

A Clean Kill (1959)

Michael Gilbert (England, 1912–2006)

About ten years ago, when I began to accumulate a checklist of milestone suspense plays, I wrote to English author Michael Gilbert with a request to provide me with information regarding his plays and their productions. The estimable Mr. Gilbert, recipient of the Mystery Writers of America Grand Master Award, replied with a handwritten letter, stating that he was "sorry to disappoint" me, but he "would much prefer that no mention at all were made of the four plays you mention." Gilbert continued, remarking that he felt that penning plays "was not my forte," and asked, "Let them rest in peace."

Michael Gilbert died in 2006 so I cannot appeal to him to change his mind. But, with pangs of an inner struggle, I decided to include one of his plays, *A Clean Kill*, in this reference book, for I believe it to be a minor masterpiece of construction and surprise, deserving renewed study and theatrical revival, a worthy epitaph.

The main character is Charles Reese, a research chemist employed by a well-known manufacturing firm. The action takes place in the living room of his solid, middle-class Victorian house in Putney, a district in South London. There is a wooden door leading to the front hall, and a double, colored-glass door opening into an elaborate laboratory. In the middle of the right-hand wall is a fireplace with several ornaments, including a heavy chiming clock on the mantelpiece. The left side of the room is clearly devoted to business pursuits, complete with a filing cabinet, a table with a typewriter, and a black oak cupboard.

Early in the first act we learn that chemist Reese has formed a private company to promote his own discovery of a cleaning fluid—the colorless, odorless chlorazolidene. At a board meeting we are introduced to Charles's neurotic, shrewish, secretly alcoholic wife, Hilda; his pretty, efficient laboratory assistant, Ann Patten; and his shrewd solicitor and friend, Mr. Schofield. At the keyhole, listening in, is the elderly, snoopy housekeeper, Mrs. Turvey. It soon becomes clear that the Reeses' relationship is strained, and that Charles and Ann are fond of each other. The meeting turns stormy when Hilda, difficult and quarrelsome, objects to the company's plan to sell the new patent to a manufacturing firm that has offered the tidy sum of five thousand pounds.

Following the meeting, Hilda corners Ann, telling the young assistant that she has hired a private detective and is aware that Ann has got her "grubby little hands" on her husband. Ann retorts coolly that upon arriving to work early this morning, she found two dirty glasses and an ashtray full of cigarette stubs—two different brands of cigarettes. She has no doubt that Mrs. Reese entertained a "boyfriend," and wryly suggests that it would be more sensible "to clear up afterwards."

Ann exits, slamming the door. The clock chimes, which reminds Hilda that she has hidden the liquor cabinet key in the clock. She goes to fetch it as a shadow appears on the glass door, and the curtain falls.

When the lights fade up on act II, we learn that Hilda Reese has passed away; at the inquest her death was ruled natural, caused by a heart attack following heavy drinking. But Mrs. Turvey, the housekeeper, reports to the police that she suspects foul play, in view of a clandestine relationship between Charles Reese and his laboratory assistant.

Soon Superintendent Morland arrives on the scene. He is "a tough, smart Cockney" whose method in a criminal investigation is "to be thoroughly offensive, so as to provoke reactions in his victim. His aim is to bring out the worst in people, because he thinks that the worst is often the truth." The superintendent tells Ann and Schofield that upon renewed examination, the police pathologist concluded that Hilda Reese died of a fatal dose of chlorazolidene that tainted her last drink of whiskey. Charles, the sole beneficiary of her will and the only person with keys to both the laboratory cabinet and the whiskey cupboard, is the main suspect. Furthermore, presses Morland with calculated brutality, Charles has been "messing round with Miss Patten." Charles contends that his relationship with Ann is platonic but admits that he is in love with her and, in good time, intends to ask for her hand.

As act III begins, Charles has been taken to police headquarters for questioning. The plot thickens when a private detective, William Senior, meets with attorney Schofield, informs him that he was hired by Mrs. Reese "to keep an eye on her husband." He adds that he has seen Mr. Reese meet the "young lady chemist" several times—"the one he plays footy-footy with among the test tubes"—and now that Mrs. Reese is dead there remains an unpaid account for the time he and his son spent on following Mr. Reese, adding up to just over eight hundred pounds. When Schofield expresses dismay at the "gall" of the request, Senior hints that "certain people" might be interested in what he knows. The blackmailing detective slinks out through the lab door, leaving Schofield puzzled and concerned.

Schofield shares his anxiety with Ann. Ann reveals to him that she has found a paper next to the typewriter which seems to be a typed codicil to Hilda's will. With the aid of a magnifying glass, Schofield reads the codicil. It leaves Hilda's share in the chlorazolidene patent to William Senior of Senior's Detective Agency "as a token of the services he has performed for me." Ann has no doubt that Senior had been Hilda's lover and that he killed her for the valuable shares. She relates to Schofield how on the morning of the board meeting she got there early and found two glasses with dredges of whiskey; Charles doesn't drink. The ashtray was full of cigarette stubs; Charles smokes a pipe. Schofield now remembers that Senior knew his way out through the laboratory and agrees with Ann's conclusions.

They call Senior to come immediately "to his advantage." As they confront him, Senior lights up a Marylands cigarette, the brand Ann found in the ashtray. Mrs. Turvey is called in. At first she says that she has never seen Senior before, but when Ann warns her that she is protecting the man who killed Hilda Reese, the housekeeper admits that Senior "has been in and out the last three months," when Charles was away.

Just when it seems that the whodunit has been solved, a surprising twist is introduced. Schofield is left alone with Ann, and begins to switch off the living room lamps. In a gradually darkened stage he extracts a confession from the young woman, who has been deeply in love with the brilliant chemist and could not bear to stand by and watch his life and career wrecked by an unstable, alcoholic wife. Superintendent Morland is waiting—and listening—behind the glass door of the laboratory.

* * *

Directed by Alistair Sim, *A Clean Kill* was first presented at the Pavilion Theatre in Bournemouth, England, on October 26, 1959. The play moved to London's Criterion Theatre on December 15. The lead roles were played by Peter Copley (Charles Reese), Rachel Roberts (Ann Patten), Hugh Latimer (solicitor Schofield), Garry Marsh (William Senior), and Andrew Keir (Superintendent Morland). "*A Clean Kill* bore evidence of a skilled legal mind," wrote *Theatre World Annual*, "which, allied with a gift for dramatic situation, produced as ingenious a thriller as London has seen for many a month."[1]

The ironically titled *A Clean Kill* ran for 140 performances and was adapted to television in 1961. In the United States, the play was seen at the Playhouse in Boothbay, Maine, on August 21, 1962. That same year, Finland's television presented *A Clean Kill* in three successive thirty-minute segments. West German television aired it the following year as a ninety-minute movie.

* * *

Michael Gilbert wrote two additional plays of suspense. *The Bargain* is a lighthearted three-act play about a family solicitor, George Selwyn, who acquires a valuable miniature and falls prey to a pair of clever blackmailers. Alistair Sim played Selwyn at West End's St. Martin's Theatre on January 19, 1961, and also directed the production.

In *The Shot in Question*, the young country doctor Colin Mayle and his wife, Elizabeth, find themselves under suspicion of murder when a patient who is also Colin's former lover is discovered dead with grains of morphine in her body. The play, directed and designed by Hendrik Baker, premiered at the Duchess Theatre, London, on May 7, 1963, with John Carson and Andree Melly as the Mayles.

Gilbert also penned the nongenre play *Windfall*, a comedy unfolding in the study of Alexander Lindsay, a housemaster at a small traditional public school, Ransfield. The school is on the verge of bankruptcy, but Lindsay is vehemently opposed to selling its ancient playing field and garden. Some hundred-year-old traditions are also in jeopardy. Furthermore, the Headmaster of Ransfield has come up with a plan to join the proud public school with a new neighboring grammar school of dubious reputation. When all seems lost, an enterprising sixteen-year-old pupil, Bernard, purchases a block of shares in a chemical company for the school's Dramatic Club, wins ten thousand pounds, and rescues Ransfield. Alistair Sim directed *Windfall*, and portrayed Lindsay, for a July 2, 1963, opening at London's Lyric Theatre.

* * *

Michael Francis Gilbert was born in Billinghay, Lincolnshire, England, in 1912 and graduated with honors from the University of London in 1937. During World War II, Gilbert served with the Royal Horse Artillery in North Africa and was captured and imprisoned in an Italian military stockade. These experiences were the inspiration for his early novel, *Death in Captivity*, aka *The Danger Within* (1952).

In 1947 Gilbert joined the London law firm of Trower, Still & Keeling, where his clients included the Conservative Party, the Sultan of Bahrain, and Raymond Chandler. He drew upon his experience with the law as source material for his novels, notably in *Smallbone Deceased* (1950), which is set in a lawyer's office; *Death Has Deep Roots* (1951), a courtroom narrative; *The Crack in the Teapot* (1966), wherein a young solicitor gets entangled with a band of racketeers; *Death of a Favorite Girl*, aka *The Killing of Katie Steelstock* (1980), highlighted by a climactic, pounding trial scene;

and *The Queen against Karl Mullen* (1991), the story of a South African security chief who comes to London on an investigative assignment and becomes a murder suspect.

Beginning with his debut novel, *Close Quarters* (1947), in which he introduced Inspector Hazelrigg, an early realistic British policeman, and spanning more than fifty years, Gilbert wrote highly regarded classical mysteries, adventure thrillers, espionage yarns, and police procedurals. Other series characters created by Gilbert include Scotland Yard's Detective Sergeant Patrick Patrella, the sleuth in many short stories and the novels *Blood and Judgment* (1959) and *Roller-Coaster* (1993); solicitor Henry Bohun, a former medical student, research statistician, and World II soldier; hard-knuckled Inspector Mercer, who leaves the force and turns into a professional criminal; Luke Pagan, a young, Russian-speaking police constable; Daniel John Calder and Samuel Behrens, two seemingly kind country gentlemen, who are in reality ruthless counterintelligence agents.

Gilbert wrote hundreds of short stories, many appearing in *Ellery Queen's Mystery Magazine*. Critic-author Anthony Boucher ranked Gilbert's *Game without Rules* (1967) as second only to Somerset Maugham's *Ashenden* as the best volume of spy stories ever written. Gilbert's last two books, both short story collections, were published by a small American house, Crippen & Landru: *The Man Who Hated Banks and Other Stories* (1997), and *The Curious Conspiracy and Other Crimes* (2002), the latter on the author's ninetieth birthday.

"Gilbert is a master of complex plotting and well-rounded characters," wrote Frank Denton in *Twentieth-Century Crime and Mystery Writers*. "With great detail and a special feel for the places he uses as settings, he delivers stories which are compelling and engage the reader immediately."[2] In a *New York Times* obituary, Marilyn Stasio hailed Gilbert's "high literary style and meticulous plot construction, elements that put him in the category of those classical masters of what is often called the golden age of the British mystery . . . who valued above all else a sturdy story with a daunting puzzle, layered with dense detail, multiple clues and schools of red herrings."[3]

Beginning in 1956 and for the next two decades, Gilbert wrote twenty-some television thrillers, including *The Betrayers* (1962), from a work by Stanley Ellin, and *Money to Burn* (1974), from a novel by Margery Allingham. He also penned many radio plays, some adapted from his own short stories.

Acting Edition: Constable.

Awards and Honors: *A Clean Kill* was a top-five selection in *Plays of the Year, 1959–1960* ("It is for you to solve the problem set by a dramatist who is ingenious and perfectly fair").[4] Michael Gilbert's short-story collection *Game without Rules* (1967) was selected by Ellery Queen for inclusion in

Queen's Quorum: The History of the Detective-Crime Short Story as Revealed by the Most Important Books Published in This Field since 1845. Gilbert's *Smallbone Deceased* (1950) was included by author-critic H. R. F. Keating in his *Crime and Mystery: The 100 Best Books.*

In 1980, Gilbert was knighted as a Commander in the Order of the British Empire (CBE). In 1988, he was named a Grand Master by the Mystery Writers of America. Two years later, he won the Life Achievement Anthony Award at the Boucheron in London. In 1994, he was awarded the Diamond Dagger for lifetime achievement by the Crime Writers Association, which he belonged to as a founding member.

NOTES

1. *Theatre World Annual,* June 1959–May 1960 (London: Barrie & Rockliff, 1960), 89.

2. John M. Reilly, ed., *Twentieth-Century Crime and Mystery Writers* (New York: St. Martin's Press, 1980), 666.

3. *New York Times,* February 15, 2006.

4. J. C. Trewin, ed., *Plays of the Year, 1959–1960* (London: Elek Books, 1961), 11.

The Blacks (1959)

Jean Genet (France, 1910–1986)

Jean Genet called his play *Les Nègres* (*The Blacks*) "a clown show." Using a play-within-a-play structure, *The Blacks* continued Genet's recurring device of pitting reality against illusion to critique contemporary civilization, already established in *Le Balcon* (*The Balcony*, 1957).

The curtain is drawn to reveal a backdrop curtain of black velvet and several tiers of different heights. On an upper level there is the Court of Justice, composed of the haughty Queen, her dwarfish Valet, the hanging Judge, the missionary Bishop, and the island Governor. Below them is a group of ordinary villagers who weave in and out of a variety of impersonations. The entire cast is black. Those of the Court wear white masks, representing the dominant white race, and are an extension of the white audience in the theatre.

In the center of the stage is a catafalque—a raised platform—covered with a white cloth, decorated with bouquets of flowers. Four black men and four black women are dancing a minuet to Mozart's *Don Giovanni*. The men's evening clothes are worn with brown shoes; the ladies' costumes—heavily spangled evening gowns—suggest fake elegance, the height of bad taste. As they dance, they pluck flowers from their lapels and bodices and lay them on the catafalque.

A garish neon light fades up on the court. The Queen wears a sad white mask with a drooping mouth. A royal crown is on her head, a scepter in her hand. The Valet wears a striped waistcoat and carries a towel on his arm. The Governor wears a uniform and is holding a pair of field glasses. The Judge wears a scarlet robe, while the Bishop is clad in a white cape and pectoral cross.

The dancers bow ceremoniously to the Court. One of the men, Archibald Absalom Wellington, introduces himself to both the Court and audience, and continues to name the other dancers. The Queen cuts him short and abruptly asks the Bishop, "Are they going to kill her?" The Bishop is taken aback: "But Madam—she's dead!"

Archibald and the group prepare to present to the Court a ritual, a ceremony, in the form of a trial for murder. He and his friends killed a white woman, an old drunkard who used to squat on a pile of rags at the entrance of the village bridge. They'll reenact the crime step-by-step.

The black villagers light cigarettes and arrange themselves in a circle. Alarmed, the Governor whispers, "They're going to cook her and eat her!" The Bishop urges the Court members to pray. The Court becomes even more alarmed when the villagers proclaim that they also did away with a milkman, a postman, a seamstress, and a government clerk.

The villagers decide to shift their attention to the rape and murder of a young, attractive woman. The local vicar, Samba Graham Diouf, dons a blond wig, a pair of white gloves, and a crude cardboard carnival mask representing a laughing white woman with big, rosy cheeks. He stands in front of the catafalque, facing the audience and knitting a pink helmet. A villager stealthily enters a bedroom lit dimly by moonlight and tells the Court: "The husband arrived too late. He'll find only his wife's corpse, disemboweled and still warm."

Edgar Alas Newport News announces that the murderer will "certainly be executed." The Queen, Judge, Bishop, Governor, and Valet leave to discuss the case and its verdict. They reenter drunk, hiccoughing and laughing. The Judge declares, "One can't hold all of Africa responsible for the death of a white woman. Nevertheless, there's no denying the fact that one of you is guilty. . . . He killed out of hatred. Hatred of the color white." The Judge adds that it doesn't matter who among the villagers committed the crime; a Negro's a Negro, and any black man will do to break his limbs and put his neck into the noose.

Mrs. Felicity, militant, confronts the Court with a warning that "everything is changing. Whatever is gentle and kind and good and tender will be black. Milk will be black, sugar, rice, the sky, doves, hope, will be black. . . ."

Suddenly several firecrackers explode off-stage, and their sparks are seen against the dark background of the set. The black villagers, who were squatting, stand up, draw revolvers, and shoot. One by one, the Governor, Judge, Bishop, Valet, and Queen fall, forming a heap in the middle of the stage.

But soon the five "dead" characters rise, take off their masks, and bow. Archibald announces to the audience that the performance has come to an end. The opening measures of *Don Giovanni* are heard. With an adieu to the spectators, the entire cast dances the minuet around the white-draped catafalque with which the play began.

* * *

MT. LEBANON PUBLIC LIBRARY

The Blacks was first performed on October 28, 1959, at the Théatre de Lutèce in Paris. The play was directed by Roger Blin, who went on to stage English-speaking productions of the play in Cambridge, Cardiff, and London, the latter opening on May 30, 1961, at the Royal Court Theatre. The Lord Chamberlain insisted on removing "blatantly shocking" words, but the critics remained harsh. Kenneth Tynan appreciated the theme—"a timeless struggle between the ins and the outs"—but felt that the play "drowns in a flood of prose poetry. . . . Genet's mind moves from image to image, never from an idea to idea."[1] Other reviewers called the production "pointless," "weary," "obscure," and "reeling."

Across the Atlantic, *The Blacks* came to off-Broadway's St. Marks Playhouse on May 4, 1961, featuring a luminous cast of black actors destined for greatness on stage and screen: Roscoe Lee Browne (Archibald Absalom Wellington), Louis Gossett (Edgar Alas Newport News), Raymond St. Jacques (Judge), Maya Angelou Make (Queen), Charles Gordone (Valet), and James Earl Jones, Cynthia Belgrave, Cicely Tyson, Godfrey M. Cambridge, and Helen Martin as some of the prominent villagers. Gene Frankel directed. The team of designers included Kim E. Swados (set), Patricia Zipprodt (costumes and masks), and Lee Watson (lighting). Howard Taubman of the *New York Times* wrote: "There is no mistaking the fierce motif that courses through M. Genet's furious flights of language encompassing obscenity and purity, violence and tenderness, hatred and love. . . . In *The Blacks*, M. Genet is not only a moralist of high indignation but also a prophet of rage and compassion."[2]

The Blacks had a whopping run of 1,408 performances. In 1963, the company traveled to Montreal, Canada, for two showings at Her Majesty's Theatre. The play was produced at the Mark Taper Forum in Los Angeles in 1962 and again in 1970. In 1964, *The Blacks* was presented at the West Berlin Festival; at the Venice Biennial; and in Darmstadt, West Germany, with white players in blackface. Additional showings of *The Blacks* were undertaken by the Seattle Repertory Theatre, Seattle, Washington (1969) and by the Black Repertory Theatre at the Kennedy Center, Washington, D.C. (1973).

In 2002, a localized version of *The Blacks* was produced in Israel, replacing African-Americans with Palestinians. The Classical Theatre of Harlem mounted the play in 2001–2002, 2002–2003 (winning four Obie Awards), and 2008, establishing the group as one of off-Broadway's most innovative companies. In 2007, *The Blacks* was revived at the Theatre Royal, Stratford East, London.

Louis Kronenberger asserts in *The Best Plays of 1960–1961*, "The Blacks was the first sophisticated play about the racial question to be written with no taboos in its use of words, images or ideas."[3]

Scholar Joseph T. Shipley writes: "No more violent attack on white su-
premacy and 'superiority' has been staged than this savage clownerie, to
use the author's term, by the lifelong rebel, Jean Genet."[4]

* * *

Born on December 19, 1910, Jean Genet was the illegitimate son of a
Parisian prostitute. He was orphaned at seven months and was brought
up in a Public Assistance institute. At the age of seven, he was placed with
a foster family. At thirteen, he stole money from his foster parents and
began a life splattered with crime. At fifteen, he was sent to a reformatory.

Young Genet joined the Foreign Legion, deserted, and spent time in
prison for petty theft and homosexual prostitution. At age thirty-two,
while serving a life sentence, he wrote *Our Lady of the Flowers*. His handwritten manuscript was smuggled out of prison and came to the attention
of André Gide, Jean Cocteau, and Jean-Paul Sartre, who lobbied vigorously for a pardon. Dozens of writers and artists petitioned for Genet's
release, and in 1948 he was pardoned.

Genet's five novels and five plays expressed sympathy for society's
dispossessed. His background as a beggar, thief, male prostitute, por-
nographer, and convict fed his writings. His first books were partially
autobiographical. *Notre-Dame-des-Fleurs* (*Our Lady of the Flowers*, 1944,
revised 1951) unfolds in a prison cell, where an inmate imagines that he
is free to roam the streets of Paris in the company of homosexuals and
criminals. The protagonist of *Miracle de la Rose* (*Miracle of the Rose*, 1946,
revised 1951) is an adolescent who is sent from a reformatory to prison
and eventually to the scaffold.

As a playwright, Genet was influenced by Luigi Pirandello's constant
juggling of illusion and reality and by Antonin Artaud's Theatre of
Cruelty. Genet's first play, *Haute Surveillance* (*Deathwatch*), was probably written in 1944 but not performed until 1949. Professor Richard N.
Coe writes that the play takes us to "the world of prisons and symbols,
flowers and criminals. . . . *Haute Surveillance* is the technical name for the
peculiarly sadistic form of detention that French criminal law prescribes
for its condemned prisoners awaiting execution."[5] The entire action takes
place in one narrow, claustrophobic prison cell, in the course of a single
afternoon. Three men are confined in the cell: Lefranc, a petty burglar;
Maurice, an adolescent delinquent; and Green Eyes, a killer facing the
death penalty (his real name is never revealed). Under the watchful eyes
of a sadistic guard, the three prisoners compete to prove their machismo;
the two small-time criminals vie for the favor of the tough murderer. The
death-fixated bickerings, recriminations, and clashes reach a climax when
Lefranc, aiming to be exalted as a bona fide killer, attacks Maurice and
strangles him.

The first American production of *Deathwatch* was mounted by five Harvard students in Cambridge, Massachusetts, in 1957. The following year, *Deathwatch* was presented at off-Broadway's Theatre East, directed by Leo Garen, with the high-powered cast of Vic Morrow (Lefranc), George Maharis (Green Eyes), Harold Scott (Maurice), and Stephen Gierasch (the Guard). David Amram provided incidental music. Critic Louis Calta of the *New York Times* found it "a generally static, drab and occasionally obscure psychological drama on the peculiar workings of the criminal mind. . . . M. Genet's unwholesome subject falls flat. It lacks the necessary theatrical impact."[6] Nevertheless, the play ran for seventy performances.

England's Foco Novo Theatre Company produced *Deathwatch* under the direction of Roland Rees at the Birmingham Repertory Theatre in February 1985, launching a tour that reached the Young Vic in London two months later. The reviews were mostly positive. Nina-Anne Kaye applauded "a still shocking, mordant piece of theatre," and direction and design "which powerfully convey the menace and sexual tension locked within the cell."[7] Andrew Risik admired a production "spare and compelling" and believed that "in the main, the tension and vigor of the piece are admirably sustained."[8]

Genet's *Les Bonnes* (*The Maids*) was inspired by the real-life case of Christine and Léa Papin, sisters and domestic servants who savagely beat their mistress and her daughter to death in Le Mans, France, in 1933. In its day, the Papin case was as sensational as the Lizzie Borden ax murders, the Lindbergh kidnapping, the killing of JonBenet Ramsey, or O. J. Simpson's alleged double murder. The crime was grisly—the victims' eyes were gouged out and their bodies mutilated. During the trial, the murderous sisters were revealed to be lovers, locked in an incestuous relationship. They were dubbed by the press "the monsters of Le Mans." The gruesome event has fascinated French writers and scholars ever since.

A ninety-minute one-act, *The Maids* unfolds in Madame's elegant bedroom. The maids Claire and Solange Lemercier indulge in make-believe games; take turns playing their glamorous young employer; and express loathing of their lowly station in society, coupled with an intense loathing of Madame. Solange tells Claire how she entered Madame's bedroom at night intending to strangle her, but she lacked the strength to follow through. The sisters vow to murder their mistress, then "carry her off to the woods, and under the fir trees cut her to bits" and "bury her beneath the flowers." They decide to put ten phenobarbital tablets in Madame's tea.

The plan fails, with Madame rushing out to meet her lover, who has been accused of theft and has just been granted bail. Instead of tea, she'll have champagne at the Hong Kong bar. The two sisters are temporarily speechless. Claire puts on an apron. It is Solange's turn to impersonate

Madame. She orders Claire to kneel and strikes her viciously. She then orders Claire to drink the tea. They will both escape servitude. Claire will die by poison, and Solange will be accused of murdering her.

The Maids was first performed at the Théâtre de l'Athénée, Paris, on April 19, 1947. Louis Jouvet produced and directed. London saw The Maids in French at the Mercury Theatre and at the Royal Court Theatre in 1952, and in English at the New Lindsey Theatre Club, four years later. The American premiere of The Maids took place at off-off-Broadway's Tempo playhouse in 1955. In 1963, the play was revived at off-Broadway's Sheridan Square Playhouse, by the Dallas Theatre Center, and broadcast by London's BBC's Third Programme. A notable production of The Maids was mounted in 1969 by the Spanish Nuria Espert Company, directed and designed by Victor Garcia, who staged the play ritualistically on a steeply raked platform inclined toward the public. It ran in Barcelona for 500 performances and went on tour to Austria, Italy, France, Yugoslavia, and Iran.

The Maids continued to enthrall audiences on world stages throughout the twentieth century and beyond. Off-Broadway groups have produced it repeatedly. In 1993, the Classic Stage Company presented The Maids with an all-male cast, as Genet originally intended; the Chocolate Factory Theatre did the same thing in 2005. An all-female cast followed a month later at the Bouwerie Lane Theatre in a Jean Cocteau Repertory production that shifted the proceedings to 1947 Los Angeles. In 2006, the Jean Cocteau produced Maids × 2, a back-to-back presentation of the play on the same evening—one with the three characters played by women, the other by men. The female version was fairly straightforward, while the male rendering was staged in the round and partially in the raw.

The Maids was filmed in the United Kingdom in 1974, starring Glenda Jackson (Solange), Susannah York (Claire), and Vivien Merchant (Madame).

The scene of Genet's Le Balcon (The Balcony) is Irma's luxury brothel, where ordinary men escape their mundane existence by masquerading as judges, bishops, and generals, and play-act perverse games. Lust, sex, and sadism have a field day. Meanwhile, outside in the streets of the city, a revolution is taking place. Soon the patrons of the "house of illusion" become involved.

Translated by Bernard Frechtman and directed by Peter Zadek, The Balcony was first performed in 1957 at London's Arts Theatre Club, a private meeting place that enabled the production to circumvent the Lord Chamberlain's ban on public showings of the play. Subsequent productions of The Balcony were staged by Hans Lietzau in Berlin (1959), Peter Brook in Paris (1960), Leon Eppin in Vienna (1961), Erwin Piscator in Frankfurt (1962), Roger Blin in Roterdam (1967), Victor Garcia in Sao Paulo (1969),

Terry Hands in London (1971), the Piccolo Theatre in Milan (1976), and the Royal Shakespeare Company in London (1977).

The first American production of *The Balcony* was presented by off-Broadway's Circle in the Square in 1960, directed by José Quintero and designed by David Hayes. The large cast included some major thespians of the era's off-Broadway scene—Nancy Marchand as Irma, the Madame with a heart of gold; Roy Poole as a Gestapo-like police chief; Arthur Malet as a masochistic judge; and Sylvia Miles, Salome Jens, and Grayson Hall as kinky trollops. The show ran for 672 performances.

The Balcony continued to be produced on both sides of the Atlantic. Richard Schechter directed an "updated" version of the play for The Performance Group in New York City in 1979. Terry Hands translated, staged, and lighted a rendering shown at London's Barbican Theatre in 1987. It was described as "limp and placid" by the reviewer of *Plays and Players*.[9] Off-Broadway's Jean Cocteau Repertory revived the play in 1999. "In this production," wrote critic J. R. Bruckner in the *New York Times*, "the director, Eve Adamson, has made it a psychological puzzle, handing on to the audience much of the task of supplying meaning."[10] Manhattan's Medicine Show Theatre reincarnated *The Balcony* in 2007.

A 1963 motion picture version of *The Balcony*, written by Ben Maddow, featured Shelley Winters as Madame Irma. Peter Falk, Lee Grant, Jeff Corey, Kent Smith, Leonard Nimoy, and Ruby Dee played the brothel's sadomasochistic clientele. In 2002, France's Aix-en-Provence Festival premiered an opera, *Le Balcon*, composed by Peter Eotvos. "High-spirited, jazz-touched, and in a sense, straight in its treatment of the original play, by Jean Genet," wrote Paul Griffiths in the *New York Times*.[11]

Les Paravents (*The Screens*), first performed at Berlin's Schlossparktheater in 1961, unfolds during the Algerian revolution. The action revolves around a pair of outcasts—an Arab couple who barely survive as thieves. *Saintete*, a ninety-minute play written by Genet in the mid-1950s and translated as *Elle*, was produced posthumously by off-Broadway's Zipper Factory in 2002. It pokes fun at the insatiable lust for fame by celebrities, centering on the pope posing for publicity pictures. Alan Cumming portrayed the pontiff wearing roller skates and a tiara marked "P." Critic Donald Lyons wrote in the *New York Post*, "Genet sets out to show, in this short, would-be shocking spectacle, that the institution of the papacy is a conscious, cynical imposition of arbitrary symbols designed to awe." Lyons found *Elle* a "coarse satire made worse by a trendy adaptation of the text and a campy production."[12] The play ran for fifteen performances.

In the 1970s, Genet joined the causes of Algerian immigrants in France, the Black Panthers in the United States, and Palestinian refugees in Lebanon. He developed throat cancer and died in 1986 in a hotel room in Paris. He is buried in the Spanish cemetery in Larache, Morocco.

Acting Edition: Samuel French, Inc.; Grove Press.

Awards and Honors: Jean Genet's *The Balcony* received an Obie Award in 1961. *The Screens* was a top-ten selection in *The Best Plays of 1971–1972*. Genet's work earned him the Grand Prix des Arts et Lettres in 1983.

NOTES

1. *New York Herald Tribune*, June 1, 1961.

2. *New York Times*, May 9, 1961.

3. Louis Kronenberger, ed., *The Best Plays of 1960–1961* (New York: Dodd, Mead, 1961), 44.

4. Joseph T. Shipley, *The Crown Guide to the World's Great Plays*, rev. ed. (New York: Crown, 1984), 249.

5. Richard N. Coe, *The Vision of Jean Genet* (New York: Grove Press, 1968), 226.

6. *New York Times*, October 10, 1958.

7. *City Limits*, London, April 12, 1985.

8. *Time Out*, London, April 25, 1985.

9. *Plays and Players*, September 1987.

10. *New York Times*, November 19, 1999.

11. *New York Times*, July 9, 2002.

12. *New York Post*, July 25, 2002.

The Andersonville Trial (1959)

Saul Levitt (United States, 1911–1977)

Based on the official record of the 1865 trial of Henry Wirz, commandant of the most notorious Confederate prisoner-of-war stockade, *The Andersonville Trial* raises the issue of passive moral conviction among military men who blindly obey the inhumane orders of their superiors.

During a hearing in Washington, D.C., Wirz was held responsible for the deaths of fourteen thousand Union soldiers. The president of the court was General Lew ("Ben Hur") Wallace.

The indictment, announced at the beginning of the play, specifies that Henry Wirz, who was in charge of the Confederate prison at Andersonville, Georgia, kept in barbarous confinement 40,000 federal soldiers without adequate shelter against the burning heat of summer and the cold of winter; that he did not provide the prisoners with sufficient food, clothing, or medical care, causing 14,000 of them to languish and die; that he instructed the prison guards stationed near the walls of the prison stockade to fire upon and kill any prisoner who might pass beyond that barrier; that he used bloodhounds to hunt down, seize, and mangle escaping prisoners of war; that through these various causes he brought about the deaths of fifty federal soldiers; and that through direct order and/or by his own hand he brought about the murder of thirteen prisoners, their names unknown.

The judge advocate, Lt. Col. N. P. Chipman, presents a parade of witnesses to relate harrowing accounts of maltreatment, hunger, lack of shelter, and a bare existence under "cruel and inhuman rules." The prosecution witnesses include a Southern official assigned to inspect the Georgia prison camp; a medical officer; the owner of a plantation adjacent to the compound, who testifies that he heard Wirz boast that he had killed more Yankees in Andersonville than Lee at Richmond; a former Andersonville inmate, who witnessed dogs tear up his companion; and another captive, who saw Wirz empty his revolver into a fellow prisoner.

Wirz's defense counsel, Otis H. Baker, artfully parries many of the accusations and demonstrates in court that Wirz, who had an injured shoulder, could not pull a trigger. Against counsel's advice, Wirz insists on taking the stand. He declares that the military code dictated that he obey orders, that he could not disobey, and that he had to keep his feelings to himself.

Prosecutor Chipman retorts that he shudders for a world that would let total obedience murder people instead of save them, and the president of the court agrees. Wirz is found guilty of all charges and condemned "to be hanged by the neck till he be dead, at such time and place as the President of the United States may direct."[1]

* * *

Saul Levitt first wrote *The Trial of Captain Wirz* for a 1957 television episode on *Climax!*, with Everett Sloane in the title role and Charlton Heston as prosecutor Chipman. Levitt's expanded version, now called *The Andersonville Trial*, opened in New York at the Henry Miller Theatre on December 29, 1959. Most of the critics greeted it with kudos. "Saul Levitt has written a striking and effective courtroom drama about a famous case in American history," stated Richard Watts Jr. "He has offered a provocative study of the moral issues involved in the conflict between man's obligation to authority and his conscience."[2] Frank Aston asserted, "Mr. Levitt has turned up a hell-raising heart searcher."[3] John Chapman found *The Andersonville Trial* "the best courtroom play since *The Caine Mutiny Court-Martial*,"[4] while Walter Kerr promised the audience "a whale of an evening."[5]

On the other hand, Robert Coleman described the play as "a worthy attempt that doesn't come off,"[6] and Brooks Atkinson felt that "the theatre was triumphing over truth by being consistently ingenious, showy and planned."[7]

The reviewers unanimously praised director José Ferrer and actors George C. Scott (Judge Advocate Chipman), Albert Dekker (Defense Counsel Baker),[8] Herbert Berghof (defendant Wirz), and Russell Hardie (General Wallace), who held court for 179 performances.

The Andersonville Trial was a success in Berlin in 1960 but was not welcome in the American South, where Captain Wirz was, and perhaps remains, a hero. Shows were cancelled in Atlanta and Birmingham for fear of protests. The play did not have a major production in the South until Theatre Atlanta's production in 1967.

Early in the twenty-first century, *The Andersonville Trial* was revived by the Finlandia University Community Theatre in Hancock, Michigan (2005), off-Broadway's The Actors Company Theatre (2008), and the Flint Youth Theatre in Flint, Michigan (2010).

In 1970, George C. Scott directed a made-for-television movie of *The Andersonville Trial*, with William Shatner stepping into the role of the prosecutor. Produced by the Public Broadcasting Service, it was a star-studded affair featuring Richard Basehart as Henry Wirz, surrounded by Cameron Mitchell, Buddy Ebsen, Albert Salmi, Jack Cassidy, Whit Bissell, and Martin Sheen.

The Andersonville Trial was presented on television in Belgium (1962), West Germany (1972), and the former Yugoslavia (1975).

The dire events at the Confederate POW camp (1861–1865) were also captured in 1996's *Andersonville*, a 200-minute television miniseries based on Mackinlay Kantor's 1955 Pulitzer Prize–winning novel of the same name, scripted by David W. Rintels and directed by John Frankenheimer, with Jan Triska as Henry Wirz.

* * *

Saul Levitt was born in Hartford, Connecticut, the son of a hatmaker. He studied at Morris High School in the Bronx and the College of the City of New York. He was planning on a career in engineering but in 1934, when he was twenty-three, his first article was published in the magazine *American Mercury* and he shifted direction. During World War II, Levitt served as a radioman in the Air Force. Because of injuries suffered in a vehicle accident, he was reassigned to *Yank Magazine*, the army's weekly publication.

In the 1940s, Levitt pursued a writing career as a freelancer and novelist. Following *The Andersonville Trial*, he focused his creativity on television, where between 1953 and 1967 he contributed episodes to *You Are There*, *Climax!*, *Ivanhoe*, *Decoy*, *The Untouchables*, *Westinghouse Presents*, and *Judd for the Defense*.

In 1967, Levitt collaborated on the screenplay of *A Covenant with Death*, in which an innocent man, convicted as a murderer, kills his hangman. Four years later, Levitt teamed with renowned pacifist Father Daniel Berrigan on *The Trial of the Catonsville Nine*, a courtroom drama about the priest's raid of a local Vietnam-era draft board in Catonsville, Maryland, setting its files on fire. It was presented under the auspices of the Phoenix Theatre at the Lyceum Theatre. Subsequently, Levitt and Berrigan joined forces on the screenplay of *The Trial of the Catonsville Nine*.

Acting Edition: Dramatists Play Service.

Awards and Honors: A top-ten choice in *The Best Plays of 1959–1960* (in spite of some misgivings by editor Louis Kronenberger: "The play offered an evening that had much in its favor in both theme and treatment, that had both effective bursts of eloquence and genuine bouts of theatre. At the same time the play lacked a certain cleanness of impact; it pounded too hard in places, it stretched out too long. . . . Vivid in so many of its parts, the play did not altogether satisfy as a whole"). [9]

Saul Levitt won an Emmy Award for Outstanding Writing Achievement in Drama for 1970's television adaptation of *The Andersonville Trial*. The show won an Emmy for Outstanding Single Program.

NOTES

1. Henry Wirz was the only man tried and executed for war crimes committed during the Civil War.

2. *New York Post*, December 30, 1959.

3. *New York World-Telegram*, December 30, 1959.

4. *Daily News*, December 30, 1959.

5. *New York Herald Tribune*, December 30, 1959.

6. *Daily Mirror*, December 30, 1959.

7. *New York Times*, December 30, 1959.

8. Born in Brooklyn, New York, Albert Dekker (1905–1968) made his professional debut with a Cincinnati stock company in 1927. The following year, he played several small roles in the Broadway production of Eugene O'Neill's *Marco Millions*. A decade of theatrical performances followed, including the parts of Baron von Gaigem in 1930's *Grand Hotel* and editor Hovstad in 1937's *An Enemy of the People*. Dekker migrated to Hollywood and appeared in some seventy films from the 1930s to the 1960s. His most memorable roles were villainous: a mad scientist in the horror movie *Dr. Cyclops* (1940), a vicious hitman in the film noir *The Killers* (1946), a shady dealer in atomic fuel in the whodunit *Kiss Me Deadly* (1955), and an unscrupulous detective in the western *The Wild Bunch* (1969). On May 5, 1968, Dekker was found dead in his Hollywood home. It was reported that there were no signs of forced entry, but money and camera equipment were missing.

9. Louis Kronenberger, ed., *The Best Plays of 1959–1960* (New York: Dodd, Mead, 1960), 12.

The Deadly Game (1960)

James Yaffe (United States, 1927–)

In a secluded Alpine retreat, three retired men of law—a judge, a prosecutor (Gustave), and a defense attorney (Bernard)—relive their glory days by playing legal charades with stranded strangers. Mr. Howard Trapp, a brash, self-assured American traveling salesman, finding shelter here during a blizzard, agrees to humor his hosts by joining their parlor game.

"Just like in the movies, huh?" laughs Trapp. "'Where were you on the night of the murder?'" The Judge smiles and assures him that their game is not so melodramatic. The prosecutor states that law is the exercise of logic and precedent; melodrama plays no part in it whatsoever.

However, *The Deadly Game* is brimming with melodrama. The setup of an isolated chalet during a night of whistling winds and heavy snow is reminiscent of *The Cat and the Canary*, *Seven Keys to Baldpate*, *The Mousetrap*, and many other unblushing stage shockers. A sense of unease creeps in when the initially amused Mr. Trapp, during a lavish dinner, learns more about the planned diversion. The Judge relates that their game is rather unusual. The three hosts undertake their former jobs in a law court. They reenact the famous trials of history: the trial of Socrates, the trial of Joan of Arc, the Dreyfus Affair. Gustave presents the evidence for the prosecution, Bernard presents the evidence for the defense, and the Judge of the court arrives at a verdict and delivers the appropriate sentence.

Trapp laughs and says that this "intellectual sort of game" might be fun. The Judge remarks that even though it is challenging to re-create famous trials of history, it is even a greater challenge to have a real person stand before their court. A month ago, he relates, they had a most interesting case. During a snowstorm, a former mayor of the province found his way to the house just as they were finishing dinner. It was a delicious meal. The poor man was unlucky to miss it. He was convicted of poisoning his first wife, and they sentenced him to hang. Naturally he was upset, but the law is the law.

The vibes of foreboding increase when at the end of act I Trapp is somberly accused of the murder of his former chief, the late Mr. Foster, and when he finds out that a fourth elderly gentleman, who has been hovering in the background, has served the municipality as its official hangman.

The prosecutor doggedly pursues the murder theory and elicits from Trapp that he was anxious to get ahead in the world by replacing the late Mr. Foster, that Foster had a dangerous heart condition and any shock might kill him, and that he deliberately carried on an affair with Foster's wife. The prosecutor maintains that Trapp intentionally spread the word about the illicit liaison, making sure that the cuckolded husband heard of it—"You struck the fatal blow, just as surely as if your hand had wielded a knife!"

The Deadly Game carries on the cynical theme that Duerrenmatt planted in *The Visit*, showing us that humanity is corrupt, that each of us is capable of committing a major crime, that it is a dog-eat-dog world. The facts may be against Mr. Trapp, says the defense attorney in his summation. He did hate his chief and coveted his job; he did make love to his chief's wife, confessed the affair to his bitter rival and ultimately caused the late lamented Foster's death by heart failure; but *in his mind* Trapp committed no murder. He started off with no grand plan which he then cunningly and cold-bloodedly set into motion; he proceeded rather by fits and starts. In this respect, declares the defense attorney, the defendant is not much different from the rest of mankind. He is *unconscious* of the implication of what he does. Granted, his behavior is mean, selfish, and ignoble. But it is also human—overwhelmingly, devastatingly human—and therefore worthy of pity, compassion, and forgiveness.

The prosecutor responds by disagreeing that the world is a battlefield occupied by unthinking, unfeeling savages. He refuses to believe it. Men do not *all* behave like brutes, but the brute is *in* us all, fighting to take control of us. The purpose of this court is to fight this brute who lies hidden inside every man, to help in a small way to stamp it out, by stamping out those individuals who have allowed it to turn them into destroyers of their fellow men. Howard Trapp is just such a destructive force, asserts the prosecutor, and demands that Trapp will pay for his crime with his life.

A few days later, Helen Trapp arrives on the scene and is told by a sympathetic trio that her husband's death was an accident: he drank a bit too much, grew somewhat confused, and rushed out into the storm. In the dark, he couldn't possibly have seen the precipice before he fell over it.

In an ironic fade-out, Helen accepts their invitation to stay for dinner. As she is offered "a very special brand" of cognac, the attorney says: "You know, it's been so long since we entertained a lady in this house, it will really be quite a novelty." And after dinner, adds the Judge, they'll think of something to amuse her, to take her mind off her troubles. Perhaps some little parlor game. . . . (The curtain slowly falls.)

* * *

The Deadly Game was initially conceived by Swiss playwright Friedrich Duerrenmatt in 1955 as a radio play—*Die Panne* (*The Breakdown*). Two years later it was adapted by James Yaffe for an episode on the American television series *Suspicion*, featuring Boris Karloff as the Judge and Gary Merrill as the traveling salesman. Subsequently, Yaffe converted it to the stage. The play was first presented at the Longacre Theatre, New York City, on February 2, 1960, to generally favorable reviews.

"Better news in the theatre for a change," wrote John Chapman. "*The Deadly Game* is a tidy, literate, well-staged and well-acted piece of dramatic make-believe."[1] Frank Aston found the play "A collegebred hair-raiser. . . . Under William Gaskill's adroit direction, all this grim jesting turns into an adult delight."[2] Richard Watts Jr. stated: "Anyone who saw the Lunts in *The Visit* knows the Swiss Friedrich Duerrenmatt's chilling ability to present his sardonic view of sin and punishment in terms of ironic melodrama. *The Deadly Game* captures his disturbing vision of human weakness and implacability with fidelity. . . . The Duerrenmatt sense of the world's evil makes *The Deadly Game* coldly haunting."[3]

John McClain and Robert Coleman savored the play with mixed feelings. "*The Deadly Game* will not be one of the season's standouts but it will enhance Mr. Duerrenmatt's status as an original and creative contributor to the modern theatre," concluded McClain.[4] "*The Deadly Game* is only intermittently gripping, though it has the potentialities for a real hair-raiser," inferred Coleman." . . . It's a play for pessimists, for those who like to watch a cat toying with a mouse. The blood in Duerrenmatt's veins must be as cold as the glaciers of his native land."[5]

The two drama deans Walter Kerr and Brooks Atkinson were disappointed. "What turns the thread of the evening inside out, I think, is an unexpected pair of theatrical vices," lamented Kerr. "The first of these is a curious lack of subtlety. Though our hearty American is supposed to be thick headed he is so conveniently quick to convict himself out of his own mouth that the very fun of the game is dissipated. Once the trial is under way, his inquisitors have much too easy a time of it. The second, and much more important, tactical error is an air of smugness that begins to hover about the Duerrenmatt vision."[6] Atkinson was more caustic: "The exposition is in the conventional style of parlor melodrama. When Mr. Yaffe finally gets to the trial, he does not write with much distinction. Although the moral issues are provocative, they are not dramatized with force. With the harshness of *The Visit* fresh in mind, *The Deadly Game* seems like commercial fiction."[7]

The entire cadre of critics, including the naysayers, complimented the cast of players. Atkinson said: "Pat Hingle vigorously describes the brassiness, cleverness and callousness of the traveling salesman."[8] Kerr wrote: "The three wise owls who glower at Mr. Hingle are all handsomely feathered. Max Adrian, the prosecutor, exposes all of his teeth in a deadly-nightshade smile and tosses his carved jester's head with a splendid arrogance. Claude Dauphin, preening himself whenever he scores a point on behalf of the client he is charged to defend, is the very picture of arthritic enthusiasm. Ludwig Donath's judge is soberly and quietly horrifying, in a fatherly way."[9]

The Deadly Game stopped playing after thirty-nine performances. London had a somewhat longer run during the 1966–1967 season.

A slightly revised version of *The Deadly Game* was presented off-Broadway at the Provincetown Playhouse on February 13, 1966, and ran for 105 performances. An added character, Nicole, a maid at the Swiss abode, contributes some glamour to the gray proceedings. Howard Trapp flirts with her quite outrageously, foreshadowing the revelation of his affair with the boss's wife, a key factor in the "guilty" verdict.

The Deadly Game was televised in India (1971), called *Silence! The Court Is in Session*; as a 1972 Italian/French production, named *The Most Wonderful Evening of My Life*, starring Alberto Sordi, Michel Simon, Charles Vanel, Claude Dauphin, and Pierre Brasseur; and in the United States (1982), with George Segal as Howard Trapp, interrogated by Trevor Howard, Robert Morley, and Emlyn Williams.

California's Hillbarn Theatre of Foster City resuscitated *The Deadly Game* in February 2001, as did The Long Beach Playhouse in January 2008.

* * *

James Yaffe was born in 1927 in Chicago, Illinois, to a middle-class Jewish family. He attended Yale University from 1944 to 1948, graduating summa cum laude. In 1948 he began to contribute episodes to television's Studio One. During the 1950s and 1960s he wrote for *The United States Steel Hour*, *The Elgin Hour*, *The Defenders*, *The Alfred Hitchcock Hour*, and *The Nurses*.

Beginning with 1953's *The Good-for-Nothing*, Yaffe published several novels, often capturing the milieu of his upbringing. That same year he began penning crime stories for the *Ellery Queen Mystery Magazine*.

Following *The Deadly Game*, Yaffe came up with two more plays of suspense, *Ivory Tower* (1969) and *Cliffhanger* (1985).

Ivory Tower, cowritten with Jerome Weidman, is a courtroom drama that played in various resident theatres but has not reached New York. The protagonist, Simon Otway, a famous American author who lived in Paris during World War II, is accused of treason for calling on the invading Allied forces, in several radio broadcasts, to lay down their arms and stop the bloodshed.

Like Henry Wirz of *The Andersonville Trial* a decade ago, Otway ignores his attorney's advice and insists on taking the stand. The proceedings, heretofore too highbrow and lacking in dramatic fireworks, now shift gears to an intense confrontation between Otway and prosecutor Harold Gutman. By the end of a grueling cross-examination, the renowned writer begins to crack and eventually, with agonized tears, admits that his broadcasts caused the death of American soldiers.

The *Citizen-Journal* of Columbus, Ohio, poses the question "Did he or did he not intentionally commit treason? . . . Simon Otway, the central figure, is so overwhelming in detail, so articulate, that he becomes the unwitting artist-on-trial and the ultimate victim of his own character. The trial brings about a kind of catharsis—a mind-bending recognition of his real motives." The *Ann Arbor [Michigan] News* found *Ivory Tower* an "intense, absorbing courtroom drama with pace, style, force and purpose."

Unlike *The Deadly Game* and *Ivory Tower*, James Yaffe's *Cliffhanger* is a conventional, old-fashioned comedy-thriller. It is the bittersweet tale of Henry Lowenthal, a gentle small-college philosophy professor, who in a moment of fit seizes a bust of Socrates and with it strikes the vindictive, ruthlessly ambitious chairperson of his department, Edith Wilshire. The panicky Henry and his wife Polly attempt to dispose of the body, but complications arise when a rather odd student, Melvin McMullen, witnesses the action and threatens exposure unless the professor elevates his F grade. "If I flunk your course," says Melvin, "my father will kill me!"

Intimidated, goaded, and losing his head again, Henry picks up the bust of Socrates and prepares to smash Melvin's head. However, in a surprise twist it turns out that Edith Wilshire was not killed when hit by the professor; she only lost consciousness. It was Melvin who did her in. "It was the wrong time to ask her about my grade, I guess. She laughed at me. . . . She just kept laughing. . . . I picked up this rock and I hit her."

Henry Lowenthal is appointed chairman of the philosophy department.

Cliffhanger was first produced at the Alliance Theatre in Atlanta, Georgia, then presented by the Lamb Theatre in New York City on February 7, 1985. Vintage Theatre, at the Glass Center of Corning, New York, included *Cliffhanger* in its Summer of Suspense '96 series. The box-office gross exceeded those of such classics as *Ten Little Indians* and *Dial "M" for Murder*. Pennsylvania's Bristol Riverside Theatre mounted *Cliffhanger* in August 2004, while Broadway Onstage Live Theatre of Eastpointe, Michigan, produced the play in January 2005.

One hopes that the deadly events of *Cliffhanger* are not autobiographical, but it should be noted that since 1981 James Yaffe has been an English professor and writer-in-residence at Colorado College in Colorado

Springs. Yaffe's series character, Mom, introduced in the *Ellery Queen Mystery Magazine* and catapulted to hardcover in *A Nice Murder for Mom* (1988), followed her son Dave from the Bronx out to Mesa Grande, Colorado, where the quick-witted Jewish mother solves crime cases over Sunday brunches and homemade chicken soup.

Shades of *Cliffhanger*, the focal point of *A Nice Murder for Mom* is the simmering rivalry between two college professors until it reaches a deadly level. A subsequent novel, *Mom Doth Murder Sleep* (1991), reveals that the hallowed community theatre is nothing but a cesspool of intrigue, mayhem, and bloodshed. The seventy-five-year-old sleuth gets entangled with the murder of an actor in a production of *Macbeth*. There are several other novels in the series, published by St. Martin's Press. The complete "Mom" short stories are collected in *My Mother, the Detective*, published in 1997 by Crippen and Landru.

Acting Edition: Dramatists Play Service.

Awards and Honors: A top-ten selection in *The Best Plays of 1959–1960*.

NOTES

1. *Daily News*, February 3, 1960.
2. *New York World-Telegram*, February 3, 1960.
3. *New York Post*, February 3, 1960.
4. *New York Journal-American*, February 3, 1960.
5. *Daily Mirror*, February 3, 1960.
6. *New York Herald Tribune*, February 3, 1960.
7. *New York Times*, February 3, 1960.
8. *New York Times*, February 3, 1960.
9. *New York Herald Tribune*, February 3, 1960.

Go Back for Murder (1960)

Agatha Christie (England, 1890–1976)

Agatha Christie's play *Go Back for Murder* was derived from her 1943 Poirot novel *Five Little Pigs*, and once again the author decided to banish the Belgian sleuth from the stage version.

In the book, the first and best of Christie's "murder in retrospect" mysteries, the daughter of a woman found guilty of poisoning her husband, a famous painter, engages Poirot years later to clear her mother's name. The play rendition has the daughter, pretty Carla Crale of London, undertaking the mission.[1]

When Carla celebrates her twenty-first birthday, Fogg, Fogg, Bambydle, and Fogg deliver a sealed letter that was written by her now dead but then imprisoned mother, Caroline, sixteen years ago. Caroline insists that she did not kill her philandering spouse, Amyas.

Carla is engaged to be married and her fiancé, Jeff Rogers, seems to be concerned about a nuptial tie with the daughter of a murderess. Solicitor Justin Fogg attempts to persuade Carla to lay the issue to rest. He urges her to be charitable toward her mother, who had been cheated on and humiliated continuously.

But Carla is determined. She gleans from Justin's files that aside from Caroline, there were five people at the house in Alderbury on the day of the tragedy: Philip and Meredith Blake, two brothers, close friends of Amyas; Angela Warren, a schoolgirl of fourteen and Caroline's half sister; the household governess, stern Miss Williams; and the father's mistress, model Elsa Greer. Carla learns that the instrument of murder was coniine, a deadly poison, introduced into a glass of beer.

In a succession of vignettes, Carla meets, one by one, the "five little pigs," a reference to the nursery rhyme Christie used as an inspiration for her play. Lawyer Justin aids Carla in gathering the "suspects" at Alderbury, and act II unfolds in the form of a flashback, reconstructing past events.

The audience follows the sketching of Elsa by the artist Amyas, their clandestine lovemaking, and a bitter clash between the brazen model and the pained wife. When Amyas asks for a bottle of cold beer, the suspense is palpable: who among the characters brings the bottle in, pours it, passes by it, has the opportunity to empty coniine into it?

In an upside-down denouement, Justin proves that it was not the wife who killed Amyas Crale but the mistress, Elsa, after she was sent packing.

A romantic subplot shifts Carla's heartstrings from her priggish fiancé to the supportive lawyer.

* * *

Go Back for Murder previewed in Edinburgh, Scotland, and came to the Duchess Theatre in London on March 23, 1960. The press reception was acrimonious and the play lasted only for thirty-seven performances. With a suitable makeup change, Ann Firbank played both Carla and Caroline Crale. She was supported by Robert Urquhart (Justin Fogg), Nigel Green (Amyas Crale), and Lisa Daniely (Elsa Greer). Hubert Gregg directed.

Go Back for Murder has had few revivals. The play had its American premiere at Players State Theatre, Coconut Grove, Florida, on April 3, 1981, running for twenty-eight performances.

Tight, turbulent, and tantalizing, *Go Back for Murder* deserves both re-evaluation and revival.

Acting Edition: Samuel French, Inc. (in manuscript form). *Go Back for Murder* is also included in *The Mousetrap and Other Plays* by Agatha Christie (New York: Dodd, Mead, 1978; Harper Paperbacks, 1993).

NOTE

1. Other Christie books in which the investigator is on a quest to solve a long-ago murder include *Sparkling Cyanide* (1945), *Ordeal by Innocence* (1958), *Elephants Can Remember* (1972), and *Sleeping Murder* (1976).

The Best Man (1960)

Gore Vidal (United States, 1925–)

During the latter part of 1959, the dirty tricks of politics took center stage with an off-Broadway revival of Robert Penn Warren's *All the King's Men* and the Broadway premiere of *The Gang's All Here* by Jerome Lawrence and Robert E. Lee.

All the King's Men is a brooding, complex, and philosophical adaptation of Warren's Pulitzer Prize–winning novel, depicting, in a kaleidoscopic style of short vignettes, the rise and fall of a political strongman. *The Gang's All Here* captures the rampaging skullduggery of President Warren G. Harding's corrupt regime.

The trend continued in 1960 when two melodramas of behind-the-scenes underhanded diplomacy became the toast of town: *The Best Man* by Gore Vidal, opening on March 31 at the Morosco Theatre for a whopping run of 520 performances; and *Advise and Consent* by Loring Mandel, based on Allen Drury's celebrated novel, debuting on November 17 at the Cort Theatre, attracting audiences for 212 showings.

The Best Man, a political shocker about character assassination and high-pressure chicanery, takes place in Philadelphia during the 1960 nominating convention of a nameless party. The action unfolds in two suites at the Sheraton Hotel, each occupied by a presidential candidate— William Russell, a former secretary of state, a man of intellect with high moral principles (enacted on Broadway by Melvyn Douglas), and Joseph Cantwell, a rugged, power-hungry businessman (portrayed by Frank Lovejoy).

The two candidates, running neck-and-neck for the nomination, solicit the endorsement of ailing former president Arthur Hockstader (Lee Tracy), whose nod will be a decisive factor. Cantwell mandates his aide, Don Blades, to arrange for an appointment with Hockstader, hinting at a looming scandal. Cantwell presents Hockstader with a file containing a psychiatrist's report: several years ago William Russell had a nervous breakdown and deserted his wife, after which their marriage has become "a phony, a political front." The report uses such political dynamite words, as "manic depressive, paranoid pattern, and attempted suicide."

Hockstader smiles: "So that's your little number, is it?" He promises Cantwell "an ugly fight" and assures him, "When I finish with you, my boy, you will know what it is like to get in the ring with an old-time killer. I am going to have your political scalp and hang it right on my belt, along with a lot of others."

Russell's doctor, Artinian, arrives on the scene to verify that apparently, somebody from Cantwell's office bribed one of their nurses; they got the whole file. However, the doctor is willing to testify that William Russell is one of the sanest men he has ever known.

An army major, Sheldon Marcus, provides Russell with a whiff of infamy about his rival: Joe Cantwell was an army captain "and . . . and sometimes when there's all those men together . . ."

HOCKSTADER: Major Marcus, am I to understand by the way you are slowly beating around the bush that Joe Cantwell is what, when I was a boy, we called de-generate?
MARCUS: Yes, sir, Mr. President, sir, that's just what I mean . . .
RUSSELL: I don't believe it. Nobody with that awful wife and those ugly children could be anything but normal!

Hockstader believes that with this piece of information they can stop Cantwell cold. But Russell overrules the weapon of personal gossip, even though his opponent uses such methods against him. He is sure that they have enough on Cantwell's public life to defeat him without going into his private life. Hockstader is furious and questions Russell's ability to make a quick decision in the White House "when maybe all our lives depended on whether you could act fast." When Russell still refuses to exercise the homosexuality card, the former president presses on with a bleak, revealing treatise about Machiavellian politics, warning Russell that power is not a children's toy but a weapon to be used by strong men; if Russell does not beat Cantwell with this opportunistic stick, then he has no business in the big league.

In a confrontation between Russell and Cantwell, the latter claims that he can prove he is in the clear and that he was the one who broke a ring of "degenerates" in the army. He even got promoted on the strength of having helped "clear those types out of our command."

Former president Hockstader dies. Confident that he is "home free," Cantwell instructs his staff to release the incriminating file on Russell to the party's delegates. As the balloting progresses off-stage, Russell loses three hundred votes but still maintains a strong following. Cantwell asks him to release the rest of his delegates to him on the next ballot, promising

Russell the vice presidency. However, stating "we cancelled each other out," Russell releases his 384 delegates to vote, not for Cantwell, but in support of a dark horse candidate—Governor John Merwin, who ends up winning the party's nomination.

* * *

"Gore Vidal's *The Best Man* was Broadway's salute to an election year," wrote Louis Kronenberger in *The Best Plays of 1959–1960*. "A lively theatre piece laid at a fanciful 1960 national convention, and concerned with a fierce struggle between two would-be nominees. . . . *The Best Man* chronicled a pretty traditional sort of struggle between a set hero and a set villain, and much of the play's interest lay in the sheer simplicity of this. . . . It contrasted ethics with opportunism, statesmanship with careerism, light with darkness. . . . If a modern-angled morality play, *The Best Man* at the same time always remembered that bad politics are a prime source of good theatre, that stage tricks pall beside political ones."[1]

The New York reviewers were unanimous in their praise. "The flagging spirits of this playgoer were lifted several notches last evening by the performance of Gore Vidal's comedy-drama about politics, *The Best Man*, at the Morosco Theatre," cheered John Chapman. "After a long, dreary round of failures, it was a pleasure to attend an excellent performance of a well-made, keen-witted play of contemporary interest. The Morosco box office has just the ticket for an election year."[2] John McClain found *The Best Man* "enormously good theatre. At last we have a drama of size, written skillfully about people who bear a quaint resemblance to living characters, performed with brilliance, directed with taste and mounted in the style it deserves. . . . Melvyn Douglas gives one of his most persuasive performances in a role magnificently tailored to him, that of a well-bred candidate. As his rough-diamond antagonist, Frank Lovejoy is tough and relentless. Lee Tracy, the former President, steals all his scenes."[3]

Richard Watts Jr. gleaned in the play "a provocative study of the flora and fauna of national politics,"[4] while Brooks Atkinson enjoyed its "breezy melodrama."[5] Walter Kerr declared that "As a piece of first-rate journalism, with a telling little editorial tucked into one corner, *The Best Man* is a knockout."[6] Frank Aston exclaimed, "*The Best Man* is more than welcome. Its sharp, jabbing entertainment is ideally tailored for the party-conscious year."[7] Robert Coleman predicted that "*The Best Man* will win in a walk at the Morosco . . . a sure candidate for box-office honors" and saluted the three lead actors—Douglas, Lovejoy, and Tracy: "Under Joseph Anthony's galloping direction, the skilled trio generate as much excitement as the returns on election night."[8]

Vidal wrote the screenplay for *The Best Man* in 1964, with Henry Fonda, Cliff Robertson, and Lee Tracy, grittily directed by Franklin Schaffner. The play was revived on Broadway at the Virginia Theatre in 2000, directed by Ethan McSweeny, featuring Spalding Gray (William Russell), Chris Noth (Joseph Cantwell), and Charles Durning (Arthur Hockstader). It garnered pro-and-con reviews, won the 2001 Drama Desk Award as Best Revival of a Play, and ran for 121 performances. In February 2011, the revival's producers announced that *The Best Man* would have another turn in the spring of 2012, to coincide with the presidential election later that year.

* * *

Born at the United States Military Academy, West Point, New York, in 1925, Eugene Luther Gore Vidal enlisted in the Army Reserves following his graduation from Phillips Exeter Academy. He wrote his first novel, the militaristic *Williwaw*, when he was nineteen, and since then built up a formidable reputation as novelist, essayist, screenwriter, and literary critic. Vidal was openly gay, and many of his stories feature homosexual characters. Perhaps the most controversial are *Myra Breckenridge* (1968) and its sequel *Myron* (1974), both featuring transsexual protagonists. Frequently identified with Democratic causes, Vidal's political novels include *Washington, D.C.* (1967), *Burr* (1973), and *Lincoln* (1984). His runs for Congress in 1960 and for governor of California in 1988 were unsuccessful.

Vidal made the Broadway scene several times. His play *Visit to a Small Planet* (1957), adapted from a 1955 television broadcast and subtitled *A Comedy Akin to a Vaudeville*, is a satire on war as seen through the eyes of Kreton, a visitor from outer space (Booth Theatre, February 7, 1957—388 performances). It was filmed in 1960 with Jerry Lewis as the alien. An adaptation of Friedrich Duerrenmatt's *Romulus* (1949) depicts the destruction of ancient Rome (Music Box Theatre, January 10, 1962—sixty-nine performances). In addition to *The Best Man*, Vidal dealt with political maneuvers in *Weekend* (Broadhurst Theatre, March 11, 1968—twenty-one performances) and *An Evening with Richard Nixon* (Shubert Theatre, April 18, 1972—sixteen performances).

For the silver screen, Vidal collaborated with Tennessee Williams on the latter's *Suddenly, Last Summer* (1959), contributed uncredited to *Ben Hur* (1959), coscripted with Francis Ford Coppola *Is Paris Burning?* (1966), and wrote an early screenplay, later revised, of the infamous *Caligula* (1979). Vidal's many television credits include episodes for *Suspense, Omnibus, Danger, Studio One, Climax!,* and *Matinee Theatre;* adaptations of the novels *Dr. Jekyll and Mr. Hyde, The Turn of the Screw,* and *A Farewell to Arms;* and the western *Billy the Kid* (1989), starring Val Kilmer in the title role.

Vidal's 1956 motion picture adaptation of Paddy Chayefsky's TV drama *The Catered Affair* starred Bette Davis as the poor mother of a girl engaged to a blue-blood fiancé. Davis called it her favorite role. A musical version of *The Catered Affair*, with book by Harvey Fierstein and music and lyrics by John Bucchino, opened at Broadway's Walter Kerr Theatre on March 25, 2008, running for 116 performances.

Under the pseudonym Edgar Box, Vidal launched three detective novels in 1952 featuring Peter Cutler Sargeant II, a Harvard graduate, former soldier, and public relations consultant: *Death in the Fifth Position* (1952), in which the prima ballerina of a Russian ballet company—a cesspool of clandestine affairs and drug addiction—falls thirty feet to her death during a performance; *Death before Bedtime* (1953), about the murder of a right-wing senator, accomplished by the special explosive Pomeroy 5X, placed behind some logs in his home's fireplace; and *Death Likes It Hot* (1954), centered around a weekend party at an East Hampton estate and the unexpected drowning of one of the guests. Chris Steinbrenner and Otto Penzler, in their *Encyclopedia of Mystery and Detection*, state, "As detective stories, they are negligible, but Vidal compensates for his shortcomings by means of his talent as a writer and satirist, and his works are highly entertaining."[9] In the late 1950s, *Death before Bedtime* and *Death Likes It Hot* were adapted for the Ellery Queen television series, starring George Nader.

Acting Edition: Dramatists Play Service.

Awards and Honors: *The Best Man* was a top-ten selection in *The Best Plays of 1959–1960*. It was nominated for a Tony Award as Best Play (1960) and as Best Revival of a Play (2001).

NOTES

1. Louis Kronenberger, ed. *The Best Plays of 1959–1960* (New York: Dodd, Mead, 1960), 18–19.

2. *Daily News*, April 1, 1960.

3. *New York Journal-American*, April 1, 1960.

4. *New York Post*, April 1, 1960.

5. *New York Times*, April 1, 1960.

6. *New York Herald Tribune*, April 1, 1960.

7. *New York World-Telegram*, April 1, 1960.

8. *New York Mirror*, April 1, 1960.

9. Chris Steinbrenner and Otto Penzler, eds. *Encyclopedia of Mystery and Detection* (New York: McGraw-Hill, 1976), 43.

Oliver! (1960)

Book, Lyrics, and Music by
Lionel Bart (England, 1930–1999)

Charles Dickens (1812–1870) penned the novel *Oliver Twist* (serialized 1837–1839) when in his twenties, introducing the style that would become his hallmark: a labyrinthian plot coated with sentiment and tension, underlined with deep concern for the underdogs of society.

In 1960, fellow Englishman Lionel Bart adapted the novel into a stage musical. He stripped away many strands and characters of the novel; however, he kept intact the key plot maneuvers.

The curtain rises on the gloomy interior of a workhouse dining hall. It is early evening. Pale-faced, starving boys file in to a large wooden table singing the ironical "Food, Glorious Food," in which they question, "Is it worth the waiting for?" They yearn for "hot sausage," "cold jelly," and "a great big steak," but they know that they'll be fed "the same old gruel." Mr. Bumble, the parish officer, and the Widow Corney, matron of the workhouse, both greedy and heartless, serve the food. The boys polish off their plates, and young Oliver musters the courage to approach Mr. Bumble to ask for more. Outraged, Bumble and Corney croon "Oliver" as they chase the child into a corner, order their assistants to lock him up, and usher the other boys to bed. Left alone, Bumble drinks his tea, wipes his lips, and kisses the widow. She pretends to be shocked, sings "I Shall Scream," and ends up sitting on Bumble's lap.

Mr. Bumble hawks Oliver through the streets of London, announcing "Boy for sale!" Eventually he takes the child to Mr. Sowerberry, the undertaker. They haggle over price and compromise on five pounds. Bumble informs Sowerberry that Oliver's mother came to his parish destitute and died when she brought her child into the world without leaving so much as a name or address.

Oliver is sent to sleep in the basement among the coffins. Lonely and fearful, he sings "Where Is Love?" In the morning, Oliver is taunted by bully Noah Claypole, the undertaker's assistant. When Claypole bad-mouths Oliver's dead mother, Oliver pummels him. Mr. and Mrs. Sowerberry run in, overpower Oliver and lock him in a coffin. When they finally release him, Oliver manages to escape. In a town square he meets Jack Dawkins, nicknamed the Artful Dodger, a very dirty youngster who wears a small top hat and a voluminous overcoat. The Artful Dodger sings "Consider Yourself at Home" and leads Oliver to the Thieves' Kitchen, Fagin's lair. Here the old scoundrel Fagin teaches boys the art of thievery.

Fagin croons "Pick a Pocket or Two," during which he places a snuff-box in one pocket of his trousers, a wallet in the other, a watch in his waistcoat, and a diamond pin in his shirt—and the boys demonstrate how to carefully take possession of the items. Fagin, the despicable villain of the original novel, is a lovable rogue in this musical adaptation. He pats Oliver on the head and sends the boys to sleep on their mattresses.

The next day, Nancy and her little sister Bet arrive for a visit.[1] Nancy drinks half a bottle of gin in one gulp and sings "It's a Fine Life," expressing her contentment with the "small pleasures" one can find, even in an environment fraught with danger. Nancy and Oliver establish an immediate rapport. She is the live-in mistress of the goon Bill Sikes, and while very much in love with him, she is also terrified of his capacity for violence.

As soon as Nancy and Bet depart, Fagin teams Oliver with the Artful Dodger for his first pickpocketing assignment. On the street, the two boys attempt to rifle the pockets of a distinguished-looking gentleman, Mr. Brownlow, but are caught in the act. A chase ensues and Oliver is captured.

At the "Three Cripples," a low-class saloon, raffish customers are drinking and flirting. Nancy leads the crowd with "Oom-Pah-Pah," a naughty number about ladies of the night. She then joins Fagin and Bet at a small table set on a raised alcove. There is a sudden hush in the room when Bill Sikes strides in. Sikes is an intense, stoutly built chap of thirty-five, who sports a three-day stubble and two scowling eyes. Singing "My Name," he walks around the room menacingly, baring his fist. Everyone cowers.

The Artful Dodger enters breathlessly and in a panic reveals that "Oliver got nabbed on the job" and was taken away by the old man they tried to rob. He ran after the coach all the way to Bloomsbury 19 at Chepstowe Gardens. Fagin is concerned: Oliver may reveal the whereabouts of his Thieves' Kitchen. Sikes offers a plan: Nancy will keep an eye on Bloomsbury 19, and they'll nab the boy the moment he steps out of the house. Nancy objects but Sikes advances, hits her without compunction, and forces her into obedience. Fagin, Sikes, and the Dodger exit. Nancy sends

Bet home and sings "As Long As He Needs Me," accepting humiliation and pain, clinging to the man she loves.

Two weeks pass. Mr. Brownlow proves to be a kindly, rich gentleman and his housekeeper, Mrs. Bedwin, takes good care of Oliver. Dr. Grimwig, a friend of Brownlow, arrives to check the boy and is satisfied with his improvement. Brownlow tells Dr. Grimwig that he finds himself "strangely attached to the child." Grimwig is cynical; he has no doubt that Oliver, who rifled Brownlow's pocket handkerchief, will steal again. Brownlow sends Oliver to return overdue books to the local library and pay a five-pound fine. Grimwig says that he'll eat his hat if Oliver returns.

Outside the house, Nancy and Bet lie in waiting. When Oliver emerges, Nancy throws her arms around his neck and tells a gathering crowd that at last she has found her missing little brother. Sikes appears with his dog, grabs Oliver, and whisks him away.

Sikes and Nancy deliver Oliver to the Thieves' Kitchen. The Artful Dodger draws from Oliver's pockets the five-pound note. Both Sikes and Fagin claim ownership of the note, and Sikes wins by plucking it from Fagin. Oliver tries to escape but Fagin's young ruffians catch him. Sikes takes off his belt to beat Oliver but Nancy vehemently objects. Fagin agrees with Nancy that there's no need for violence. Sikes pushes Oliver out through the door and all follow. Left by himself, Fagin hurriedly collects his hoard but stops to ponder his future in the humorous song "Reviewing the Situation." He considers going straight, but remains skeptical about changing his stripes.

Back at the workhouse, Mr. Bumble and Widow Corney, now unhappily married, scrutinize a gold locket left by Oliver's mother when she died in childbirth. Bumble and Corney read in a newspaper advertisement that a Mr. Brownlow is searching for Oliver. Bumble goes to Brownlow's home, exhibits the locket, and asks for payment. Brownlow throws him out. In one of those happy coincidences that prevail in Dickens's works, Brownlow recognizes a picture of his daughter Agnes in the locket. Agnes had years earlier eloped from home with a lover who later jilted her. Brownlow now realizes that Oliver is actually his grandson.

Nancy, concerned about Oliver, knocks on the door and bursts in. She confesses to Brownlow that she was the girl who took young Oliver away, but even though she is jeopardizing her own life, she felt the need to notify Mr. Brownlow that Oliver is imprisoned at Fagin's place. Brownlow wants to summon the Bow Street Runners for immediate action, but Nancy explains that she has to protect her lover. She'll bring Oliver to the London Bridge tonight, between 11:00 p.m. and midnight.

It is 10:45 at night. A clock chimes the three-quarter hour as Nancy hurries to the bridge with Oliver while looking over her shoulder. She stops at a recessed embrasure. They are waiting, silhouetted against the night sky, when the shadow of a burly man falls across the scene. Bill Sikes suddenly appears behind Nancy. She attempts to explain that she never betrayed him, but Sikes brutally clubs her to death.[2] He then grabs Oliver and hastily leads him away. Brownlow enters in time to see Sikes disappearing and notices Nancy's sprawled body. He calls for help and a night watchman appears.

The pace of the proceedings accelerates. Sikes bangs on the Thieves' Kitchen door and he and Oliver disappear inside. A crowd gathers on the bridge around Brownlow. Bet enters and kneels, sobbing, by Nancy's corpse. A Bow Street Runner squeezes through the people. Brownlow says that as he crossed the bridge, he saw someone disappearing in the other direction, a broad-shouldered, heavily built man wearing a blue coat and a tall hat. A woman whispers, "Bill Sikes!" Another woman screams, "It's Nancy, he's murdered Nancy!" This causes a sensation in the crowd. They notice Sikes's dog and, yelling for blood, follow the dog until they reach the Thieves' Kitchen.

The crowd attacks the door with a battering ram. A wild shout suddenly goes up as they see Sikes tottering on the roof with a rope in his hand. Oliver is tied to the other end of the rope. The crowd surges forward. Sikes shouts, "Stand back, or I'll kill the boy!" A police officer aims a gun and fires. The crowd roars as Sikes falls.[3]

Several Bow Street Runners continue to ram the door and enter the house. They soon leave, disappointed that Fagin is not there. Someone suggests that Fagin may be at the Three Cripples Pub, and the crowd, roaring, disappears.

Oliver is brought to Mr. Brownlow. Mrs. Bedwin enters and embraces the boy. "Come, Oliver, we'll take you home now," says Brownlow, and the threesome saunter out happily. Fagin takes off the masquerading uniform of a Bow Street Runner, reprises "Reviewing the Situation," and dances his way into the dawn.[4]

* * *

Directed by Peter Coe, designed by Sean Kenny, and choreographed by Malcolm Clare, *Oliver!* opened at London's New Theatre on June 30, 1960, received sixteen or twenty-three curtain calls (sources vary), garnered rave reviews, and ran for 2,618 performances. The leading actors were Ron Moody (Fagin), Georgia Brown (Nancy), Danny Sewell (Sikes), and Keith Hamshere (Oliver). Clive Revill took over the role of Fagin and Bruce Prochnik played Oliver when the show was exported to San Francisco, Los Angeles, and finally to Broadway's Imperial Theatre, where it opened on January 6, 1963.

The New York reviewers offered pro and con assessments of the show. "Scrumptious," wrote John McClain. "It represents a breakthrough for the British in a field which has so long been dominated by Americans. . . . Never before have so many gifted urchins filled a stage to better effect."[5] Norman Nadel called *Oliver!* "a work of art" and lauded playwright-composer-lyricist Lionel Bart, who "has taken more liberties with Charles Dickens' *Oliver Twist* than a drunken earl with a tavern wench, but has kept a core of hard truth that gives backbone to the bold new musical at the Imperial Theatre."[6] Richard Watts Jr. admired "the frankness and expertness of its showmanship. Its beauty, melodiousness, humor and occasional pathos are shrewdly combined in a pattern that isn't ashamed to be good fun, and the versatility of Mr. Bart in writing the music, lyrics and libretto with so much skill demonstrates his importance in the popular musical theatre."[7] John Chapman declared, "It is one of the most impressive British products to be imported here since the first Rolls Royce."[8] John Coleman agreed: "Everything about *Oliver!* is top drawer. The book has dramatic impact, the lyrics are clever, and the score haunting. Sean Kenny has designed a semi-constructivist set that permits the action to flow like quicksilver, while director Peter Coe has assembled a perfect cast."[9]

Critics Howard Taubman and Walter Kerr were less impressed. Taubman appreciated songs that "are catching," staging that "pulls out all the stops," and sets "evoking the atmosphere of London," but felt that "too often" the production "settles for stridency, smoke, easy laughs and facile show-business razzmatazz."[10] Kerr concluded that "in general, *Oliver!* is like looking at a comic book condensation of a Dickens classic with the radio on. The colors are bright, the action is constant, but the pace falters for lack of any genuine emotional involvement."[11]

Oliver! received ten Tony Award nominations, including Best Musical, and ran for 774 performances. A return engagement of sixty-four performances came to Broadway's Martin Beck Theatre on August 2, 1965, featuring Robin Ramsey (Fagin), Maura K. Wedge (Nancy), Victor Stiles (Oliver), and bringing back Danny Sewell as Bill Sikes.[12]

British producer Cameron Mackintosh revived *Oliver!* in 1977 at London's Albery Theatre (now the Noel Coward Theatre), featuring Roy Hudd as Fagin, a production that ran for two years. Mackintosh returned with *Oliver!* in 1983 for a limited five-week Christmas production at West End's Aldwych Theatre, directed by Peter Coe, and bringing back Ron Moody in the role of Fagin. The original set designs by Sean Kenny were used. The following year, the show moved to Broadway's Mark Hellinger Theatre with one notable cast change: Patti LuPone took over the part of Nancy. It ran for only seventeen showings. In her *Patti LuPone: A Memoir*, the actress-singer relates, "We were given the blocking from the original production. There was no exploration, no discovery, no nothing."[13]

Ten years later, on December 8, 1994, Sam Mendes staged a lavish production of *Oliver!* at the London Palladium. Jonathan Pryce played Fagin. A four-year run culminated on February 21, 1998. Rupert Goold (director), Matthew Bourne (choreographer), and Anthony Ward (designer) teamed on an extravagant *Oliver!* that opened on January 14, 2009, and ran through January 8, 2011, at the Theatre Royal Drury Lane. Ben Brantley of the *New York Times* wrote, "For old-fashioned, picture-postcard prettiness, it's hard to top *Oliver!* . . . The comedian Rowan Atkinson miraculously stands out—and even hunched, stands tall—on a crowded stage with a vivid performance as an anxious, epicene Fagin."[14] In July 2009, Atkinson was replaced by stand-up comedian Omid Djalili, a British-born Iranian. The casting of "a man with parents from an Islamic republic, one whose current president makes his feelings about the state of Israel starkly clear, playing one of the best-known Jewish characters in literature" caused a furor.[15] The production garnered three 2010 Olivier Award nominations, including Best Revival of a Musical.

During the first decade of the twenty-first century, British touring companies of *Oliver!* tracked to Sydney, Singapore, and most major venues in the United States. Estonian productions were mounted in the early 1990s and in November 2003. A Hebrew translation of the musical was presented in Israel twice—by the Habimah National Theatre in 1966, starring Shraga Friedman and Rivka Raz, and at Beit Lessin in 2008, featuring Sasson Gabai and Anya Bukshtein. Critics in Israel were cool to *Oliver!*, although anti-Semitism was not an issue. The English-language *Jerusalem Post* said that Fagin was "a villain you could not hate even if you try." But the paper's reviewer opined that "the musical could not decide whether to take itself seriously or mock the Dickensian schmaltz."[16]

Directed by Carol Reed,[17] *Oliver!* was converted to the screen in 1968, starring Ron Moody (the original Fagin), Mark Lester (Oliver), Oliver Reed (Sikes), Shani Wallis (Nancy), Joseph Connor (Mr. Brownlow), and Harry Secombe (Mr. Bumble). Considered one of the rare films that is superior to the original show, *Oliver!* was nominated for eleven Academy Awards, winning for Best Picture, Best Director, Best Score, Best Art Direction, and Best Sound. Onna White won an Honorary Oscar for her choreography. *Oliver!* also garnered two Golden Globe awards: Best Film in the category of Musical/Comedy and Best Actor in the same category, Ron Moody.

* * *

Lionel Bart was born in 1930, the son of a Jewish tailor and the youngest of seven siblings. His birth name was Lionel Begleiter. The family lived in London's Stepney, a working-class district. When Bart was six years old, a teacher told his parents that he was a musical genius, but at the age of sixteen Bart obtained a scholarship to St. Martin's School of Art, aiming to become a painter.

Without ever learning to read or write musical notations, Bart eventually changed course and began writing songs for amateur theatre groups and the Sunday BBC radio programs. In the 1950s he contributed material for Unity Theatre, including a version of *Cinderella* and a version of *Volpone*, called *Wally Pone*. He began to gain recognition when composing pop and rock 'n' roll songs for Cliff Richard and Tommy Steele.

Bart's first West End musical was 1959's *Lock Up Your Daughters*, an adaptation by Bernard Miles of the eighteenth-century comedy *Rape upon Rape* by Henry Fielding. The lyrics were written by Bart, the music by Laurie Johnson. The farcical plot revolves around two cases of dubious rape tried by a corrupt justice in 1735 London. Directed by Peter Coe and designed by Sean Kenny, the show ran at the Mermaid Theatre for 328 performances. A 1962 revival at the same theatre ran for 664 showings. Staged by Alfred Drake, *Lock Up Your Daughters* was planned for Broadway, but closed on the road in 1960. A 1969 movie version was given an "X" rating by the UK censor.

Next, Bart wrote the music and lyrics of *Fings Ain't Wot They Used T' Be* for Joan Littlewood's Theatre Workshop. The Cockney comedy was populated with gamblers, petty thieves, prostitutes, and crooked cops. A success, the musical was moved to West End's Garrick Theatre in 1960, where it ran for nearly two years. Bart's follow-up musical was *Blitz!*, focusing on a Jewish woman and a Cockney man whose romance blossomed during the bombings of London during World War II. *Blitz!* opened at the Adelphi Theatre in 1962, while *Oliver!* was running successfully at the New Theatre. Its enormous set included an overhead bridge. It was at the time the most expensive West End musical ever produced. *Blitz!* ran for 568 performances. It never came to Broadway but was performed in Australia in 1985, directed by Bart, and revived at London's Playhouse Theatre in 1990.

Maggie May, for which Bart wrote music and lyrics, spotlights a Liverpool streetwalker, Margaret May Duffy, after her lover dies. The show opened in 1964 at London's Adelphi Theatre and ran for 501 performances. *Twang!*, the story of Robin Hood and his merry men, is famous for its backstage tensions (coproducer/director Joan Littlewood left the production a day before the opening), a booed opening night, and the universal scorn heaped by the critics. It ran in 1965 for forty-six showings at the Shaftsbury Theatre. Bart invested his personal fortune in *Twang!* (including his rights in *Oliver!*) and lost everything.

Bart's *La Strada* is based on the highly regarded 1954 Frederico Fellini movie of the same name. It is the bleak account of a young girl, Gelsomina, who is sold by her impoverished mother to a brutal circus strongman, Zampanô. She demonstrates her talent as a clown and soon becomes the star of the show. Gelsomina falls in love with Zampanô, but when she befriends Mario, a circus clown, Zampanô kills Mario in a fit of jealousy. Eventually, Zampanô moves on, leaving Gelsomina to die on the road. Directed by Alan Schneider and choreographed by Alvin Ailey, the musical tried out in Detroit, Michigan, opened at Broadway's Lunt-Fontanne Theatre on September 14, 1969, played for fourteen previews, and famously closed after just one performance, losing its $65,000 investment.

For the movies, Bart composed the energetic tunes of several Tommy Steele vehicles; the haunting theme of *From Russia with Love*, the 1963 James Bond movie; and the background music for 1964's *Man in the Middle*, a filmization of Howard Fast's novel *The Winston Affair*, about an American military officer charged with homicide. Bart's musical numbers were incorporated into many television shows on both shores of the Atlantic, including *The Ed Sullivan Show*, *The Red Skelton Hour*, *Sesame Street*, *The Julie Andrews Hour*, *The Brady Bunch*, and *Mystery Science Theatre 3000*.

By 1972, Bart was bankrupt and in debt. He turned to drink, damaged his health, had affairs with men, and, after a long struggle, died of cancer in 1999. His funeral took place at Golders Green Crematorium in Hoop Lane, London.

A three-part series, *A Handful of Songs: The Lionel Bart Story*, was aired on BBC's Radio 2 in August 2005. A musical based on Bart's life and using his songs, *It's a Fine Life*, was staged at the Queen's Theatre, Hornchurch, East London, in 2006. Written by Christopher Bond, it follows Bart's journey from East Side rags to West End's riches and back again.

Acting Edition: Tams-Witmark Music Library.

Awards and Honors: *Oliver!* was nominated for nine 1963 Tony Awards. Lionel Bart won as Best Composer/Lyricist; Sean Kenny won for Best Scenic Design; Donald Pippin won as Best Conductor/Musical Director. In 1960, Bart was given the Variety Club Silver Heart for Show Business Personality of the Year. Four years later, Bart's musical *Maggie May* won the Ivor Novello Award for outstanding score. In 1986, Bart received a special Ivor Novello Award for life achievement.[18]

NOTES

1. In the original novel, Bet is Nancy's best friend, not her sister.

2. In alternate stagings of *Oliver!*, Bill Sikes strangles Nancy, stabs her, or slits her throat. The musical's original libretto follows the Dickens novel in having Nancy beaten to death.

3. In the original novel, Sikes accidently hangs himself while fleeing across a rooftop from the angry mob.

4. In *Oliver Twist*, Fagin is arrested and condemned to the gallows.

5. *New York Journal-American*, January 8, 1963.

6. *New York World-Telegram*, January 8, 1963.

7. *New York Post*, January 8, 1963.

8. *Daily News*, January 8, 1963.

9. *The Mirror*, January 8, 1963.

10. *New York Times*, January 8, 1963.

11. CBS TV, January 7, 1963.

12. Danny Sewell's main competition at audition for the role of Bill Sikes was Michael Caine, who later revealed that he "cried for a week" after failing to secure the part.

13. Patti LuPone, *A Memoir* (New York: Crown Archtype, 2010), 155.

14. *New York Times*, July 8, 2009.

15. *New York Times*, July 18, 2009.

16. Quoted in the *New York Times*, February 5, 1966.

17. English film director Carol Reed (1906–1976) began his professional career when staging several Edgar Wallace thrillers on the London stage, including *The Squeaker* (1928), *Persons Unknown* (1929), and *Smoky Cell* (1930). For the next four decades, Reed directed thirty-three motion pictures, many with suspense elements: *Laburnum Grove* (1935), a whodunit based on a play by J. B. Priestley; *Night Train to Munich* (1940), in which a British intelligence agent rescues a Czech scientist from the Nazis; *Odd Man Out* (1947), a masterful account of an Irish rebel leader hunted by the police after a bungled robbery; *The Fallen Idol* (1948), from a story by Graham Greene, about a household butler who is suspected of murdering his wife (New York Critics Circle Award for Best Director); *The Third Man* (1949), the classic film noir about the search by a pulp-writer for the mysterious Harry Lime in post–World War II Vienna (Grand Prize of the Cannes Film Festival); *The Man Between* (1953), depicting black-marketing in post–World War II Berlin; and *Our Man in Havana* (1959), a satirical spy yarn, adapted by Graham Greene from his novel about a vacuum cleaner salesman who becomes a British agent.

18. Ivor Novello was a Welsh composer, singer, and actor who became one of the most popular British entertainers of the early twentieth century. The Ivor Novello Awards are prizes for songwriting and composing. They are presented annually by the British Academy of Songwriters, Composers, and Authors (BASCA).

Settled out of Court (1960)

William Saroyan (United States, 1908–1981) and Henry Cecil (England, 1902–1976)

It may seem truly surprising that William Saroyan, the Pulitzer Prize–winning dramatist whose writings epitomize American life in his native Fresno, California, appears within the covers of a book dedicated to plays of crime, mystery, and detection. Even more surprising, he cowrote a thriller that is singularly English in environment, plot, and characters.

But there is no mistake. Saroyan joined Henry Cecil, a British county court judge and prolific detective-story writer, in dramatizing Cecil's 1959 novel, *Settled out of Court*, a credit missing from most, if not all, bibliographical listings of Saroyan's works.

The three acts of *Settled out of Court* unfold in the study of Sir George Halliday, a High Court judge. The room is described as "impressive in its mixture of spaciousness and solidity." There are double doors leading to the hall and staircase. A window overlooks the grounds. The walls are lined with bookcases full of law books. In an alcove are a china cabinet and a grandfather clock.

When the curtain rises, Sir Halliday, a distinguished old man, is posing in wig and gown for his portrait. Charles Brandy, more or less the same age as Sir George, is painting at an easel, working slowly and thoughtfully. Soon Sir George gets up, stretches, and crosses to his desk for a cigarette. Brandy puts down his palette and brushes. As they relax smoking, Brandy asks Sir George what he thinks about when he sits on the bench, dressed in his robes, and if he ever sympathizes with "the poor chap in the dock."

Sir George states that if the man is innocent, he'll get off, 999 times out of a thousand—though, admits the judge, "laws made by man must be fallible; mistakes must occasionally occur."

The doorbell rings, and the housekeeper, Mrs. Parsons, ushers in a man wearing a policeman's uniform. "Judge Halliday, I presume," he says, and introduces himself as "Officer Banks." The play now casts off its cozy beginning when suddenly Officer Banks draws a revolver, orders the judge to sit on the settee, and blows a whistle.

A tall man enters from the hall. He tells the judge that his name is Mr. I—for the ninth letter in the alphabet, he explains, as this is his ninth "production" as an international crook. Mr. I declares, "Your house has been seized and occupied"; other members of the gang enter and search the rooms. Mrs. Parsons is ordered to stay in the kitchen. Judge Halliday is astonished to learn that Charles Brandy, the artist who has painted his portrait, is Mr. I's henchman.

Enter Angela Walsh, the attractive daughter of Lonsdale Walsh, a man sent to prison for murder by Judge Halliday. Walsh had been found guilty of causing the death of his business associate, Thomas Barnwell, by running him down with a car. Angela tells the judge that the witnesses at her father's trial have been coaxed to come to the judge's home. She intends to conduct a "retrial" and prove that they were lying and that her father is innocent.

The assembled witnesses prove to be a motley group. Josephine Barnwell, the widow of the victim, "a handsome woman with a great deal of physical appeal," complains that she was lured to an ambulance by the false message that her young brother had been taken to the hospital and was dangerously ill. Harold Allwinter, a young, soft-spoken artist, was conned with an offer to paint Sir George Halliday's portrait. He is curious about the judge's chauffeur—how did he get that terrible scar from the top of his forehead to the bottom of his neck? Miles Hampton, a bit-part film actor, believes that he was cast in a movie. Mrs. Meadows, "a very large lady," was told that she won a hefty sum in a football pool. Herbert Adams, "a little fellow of the streets," thought that the two coppers who accosted him in Hyde Park were taking him to a police station. He demands to know, "What's the charge?"

Lonsdale Walsh enters, dressed in a torn prison uniform. He tells his daughter that "apart from a little difficulty in getting over the wall, everything was perfect."

SIR GEORGE: The police will be searching for you in every corner of the country.
WALSH: I'm sure they will—except here. Your house is the safest place for me, don't you think?

Walsh tells the judge that he was convicted on perjured evidence. He would like to reexamine the case and prove that there was a miscarriage of justice at his trial. The judge vehemently objects, but changes his mind when Walsh promises to give himself up whatever the verdict.

Lonsdale Walsh acts as his own attorney and cross-examines the witnesses. Harold Allwinter testifies that he saw Barnwell come out of a house and start to cross the road. Suddenly, a very fast car seemed to come from nowhere and struck him flat. He saw the car drive off but didn't see the face of the driver, didn't think of getting the car's license tag number—but he is certain that it was a premeditated murder.

"Has it occurred to you that the driver of the car might not have seen him?" asks Walsh. He instructs Angela to take a small container of black pepper from her briefcase and have Allwinter sniff it. Allwinter is overcome and sneezes. During the sneeze, Walsh crosses away, making a point of the fact that the artist did not see him move.

The widow, Josephine Barnwell, testifies that her late husband and Thomas Walsh were not on speaking terms before he was killed; they were fighting for control of one of the biggest companies in the country, Midland Consolidated. Her husband had filed a motion to remove Walsh from the company's board.

Miles Hampton and Herbert Adams relate that prior to the death of Thomas Barnwell, they were sitting on a bench in Hyde Park. A man came along wearing a bowler hat, a black jacket, and striped trousers. He walked down the path, says Hampton, and threw a newspaper into the litter basket. Adams got up, retrieved the newspaper and started to read. Both Hampton and Adams noticed that the newspaper was curiously mutilated. Parts of it had been torn out. The man also dropped a pigskin glove by the litter basket. After reading of the car homicide, an account that included an item about a missing glove, they went to the police.

The last witness, Mrs. Meadows, admits that her late husband, Kenneth Meadows, was a hardened criminal with many previous convictions and jail time. Knowing that he had a short time to live, Meadows went to the police and later testified at the trial, that three days before Barnwell was killed, Walsh approached him with an offer of a hundred pounds to drive his car over a man. Meadows refused. He died a few days after the trial ended. Walsh categorically denies that he was the one who spoke with Meadows.

Judge Halliday tells Walsh that so far he hasn't produced "one little, iota, scintilla of additional evidence. All you say is that you were framed. Anyone can say that."

However, when Walsh interrogates Miles Hampton again, with machine-gun pace, the actor breaks under the rapid grilling, and admits to being paid for his testimony. One by one, the witnesses admit that they had succumbed to bribes by Josephine Barnwell and had provided false testimonies at trial.

Sir George is now persuaded that a grave miscarriage of justice has taken place and that Lonsdale Walsh is innocent of the crime. Thomas Barnwell was probably killed accidently, and it was made to look to be murder afterward.

Mr. I and his band depart. Walsh corners Josephine Barnwell and assures her that there is no evidence that she is the one who framed him. Messrs. Hampton, Adams, and company wouldn't dare speak out, for they're involved themselves. "You'd have been amused if you could have seen me collecting the little fellows and rehearsing them in their parts," chuckles Josephine.

In a surprising twist, Walsh admits to Josephine that he actually drove the homicidal car himself. There is nothing she can do about it, for no one will believe her. He tells her that he now intends to take a trip around the world.[1]

Walsh cheerfully says "good-bye" and moves toward the double doors. "No, Lonsdale, not quite good-bye," intones Josephine. He may not see her again, but she shall certainly see him. Wherever he goes, somewhere, sometime, he'll have to cross a road.

* * *

Settled out of Court opened at London's Strand Theatre on October 19, 1960. Nigel Patrick directed and played Lonsdale Walsh. The *New York Times* reported that "the newspaper critics differed only in the intensity with which they disliked it."[2] The *Times* of London said, "Mr. William Saroyan is named in the program as Mr. Cecil's co-adapter, but of the American's easily identifiable thumb-mark there is not a trace."[3] Critic Robert Muller of the *Daily Mail* concurred: "What but dire and undeserved poverty could have persuaded Saroyan to lend his gifts, not alone his name, to the concoction of this dusty clutter of a play which calls itself a 'comedy thriller'?"[4] Bernard Levin of the *Daily Express* called *Settled out of Court* "a surprisingly preposterous play . . . ludicrous even within its own terms of reference."[5]

However, disagreeing with the London critics, the public clamored to see *Settled out of Court,* and the play ran for the best part of a year.

* * *

Born in London in 1902, Henry Cecil Leon was educated at St. Paul's School, London; King's College, Cambridge; and Gray's Inn, London. He was called to the bar in 1923. During World War II he served in the Middle East. In 1949 he was appointed a county court judge, a position he held until 1967. He was chairman of the British Copyright Council from 1973 to 1976, the year he died.

Cecil used his legal expertise as inspiration for his twenty-five novels, three volumes of short stories, eight plays, half-a-dozen radio dramas, and several television episodes. In his writings, he often attempted to prove that the law is an ass, poking fun at the British legal system.

For the stage, he coadapted, with Ted Willis, one of his most celebrated novels, 1955's *Brothers in Law,* for an opening at the New Theatre, Brom-

ley, in February 1957. *Brothers in Law* relates the experiences of a young
barrister, Roger Thursby, during his first year in chambers. Also in 1957,
the book was made into a film by the Boulting brothers, Roy and John,
starring Ian Carmichael as Roger. Five years later, *Brothers in Law* was
converted into a television series, featuring Richard Briers. In 1970, Briers
reprised the role in a long-running radio program.

Cecil teamed with Felicity Douglas and Basil Dawson to dramatize his
1960 novel, *Alibi for a Judge*, in which Mr. Justice Gerald Carstairs cannot
make up his mind whether Lesley Burford is lying in an attempt to save
her husband from a ten-year prison sentence, or whether she is telling the
truth by supplying him with an alibi. *Alibi for a Judge* premiered at the
Savoy Theatre, London, on August 5, 1965, with Andrew Cruickshank as
the judge and Amanda Grinling as Lesley. Reviewer John Russell Taylor
of *Plays and Players* sniffed: "Why this mish-mash took three writers to
compile from one book I cannot imagine; maybe it is just a classic demonstration of too many cooks spoiling the broth."[6] However, the play was
chosen by J. C. Trewin to be included in his *Plays of the Year* and ran for
more than three hundred performances. Two years later, Cecil, Douglas,
and Dawson collaborated on another dramatization of a Cecil novel,
1954's *According to the Evidence*, scoring a 260-performance run. The play
featured Ambrose Low, a former criminal, and Colonel Brain, an ex-army
officer, recurring Cecil characters, combining forces to get the murderer
of a murderer acquitted.

In 1970, Cecil's dramatization of his 1967 novel *A Woman Named Anne*
played at West End's Duke of York's Theatre. This "courtroom comedy"
is about a trio of foxy lawyers who grill the title character in a divorce
case with a string of questions about her secret love life. Reviewer Peter
Ansorge of *Plays and Players* reported that he left the theatre "feeling that
everyone involved would have had a much better time on a big dipper
or inside a little cinema, or even in the dock of a real-life divorce court."[7]

Cecil was also the author of the nonfiction guides for the layman, *Brief
to Counsel* (1958, revised 1972), *Know about English Law* (1965, revised
1974), and *The English Judge* (1970, revised 1972). His autobiography, *Just
within the Law*, was published in 1975. His manuscripts are housed at Mc-
Master University, Hamilton, Ontario, Canada.

"Mystery literature abounds with excellent writers who, because they
are stereotyped as 'mystery writers,' fail to acquire the larger audience
they deserve," writes Donald J. Pattow in the *St. James Guide to Crime and
Mystery Writers*. "Henry Cecil is one of these writers. Cecil wrote a number of works, of which almost all manage to keep a fine balance; while
they are thoughtful and thought-provoking, they maintain a healthy view
of society's more curious foibles. Though one might not always agree
with Cecil's views, he is always provocative and entertaining. . . . Though

he is obviously very knowledgeable about law and the legal system, he is never (well, almost never) pedantic. Though he has strong feelings, they are tempered with a humaneness and humor that are rare today."[8]

* * *

William Saroyan was born in Fresno, California, to Armenian immigrants. His father died when he was three, and Saroyan was placed in an orphanage in Oakland, California. He grew up supporting himself with odd jobs and was self-educated. He began his writing career with articles published in *Overland Monthly* and short stories that appeared in the Armenian journal *Hairenik*. Many of his stories were based on his childhood experiences among the Armenian-American fruit growers of the San Joaquin Valley. The short story collection *My Name Is Aram* (1940), about a young boy and his immigrant family, became an international bestseller.

Saroyan made his breakthrough with *The Daring Young Man on the Flying Trapeze*, published in *Story* magazine in 1934, the tale of a young writer trying to survive during the Depression. He continued to write rapidly and intensely, drinking and gambling away much of his earnings. Some of his essays depicted the people he had met on travels in Europe, such as Finnish composer Jean Sibelius, playwright George Bernard Shaw, and actor-director Charlie Chaplin.

In 1939, Saroyan had his first plays produced on Broadway: *My Heart's in the Highlands*, a comedy about a young boy and his Armenian family, set in Fresno, California (Guild Theatre, April 13, 1939—forty-four performances), and *The Time of Your Life*, a character study set in a San Francisco waterfront saloon (Booth Theatre, October 25, 1939—185 performances), which won both the Pulitzer Prize for Drama and the New York Drama Critics Circle Award. Staged by Eddie Dowling, the cast included several actors who would migrate to Hollywood: William Bendix, Celeste Holm, Gene Kelly, Curt Conway, Edward Andrews, and Tom Tully. The play was revived in New York in 1955, featuring Franchot Tone, Biff McGuire, John Carradine, Myron McCormick, John Randolph, and Clifton James; in 1969, with McGuire, James Broderick, and Philip Bosco; and in 1975, with Nicolas Surovy, Kevin Kline, Patti LuPone, and David Schramm. It was adapted to the screen in 1948, starring James Cagney, supported by William Bendix, Wayne Morris, Jeanne Cagney, Broderick Crawford, and Ward Bond.

Other Broadway productions by Saroyan include *Love's Old Sweet Song*, a screwball comedy of mistaken identities taking place in 1939 Bakersfield, California, at the start of World War II (Plymouth Theatre, May 2, 1940—forty-four performances); *The Beautiful People*, written, produced, and directed by Saroyan, about an alcoholic father living with his adolescent son and daughter in a decaying mansion on San Francisco's Red

Rock Hill (Lyceum Theatre, April 21, 1941—120 performances); and *Get Away Old Man*, a satire about Hollywood (Cort Theatre, November 24, 1943—thirteen performances).

Saroyan's poignant one-act play *Hello Out There* was accompanied by G. K. Chesterton's *Magic* as a double bill presented at the Belasco Theatre on September 29, 1942, for forty-seven showings. The protagonist of *Hello Out There* is a young man who is held in the jail of a small Southern town for an alleged rape. He enlists a local maid, who is sympathetic to his plight, to help him escape, so that they can run away to San Francisco together. However, his victim, her husband, and their friends arrive at the jail to lynch him. Famed director James (*Frankenstein*) Whale directed a forty-one-minute film version of *Hello Out There* in 1949. The film was never released because its producer, Huntington Hartford, was dissatisfied with it. *Hello Out There* was televised by BBC-TV on March 17, 1950.

In the early 1940s, Saroyan worked in Hollywood on the screenplay of *The Human Comedy*, a slice-of-life drama taking place in a small California town during World War II. The focus is on young Homer Macauley, a telegraph messenger, who witnesses the joys and sorrows of his neighbors. Homer was played by Mickey Rooney, and the typical Macauley family was enacted by Jackie "Butch" Jenkins, Fay Bainter, Ray Collins, Van Johnson, and Donna Reed. It is reported that Louis B. Mayer, head of MGM, balked at the film's length and removed Saroyan from the project. Saroyan then turned the script of *The Human Comedy* into a novel. The novel served as a basis for a Broadway musical (Royale Theatre, April 5, 1984—twenty previews and thirteen performances).

Saroyan's last play of note was *The Cave Dwellers*, set in an abandoned theatre on the Lower East Side of New York, populated by homeless, down-on-their-luck men and women (Bijou Theatre, October 19, 1957—ninety-seven performances). The manuscripts of Saroyan's plays are housed at Stanford University.

Saroyan died in Fresno in 1981 at the age of seventy-two. The cause was prostate cancer. Half of his ashes were buried in California, and the remainder in Armenia at the Pantheon.

Acting Edition: Samuel French, Inc. (in manuscript form).

Awards and Honors: William Saroyan's *The Time of Your Life* was a top-ten selection in *The Best Plays of 1939–1940*. It also won the 1940 Pulitzer Prize for Drama and the New York Drama Critics Circle Award.

NOTES

1. The unexpected turnaround ending is reminiscent of George Pleydell's classic *The Ware Case* (novel, 1913; play, 1915), wherein the protagonist, Sir Hubert

Ware, accused of the murder of his wife's brother, gains the sympathy of the jury (and the audience) as a victim of circumstances and is found not guilty. Prior to the final curtain he confesses to the deed. (*The Ware Case* is detailed in Amnon Kabatchnik, *Blood on the Stage, 1900-1925* (Lanham, MD: Scarecrow Press, 2008), 233–237.

2. *New York Times*, October 20, 1960.

3. *Times* of London, October 19, 1960.

4. *Daily Mail*, October 19, 1960.

5. *Daily Express*, October 19, 1960.

6. *Plays and Players*, October 1965.

7. *Plays and Players*, April 1970.

8. Jay P. Pederson, ed., *St. James Guide to Crime and Mystery Writers*, 4th ed. (Detroit, MI: St. James Press, 1996), 164.

Advise and Consent (1960)

Loring Mandel (United States, 1928–)

President Nixon's Watergate woes and President Clinton's Monica Lewinsky scandal seem negligible indeed when compared to the Washington intrigues festering in *Advise and Consent*, a political melodrama set "sometime in the future."

Adapted from Allen Drury's Pulitzer Prize–winning novel (1959), Loring Mandel's play depicts venomous backstabbing, dirt digging, and character assassination in the U.S. Senate and the Oval Office, triggered by the president's nomination of William A. Huntington, director of the Office of Defense Mobilization, to the position of secretary of state. A subcommittee of the Senate Foreign Relations Committee, chaired by Senator Brigham Anderson of Utah, is to conduct hearings and vote on the nomination. Some senators are dubious about the president's choice in view of Huntington's philosophy of "creative negotiations with the communists."

"Before the hearings are over," wrote Walter Kerr in the *Herald Tribune*, "blackmail will be as common as starlings in the capital, reputations will be disemboweled and some blood will be shed."[1]

During the subcommittee's sessions, Senator Seab Cooley of South Carolina produces a witness, Herbert Gelman, who testifies that he studied with Huntington at the University of Chicago and that the professor invited him to his roominghouse on several occasions and suggested that he join the Communist Party.

Upon cross-examination, Gelman falters. He reluctantly admits that he was not actually a registered student in Huntington's course and that in his senior year he suffered a nervous breakdown.

The young, ambitious senator from Wyoming, Fred Van Ackerman, who advocates "crawling to Moscow on our knees rather than perish under an atomic bomb," is a supporter of Huntington. Upon a visit to Brig Anderson's office, while searching for matches, he finds in a desk drawer a photograph with a letter clipped to it. He stuffs the materials in his pocket.

When Anderson intends to ask the president to withdraw Huntington's nomination, Van Ackerman informs the White House of his findings. The president gives him the green light to strong-arm Anderson into approving his designee.

Anderson searches for his letter and photograph in his desk drawer and realizes that they are gone. Anonymous phone calls, an unsigned letter, and a telegram signed "Old Friend" arrive at his home—all threatening to expose his liaison with a man. Anderson relates to his wife Mabel that it was just a passing fling while he was stationed at a Navy communication detachment in Honolulu. In spite of Mabel's assurance of her love and support, Anderson goes to his office, scribbles a note, takes a revolver from his pocket, and presses the barrel to his forehead.

The suicide of Brig Anderson yields "ethical cleansing" in the Senate. During the subcommittee's final meeting, Senator Van Ackerman is put in his place by more seasoned members. Anderson's friend, Senator Orrin Knox, resisting pressure from the White House, eloquently addresses his colleagues, pointing out that when the senator from Utah, who objected to the president's nominee, was threatened with "a very old and very tired sin," he chose not to bend and be silent but did what he thought was necessary, right and honorable.

The nomination of Huntington is rejected.

* * *

Opening on November 17, 1960, at New York's Cort Theatre, *Advise and Consent* was trumpeted by most of the critics. "I found it absorbing, exciting and disturbing—and a remarkable piece of stage craftsmanship," declared John Chapman.[2] Frank Aston advised his readers to "check political prejudice at the door of the Cort and you will be stampeded by Loring Mandel's *Advise and Consent* which opened last evening. . . . Mr. Mandel's drama is full of fury and fevers, so much so that I almost jumped out in the aisle to start a demonstration."[3] Robert Coleman called the play "a rip-roaring melodrama about politics. There's a lot in it that's hard to swallow, yet taken on its own terms it spells exciting theatre."[4]

Howard Taubman cast a negative vote: "No one can question the high principle enunciated by *Advise and Consent* that integrity rather than expediency should inform the decisions of the President and the Senate. One doubts, however, that the play proves this point as convincingly as its authors seem to believe."[5] Richard Watts Jr. said: "Whatever Allen Drury's successful *Advise and Consent* may be as a novel of Washington's politics, it comes over on the stage as a curiously hollow melodrama. The dramatization by Loring Mandel is unquestionably vigorous and well acted, and it whips up quite a bit of excitement from time to time, but its characters are so vague and its viewpoint so shadowy that what it has to tell about the skullduggery behind the President's attempt to appoint a new Secretary of State struck me as virtually meaningless."[6]

All the reviewers heaped praise on veteran thespians Ed Begley, Richard Kiley, Henry Jones, Chester Morris, Staats Cotsworth, and Kevin McCarthy for their interpretation of various VIPs. (None of them, though, were recruited for the 1962 motion picture version, directed by Otto Preminger. Instead, the stellar movie cast included Henry Fonda, Charles Laughton, Walter Pidgeon, Franchot Tone, Lew Ayres, Burgess Meredith, Don Murray, and George Grizzard.)

Louis Kronenberger, in *The Best Plays of 1960–1961*, summed up the strengths and weaknesses of *Advise and Consent*: "In terms of substance, the play was vague when not downright vaporous; but in terms of that feedbox of theatre, political maneuverings, it could be brisk and at moments tense. Equipped with an all but complete set of political chessmen, the play pushed rooks and pawns about with gusto, kept crying Check! with relish, and in the course of the evening made almost every known move on the board. . . . Not only were the play's few personal scenes weak, but it far oftener invoked the laws of melodrama than it shed light on political depths—so much so that *Advise and Consent* not only lacked thematic point, but had a rather bewildering plot. . . . Though the play wholly lacked political meaning, of political methods it had something to show."

Advise and Consent ran for 212 performances.

* * *

Allen Drury was born in Houston, Texas, on September 2, 1918. He conveyed firsthand knowledge when painting the political milieu of *Advise and Consent*, his first novel. For twenty years, Drury served as a Washington correspondent for United Press International, the *Washington Evening Star*, and the *New York Times*, covering Congress, the Supreme Court, and a dozen presidential campaigns. During a span of close to forty years, Drury penned numerous best sellers, several of which have continued to dwell on the *Advise and Consent* theme, notably the sequels *A Shade of Difference*, *Capable of Honor*, and *Preserve and Protect*. Additional political novels by Drury, all set against the Cold War, include *Come Nineveh, Come Tyre*, *The Promise of Joy*, *Mark Coffin U.S.S.*, *The Hill of Summer*, and *The Roads of Earth*.

Drury died in San Francisco, California, on September 2, 1998, his eightieth birthday.

Born in Chicago, Illinois, on May 5, 1928, Loring Mandel graduated from the University of Wisconsin, Madison, in 1949. During a span of more than fifty years, he has written for radio, television, film, and the stage. He contributed episodes for *Lux Video Theatre*, *Studio One*, *The Raider*, *Ambassador at Large*, *Benjamin Franklin*, and *The DuPont Show of the Week*.

Several full-length dramas that Mandel penned for television contain suspense ingredients: *Particular Men* (WNET, New York, 1972) is the tale of a physicist whose opposition to nuclear research for the military prompts a security hearing; *The Trial of Chaplain Jensen* (Twentieth Century–Fox Television, 1975) tells the true story of Chaplain Andrew Jensen, the only U.S. Navy chaplain ever court-martialed on charges of adultery; the title character of *The Lost Honor of Kathryn Beck* (CBS TV, 1984) is a businesswoman who meets a runaway thief at a party, invites him to her apartment, and is shocked (or is she?) when the police come knocking on the door in the morning. *The Little Drummer Girl* (Pan Arts, Warner Brothers, 1984), based on the novel by John Le Carré, is an American actress who is recruited by Mosad, the Israeli intelligence agency, to trap a Palestinian bomber; *Conspiracy* (BBC, 2001) is a dramatic re-creation of the Wannsee Conference where the Nazi Final Solution phase of the Holocaust was devised.

Acting Edition: Samuel French, Inc.

Awards and Honors: Allen Drury's 1959 novel, *Advise and Consent*, won the Pulitzer Prize for Fiction. Loring Mandel has received five Emmy nominations and was twice awarded that prize for his original dramas. He has also won the Sylvania Award and two Peabody Awards. Mandel's TV film *Conspiracy* (2001) won the BAFTA.

NOTES

1. *New York Herald Tribune*, November 18, 1960.
2. *Daily News*, November 18, 1960.
3. *New York World-Telegram*, November 18, 1960.
4. *New York Mirror*, November 18, 1960.
5. *New York Times*, November 18, 1960.
6. *New York Post*, November 18, 1960.

The Devil's Advocate (1961)

Dore Schary (United States, 1905–1980)

A theological detective story, *The Devil's Advocate* unfolds in an Italian village, at the foot of the age-old Calabrian mountains. Englishman Blaise Meredith, a monsignor dying of cancer, arrives on the scene to investigate whether or not sainthood should be conferred upon a mysterious Britisher who called himself Giacomo Nerone and who was executed by the Nazis during World War II. It is said that Nerone was a deserter from the British army during the war and lived in sin with a woman. But it is also reported that Nerone performed miracles in this remote area. Was he a holy man or a sinner?

Meredith attempts to put the pieces together by interviewing various villagers who knew Nerone—his passionate lover, Nina Sanduzzi, who bore him a child; the local Jewish doctor, Aldo Meyer; the neurotic Contessa, Anne Louise De Sanctis; the homosexual painter, Nicholas Black; and the liberal-minded Bishop Aurelio.

As he weighs the worth of another man's life, Meredith gropes for the meaning of his own.

* * *

Dore Schary dramatized *The Devil's Advocate* from a 1959 novel by Morris L. West (1916–1999). Schary produced and directed his adaptation at New York's Billy Rose Theatre on March 9, 1961. With Leo Genn as Monsignor Meredith, Edward Mulhare as Giacomo Nerone, Sam Levene as Dr. Meyer, Olive Deering as the Contessa, and Eduardo Ciannelli as Bishop Aurelio, the ecclesiastic drama won the hearts of most reviewers— "superlative," Frank Aston;[1] "powerful," Howard Taubman;[2] "effective," Richard Watts Jr.;[3] "inspiring," John Chapman.[4]

Dissenting voices came from John McClain—"The narrative is such that it defies graceful telling on stage";[5] Walter Kerr—"*The Devil's Advocate* is nearly always intriguing as a dossier; what it cannot do is make a firm, tight fist";[6] and Justin Gilbert—"The play lacks strength and significance."[7]

372

The Devil's Advocate ran for 116 performances. In 1977, it was adapted to the screen as a German-British coproduction, starring John Mills.

* * *

Born in Newark, New Jersey, to Russian Jewish parents, Dore Schary worked at his family's kosher catering business and as a stockbroker before he turned his attention to the theatre, writing plays for a local company. In 1928 he joined a traveling troupe, playing supporting roles in a variety of productions, and began penning screenplays. Columbia Pictures became interested in his work, and in 1932 Schary relocated to the West Coast.

Schary's long career in Hollywood encompassed some thirty-five screenplays for Paramount, Warner Brothers, and Columbia during 1933–1937 before joining Metro-Goldwyn-Mayer, where he won the Academy Award in 1938 for *Boys Town*.[8] In 1942, Schary was placed in charge of MGM's B-picture unit, and that year he produced such excellent suspense films as *Grand Central Murder*, *Kid Glove Killer*, and *Eyes in the Night*. When in 1951 Louis B. Mayer was ousted from MGM after a power struggle, Schary became the studio's head of production, a position he held for five years until another power struggle forced him out.

Schary returned to New York and became active on Broadway as a writer, director, and producer. His plays include *Sunrise at Campobello* (1958), a portrait of Franklin Delano Roosevelt that earned five Tony Awards; *The Highest Tree* (1959), an anti-bomb drama; *One by One* (1964), a love story between two paraplegics; and *Brighttown* (1970), the examination of a famous author who suffers a mental breakdown and commits suicide.

Schary produced and staged the works of other playwrights: *A Majority of One* (1959), *Portrait of a Madonna* (1959), *Pound on Demand* (1959), *On the Harmful Effects of Tobacco* (1959), *Bedtime Story* (1959), *The Unsinkable Molly Brown* (1960), *Something About a Soldier* (1962), *Love and Kisses* (1963), *The Zulu and the Zayda* (1965).

Acting Edition: Samuel French, Inc.

Awards and Honors: Dore Schary served as National Chairman of the B'nai B'rith's Anti-Defamation League. In 1982, to honor his memory, the League established the Dore Schary Awards, given to young filmmakers promoting human rights or combating bigotry and prejudice.

NOTES

1. *New York World-Telegram*, March 10, 1961.
2. *New York Times*, March 10, 1961.
3. *New York Post*, March 10, 1961.

4. *Daily News*, March 10, 1961.

5. *New York Journal-American*, March 10, 1961.

6. *New York Herald Tribune*, March 10, 1961.

7. *Daily Mirror*, March 10, 1961.

8. During the early phase of Dore Schary's busy career in Hollywood, he managed to pen one play for Broadway: *Too Many Heroes* (1937), the story of a lynching in a small American town, provoked by the savage kidnapping and murder of a young girl by two drunken mill hands. The grim drama ran for sixteen performances.

A Shot in the Dark (1961)

Marcel Achard (France, 1899–1974)

Paul Sevigne, a young, idealistic examining magistrate who has just been promoted to a post in Paris, is assigned his first case—seemingly a cut-and-dried murder. The prime suspect, Josefa Lantenay, is a sexy parlor maid who was found unconscious, nude, and clutching a gun alongside her dead lover, the chauffeur. Since their employer, Benjamin Beaurevers, is a powerful banker, Sevigne is pressed by his superiors to "get a confession from the girl—a short one, if possible, and you'll be home in time for an early dinner."

But as the investigation of *A Shot in the Dark* progresses, Sevigne concludes that the earthy, guileless, babbling Josefa could not have committed the crime. There is a curious naiveté about the girl who readily admits to a summer affair with the Spanish chauffeur, Miguel Ostos ("The heat, you know, and to tell you the truth, I wasn't wearing very much. I mean, underneath"), to discarding Miguel for another man, and to devoutly protecting her latest lover, who is Monsieur Beaurevers, no less.

"If she talks long enough—the idiot!—" says Sevigne, "she'll chatter herself right up the steps to the guillotine."

Against all odds and despite objections from despotic chief prosecutor Lablache, jaded court clerk Morestan, and his petulant bride, Antoinette, Sevigne persists in unraveling the naughtiness of an aristocratic Parisian household. He interrogates the pompous Beaurevers, who took an instant dislike to the victim for being taller than himself, then swings the pendulum of suspicion toward the banker's arrogant wife, Dominique, "who descended in direct line from Attila the Hun," and who, it turns out, shot Miguel in the dark believing it was her husband carousing with the maid. If it weren't for that mistake, "my wife would now be a rich, beautiful, young widow, free to marry her lover, Monsieur de Bennoit," muses Beaurevers. "He and my wife were inseparable due to their mutual passion for horses—or so I thought. Now I remember how many times, when they came back from the trails, they were exhausted, and the horses were fresh."

Josefa offers to pay Sevigne for having rescued her in the only way she knows how, but he shyly declines. In parting, she promises to mend her ways—get "a good job" and make "a nice fellow happy."

* * *

Marcel Achard's *L'Idiote* premiered in September 1960 at the Theatre Antoine, Paris, achieving acclaim with Annie Girardot as Josefa and Jean-Pierre Cassel as Sevigne. "M. Achard's method is light and ironic. His piece is meant for laughs, and it gets them," dispatched the *New York Times* correspondent.[1] Following a U.S. tryout (during which Joel Thomas took over the role of Benjamin Beaurevers for the late Donald Cook, only to be replaced by Walter Matthau), an adaptation by Harry Kurnitz, called *A Shot in the Dark*, directed by Harold Clurman, opened on October 18, 1961, and ran for 389 performances at the Booth Theatre.

The reviewers adored Julie Harris's "flamboyant" impersonation of Josefa, admired Walter Matthau's "disdainful banker," praised William Shatner's "vulnerable judge," and complimented Diana van der Vlis's "wholesome" young wife, Gene Saks's "deadpan" court clerk, and Louise Troy's "haughty" Dominique.

But the critics were split regarding the brew of infidelities and crimes. "A saucy and classy little French-American sex comedy," declared John Chapman.[2] "It is written with humor, dramatic effectiveness, emotional force and deft expertness," gushed Richard Watts Jr.[3] "Whether Achard is the French Kurnitz or Kurnitz the American Achard doesn't really matter. With *A Shot in the Dark*, the two have hit the target," stated Norman Nadel.[4]

The naysayers were Howard Taubman, who found that "the light, tasty soufflé rises only a little,"[5] and Robert Coleman, who claimed that "the result is hit-and-miss."[6]

Judi Dench was cast as Josefa in a subsequent London production. *L'Idiote* was revived in Paris with great success during the 1970–1971 season. In the mid-1990s, the play still proved its bittersweet potency when presented by Vintage Theatre in Elmira, Corning, and Ithaca, New York. A 1964 movie version, scripted by director Blake Edwards and William Peter Blatty, evolved into the second Inspector Clouseau–Peter Sellers comedy, preserving from the original play one motif only—the great detective is out to prove the innocence of Elke Sommer in a murder case despite all evidence to the contrary.

* * *

Prior to his theatre and film career, Harry Kurnitz (1909–1968) wrote several detective novels under the nom de plume of Marco Page. His first mystery, *Fast Company* (1937), depicts murder in the world of rare books; it won Dodd, Mead's Red Badge Award. In *The Shadowy Third* (1946), the theft of a Stradivarius violin leads to bloodshed. Murder strikes during an investigation of art forgery in *Reclining Figure* (1952) and during the making of a criminous movie in *Invasion of Privacy* (1955). Adapting *Reclining Figure* for the stage, Kurnitz kept—lightheartedly—the element of skullduggery swirling around a faked Renoir but eliminated the gore. Emphasis was placed on a romantic attachment between an idealistic art dealer and the spunky daughter of an eccentric collector. *Reclining Figure* opened at the Lyceum Theatre on October 7, 1954, and ran for 116 performances.

Other Broadway offerings by Kurnitz include *Once More, with Feeling*, a farcical assault on the realm of music (National Theatre, October 21, 1958—263 performances) and the book of the musical *The Girl Who Came to Supper*, based on Terence Rattigan's *The Sleeping Prince*, with music and lyrics by Noel Coward (Broadway Theatre, December 8, 1963—112 performances).

Kurnitz converted his debut novel, *Fast Company*, to an MGM movie in 1938, the first in a series of rare-book hijinks—*Fast and Loose* (1939) and *Fast and Furious* (1939). Since then he wrote, often in collaboration, numerous screenplays, including the genre's *The Shadow of the Thin Man* (1941), *The Thin Man Goes Home* (1944), *The Web* (1947), *Witness for the Prosecution* (1957), and *How to Steal a Million* (1966).

Kurnitz also penned a Bob Hope spy yarn, *They Got Me Covered* (1942), and a Danny Kaye satire on Russian bureaucracy, a musical adaptation of Gogol's play *The Inspector General* (1949).

The screenwriter's versatility is amply demonstrated in such varied fare as the army comedy *See Here, Private Hargrove* (1944), the fantasy *One Touch of Venus* (1948), the swashbuckling *The Adventure of Don Juan* (1949), the East-West political *The Man Between* (1954), the biblical *Land of the Pharaohs* (1956), and the cinematization of his own battle-of-the-sexes play, *Once More, with Feeling* (1962).

* * *

The career of the French dramatist and screenwriter Marcel Achard (pseudonym of Marcel-Auguste Ferreol, 1899–1974) spans the early 1920s to the end of the 1950s. His first play, *Voulez-vous jouer avec mod?* (1923), a poetic commedia dell'arte about circus clowns, was presented off-Broadway at the York Playhouse on April 30, 1959, in a musical adaptation by Tamara Geva and Haila Stoddard called *Come Play with Me*, for four performances. Other American productions of Achard plays include *Domino* (1932), depicting the misadventures of a jealous husband, translated into English by Grace George and shown—with Achard attending as a guest of honor—at Atlantic City's Apollo Theatre during the first week of

August 1932, then transferred to the Playhouse in New York on August 16 for seven performances; *Jean de la Lune* (*The Dreamer*, 1929), a comic fantasy, presented by the French Theatre of New York at the Barbizon Plaza Theatre on December 13, 1937, for a limited run; *Aupres de ma blonde* (1947), adapted by S. N. Behrman under the title *I Know My Love*, starring the Lunts as a couple celebrating their silver anniversary, reminiscing about their life together (Shubert Theatre, November 2, 1949—246 performances); and *Palate* (1957), about a heel and his fall guy, adapted by Irwin Shaw (Henry Miller's Theatre, October 28, 1958—seven performances; a subsequent London production, in 1960, was called *Rollo*).

Among Achard's thirty-some plays, the more fashionable efforts were *La vie est belle* (*The Most Beautiful Life*, 1928); *La belle mariniere* (*The Beautiful Barge Woman*, 1929); *La femme en blanc* (*The Woman in White*, 1933); *Petrus* (1933), in which a chorus girl is accused of killing her lover, but is cleared; *Le Corseire* (*The Corsair*, 1938); *Adam* (1938); *Les Compagnons de la Marjolaine* (*The Companions of Marjolaine*, 1952).

In 1950, Achard adapted into French Mary Chase's *Harvey*, and in 1957 he wrote the musical *La Petite Lill* for Edith Piaf.

Achard penned thirty-seven screenplays, mostly in collaboration, notably *La Veuve joyeuse*, a version of *The Merry Widow* (1934); *Mayerling* (1936); *Mademoiselle Doctor* (1937); *Orage* (1938); *Felicie Mantevil* (1942); *Mademoiselle X* (1945); *Madame de . . .* (1953); and *Sophie et le crime* (1955).

Among his directors were Ernst Lubitch, Anatole Litvak, Julien Duvivier, Max Ophuls, and Marcel Carne.

"Without considering too seriously the larger political and social aspects of life, but with a tolerance and humanist spirit, Achard gives us play after play based on the joy of life and of love," writes Karel Tobey.[7]

Acting Edition: Samuel French, Inc.

Awards and Honors: Marcel Achard—Member, Academie Francaise, 1959; Officer, Legion of Honor. Tony Award—Walter Matthau as Benjamin Beaurevers—Best Supporting Actor.

NOTES

1. *New York Times*, September 26, 1960.

2. *Daily News*, October 19, 1961.

3. *New York Post*, October 19, 1961.

4. *New York World-Telegram*, October 19, 1961.

5. *New York Times*, October 19, 1961.

6. *New York Mirror*, October 19, 1961.

7. *The International Dictionary of Films and Filmmakers*, vol. 4, *Writers and Production Artists* (Chicago: St. James Press, 1987), 1.

Write Me a Murder (1961)

Frederick Knott (China-born, England– United States, 1918–2002)

In 1952, Frederick Knott scored big with *Dial "M" for Murder*. It took him nine long years to come up with another "foolproof" murderous drama, this time called *Write Me a Murder*.

Once again, the action takes place in England, unraveling in five-hundred-year-old Rodingham Manor, located about two hours from London. Here, too, the narrative is not a whodunit; the audience is privy to the planning, method, and execution of a pistol-shot homicide. And, in cloning *Dial "M" for Murder*, the main interest is the deciphering of the culprit's mistake, a slip that will deliver him into the hands of Scotland Yard.

The principal difference between *Dial "M" for Murder* and *Write Me a Murder* lies in the characters. Tony Wendice of *Dial "M"* is a rotter who almost succeeds in eliminating his sympathetic, unsuspecting wife. In *Write Me a Murder*, David Rodingham and Julie Sturrock are agreeable, victimized figures who first combine forces to concoct a fictional crime yarn, then translate it into real-life action against two despicable blackguards.

It all begins when Baron Rodingham dies, and his elder son, Clive, a reckless playboy, peddles the estate to a shrewd entrepreneur, Charles Sturrock. Clive's younger brother, David, a well-known author, is against the sale, but to no avail. Clive sails to America, chasing a Texas girl who "can swim like a fish and ski like a bird." Perhaps more importantly, "the girl's mother has eighty million dollars."

Charles Sturrock, the new lord of the manor, reveals to his young wife, Julie, that the purchase of the Rodingham estate is the first step in gobbling up the entire area. He plans to buy up every acre he can get his hands on, bring in some quick middle-class money, and then, when the whole place is booming, he'll sell little quarter-acre plots, thousands of them, all jammed up together with his own bus line to race the people in and out of London. And he'll get a percentage of all the pickings, the laundries, and the supermarkets. He'll make a killing!

Julie, unhappy in the loveless marriage to begin with, is jolted by Charles' greedy attitude. "Why did you marry me?" she asks. The cruel answer is: "Because you were a lady. And I didn't have too much choice."

A novice writer, Julie meets David Rodingham for advice about a murder tale. The collaboration yields not only an ingenious little yarn, but also a romantic attachment. David and Julie decide to utilize the lethal technique they had hatched for an actual plot to kill Charles Sturrock. It is a complicated scheme incorporating a silencer-pistol, a second shot triggered by a bang-contraption, and revolvers hidden under a terrace sundial, seen upstage through French windows. However, before David and Julie can activate their plan, Charles dies in an automobile accident.

A year passes. David and Julie get married. Clive returns from America, sans wife and funds, aiming to regain possession of the mansion. While Julie is in London for the night, David resuscitates the scrapped murder plan, shooting Clive. In an ironic twist, Julie returns home happily and relates to David that she has won first prize in an *Evening News* competition with their crime story.

As the shocked David is perusing the incriminating tale, two men from Scotland Yard appear on the terrace and begin to inspect the sundial. One of them keeps referring to a damp copy of the evening paper.

* * *

Write Me a Murder opened at New York's Belasco Theatre on October 26, 1961. Invariably, the critics measured it against *Dial "M" for Murder*. "This one doesn't belong in the same league as its predecessor," wrote Robert Coleman. "In this instance, you can call the author's shots before he makes them, and you don't have to be very bright to do it."[1] On the other hand, Norman Nadel found the play "every bit the match of his 1952 success, and in at least one respect, it is even better. . . . Where he has surpassed *Dial "M"* is in the subtle technique of character revelation."[2] Richard Watts Jr. stated, "In *Dial "M"* there was consistent suspense in watching the slow, inexorable process of entrapping the culprit, but this time the killing is delayed interminably, there is no discernible reason for caring if the slayer is caught, and a minimum of suspense is managed over the manner of the detection."[3] However, John McClain was ecstatic: "Goody, Goody, Gumdrop! After all these years since *Dial "M" for Murder* we've got a good sneaky homicide mystery going for us."[4]

Thumbs up were rendered by John Chapman, who commented, "*Write Me a Murder* is sort of a criminal switch on *The Cherry Orchard*, and it has enough twists of story and character to make a pleasant evening for the bloodthirsty."[5] Howard Taubman claimed that "Frederick Knott, the polished technician who wrote *Dial "M" for Murder*, has set himself some challenging problems in *Write Me a Murder* and has solved them with the smoothness of Scotland Yard's best."[6] Walter Kerr said, "Mr. Knott meets the basic tests of his peculiar calling. Does he surprise you? Yes. Does he surprise you logically? Yes. Does he throw in enough plausible small talk along the way to keep the whole business casual and decently folksy while the fidgets mount? He does, does Mr. Knott."[7]

Write Me a Murder ran for 196 performances on Broadway, followed by a long streak in London.

Acting Edition: Dramatists Play Service.

Awards and Honors: A top-ten selection in *The Best Plays of 1961–1962*. ("In his first play since *Dial "M" for Murder* Frederick Knott again devised an ingenious murder method, and a victim who well deserved his fate."[8]) Recipient of the Mystery Writers of America's Edgar Allan Poe Award as Best Play, 1962.

NOTES

1. *New York Mirror*, October 27, 1961.
2. *New York World-Telegram*, October 27, 1961.
3. *New York Post*, October 27, 1961.
4. *New York Journal-American*, October 27, 1961.
5. *Daily News*, October 27, 1961.
6. *New York Times*, October 27, 1961.
7. *New York Herald Tribune*, October 27, 1961.
8. Henry Hewes, ed., The *Best Plays of 1961–1962* (New York: Dodd, Mead, 1962), 12.

Daughter of Silence (1961)

Morris L. West (Australia, 1916–1999)

At the end of a quick prologue, a young woman named Anna Albertini crosses the village square of San Stefano and knocks on the door of Mayor Rosati's home. Without a word she fishes a pistol from her handbag and shoots him in the chest.

Daughter of Silence is set in the Province of Tuscany, Italy, a decade after World War II. The courtroom drama revolves around the question of why a nineteen-year-old girl killed the buffoonish mayor of a small, quiet town. It turns out to be an act of revenge. At the age of eight, Anna witnessed the rape and execution of her mother, falsely accused of collaborating with the enemy.

On a deeper level, according to Walter Kerr in the *New York Herald Tribune*, the author is determined "to peel its bloodthirsty surface away until every last social, legal and moral implication of the insane act is uncovered."[1]

An inexperienced lawyer, Carlo Rienzi, undertakes Anna's defense in an attempt to prove himself before his capricious, unfaithful wife, Valeria, and become free from the shackles of his domineering father-in-law, Alberto Ascolini, a famous legal authority. "You have no hope at all of winning," says Ascolini. "Your first case! They'll butcher you for a summer holiday and I'll be there to watch it!"

Carlo faces numerous obstacles, including a hostile police force and a conspiracy of silence by the villagers. However, he manages to call witnesses who reveal the victim's shady past: Father Bonifacio testifies that many of Gianbattista Rosati's actions were dictated not by the needs of the war but by a desire for private vengeance or private gain. Ignazio Carrese, Rosati's number two, relates that the late mayor was mad at the "Moschetti bitch," once exclaiming, "Nobody slaps Rosati and gets away with it!"

"Who killed Rosati—this woman, or a child of eight?" asks Carlo in court. In his summation, he requests "a minimum penalty . . . on the grounds of partial mental infirmity." The president of the court agrees and sentences Anna to serve a sentence of three years in a medical institute.

In an unexpected, unnerving ending, Anna reverts to her mad quest for vengeance by attacking Carlo: "You killed her! You killed my mother!" The guards rush in and carry her out. On a mellower note, Valeria makes amends with the distraught lawyer and they proceed to give their marriage another try.

* * *

Daughter of Silence, dramatized by Morris L. West from his novel, opened at the Music Box Theatre on November 30, 1961, to a gamut of opinions. Robert Coleman raved: "It's an intelligent drama . . . an arresting, stirring vehicle. . . . Here is a literate and exciting excursion into the world of illusion. Don't miss it."[2] Norman Nadel scoffed: "*Daughter of Silence* is too predictable to generate much suspense. . . . It would take a combination of rewriting, recasting and redirecting, with only Oliver Smith's sets retained intact, to lift this new drama to mediocrity."[3]

Positive reactions were expressed by Howard Taubman, who called it "a richly satisfying drama,"[4] and John Chapman, who called it "a distinguished play."[5] Less receptive were Richard Watts Jr., who found it "powerful but a little dissatisfying,"[6] and John McClain, who theorized, "And, as the book takes form as a play, it seems the author has been caught between two themes."[7]

Emlyn Williams as Ascolini, Rip Torn as Carlo, Joanne Linville as Valeria, and newcomer Janet Margolin as Anna stirred audiences for thirty-six performances.

* * *

Morris Langlo West was represented on Broadway earlier in 1961 via a faithful adaptation by Dore Schary (1905–1980) of his novel *The Devil's Advocate* (1959), a religious thriller.

Born in St. Kilda, Victoria, West graduated from the University of Melbourne in 1937, worked as a teacher in New South Wales and Tasmania, and spent twelve years in a monastery of the Christian Brothers. In 1941 he left without taking his final vows, got married, and enlisted in the Royal Australian Air Force. He left Australia in 1955 to write, lived in Austria, Italy, and the United States, was the Vatican correspondent for the *Daily Mail*, and finally returned to Australia in 1980.

West won international acclaim with a succession of worldwide best sellers, including *Children of the Shadows* (1957), *Navigator* (1976), *The World Is Made of Glass* (1983), *Master Class* (1988), *The Lovers* (1993), and the Vatican Trilogy: *The Shoes of the Fisherman* (1963; filmed 1968), *The Clowns of God* (1981), and *Lazarus* (1990).

His novels of intellectual suspense are comprised of *The Big Story* (U.S. title *The Crooked Road*, 1957; filmed 1965), *The Second Victory* (U. S. title *Backlash*, 1958; filmed 1986), *Ambassador* (1965), *The Tower of Babel* (1968), *Summer of the Red Wolf* (1971), *The Salamander* (1973; filmed 1981), *Harlequin* (1974), *Proteus* (1979), *A West Quartet, Four Novels of Intrigue and High Adventure: The Naked Court, Gallows on the Sand, The Concubine, Kundu* (1981), and *Vanishing Point* (1996).

West contributed pulsating TV episodes to UK's *Armchair Theatre* (1958) and *ITV Television Playhouse* (1961) and to Australia's *Whiplash* (1961). In 1989 he penned the thriller *Cassidy* for Australian television.

West died of a heart attack in 1999 in Clareville, New South Wales, while working on his novel *The Last Confession*, about Giordano Bruno, an Italian philosopher who in 1600 was burned at the stake for heresy by the Roman Inquisition. West has long been fascinated with the figure of Bruno. In 1970, West's blank-verse play, *The Heretic,* on the same subject, was produced in London, and in 1998 he converted it into a libretto for an opera. West's family published the unfinished novel in 2000 without editing, letting the reader imagine how the story might have ended.

Acting Edition: Samuel French, Inc.

Awards and Honors: Morris L. West was appointed chairman, Council of the National Library of Australia. In 1959 he was awarded the James Tait Black Memorial Prize for *The Devil's Advocate*.

NOTES

1. *New York Herald Tribune*, December 1, 1961.
2. *New York Mirror,* December 1, 1961.
3. *New York World-Telegram*, December 1, 1961.
4. *New York Times*, December 1, 1961.
5. *Daily News*, December 1, 1961.
6. *New York Post*, December 1, 1961.
7. *New York Journal-American*, December 1, 1961.

The Spiral Staircase (1962)

F. Andrew Leslie (United States, 1927–)

First came the 1933 novel *Some Must Watch* by British detective story writer Ethel Lina White. In 1946, screenwriter Mel Dinelli adapted the novel to the silver screen, under the title *The Spiral Staircase*. And in 1962, F. Andrew Leslie adapted the film to the stage, confining the action to one set and eliminating some of the characters, but otherwise remaining faithful to the Dinelli scenario.

The time is the early 1900s. The setting is a gloomy mansion located on the outskirts of a small Massachusetts city. The stage harbors two rooms: a front parlor, which takes most of the space, and the small bedroom of the mistress of the house, Mrs. Warren. The action is continuous, beginning in the late afternoon of an autumn day and carrying into that evening. A violent storm rages outside, punctuated by thunder and lightning. Heavy rain beats against the windows.

The curtain rises on a knocking on the street door. Mrs. Oates, the housekeeper, "graying and hearty-looking," enters the parlor and snaps on several lamps. She crosses to the door, unlocks it, and swings it open to admit the town's constable, Williams, a short and stocky middle-aged man, who steps into the room, dripping.

The constable informs Mrs. Oates that there has been another murder, the third. "This time it was a crippled girl," says Williams. "It's always a girl—one with an imperfection of some kind." Mrs. Oates expresses concern for Helen Capel, the live-in companion for bedridden Mrs. Warren. Helen, who left earlier for town, has been mute ever since she saw her parents die in a fire, the sort of affliction that may tempt the elusive murderer.

A door opens on top of the stairs and Professor Albert Warren descends partway. He is a tall, commanding elderly man with thick white hair. The constable asks him if he knows when and where Helen has gone. Professor Warren doesn't know because he has been in his study most of the day, but he refers the constable to his stepmother, Mrs. Warren.

At that moment they hear a key inserted in the lock. The street door opens and Helen Capel enters, followed by Doctor Brian Parry. She is a young girl of twenty, simply dressed, "and while small and rather pale there is a certain luminous glow about her." Dr. Parry, handsome and personable, carries his doctor's bag. Relieved, Mrs. Oates rushes to Helen and throws her arms around her. Professor Warren suggests that they drink "something to warm them inside" and goes upstairs to his study. The constable departs, and Mrs. Oates exits to the kitchen.

Dr. Parry tells Helen that he'll be going to Boston the next day and, believing that she can be cured, took the liberty of making an appointment for her with an expert, Dr. Fleming. Mrs. Oates returns carrying a tray with three glasses on it. They drink. Helen makes a face at the strength of the liquor. Dr. Parry says that he'll be back for her at ten o'clock the next morning and departs.

Suddenly, there is a rapping sound off-stage, behind the door leading to the rear of the house. Helen's hand goes to her mouth in alarm. Mrs. Oates crosses, opens the door slowly, and asks nervously, "Who's there?" There's no answer and she exits cautiously. After a short pause, her voice is heard, "Blast that cat!" followed by the sound of a window being pulled shut.

Mrs. Oates reappears and explains that the wind must have opened the window and let the cat in. Mrs. Oates and Helen leave for the kitchen and the stage is empty for a moment. Then a figure in a nurse's uniform appears at the top of the stairs. It is Nurse Barker, "an efficient looking woman in her late twenties." The nurse comes down, goes to the bookcase and selects a book. She sits in an armchair and leafs through it. Helen enters carrying a small tray with a cup of broth on it. Nurse Barker warns Helen that Mrs. Warren's mood this morning is foul.

The lights come up on the small bedroom. Mrs. Warren, "an old woman with the pallid grayness of the chronic invalid," sits upright in a four-poster bed, propped up by several large pillows. Helen enters and gives her the broth, which Mrs. Warren sniffs at critically before sipping it. Helen writes a note, asking Mrs. Warren's permission to go to Boston tomorrow with Dr. Parry. The old woman surprises Helen by urging her to go away now, immediately.

Meanwhile, a knock is heard at the front door and Nurse Barker admits the constable. He asks the nurse to gather everyone in the house for emergency instructions. Nurse Barker knocks brusquely on Mrs. Warren's door and summons Helen. Professor Warren comes down the stairs, followed by his young, casually dressed assistant, Stephen Rice. The constable says that he'll proceed without Mrs. Warren as he's aware that she has been bedridden for many years, and he announces that there is reason to believe that the murderer might be in the neighborhood. He asks that they make sure the house is locked tight. If they see anyone suspicious, they should call him on the telephone right away.

On his way to the door, the constable whispers to Professor Warren a request that he keep a close eye on Helen, as each of the murdered girls has had some sort of a physical affliction. The professor assures him that he'll arrange it so that Helen will be carefully watched for the next few days.

Helen returns to Mrs. Warren's bedroom. The old woman asks Helen to retrieve a package from the drawer of the desk. Helen searches for the object in question and finds it—a revolver hidden beneath a silk scarf. She refuses to hand the weapon to Mrs. Warren, who begins to gasp and claws at her throat. Helen, terrified, drops the gun and rushes out for help. She hurriedly enters Professor Warren's study and soon both she and the professor come down the stairs and enter the old woman's room. Professor Warren takes her hand and feels for her pulse. "Get the ether, Helen," he says. She gives the can to the professor. He unscrews the top, takes a clean handkerchief from the bedside table, carefully puts a few drops on it, and holds the handkerchief near Mrs. Warren's face. She stirs and seems to revive, but it's almost as if she's giving a performance—her gestures seem calculated, her sighs and moans measured.

Haltingly, Mrs. Warren blames Helen for the heart attack: "Stupid girl . . . she's to blame. . . . She deliberately refused to give me my spectacle case." Helen picks the scarf-wrapped gun from the floor and intends to give it to the professor, but Mrs. Warren snatches it and quickly slips it under the pillow. Helen shakes her head violently and attempts to warn the professor. He turns toward his stepmother, who smugly produces a spectacle case from behind the pillow, and throws it toward them. "There!" she says. "You're welcome to it."

Mrs. Warren asks Helen and the professor to leave. As they reach the door, she whispers, "There's been another murder, hasn't there?" The professor looks accusingly at Helen, who shakes her head. "Nobody told me," says the old woman. "I know."

The second act unfolds later that evening, after dinner. Stephen and Nurse Barker play a game of checkers with rapt concentration. They are interrupted by Professor Warren, who demands to know where his assistant spent the afternoon; he went over Stephen's papers and found no progress. Stephen coldly volunteers to resign, but Barker confides that Stephen was with her that afternoon. The professor says that he'll take her word for it, but insists on dismissing Stephen, effective immediately. Stephen goes upstairs to pack, the professor exits to his office, and the nurse leaves for her quarters. Helen enters and is puzzled by the empty room. Mrs. Oates appears from the kitchen, her face flushed, and it is evident that she had too much to drink. She puts away the checkerboard when there is a knock on the front door.

It is Dr. Parry. He asks the nurse about his patient, and Barker says wryly that she's kept out of Mrs. Warren's room most of the time. The lights come up in that area. Mrs. Warren asks Dr. Parry to take Helen to Boston immediately. She begins to mumble and gasp for breath. Dr. Parry sends Helen for the ether and checks Mrs. Warren's pulse. Helen can't find the ether. Dr. Parry calls Nurse Barker, who looks around and says that Professor Warren used it on his stepmother a few hours ago. "You took the ether, Nurse Barker," snaps Mrs. Warren suddenly. The nurse negates the accusation. Dr. Parry asks her to get the professor, who is surprised at the missing ether but agrees to send Mrs. Oates into the village to fetch some more. Mrs. Warren closes her eyes and seems to sleep heavily, while Nurse Barker sits quietly at her bedside.

Dr. Parry informs Professor Warren that after he visits several other patients, he'll be back for Helen and will drive her in his carriage to a specialist in Boston. He believes that Helen's condition is due to shock, and a new mental therapy can restore her voice. Professor Warren argues that the doctor is taking upon himself a tremendous responsibility and is probably building up false hopes, making Helen believe that her trip to Boston will perform some sort of "messianic miracle." The professor says pointedly, "Are your humanitarian instincts restricted only to people with various serious afflictions?" and mounts the stairs to his study.

Dr. Parry writes on a prescription pad a list of places he'll visit in the next couple of hours before he returns for Helen. If Helen needs him for anything before he gets back, Nurse Barker is to call him. He'll return before eleven o'clock. She should bar the door behind him and not let anyone in. He smiles: "Not even me."

Dr. Parry leaves. In the bedroom Mrs. Warren points a finger at Nurse Barker and orders her out. Angrily, the nurse exclaims that she had enough, that she is packed anyway, and stalks to her room. She soon reappears, suitcase in hand, an overcoat thrown over her uniform. Helen attempts to stop her, but Nurse Barker states that she's not willing to be insulted again; she quickly unbars the front door and exits into a gust of wind. Helen goes to the bedroom and sits near Mrs. Warren. Mrs. Oates, wearing a coat and hat, enters from the kitchen, her face flushed, her walk unsteady, betraying the fact that she has been at the brandy again. She puts on rubber boots with difficulty and crosses to the door. Stephen Rice comes down the stairs, dressed for travel and carrying a suitcase. Mrs. Oates consents to give him a ride.

In Mrs. Warren's room, the old lady opens her eyes and there's a wild look on her face as she leans forward and tells Helen, "I want to keep an eye on you, do you hear me? Come here, nearer to me!" She extends a bony hand toward Helen, her face turning scarlet, and falls back, motionless. Helen is petrified. She rushes to the parlor, reaches into her pocket and brings out the paper which Dr. Parry had left with her. She picks up the receiver and the operator's voice is heard: "Number please." Helen stares into the mouthpiece, her lips begin to move, but there's no sound. Her knuckles grow white as she grips the instrument. There's a look of panic on Helen's face now; she is isolated and cannot make contact with the outside world. She slowly puts the receiver back on the hook.

Professor Warren comes out of his study and watches Helen for a moment. "What's the matter, Helen?" he says quietly. Helen turns sharply at the sound of his voice, then relaxes and runs toward him, a smile of relief on her face. She hurriedly scribbles a note on a pad. He reads it and mutters, "An attack." He sends Helen to fetch some brandy from the kitchen, then reaches into his coat pocket and extracts a pair of thin black gloves.

There is a knock at the front door. The professor quickly removes the gloves and stuffs them in his pocket. He crosses rapidly to the door. "Who is it?" he asks. Constable Williams's voice comes from the outside, raised against a gust of wind. He is on his way back into town and is checking to make sure that everything is all right. Professor Warren assures him that all is well, and Williams leaves.

Professor Warren removes the key from the lock. Methodically he pulls his black gloves on, wriggling his fingers into place and snapping the gloves at the wrist. Helen reenters. The professor takes a step toward her and says, "You might as well know, Helen. . . . Things will be easier for you my way." He takes another step, and she shrinks back. He points at a wall mirror: "Look at yourself, Helen. . . . You're imperfect, and there's no room for imperfection in the world. . . . It is my sacred duty to dispose of imperfect girls before they bring more of their own kind into the world."

Helen, terrified, backs up the stairs. Professor Warren puts his foot on the bottom step when suddenly there is the loud sound of a shot fired from across the room. The professor lurches and stiffens, his arms jerk back spasmodically. Then there is another shot, and the professor stumbles backward and falls heavily to the floor. Across the parlor, Mrs. Warren stands in the bedroom door, a smoking revolver in her hand. She speaks in a halting, raspy voice, "I didn't want to believe it for a long time . . . but I knew, I knew. . . . I made myself an invalid years ago, so I could be in the house near him, so I could watch him . . ."

Mrs. Warren begins to sway and then stumbles forward on the floor. Helen moves quickly to her, kneels, and cradles Mrs. Warren in her arms. She soon lets her down gently as she realizes that the old woman is dead. There is a pounding on the door and Dr. Parry's voice is heard, "Helen, are you all right?" Helen crosses toward the door, her lips moving hesitantly, and then she speaks, "Yes, oh, yes, I'm all right, I'm all right!" She reaches the door and falls against it, sobbing with relief and joy as the curtain falls.

* * *

Ethel Lina White was born in Abergavenny, Monmouthshire, a small town on the Welsh border, in 1877. She was raised in Wales, one of a family of twelve. She served for several years at the Ministry of Pensions and turned to writing in the 1920s. She began by contributing essays, poems, and short stories to children's magazines. After penning three mainstream novels—*The Wish-Bone* (1927), *'Twill Soon Be Dark* (1929), and *The Eternal Journey* (1930)—White switched to the mystery genre. Beginning with *Put Out the Light* (aka *Sinister Light*, 1931), she wrote thirteen highly regarded suspense novels in as many years.

"A writer with a Gothic touch," asserts Mary Groff in *Twentieth-Century Crime and Mystery Writers*, "Ethel Lina White wrote about the defenseless female—whether the young rich girl needing protection from fortune hunters or the poor and underpaid governess or companion left to the torments that only spiteful employers can devise. They are wretched creatures trying to exist in gloomy situations, in decaying atmospheres full of unearthly threats, or earthy ones that are even worse, and trying bravely to cope with these real or imaginary terrors. The most horrifying story must surely be *Some Must Watch*. . . . Not merely the loneliness of her life and the lack of family or a trustworthy friend, but also the total inability to communicate her fear, plunge the White heroine into situations that most sensible people would wish to avoid. . . . While romance frequently plays a part, and there is always a lingering belief in the benefits of true love, it does not dominate these books. The plots are based on a mighty sense of fortune, usually threatening. Threats play a strong part in the books, emotions seem to become characters, and the result is nearly always a very high level of tension."[1]

In addition to *Some Must Watch* (*The Spiral Staircase*), two other works by White were made into noteworthy movies: *The Wheel Spins* (1936) was filmed by Alfred Hitchcock two years later under the title *The Lady Vanishes*, the story of a kidnapped lady who is saved by a young Englishwoman.[2] *Midnight House* (1942, aka *Her Heart in Her Throat*), a haunted house yarn released as *The Unseen* (1945), was coscripted by Raymond Chandler and Hagar Wilde and directed by Lewis Allen.

Ethel Lina White died in London in 1944 at the age of sixty-eight. During the 1930s and 1940s she was hailed as one of the era's best crime writers, but today she's all but forgotten. However, White has enjoyed a revival of sorts at the dawn of the twenty-first century, with a stage adaptation of *The Lady Vanishes* that toured England from March to July 2001, and a broadcast on BBC Radio 4.

* * *

The stark proceedings of Ethel Lina White's novel *Some Must Watch* take place in a Welsh border town. Screenwriter Mel Dinelli (1912–1991) shifted the locale to a small New England city. Dinelli provided thrills on radio and television before penning the scenarios of *The Spiral Staircase* (1946) and his second suspense film, *The Window* (1949), the latter based on a short story by Cornell Woolrich.[3] Robert Siodmak, a master of stylish suspense,[4] directed *The Spiral Staircase* with spine-tingling flair. The movie featured Dorothy McGuire (Helen Capel), George Brent (Professor Albert Warren), and Ethel Barrymore (Mrs. Warren), who was nominated for an Academy Award as Supporting Actress. Kent Smith played Dr. Brian Parry, Elsa Lanchester enacted Mrs. Oates, and Sara Allgood portrayed Nurse Barker. Roy Webb composed a haunting musical score. Nicholas Musuraca provided atmospheric black-and-white cinematography, highlighted with a thrilling close-up of the frantic eye of the elusive killer. Albert S. D'Agostino designed the shadowy, creepy Warren mansion.

In 1946, following the release of the motion picture, the original novel *Some Must Watch* was published under the title *The Spiral Staircase* in hard cover by World Publishing and in soft cover by Popular Library.

The Spiral Staircase was adapted as a half-hour radio play on the November 25, 1949, broadcast of *Screen Director's Playhouse*, with Dorothy McGuire reprising the role of Helen. A disappointing 1975 feature remake starred Jacqueline Bisset, and a 2000 made-for-television movie cast Nicollette Sheridan.

* * *

Frederick Andrew Leslie specialized in stage adaptations from screenplays and novels by other hands. Leslie's 1962 *The Spiral Staircase* is arguably his standout achievement. In the 1980s the play was presented with great success by Vintage Theatre in various venues across the Finger Lakes area of central New York State. Other dramatizations by Leslie that are based on motion pictures include *The Boy with Green Hair* (1961), an allegory about a twelve-year-old war orphan who becomes a social outcast because his hair changes color; *The Haunting of Hill House* (1964), detailing the investigation of a broody, isolated mansion by a team of scientists; *Splendor in the Grass* (1966), which describes school sweethearts who are plunged into tragic events that dash their plans; *Lilies of the Field* (1967), which focuses on a relationship between a discharged soldier who is headed West, and a Mother Superior who convinces him to stay and help build a chapel; *The People Next Door* (1969), which tells of a troubled New

York household where the parents of a drug-addicted daughter are trying desperately to rehabilitate her. In 1978, Leslie dramatized *The Hound of the Baskervilles*, a version generally faithful to Arthur Conan Doyle's Sherlock Holmes novel.

On a lighter note, Leslie adapted to the stage three motion picture comedies. *The Bachelor and the Bobby-Soxer* (1961) spotlights the dilemma of a playboy who is romantically pursued by a persistent teenager while his heart belongs to her older sister, a severe, no-nonsense judge. *The Farmer's Daughter* (1962) is the story of a Scandinavian immigrant, a naive, straight-arrow maid at the home of a powerful senator—who winds up as a candidate of the opposition party. *Mr. Hobbs' Vacation* (1963) pictures the misadventures of a family—father, mother, and college-age daughter—renting a summer cottage at an island off the coast of New England.

Acting Edition: Dramatists Play Service.

NOTES

1. John M. Reilly, ed., *Twentieth-Century Crime and Mystery Writers* (New York: St. Martin's Press, 1980), 1473.

2. George Axelrod scripted and Anthony Page directed a pale remake of *The Lady Vanishes* in 1979.

3. Mel Dinelli had one play produced on Broadway, *The Man*, a psychological thriller in which a deranged handyman imprisons and terrorizes a kind landlady (Fulton Theatre, January 19, 1950, featuring Dorothy Gish and Don Hanmer—ninety-two performances; filmed in 1952 under the title *Beware, My Lovely*, starring Ida Lupino and Robert Ryan).

4. Robert Siodmak (1900–1973) was born to a Polish Jewish family in Dresden, Germany. He launched his show business career as a stage director, and at the age of twenty-six began to dabble in silent films. His first directing feature was *Menschen am Sonntag* (*People on Sunday*, 1929), based on a script written by his younger brother, Curt Siodmak. With the rise of Nazism, the Siodmak brothers left Germany for Paris and then Hollywood. Robert made several B films for various studios before gaining a seven-year contract with Universal Studios. His initial motion pictures for Universal were *Son of Dracula* (1943), a top-notch horror film written by his brother Curt; *Cobra Woman* (1944), a Maria Montez–Jon Hall–Sabu costume extravaganza; and *Christmas Holiday* (1944), a crime yarn with Deanna Durbin and Gene Kelly. Siodmak established his reputation with the film noirs *Phantom Lady* (1944), based on the novel by Cornell Woolrich; *The Suspect* (1944), inspired by Jeffrey Dell's drama *Payment Deferred*; *Uncle Harry* (1945), from a murder play by Thomas Job; *The Killers* (1946), from a story by Ernest Hemingway; *The Dark Mirror* (1946), a psychological thriller in which Olivia de Havilland plays two sisters implicated in murder; *Cry of the City* (1948), about childhood friends who part ways when one becomes a criminal, the other

a policeman; *Criss Cross* and *The File on Thelma Jordan*, both made in 1949, each depicting a romantic, dangerous, deadly triangle. In 1952, Siodmak returned to Germany, where he made *Die Ratten* (*The Rats*), which went on to win the Golden Bear at the 1955 Berlin Film Festival, and *Nachts, wenn der Teufel cam* (*The Devil Came at Night*), which was nominated in 1957 for an Academy Award as Best Foreign Language Film.

Sequel to a Verdict (1962)

Philip Dunning (United States, 1890–1968)

In 1954, the British playwright-journalist Ludovic Kennedy wrote the drama *Murder Story* as a protest against capital punishment, which he called "legal killing." Eight years later, American Philip Dunning came out with the courtroom drama *Sequel to a Verdict*, also condemning the practice.

The action of the play takes place in an imaginary Connecticut town, Nortonberg, in the 1920s. On trial is Otto Ludwig Grossmeir, a carpenter accused of kidnapping and murdering an infant girl. The newspapers deemed it "the crime of the century." The circumstances of the case are reminiscent of the Charles Lindbergh tragedy. In that case, Charles August Lindbergh Jr., baby son of aviator Charles Lindburgh, was abducted from his crib in a New Jersey home on March 1, 1932. A ransom note was left behind, peppered with spelling mistakes and grammatical errors. Two months later, the body of the toddler was discovered a short distance from the Lindbergh home. After a two-year investigation, Bruno Richard Hauptmann was arrested and charged with the crime. The 1935 trial culminated with the death sentence. Hauptmann, who proclaimed his innocence to the very end, was executed by electric chair on April 3, 1936. However, Dunning included a special note in the published edition of *Sequel to a Verdict*, declaring that "the court trial is purely imaginary" and that "all the characters are fictitious and have no relation to any person living or dead."[1]

State Attorney Floyd Warren, "forceful and ambitious and just a bit of a show-off," calls to the stand the first witness for the prosecution—the grieving mother of the dead infant, Mrs. Brundage, who testifies that she, her husband, Frank, and the nursemaid, Abbie Lee, found the baby's crib empty. Frank Brundage, an architect, relates how he came upon a ransom note on the windowsill of the room. Prosecutor Warren exhibits the note to the jury members, emphasizing that the dollar sign is after the numbers (50,000$), and that the handwritten message is riddled with misspellings—"anyding" instead of "anything," "gut" instead of "good," "signnature" instead of "signature."

State Trooper Rouls testifies that he saw dirt tracks leading from the window toward the crib, and that there were footprints on the soft ground outside, next to a ladder.

Prosecutor Warren summons an array of witnesses, including the nursemaid, who confirms the evidence given by her employers; a neighbor of the Brundages, Adolph Nockheiser, who testifies seeing the accused in the neighborhood on the eve of the kidnapping; a handwriting expert, Andrew Campbell, who verifies that the writing on the ransom note matches Grossmeir's scribbling in his account book; Department of Justice Agent Daniel Knapp, who reveals that he found the ransom money hidden in a shoebox under the wooden floor of Grossmeir's garage.

Defense Attorney Martin calls upon Otto Ludwig Grossmeir to rebut the prosecution's case. A carpenter by trade, the defendant denies that he built the ladder that was used to enter the baby's room, and says in derision: "It looks like a musical instrument of some kind, to me." Grossmeir insists that an acquaintance, Emil Spitzer, asked him to store the shoebox before leaving for Europe, and he never knew that it contained money. At a police station on Greenwich Street, Brundage's neighbors could not identify Grossmeir in a lineup.

In his summation, Counsel Martin maintains that the kidnapping was an inside job. He points out that there are six rooms on the second floor of the Brundage home and scoffs, "How in the name of heaven could any stranger know exactly the window that led to the nursery?" And, argues Martin, "Why didn't the baby cry? Why didn't the dog bark?" However, the jury finds the defendant guilty, and Judge Pritchart sentences Grossmeir to death in the electric chair.

In a short epilogue, a Story Teller addresses the audience with the notion that "maybe it's time to abolish capital punishment. There might be some better way—anyhow think it over."

* * *

Philip Hart Dunning began his theatrical career as a performer. At an early age he left his Meriden, Connecticut, home to join a carnival show as a magician's assistant. He sang and danced in vaudeville, and appeared in stock and in New York in the early 1920s. He also managed a Marilyn Miller musical before finding himself a celebrated dramatist with the 1926 melodrama *Broadway*, which he cowrote with George Abbott. *Broadway*, a potpourri of cabaret entertainment, gangland territorial war, and true love blossoming in the midst of sleaze, ran for 603 performances. In 1932, Abbott and Dunning teamed on *Lily Turner*, picturing the romantic escapades of a circus barker's wife, and coproduced the Ben Hecht–Charles MacArthur hit comedy *Twentieth Century*.

Dunning followed *Broadway* with another speakeasy melodrama, *Night Hostess* (1928), interweaving illegal gambling, racketeering, and murder, all taking place in the bustling "Little Casino." *Night Hostess* ran for 117 performances, introduced Katharine Hepburn (billed as Katherine Burns) in a small role as a hostess, and was filmed in 1930 under the title *The Woman Racket*.

Dunning's *Sweet Land of Liberty* (1929) also unfolds in a shady night club operating on bootlegging and "protection" payoffs. Two liquor dealers witness the shooting of a federal Prohibition agent and find themselves in hot water when they agree to tell what they saw to the grand jury. *Kill That Story* (1934) exposes crooked newspaper deals. In *Page Miss Glory* (1934), James Stewart played a hustling promoter who submits a composite photo of Hollywood beauties to a contest for "the most beautiful girl in America," wins the award, and then has to produce the girl. Complications ensue when a pair of petty criminals mistake a hotel chambermaid for the nonexistent celebrity and kidnap her for ransom. *Page Miss Glory* was filmed in 1935.

Acting Edition: Dramatists Play Service.

NOTE

1. Philip Dunning, *Sequel to a Verdict* (New York: Dramatists Play Service, 1962), 3.

Prescription: Murder (1962)

William Link (United States, 1933–) and Richard Levinson (United States, 1934–1987)

In their three-act play *Prescription: Murder*, William Link and Richard Levinson introduced Lieutenant Columbo (no first name), the rumpled, stub-cigar-chewing police investigator made famous by the later TV series, whose bumbling, apologetic, and inept demeanor masks a shrewd professional with a deep knowledge of human nature.

The action of *Prescription: Murder* takes place in New York City. The curtain rises on the plush reception room and office of Dr. Roy Flemming, a society psychiatrist. Miss Petrie, a pleasant, efficient receptionist in her fifties, is on the phone, setting an appointment with a talkative patient. Enter Dr. Flemming, a polished, urbane man of forty. The doctor exchanges a few words with Petrie and crosses to his office, where he opens an attaché case and removes a folded cloth bundle. He shakes it out and we see that it's a woman's gray wool dress. He studies it reflectively, holding it at arm's length.

The door to the reception room opens and Claire Flemming walks in, wearing sunglasses and carrying a pair of white gloves. She is a chic woman in her late thirties. Miss Petrie buzzes Dr. Flemming and informs him that his wife is here. The doctor quickly folds the dress and puts it in his attaché case. During the ensuing scene, Claire inquires why her husband came home at 3:00 a.m. and admits that she is "bitchy sometimes" out of jealousy. Dr. Flemming soothes her, and they make plans to spend the weekend at their cottage in upstate New York where there will be no phone calls, no interruptions, not even the Sunday *Times*.

Claire leaves, passing a newly arrived patient, Susan Hudson, a young, attractive brunette actress. As soon as Susan enters Flemming's office and the door closes behind her, they fall into each other's arms and kiss passionately. He then reminds her that his wife has refused his persistent requests for a divorce, and insists that they proceed with their plan. Though apprehensive, Susan tries on the gray dress and studies Claire's picture, making note of her pulled-back hair and heavy use of an eyebrow pencil and lipstick. She is to arrive at the Flemming apartment that night at ten o'clock.

After Susan's departure, Flemming folds Claire's dress and puts it back in the attaché case. He removes a small tissue-paper package from his jacket pocket, revealing a pair of gloves. He tries them on, inching them down each finger as the lights go out.

Scene 2 unfolds in the living room of the Flemming apartment in Manhattan's East Seventies. Claire, wearing a negligee, happily tells her husband that she has finished packing and is looking forward to their weekend upstate. She mixes a drink and does not notice that Roy is putting on gloves while approaching her. His hands suddenly shoot around her neck, the fingers closing. Claire begins to struggle as the telephone rings. Flemming frantically increases his pressure, finally lets her slide to the floor, and snatches the receiver. He tells his friend Dave Gordon that he and Claire will be away for the weekend.

Flemming now moves to make it look as if a burglar entered the room from the garden. He shatters the glass panel of the French window, scattering silverware and knick-knacks. The doorbell rings. It is Susan, made up to look like Claire—her hair is pulled back, her lipstick and eyebrow lines are emphasized. When Susan sees Claire's body she utters an involuntary gasp. Trembling, she strips and puts on Claire's gray dress. Flemming stuffs his gloves into his breast pocket and gathers some pieces of jewelry in a knotted handkerchief, which he intends to drop into a lake near the upstate lodge. He then wraps a handkerchief around the receiver of the telephone, dials and hands it to Susan. Susan identifies herself as Mrs. Flemming of apartment 6-K, 23 East 72nd Street, and says that she'll be leaving a bundle of laundry for cleaning outside the door to be picked up the first thing in the morning.

There is a moment of tension when Susan searches her large bag for a pair of sunglasses. She finally finds them and puts them on. Flemming hands her the gloves that Claire always wore with the gray dress.

Finally, Flemming reviews with Susan the staged quarrel that will ensue when they take their seats in the plane. She is to stalk out angrily and leave him to fly by himself. She will take a cab, return to the apartment, add the dress to the pile of laundry, and go home.

They exit, glaringly leaving behind the white handkerchief wrapped around the telephone receiver. This must be their one fatal mistake! Suddenly, the door opens and Flemming returns. He strides to the phone, whips out the handkerchief, and stuffs it in his breast pocket. He takes a last look around and hurries to the door as the curtain falls.[1]

We meet Lieutenant Columbo of the NYPD in the second act as he waits for Dr. Flemming's return. The lieutenant is described as "lumbering and homely, of indeterminate age." The day is warm but he wears a dusty topcoat and a battered felt hat. He chews on an "ancient cigar" and "some of its ashes have descended like dandruff to his shoulders and lapels." His manner is deferential, almost humble. At times he seems a bit vacant and distracted, but we learn later that he is very much aware of his surroundings.

Columbo makes a mental note of a curious omission: when Flemming walks into the apartment, he makes no effort to call out to his wife.

The lieutenant checks the French windows and expresses to Dr. Flemming his surprise that the thief obviously went on to culminate his robbery instead of fleeing the scene after strangling Flemming's wife. Flemming keeps his cool when informed that his wife has not died but is in a coma in the hospital. However, soon word comes that Claire has passed away. She was conscious at the end. The last thing she called out was her husband's name.

A cat-and-mouse duel of wits develops between the investigator and the doctor. Columbo hounds Flemming with questions and corners him with a gamut of sly tactics. He seems to be on the losing end when an airline stewardess identifies a picture of Claire Flemming as the quarreling lady in the gray dress who left the plane in a huff. The dress itself is returned by the cleaners.

At last the tenacious lieutenant finds a weak link in Flemming's defense. Realizing that the doctor's mistress, Susan Hudson, is increasingly agitated, he subjects her to a harsh interrogation and uses her to trap the doctor. In a ruse, Columbo tells Flemming that Susan has cracked under the pressure and committed suicide in order to protect her lover. Flemming, touched, confesses to the crime.

* * *

Prescription: Murder originated as a short story, "May I Come In," penned by two boyhood friends from Philadelphia, William Link and Richard Levinson. The story was published in the *Alfred Hitchcock Mystery Magazine* under the title "Dear Corpus Delecti," and was adapted for a one-hour episode on NBC's *The Chevy Mystery Show*, this time called "Enough Rope."

Link and Levinson plucked some elements of the tale, notably Dr. Flemming's alibi, for their play *Prescription: Murder*. It was first presented at the Curran Theatre in San Francisco on January 20, 1962. The cast included renowned screen actors Thomas Mitchell (Lieutenant Columbo), Joseph Cotten (Dr. Roy Flemming), Patricia Medina (Susan Hudson), and Agnes Moorehead (Claire Flemming). "Mitchell was terrific, but we didn't get good reviews," said Link. "It needed work. But it went on tour for twenty-five weeks in the United States and Canada, and it made a fortune."[2]

Link and Levinson were surprised by the fact that even though Joseph Cotten was the star of the show, audiences gave warmer ovations to Thomas Mitchell. So when the writers converted the play to television, the role of Lieutenant Columbo became central. Mitchell passed away in December 1962; Bing Crosby and Lee J. Cobb were considered, but when Peter Falk called to say, "I would kill to play the cop," the plum role was given to him without even a screen test.

Airing on February 20, 1968, the ninety-minute *Prescription: Murder* had the following cast: Lt. Columbo—Peter Falk; Dr. Ray Fleming (instead of Roy Flemming)—Gene Barry; Joan Hudson (instead of Susan Hudson)—Katherine Justice; Carol Fleming (instead of Claire Flemming)—Nina Foch. The locale was shifted from New York to Los Angeles to reduce production expenses.

Link and Levinson followed *Prescription: Murder* with a second Columbo TV movie, *Ransom for a Dead Man*, continuing the "inverted mystery" motif in which the audience is privy to the murder as planned, committed, and covered up by the murderer. Suspense is achieved thanks to the methods employed by Lt. Columbo to entrap the clever culprit.[3] The two television movies spawned a most successful series, *Columbo*, which ran on NBC from 1971 to 1978—ninety-minute episodes presented in rotation with two other mystery shows, *McMillan and Wife* (starring Rock Hudson and Susan Saint James) and *McCloud* (starring Dennis Weaver). Several segments of *Columbo* were novelized and published as original paperbacks.

* * *

Both William Link and Richard Levinson were born in Philadelphia, Pennsylvania, attended the Elkins Park Junior High School, and enrolled at the University of Pennsylvania, where they earned B.S. degrees in economics at the famous Wharton School in 1956. Mark Dawidziak wrote in *The Columbo Phile* that "each had grown up on a diet of pop culture served at the local movie houses, through the radio airwaves, between the covers of pulp magazines and in the panels of brightly inked comic books. Each's tastes were formed by cherished sessions with Captain Marvel, Superman, Saturday afternoon serials, Walt Disney, Abbott & Costello, Dashiell Hammett, Raymond Chandler, Ellery Queen, Erle Stanley Gardner and such radio shows as *Jack Armstrong*, *Inner Sanctum*, *Lights Out* and *Suspense*."[4]

Together, Link and Levinson headed to New York and began their literary career by contributing short stories to *Playboy*, *Alfred Hitchcock Mystery Magazine*, and other publications. At the age of twenty-four, they made an auspicious debut on television with an army drama called *Chain of Command*. In 1959 they traveled to California, signed a contract with Four Star

Television, and submitted scripts for the series *Michael Shayne* and *Richard Diamond, Private Eye.*

Soon Link and Levinson expanded their scope, contributing episodes to such series as *McCloud, The Fugitive, Burke's Law, The Rogues, The Man from U.N.C.L.E.,* and *The Alfred Hitchcock Hour.* Becoming one of the medium's most successful writing teams, Link and Levinson launched *Mannix* (CBS), *The Adventures of Ellery Queen* (NBC), *Murder She Wrote* (CBS), and many other milestone shows. They branched out to topics of social conscience, but continued to pen mysteries-for-television—*Murder by Natural Causes* (1979),[5] *Rehearsal for Murder* (1982), *Guilty Conscience* (1985),[6] and *Vanishing Act* (1986).[7]

Link and Levinson cowrote the book for the Broadway musical *Merlin,* with music by Elmer Bernstein and lyrics by Don Black. The fairytale plot had the legendary wizard, Merlin, as a still-young apprentice learning sleight-of-hand magic. Merlin (played by illusionist Doug Henning) is the only obstacle in the nefarious scheme of a wicked queen (Chita Rivera) to install her idiot son (Nathan Lane) on the English throne. *Merlin* played sixty-nine previews before opening at the Mark Hellinger Theatre on February 13, 1983. It was snubbed by critics and ran 199 performances.

Link and Levinson went through a Broadway setback, but their creation, Lieutenant Columbo, took another career leap when in the 1990s writer and former criminal lawyer William Harrington was authorized to pen two Columbo novels, published in hardcover by Forge: *The Grassy Knoll* (1993), in which the persistent lieutenant tackles the JFK assassination, and *The Helter Skelter Murders* (1994), taking on the Charles Manson affair.

In 2007, Link penned the play *Columbo Takes the Rap* for a presentation at the International Mystery Writers' Festival in Owensboro, Kentucky, and in 2010 he extended Lt. Columbo's career through a volume of original short stories, *The Columbo Collection,* published by Crippen & Landru. In conjunction with the publication of the book, Link was interviewed by Tom Nolan for *Mystery Scene* magazine, and said: "Our template for Columbo was Petrovich, the detective-inspector in *Crime and Punishment,* Dostoevsky's great novel; Dick and I read it in college. . . . And Peter Falk, you know, gave it a whole new spin, because the cop in the Dostoevsky book was not humorous at all. . . . In this one man, you have both Sherlock Holmes and Watson. There's the intellectual, the very clever, great detective Sherlock Holmes; and then you have the everyman Watson. . . . He's the regular working-class guy—who's got a brilliant mind but doesn't really tout it, you know. He's humble, even to the murderer! And people identify with that; they like that."[8]

Acting Edition: Samuel French, Inc.

Awards and Honors: William Link and Richard Levinson received an Emmy Award for Outstanding Writing Achievement in Drama two years in a row—in 1970 for *My Sweet Charlie* and in 1971 for *Columbo: Death Lends a Hand*; the Golden Globe Award, 1972, for both Best Television Show, Drama—*Columbo*, and Best Television Movie—*That Certain Summer*; Peabody Award, 1974, for Meritorious Service to Broadcasting—*The Execution of Private Slovik*; Distinguished Service recognition by the board of governors, Academy of Television Arts and Sciences, 1976–1977; three Edgar Awards, Mystery Writers of America, for Best TV Feature or Miniseries—*Murder by Natural Causes* (1980), *Rehearsal for Murder* (1983), and *Guilty Conscience* (1986). They were inducted into the Academy of Television Arts and Sciences Hall of Fame, 1984; they received the Paddy Chayefsky Laurel Award, Writers Guild of America, 1986; and the Ellery Queen Award, Mystery Writers of America, 1989, for lifetime contribution to the art of the mystery. William Link received the Marlowe Award, Southern California Chapter of the Mystery Writers of America, "in honor of [his] many and significant contributions to our genre," 2001. He was also elected national president of the Mystery Writers of America in 2002 and garnered Malice Domestic's Agatha Christie "Poirot" award in 2010.

NOTES

1. The gambit of leaving behind an incriminating item, suspensefully playing upon the emotion of the audience, is a variation on the hat forgotten by Inspector Rough in Patrick Hamilton's 1938 *Gaslight* (*Angel Street*), when the inspector returns in the nick of time to retrieve his hat and exit just as the villainous Mr. Manningham makes his entrance.

2. Mark Dawidziak, *The Columbo Phile: A Casebook* (New York: Mysterious Press, 1989), 21.

3. The invention of the "inverted mystery" is credited to R. Austin Freeman (1862–1943), an English detective story writer. In his novel *The Red Thumb Mark* (1907) and the short-story collections *John Thorndyke's Cases* (1909) and *The Singing Bone* (1912), the reader is witness to the crime and follows Dr. John Evelyn Thorndyke, Freeman's scientific detective, as he identifies, one by one, the mistakes made by the murderer. Another Englishman, A. A. Milne (1882–1956), immortalized by his *Winnie the Pooh* children's stories, introduced the "inverted" form to the stage—in 1928's *The Fourth Wall* (aka *The Perfect Alibi*). Instead of waiting to learn the solution until 11:00 p.m., the audience follows the execution of a murder committed in act I by two malefactors, who claim a touch of genius by clearing all evidence after them. For the balance of the play, the investigative process sifts the truth by pinpointing the killers' missteps. In the 1920s, the golden age of the chess-like who-done-it (note Agatha Christie in England and S. S. Van Dine in the United States, as well as last-minute unmasking of clever criminals in numerous stage melodramas), A. A. Milne's approach was a novelty. A detailed description

of *The Fourth Wall* and its production data are set forth in Amnon Kabatchnik, *Blood on the Stage, 1925–1950* (Lanham, MD: Scarecrow Press, 2008), 165–167.

4. Mark Dawidziak, *The Columbo Phile*, 15.

5. The teleplay *Murder by Natural Causes* was adapted to the stage in 1985 by Tim Kelly, a prolific playwright. The play's lead characters are Arthur Sinclair, a mentalist, and his greedy wife, Allison, each concocting a scheme to get rid of the other. Three or four plot twists unravel before the final curtain.

6. William Link and Richard Levinson first wrote *Guilty Conscience* as a play in two acts. Richard Kiley and Rosemary Murphy starred in the world premiere, which took place at the Parker Playhouse in Fort Lauderdale, Florida, on April 22, 1980. The play added new wrinkles to the husband-wife-mistress triangle with surprising turns and twists. The husband, Arthur Jamison, a defense attorney, confides his homicidal plans to an alter ego—an imaginary prosecutor with whom Jamison shares his plans to get rid of his wife. However, he is not aware that the wife, Louise, and the mistress, Jackie, have plans of their own.

7. Link and Levinson based their teleplay *Vanishing Act* on the twisty *Trap for a Single Man* by Frenchman Robert Thomas, a thriller about a missing wife, which boasts one of the most surprising denouements in the annals of the stage mystery.

8. *Mystery Scene* 115, Summer 2010.

The Physicists (1962)

Friedrich Duerrenmatt
(Switzerland, 1921–1990)

In 1956, *The Visit* demonstrated Friedrich Duerrenmatt's unique blend of ambiguous, paradoxical, and grotesque elements. *The Physicists*, a black comedy of murder and espionage within the walls of a mental institution, follows suit.

The only three patients in the private sanatorium known as Les Cerisiers are Herbert Georg Beutler, who declares that he is Isaac Newton; Ernst Heinrich Ernesti, who claims to be Albert Einstein; and Johann Wilhelm Möbius, who alleges profound friendship with King Solomon. A few months ago, Newton strangled his nurse Dorothea with a curtain cord, and now Einstein has garroted his nurse Irene with the cable of a standard lamp.

Police Inspector Richard Voss arrives on the scene. The ironic thrust of the play is evident when the inspector confronts the institution's matron, Marta Boll. She denies his request to interview the assailant Ernesti/Einstein, for he cannot be disturbed while playing the fiddle. When the inspector asks to see the doctor in charge, he is told that's impossible too because Fräulein Doktor is accompanying Einstein on the piano. The inspector sighs. Three months ago, when he was investigating the strangulation of the nurse Dorothea, he could not interrogate the patient Newton, who was playing chess with Fräulein Doktor.

Inspector Voss insists, and at long last he is ushered to the office of the head of the institution, Fräulein Doktor Mathilde von Zahnd. The doctor is middle-aged, hunchbacked, dressed in white topped by a surgical coat, a stethoscope around her neck. The inspector informs her that the public prosecutor is fuming at the lack of cooperation in the matter of two murders. No doubt the safety precautions at Les Cerisiers are lax. Doktor von Zahnd responds coolly. The incidents could not have been foreseen, she says. Medically speaking, there is no explanation for what has happened. However, continues von Zahnd, the patients, Newton and Einstein, are both nuclear scientists, doing research on radioactive materials; perhaps that activity affected their brains to the point of becoming dangerous.

Even though the doctor assures the inspector that the third patient, Möbius, is harmless, at the end of the first act, unexpectedly, Möbius responds to Nurse Monika's declaration of love ("I want to sleep with you, I want to have children by you") by choking her to death with the tassled twine of a window curtain.

Doktor von Zahnd and Inspector Voss interrogate Möbius. The patient explains that King Solomon ordained the strangulation of the nurse. He was standing at the window staring out at the falling dusk when the king floated up out of the park and whispered his command through the windowpane. The Inspector, nonplussed, asks Möbius to deliver his "kindest regards" to Einstein and Newton and his "respects" to King Solomon, and hurriedly departs.

With that satirical barb at the impotence of justice, the official investigation of the three murders is closed.

The proceedings take a surprising turn when Einstein and Newton reveal to Möbius their true identities: both are scientist-spies for two competing Cold War Intelligence Services, American and Russian. In order to maintain their cover of insanity, they killed their nurses, who had become suspicious. Einstein and Newton attempt to recruit Möbius to their cause, but Möbius talks of the danger to the planet, the potential destruction of humanity. We know what the world has done with the weapons it already possesses, he argues. We can imagine what it would do with those which his research will make possible. He was offered a position at a university and a great deal of money from industry, but a sense of responsibility compelled him to choose another course. He relinquished an academic career, said no to industry, abandoned his wife and three children, and took on the masquerade of a madman conversing with King Solomon.

Möbius asserts that for the salvation of mankind, Newton and Einstein must remain with him in Les Cerisiers. Their knowledge has become a frightening burden, their researches are perilous, their discoveries lethal. Through their secret radio transmitters they should inform their superiors that they have made a mistake.

Newton and Einstein object to remaining in the institute; they are not mad. But Möbius points out that they *are* murderers. Each of them killed his nurse—Newton and Einstein so as not to endanger the outcome of their secret mission; and he, because Nurse Monika thought he was an unrecognized genius and he could not take a chance of her spreading the word.

Newton and Einstein agree to remain with Möbius in the institute— forever. But this flicker of optimism is snuffed and the sacrifice of the scientists comes to naught. Doktor von Zahnd is unmasked as an oppor-tunistic, power-hungry monster who has eavesdropped on the scientists' conversations, duplicated their notes, and driven the three nurses into their arms predicting the deadly outcome, thus imprisoning them forever. Fräulein Doktor is establishing a worldwide operation of destructive atomic weapons.

* * *

Mark R. McCulloh, in *Masterplots II, Drama Series*, points out that von Zahnd "eventually succeeds in obtaining from Möbius that which he set out to conceal, and thereby the traditional tragic conclusion is achieved (as in the case of Sophocles' *Oedipus Rex*) with the hero's attainment of the very opposite of what he intended. Paradoxes such as these (noble intentions leading to disaster, the apparent insanity of the 'sane,' the search for freedom in confinement and isolation from the world, and so on) represent the essence of Duerrenmatt's dramatic motivation. . . . In many ways, *The Physicists* is a very traditional tragedy. It maintains the classical unities of action, time, and place; the entire play takes place in-side one ward at 'Les Cerisiers' within one twenty-four-hour period. The ending, Duerrenmatt's tragicomic innovations notwithstanding, follows the pattern of traditional Greek tragedy, with the hero's nullification of his own efforts."[1]

In another *Masterplots II* essay, William S. Brockington Jr. asserts, "All Duerrenmatt's plays are fundamentally pessimistic, reflecting his anxiety regarding the future of the world."[2]

Die Physiker was first produced at the Schauspielhaus of Zurich, Swit-zerland, on February 21, 1962. Translated from the German by James Kirkup and directed by Peter Brook, *The Physicists* was presented by the Royal Shakespeare Company at London's Aldwych Theatre, previewing at the end of 1962 and opening officially on January 9, 1963. Irene Worth appeared as Doctor von Zahnd; Diana Rigg portrayed Nurse Monika; Michael Hordern, Alan Webb, and Cyril Cusack enacted, respectively, scientists Newton, Einstein, and Möbius. Critic Kenneth Tynan wrote: "Eagerly abetted by Mr. Brook, Duerrenmatt plays on our nerves and through them reaches our brains, using the techniques of detective fiction to convey an apocalyptic message. . . . Beneath the Arctic cap of the argu-ment there simmers a passionate concern for human life."[3]

Peter Brook also staged a New York production of *The Physicists* at the Martin Beck Theatre, opening on October 13, 1964, featuring Jessica Tandy as von Zahnd, and Hume Cronin, George Voskovec, and Robert Shaw as the "mad" scientists. Reviewer Norman Nadel was impressed: "It takes a play like *The Physicists*—and, believe me, there aren't many like it—to remind us what an adventure of spirit and mind the theatre can be."[4] Walter Kerr, however, felt that *"The Physicists* does not so much dramatize its debate as postpone it with bizarre performing tricks."[5] The play ran for fifty-five performances.

Productions of *The Physicists* were mounted in Paris and Tel Aviv (1963); Manchester, England (1964); Houston, Texas (1967); Sarasota, Florida (1970); off-Broadway (Ethical Culture, 1975); Princeton, New Jersey (1977); and Washington, D.C. (1981). A flurry of revivals occurred during the first decade of the twenty-first century, with shows by off-off-Broadway's Oberon Theatre Ensemble (2001); Burton Taylor Theatre, Oxford, England (2004); The Williamstown Theatre Festival, Williamstown, Massachusetts (2007); and the Los Angeles Theatre Works (2009), among others.

The Physicists was televised in West Germany (1964), Belgium (1970), Argentina (1972), and Norway (1988).

Acting Edition: Samuel French, Inc.

NOTES

1. Frank N. Magill, ed., *Masterplots II, Drama Series* (Pasadena, CA: Salem Press, 1990), 1246.
2. Frank N. Magill, *Masterplots II, Drama Series*, 1693.
3. London *Observer*, January 3, 1963.
4. *New York World-Telegram*, October 14, 1964.
5. *New York Herald Tribune*, October 14, 1964.

Calculated Risk (1962)

Joseph Hayes (United States, 1918–2006)

Who among the directors of a New England textile company is supplying inside information to an unscrupulous corporate raider?

Julian Armstone, president of Armstone Mills, conducts a dogged whodunit investigation, in which suspicion veers from one member of the board to another. Just prior to the final curtain, Julian unmasks the inner-circle traitor and saves the firm from a takeover.

Calculated Risk, based on the English play *Any Other Business* by George Ross and Campbell Singer, detours sporadically to the marital crises of company president Julian and his younger brother Quentin. However, the main punch of the proceedings occurs during board meetings, where it soon becomes ominously clear that a mole has joined forces with an adversary stock market manipulator.

Is it Clyde Norman, the elderly chairman of the board? Malcolm Turnbull, vice president in charge of sales? Walter Dodds, manager of the mill? Jonathan Travis, the products' designer? Congressman Roger Parkhurst, who is also an active board member? Harrison Bellows, the local bank president? James McQueen, attorney for Armstone Mills? Quentin Armstone, the secretary-treasurer? Or perhaps Rhoda Andrews, Julian's efficient secretary?

In conjunction with its intriguing premise, *Calculated Risk* provides fascinating tidbits about wheeling-dealing in the business world, its behind-the-scene machinations, and its dog-eat-dog demeanor. Perhaps that facet of the play, and no doubt the drawing power of stars Joseph Cotten and Patricia Medina as Julian and Helen Armstone, is what kept the show on Broadway for 221 performances, in spite of a lukewarm reception by most critics.

"*Calculated Risk* is a damp little 'suspense play,'" wrote Walter Kerr following the premiere at the Ambassador Theatre on October 31, 1962.[1] "The drama lapses into a banal mishmash of domestic relations," complained Norman Nadel. "The only suspense during those scenes is over which will turn out to be worse—the writing or the acting. It's a draw."[2] Richard Watts Jr. stated, "*Calculated Risk* is never completely ineffectual, and it works up to some admirable moments of suspense, but it isn't steadily satisfying."[3] Robert Coleman lamented, "There is all too much razzle-dazzle chicanery in this one for credibility."[4]

John McClain wrote a more favorable review: "The fact that I cared and, in fact, settled on the wrong character, is a tribute to the author; to the efforts of an excellent cast; and the staging of Robert Montgomery. . . . *Calculated Risk* does not pack the punch of Mr. Hayes' earlier thriller, *The Desperate Hours*, but it still is an engrossing and unexpectedly exciting experience—and is hence recommended."[5] Howard Taubman gushed, "How rare and satisfying to encounter a knowledgeable and gripping play about the world of business! . . . *Calculated Risk* has elements of the mystery tale and courtroom stories as well as shrewd observation of the motives of men in crisis. . . . Mr. Hayes does not forget that livelihoods and communities hang in the balance when a power struggle takes place. *Calculated Risk* is not only a lively thriller but also a valid contemporary document."[6]

Years later, in the 1980s, the pendulum would swing back to the motif of business-world intrigue with two devastating plays: *Glengarry Glen Ross* by David Mamet, winner of the 1984 Pulitzer Prize for Drama, populated with cutthroat real estate salesmen competing against each other, and *Other People's Money* by Jerry Sterner, an Outer Critics Circle Award winner in 1989 as Best Off-Broadway Play. In it, a vulnerable New England company, Wire & Cable, is in the clutches of an unsavory corporation raider.

Acting Edition: Samuel French, Inc. (in manuscript form).

NOTES

1. *New York Herald Tribune*, November 1, 1962.
2. *New York World-Telegram*, November 1, 1962.
3. *New York Post*, November 1, 1962.
4. *New York Mirror*, November 1, 1962.
5. *New York Journal-American*, November 1, 1962.
6. *New York Times*, November 1, 1962.

Rule of Three (1962)

Agatha Christie (England, 1890–1976)

Agatha Christie ventured into the one-act format with a triple bill of playlets first produced under the collective title *Rule of Three*. *The Rats*, *Afternoon at the Seaside*, and *The Patient* have no intrinsic linkage and can be performed individually.

The Rats unfolds in a one-room flat in Hampstead during a summer evening. The furniture and knick-knacks indicate a Middle East connection. By the window there is a big casket of the type known as a Kuwait bride chest, dark wood studded with brass nails. Scattered about are pieces of Persian pottery and figurines from Baghdad. A line of Kurdish knives shines on the wall.

It soon becomes clear that the owners of the apartment, the Torrances, are away in the south of France. Sandra Grey, a young and attractive married woman, and her lover, David Forrester, are lured into the place by a bogus invitation to a party. Has Sandra's husband, John, suspected an illicit relationship and concocted a plan to catch them in the act?

A friend, Alec Hanbury, arrives on the scene dressed fashionably. When informed that there is no party, Alec chuckles happily, admitting that he finds those mysteries intriguing. He leaves, locking the door behind him.

After a while, Sandra and David realize that the door is fastened. The situation becomes more ominous when they find John's body crumpled in the Kuwait chest. Sandra's husband has been stabbed to death.

"Did you do it?" queries David, as a quarrel ensues between the lovers. Sandra believes that it must have been Alec who killed John and has trapped them with the corpse to frame them.

Sandra confides that Alec was devoted to her first husband, Barry, perhaps in an unnatural way, and that he has never believed that Barry's death was accidental. David pounds on Sandra and she admits to having pushed Barry over a cliff.

The telephone rings. Hesitant, David picks it up. It is Alec, telling them that the police are on the way. Sandra and David begin to engage in a fierce war of words, gradually exposing layers of hatred rather than love.

There is a knock at the door, and a voice is heard: "Open up. It's the police."

* * *

In contrast to the stark, claustrophobic melodrama of *Rats*, *Afternoon at the Seaside* is a lighthearted, sunny piece taking place on a spacious public beach. "The real charm of *Afternoon at the Seaside*," writes Charles Osborne, "lies in its curiously old-fashioned, pre-war picture of the lower-middle-class relaxing on a crowded beach at a resort called, improbably, Little Slyppings-on-Sea."[1]

The MacGaffin of the play is an emerald necklace stolen by a gang of cat burglars from the Esplanade Hotel. A witness saw a woman sneaking around the bathing huts on the beach and soon Inspector Foley, a tall, uniformed figure, arrives to conduct a search. The prime suspect is an exotic girl wearing a daring bikini and sporting a foreign accent, but she turns out to be a policewoman on the case. Alice Jones fails to find the necklace but wins the heart of a nice young man, Percy Gunner, and helps him escape the clutches of a controlling mother.

The cat burglars masquerade as typical seaside revellers and outwit the authorities by planting the stolen necklace in a sand castle.

* * *

The Patient is set in a nursing home. The title character is Mrs. Jennifer Wingfield, a wealthy socialite totally paralyzed following a recent fall from her second-story balcony.

Inspector Cray, described as "a middle-aged man of delusively mild appearance," is assigned to verify whether Mrs. Wingfield fell accidentally or was pushed. The four people who were at the house at the time of her fall are assembled by the inspector in a private room at the nursing home: Bryan Wingfield, the patient's husband, a womanizing, stocky man of about thirty-five; his young secretary, Brenda Jackson, tall and extremely pretty; William Ross, the patient's brother, short, dark, rather mercurial in temperament; and a sister, Emmeline, a gaunt, grim-faced woman of forty.

The tragic fall occurred in the afternoon, when Jennifer, perpetually sick and fragile, was supposed to be resting in her room. The nurse, Miss Bond, took her off-duty break, so, stresses the inspector, "nobody who was in the house can tell us exactly what happened."

Dr. Ginsberg and the nurse bring the patient in on a trolley. Jennifer's head is visibly bandaged. Her eyes are open but she does not move. Dr.

Ginsberg explains that slight movement was detected in the fingers of the patient's right hand. An electrical apparatus will be placed within reach and Jennifer can answer questions by pressing a lever. The slightest pressure will ignite a red light on top of the contraption.

Dr. Ginsberg ascertains that the bandaged woman understands the proceeding: when an answer to a question is "yes," she will press the lever once; if the answer is "no," she will press it twice.

Through a succession of queries, Jennifer indicates that she was intentionally pushed over the railing of a balcony. By the time the doctor attempts to elicit the name of the person who has done the deed, the patient collapses. The strain of the interview has been too much for her. Dr. Ginsberg suggests that they resume in half an hour.

The high-strung family members confront one another with recriminations. Emmeline reproaches Bryan for having an affair with Brenda, his secretary; he lashes back, pointing out that she is the one who stands to gain by Jennifer's death. They are ushered out to a lobby downstairs.

Dr. Ginsberg and Inspector Cray approach the trolley and thank the patient for her effort. We learn that Jennifer has just regained her power of speech but did not in fact see who pushed her off the balcony. Now comes the crucial moment in the experiment to trap the assailant. "Mrs. Wingfield," says Cray, "we are about to leave you here, apparently unguarded. . . . Someone will almost certainly enter this room. . . . We shall be close at hand."

A figure enters in the dark with a small syringe. The patient calls for help. Cray and Ginsberg rush in. They face Bryan Wingfield's clandestine lover—Nurse Bond.

* * *

Rule of Three premiered in Aberdeen, Scotland, moving to the Duchess Theatre, London, on December 20, 1962. The cast of each of the one-act plays included the same principal thespians—Betty McDowall, Mercy Haystead, David Langdon, and Raymond Bowers. The director was Hubert Gregg, who had previously staged Agatha Christie's *The Hollow* (1951), *The Unexpected Guest* (1959), and *Go Back to Murder* (1960).

The triple bill received assorted reviews, ranging from "as rich and succulent a mixed grill as we've had in the theatre for a long, long time" to "bricks cannot be made without straw, and this commodity Miss [sic] Christie has surprisingly failed to provide."[2] *Rule of Three* ran for ninety-two performances.

In New York, *The Rats* was performed off-off-Broadway at the Impossible Ragtime Theatre on December 11, 1975, while *The Patient* was presented that same week by Lunchtime Theatre. *The Rats* and *The Patient* were united by the Academy Arts Theatre Company in 1977. Food for

Thought exhibited *The Patient* in 2002, *The Rats* in 2003 (with the participation of Kathleen Turner), and *Afternoon at the Seaside* in 2004.
  Acting Edition: Samuel French, Inc.

NOTES

  1. Charles Osborne, *The Life and Crimes of Agatha Christie* (London: Collins, 1982), 198.
  2. Charles Osborne, *The Life and Crimes of Agatha Christie*, 199.

A Case of Libel (1963)

Henry Denker (United States, 1912–)

Inspired by the once-celebrated Quentin Reynolds–Westbrook Pegler lawsuit (as recounted in the first chapter of Louis Nizer's 1961 book *My Life in Court*), *A Case of Libel* is about an ace war correspondent's litigation against a widely syndicated columnist. The names have been changed, but the facts remain true to the real-life case.

The correspondent, Dennis Corcoran, a political liberal, and columnist Boyd Bendix, a right-winger, had once been friends. The relationship sours when Corcoran reviews a biography of Bendix titled *Hangman on Horseback*, which, albeit favorable, points out his faults and eccentricities. Bendix retaliates with a barrage of poisonous columns, questioning Corcoran's patriotism, accusing him of being a war profiteer, and branding him a "drunken, immoral, yellow-bellied degenerate" who engages in sexual vulgarities of all sorts.

Corcoran asks famed attorney Robert Sloane (a fictional name for Louis Nizer) to represent him. Sloane warns him of the danger in taking on the most powerful news syndicate in the world, arguing that it has millions to spend and batteries of the best lawyers on retainer. But Corcoran insists that he is not going "to run and hide."

Reluctantly, Sloane agrees to take the case. In court, a battle royale develops between him and Paul Cleary, Bendix's defense counsel. When Boyd Bendix takes the stand in his own defense, Sloane subjects him to a grueling cross-examination about sex and politics. The clash reaches its boiling point when Sloane waves sheets of paper and quotes passages from articles by Corcoran. Bendix characterizes the quotes as Red propaganda, Communist inspired, not realizing that midway Sloane has begun to quote statements from his own writings.

Sloane coaxes Bendix to declare that the writer of the articles is without a doubt a Communist. Sloane brandishes the papers and submits in evidence "certain writings from the columns of Boyd Bendix!"

The verdict is predictable.

Defendant News International is ordered to pay the plaintiff Dennis Corcoran punitive damages in the sum of $500,000, and Boyd Bendix is to pay him $100,000.

* * *

A Case of Libel, staged by Sam Wanamaker, opened at New York's Longacre Theatre on October 10, 1963. It featured Van Heflin as attorney Sloane, John Randolph as plaintiff Corcoran, Larry Gates as columnist Bendix, and Sidney Blackmer as defense lawyer Cleary.

The reception by the critics was mostly positive. John McClain began his review with a dissertation on the role of courtroom dramas in world theatre "since the first time Portia haggled with Shylock over a pound of Antonio's prime filet" and concluded that "Henry Denker made good use of all these elements in fashioning *A Case of Libel*. . . . This is engrossing stuff, and Mr. Denker has endowed it with the proper amount of hokum. . . . There are a reasonable number of tricks of the trade, employed by the dedicated counsel for the plaintiff, but in the final summation it comes down to the fact that the defendant has been irresponsible in his research and is hence threatening the freedom of the press."[1]

Richard Watts Jr. found "Henry Denker's documentary dramatization of the trial frank in its partisanship, detailed in its report, and, of course, you know how it is going to turn out, but it has the almost inevitable effectiveness of courtroom dramas on the stage and provides the emotional satisfaction of seeing justice score a triumph."[2]

"Despite its periodic flaws, *A Case of Libel* is suspenseful, even if you know how it will turn out," wrote Norman Nadel. "Most of the dialogue—tracing back to Nizer, Pegler, Reynolds and the others in the true case—has an impact and a vividness that set this play above the run of courtroom dramas."[3] Howard Taubman enumerated flaws and virtues in *A Case of Libel*, concluding: "If you're a soft touch for courtroom drama, as I am, and if you enjoy seeing an extremist get his comeuppance, as I do, you should find *A Case of Libel* lively theatre, especially when it warms up to its business."[4]

Walter Kerr hailed the performances of several actors: "Mr. Heflin does not win by a show of power. He wins by fiddling. . . . He is splendid." "Mr. Blackmer is gracious. Mr. Blackmer is genial. Mr. Blackmer is fun." "You will hate Mr. Gates, which is to say he is very good."[5]

In the negative corner was John Chapman, who stated bluntly, "There is a lack of suspense in *A Case of Libel*. . . . In Denker's play—and Denker is a lawyer as well as a dramatist—it is certain that the plaintiff has been libeled before the stage trial begins. So there isn't much for an audience to do but listen as the evidence is carefully built—and I think the audience has reached its decision many scenes before the unseen jury delivers its verdict in the courtroom in the Longacre."[6] Robert Coleman said: "*A Case of Libel* suffers somewhat from being too literal. As George Kelly once pointed out, life itself can be unconvincing behind the footlights."[7]

Henry Denker, a member of the New York bar, had scored previously with the hit military-court drama *Time Limit!* (1956). The civil suit of *A Case of Libel* drew spectators for 242 performances and was adapted to television in 1968 (with Lloyd Bridges as Dennis Corcoran, José Ferrer as Boyd Bendix, and Van Heflin repeating his role of Robert Sloane), and in 1984 (with Gordon Pinsent, Daniel J. Travanti, and Edward Asner).

Acting Edition: Samuel French, Inc.

NOTES

1. *New York Journal-American*, October 11, 1963.
2. *New York Post*, October 11, 1963.
3. *New York World-Telegram*, October 11, 1963.
4. *New York Times*, October 11, 1963.
5. *New York Herald Tribune*, October 11, 1963.
6. *Daily News*, October 11, 1963.
7. *Daily Mirror*, October 11, 1963.

The Murder of Maria Marten, or The Red Barn (1963)

Brian J. Burton (England, 1922–)

Brian J. Burton's musical melodrama *The Murder of Maria Marten, or The Red Barn* is inspired by a true story. Maria Marten, the attractive daughter of a molecatcher, was born in Polstead, Suffolk, England, in 1801. When Maria was twenty-four, she met William Corder, the son of a local farmer, and they had an out-of-wedlock child who died in infancy (later it was rumored that the child was murdered). On Friday, May 18, 1827, Corder suggested to Maria that they elope and get married in London. Maria set out to meet him at the red barn, a local landmark. This was the last time she was seen alive.

For a while it was believed that Maria and Corder lived abroad. Legend has it that Maria's stepmother began to have a recurring dream in which the girl had been murdered and buried in the red barn. Maria's father, Thomas Marten, went to search the barn and discovered there, in a dug hole, the body of his daughter. Corder, who meanwhile had gotten married to someone else in London, was arrested, tried, and convicted of the crime. On August 11, 1928, he was executed at Bury Gaol in front of a huge crowd.

Many plays have been written about the case, penned by anonymous hands. Even during the sensational trial of Corder, *The Late Murder of Maria Marten* was produced in Polstead. At Weymouth, playgoers flocked to see the lurid *The Red Barn, or The Gypsy's Curse*. London had two versions running simultaneously, *Advertisement for Wives*, and *The Red Barn, or The Mysterious Murder*. A four-act melodrama, *Red Barn, or The Prophetic Dream*, was presented at Lincoln in 1830. Maria Marten's death was the most frequently performed topic of plays in nineteenth-century England.

During the 1920s, several theatrical treatments of the case were again mounted in London. An anonymous version, *Maria Marten, or The Murder in the Red Barn*, was presented, for one performance, at the Globe Theatre on November 29, 1925. William Corder was played by Robert Atkins and

Maria Marten by Jack Hobbs. The same cast appeared, for two performances, in a revival at the Globe the following year. In 1927, Tom Slaughter staged *Maria Marten* at South London's Elephant Theatre, where it
played to packed houses for five months.[1] A new adaptation, by Frank
H. Fortescue, was produced at the Royal Theatre on March 10, 1928, for
twelve showings. Edmund Blake portrayed Corder and Peggy Mortimer
enacted Maria. On November 24, 1942, another anonymous replica of the
play, directed by Alec Clunes, opened at the Arts Theatre, featuring Julian
Somer (William Corder), Joanna Horder (Maria Marten), and Richard
Attenborough (Tim Bobbin). On July 11, 1951, the Old Vic presented one
midnight performance of Alfred Denville's version of the play, directed
by Russell Thorndike, who also starred as William Corder.

Surprisingly, there have been few published manuscripts of *Maria
Marten*. The first printed version was that of a short one-act, called *Maria
Martin* (note the spelling of the surname), *or The Murder in the Red Barn*,
performed at the Star Theatre, Swanson, England, in 1842. A version
by Montague Slater, in 1928, had the ghost of Maria appear at the scaf-
fold, frightening Corder before he is hung. Written and directed by Alec
Clunes, *Maria Marten; Or, The Murder in the Old Red Barn* opened at London's Arts Theatre on December 19, 1952, and ran for forty-five performances. A one-act by Constance Cox, *Maria Marten, or Murder in the Red
Barn*, won the Advanced Cup and the Highest Marks in the 1969 Drama
Festival of the Sussex Federation, and was published that year by Samuel
French, Inc. The entire action of this playlet unfolds outside the Martens'
cottage. In the climax, William Corder dooms himself with a slip of the
tongue, mentioning that the body of Maria is buried "in the old Red Barn"
though no one had mentioned that fact to him before.

Brian J. Burton's treatment of the subject, "based on various anonymous
Victorian texts" and peppered with songs, was first published in 1964
and went through two revisions. The curtain rises on the village green
at Polstead, Suffolk, during an afternoon in the 1820s. At center stage is
a maypole, around which young villagers are dancing. Sisters Maria and
Ann Marten are partnered with Johnny Badger and Tim Bobbin. Soon
the group exits to Thomas Marten's cottage for food and drinks. Maria
remains behind, and sitting on a bench establishes the presentational style
of the proceedings by breaking through the fourth wall and addressing
the audience directly. The young, pretty girl confides that though Johnny
Badger is "the most gentle and kind of men," she is not in love with him
and hopes to someday meet "a handsome, wealthy gentleman" whom
she will marry and live happily with for the rest of her days.

Enter Nell Hatfield, a middle-aged gypsy. She asks Maria for some
water as she walked twenty miles today in the hot sun. When Maria exits
to fetch water, Nell moves downstage and tells the viewers that she came

to Polstead in her quest to avenge the death of her little sister, Zella, who perished heartbroken and neglected at the hands of a dastardly seducer. Nell's brother, Pharos, is also seeking vengeance on the villain who had ruined their dear sister.

Maria returns with food and drink. The outline of a revenge plot crosses the gypsy's mind. She reads Maria's palm and predicts a fortunate marriage to a young, handsome, and rich man. Maria sings "Love at Last," looking forward to "the joy of living true love can impart."

In an aside, Nell reveals that the first part of her plan has been carried out. She will now seek out the villain, William Corder, and will lead him on, step by step, "until he mounts the scaffold."

Later that day, in a clearing of an adjacent wood, Nell awaits William Corder. The suave, mustached aristocrat enters. He croons "Three Hisses of Villainy," in which he boasts that

> No maiden is safe within miles of me
> For I simply revel in salacity . . .
> Infamy, perfidy, carnality,
> Lechery, treachery, dishonesty,
> All these I practice with dexterity.

Nell draws Corder's attention to the lovely Maria Marten, elder daughter of old Thomas Marten, the molecatcher. Rumor has it, says the gypsy, that Maria is enamored with the handsome Corder.

A week later, the day of the Polstead Fair, Corder introduces himself to Maria as the son of her father's landlord, and confesses to being in love with her. "Nonsense, do not be so foolish," says Maria, but her heart is thumping—all is happening as the gypsy predicted. Corder promises Maria marriage and "the gay sights of London—the balls, the concerts, the theatres and all the joys that make life worth living."

Twelve months later Corder asks the gypsy Nell to procure poison for him. The illegitimate child that Maria bore him must die, before the villagers find out about it. He will bury it in the woods. Nell, exalted, tells the audience, "now my revenge is about to triumph."

Inside her cottage, Maria bemoans, "I am a betrayed, ruined woman scorned by all who know my shame." She sits beside the cradle of her sick child and sings "Deserted and Lonely." Her sister Ann and her beau Tim arrive for a visit, followed by her parents, and they all fall into each other's arms crying.

Later in the day, Corder enters. He tells Maria that he brought with him medicine prepared by the village apothecary. Maria fetches a spoon and administers the drops to the baby. She soon realizes that the infant is dead. She checks the medicine bottle and sees to her horror that it is marked "poison." Corder curses in an aside the gypsy woman who has

MT. LEBANON PUBLIC LIBRARY

labeled the bottle thus, then strikes his head with his hands and cries in an assumed anguish that it was all a dreadful mistake: when he purchased the medicine for the child he also acquired some poison for rats; it was the rat poison that he gave Maria by error. They must now bury the child secretly "where none will find it."

At night, under a dim moonlight, Corder returns to the woods with a spade. He is followed by Maria who is clasping a small bundle. He begins to dig, assures Maria that "the child will sleep peacefully here as in a graveyard," puts the bundle in the hole and covers it over. Maria kneels with a prayer, but Corder rushes her away.

Murder begets murder. Corder overhears Nell telling her brother Pharos Lee that she is aware of the murder of the baby and is intent to notify the law. He corners the gypsy woman, produces a pistol, and shoots her to death. And when the blackguard discovers that Maria has been making inquiries of the apothecary, he entices her to meet him at a local landmark, the old, isolated red barn, where he shoots her and disposes of the body in a deeply dug grave so that "no clue will then remain to risk discovery."

The murder of Maria Marten would have remained a mystery if it weren't for a nightmare dreamed by her mother. The dream is made visible to the audience. Accompanied by soft music, the lights fade up slowly on the interior of the red barn. Corder and Maria are seen in a mimed quarrel. He draws a pistol and shoots her. He then drags the body and is about to lower it into a grave when Mrs. Marten wakes with a scream.

Thomas Marten and Tim Bobbin search the red barn, find a stained spade, a discarded pistol, and Maria's necktie.[2] They dig feverishly and discover the body. At first horrified, Marten recovers and vows to bring the murderer to justice. He rushes off. In a comedic bit, Tim realizes that he is alone by the grave, calls out "Don't leave me," and runs to the door.

The play could have ended soon thereafter, but playwright Burton borrows from the real-life case one more plot maneuver: William Corder advertises in the *Times* for a wife and gets married to a woman running a boardinghouse. This does not sway him from flirting with his newly engaged household maid, Alice Rumble. He calls Alice "a comely wench" and places her onto his knee. She struggles to get away when the doorbell chimes. At the door is Pharos Lee, who introduces himself as a Bow Street Officer and charges Corder with the murder of Maria Marten. Lee announces that following the death of his sister Nell, he swore vengeance and joined the Law to complete his task. He handcuffs Corder and leads him to the Lambeth Police Office.[3]

In a cell for the condemned, several weeks later, Corder falls asleep and Maria's spirit appears. "Thy poor Maria pities and forgives thee—her murderer," says the specter. Touched, Corder writes rapidly on a piece of paper. When Lee arrives at the hour of the execution, Corder gives him the paper, falls on his knees, and says, "This is my confession. I am—I am the murderer of Maria Marten. . . . May innocence and virtue pray for the peace of my departing soul."

A bell tolls as the curtain descends.

* * *

Brian J. Burton's *The Murder of Maria Marten, or The Red Barn* was first presented by the White Rose Repertory Company at the Opera House, Harrogate, England, in December 1963. A revised version of the play premiered at the Leicester Little Theatre on November 9, 1964. The lead roles were played by Tony Ward (William Corder) and Penelope Clarke (Maria Marten). A second revised version, directed by the author, premiered at the Swan Theatre, Worcester, England, on December 6, 1978, featuring Peter Jones (William Corder) and Chris Carmichael (Maria Marten).

Burton inserted detailed production notes in the published acting version of his play. He warns performers to avoid a style of mockery or burlesque: "The audience must never be aware that you are laughing at the characters being portrayed. . . . Movement and gesture should be exaggerated rather like the old silent films. . . . There should be a good overall pace so that the audience are not allowed to realize how absurd the situation is before they are whisked on to the next improbability. . . . As with other melodramas played today, audience participation is essential and should be encouraged by every possible means."[4]

The Maria Marten case was the topic of several motion pictures made during the silent era, notably 1928's *Maria Marten*, produced in England under the direction of Walter West, featuring Warwick Ward (William Corder) and Trilby Clark (Maria Marten). A sixty-five-minute version, *Murder in the Red Barn*, was filmed in 1935, directed by Milton Rosmer and starring Tom Slaughter and Sophie Stewart. The British Board of Film Censors passed it on the condition that the execution scene be eliminated. When distributed in the United States, scenes emphasizing Maria's pregnancy were cut. A fictionalized account of the murder was aired in 1953 by the CBS radio series "Crime Classics." BBC televised *Maria Marten* in 1980, with Kevin McNally as Corder and Pippa Guard as Maria. Musicians inspired by the incident include the Albion Country Band, who in 1971 included the song "Murder of Maria Marten" in their album *No Roses*; Tom Waits, whose song "Murder in the Red Barn" is part of the 1992 album *Bone Machine*; and Kathryn Roberts and Sean Lakeman, with "The Red Barn" included in their 2004 release, *Album 2*.

The Swavesey Village College Theatre Company, in Swavesey, Cambridgeshire, England, mounted *Murder in the Red Barn*, by John Latimer, in 2000, and revived the production for a tour in 2006, to critical acclaim and several awards, including a Best Actress nod for Kate Summers in the role of Maria Marten at the Cambridge Drama Festival. In its sixty-fourth year, The Blackburn Drama Club of Blackburn, Lancashire, England, presented a new version of *Maria Marten: Murder in the Red Barn*, by Paul Mason, at the Thwaltes Empire Theatre, December 3–6, 2008.

* * *

Brian J. Burton was born in Birmingham, England, in 1922. He started acting at the age of twelve and directed his first play when he was sixteen, the same year he wrote his first full-length play. Since then he has been active in various areas of theatre as actor, director, stage manager, lecturer, teacher, and drama critic. He was art director of the Crescent Theatre in Birmingham for four years.

In addition to *The Murder of Maria Marten, or The Red Barn*, Burton's often-performed melodramas include *Sweeney Todd the Barber* (1962), which he adapted from George Dibdin Pitt's Victorian version of the legendary drama; *East Lynne, or Lady Isabel's Shame* (1965), based on the 1861 best-selling novel by Mrs. Henry Wood (1814–1887), a tale of jealousy, deceit, and murder; *Lady Audley's Secret, or Death in Lime Tree Walk* (1966), from the popular 1862 novel by Mary Elizabeth Braddon (1837–1915), focusing on an ambitious, unscrupulous woman who, in order to climb up society's ladder, is prepared to murder her husband and plant his body in the garden well; and *The Drunkard, or Down with Demon Drink!* (1969), a temperance tearjerker based on a nineteenth-century play by William Henry Smith (1806–1872).

Burton's *Three Hisses for Villainy!!!* (1979), subtitled *An Evening of Victorian Entertainment*, contains three short original melodramas with popular themes of the genre. *One Month to Pay, or The Sailor's Return* focuses on the traditional battle between a wicked landlord who carries a riding crop and a beautiful, helpless wife. Another long-suffering wife is the heroine of *The Drunkard's Wife, or The Tables Turned*. A young fortune-telling gypsy girl falls prey to the machinations of an aristocratic country squire in *The Gypsy Curse, or The Flower of the Tribe*.

More original one-act melodramas by Burton are featured in *Cheers, Tears and Screamers!!* (1982) and in *Foiled Again!* (1989), proving that virtue, of course, triumphs in the end. In *Murder Play* (1981), a scorned wife kills her husband with a hat pin. *Being of a Sound Mind* (1981) is the story of a London couple who rent a cottage in France for a holiday and find themselves in the center of terrifying events. *Ghost of a Chance* (1985) is a haunted house yarn.

Acting Edition: Combridge Jackson Ltd.

NOTES

1. Tom Slaughter (1885–1956) was an English actor best known for playing melodramatic villains on stage and screen. Born as Norman Carter Slaughter in Newcastle, he launched his stage career at the age of twenty, initially playing leading man roles and young heroes like Sherlock Holmes and d'Artagnan in *The Three Musketeers*. During World War I he served in the Royal Flying Corps. After the war, he managed several theatres and established a company that concentrated on Victorian blood-and-thunder melodramas. In 1931 he won acclaim playing Long John Silver in *Treasure Island* and body snatcher William Hare in *The Crimes of Burke and Hare*. Soon thereafter he garnered kudos in the title role of *Sweeney Todd, the Demon Barber of Fleet Street*, and, like Lon Chaney, Boris Karloff, and Bela Lugosi, his subsequent career became geared to macabre fare. During World War II he appeared on stage performing *Jack the Ripper, Landru*, and *Dr. Jekyll and Mr. Hyde*. In 1935, Slaughter made his first motion picture, *Maria Marten, or Murder in the Red Barn*, in the role of William Corder, and the following year reprised on screen another of his stage triumphs, *Sweeney Todd, The Demon Barber of Fleet Street*. Adding to his gallery of flamboyant villains was *The Crimes of Stephen Hawke* (1936), in which Slaughter portrays a kind moneylender by day who, masquerading as the Spine Breaker, is a ruthless murderer by night. In *The Ticket-of-Leave Man* (1937), Slaughter appears as an archcriminal concocting a bank robbery, while in *Sexton Blake and the Hooded Terror* (1938) he is The Snake, the elusive leader of a band of masked criminals. *Crimes at the Dark House* (1939), loosely based on Wilkie Collins' *The Woman in White*, has Slaughter as the cunning Sir Henry Glyde, who disposes of his wealthy wife and replaces her with a look-alike. In *The Face at the Window* (1939), Slaughter leads a double life as a Parisian aristocrat and as the notorious killer nicknamed The Wolf. He returned to the character of Sweeney Todd in *Bothered by a Beard* (1945) and to the role of a grave robber in *The Greed of William Hart* (1948).

2. In the real-life case of Maria Marten, during the inquest her sister Ann identified the victim's hair and some clothing. The tooth she was known to be missing was also missing from the jawbone of the corpse. One of the pieces of evidence to implicate Corder in the crime was his green handkerchief, discovered around the body's neck.

3. In the real-life case, the arresting officer of William Corder was a member of the London police force named James Lea.

4. Brian J. Burton, *The Murder of Maria Marten, or The Red Barn*, 2nd ed. (Birmingham, England: Combridge Jackson Ltd., 1980), 60.

Hostile Witness (1964)

Jack Roffey (England)

While not on a par with such milestone courtroom dramas as *On Trial* (1914), *The Trial of Mary Dugan* (1927), or *Witness for the Prosecution* (1953), *Hostile Witness* rewards its viewers with colorful glimpses of the pomp and ceremony of the British judicial system, the unusual dilemma of a famous barrister finding himself accused of murder, and a last-minute surprise resolution.

Hostile Witness premiered in Brighton, England, in 1964, moved to London in 1965, and came to New York in 1966, starring Ray Milland as Simon Crawford, Q.C., a no-nonsense lawyer. Crawford is a widower. Some months ago his daughter Jill was killed by a hit-and-run driver. In his grief, Crawford swore that he would find the driver and kill him.

Allegedly, the driver was a neighbor, Judge Anthony Gregory, who is found lying dead on the floor of his study with a knife in the chest. Crawford maintains that someone attacked him that night, on the way home, and knocked him out by bashing the back of his head. However, Crawford is incriminated by overwhelming physical evidence. His fingerprints are found on the fatal weapon, scrapings from the dead man's nails show fibers and threads identical with his overcoat, patches of blood on the coat correspond with the blood type of the deceased, Group A.

Crawford's defense attorney, Sir Peter Grossman, counters the prosecution's witnesses with a theory of his own: suppose someone was waiting in the shadows that night for Crawford to return home, and hit him on the back of his head as he was about to open his front door. Suppose he or she then carried or dragged him into the judge's house where the judge was already lying dead—or alternatively brought the necessary objects out into the mews—pressed Crawford's hands round the knife with which the old man had been killed, then scraped the dead man's hands down the coat Crawford was carrying, so that fibers and threads from it lodged beneath the torn nails. In that case blood would have been transferred onto the coat itself for all to see. Would not the scientific evidence available in those circumstances be identical with the scientific evidence now being produced by the Crown?

When Crawford insists on calling a witness to establish his alibi, Sir Peter withdraws from the case. Crawford undertakes his own defense with the help of his junior assistants, but his alibi is shattered by the calculation of Daylight Saving Time.

Just when the situation seems hopeless and Crawford's team believes that "he hasn't a ghost of a chance," a connection is established to the case of a convict named John Logan who, before being taken to prison on an armed robbery charge, pointed at Mr. Justice Gregory and at prosecuting counsel Mr. Crawford and threatened to kill both of them. Crawford cannot recall what Logan looked like, but he remembers that the man was color-blind. That's what led to his arrest. The driver of the getaway car was injured by an enemy's bombing raid, so Logan drove the car himself. Being color-blind, he drove through a red light and was stopped by the police. It was only a routine stop, but they saw the injured driver in the back—and that was that.

Logan's affliction is instrumental in identifying him when Crawford summons his chief of staff, Charles Milburn, to the stand. Milburn delivered to chambers a letter in an envelope typed in red and admits that he is color-blind. Under Crawford's pounding cross-examination, Milburn makes a crucial slip of the tongue when he blurts that he could not be Logan, as Logan is dead. Crawford jumps at him with the query, "How do you know that Logan is dead?"

Milburn breaks down and admits that he is Logan. He became a clerk in Crawford's chambers and for years studied his employer and Judge Gregory. When Crawford's daughter was killed in a car accident, he saw his opportunity.

"That is the case for the Defense," says Crawford, and the curtain descends.

* * *

Hostile Witness opened at the Music Box Theatre in New York on February 17, 1966, and was greeted with hostility by critics Douglas Watt, who found it "so rickety and inept a piece of playwriting that the bubbles have turned to vinegar long before the payoff, which is, of course, merely arbitrary,"[1] and John McClain, who sniffed, "This is a singularly sad occasion. . . . I'm afraid it will take a hung jury to save it from early execution."[2]

Other critics, however, welcomed the play. "Jack Roffey's *Hostile Witness* is strictly courtroom fun and games of the don't-you-believe-it-for-a-moment variety, and as such it's pleasantly tricky entertainment," wrote Walter Kerr.[3] "Sturdy and serviceable . . . has the necessary cliff-hangers at curtain times and the necessary credible twist at the end," stated Stanley Kauffman.[4]

Hostile Witness ran on Broadway for 157 performances. In his introduction to the Samuel French acting edition, playwright Jack Roffey maintains that "stock companies and amateurs are the life-blood of the theatre," but the sixteen speaking roles, courtroom extras, three sets, and wigs and gowns, place this play beyond reach of most shoe-string troupes.

Jack Roffey penned the screenplay of *Hostile Witness*. The movie was distributed in 1968, with Ray Milland directing and repeating his stage role as Simon Crawford. Roffey also collaborated on the scripting of the whodunit *Eight O'Clock Walk* (1953), about a London taxi driver, played by Richard Attenborough, who is accused of murdering a little girl.

During the 1950s and 1960s, Roffey, a real-life court official, contributed numerous suspenseful episodes to the British television series *Boyd Q.C.* (1956–1964), in which barrister Richard Boyd, a counterpart of the American Perry Mason, appeared in court as counsel for the defense. Notable among Boyd's cases were *By Gas: That's Murder*, *The Open and Shut Case*, *Nylon Spells Murder*, *Thread of Evidence*, and *The Case of the Lazy Eye*. Simultaneously, Roffey had three criminous plays produced in London: *No Other Verdict* (1953), *Night of the Fourth* (1956), and *Justice Is a Woman* (1966), the latter starring Flora Robson as a Queen's Counsel called upon to defend an English boy accused of murder.

Acting Edition: Samuel French, Inc. (in manuscript form). *Hostile Witness* is also included in *Ten Classic Mystery and Suspense Plays of the Modern Theatre*, edited by Stanley Richards (New York: Dodd, Mead, 1973).

NOTES

1. *Daily News*, February 18, 1966.
2. *New York Journal-American*, February 18, 1966.
3. *New York Herald Tribune*, February 18, 1966.
4. *New York Times*, February 18, 1966.

Blues for Mr. Charlie (1964)

James Baldwin (United States, 1924–1987)

James Baldwin's *Blues for Mr. Charlie*[1] begins with a murder. The curtain rises on a dark stage and we hear a shot. Lights come up slowly on Lyle Britten as he looks around, bends down, and picks up the body of Richard Henry. As he carries Henry off, Lyle mumbles, "And may every nigger like this nigger end like this nigger face down in the weeds."

Lyle Britten is a white grocery-store owner in a small town, circa the 1960s. Richard Henry was a young, rebellious African American musician who went north, became a junkie, kicked the habit, and returned home. The murder scene will be repeated several times as the play progresses through a series of flashbacks in which the action moves between past and present.

A skeletal set divides the proceedings between Whitetown and Blacktown. The action among the whites takes place on one side of the stage, the action among the blacks on the other. The church is divided by an aisle. The courthouse is segregated.

Reverend Meridian Henry, the father of Richard, returns home from a rally, accompanied by his students. They are exhausted, disheveled, wounded. They carry placards bearing such statements as "Freedom now"; "One man, one vote"; "We want the murderer." Pete, a militant student, wonders how the authorities will explain "what Richard's body was doing in them weeds." Reverend Henry says that he'll not rest "until they bring my son's murderer to trial," but the student Lorenzo complains that "the cops ain't going to protect us," and reminds the reverend that the suspected killer, Lyle Britten, once killed another black man and "the sheriff just shoveled the body into the ground and forgot about it."

A friendly white man, Parnell James, editor of the local newspaper, enters and informs the group that a warrant has been issued for Lyle's arrest. Juanita Harmon, lover of the deceased, pooh-poohs the possibility that Lyle will be convicted.

In Whitetown, Parnell pays a visit to Lyle's home. Lyle is playing with his infant son, whom he soon hands over to his wife, Josephine, for a change of diapers. Parnell tells Lyle that he'll soon be arrested, for according to the testimony of Joel Davis, otherwise known as Papa D, the owner of the local juke joint, Lyle was the last person to see Richard alive. Lyle says calmly that he is not concerned; Richard was probably killed by "some other nigger, they do it all the time."

In a flashback, Richard tells his grandmother, Wilhelmina Henry, of his suspicion that his late mother did not fall down hotel steps by accident, but was pushed by a white man. Grandma Henry maintains that the steps were slippery and that her daughter fell. "You can't start walking around believing that all the suffering in the world is caused by white folks," she states. Richard contends that "the only way the black man's going to get any power is to drive all the white men into the sea." He takes a small sawed-off pistol from his pocket and announces, "This gun goes everywhere I go."

At Papa D's tavern, Richard, Juanita, and Pete sit at a table. Over loud music, Juanita tells Richard, who has been away in New York for eight years, that Lyle Britten shot a black man a few years back and nothing was done about it. Pete explains that the victim was Bill Walker, whom everybody called Old Bill. Bill's wife, "a pretty little thing," was coveted by Lyle. Following Bill's death, his wife disappeared, went North somewhere. Richard chats about his New York experience, living in bohemian Greenwich Village, and describes his conquest of "a whole gang of white chicks." Richard exhibits girls' pictures and says, "I take their money and they love it." Papa D comes over nervously and requests that Richard put the pictures away. As they eat and drink, Richard confesses that he was addicted to dope, got busted, but has since recovered.

Richard and Juanita go to the dance floor when Lyle Britten enters and crosses to the counter. He gets cigarettes out of the machine, watches the dancers for a moment, and on the way out jostles Juanita. Richard and Lyle stare at each other. Lyle apologizes and exits.

In a shift to the present, Parnell advises Reverend Henry that circumstantial evidence is not reliable and there's no proof that Lyle Britten killed Richard. He has known Lyle for many years and he does not believe that he is a wicked man. The truth will come out in the trial. However, Henry feels that the jury will never convict Lyle.

In church, Reverend Phelps assures Lyle that he is supported by every white person in town. A member of the congregation, Ellis, complains that there is an attempt "to put niggers on the jury." Parnell opines that this is only fair as the town's population is 44 percent black. Josephine Britten corners Parnell and asks him about the rumors that her husband lusted after Old Bill's wife and that's why he shot the old man. She's puzzled about the attraction of white men to women of color. Parnell confides to Josephine that when he was eighteen years old he fell in love with an adolescent black girl, Pearl. One day they were sitting in the library kissing, when Pearl's mother came in. The mother didn't say a word, took her daughter by the hand, and they left. He never saw Pearl again. Her mother sent her away. If he ever found Pearl again he'd marry her.

Josephine becomes agitated: if Lyle felt that way about Old Bill's wife, he could have shot him, and if he could have killed Old Bill, he could also have killed Richard.

That evening Parnell goes to Lyle's store and asks him point blank about Willa Mae, Old Bill's wife. Lyle, a little inebriated, admits that he had a liaison with Willa Mae, who was much younger than her sixty-year-old husband. At first he took her by force, but later "she liked it as much as me." Lyle believes that it was Papa D who told Old Bill of the affair. He noticed that the old man began looking at him murderously. Parnell prods Lyle for more details, but Lyle says nothing.

A crucial flashback unfolds in the Britten store. Lyle is hammering nails in the back, fixing the baby's carriage, and Josephine is minding the store when Richard and his friend Lorenzo enter from the road and purchase two bottles of Coca Cola. "That will be twenty cents," says Josephine. Richard says that all he has is a twenty-dollar bill. Josephine calls Lyle, who enters carrying the hammer. A quarrel ensues, leading to a physical confrontation. As Lyle raises the hammer, Richard grabs his arm and knocks Lyle down. Richard chuckles, "Now, who do you think is the better man? Ha-ha! The master race!" He points at Josephine and smirks: "You let me in that tired white chick's drawers, she'll know who's the master!" He walks out laughing, followed by Lorenzo.

The proceedings now take place in the courtroom, two months later. Attending the segregated hearings are black and white townspeople, the jury, journalists, photographers. Scattered about are television cameras and microphones. The judge's chair is center stage, the witness stand downstage. The playwright suggests that each witness be revealed behind a scrim when called. The testimonies are supported by flashback episodes. [2]

The first witness called by the state is Josephine Britten, wife of the accused. She relates the incident in which Richard Henry came to the store to buy two Cokes. "He acted like he was drunk or crazy or maybe he was under the influence of dope," she says, and adds that Richard pushed himself against her "real close and hard," behaving "like an animal." When her husband, Lyle, came to her rescue, Richard and his friend jumped on him and knocked him down. She and Lyle decided not to report the incident because there was already so much trouble in town. On the morning of August 24, the day Richard was found dead, she and her husband were at home.

The clerk calls Joel Davis to the stand. Davis ("Papa D") testifies that
Lyle and Richard clashed face-to-face in his juke joint, after which he
never saw the boy again, and he has no doubt that Lyle killed him.
Juanita Harmon concurs. By the time she persuaded Richard to take her
away "from this terrible place," it was too late. Lyle killed him "like they
been killing all our men, for years, for generations!" Wilhelmina Henry
denies that her grandson carried a gun or that he was ever under the
influence of hard drugs. Under cross-examination, Reverend Meridian
Henry rejects the supposition that his son was a pimp, dope addict, and
rapist. Editor Parnell James testifies of his awareness that racial dynam-
ics have been greatly strained of late, but to his knowledge the black
population has not armed itself. As to the accusation by Mrs. Britten of
Richard's misbehavior, it may be, says Parnell, that she misconstrued
the boy's actions; he had been in the North for a long time, his manner
was free and bold.

After deliberating, the foreman of the jury announces, "Not guilty,
Your Honor," and there's cheering in Whitetown. Lyle is congratulated
and embraced. The stage is taken over by reporters, photographers,
townspeople. Slowly they file out until only a few people remain on
stage. Reverend Henry approaches Lyle and asks, "Did you kill him? . . .
What was the last thing my son said to you before you shot him down
like a dog?" A flashback illustrates the final encounter between Lyle and
Richard on the road outside Papa D's joint. Lyle demands that Richard
apologize for insulting his wife the other day. Richard refuses and Lyle
insists, producing a gun. Richard flashes with anger, calls Lyle "sick," and
goes into a tirade about white women. Lyle shoots. Richard cries "Juanita!
Daddy! Mama!" and falls.

The play ends on an ominous note when Reverend Henry says to his
students, "You know, for us, it all began with the Bible and the gun.
Maybe it will end with the Bible and the gun." He announces that he has
kept Richard's gun in the pulpit, under the Bible.

* * *

Blues for Mr. Charlie was the first Broadway play to express black mili-
tancy.[3] Produced by the Actors Studio, it opened at the ANTA Theatre on
April 23, 1964. Burgess Meredith directed a glittering cast that included
Rip Torn (Lyle Britten), Ann Wedgeworth (Josephine Britten), Al Free-
man Jr. (Richard Henry), Percy Rodriguez (Reverend Meridian Henry),
Rosetta Le Noire (Mother Henry), Diana Sands (Juanita), Pat Hingle
(Parnell James), and future stars Ralph Waite and Jon Don Baker in small
roles. Scenery and lighting were designed by Feder.

The morning-after reviewers were divided. Leonard Harris lauded
playwright Baldwin for refusing "to create abstract symbols, Negro or

white. All his people have blood, and when that blood spills, it makes you want to cry rather than picket." Harris also commended the technique of maneuvering "movements forward and backward in time" with ease and lucidity. "His dramatic situation is lively and builds in intensity," wrote Harris.[4] Howard Taubman also liked the use of "a free form which weaves in and out of the present and the past" in a play penned "with fire of fury in its belly, tears of anguish in its eyes and a roar of protest in its throat."[5]

On the other hand, Richard Watts Jr. believed that "the play's technique, which includes flashbacks and occasional speeches and meditations directly aimed at the audience, hasn't been quite mastered. . . . It makes for initial confusion. . . . Mr. Baldwin remains essentially a novelist."[6] John McClain asserted that "the civil rights issue is certainly the most important problem facing our nation today and I'm afraid that James Baldwin's *Blues for Mr. Charlie* doesn't have the size to advance the cause appreciably. . . . For reasons which I found difficult to understand, most of the story is told in reverse, or certainly in the most confusing order. . . . It seemed a cumbersome way to tell a plot which could just have easily followed a chronological pattern."[7] John Chapman admired Baldwin's hopes for "harmonious life between colored and white people," but believed that the playwright's methods as a dramatist were "oddly anachronistic. . . . *Blues for Mr. Charlie* has been couched in the scenery-chewing terms of the turn of the century. . . . As the play digs into a rather obvious story of Southern justice, it doesn't dig in a straight line; it zigs and zags and meanders through a series of flashbacks and flashforwards which makes it difficult to remember whether a certain character is supposed to be dead or alive."[8]

The production elements were universally admired. Walter Kerr applauded "a few most intelligently used geometric designs under the ghostly spill of light magnetically arranged by Feder" and declared that "Burgess Meredith has directed superbly."[9] The cast was hailed by the entire cadre of critics.

Blues for Mr. Charlie ran for 148 performances. In summing up the theatrical season in New York, Otis L. Guernsey Jr. wrote in *The Best Plays of 1963–1964*: "Instead of presenting us with a well-behaved Negro who is unjustly killed by a bigoted white man, Mr. Baldwin offers us a young militant, who, on returning South from New York, feels compelled to assert himself by using bad language and publicly mocking and insulting the whites. . . . One feels that this man, Richard, is the natural reaction to a long period in which previous generations of Negroes persisted up a blind alley of patience and hope. That generation is represented by Richard's father, the Reverend Meridian Henry, who now finds himself questioning Christianity."[10]

MT. LEBANON PUBLIC LIBRARY

Blues for Mr. Charlie came to London in 1965 and drew a hostile reaction from the critics. The *Times* of London said that the playwright was "exchanging creative writing for demagogic oratory" and that the Actors Studio's company "far from deepening the play, were broadening and coarsening it even more."[11] The *Financial Times* complained that "throughout the whole first act the players gave a display of uniformly bad acting."[12] The *Daily Mail* called the Actors Studio display of method acting "a sorry disappointment."[13] Lee Strasberg, the artistic director of the Actors Studio, said at a press conference that "the unclarity was partially our fault, partially the author's."

* * *

James Arthur Baldwin was born to a poor family in Harlem, New York, in 1924. His adoptive father, David Baldwin, was a preacher. Baldwin attended DeWitt Clinton High School in the Bronx, where he wrote for the school magazine. At the age of fourteen, Baldwin joined the Pentecostal Church and became a child preacher, but at seventeen he turned away from his religion and moved to Greenwich Village, a bohemian neighborhood in Manhattan. He studied at the New School and began writing essays, book reviews, and short stories.

A homosexual, Baldwin became disillusioned by American prejudice against blacks and gays, and in 1948 departed for Paris, France, where he was soon embedded in the cultural radicalism of the Left Bank and contributed articles to various literary magazines, most notably *Zero: A Review of Literature and Art*.

During the 1950s, Baldwin published his autobiographical novel, *Go Tell It on the Mountain* (1953); a first collection of essays, *Notes of a Native Son* (1955), the title referring to his mentor Richard Wright, author of the novel *Native Son*; and a second novel, *Giovanni's Room* (1956), controversial due to its homoerotic content. In the 1960s, Baldwin wrote mainly about the restive civil rights movement. His lengthy essay *No Name in the Street* discussed the assassination of his personal friends Medgar Evers, Malcolm X, and Martin Luther King Jr. In the 1970s, Baldwin penned two novels, *If Beale Street Could Talk* and *Just above My Head*, advocating the importance of nurturing black families, and a series of essays offering provocative studies of American society through an analysis of various motion pictures, including *A Tale of Two Cities, You Only Live Once, Dead End, Rebel without a Cause, The Birth of a Nation, In the Heat of the Night, In This Our Life, The Defiant Ones, Home of the Brave*, and *Guess Who's Coming to Dinner*. In the 1980s, Baldwin concluded his literary career with a nonfiction book, *The Evidence of Things Not Seen*, covering the Atlanta child murders. He focused on the two-year period

1979–1981, during which at least twenty-eight African Americans were murdered in Atlanta, Georgia.

Politically, Baldwin aligned himself with the ideals of the Congress of Racial Equality (CORE). In 1963, along with prominent figures like Harry Belafonte and Lorraine Hansberry, Baldwin met with then attorney general Robert F. Kennedy to voice the concerns of the black community. He appeared at the civil rights march in Washington, D.C., on August 28, 1963, accompanied by Belafonte, Sidney Poitier, and Marlon Brando. Among Baldwin's associates and friends were fellow writers Langston Hughes and Maya Angelou, singer Nina Simone, and French painter Philippe Derome.

Besides *Blues for Mr. Charlie*, Baldwin's only other contribution to the Broadway scene was the drama *The Amen Corner*, previously produced at Howard University (1953) and at the Robertson Playhouse in Los Angeles, California (1964). It arrived at the Ethel Barrymore Theatre on April 15, 1965. The protagonist of *The Amen Corner* is Margaret Alexander, the pastor of a small church in Harlem. Margaret loses her son, husband, and congregation before realizing that in her fervent devotion to the service of God, she neglected her duty to her family. Bea Arthur enacted Sister Margaret. Frank Silvera produced and directed. Howard Taubman said in the *New York Times*, "The structure of the play is elementary. The characterization is halting, and points are made obviously and repetitively," but the critic asserted that the play "throws some light on the barrenness of the lives of impoverished Negroes who seek surcease from their woes in religion."[14] *The Amen Corner* ran for eighty-four performances and, headed by Claudia McNeil in the role of Sister Margaret, went on an extensive tour to Vienna, Paris, Zurich, Amsterdam, Rotterdam, Munich, Turin, Milan, Budapest, Tel Aviv, and the Edinburgh Festival in Scotland.

Baldwin died on November 30, 1987, from esophageal cancer in Saint-Paul de Vence, France. He was buried at Ferncliff Cemetery in Hartsdale, near New York City. More than twenty years later, in 2010, Pantheon Books published *The Cross of Redemption*, a 300-page assembly of previously uncollected Baldwin speeches, book reviews, lectures, letters, and essays. Reviewing the book in the *Los Angeles Times*, English professor Lynell George writes of Baldwin: "Language written and spoken was his blade, and it was his balm."[15]

Acting Edition: Samuel French, Inc.

Awards and Honors: In 1987, the National James Baldwin Literary Society was founded. In 1992, Hampshire College in Amherst, Massachusetts, established the James Baldwin Scholars program. In 2002, scholar Molefi Kete Asante included Baldwin among the *One Hundred Greatest African Americans: A Biographical Encyclopedia*.

NOTES

1. Mr. Charlie was an early-twentieth-century phrase used by African Americans to refer to Southern whites.

2. The first play to illustrate the testimony of court witnesses via flashbacks was *On Trial* (1914) by Elmer Rice. The device, considered revolutionary at the time, has been used sporadically ever since.

3. On March 24, a month prior to the Broadway opening of *Blues for Mr. Charlie*, another explosive play with racial overtones, LeRoi Jones's one-act *Dutchman*, was presented at off-Broadway's Cherry Lane Theatre. *Dutchman* pictures an incident taking place in a New York subway. Lula, an attractive thirty-year-old white woman, flirts with Clay, a studious black man ten years her junior, arouses him by dancing sensuously in the subway car, taunts him about his skin color, and then, unexpectedly, pulls out a knife and stabs him to death. Jennifer West and Robert Hooks portrayed Lula and Clay under Edward Parone's direction.

4. *New York World-Telegram*, April 24, 1964.

5. *New York Times*, April 24, 1964.

6. *New York Post*, April 24, 1964.

7. *New York Journal-American*, April 24, 1964.

8. *Daily News*, April 24, 1964.

9. *New York Herald Tribune*, April 24, 1964.

10. Otis L. Guernsey Jr., ed., *The Best Plays of 1963–1964* (New York: Dodd, Mead, 1964), 7.

11. Quoted in the *New York Times*, May 5, 1965.

12. Quoted in the *New York Times*, May 5, 1965.

13. Quoted in the *New York Times*, May 5, 1965.

14. *New York Times*, April 16, 1965.

15. *Los Angeles Times*, August 22, 2010.

In the Matter of
J. Robert Oppenheimer (1964)

Heinar Kipphardt (Germany, 1922–1982)

A new dramatic trend arose in Germany during the 1960s—the political docudrama. Associated primarily with Rolf Hochhuth, Peter Weiss, and Heinar Kipphardt, the playwrights examined recent historical events by using official documents and court records. Hochhuth's *The Deputy* (1963) questions the failure of Pope Pius XII to speak out against the Nazi slaughter of Jews. In *The Investigation* (1965), Weiss re-creates the horrific events at the Auschwitz concentration camp. Kipphardt's *In the Matter of J. Robert Oppenheimer* (1964) goes back to the hysterical era of McCarthyism when in 1954 J. Robert Oppenheimer, "the father of the atomic bomb," was summoned to a congressional hearing regarding his security clearance.

Kipphardt sifted through 3,000 typewritten pages before condensing the records about Oppenheimer into a two-act, three-hour play. In an introduction to the published edition of *In the Matter of J. Robert Oppenheimer*, Kipphardt states that he deliberately confined himself to drawing upon historical data for the facts presented. "The author exercised his freedom only in the selection, the arrangement, formulation, and condensation of the material," he wrote.[1]

"Films and slides are utilized in this production as documentation of real events and a continuing reminder of this as fact," writes Gordon Davidson, who staged the play's initial U.S. productions in both Los Angeles and New York. "The action on the stage is merely an abstraction of ideas embodied in human behavior; the film is a shadow of reality; the actor on stage is the three-dimensional existence of illusion. The play answers no questions, rather it begs the question and poses problems with which the audience itself must wrestle."[2]

The time: April 12–May 6, 1954. The place: Room 2022, Building T3, Atomic Energy Commission, Washington, D.C. The room, "a small ugly office," has been temporarily furnished for the purpose of the investigation. On a raised platform, back center, is a table surrounded by three black leather armchairs for the members of the Personnel Security Board—Gordon Gray, Chairman; Ward Evans; and Thomas Morgan. In front of the platform, floor level, the stenographers are seated with their equipment. At a table on the right, Roger Robb and C. A. Rolander, counselors for the Atomic Energy Commission, are busying themselves with stacks of documents. Opposite are Lloyd Garrison and Herbert Marks, Oppenheimer's attorneys. There is an old leather sofa in the corner. A swivel chair for witnesses is also prominent.

As the lights fade up, a huge picture of Joseph McCarthy is projected on white screens at the back of the stage. J. Robert Oppenheimer enters the room by a side door. An official leads him to the sofa. He sets down his smoking paraphernalia, steps forward, and introduces himself to the audience as a "Professor of Physics at Princeton, formerly Director of the Atomic Weapons Laboratories at Los Alamos." He explains that he has been summoned to answer questions put to him by the Personnel Security Board concerning his views, his associations, his actions, and the suspicion that he has been disloyal.

Chairman Gray announces that "this is not a trial" and "shall be strictly confidential." Counsel Robb begins the interrogation. Oppenheimer denies that he had a major part in the decision to drop the A-bomb on Japan—that was "a political decision," not his. Once the decision was made, however, he advised on the choice of targets (photographs of several Japanese cities are projected on the background screens). After the bombing of Hiroshima, he had "terrible moral scruples" but believes that by bringing the war to an end as soon as possible many lives were saved.

Roger Robb steps forward and reports that the FBI suspected that Oppenheimer was "probably a camouflaged Soviet agent," which caused President Eisenhower to order "an impenetrable wall between Oppenheimer and all government secrets." It is in the sphere of energy, says Robb, "we came across the new type of traitor—the traitor for ideological, ethical motives."

The text "Guilty through Association" is projected on the wall screens, and the following interrogation focuses on Oppenheimer's wife, who was first married to a Communist, and his brother Frank, who was a member of the Communist Party until 1941. Oppenheimer's former fiancée, Dr. Jean Tatlock, was also a member of the Party on an "on again, off again" basis. Interrogator Robb presses the point that Oppenheimer, the man responsible for the atomic weapons project in Los Alamos, spent the night with a female Communist. Oppenheimer responds that Tatlock came to him at a time of severe emotional crisis and a few days later committed suicide.

The board's only scientist, Professor Ward Evans, comes forward and declares to the audience that he is disturbed by both queries. He believes that they are humiliating to a scientist. He is also incensed by the state's increasing control over scientists, demanding their conformity.

The industrialist on the panel, Thomas Morgan, asks Oppenheimer if he was aware that in 1943 the Communist Party was an instrument of espionage in the United States. Oppenheimer answers in the negative; at the time the Russians were lauded allies who had just beaten Hitler at Stalingrad. C. A. Rolander, a security expert and Robb's associate, insists that the issue is whether Oppenheimer is a security risk today, when the enemy is not Nazi Germany but Communist Russia. Rolander questions Oppenheimer about his recommendation of physicians with left-wing views for employment at Berkeley and Los Alamos. Yes, admits Oppenheimer, a few of his pupils were in fact Communists but his endorsement of them was purely professional, as they were good scientists.

Professor Evans cannot understand why so many physicists are attracted to radical political ideas. It's because they are open-minded and don't have preconceived notions, says Oppenheimer. They want to probe into things that don't work and ask why hunger, joblessness, and cruelty persist.

The tenth day of the hearing is Oppenheimer's fiftieth birthday. Projected on the hangings is the text "Is there such a thing as hundred-percent security?"

Major Nicholas Radzi, a security officer specializing in counterespionage, is called to the witness stand. Radzi testifies that in 1943 he was assigned to investigate a possible case of espionage at the University of California at Berkeley. It seemed strange, said Radzi, that everybody they suspected had some sort of connection to Dr. Oppenheimer. He recommended to his superiors at the Pentagon that Oppenheimer be completely removed from any employment by the U.S. government, but his recommendation was rejected. Dr. Evans asks Radzi whether, with reference to a secret war project, it is possible to achieve 100 percent security. No, Radzi admits, but 95 percent would be possible if scientists would cooperate. Says Radzi: "If we want to defend our freedom successfully, we must be prepared to forego some of our personal liberty."

John Landsdale, a former security officer, is questioned by Garrison, one of Oppenheimer's attorneys. Landsdale's conclusion is the opposite of Radzi's; he believes that the hysteria over Communism is a danger to democracy. Landsdale has no doubt that Oppenheimer should regain his clearance no matter what the FBI reports said.

In act II, the panel shifts focus to the matter of the hydrogen bomb. Dr. Oppenheimer was widely criticized for delaying the development of the hydrogen bomb in a manner which allowed the USSR to gain ground on the United States in the nuclear arms race. Projected on the background screens is an October 31, 1952, test explosion of the first hydrogen bomb in the Pacific (the isle of Elugelab disappeared within ten minutes) and an August 8, 1953, test explosion of the first Russian hydrogen bomb (alleged to be superior to the American model).

Chairman Gray announces that their secret hearing has been leaked to the *New York Times* and the case of Dr. J. Robert Oppenheimer "dominates the headlines and public discussion all over America."

Questioned by Robb and Rolander, the counsels for the commission, Oppenheimer tells of his "terrible scruples" after Hiroshima and his fear that in a third world war the awesome weapon of a hydrogen bomb will destroy 98 percent of humankind. When the president made the decision to produce it, he helped only as an adviser. It was Dr. Edward Teller who earned the soubriquet "father of the hydrogen bomb."

Dr. Teller is called and sworn in as a witness. In 1945, he wanted to develop a hydrogen bomb, says Teller, but Dr. Oppenheimer did not warm up to the idea. Teller realized that a U.S. hydrogen program would have to take place without Oppenheimer's contribution. No, Teller wouldn't take away Oppenheimer's clearance, but he personally would feel more secure if the vital interests of this country did not rest in his hands. Oppenheimer and Teller look at each other momentarily, and after a slight hesitation Oppenheimer rejects an offer to question Dr. Teller.

The next two witnesses provide contradicting testimonies. David Griggs, chief scientist of the Air Force, believes that Oppenheimer led a silent conspiracy among prominent scientists against the development of the hydrogen bomb. Isador Isaac Rabi, professor of physics at Columbia University, supports Oppenheimer in every way and calls him "the most loyal person I know, including myself."

On the morning of May 6, 1954, the commission concludes the interrogation of forty witnesses. Ward Evans, in his minority report, announces his complete confidence in Dr. Oppenheimer's loyalty, and sees no reason why his security clearance should be revoked. Chairman Gordon Gray reads the board's majority decision. He and Thomas Morgan find "no indication of disloyalty" but are concerned about Dr. Oppenheimer's "ambiguous and disquieting" attitude toward the development of the hydrogen bomb. Therefore, Dr. Oppenheimer can no longer enjoy "the unreserved confidence of the government and the Atomic Energy Commission." He does not receive security clearance.

Oppenheimer rises to his feet and requests that the Atomic Energy Commission review the decision, although he vows never to work on war projects again, as it is "the work of the devil."

* * *

The world premiere of *In der Sache J. Robert Oppenheimer* took place at West Berlin's Freie Volksbühne in 1964 under the direction of Erwin Piscator (1893–1966), innovator of epic theatre and master of the documentary drama.[3] The play performed all over Europe and reached London on October 17, 1966, running for seventy-six performances at the Hampstead Theatre Club. Translated by Ruth Spiers, *In the Matter of J. Robert Oppenheimer* was first produced in America on May 24, 1968, by Los Angeles's Center Theater Group at the Mark Taper Forum. Gordon Davidson directed a cast headed by Joseph Wiseman in the role of Dr. Oppenheimer. The *New York Times* reported that "the first-night audience and critics alike found it distinguished treatment of essentially undramatic material."[4] Critic Walter Kerr provided a second opinion in the *Times*, in which he praised a performance "spare, dry, controlled, quietly intelligent," but at the final curtain remained unclear as to what has been real-life documentation and what has been manipulated by the playwright: "We are not truly certain what we have seen, how responsible or how manipulated the ending has been, how representative the residue may be taken to be."[5] *In the Matter of J. Robert Oppenheimer* ran at the seven-hundred-seat Mark Taper for seven weeks to sold-out houses and was taken to New York, where it was hosted by the Repertory Theater of Lincoln Center on March 6, 1969.

Most of the morning-after reviews were laudatory. "It is a talkative, stimulating and intellectually engaging evening," wrote Clive Barnes. "It is good to have a play in town that offers a little nourishment for thought and discussion."[6] Richard Watts Jr. raved: "The documentary drama by Heinar Kipphardt . . . is intellectually interesting and astonishingly engrossing theatrically, and it is being given a brilliant production filled with stunningly effective performances."[7] Martin Gottfried asserted that the play "is as important as theatre can get," and applauded the "cohesive" direction by Gordon Davidson as well as the "excellent frigid-warm courtroom set" designed by Peter Wexler.[8]

The television critics were less enthusiastic. Leonard Harris of WCBS TV2 complained of "imbalance. It stacks the deck in favor of Oppenheimer and against McCarthy witchhunts. . . . You can tell the good guys from the bad guys without a program, and there was more to the Oppenheimer affair than that."[9] Edwin Newman of NBC TV4 frowned: "It's an interesting work, though not a gripping one. . . . The play in its nature can have no surprises. The story is known. Also, it has no climax. It merely subsides at the end."[10]

The cast was received with kudos, notably Eduard Franz as Ward Evans, the sympathetic member of the board; Philip Bosco as Gordon Gray, the skeptical chairman; and Herbert Berghof as Edward Teller, the opposing scientist. Joseph Wiseman, in the role of Dr. Oppenheimer, garnered unanimous praise. "A fine choice," "Altogether superb," "Calmly dominates the evening," wrote the critics.[11]

In the Matter of J. Robert Oppenheimer ran for sixty-four performances. The play returned to Lincoln Center on June 26, 1969, with Paul Sparer portraying Dr. Oppenheimer, for 108 showings. On October 13, 1969, it began a tour at the National Theatre in Washington, D.C., and closed in San Francisco on January 10, 1970. The Seattle Repertory Theatre of Seattle, Washington, included *In the Matter of J. Robert Oppenheimer* in its 1969–1970 season. Almost four decades later, in 2006, the play was mounted by off-Broadway's Keen Company, a troupe dedicated to plays that are "generous in spirit" and are "saying anything optimistic or positive about humanity."

Other playwrights to tackle the Oppenheimer saga are Joseph Boskin (*The Oppenheimer Affair*, 1968) and Carson Kreitzer (*The Love Song of J. Robert Oppenheimer*, 2004).

Produced by England's BBC TV in 1980, *Oppenheimer: Father of the Atomic Bomb*, a seven-episode miniseries, featured Sam Waterston as the physicist and David Suchet as his nemesis, Edward Teller. A year later, the documentary *The Day after Trinity* covered scientists involved in the creation and testing of the first atomic bomb, including J. Robert Oppenheimer as himself. In 2005, *Doctor Atomic*, John Adams's operatic treatment of J. Robert Oppenheimer and his wife, Kitty, premiered in San Francisco under the direction of Peter Sellars. A slightly revised version was presented by Lyric Opera of Chicago in 2007 and the following year by New York's Metropolitan Opera. Gerald Finley starred in the title role. *Doctor Atomic* follows the last twenty-four hours in the creation of the atom bomb at Los Alamos, New Mexico. Made by ITVS in 2008, *Wonders Are Many: The Making of Doctor Atomic* traces the creation of the opera. A television documentary *The Trials of J. Robert Oppenheimer*, a two-hour brew of archive footage, interviews, and dramatization, was aired by PBS on January 26, 2009. In 2010, film director Lucy Walker mixed newsreel footage, graphics, and interviews with scientists and politicians in the documentary *Countdown to Zero*, a disturbing testament to the horrors of the nuclear bomb. Included is a haunting clip of J. Robert Oppenheimer emoting his mea culpa, "Now I have become Death, the destroyer of worlds."

* * *

Heinar Mauritius Kipphardt was born in Heidersdrof, Upper Silesia, Germany, in 1922. When he was eleven years old, his father, a dentist, was sentenced to five years in the Dürrgoy concentration camp for expressing anti-Nazi views. During World War II, Kipphardt served in the German army, by then in full retreat before the Russian advance. Both experiences impacted him profoundly and his politics became radically left-wing.

Kipphardt studied medicine in Düsseldorf and practiced as an MD, but he shifted his career direction in 1950, becoming literary adviser and chief dramatist for the Deutsches Theater in East Berlin. In 1959 he moved to West Berlin and served in a similar capacity at the Munich Kammerspiele (Intimate Theatre). Kipphardt's first major play, *Der Hund des Generals* (*The General's Dog*, 1962), deals with inhumane treatment of infantrymen by the generals. A sentry accidently shoots the general's favorite dog. The general is so angry that he sends an entire company to an untenable position where they are completely wiped out. *Joel Brand* (1964) and *Bruder Eichmann* (*Brother Eichmann*, produced posthumously in 1983) focus on the genocide of the Jews in Nazi Germany. Kipphardt adapted *Joel Brand* and *Bruder Eichmann* to television, and he penned for German TV two versions of *In the Matter of J. Robert Oppenheimer*.

Acting Edition: Hill & Wang.

Awards and Honors: A top-ten selection in *The Best Plays of 1968–1969*. Heinar Kipphardt was the recipient of the East German national prize, 1953; Schiller Memorial prize, 1962; Gerhart Hauptmann prize, 1964; Adolf Grimme prize, 1965; German Academy of Representational Arts television prize, 1975; Society of German Doctors film prize, 1976; Prix Italia, 1976; and Bremen Literature prize, 1977.

NOTES

1. Heinar Kipphardt, *In the Matter of J. Robert Oppenheimer* (New York: Hill & Wang, 1968), 5.

2. Otis L. Guernsey Jr., ed., *The Best Plays of 1968–1969* (New York: Dodd, Mead, 1969), 235.

3. A year earlier, in 1963, Erwin Piscator staged in Berlin the controversial political drama *The Deputy* by Rolf Hochhuth. Piscator was one of the first directors to use filmstrips in conjunction with live actors. His influence was apparent in the work of Joan Littlewood at Theatre Workshop in England and in that of the Living Theatre in the United States.

4. *New York Times*, May 27, 1968.

5. *New York Times*, June 9, 1968.

6. *New York Times*, March 7, 1969.

7. *New York Post*, March 7, 1969.

8. *Women's Wear Daily*, March 7, 1969.

9. WCBS TV2, March 6, 1969.

10. NBC TV4, March 6, 1969.

11. Born in 1918 in Montreal, Quebec, Canada, Joseph Wiseman began acting in summer stock as a teenager and made his Broadway debut playing a bit part in Robert E. Sherwood's *Abe Lincoln in Illinois*. During the 1940s he enacted feature roles in Maxwell Anderson's *Candles in the Wind* and *Joan of Lorraine*, William Shakespeare's *Antony and Cleopatra*, and Sidney Kingsley's *Detective Story*. His other Broadway credits include appearances in Jean Anouilh's *The Lark*, Arthur Miller's *Incident at Vichy*, and revivals of Clifford Odets's *Golden Boy* and

Paddy Chayefsky's *The Tenth Man*. In Hollywood, Wiseman made a dozen movies, including *Detective Story* (1951), *Viva Zapata!* (1952), *Les Miserables* (1952), *The Garment Jungle* (1957), and *The Unforgiven* (1960), before playing the role he is most remembered for, the sinister title character in *Dr. No* (1962), the first James Bond movie. "I had no idea it would achieve the success it did," Wiseman told the *Los Angeles Times* in 1992. "As far as I was concerned, I thought it might be just another grade-B Charlie Chan mystery." On television, Wiseman played the recurring role of crime boss Manny Weisbord in the 1980s series *Crime Story*. Over the years he was featured on series such as *Danger, Suspense, Justice, On Trial, The Untouchables, The Streets of San Francisco*, and *Law & Order*. In 2001, Wiseman returned to Broadway in a production of Abby Mann's *Judgment at Nuremberg*. He died at his home in Manhattan in 2009. His daughter, Martha, said that Wiseman viewed *Dr. No* with disdain. "He was horrified in later life because that's what he was remembered for. Stage acting was what he wanted to be remembered for." *Los Angeles Times*, October 21, 2009.

Home Is the Hunter (1964)

Helen MacInnes (Scotland-born American, 1907–1985)

Helen MacInnes, mistress of romantic suspense, went to Greek mythology and adapted the story of Ulysses, hero of the Trojan War, into a rip-roaring melodrama, both saluting and lampooning legendary fables.

The action takes place in Ithaca, Greece, in 1177 BC, ten years after the fall of Troy to the Greek legions. Penelope, Ulysses' beautiful wife, does not believe the rumors that her husband is dead. A gang of eleven dangerous ruffians has taken hold of her home and she has barely managed to stay unharmed by promising to marry one of them when she finishes embroidering a set of seven chair covers. They are not aware that Penelope and her old nurse, Clia, are removing stitches at night.

Ulysses returns, masquerading as a hunchbacked beggar. With the help of his courageous seventeen-year-old son Telemachus, the devoted swineherd Eumaeus, and the stableman Philitius, all armed with knives, spears, and bows, Ulysses manages to outwit, divide, and liquidate the usurpers, whose bodies are carted away to be thrown over a cliff.

Homer, a white-haired poet who serves as the comic foil of the proceedings, records the events. The goddess Athena appears and confides to the audience that Homer will embellish the facts, as poets tend to do, in his upcoming composition *The Odyssey*, a poetic narrative that "will last 3000 years and more."

* * *

Born in Glasgow, Scotland, in 1907, Helen Clark MacInnes earned a master's degree in French and German from the University of Glasgow in 1928, and a diploma in library science from University College, London in 1931. During 1934–1937, MacInnes became involved in amateur theatricals at Oxford, where her husband, Gilbert Highet, was a classics professor. She acted with the university's Dramatic Society and with the Oxford Experimental Theatre. In 1937, when Highet was invited to lecture at Columbia University, the family crossed the Atlantic and settled in New York, becoming naturalized U.S. citizens in 1951.

The heroes of MacInnes's first novel, 1939's *Above Suspicion*, are an Oxford don and his wife who are persuaded by British Intelligence to undertake a dangerous mission in prewar Nazi Germany. The novel became a best seller and was adapted to the screen by MGM in 1943, starring Fred MacMurray and Joan Crawford. A distinguished supporting cast included Conrad Veidt, Basil Rathbone, and Reginald Owen. William L. DeAndrea writes in *Encyclopedia Mysteriosa* that *Above Suspicion* set the tone for subsequent MacInnes novels: "The heroes are frequently amateurs drawn more or less willingly into international intrigue, and the villains represent totalitarian regimes, with Communists and neo-Nazis prominent in the postwar years. The morality is unambiguous, and the entertainment value high."[1]

MacInnes's follow-up novel, *Assignment in Brittany* (1942), set during World War II, is the story of a French Resistance fighter who infiltrates high Nazi echelons to locate a secret submarine base. Jean-Pierre Aumont made his American debut in the 1943 movie version. Spanning four decades, from 1944 to 1984, MacInnes published eighteen more espionage novels, of which *The Venetian Affair* (1963) was filmed four years later, and *The Salzburg Connection* (1968) was made into a movie in 1972.

MacInnes, whose books sold more than twenty-five million copies, was dubbed "the queen of spy thrillers," "reigning queen of suspense," and "master teller of spy stories." *Home Is the Hunter* is her only play. It was copyrighted in 1964. Domino Theatre of Kingston, Ontario, Canada, included *Home Is the Hunter* in its 1975–1976 season.

Acting Edition: Samuel French, Inc. (in manuscript form).

Awards and Honors: In 1966, Helen MacInnes won the Columbia Prize in Literature at Iona College, New Rochelle, New York.

NOTE

1. William L. DeAndrea, *Encyclopedia Mysteriosa* (New York: Prentice Hall, 1994), 221.

East Lynne, or
Lady Isabel's Shame (1965)

Brian J. Burton (England, 1922–)

Written by an English novice writer known as Mrs. Henry Wood, *East Lynne*, a sentimental Victorian novel peppered with criminous elements, was serialized in *Colborn's New Monthly Magazine* during 1860–1861. Its appearance in book form was rejected by publishers concerned about "sensational" and "foul" elements. When *East Lynne* was finally accepted and published by Richard Bentley at the end of 1861, the *Times* of London gave it a favorable review. A French translation quickly followed, versions in other European languages were soon available, and the novel was pirated by two dozen American publishers. *East Lynne* became one of the most successful books of the nineteenth century, selling 500,000 copies in England by 1900 and over a million copies during the author's lifetime.[1]

Ever since 1863, numerous stage adaptations of *East Lynne* have been written and produced on both sides of the Atlantic. Brian J. Burton, a prolific British playwright, dramatized Mrs. Wood's book in 1965. In an introduction to his published manuscript, *East Lynne, or Lady Isabel's Shame*, Burton relates that his version is not based on any previous plays but directly on the original novel. "Nevertheless," writes Burton, "I have included one or two lines from the Victorian versions where they do not appear in the novel yet have become an essential part of any dramatization of *East Lynne*. An example is the famous 'Dead, dead and never called me Mother' which was the invention of T. A. Palmer [1874] and not of Mrs. Henry Wood. What play of *East Lynne* would be complete without this immortal line?"[2]

Burton confined the sprawling proceedings to one set, the sitting room of lawyer Archibald Carlyle's residence at East Lynne, and eliminated a number of characters. The time is June 1850. The curtain rises on a late Friday evening. Cornelia Carlyle, "a tall angular woman in her late forties," immediately sets the presentational style of the melodrama by breaking through the fourth wall and addressing the audience directly, expressing

445

her dismay at the marriage of her brother Archibald. She is bitter at having been "discarded with contemptuous indifference." Cornelia assures the viewers that she intends to stay at East Lynne for the duration. She sees no reason "to keep up the expense of two establishments."

Archibald Carlyle and his wife Isabel arrive by carriage. He is "in his late twenties—a handsome, gentle man." She is "little more than a girl, very beautiful with fair hair and a pale complexion." Cornelia makes it clear that she'll remain as a housekeeper and take charge of all the domestic needs. She will adhere to the maxim "To be thrifty is a virtue; to squander is a sin."

A month has passed. It is evident that Archibald and Isabel are very much in love. The household is a happy one, but a cloud arises when a former acquaintance of Archibald, Barbara Hare, "a very pretty girl of twenty-three," arrives on the scene. With a teary aside, Barbara confides to the audience that Archibald was her true love.

The second act takes place a few years later. The Carlyles have a boy, William, and a girl, Lucy. The villain of the piece, Captain Francis Levison, "a tall, handsome man of thirty with a polished, suave manner" has just arrived from Europe. Archibald invites Levison to stay at East Lynne while seeing to his business affairs. Levison shares with the audience his pleasure of being "under the same roof as the fair Isabel." He plans to play his cards "cunningly" and is certain that she will soon be his.

Levison's opportunity comes when Barbara Hare pleads for Archibald's help to save her brother Richard from a false accusation of murder. Richard, hounded by the police, enters stealthily through the French window and tells Archibald that upon knocking on the door of his beloved Afy (short of Aphrodite) Hallijohn, she refused to see him. With a pang of jealous suspicion he hid behind trees outside the cottage and saw Afy's brother, George, come up the path and enter the house. Not long afterward, he heard a shot and a man known locally as Thorn came running out. Soon Richard heard the sound of a horse's hooves galloping away. He leaped up the stairs and fell over the prostrate body of George Hallijohn. "He was lying just within," says Richard, "on the kitchen floor—dead. Blood was around him, and my gun, one that I loaned him, was thrown near him." People began to gather and, in panic, Richard picked up the gun and fled. To his horror, he was taken for the murderer. [3]

Archibald chides Richard for acting like a guilty man by escaping the scene of the crime, but he promises to keep the matter quiet and come to his aid. It is not an easy task, for Thorn has disappeared. During the next few weeks Barbara acts as a go-between for the lawyer and her brother. Levison points out to Isabel that her husband and Barbara have been meeting clandestinely. "Oh, I am wretched, jealous, mad," sighs Isabel. She leaves behind husband and children, and goes with Levison.

A few more years pass. It is believed that Isabel, deserted by Levison, has died in a train crash in France. To the chagrin of Cornelia, Archibald marries Barbara Hare. Her brother Richard recalls "a peculiar motion of the hand" as a clue to the identification of the elusive Thorn, and it is thus proven that Hallijohn's murderer is none other than Sir Francis Levison. Richard is exonerated and Levison is arrested and hanged.

A new governess, Madame Vine, is hired to take care of the children. Her hair is white, she walks with a limp, and she wears dark glasses. No one recognizes her as the former mistress of the house, Isabel Carlyle. However, when little William dies of consumption, his mother cries, "Oh, Willie, Willie my child! He is dead, dead, dead. And he never knew me— never called me mother!"

Her true identity revealed, Isabel tells Archibald that she recovered from the railway accident, but her appearance changed "dreadfully." Feeling guilty for leaving husband and children, she found a way of coming back. Coughing, Isabel dies in Archibald's arms. He raises his eyes to Heaven as the curtain falls.

* * *

Ellen Price (1814–1887), the daughter of an affluent glove manufacturer, was born in Worcester, England, with a deformed spine. Her mobility restricted, young Ellen became a voracious reader, and began writing at an early age. In 1836 she married Henry Wood, a banker, and continued to write profusely under the pen name Mrs. Henry Wood. At first she concentrated on short stories, many of which were published in *New Monthly Magazine* and *Bentley's Miscellany*. *East Lynne* proved her to be in command of the long narrative. She continued to write more than thirty romantic and sensational novels, some spiced with crime and detection. Henry Wood died in 1866. Soon thereafter his widow purchased a struggling monthly magazine, *Argosy*, and under her management the monthly circulation reached 20,000, three times as much as the more reputable magazines of the era. Between 1868 and 1873, the main feature of *Argosy* was a serial by Wood.

Graham Greene and Dorothy Glover list several criminous works by Mrs. Wood in their compilation *Victorian Detective Fiction*, including *Mrs. Halliburton's Troubles* (1862), which features Sergeant Delves, a local policeman. Scotland Yard investigators include Totton in *Within the Maze* (1872), George Byde of *The Passenger from Scotland Yard* (1887), and Toppin as *The Englishman of the Rue Cain* (1888), a Yard representative at the Sûreté. *The Master of Greylands* (1873) highlights the deductive prowess of an early female sleuth, Madame Charlotte Guise. The six volumes in a series titled *Johnny Ludlow* (1874–1899), some published posthumously, cover the escapades of the title detective, told in the first person. Also published posthumously was *The Story of Charles Strange* (1888), in which Mrs. Wood wove together no less than five distinct problems and dealt artfully with their ultimate solution.

Bruce F. Murphy, in *The Encyclopedia of Murder and Mystery*, adds the crime-tinted *The Channings* (1862) and *Trevlyn Hold* (1864). Allen J. Hubin lists eighteen short-story collections by Wood in his *Bibliography of Crime Fiction, 1749–1975*.

Mrs. Wood's thirty-some novels and hundreds of short stories are all but forgotten today. Only *East Lynne* weathered the passage of time. Upon the occasion of reprinting the novel in October 2000, Professor Dinah Birch of Liverpool University wrote in the *London Review of Books* that the appeal of *East Lynne* can be traced to its power to affect the reader's emotions and to the fact that "much of the narrative is unexpectedly down to earth, concerned with money, houses, clothes, food, the day-to-day business of life." Birch also asserts that "concealed crime, sorrow and death were then as now what people wanted from their fiction. Ellen Wood knew how to satisfy the market."[4]

In her milestone study *The Development of the Detective Novel*, A. E. Murch theorizes, "Within the extensive framework of this romance is a well-constructed murder mystery. The problem is difficult, for years have elapsed since the crime, and an innocent man was, at the time, convicted on circumstantial evidence. New information is gradually discovered, an alias penetrated and an alibi proved false. Material witnesses must be traced before the case can be re-opened and the truth established."[5]

When she was seventeen years old, the American actress Lucille Western paid actor-manager-playwright Clifton W. Tayleure $100 to adapt *East Lynne* to the stage. The play was produced in 1860 at Baltimore's Holiday Street Theatre with great success. On March 23, 1863, Western brought the melodrama to New York's Winter Garden Theatre, where it ran approximately twenty performances. *East Lynne* served Western as a vehicle for ten years and became a favorite of touring and stock companies.[6] In 1865, *East Lynne* was performed at Brooklyn's Academy of Music with Ada Gray as Lady Isabel. Gray toured with the play constantly in the provinces and it is reported that she performed the role more than four thousand times. Boston's theatergoers flocked to see the play in 1865, 1867, and 1869. Dallas's first Opera House opened its doors in 1873 with a gala performance of *East Lynne*. The great Modjeska played Lady Isabel for a week in 1879 at the Grand Opera House in Manhattan. "Actresses loved the play because Lady Isabel was such a tremendous role—virtually two roles, considering the disguise," writes Sally Mitchell in her introduction to a publication of *East Lynne* by Rutgers University Press, "with opportunities to display love, flirtatiousness, anger, grief, and determination as well as the pathos that brought such a satisfactory response from the audience."[7] Mary Pickford and Lillian Gish made their stage debuts in the role of Little Willie.

There were twenty-seven revivals of *East Lynne* in the United States by the turn of the twentieth century. The play became a staple of touring and stock companies, and whenever the box office needed a lift, a sign went up proclaiming, "Next week, *East Lynne*." Sometimes there were setbacks. In 1901, a dramatization of *East Lynne* by and starring Agnes Burroughs was produced at the Harlem Opera House to hisses and catcalls from the gallery. The *New York Times* reports that "before the play ended less than fifty people remained in the theatre. Boys rolled their programmes into balls and pelted the actors."[8]

A parody of *East Lynne* was presented for thirty-five showings at off-Broadway's Provincetown Playhouse on March 10, 1926. The reviewer of the *New York Times* was not happy with the general level of the performance but singled out Stanley Howlett as Sir Francis Levison: "Well fortified behind a black mustache gracefully curled at the ends, toying with a monocle, smoking a rakish cigar, tapping his top hat with a defiant, mocking gesture, Mr. Howlett enacts his base, perfidious scoundrel almost honestly. . . . Most of the other actors seem too conscious of the ridiculousness of their roles."[9]

In 1929, when purchasing a property that would become their theatre for the next sixty years, the Tulsa, Oklahoma, Little Theatre inaugurated its new location with a production of *East Lynne* in a tent. Almost twenty years later, in 1948, off-Broadway's troupe On-Stage resuscitated the play for six performances, playing it straight with no spoofing. Three decades hence, in 1978, *East Lynne* was performed broadly for laughs by the Halcyon Repertory Company of Chicago, Illinois. Critic Richard Christiansen of the *Chicago Tribune* described the presentation as "a camped-up staging of the venerable sentimental melodrama padded out with an olio of song-and-dance vaudeville routines by members of the cast."[10] Also in 1978, *East Lynne* was revived by off-off-Broadway's Academy Arts Theatre Company.

In England, inadequate contemporary copyright laws meant that Mrs. Henry Wood could not stop a flood of adaptations based upon her novel. A version by W. Archer was staged at the Effingham Theatre in Whitechapel in 1864. Two years later, an adaptation by George Conquest, titled *East Lynne; or, The Divorced Wife* was presented at London's Grecian Theatre. A dramatization by John Oxenford proved to be very popular, opening at the Lyceum Theatre in May 1867 and running at various venues until April 1897. T. A. Palmer's adaptation was first performed in Nottingham in 1874 and toured the country with great success. A replica by Harry St. Maur, who also played Captain Levison, premiered at the Haymarket Theatre in September 1896. Since then, at least sixteen different versions have been licensed by England's Lord Chamberlain for public performance. West End theatres presented notable productions of the play in 1909 (adapted by Eric Mayne), 1929 (by J. Pitt Hardacre), 1933, and 1954 (both by Edgar K. Bruce). A highly praised dramatization by Lisa Evans was mounted by the Birmingham Rep Studio on December 17, 1992, with a cast of five doubling in contrasting roles.

Edna Ferber mentions *East Lynne* as an example of a typical stage melodrama in her 1926 novel *Show Boat*, and scenes from the play are enacted, burlesque style, in several movie adaptations of the novel.

Also available in print today, in addition to Brian J. Burton's version, is *East Lynne* by Ned Albert (a pen name for Wilbur Braun), subtitled "A Spirited and Powerful Mellow Drammer in Three Acts" and advertised as "a brand new, sparkling and streamlined play." Written in 1941, the Albert adaptation divides the action into several locales and keeps the character of ailing Little Willie on stage. In 1990, Bruce Cutler penned a new version of *East Lynne*, basing it on the novel by Mrs. Henry Wood and the play by Clifton W. Tayleure.

East Lynne was filmed several times during the silent era, beginning with a 1912 Thanhouser production and followed by a five-reel 1913 British endeavor with Blanche Forsythe in the role of the long-suffering Lady Isabel, Fred Paul as her befuddled husband Archibald Carlyle, and Fred Morgan as the dastardly Captain Francis Levison. The first American screen adaptation was made in three reels by Biograph Company in 1915. A 1916 Fox film featured Theda Bara (Lady Isabel), Ben Deeley (Archibald), and Stuart Holmes (Levison). A 1921 replica remained faithful to the plot but shifted the proceedings from England to America. The leads were played by Mabel Ballin, Edward Earle, and Henry G. Sell. Four years later, Alma Rubens, Edmund Lowe, and Lou Tellegen undertook the triangular roles. In 1930, writer-director Victor Halperin based his movie *Ex-Flame* on *East Lynne*, albeit with drastic changes. The following year, *East Lynne* was remade again, with some story variations, starring Ann Harding, Conrad Nagel, and Clive Brook. This film was nominated for an Academy Award as Best Picture.

In 1982, the melodrama was converted to British television with Lisa Eichhorn, Martin Shaw, and Tim Woodward. Five years later, to mark the centenary of Mrs. Wood's death, BBC Radio 4 broadcast seven hour-long episodes based upon *East Lynne*, playing it straight and proving that this Victorian novel could still be effective and captivating.

Acting Edition: Samuel French, Inc.

NOTES

1. Mrs. Henry Wood's *East Lynne* (1861) was one of three crime-oriented best sellers that were published in England within a very short period of time, the others being Wilkie Collins's *The Woman in White* (1860) and Mary Elizabeth Braddon's *Lady Audley's Secret* (1862).

2. Brian J. Burton, *East Lynne, or Lady Isabel's Shame* (Birmingham, England: C. Combridge Ltd, 1965), unpaginated.

3. This is an early use of the plot device depicting an innocent man found by the body of a murdered victim with a weapon in his hand, thus accused of the foul deed. A variation on the theme has become a staple of detective literature ever since.

4. *London Review of Books* 23, no. 3, February 8, 2001.

5. A. E. Murch, *The Development of the Detective Novel* (London: Peter Owen Limited, 1958), 153.

6. Actress Pauline Lucille Western (1843–1877) was born in New Orleans, Louisiana, and made her first appearance on the stage at her father's theatre in Washington, D.C. Her role as Lady Isabel in *East Lynne* was her first success. She continued to appear with traveling troupes, playing such roles as Nancy Sikes in *Oliver Twist* and the title character in *Lucretia Borgia, Jane Eyre,* and *Mary Tudor.* Clifton W. Tayleur (1831–1887) began his career as an actor, specializing in the parts of old men. His interest shifted to writing melodramas—*Horseshoe Robinson* (1856), *A Woman's Wrongs* (1874), *Rube; or, The Wall Street Undertow* (1875), *Parted* (1876)—all undistinguished. By the late 1860s he became the manager of several Broadway theatres, including the Olympic and the Grand Opera House.

7. Mrs. Henry Wood, *East Lynne* (New Brunswick, NJ: Rutgers University Press, 1984), xiv.

8. *New York Times*, October 8, 1901.

9. *New York Times*, March 11, 1926.

10. *Chicago Tribune*, July 15, 1978.

Baker Street (1965)

Book by Jerome Coopersmith (United States, 1925–), Music and Lyrics by Marian Grudeff (Canada, 1927–2006) and Raymond Jessel (United States, 1930–)

The world's foremost consulting detective—Sherlock Holmes—first appeared on stage in a one-act musical satire, *Under the Clock*, part of a triple bill produced at London's Royal Court Theatre on November 25, 1893. The dialogue was written by Charles H. E. Brookfield (who played Sherlock Holmes) and Seymour Hicks (who played Dr. Watson). Brookfield and Hicks impersonated Holmes and Watson as a front for throwing acid darts at some eminent colleagues in the acting profession. *Under the Clock* enraged London for seventy-eight performances. Photographs of the era depict Brookfield's Holmes in black tights with a short striped cape over his shoulders, a stubby beard, a thick moustache, and rumpled hair. Seymour's Watson sports a monocle on his right eye, a black high collar around his neck, eyebrows that are darkened toward the center and arched to touch his nose, and lips uplifted and highlighted in the middle.

The next musical to be graced, sort of, by the characters of Holmes and Watson was *The Red Mill*, which opened at Broadway's Knickerbocker Theatre on September 24, 1906. With music by Victor Herbert, and book and lyrics by Henry Blossom, two famous comedians of the era, Fred Stone and David Montgomery, appear as touring Americans who masquerade as Holmes and Watson when they are summoned by the burgomaster of a small Dutch town to find his missing daughter.

A musical spoof of the Conan Doyle heroes, titled *The Great Detective*, came to London's Sadler's Wells on January 21, 1953. Kenneth MacMillan played both the title role (Sherlock Holmes) and The Infamous Professor (Moriarty). Stanley Holden portrayed the Great Detective's Friend (Dr. Watson). The cast of characters included Innocent Suspects, Unfortunate Victims, Murderous Villains, Distressed Ladies, Respectable Folk, and the Infamous Professor's Human Marionettes.

The first bona fide Sherlock Holmes musical is *Baker Street* (1965), with book by Jerome Coopersmith, and music and lyrics by Marian Grudeff and Raymond Jessel.

"A musical Sherlock Holmes? Well, why not? He had been morphed into a play, a ballet, an early TV series and of course lots of movies. Perhaps the time for a Sherlock Holmes musical has come. That was my self-imposed challenge in the 1960's," recalls Jerome Coopersmith, a devout Sherlockian.[1]

Coopersmith tried to secure the rights from the Conan Doyle estate but was turned down several times. Taking a gamble, he spent four months working on *Baker Street*—a mélange from several of Doyle's stories, including *A Scandal in Bohemia*, *The Final Problem*, and *The Empty House*—and submitted the manuscript to flamboyant Broadway producer Alexander H. Cohen. Cohen liked what he read, optioned the play, and negotiated for a production license.[2]

Harold Prince was hired to direct the extravaganza, budgeted at a then-lavish $650,000; Fritz Weaver was to play Sherlock Holmes—"His lean, sharp features, and precise articulation fit in perfectly with our concept of the great detective. And he sang."[3] Englishman Peter Sallis was cast as Watson; Inga Swenson as "The Woman," Irene Adler; and Martin Gabel as Professor Moriarty. Moriarty's henchmen were played by Christopher Walken (who went on to epitomize evil in the cinema) and Tommy Tune (destined to become a prominent dancer-choreographer on Broadway).

The curtain rises on a dark, foggy street. A drunk who lies sprawled in a doorway suddenly leaps to his feet, draws a pistol, aims it at the silhouette of Sherlock Holmes behind a large bow window, and fires twice. There is the sound of shattered glass. The "drunk" starts to flee but is blocked by an elderly, hunchbacked organ-grinder who flings him to the ground and rips off a disguise to reveal himself to be Sherlock Holmes.[4]

The scene now shifts to the Baker Street flat. Robert Gregg, a handsome young man, knocks on the door. Holmes croons "It's Simple" while deducing that Gregg is an army captain ("That handkerchief tucked in your sleeve—a military custom, I believe?") who serves in the palace guard ("The line of your sunburn . . . what type of headgear could possibly do that?—a brimless bearskin hat!"). Gregg needs Holmes's help in securing a number of love letters he sent to the American actress Irene Adler, during their past romance.[5] Gregg is now engaged to a lady of the nobility and is concerned about a potential scandal; Miss Adler has threatened to publish the incriminating letters.

Backstage at the Theatre Royal, Holmes offers Adler a hundred pounds. Irene responds, "You may tell your client I will *give* him his letters as a wedding gift—on the pages of the *Pall Mall Gazette*." Holmes concludes that "Miss Adler is not a simple blackmailer, but indeed may be connected to a larger crime, perhaps to the Moriarty group itself."

Holmes assigns the Baker Street Irregulars, a band of rugged urchins, to remove a packet of letters from the home of a woman in Serpentine Lane.

The youngsters, cajoled by their leader Higgins, sing and dance energetically, assuring Holmes, "Leave it to us, guv, leave it to us!"

At her house, Irene Adler peruses stories penned by Dr. John Watson—*The Case of the Sussex Vampire, The Man with the Twisted Lip, The Adventure of the Engineer's Thumb*—when Higgins calls from off-stage, "Open up, ma'am! A man's been hit by a carriage!" The Irregulars carry in Holmes, disguised as an Anglican deacon, and place him on the sofa. Smoke begins to pour into the room. Irene sends Higgins for the fire brigade, rushes to a wall safe, and removes a catchall box containing mementos and letters. The smoke evaporates, and Irene realizes that "the fire" was but a gambit to discover the whereabouts of Captain Gregg's letters.[6]

Later that day, the letters disappear. Irene requests that Inspector Lestrade of Scotland Yard arrest Sherlock Holmes for "fraud, deception, torts, encroachment, vile misrepresentation—and theft!" Holmes assures her that, though tempted, he did not steal the letters. He believes that they have fallen into the hands of "a sinister organization."

Holmes is ill at ease when alone with Irene Adler. Wondering how to cope with a female guest, he offers her a cigar. She strolls about his flat, picks up an object covered by a glass bell (a fang from the giant rat of Sumatra), and scrutinizes the blowgun that killed Bartholomew Sholto in the case of *The Sign of Four*. She comments that Holmes should have been on the stage and he informs her that he used to be an actor: "My *Hamlet* was quite unique as I had devised a method of achieving the utmost reality in acting—a method I unfortunately confided to that young Stanislavsky chap in Moscow." Irene asks whether he has ever kissed a woman, and Holmes sings the praises of "the Cold, Clear World of the Intellect."

Impersonating crude underworld characters, Holmes and Adler wander through murky alleys, dingy cafés, opium dens, and waterfront piers, where three ruffians leap upon the detective and drag him off.

Holmes finds himself in the cabin of a private yacht docked on the river Thames. There is the sound of an oriental gong, and a bejeweled Buddha statue swings around to disclose an enthroned Professor Moriarty. A battle of wits ensues. Holmes informs the Napoleon of crime that he is aware of the scheme to steal the Queen's Diamond Jubilee gifts. Moriarty chuckles and reveals that his people, in the guise of two reporters and a photographer, will enter the palace at the height of the parade "with the aid of the good Captain Gregg, who believes he is doing nothing more than assisting three enterprising journalists, a minor infraction to be sure in exchange for his stimulating letters." When they leave, the photographer's satchel will be bulging with two million pounds worth of glittering gems. The gang will escape from England by balloon.

Watson is hauled in by two strongmen who tie him and Holmes to their chairs. Moriarty unveils a time bomb, croons, "I Shall Miss You, Holmes," and exits. The deadly contraption seems to tick louder and louder as the curtain falls.

The second act begins with the Diamond Jubilee parade, executed by the Bill Baird marionettes. On the yacht's deck, Irene, Wiggins, and the Irregulars clash with the three henchmen and toss them into the river. Irene descends to the cabin. Holmes warns her not to touch the bomb, drops off his bonds ("When your hands are clasped in that manner, it is quite impossible to bind them securely"), lowers a wire into the mechanism of the bomb, twists—and the ticking stops.

Holmes rushes after Moriarty in a cutaway of a horse-drawn carriage.

On the cliffs of Dover (substituting the Reichenbach Falls), the two adversaries struggle for several moments, then both fall into the precipice.

In the last scene we learn that Holmes saved himself by grasping a vine, holding on for dear life, and tossing his coat over the side of the cliff to signify his demise. By doing so, Holmes believes that Moriarty's dangerous lieutenants will now become careless, thus easier to catch.

Holmes guides Lestrade and his officers to a funeral chapel where the criminal mourners are eulogizing the late Moriarty. The gang is rounded up and hustled to headquarters. Holmes approaches the boy organist—"You may remove your disguise. I know who you are." It is Irene, who informs the Great Detective that she will be sailing back to America on the midnight steamer. "Mr. Holmes," she says, "you are a fool! . . . I could have given you an adventure beyond your wildest dreams. In feelings you have never known before. . . . What a pity that Sherlock Holmes has chosen to leave a mystery unsolved."

Irene exits. Sherlock remains silent. Suddenly the voice of Moriarty echoes. Holmes and Watson search the chapel frantically for the source of the voice and find a recording cylinder hidden underneath the keyboard of the organ. "Of course he would be alive!" exclaims Holmes. "If one vine, why not two! . . . I heard a scream diminishing into the distance. Of course—a simple ventriloquist's trick!"

Holmes conjectures that Moriarty has managed to escape from England and vows: "I shall find him if I have to search the four corners of the earth." Holmes will catch the midnight steamer—to America.

* * *

Rehearsals for *Baker Street* began in November 1964. A press release from the offices of Alexander H. Cohen announced that "actor Fritz Weaver departs for London this week to do 'homework' for his characterization of Sherlock Holmes. . . . Weaver will visit the London pubs and hangouts which are closely identified with the famed fictional sleuth."

Baker Street began a three-week pre-Broadway tryout at the Shubert Theatre, Boston, on December 28, 1964. The critics were divided. Elinor

Hughes called it "an excellent musical show . . . a production that is handsome, amusing and in keeping with the spirit of Sherlock Holmes,"[7] and Guy of *Variety* threw bouquets at "a cinch hit . . . a musical melodrama with a twist that lifts it into the *My Fair Lady–Around the World in 80 Days* class."[8] However, Elliot Norton found the show "presently cluttered and often clumsy"[9]and Kevin Kelly frowned at an endeavor "badly bungled, confused and steadily confusing."[10]

Baker Street continued its refinement at the O'Keefe Centre, Toronto, Canada, January 20–February 6, 1965, garnering such varied reviews as "should prove to be paved with gold" to "crowded, garbled and pedestrian." The show landed at New York's Broadway Theatre on February 16, amid the blitz of a promotional campaign orchestrated by producer Cohen. It was announced that the advance sale set "an all time record" of over one million dollars, and that the box office, staffed by five treasurers, will open daily from eight a.m. to midnight; Metro-Goldwyn Mayer will produce the motion picture version; a collection of rare manuscripts and first editions of works by Arthur Conan Doyle will be exhibited in the theatre lobby—housed in six glass-enclosed display cases, locked, insured, and guarded day and night; the slogan "Sherlock Holmes of Baker Street Taught James Bond Everything He Knows" will be emblazoned on the marquee, alongside an animated complex of moving figures, replicas of Holmesian characters; supplementing the regular corps of ushers will be a half-dozen London bobbies, posted for the express purpose of answering customer queries "with traditional English courtesy."

The press reception of *Baker Street* was mixed. John Chapman called the show "an absolutely captivating entertainment,"[11] while Richard Watts Jr. complained of a "curious flatness of the whole ambitious enterprise."[12] Norman Nadel hailed playwright Coopersmith for endowing the material with "the flavor, the purposeful pace and the piquant surprises of a Conan Doyle original,"[13] but the *Saturday Review* opined that "Jerome Coopersmith's embellishments of Sir Arthur Conan Doyle's stories do no more than remind us that they are just that. He has not succeeded in making us care about the story or about his heroine's emotional involvement with Holmes."[14] Emory Lewis chirped, "*Baker Street* offers an enchanted, imaginative and very funny evening of pure joy."[15] John McClain scowled, "The thing quickly got into the realm of farce and Holmes became a comic page detective."[16] Sothern Hip applauded "first-rate acting, admirable singing and dancing, spectacular sets and the glow of perky, faintly tongue-in-cheek treatment."[17] *Newsweek* countered, "There are no songs distinguishable as songs, no dancing distinguishable from third-rate *West Side Story* or second-rate *Oliver!* And no staging distinguishable from *Golden Boy* or a summer-stock *Threepenny Opera*."[18]

Baker Street ran for 313 performances, with David Thayer taking over the role of Moriarty midway, then embarked on an extensive national tour in eighteen cities. Scene designer Oliver Smith won a Tony Award and Motley was pronounced Best Costume Designer by the New York Drama Critics. Backers of the show lost $350,000, about half of their investment. MGM, which had a sizable slice of it, never made a *Baker Street* screen version.

Baker Street resurfaced, in a staged concert performance, at off-Broadway's York Theatre on January 19–21, 2001, with Simon Jones playing Sherlock Holmes, supported by Tom Toner (Dr. Watson), Dee Hoty (Irene Adler), and Randall Duk Kim (Professor Moriarty).

* * *

Born in Manhattan in 1925, Jerome Coopersmith has been fascinated with show business since childhood. At sixteen he became an office boy for the Shubert Theatrical Company. During World War II, Coopersmith went overseas and was awarded the Purple Heart. Following his army service, he completed his formal education at New York University. Then he began writing for television.

Coopersmith helped originate the *Armstrong Circle Theatre*, won the Robert E. Sherwood Award for the teleplay *I Was Accused*, and contributed to the *United States Steel Hour, Alcoa-Goodyear Theatre, Kraft Mystery Theatre, Brenner, The Great Adventure, Spenser for Hire*, and *Hawaii-Five-O*, for which he penned thirty-two episodes. Coopersmith's made-for-TV movies include *The Cradle Will Fall* (1983), based on the novel by Mary Higgins Clark.

In addition to *Baker Street*, Coopersmith was attached to another Broadway venture, *The Apple Tree*, a musical based on three short tales by Mark Twain, Frank R. Stockton, and Jules Feiffer. Coopersmith was engaged to write the book, but during preproduction, the composers Jerry Bock and Sheldon Harnick readapted the libretto, explaining that "the show turned out to be more musical than anything else." Coopersmith received program billing for "additional material." *The Apple Tree* opened at New York's Shubert Theatre on October 18, 1966, and ran for 463 performances.

Coopersmith wrote the book for the operatic *Mata Hari*, about the infamous German spy, with music by Edward Thomas and lyrics by Martin Charnin. It premiered in Washington, D.C., in November 1967 and was subsequently staged (as *Ballad for a Firing Squad*) at off-Broadway's Theatre de Lys (1968) and (reverting to its original title) at the

York Theatre (1995). The three-decade efforts were futile, according to reviewer Stephen Holden in the *New York Times*: "Over the years *Mata Hari* has acquired notoriety as a legendary flop. . . . *Mata Hari* reveals itself as not a spoof but a deadly serious and lethally dull musical peddling a garbled message about the futility of war."[19]

Coopersmith's theatrical contributions include the dialogue for the Bill Baird puppet show *Pinocchio*; the book for the musical *Eleanor*, depicting a young Eleanor Roosevelt; a collaboration with Lucy Freeman on *The Mystery of Anna O*, a drama that travels back to 1880's Vienna and the pioneering days of psychoanalysis, produced at the John Houseman Theatre, Manhattan (1992); and an award-winning thriller, *Reflections of a Murder*, presented by the Arena Players Repertory Theatre, Long Island, New York (1998).

A one-act play, *The Other Side*, describes a clash between Houdini and Sir Arthur Conan Doyle on the topic of spiritualism. The playlet premiered in 2008 at the New York Bar Association under the auspices of the Baker Street Irregulars and performed a year later across the Atlantic, sponsored by the Sherlock Holmes Society of London.

Coopersmith is currently an adjunct professor in the Radio and Television Department of Brooklyn College.

* * *

Born in Toronto, Canada, Marian Grudeff studied piano with her mother and made her first appearance in Listz's *Hungarian Fantasy* with the Toronto Symphony Orchestra at the age of eleven. She performed recitals extensively in Canada and in 1946 played with the New York Philharmonic. Four years later she appeared in Carnegie Hall.

Grudeff toured British Columbia and Europe, taught at the Royal Conservatory of Music, and during the 1950s and 1960s contributed her talents to Toronto's theatrical revue *Spring Thaw*.

Following *Baker Street*, Grudeff and her collaborator, Raymond Jessel, were assigned by producer Alexander H. Cohen to work on the musical *Hellzapoppin*. The show closed out of town. Jessel shifted gears and from a theatrical songwriter became a writer-producer for television. He was a creative consultant on *The Jacksons* (1976), story editor on *The Love Boat* (1977), and musical director for *Comedy Factory* (1985) and *Head of the Class* (1987–1991). Among his other credits are *The Bob Newhart Show*, *The Carol Burnett Show*, and *The Dean Martin Show*.

Jessel made one more transition, to that of performer. He is currently enjoying a whole new career as a cabaret headliner, crooning his own songs, which range from Noel Coward–style witticisms to sentimental ballads.

Acting Edition: Doubleday & Company.

NOTES

1. *Mystery Scene* 86 (Fall 2004).

2. Alexander Cohen launched his distinguished Broadway career with the hit production of another criminous "street"—*Angel Street* by Patrick Hamilton (John Golden Theatre, December 5, 1941—1295 performances).

3. *Mystery Scene* 86 (Fall 2004).

4. A silhouetted wax dummy was the device utilized by Holmes to trap Colonel Sebastian Moran—an associate of Moriarty—in *The Adventure of the Empty House*. The stratagem was duplicated as the climax of several plays, but here is executed in the prologue.

5. Irene Adler, the one and only woman to touch Holmes's heart, is described in *A Scandal in Bohemia* as a New Jersey–born, retired opera prima donna who presently lives in London.

6. The scene is borrowed from the story *A Scandal in Bohemia*—*Strand*, July 1891; collected in *The Adventures of Sherlock Holmes* (1892).

7. *Boston Herald*, December 29, 1964.

8. *Variety*, December 30, 1964.

9. Boston *Record American*, December 29, 1964.

10. *Boston Globe*, December 29, 1964.

11. *Daily News*, February 17, 1965.

12. *New York Post*, February 17, 1965.

13. *New York World-Telegram*, February 17, 1965.

14. *Saturday Review*, March 6, 1965.

15. *Cue*, February 27, 1965.

16. *New York Journal-American*, February 21, 1965.

17. *Newark Evening News*, February 28, 1965.

18. *Newsweek*, March 1, 1965.

19. *New York Times*, January 26, 1996.

Catch Me If You Can (1965)

Jack Weinstock (United States, 1907–1969) and Willie Gilbert (United States, 1916–1980)

As the curtain rises on a summer Catskill lodge, Daniel Corban, an advertising man from Detroit, is calling the local police for help. His bride of two weeks, Elizabeth, has stormed out in a tiff, driven off in a yellow Marlin, and vanished. Inspector Levine, a borscht-circuit Columbo, dismisses the disappearance. He relates to Corban that his wife's gone too, to the seashore; she's in Rockaway with her sister. In 96 percent of these cases, maintains Levine, they come back. Corban retorts: "Just what I need—another Keystone cop!"

Catch Me If You Can is based on a 1959 twisty comedy-mystery that originated in France, *Piège pour un homme seul* (*A Trap for a Lonely Man*) by Robert Thomas, but this time, the action is transplanted to the Catskills. The first curve occurs when a pretty red-haired girl is escorted in by the parish priest, Father Kelleher, and asks Corban's forgiveness. "I know I was foolish," she says, kissing him, and she goes into the bedroom to change.

"Father," exclaims a dumbfounded Corban, "that woman is not my wife . . . she's not Elizabeth. I have never seen her before in my life."

It soon becomes apparent that "Elizabeth" is an impostor, in cahoots with Father Kelleher, intending to declare Corban a mental case who belongs in a sanitarium. Failing that, they plan an "accidental death" in order to collect his $100,000 life insurance and his wife's $430,000 inheritance. "You're not worth anything—alive," says Elizabeth to Corban, while lacing his drink with nicotine and twirling a gun with Wild West expertise.

Inspector Levine pouts, "When there's insurance—cherchez le hanky-panky"—but, torn between the two, he is not sure whom to believe. Exasperated, he tells Corban, "If a gorgeous girl—with a build like that—says she was my wife, you know what I'd do? I'd force myself." When at long last Corban finds a witness who can identify his real wife, a nearby kosher caterer named Sidney who has come to deliver brunch, Kelleher stabs the caterer savagely for a second-act curtain.

The wheels of *Catch Me If You Can* keep turning as Corban, cornered, shoots Kelleher and is accused of two murders. And just as Corban manages to prove Elizabeth's dastardly schemes, he finds himself covered by a gun—it is Levine. "Oh, my God!" he stammers, "The Police Inspector himself. You! You arranged everything . . . the alibis . . . the phone calls . . . everything to drive me crazy. And in your official position you could get away with murder."

But there is another surprise in store. Pressured by Levine, Corban makes a slip-of-the-tongue about his missing wife: "She's in my car! . . . off Mountain View Road . . . the sharp curve." We now learn that Levine, Elizabeth, Father Kelleher, and Sidney have combined forces to trap Daniel Corban into confessing that he murdered his wife. Levine explains that the car with the wife's body was found three nights ago. It looked like an accident, says the inspector, but there was one disturbing fact: Elizabeth's glasses were in her bag even though her license said she had to wear them while driving. Why would a nearsighted woman drive at high speed on a strange curving mountain road without her glasses—unless she wasn't driving? His suspicion aroused, Levine and his associates hatched a plan to gather proof, or a confession.

Levine praises his assistant, "Elizabeth," and his deputy, "Father Kelleher," for performing their roles superbly, and thanks Sidney for agreeing to play his death scene on condition he could use his own secret ketchup for blood.

One last twist is left for the final curtain: when Corban is led off handcuffed, "Elizabeth" (Florence) plants a kiss on Levine's mouth: "That's for all the compliments you paid me . . . about my hair . . . my legs . . . my 'build.' After ten years of marriage, I thought you had forgotten." Evidently, Levine's wife did not go to Rockaway's seashore but remained in the Catskills to aid her husband with the capture of a clever murderer.

* * *

According to Robert Thomas in a program note dated May 12, 1962, for an Israeli production of *Piège pour un homme seul* (entitled in Hebrew *The Trap*), the play ran for about six thousand performances around the world. Adapted by Jack Weinstock and Willie Gilbert as *Catch Me If You Can*, it opened on March 9, 1965, at New York's Morosco Theatre. A billboard in the lobby pleaded, "Mum's the word—don't give away the ending," and a show program promised mystification by listing the actors but not the roles they played.

The critics, by and large, were not impressed. "A murder mystery should race and tingle with surprises," opined Howard Taubman. "*Catch*

Me If You Can dawdles and drones for a long time. As a thriller it's a short short."[1] John McClain frowned: "This one is just too preposterous. . . . There is an atmosphere of unreality about the entire proceedings."[2] Walter Kerr believed that "The last two twists are truly surprising. The catch in *Catch Me If You Can* is that you have to see the whole play to be surprised by them."[3] "A little thin . . . this kind of business is quicker and easier on television," decreed John Chapman.[4] However, die-hard mystery aficionado Richard Watts Jr. found here "a cheerful game of homicide and red herrings,"[5] while Norman Nadel applauded "an evening of polished lines, skillfully timed action, cleverly spaced surprises, satanic plotting and a few medium-voltage shocks."[6]

Guided by director Vincent J. Donehue, the actors—Dan Daily as Daniel Corban, Tom Bosley as Inspector Levine, Bethel Leslie as Elizabeth, and George Mathews as Father Kelleher—played their corkscrew parlor game for 103 performances.[7]

Piège pour un homme seul was revived in Paris during the 1970–1971 season with the author in the cast. The play was adapted to television in Austria (1960), Switzerland (1960), the United States (1969, called *Honeymoon with a Stranger*; 1976, called *One of My Wives Is Missing*), Spain (1977), France (1979), the United States again (1986, called *Vanishing Act*), and the Soviet Union (1990).

* * *

Prior to *Catch Me If You Can*, Jack Weinstock and Willie Gilbert wrote comedy material for television and collaborated on two musicals: the Pulitzer Prize/Drama Critics Circle Award winner *How to Succeed in Business without Really Trying* (Forty-sixth Street Theatre, October 14, 1961—1,417 performances) and *Hot Spot* (Majestic Theatre, April 19, 1963—forty-three performances).

Robert Thomas (France, 1927–1989) enacted small roles in variety shows and operettas while penning eight plays that were never produced. Then, during the Christmas of 1959, *Piège pour un homme seul* received the nod. The thirty-two-year-old Thomas followed the universal success of his comic thriller with another detective play, *Huit femmes* (*Eight Women*), which premiered at the Henry VII Theatre on August 28, 1961, and found himself the toast of Paris. The eight women of the title become entangled in the murder of their family patriarch in an isolated countryside mansion. The victim's wife, sister, sister-in-law, mother-in-law, two daughters, housekeeper, maid—each had a motive, each has a secret, each is a suspect.[8]

Thomas continued to pen a succession of clever mysteries: *Le deuxieme coup de feu* (*The Second Shot*)—1964–1965; *Les assassins associés* (*Murder Inc.*)—1965–1966; *La perruche et le poulet* (*The Budgerigar and the Cop*)—1966–1967; *Freddy*—1968–1969; *Le marchand de soleil* (*The Sun Merchant*)—1969–1970; and *La poulette aux oeufs d'or* (*The Chicken with the Golden Eggs*)—1969–1970.

Double jeu (*Double Game*), produced in Paris in 1970–1971 and translated into English by Mawby Green and Ed Feilbert as *Ding Dong Dead*, is the wheels-within-wheels story of a delicate, frightened, and wealthy wife who is placed in mortal danger by her sadistic husband and his deadly associates—only to turn the tables on them a few minutes before the final curtain.

The title character of *Aurelia*, produced 1972–1973, arrives in England from Africa with a scheme to kill her husband's rich aunt for the inheritance. But other forces come into play, weaving a tangled web of deceit—her husband's former lover, a greedy maid, a ruthless blackmailer, and a band of serial burglars. As typical with Thomas, a whirlwind of twists culminates with bitter irony.

Considered France's premier writer of thrillers, in 1969 Thomas adapted into French Agatha Christie's *The Unexpected Guest*.

Acting Edition: Samuel French, Inc. (in manuscript form).

NOTES

1. *New York Times*, March 10, 1965.
2. *New York Journal-American*, March 10, 1965.
3. *New York Herald Tribune*, March 10, 1965.
4. *Daily News*, March 10, 1965.
5. *New York Post*, March 10, 1965.
6. *New York World-Telegram*, March 10, 1965.
7. Thirty years later, during the 1990s, Vintage Dinner Theatre presented *Catch Me If You Can* at various country clubs, restaurants, hotels, and colleges throughout the Finger Lakes region of New York State. Without fail, audiences reacted with oohs and ahs, especially during the final trick revelations. "A gem of a play," wrote reviewer Nancy MacCaig, "a suspenseful fun-packed 90 minutes." *The Corning Leader*, November 21, 1992.
8. *Eight Women* was made into an internationally successful movie in 2002, scripted and directed by François Ozon, featuring a stellar cast that included Danielle Darrieux, Catherine Deneuve, Isabelle Huppert, and Fanny Ardant.

Frankenstein (1965)

The Living Theatre Ensemble

In the mid-1950s, the avant-garde Living Theatre Company, founded by the married couple Julian Beck and Judith Malina and known for its off-beat productions of *The Connection* and *The Brig*, began to rehearse their interpretation of *Frankenstein* while on a European tour. It was a sharp departure from the original novel. Pierre Biner, in his book *The Living Theatre*, cites that for Beck and Malina "the play's philosophical foundation is embedded in the idea that the world must be changed, that a new man must evolve, and all human suffering must be eliminated. The motives of Dr. Frankenstein are to be found in that idea."[1]

Initially a six-hour show, the play evolved from a skeletal script developed by actors' improvisations during rehearsals. The curtain rises as a girl is tossed into a coffin. The girl's executioners hoist the coffin upon their shoulders and carry it down the aisle among the spectators. The cries of the girl, buried alive in the coffin, echo from within. The executioners return to the stage and become victims themselves. One by one they too are killed by various forms of capital punishment: beheading, quartering, crucifixion, electric chair, iron maiden, garrote, guillotine, firing squad. Dr. Frankenstein (played by Julian Beck) is anguished. "How can we end human suffering?" he emotes, and begins to dismember the remains of the scattered bodies. He sets out to create a New Man, free from the omnipresence of society's injustice.

Dr. Frankenstein's laboratory is pentagonal, containing an operating table that slopes in the direction of the audience. A corpse lies on it. The doctor and his assistants don white gowns and masks. They attach plastic tubes equipped with interior lights to the executioners' bodies. Blood is pumped. Instruments are passed. A mystical third eye is transplanted to the Creature's naval. "Slowly, with a sort of whistling of lungs," writes Pierre Biner, "the dead begin to detach themselves from the lit ground, and create in Chinese shadow silhouette the effect of a three-storied monster with red eyes. The curtain slowly descends."[2]

In the second act we meet Fritz, a hanged man who survived because the rope broke. Fritz becomes Dr. Frankenstein's man Friday. His main task is to supply the master with sacks of bloody organs.

The Creature (played in various performances by Steven Ben Israel and by Henry Howard) opens his eyes and is gradually coming to life. He dreams of the sea. On an upper level of the stage a ship collides with an iceberg. The coffin becomes a lifeboat. The actors imitate the sound of the wind, sit on the coffin, and row. They fall into the water, lie down on their backs, and turn into waves, moving their arms in patterns.

The Creature wakes up. A girl sitting behind a desk reads to him headlines taken from English-language newspapers. Through a control booth he learns the history of the world. The actors move about to illustrate such diverse legendary stories as those of Icarus, the Minotaur, Theseus, and the Four Horsemen of the Apocalypse. Armed with an elaborate set of earphones, Frankenstein himself imparts to the Creature the mythology and wisdom of the ages, emphasizing the teachings of Buddha.

Naive, the doctor does not foresee that his noble aspirations will ultimately be corrupted. The Creature soliloquizes the account from Mary Shelley's novel of how it made the discovery of light, darkness, fear, fire, and pain, and its observation of the viciousness of humans, the hypocrisy of governments, the stupidity of laws, and the falsehood of religions. Soon the Creature strangles a policeman who attempted to seize him, and steps upon Fritz, who taunted him with a blazing torch (a sequence borrowed from the classic 1931 movie). More acts of violence follow.

Act III unfolds in a prison. The executioners look for (planted) victims in the auditorium, haul them to the stage, take their fingerprints, and dispatch them to solitary cells. A whistle blows, lights go out, and the prisoners move from one cell to another in a sort of a perpetual motion. Dr. Frankenstein is captured and incarcerated. He leads the prisoners in a revolt, but once again he triggers violence and death. To distract the guards, he starts a fire in his cell. It spreads out of control. Behind a wall of smoke are heard the cries of dying prisoners. The smoke clears to reveal a row of corpses.

The "dead" drag themselves toward the center and slowly they form the silhouette of the Creature. The Creature accuses Frankenstein of having killed innocent people but, in a sort of mea culpa, their enmity results in mutual forgiveness and exchanging kisses. The entire cast chants, "No more violent untimely deaths . . . no more sad scenes of violence, and wars, and early deaths . . . until happiness succeeds man's ancient need for hate." So, surprisingly, in this unique, expressionistic, nightmarish version, the saga of Dr. Frankenstein and his Monster ends on a hopeful, optimistic note.

* * *

When the Living Theatre's *Frankenstein* premiered at the Teatro La Perla in Venice, Italy, on September 26, 1965, the running time of the production was six hours. A second version, five hours in length, opened at the Festival of Cassis, Provence, France, in the summer of 1966. A considerably shorter third rendering of *Frankenstein* emerged at Dublin's Olympic Theatre in October 1967.

On September 9, 1968, the Living Theatre ensemble arrived back in New York aboard the Italian liner *Aurelia*. Upon the opening of *Frankenstein* at the Brooklyn Academy of Music, in repertoire with three other productions, *New York Times* critic Clive Barnes wrote, "The evening is at times repetitious, at times banal, here and there (and only here and there) a little boring. But the overwhelming impression is of a new physical style of theatre, raw, gutsy and vital."[3] The production won an Obie Award.

During 1968 and 1969, the Living Theatre went on a national tour. A performance of *Frankenstein* at the University of Chicago on January 9, 1969, elicited a gushing review from Glenna Syse of the *Chicago Sun-Times*: "It is completely unique, often totally theatrical, funny, devastating and notably ingenious."[4] On the other hand, when *Frankenstein* played for a single night at the University of Southern California, Los Angeles, on February 25, 1969, reviewer Dan Sullivan complained that "the Living Theatre's tendency to do its own thing no matter what makes *Frankenstein* a much deader show than it should be. The company's penchant for animal cries, for example, becomes very wearing after a time and too many scenes go on long, long after you have got the point. . . . I am afraid that more than one nap was taken in USC's Bovard Auditorium Tuesday night as *Frankenstein* lumbered along to midnight."[5]

The Living Theatre continued to mount the three-ton scenery of *Frankenstein* at the Yale School of Drama in New Haven, Connecticut; MIT, Cambridge, Massachusetts; the YM-YWHA, Philadelphia, Pennsylvania; Playhouse-in-the-Park, Cincinnati, Ohio; Detroit Institute of Art, Detroit, Michigan; Fox Forum, Bronx, New York; Lawrence University, Appleton, Wisconsin; University of Colorado, Boulder, Colorado; Berkeley Community Theatre, Berkeley, California; and Nourse Auditorium, San Francisco, California.

In her book *The Living Theatre: USA*, columnist Renfreu Neff describes *Frankenstein* as "a collage of pop art, mytho-science-fiction, and the Late Late Show, all of it buttressed by political dogma and moral polemic. It is essentially naïve and corny in plot concept, yet it is so theatrically spectacular, so brilliantly mounted and performed that a kinetic tension is produced, an existing force that is truly electrical. . . . It is a virtuoso achievement that will never be duplicated by others."[6]

* * *

The daughter of an actress and a rabbi, Judith Malina was born in Kiel, Germany, in 1926. When she was three years old, the family moved to New York City. Interested in acting from an early age, Judith attended the New School for Social Research to study theatre under Erwin Piscator, an exponent of epic theatre. In 1943, when she was seventeen, Judith met Julian Beck (1925–1985), a New Yorker who dropped out of Yale University to pursue the career of a painter. Judith and Julian shared a passion for unconventional drama, founded the experimental Living Theatre as an alternative to the commercial theatre, and got married.

The Living Theatre's choice of political, anarchistic material and shock techniques brought upon it the ire of the authorities. In 1946, their very first venue, a basement at downtown's Wooster Street, was closed by the police department on the charge that it was a front for a brothel. When performing at off-Broadway's Cherry Lane Theatre (August 1951–August 1952), the building was shattered by the fire department. Upon moving to a loft on One Hundredth Street (March 1954–November 1955), they were stopped by the building department. Their theatre at Fourteenth Street and Sixth Avenue (July 1959–January 1964) was sealed by the IRS. Following the last encounter, Beck, Malina, and their company spent the next five years in self-exile, touring in Europe, creating increasingly radical works, dedicating their efforts to further social change.

Initially, the Living Theatre tackled poetic works by Gertrude Stein, Kenneth Rexroth, Paul Goodman, Federico Garcia Lorca, T. S. Eliot, Alfred Jarry, and W. H. Auden. Laced with violent, bloody elements are Stein's *Doctor Faustus Lights the Lights*, in which Mephisto sends Faust to kill a dog and a little boy; Rexroth's *Beyond the Mountains*, a verse adaptation of *The Oresteia*, replicating its multiple assassinations; and Goodman's *Faustina*, depicting the ritual murder of a young, handsome man. Next came interpretations of August Strindberg's *The Spook Sonata*, Jean Cocteau's *Orpheus*, Luigi Pirandello's *Tonight We Improvise*, and Jean Racine's *Phèdre*. The lasting reputation of the company rests with the presentations of modern plays: Jack Gelber's *The Connection*, Bertolt Brecht's *In the Jungle of Cities* and *Man Is Man*, and Kenneth H. Brown's *The Brig*.

The Connection (July 15, 1959) deals with a group of addicts, among them four jazz musicians, waiting in a shabby apartment for their "connection," a drug pusher nicknamed Cowboy. The down-to-earth dialogue is interspersed sporadically with improvised jazz tunes. Under a naked bulb hung on a long wire over center stage, the men tell their stories and express their desperation. When Cowboy arrives, one by one the addicts exit to the bathroom for their fix. In a tense climax, the owner of the apartment, Leach (played by Warren Finnerty), takes an overdose. It is reported that during the three-year run of the play, a total of about fifty spectators fainted at the sight of Leach sticking a hypodermic in his arm. Under the direction of Judith Malina, the actors broke through the fourth wall with asides directed at the viewers, making entrances and exits through the aisles, and mingling with the audience during the intermission to solicit money for cocaine. *The Connection* was savaged by the morning-after newspaper reviewers ("A farrago of dirt, smalltime philosophy, empty talk," wrote the *New York Times*),[7] but hailed in various magazines by such authorities as Robert Brustein, Harold Clurman, and Henry Hewes. In 1960, *The Connection* won an Obie Award for Best New Play. It ran for over seven hundred performances and was the backbone of the Living Theatre's repertory for more than two years. With a screenplay by Jack Gelber and featuring many members of the original cast, the play was filmed in 1962 under the direction of Shirley Clarke.

Judith Malina directed and Julian Beck designed a 1960 revival of *In the Jungle of Cities*, Bertolt Brecht's 1920s melodrama about money and its affecting corruption. Garga, a romantic boy from the prairies, falls under the influence of Shlink, a wealthy lumber dealer in Chicago of 1912, and turns into a demon. The critics by and large found the Brecht play enigmatic and without focus, but Robert Brustein, in an article in *New Republic*, commented: "It has a diabolical brilliance and hypnotic power which is quite overwhelming and it leaves its mark on you like a wound." Brustein, however, had this to say about the production: "While the Living Theatre has very effectively evoked that weird gallery of gangsters, coolies, pimps, whores, sailors, and salvationists which make up the grotesque population of this play, the essence of the work has escaped them."[8]

In September 1962, the Living Theatre added to its repertoire a second Brecht play, also written in the 1920s. Set in India, *Man Is Man* is the story of Galy Gay, an innocent, gullible day laborer who is tricked by three British soldiers and a seductive camp-following widow to impersonate a captured soldier. He gradually turns into a human fighting machine, enthusiastically firing the cannon that destroys the enemy's fortress. Jamie Edward Rader, in his MFA thesis, writes: "*Man Is Man* embodies Brecht's ideas about the frailty of human identity, the dehumanizing effect of military life, and the senselessness of war. It is a savage clown show which uses slapstick, shock, music, direct speeches to the audience, and other devices to demonstrate his feelings about the total insignificance of the individual personality in the modern world."[9]

Another play about the dehumanizing effect of military life is Kenneth H. Brown's *The Brig*. In his article "Storming the Barricades," Julian Beck relates: "*The Brig* arrived in the mail. I opened it. Knew instantly that it was the next play we would do. Read it that night. It was as if everything in my life had led to the occasion."[10] The playwright, Kenneth H. Brown, had been in the Marines for three years, from 1954 to 1957, stationed at

the base of Mount Fujiyama in central Japan. One night, when he returned from leave four hours late, he had been declared AWOL and was
confined in the Marine brig for thirty days. Brown based *The Brig* on his
experience, recapturing the harrowing existence of prisoners who had
their heads shaved, were forbidden to speak to each other, were called
"maggots," punched in the stomach, and constantly belittled, degraded,
and humiliated. "The action of *The Brig* was simple, repetitive, and hellish," writes professor of English John Tytell in *The Living Theatre: Art,
Exile, and Outrage*. "Its emphatic point was that sane prisoners had been
conditioned to behave like madmen. Implicitly, it suggested that the
world was a prison. Brown showed the progress of a day from sunrise
to bedtime, arranging the action in a series of dehumanizing episodes
where the excruciatingly boring routine of the prisoners was interrupted
by the torture imposed by the guards. . . . The prisoners in *The Brig* were
so spiritually defiled and beaten that they were always in danger of snapping, losing all mental control, and breaking down like the prisoner at the
end of the play."[11] Designer Julian Beck replaced the conventional curtain
with a barbed-wire fence.

"*The Brig* is a structure. The precision of the description of this structure
is the key to *The Brig*," asserts Judith Malina in her essay "Directing *The
Brig*." She proceeds to describe how she created an autocratic discipline
during the rehearsals, demanding that the cast members study *The Guide-
book for Marines* and adhere to rigid rules "such as promptness. Proper
dress, silence. . . . Actors will sign in before Rehearsal Time. . . . No eating
during rehearsal time. . . . All actors and crew will maintain a respectful
and serious attitude toward one another. There will be no joking toler-
ated during Rehearsal Time, especially in reference to the relationships
of guards and prisoners."[12] As all the moves of the prisoners must be
executed at a running pace, much of the rehearsal time was dedicated to
drill. A lobby of the theatre was cleared, and the actors marched endless
hours on the tile floors.

The Brig premiered on May 15, 1963, and, like *The Connection*, was
generally lambasted by the critics. They called the play "mindless" and
"self-conscious." Some thought that "it makes a painful evening in the
theatre" while others dismissed it as "totally self-contained; the audience
might just as well not be there." But, like *The Connection*, with the passage of time *The Brig* garnered a cult reputation in the annals of modern
American drama. Scripted by Kenneth H. Brown and directed by Jonas
and Adolfas Mekas, the play was filmed in 1964.

In addition to *Frankenstein*, the Living Theatre's tour of Europe consisted of several dark and criminous plays. The nine improvised, un-
connected episodes of *Mysteries and Smaller Pieces* include a sequence of
piling corpses, apparently the victims of a nuclear holocaust. Sophocles'

Antigone, adapted by Brecht, continues the Living Theatre's trademark of heroic rebellion against evil authority as the title character buries her brother in violation of the king's edict, and pays with her life. Jean Genet's *The Maids*, based on a real-life case, is the story of the sisters Lemercier, domestic servants Claire and Solange, who spend their time play-acting the role of their hated Madame and fail in their scheme to poison her by mixing lime tea with pills of phenobarbital.

* * *

Julian Beck died of stomach cancer in 1985. Hanon Reznikov, a veteran company member who had become Malina's lover, and later her husband, assumed coleadership of the Living Theatre until his death in May of 2008. In 2009, Malina was invited to the Yale University School of Drama for a two-day residency that included a series of classes and workshops. Still going strong at the age of eighty-four, Malina runs the Living Theatre at the Lower East Side of Manhattan. In December of 2009, she directed *Red Noir* by poet Anne Waldman, "a detective thriller based on film noir techniques and themes." True to form, the play begins with a chorus of twenty or so chanting "Anarchy! Anarchy!" and then stepping into the auditorium, surrounding the audience. The lead character, Ruby (played by Sheila Dabney), is a private eye in a red dress assigned to find a missing valise. Reviewer Andy Webster of the *New York Times* found the proceedings "tough to follow" but liked the chorus members: "The energy these performers bring to this abstract, scattershot, elaborately choreographed ramble of a play is impressive. And their youthful hunger for guidance from a formidable visionary like Ms. Malina is palpable. Who will remain in this shifting neighborhood to inspire them when she is gone?"[13]

Awards and Honors: Judith Malina was the recipient of a Lola D'Annunzio Award (1959), Page One Award (1960), seven Obie Awards (1960, 1964, 1969, 1975, 1987, 1989, and 2007), Creative Arts Citation from Brandeis University (1961), Grand Prix du Théâtre des Nations (1961), Paris Critics Circle medallion (1961), Prix de l'Université de Paris (1961), New England Theatre Conference Award (1962), Olympio Prize (1967), and a Guggenheim Fellowship (1985). Julian Beck won the Creative Arts Citation from Brandeis University (1961), Prix de l'Université de Paris (1961), and six Obie Awards.

NOTES

1. Pierre Biner, *The Living Theatre* (New York: Horizon Press, 1972), 111.
2. Pierre Biner, *The Living Theatre*, 123.

3. *New York Times*, October 3, 1968.

4. Quoted in Donald F. Glut, *The Frankenstein Legend* (Metuchen, NJ: Scarecrow Press, 1973), 51.

5. Quoted in Donald F. Glut, *The Frankenstein Legend*, 53.

6. Renfreu Neff, *The Living Theatre: USA* (New York: Bobbs-Merrill, 1970), 66.

7. *New York Times*, July 16, 1959.

8. *New Republic*, January 9, 1961.

9. Jamie Edward Rader, "Representative Productions of The Living Theatre, 1959–1963" MFA thesis, Ohio University, 1968, 49.

10. Kenneth H. Brown, *The Brig* (New York: Hill & Wang, 1965), 4.

11. John Tytell, *The Living Theatre: Art, Exile, and Outrage* (New York: Grove Press, 1995), 180, 181.

12. Kenneth H. Brown, *The Brig*, 92, 93, 94.

13. *New York Times*, December 25, 2009.

The Playroom (1965)

Mary Drayton (United States, 1905–1994)

In a deserted attic of the Montana, a fashionable apartment building over-looking Central Park in New York City, a group of privileged, spoiled teenagers, who call themselves The Filthy Five, assemble to booze, smoke weed, play strip poker, croon reviling songs, and, when bored, plot das-tardly schemes. The three boys and two girls are united in their hostility toward their parents.

The Playroom weaves a tale fraught with terror when one of the teens, Judy Michaels, who bitterly resents the recent marriage of her father, pro-poses that the gang kidnap her stepmother's ten-year-old daughter, El-len. They proceed to imprison the little girl in the attic, bug the Michaels' apartment with an intercom, and as a lark send a ransom note for $10,000. Ellen, clinging to her stuffed panda, is innocently delighted with her new-found friends—her lovely stepsister Judy; chubby Paulie; effeminate Eric; sophisticated Peter; and the cool Charlot from France.

The new Mrs. Michaels calls the police, and the malevolent youths realize that the repercussions of their playful plot may be serious. Their gruesome solution is to "eliminate" the captive by plying her with sleep-ing pills and wrapping the body in an airtight plastic garment bag. Dur-ing a tense climax, Judy has a change of heart, struggles with the boys, and pulls Ellen out, shaking her and crying, "Wake up, wake up. Don't be dead. You mustn't be dead! Oh, God. Dear God. Make her all right. Let her be all right."

Ellen is still breathing and will recover. Judy will face the reverberation of her fling at crime.

* * *

The Playroom, staged by Joseph Anthony, opened at New York's Brooks Atkinson Theatre on December 5, 1965. The morning-after reviewers were split. John McClain found the play "the most tingling, tantalizing and suspenseful bone buckler to have been presented within the limits of my faltering memory,"[1] while John Chapman declared, "*The Playroom* strikes me as being out of style, for all its up-to-the-minute gimmicks."[2] Richard Watts Jr. applauded "an ingenious and entertaining tale of menace and seemingly impending horror,"[3] but Howard Taubman opined, "There are enough holes in *The Playroom* to equip a large swiss cheese."[4] Walter Kerr recommended the thriller as "a good scare,"[5] and Norman Nadel was spellbound by its "compelling atmosphere of evil";[6] however, actors Karen Black, Bonnie Bedelia, Richard Thomas, Peter Kastner, and Alan Howard, as The Filthy Five, occupied the attic of the Montana for only thirty-three performances.

* * *

Born in Hope, Arkansas, Mary Drayton was an actress until an auto accident in the 1940s cut short her career and she turned to playwriting. Prior to *The Playroom*, her play *Debut*, based on Isabel Dunn's novel *Maria and the Captain*, premiered at Broadway's Holiday Theatre on February 22, 1956. The comedy, about a South Carolina belle (played by Inger Stevens) who falls in love with a visiting Boston writer (Tom Helmore), ran a mere four performances. However, the occasion had a happy turn, for playwright Drayton wed actor Helmore, a marriage that lasted till her death in 1994.

Acting Edition: Samuel French, Inc.

NOTES

1. *New York Journal-American*, December 6, 1965.
2. *Daily News*, December 6, 1965.
3. *New York Post*, December 6, 1965.
4. *New York Times*, December 6, 1965.
5. *New York Herald Tribune*, December 6, 1965.
6. *New York World-Telegram*, December 6, 1965.

Wait until Dark (1966)

Frederick Knott (China-born, England–United States, 1918–2002)

Lightning struck thrice for Frederick Knott. In 1952 he came out with *Dial "M" for Murder*, which according to Stanley Richard's preface in *Best Mystery and Suspense Plays of the Modern Theatre* was "unquestionably one of the most internationally performed suspense plays of the mid-century."[1] In 1961, *Write Me a Murder* was his second major hit both on Broadway and the West End, and five years later he penned another blockbuster with *Wait until Dark*.

The almost-continuous action takes place in a Greenwich Village basement apartment. Sam Hendrix, a commercial photographer, is sent on assignment. Unbeknownst to him, it is only a ruse to get him out of the way. Upon a recent trip to Montreal, a strange woman at the airport entrusted Sam with a rag doll for safekeeping. Now, three shady characters descend upon the apartment determined to obtain the doll, which is stuffed with uncut heroin worth $50,000. The only obstacle that stands in the mobsters' way is Sam's blind wife, Susy.

The unholy trio devise an elaborate charade of pretense, claiming to be Sam's wartime buddy, a police sergeant, and a father and son masqueraded by the leader of the gang, Harry Roat Jr. They hope to gain Susy's confidence so that she will unwittingly steer them to the hidden doll. The lonely blind woman, whose other senses are very acute, perceives that something is wrong. Against all odds, she wages a war of wits against the thugs.

After a harrowing cat-and-mouse encounter, during which Roat kills his two more humane associates, Susy, frightened and desperate, is left to face him. Roat takes from his zip bag a metal can of gasoline and sprinkles it all over the carpet and around the bedroom door. Susy feels the tabletop until she finds a box of matches. She manages to switch off the lights. In the dark she finds the can of gasoline. When Roat strikes a match, Susy goes straight for him. He extinguishes the flicker, shouting, "No! I've blown it out. It's out!"

Susy seems to be in control of the situation. But in one of the play's most fearful moments, Roat suddenly opens the refrigerator, throwing a wide beam of light straight across at Susy.

"So you see—it's all finished," he says. "You can relax now, Susy. It's all over."

He grabs a kitchen knife. A struggle ensues, during which Roat is stabbed. Susy crawls toward the refrigerator in an attempt to close its door. Roat plunges his knife into the floor ahead of him, pulling himself along after Susy, sliding like a reptile. She makes a frenzied effort to find the refrigerator cord. Roat reaches the refrigerator and hauls himself up, using the inside trays like a ladder. Just as he raises his knife, Susy tugs the cord. When Sam Hendrix and the police arrive on the scene, they find Roat in a grotesque position, slumped over the refrigerator door, apparently dead. Susy emerges from the terrifying ordeal dazed but unscathed.

* * *

Wait until Dark premiered at the Ethel Barrymore Theatre on February 2, 1966. It was directed by Arthur Penn, with Lee Remick as blind Susy, Robert Duvall as the sadistic Roat, and Mitchell Ryan and Val Bisoglio as his ill-fated collaborators. The critics were divided. Stanley Kauffmann acknowledged "some pretty good scares in the final scene of *Wait until Dark*," but complained that "Frederick Knott, the author, makes us pay for the chills in that scene with a slow start, unnecessary complicated action and some weak motivation."[2] Walter Kerr opined that "Author Knott has tied too simple, too tenuous, and therefore too exasperating a knot. He makes you dismiss both the criminals and the victim as clods."[3]

Other reviewers gave *Wait until Dark* their stamp of approval. "Mr. Knott has an ingenious way with his plots and his people, and here he has pitted a psychopathic killer and two jailbirds against a single blind girl and contrived to have her emerge the winner," lauded John McClain.[4] Richard Watts Jr. danced in the aisle: "It is a rousing example of the school of chilling menace that deserves the popular welcome it seems certain to capture. . . . *Wait until Dark* is the suspense drama we've long awaited eagerly."[5] Norman Nadel nodded appreciatively: "At a sudden, violent movement on the darkened stage, every man and woman in the audience gasped audibly, exclaimed, screamed, shouted a warning, or at least gulped air."[6]

Wait until Dark played on Broadway for 373 performances. Lee Remick was nominated for a Tony Award as best actress. Shirley Jones and Ann Blyth also portrayed Susy Hendrix during the long run. The thriller had a two-year stay in London, with Honor Blackman, and a sparkling reception in Paris, with Annie Girardot.

Following a tryout engagement in Boston (Wilbur Theatre, March 12–March 22, 1998), a revival of *Wait until Dark*, directed by Leonard Foglia, arrived at New York's Brooks Atkinson Theatre a week later for a series of previews and an official opening on April 5, 1998. Marisa Tomei starred as Susy, with Quentin Tarantino portraying Harry Roat. Reviewer Ben Brantley roasted Tarantino as "menacing to nothing except possibly Mr. Knott's script," and sneered at a play that "today comes across as a tediously contrived wind-up toy that yells 'Boo!' just before it runs down."[7] *Wait until Dark* went dark after a three-month run.

A 1967 screen version, directed by Terence Young, had Audrey Hepburn menaced by Alan Arkin, Richard Crenna, and Jack Weston. Hepburn was nominated for an Academy Award as best actress. Critic Leonard Maltin called the film "a solid shocker" and "a memorable nail-biter."[8] William L. DeAndrea stated in *Encyclopedia Mysteriosa*: "Hepburn's attempt to combat her attackers in the pitch-black apartment is one of the most suspenseful scenes ever filmed."[9]

In 1982, *Wait until Dark* was presented on television with Katharine Ross as Suzy Hendrix and Stacy Keach as Harry Roat.

Acting Edition: Dramatists Play Service.

NOTES

1. Stanley Richards, ed., *Best Mystery and Suspense Plays of the Modern Theatre* (New York: Dodd, Mead, 1971), 101.

2. *New York Times*, February 3, 1966.

3. *New York Herald Tribune*, February 3, 1966.

4. *New York Journal-American*, February 3, 1966.

5. *New York Post*, February 3, 1966.

6. *New York World-Telegram*, February 3, 1966. As one who has staged *Wait until Dark* for the New London Players, New Hampshire, and at Elmira College, Elmira, New York, I can verify that an unexpected, murderous leap executed by the wounded Roat, in semi-darkness, toward his cowering victim, Susy, still yields shrieks of alarm from the unnerved spectators.

7. *New York Times*, April 6, 1998.

8. *Leonard Maltin's 1997 Movie and Video Guide* (New York: Signet, 1996), 1449.

9. William L. DeAndrea, *Encyclopedia Mysteriosa* (New York: Prentice Hall, 1994), 367.

It's a Bird . . . It's a Plane . . . It's Superman (1966)

Book by David Newman (United States, 1937–2003) and Robert Benton (United States, 1932–), Music by Charles Strouse (United States, 1928–), Lyrics by Lee Adams (United States, 1924–)

Superman, a comics superstar and cultural icon, was created by American writer Jerry Siegel and Canadian-born artist Joe Shuster in 1932. The character first appeared in the June 1938 issue of *Action Comics #1*.[1] Subsequently, the Man of Steel was presented in radio serials, television programs, motion pictures, newspaper strips, and video games. On Broadway, he made an appearance only once—in the 1966 musical *It's a Bird . . . It's a Plane . . . It's Superman.*

Divided into two acts and many short scenes, the musical begins with a raucous sequence unfolding on a Metropolis street. A car, its motor purring, is parked next to a facade of a bank. Seven crooks emerge from the bank carrying bags of money and brandishing guns. They run for the getaway car, followed by security guards. The crooks shoot at the guards, killing them.

Suddenly on the scene, arriving from above (by means of a rigged contraption of invisible wires), is a figure dressed in outlandish tights and a cape marked with the letter S. Superman lands, rushes to the rear of the car and grabs it by the back fender. He lifts the car and flings it into the sky, off-stage. Then, while donning his alter ego disguise as Clark Kent, a timid, bespectacled newspaper reporter, Superman sings "Doing Good," happy in his mission of "averting murder, larceny and rape."[2]

At the offices of the *Daily Planet* we meet Clark Kent's colleagues—editor Perry White, columnist Max Mencken, and reporter Lois Lane, who keeps getting into scraps and being saved by Superman. Secretary Sydney is in love with Max, but the columnist is concentrating on advancing his career. He believes that exposing the identity of "the scarlet-caped show-off with an S on his chest" will boost his reputation. When the dejected Sydney calls Max "a low, rotten, lying, cheating rat," he coolly answers, "Well, nobody's perfect."

Clark tells Lois that he was promoted from doing basketball scores to Shipping News. Lois shares with him her frustration about Superman, who has often saved her life but has never "said I'm attractive." She sighs and croons the ballad "Superman," in which she confesses her love for her protector but believes that she may have to look for "a guy with both feet on the ground."

Enter Dr. Abner Sedgwick, head of MIT—Metropolis Institute of Technology. He informs Lois that the institute's $20 million nuclear reactor is flashing a red warning light that signifies a "dangerous buildup of negative radioactive electrons." If something isn't done immediately to halt this deadly accumulation, the entire city "will be a graveyard by tomorrow." Clark, who has been eavesdropping, hurriedly exits.

Slipping into a telephone booth in front of a drop curtain, Clark Kent strips and steps out in full Superman regalia. He whoops, "Up, up, and awayyy!" and flies off stage.[3]

Lois, Dr. Sedgwick, and his assistant Jim Morgan enter the outer chamber of the nuclear reactor at MIT, a vast open room with a large arrow marked DANGER. A red light is on, signifying the precarious situation. Superman flies in, and with his x-ray vision identifies the problem in the gamma chamber. He enters the chamber and the door clangs shut behind him. After a tense moment, a boom is heard from inside the reactor and the red light goes off. Superman emerges, tells Dr. Sedgwick that he always "wanted to have a look at one of these gizmos up close," and flies away. Jim Morgan flirts with Lois and offers her a ride to Metropolis. Left by himself, Dr. Sedgwick is revealed as the villain of the piece, a mad scientist who has repeatedly lost the Nobel Prize and is now seeking revenge. He vows to destroy the world's symbol of good—Superman!

Vengeful Dr. Sedgwick and ambitious Max Mencken join forces to trap Superman. They solicit the help of the Flying Lings, a father and five sons who work as acrobats. "I require superior strength, exceptional mobility, and team spirit," says Dr. Sedgwick to Father Ling, and sends the acrobats to City Hall Tower, the highest building in Metropolis, to blow it to smithereens with sticks of dynamite. When City Hall explodes, the citizens of Metropolis are disappointed that Superman failed to save it.

Dr. Sedgwick and Max Mencken decipher the identity of Superman. The scientist tells Clark that he is aware of his "unfortunate childhood," when he was "rejected" by Kryptonian parents who left him adrift, alone, on another planet, and convinces Superman that his heroic deeds were not executed for the benefit of humanity but to satisfy his ego, "to win the adulation of millions." Superman is shaken, his confidence shattered.

Sedgwick and Max are elated, but unexpectedly the leader of the Lings wheels around, his normal placidity now gone, and points a revolver at

Max. He then pins a medal on Sedgwick "on behalf of People's Republic of China." Ling declares that within minutes an off-shore submarine will launch a missile of atomic warheads toward Metropolis.

Lois attempts to draw Superman's attention but he remains indifferent and immobile. It is only when Ling slaps Lois viciously and shoots at Max, that Superman begins to break through the fog. He mutters, "I'll never stop doing good," and whips into action. A choreographed battle ensues. The Flying Lings make spectacular leaps, using every dirty trick in the book, attacking Superman from all sides, using karate, judo, knives, crowbars, sledgehammers, and battering rams. Through this barrage, Superman sings "Pow! Bam! Zonk!" and fights them off. By the end of the melee, the Lings are piled up at his feet.

Dr. Sedgwick, realizing that all is lost, holds Lois hostage as he escapes up the stairs to the top of the water tower. Lois screams for help and Superman follows. Sedgwick fires at Superman, who advances steadily. Suddenly, the sound of loud motors is heard and a helicopter appears overhead. A rope drops down. Sedgwick flings Lois away and leaps for the rope. He misses and plummets to his death.

Policemen arrive to herd the Lings away. Sydney hugs Max, who is only slightly wounded. Lois and Superman embrace, but when a cop announces, "There's a missile heading this way!" the Man of Steel exclaims, "This is a job for Superman! Up, up, and awayyy!"

* * *

Produced and directed by Harold Prince, *It's a Bird . . . It's a Plane . . . It's Superman* previewed in Philadelphia on February 12 and 14, 1966. The audiences responded with standing ovations but the critics savaged it. Ron Snyder of local station KYW TV proclaimed, "It's a bird, it's a plane, it's a bomb."[4] With some rewrites and cast replacements, the musical opened at New York's Alvin Theatre on March 29, 1966. The next morning, there were pro and con reviews. Richard Watts Jr. pointed out that authors David Newman and Robert Benton followed "the spirit and letter of the famous strip" and found the production "ingenious."[5] John McClain admired the show's "style and speed" and promised audiences "a good time."[6] Stanley Kauffmann applauded "brisk lyrics, some clever staging and some very engaging performers."[7]

However, Douglas Watt sniffed at "an exercise in low camp";[8] Norman Nadel believed that "the show has trouble sustaining its comic level";[9] Walter Kerr bemoaned a promising endeavor that "runs out of cheek . . . is lame where it daren't be . . . is on the whole only half-sly vaudeville. . . . Its wit is on the lazy side."[10]

The actors-singers were unanimously praised—Bob Holiday (Superman/Clark Kent), Patricia Marand (Lois Lane), Jack Cassidy (Max

Mencken), Linda Lavin (Sydney), and Michael O'Sullivan (Dr. Abner Sedgwick). Bruce Scivally relates in *Superman on Film, Television, Radio and Broadway* that during one performance, as the six-foot-four-inch Holiday was flying in on an entrance, "the shackle of his flying harness broke. Holiday fell about six feet on the stage. Without breaking character, he sprang to his feet, put his hands on his hips, looked into the audience and said, 'That would have hurt any mortal man!' The audience screamed, cheered and gave Holiday a standing ovation."[11] *It's a Bird . . . It's a Plane . . . It's Superman* ran for 129 performances. Two revivals were mounted the next year—at the St. Louis Municipal Opera and the Kansas City Starlight Theatre. Bob Holiday reprised the title role in both productions, with Charles Nelson Reilly as Dr. Sedgwick. In 1992, the musical was reincarnated by the Goodspeed Opera House, East Haddam, Connecticut, with Gary Jackson as Superman. The Flying Lings were now an Arabian tumbling troupe. A concert version of *It's a Bird . . .* was presented in Los Angeles in 2007, featuring Cheyenne Jackson as Superman and Patrick Cassidy in his father's role of Max Mencken, before moving to Manhattan's York Theatre with some cast replacements. The Dallas Theatre Center performed a revised version of *It's a Bird . . .* with a new book by Roberto Aguirre-Sacasa, in June and July 2010. The show had an $800,000 budget, a cast of twenty-four and more than a hundred costume changes. According to the *New York Times*, "the creative team admits it has one eye on Broadway."[12]

It's a Bird . . . was adapted into an ABC television special on February 1, 1975, with the evil band of Chinese acrobats transformed to Mafia gangsters. It starred David Wilson (Superman/Clark Kent), Lesley Ann Warren (Lois Lane), David Wayne (Dr. Abner Sedgwick), and Loretta Swit (Sydney). David Newman and Robert Benton were among the cadre of writers of the Superman film quartet that starred Christopher Reeve (1978, 1980, 1983, and 1987).[13] However, Newman and Benton were not connected to the later *Superman Returns* (2006), featuring Brandon Routh.

* * *

Besides *It's a Bird . . . It's a Plane . . . It's Superman*, librettists David Newman and Robert Benton's only other contribution to Broadway consisted of a sketch in *Oh! Calcutta!* (1969), an X-rated revue dedicated to sex-related topics.[14] The following year, the notorious show opened at London's fringe Roundhouse Theatre and was transferred to West End's Royalty and Duchess Theatres for a total of 3,918 showings. In 1976, it was revived at New York's Edison Theatre for 5,959 performances, the longest-running revue in Broadway history.

David Newman worked as the magazine editor and Robert Benton was the art director of *Esquire* where they met and began their fruitful collaboration. Following their Broadway ventures, they migrated to Hollywood, where both made a name for themselves as screenwriters and directors. Their first team effort was the screenplay of *Bonnie and Clyde* (1967), a milestone crime drama about the famous pair who robbed banks during the Great Depression (the movie was selected for preservation in the United States National Film Registry). Newman and Benton followed this with the prison caper *There Was a Crooked Man* (1970), the screwball comedy *What's Up, Doc?* (1972), the western *Bad Company* (1972), *Superman* (1978), and the psychological thriller *Still of the Night* (1982).

Newman and Benton broke their partnership but continued to pursue their motion picture careers. Newman scripted *Superman II* (1981) with Mario Puzo; *Jinxed!* (1982), a Las Vegas black comedy, with Bert Blessing (a pen name for Frank D. Gilroy); and, on his own, *Santa Claus* (1985), the tale of a greedy toy manufacturer. Benton teamed with other writers on the scenarios of *The Late Show* (1977), a moody whodunit about an aging private eye who traces the murderer of his partner; *Kramer vs. Kramer* (1979), the story of a complicated divorce (an Oscar winner as Best Picture); *Places in the Heart* (1984), a nostalgic look at a small Texas town during the 1930s (for which he won the Academy Award for Best Original Screenplay); and *The Ice Harvest* (2005), a noir adventure that pivots around a duffle bag full of stolen money.

Mastering a variety of genres, Benton directed the comedy *Nadine* (1987), the gangster saga *Billy Bathgate* (1991), the domestic drama *Nobody's Fool* (1994), the murder thriller *Twilight* (1998), and the romantic *Feast of Love* (2007).

* * *

Prior to *It's a Bird . . . It's a Plane . . . It's Superman*, New York–born composer Charles Strouse and Ohio-born lyricist Lee Adams collaborated on the 1960 hit *Bye Bye Birdie*, for which they won their first Tony Award. They also created *All American* (1962) and *Golden Boy* (1964), starring Sammy Davis Jr. In 1970, Strouse and Adams teamed on *Applause*, starring Lauren Bacall, for which they garnered their second Tony (Strouse was awarded a third Tony in 1977 for another comic strip, *Annie*). Strouse, who admits to inspiration by Jerome Kern, Cole Porter, and Stephen Sondheim, has written fourteen scores for Broadway, including *Charlie and Algernon* (1979), *Rags* (1986), *Annie 2* (1989), *Nick and Nora* (1993), and *Minsky's* (2009). Strouse composed the film scores of *Bonnie and Clyde* (1967), *The Night They Raided Minsky's* (1968), *There Was a Crooked Man*

(1970), *Just Tell Me What You Want* (1980), *Ishtar* (1987), and the animated *All Dogs Go to Heaven* (1989).

Strouse and Adams also cowrote "Those Were the Days," the opening theme to CBS TV's situation comedy *All in the Family*.

Acting Edition: Tams-Witmark Music Library.

Awards and Honors: A top-ten selection in *The Best Plays of 1965–1966* ("It was not camped, but played as straight as possible in a good laugh at our secret longing for a hero who could solve all problems, defeat all enemies. . . . This Superman is almost human. What is he but a knight-errant of the space age who can 'fight the unbeatable foe' and win, who *can* reach the unreachable star? Superman is Don Quixote's dream come true; and Don Quixote's dream, though it may be laughable, is never ridiculous. The same goes for Superman in his welcome arrival in a stage version").[15]

Composer Charles Strouse was the recipient of the Rodgers and Hammerstein Award, and he is a member of the Songwriters Hall of Fame (inducted 1985) and the Theatre Hall of Fame (inducted 2001). Lyricist Lee Adams was inducted into the Songwriters Hall of Fame in 1989.

NOTES

1. The June 1938 issue of *Action Comics #1* originally cost 10 cents. In February 2010 it sold for $1 million.

2. Superman/Clark Kent continues the tradition of literary heroes who establish a counterpart persona to baffle their foes. Others include Sir Percy Blakeney/The Scarlet Pimpernel, the Duke of Charnerace/Arsène Lupin, Don Diego/Zorro, Pierre Birabeau/The Red Shadow (in the musical *The Desert Song*), Bruce Wayne/Batman, Selina Kyle/Catwoman, and Tony Stark/Iron Man.

3. In the published version of the musical, the authors suggest that stock and amateur groups who desire to produce *It's a Bird . . . It's a Plane . . . It's Superman* may dispense with the flying effect and "the actor portraying Superman need merely cry, 'Up, up and away!' and dash off stage while those left on stage can look and point upward. . . . The audience, knowing the legend of Superman, will accept the fact that he can fly without having to see it before their eyes."

4. Quoted in Bruce Scivally, *Superman on Film, Television, Radio and Broadway* (Jefferson, NC: McFarland, 2008), 67.

5. *New York Post*, March 30, 1966.

6. *New York Journal-American*, March 30, 1966.

7. *New York Times*, March 30, 1966.

8. *Daily News*, March 30, 1966.

9. *New York World-Telegram*, March 30, 1966.

10. *New York Herald Tribune*, March 30, 1966.

11. Bruce Scivally, *Superman on Film, Television, Radio and Broadway*, 69.

12. *New York Times*, July 4, 2010.

13. David Newman and Robert Benton were not involved with the previous movie *Superman and the Mole Men*, aka *The Unknown People* (1951), a fifty-eight-minute low-budget feature made as a pilot for the long-running television series *Adventures of Superman* (1952–1958) with George Reeves as the Man of Steel.

14. *Oh! Calcutta!* premiered at off-Broadway's Eden Theatre in 1969 and was transferred to Broadway's Belasco Theatre for a total of 1,314 performances.

15. Otis L. Guernsey Jr., ed., *The Best Plays of 1965–1966* (New York: Dodd, Mead, 1966), 16–18.

We Have Always
Lived in the Castle (1966)

Hugh Wheeler
(England-born American, 1912–)

The dark happenings of *We Have Always Lived in the Castle* unfold in an isolated Vermont home, where a multiple murder was committed six years earlier. Nearly everyone in the Blackwood family—father, mother, aunt, and young boy—died after sugar mixed with arsenic was sprinkled on their blackberries.

The older daughter, Constance, was accused of the mass poisoning but was acquitted. Since then, Constance has feared the nearby villagers who have composed a nasty chant about her: "Father, Father, quick, quick, quick. Mother dear, we're up the creek. Constance fed us arsenic."

As a result, Constance becomes a recluse, never wandering from her "castle." She spends each day caring for a fifteen-year-old sister, Merricat, who seems to carry ghosts of her own; a crotchety old uncle, Julian, who scribbles his memoirs while confined to an electric wheelchair; and a tiny black boy, Jonas, adopted from an orphanage, who likes to hide in the dumbwaiter and emit weird sounds.

A youthful cousin, Charles, arrives from abroad and serves as the catalyst for the dire events that follow. Charles and Constance fall in love, to the chagrin of Merricat, who is fiercely possessive of her sister. We discover that it was Merricat who poisoned the family in a fit of rage, and now the kid sister embarks on another homicidal quest, first dropping the boy Jonas to the bottom of the dumbwaiter shaft as an eerie "sacrifice," then lacing Charles's strawberry dessert with rat poison. It was the only suitable way, confides Merricat to Constance. She assures her sister that there is no need to worry. They'll bury Jonas and Charles in the lawn, and everyone will think that they went away. She'll plant a flower on the grave as a marker. Perhaps a yellow rose.

Surrounded by spirits of the dead, the two sorrowful sisters will always live in the castle.

* * *

We Have Always Lived in the Castle was dramatized by Hugh Wheeler from a 1962 novel by Shirley Jackson (1919–1965), mistress of the modern gothic. The play premiered at the Ethel Barrymore Theatre on October 19, 1966, a year after Jackson's death. The reviews were devastating. "One of the sloppiest written, drudgiest directed and carelessly acted plays I have ever seen," snarled Martin Gottfried.[1] "The mayhem doesn't get moving until after we have given up . . . without sugar or spice or even arsenic to make things tastier for us," lamented Walter Kerr.[2] "Mr. Wheeler's adaptation just misses as a grisly hall of satisfying horrors," concluded Richard Watts Jr.[3] "It is on the frail side for the rough-and-tumble of Broadway," agreed John Chapman.[4]

Directed by Garson Kanin, and featuring Shirley Knight as Constance, *We Have Always Lived in the Castle* lasted only nine performances. It is a moody piece, tinged with subtle horrors, that deserves renewed interest and another chance across the footlights. The two main characters, Merricat and Constance, were conceived by Jackson as separate personalities who are actually "two halves of the same person." Merricat "wants to see the world, with always one foot on base at home; the other, Constance, never wants to leave home. . . . Together they are one identity, safe and eventually hidden."[5] With such Freudian nuances, the staging of *We Have Always Lived in the Castle* offers intriguing possibilities.

Early in 2010, Yale University's Center for New Theatre commissioned playwright Adam Bock and composer Todd Almond to create a darkly humorous musical based on *We Have Always Lived in the Castle*. The show was presented by the Yale Repertory Theatre from September 17 through October 9, 2010. Critic Charles Isherwood of the *New York Times* was disappointed, asserting that Bock and Almond "have thrown open the shutters and let in the sunshine," dissipating "the haunting atmosphere of the book" and letting "the all-important aura of mystery, of submerged madness and pervasive dread, evaporate almost entirely from the stage version, directed by Anne Kauffman."[6]

* * *

Shirley Jackson's *The Haunting of Hill House* (1959), another yarn about a hidden past uncovered in a brooding mansion, was adapted to the stage in 1964 by F. Andrew Leslie. The supernatural proceedings were effectively transformed to the screen in *The Haunting* (1963), directed by Robert Wise.

The Lottery, Jackson's 1948 classic short story depicting the traditional rite among the villagers of a small New England town to select, by a drawing, an innocent victim who will be stoned to death, was dramatized by Brainerd Duffield in 1953. Duffield also converted to the stage, in 1970,

Jackson's tale *The Summer People* (1950), in which New York vacationers face an ominous reception in rural New England.

In 1958, Jackson penned the book and lyrics of a one-act musical, *The Bad Children* (with Allan Jay Friedman composing the score), an enchanting variation on the Hansel and Gretel fairytale.

"Although Shirley Jackson's fiction draws on many elements of classic Gothicism (madness, mansions, and murder *inter alia*), the mysteries with which she deals are those of the mind, of reality, and of truth," writes Jane W. Stedman in *Twentieth Century Crime and Mystery Writers,*[7] a maxim amply illustrated in all of Jackson's stage works.

Jackson's literary output includes the following crime novels: *The Road through the Wall* (1948), also published as *The Other Side of the Street* (1956); *Hangsaman* (1951); *The Bird's Nest* (1954), also published as *Lizzie* (1957); and *The Sundial* (1958). Short tales of ominous suspense are featured in *The Lottery; or, The Adventures of James Harris* (1949), and *Come Along with Me* (1968).

In 2010, Library of America published *Shirley Jackson: Novels and Stories*, edited by Joyce Carol Oates, an 827-page volume containing the novels *We Have Always Lived in the Castle* and *The Haunting of Hill House*, as well as forty-six short stories.

* * *

Hugh Callingham Wheeler had his ups and downs on Broadway. Generally, his dramas and comedies did not fare well: *Big Fish, Little Fish* (ANTA Theatre, March 15, 1961—101 performances), is about a small-press editor surrounded by hangers-on. *Look: We've Come Through* (Hudson Theatre, October 25, 1961—five performances), depicts the developing relationship between a girl-with-a-past and a young man with a homosexual history. *Rich Little Rich Girl*, based on a play by Miguel Mihura and Alvaro de Laiglesia (a pre-Broadway tryout, for two weeks, at the Walnut Street Theatre, Philadelphia, October 26, 1964), is a comedy of murder involving a South American dictator. *Truckload* (Lyceum Theatre, September 6, 1975—closed after a week of previews) tells of hitchhiking across the country in trucks.

Wheeler did, however, contribute the libretto for some very successful musicals, winning Tony, Drama Critics Circle, and Drama Desk Awards: *A Little Night Music* (Shubert Theatre, February 25, 1973—600 performances), based on the 1955 Ingmar Bergman film *Smiles of a Summer Night*, about a weekend of romance and sex at a country estate; *Irene* (Minskoff Theatre, March 13, 1973—604 performances), an adaptation of a 1919 musical focusing on the behind-the-scenes romance between a fashion designer and his female associate; *Candide* (Chelsea Theatre Center of Brooklyn, December 11, 1973—forty-eight performances; transferred to the Broadway Theatre, March 10, 1974—740 performances), a revised book of the 1956 musical based on Voltaire; *Pacific Overtures* (Winter Garden, January 11, 1976—193 performances), additional material to the book by John Weidman regarding Admiral Perry's arrival in 1853 to isolated Japan; and *Sweeney Todd, the Demon Barber of Fleet Street* (Uris Theatre, March 1, 1979—557 performances), founded on a version of *Sweeney Todd* by Christopher Bond, concerning a London barber who soothes an ire at society by slitting his customers' throats and consigning them to a pastry cook who then sells them baked in her pies.

For the cinema, Wheeler cowrote the screenplays for *Five Miles to Midnight* (1962), *Something for Everyone* (1969), *Cabaret* (1972), and *Travels with My Aunt* (1973).

Prior to his stage and screen career, from 1936 to 1957, Wheeler jointly penned, with Richard Wilson Webb and other collaborators—under the pseudonyms Patrick Quentin, Q. Patrick, and Jonathan Stagge—thirty-three highly regarded detective novels, a true-crime paperback original (*The Girl on the Gallows*, 1954), and a collection of criminous tales, *The Ordeal of Mrs. Snow and Other Stories*, for which he won the Mystery Writers of America's Edgar Allan Poe Award in 1963.

Acting Edition: Dramatists Play Service.

Awards and Honors: Shirley Jackson was the posthumous recipient of the Mystery Writers of America Edgar Allan Poe Award, 1966, for her short story *The Possibility of Evil*.

NOTES

1. *Women's Wear Daily*, October 20, 1966.

2. *New York Times*, October 20, 1966.

3. *New York Post*, October 20, 1966.

4. *Daily News*, October 20, 1966.

5. Judy Oppenheimer, *Private Demons: The Life of Shirley Jackson* (New York: Putnam, 1988), 233.

6. *New York Times*, September 28, 2010.

7. John M. Reilly, ed., *Twentieth Century Crime and Mystery Writers* (New York: St. Martin's Press, 1980), 851.

Loot (1966)

Joe Orton (England, 1933–1967)

Joe Orton, the *enfant terrible* of the British theatre, completed *Funeral Games*, a first draft of his dark comedy *Loot*, in October 1964. An unruly satire lambasting detective fiction, investigative methods of the police, and the Roman Catholic Church, the play, directed by Peter Wood, opened in Cambridge in February 1965 to hostile reviews and outraged audiences. Orton continued to rewrite his work during an ensuing run in the provinces and under the title *Loot*, staged by Charles Marowitz, it came to the Cochran Theatre in Holborn in September 1966. Two months later, *Loot* was transferred to West End's Criterion Theatre, garnering rave reviews, winning the *Evening Standard* Drama Award as best play of the year, and running for 275-plus performances. Since then it has gained the reputation of a comic masterpiece.

The curtain rises on a room in McLeavy's house. A coffin containing Mrs. McLeavy's body stands on a trestle. McLeavy, dressed in mourning attire, sits beside an electric fan. Fay McMahon, in a nurse's uniform, enters. She removes her slippers and puts on a pair of the dead woman's shoes, claiming that Mrs. McLeavy wouldn't mind her having them. Fay pins a flower on McLeavy's coat and says: "You've been a widower for three days. Have you considered a second marriage yet?" She offers herself as an ideal choice.

Fay tries to open the wardrobe but it is locked. McLeavy says that his son Harold has the key. The young man enters, stands beside the coffin, and crosses himself. He tells Fay that he keeps the wardrobe locked because he has personal property inside it. Fay rebukes Harold for his thieving from slot machines, deflowering young women, and loafing without a job or prospects. Harold says that he intends to pursue opportunities abroad with his good friend, Dennis, an undertaker's assistant.

McLeavy picks up a newspaper and exclaims: "Another catastrophe has hit the district! Bank robbers have got away with a fortune . . . next door to the undertakers. They burrowed through . . . demolished a wall, they did."

The front doorbell chimes and Harold exits to meet his friend. Fay returns to the topic of matrimony and tells McLeavy that since the age of sixteen she has had seven husbands; all have died, an average of one per year.

Dennis, Harold's friend, enters carrying a screwdriver. McLeavy and Fay exit, leaving Harold and Dennis to unlock the wardrobe and bring out bundles of money. Apparently Harold and Dennis are the elusive bank robbers. They decide to hide the loot in what they consider a safe place. They lift the coffin from the trestles, tip it and shake the corpse into the wardrobe. They lock the wardrobe and pack the money into the coffin. Dennis takes chewing gum from his mouth, sticks it under the coffin, and screws down the lid. Harold kneels in prayer and bows his head as Fay enters with a mourning veil over her hair. Her dress is unzipped in the back. She crosses to the coffin and bows her head over it. Harold, still kneeling, zips her dress up. Fay places an embroidered text on the coffin and says, "Here, the Ten Commandments. She was a great believer in some of them."

Harold and Dennis lift the coffin and go out; it is to be driven soon by McLeavy to church before the funeral. Fay throws back her veil. Jim Truscott enters and introduces himself as an official of the metropolitan water board. He has come to inspect the main supply. He tries the wardrobe door and finds it locked. When Fay tells him that the pipes are outside in the garden, he comments, "Most ingenious."

Truscott chews on his pipe and surprises Fay by going through her systematic disposal of seven husbands in less than a decade. "There's something seriously wrong with your approach to marriage," he admonishes her. He's certain that she's contemplating an eighth engagement—she's wearing another woman's dress, probably one that belonged to the late Mrs. McLeavy—elementary detection: the zip is the type worn by elderly ladies.

Fay corners McLeavy and informs him that she poisoned Mrs. McLeavy, but not before the old woman changed her will and left all her money to her—19,000 pounds, including bonds and jewels. McLeavy sighs: "Employing you has cost me a fortune. You must be the most expensive nurse in history." Fay suggests that they get married and open a joint bank account. McLeavy is concerned: "I'm too old. My health wouldn't stand up to a young wife." But Fay assures him, "I'm a qualified nurse."

However, after Harold reveals to Fay that he and Dennis possess a great deal of money, she begins to turn her attention to Dennis as "a more interesting proposition."

Harold opens the wardrobe. Fay looks in, and screams. "This is unforgivable," she says. "I shall speak to your father." They lift the corpse and lay it on the bed. They place a screen around the bed and, unseen, Fay undresses the dead woman. From behind the screen she hands Harold a pair of shoes, stockings, a slip, a pair of corsets, a brassiere, a pair of knickers, and a pair of false teeth. Harold piles them into a sheet which is spread on the floor.

Truscott knocks on the door. Harold stuffs the sheet and clothes into the bedpan attached to the invalid's chair. Fay opens the door for Truscott. He takes a pipe from his pocket and plugs it with tobacco. He asks Harold to open the wardrobe, puts on a pair of spectacles, and stares at what is inside. He shakes his head, goes to the screen, folds it, and the corpse is revealed, swathed in the mattress cover and tied with bandages. Fay convinces Truscott that this is not a mummy but a dummy. "I used to sew my dresses on it," she says. The investigator puts the pipe in the corner of his mouth, takes out a notebook, makes several notes, and declares, "Sounds a reasonable explanation."

Truscott asks Harold what he was doing Saturday night. Harold tries to avoid telling the truth and stares at Fay with a look of agony on his face. After a long pause he confesses, "I had a hand in the bank job." Truscott laughs, but he soon scrutinizes Harold carefully and asks, "Where's the money?" When Harold answers truthfully, "In church," Truscott kicks him viciously and barks, "Don't lie to me." Harold persists, "In church! My dad's watching the last rites of a hundred and four thousand quid," and Truscott keeps beating and punching him.

McLeavy enters the house heavily bandaged. He falls into a chair and relates that on the way to the cemetery, a lorry, clearly out of control, came hurtling down, struck the first car, killed the undertaker, and left the cortege in smoking wreckage. He himself was flung to the ground and was bitten on the face and hands by a fear-crazed afghan hound. Fortunately, the coffin was not seriously damaged; his wife is safe. Harold and Dennis carry in a charred, blackened, and smoking coffin.

The first act ends with Truscott finding a glass eye on the floor, and, puzzled, examining it with a magnifying glass. In the second act, he reveals himself as Truscott of the Yard, "the man who tracked down the limbless girl killer." Truscott tells McLeavy that he has reason to believe that a number of crimes have been committed under his roof, of which the least important is murder. Fay announces that she had "a psychic experience last night," during which the late Mrs. McLeavy materialized and accused her husband of murder. However, Truscott says that he cannot accept the testimony of a ghost. Besides, he's well aware of Nurse Fay's checkered past. Using an assumed voice and being a master of disguise, he has followed Fay for years. He knows that "she's practiced her own form of genocide for a decade and called it nursing." Upon Truscott's signal, Deputy Meadows kisses Fay's hand, handcuffs her, and leads her out.

Dennis tells the inspector that during the road accident an explosion occurred, the lid of the casket was forced open, and the contents of his mother's stomach were destroyed. Truscott shakes his head, bowled over, and sadly asserts that without the victim's stomach there is no evidence on which to convict. He quickly sends a deputy to bring Fay back before she sues for wrongful arrest.

Truscott has one clue left—the glass eye he found on the floor. McLeavy believes that it belonged to his wife, who had glass eyes. He fetches a screwdriver, opens the coffin's lid, looks inside, grunts in disbelief, and staggers back, incredulous. "Oh, the end of the world is near when such crimes are committed," he gasps. Fay explains to Truscott that the condition of the corpse has deteriorated due to the accident. She asks the inspector whether he wishes to verify it, but Truscott shudders and declines.

Truscott insists on taking the casket to police headquarters. As he lifts it, the lid swings open and the bundles of bank notes fall to the floor. The inspector stares silently at the notes scattered at his feet. Harold asks Truscott if he's married. The answer is yes, and Harold says that as his wife is a woman, the inspector certainly needs a larger income; he's about to offer a bribe. Truscott removes his pipe. "How much?" he asks. "Twenty percent," offers Harold. They haggle and agree on 25 percent.

McLeavy, dumbfounded, threatens to denounce all of them and stalks out. Harold and Dennis are concerned, but Truscott assures them that there's no need to worry. He was exposed before and arrested the accuser, who's currently doing twelve years.

Truscott picks up the casket, tells Harold and Dennis that the safest place for it is in his station locker, hands Fay a calling card, and, smiling, goes off. Harold comments that it is comforting to know that the police can still be relied upon when people are in trouble. Fay decrees that she and Dennis will soon get married. At the end of the play, Dennis and Harold stand on either side of the coffin, with Fay above it, and the threesome bow their heads, with lips moving in a silent prayer.

* * *

The 1966 London production of Loot was praised by scholar Martin Esslin in Plays and Players. Esslin found Loot "harmless, old-fashioned fun," complimented director Charles Marowitz for "grasping the nature of the play very well," and applauded the "first rate" cast: Gerry Dugan "as the outraged father and bereaved husband"; Sheila Ballantine as the nurse who has "a lovely crispness, a sort of mechanically efficient sex appeal"; Kenneth Cranham and Simon Ward "as the son and his friend, who hide their loot from a bank robbery in the mother's coffin"; and Michael Bates, "the archetype of all policemen, the father-figure of father-figures," who "cruelly shatters that message with what deliciously sadistic leers, with what nonchalance in pocketing the bribe!"[1]

The Best Plays of 1966–1967 said: "Orton is a unique stylist. In his outrageous farces he blends plots of extreme sordidness, bordering on depravity, with dialogue of the most polished formality and epigrammatic Wildean elegance. The pivot of *Loot* is the corpse of Mrs. McLeavy, murdered by her nurse, whose delinquent son requires the coffin for stowing away the proceeds of a bank robbery. Michael Bates, as an over-zealous, totally unimaginative detective investigating this cesspool, gave the funniest performance of the year. Orton, like oysters, is an acquired taste."[2]

The first American production of *Loot* was presented at the Biltmore Theatre in New York on March 18, 1968. It was directed by Derek Goldby, with scenery and lighting by William Ritman. The cast included Liam Redmond (McLeavy), Kenneth Cranham, recruited from the London show (Harold), James Hunter (Dennis), Carole Shelley (Fay), and George Rose (Truscott). By and large, the critics panned the play but some found merit in the production elements. Clive Barnes wrote, "There is something for everyone to detest in Joe Orton's outrageous play, *Loot*. . . . The quite deplorable story is about death, religion, money and the police. . . . The work is sacrilegious and blasphemous, and, indeed, some of it is also distasteful." Barnes praised director Goldby for keeping "the mannered, staccato dialogue stabbing across the scene like machine-gun fire," and for adroitly handling "the sheerly mechanical farce business."[3] Douglas Watt believed *Loot* to be "a witless, headlong enterprise . . . a Feydeau farce masquerading as social commentary."[4] Martin Gottfried concluded that "*Loot* didn't quite make it at the Biltmore Theatre last night . . . because Derek Goldfry, the director, wasn't able to translate the visual energies of ordinary farce to serve the purposes of verbal farce . . . He blundered the timing. Instead of contrast, clicking dialogue there was line, pause, line, pause, line, and so on. He also should have used a real actress for the mother's corpse."[5] Richard Watts Jr. gleaned in the play "a number of amusingly wild and outrageous moments of farcical humor," but felt that "Mr. Orton's play runs into the doldrums too frequently, especially towards the end."[6] Walter Kerr opined that *Loot* was "closest to success with Mr. Rose's manic inspector. . . . When he is ostentatiously revealing himself to be the policeman everyone has known he was from the beginning (he has a notion that wearing a hat disguises him), he is on the verge of delighting us with his owlish miss-management of the obvious. But what, we now wonder, is being satirized? Sherlock Holmes? . . . Does the evening have a target, or even an environment? . . . Eventually it is plain the assault on our conventional expectations is not headed for any real goal. . . . The play gasps, backed to the wall."[7]

Loot ran for twenty-two performances. The New York Drama Critics selected Derek Goldby as Best Director of the year for his staging of both *Loot* and Tom Stoppard's *Rosencrantz and Guildenstern Are Dead*.

Loot continued to be performed on both shores of the Atlantic. In June 1975, Albert Finney directed the play at London's Royal Court Theatre as part of its Joe Orton Festival. John Tillinger staged *Loot* at the Manhattan Theatre Club in February 1986. The lead actors were Kevin Bacon (Dennis), Zeljko Ivanek (Harold), Zoë Wanamaker (Fay), Charles Keating (McLeavy), and Joseph Maher (Truscott), the latter winning a Drama Desk Award for his performance. The production transferred to Broadway's Music Box Theatre on April 7, 1986, with Alec Baldwin replacing Kevin Bacon. It ran for ninety-six performances and was awarded the 1986 Outer Critics Circle Awards for Best Revival and Best Director. The Hartford Stage Company of Hartford, Connecticut, presented *Loot* in March 1996, directed by Bartlett Sher. A Noise Within of Glendale, California, mounted the play in May 2007, staged by Geoff Elliott and Julia Rodriguez.

In London, *Loot* was revived at the Lyric Hammersmith Theatre on May 7, 1992, and at the Tricycle Theatre on December 11, 2008, transferring to Theatre Royal, Newcastle, on February 2, 2009, for a short run.

Loot was made into a film in England in 1970, directed by Silvio Narizzano, starring Richard Attenborough (Truscott), Milo O'Shea (McLeavy), and Lee Remick (Fay). Spanish television presented *El botí* in 1990.

* * *

John Kingsley (Joe) Orton was born in Leicester, England, in 1933 to a working-class family. He attended the Mariott Road Primary School, but after failing his exams due to extended bouts of asthma, took a secretarial course at Clark's College in Leicester from 1945 to 1947. He then began working as a junior clerk for three pounds a week.

In 1949, Orton became interested in performing in the theatre and joined several dramatic societies. He applied for a scholarship at the Royal Academy of Dramatic Art, was accepted, and left for London in 1951. At RADA he met Kenneth Halliwell, a student seven years older than him and of independent means, and soon they became lovers. They collaborated on a number of novels, all rejected. Subsisting on Halliwell's money, they began to amuse themselves with pranks and hoaxes. They would steal books from the local library and modify the cover art before returning them. They were eventually discovered and prosecuted in 1962, charged with five counts of theft and malicious damage. They were jailed for six months and fined 262 pounds each.

Prison proved to be a formative experience for Orton. The isolation from Halliwell allowed him to break free of him creatively, and, as he put it, "It affected my attitude towards society. Before I had been vaguely conscious of something rotten somewhere; prison crystallized this. The old whore society really lifted up her skirts and the stench was pretty foul."

Orton began to write plays in the early 1960s. In 1963, the BBC paid him sixty-five pounds for the radio play *The Ruffian on the Stairs*, broadcast on August 31, 1964, and subsequently written for the stage as a one-act. The mystifying plot concerns a poor London couple, Mike and Joyce, who are visited by a young, good-looking man named Wilson. Wilson terrifies Joyce and pretends to make love to her, goading Mike to shoot him dead. The playlet came to off-Broadway's Astor Place Theatre in October 1969, earning a positive nod from Clive Barnes of the *New York Times*: "A strange play, an uncertain, even unfinished play, yet impressive,"[8] and a negative one from Walter Kerr in the same newspaper: "*The Ruffian on the Stairs* went on too long, well past our fascination with David Birney's malicious visitor, or Richard Dysart's fatuously contented killer, and its tensions were often wantonly sacrificed to those easy and obvious half-jokes, mere upended platitudes, that Mr. Orton would not weed out."[9]

In London, *The Ruffian on the Stairs* was double-billed with another one-act play of menace, Harold Pinter's *The Dumbwaiter*, during the 1973–1974 season. The playlet was shown on Austrian television in 1970, on British television in 1973, and on Spanish television in 1987.

Orton's first full-length play, *Entertaining Mr. Sloane*, previewed at the New Arts Theatre on May 6, 1964, and endorsed by playwright Terence Rattigan, was transferred to West End's Wyndham Theatre on June 29. The action unfolds in an isolated house, symbolically built on a garbage dump. A blond, handsome, and completely amoral lodger, Sloane, is seduced by the landlady, Kath, an oversexed old maid, and in turn by her stalwart, wealthy brother, Ed. Brother and sister vehemently compete for the favors of Sloane. Eventually they reach a compromise, agreeing to cover up the fact that Sloane killed their old father, Kemp, and to share him, with each "entertaining Mr. Sloane" for six months at a time.

Entertaining Mr. Sloane was voted by the London Drama Critics the best new play of 1964. But when *Sloane* migrated to New York's Lyceum Theatre on October 12, 1965, directed by Alan Schneider and designed by William Ritman, it was savaged by the critics. Norman Nadel sniffed at a comedy that "has the sprightly charm of a medieval English cesspool."[10] John McClain believed the endeavor to be "a dreary British import."[11] Howard Taubman called it "a singularly unattractive play."[12] Richard Watts Jr. shrugged off "a tedious effort to combine sardonic humor with macabre drama."[13] Only John Chapman favored "Joe Orton's subtle and sinister comedy" and found Sheila Hancock, in the role of Kath, "enormously funny—and crafty and a bit scary too."[14]

Entertaining Mr. Sloane closed after thirteen showings. It was revived ten years later at London's Royal Court Theatre as part of the "Joe Orton Festival" and subsequently moved to the Duke of York's Theatre. The high-powered cast consisted of Beryl Reid (Kath), Malcolm McDowell (Sloane), Ronald Fraser (Ed), and James Ottaway (Kemp). Roger Croucher directed. London theatergoers had another opportunity to see the triangular intrigue of *Entertaining Mr. Sloane* at the Lyric, Hammersmith Theatre in an acclaimed production that ran from March 18 through April 11, 1981, while Manchester audiences had to contend with a *Sloane* that was snubbed by the critics when it opened at the Manchester Royal Exchange Theatre on May 16, 1985, for a six-week run.

Off-Broadway's Classic Stage Company revived *Entertaining Mr. Sloane* in 1996, with Ellen Parker and Brian Murray as the quarreling brother and sister. The Roundabout Theatre Company tackled the play in 2006, featuring Alec Baldwin (Ed), Chris Carmack (Sloane), Jan Maxwell (Kath), and Richard Easton (Kemp). Australia's Melbourne Theatre Company produced *Entertaining Mr. Sloane* a year later. The Trafalgar Studios in London mounted it in 2009. Mathew Horne, who played Sloane, collapsed and died during a performance on April 2, 2009, from a suspected virus.

Entertaining Mr. Sloane was telecast by England's ITV in 1968 and by Swedish television in 1981. A 1970 feature film, scripted by Clive Exton and directed by Douglas Hickox, starred Beryl Reid (Kath), Peter McEnery (Sloane), Harry Andrews (Ed), and Alan Webb (Kemp).

Orton's companion, Halliwell, felt increasingly isolated by the playwright's success and reportedly had come to rely on antidepressants and barbiturates. During the night of August 9, 1967, Halliwell bludgeoned Orton to death with nine hammer blows to the head and then committed suicide with an overdose of Nembutal tablets.

Orton's last play, *What the Butler Saw*, was produced posthumously on March 5, 1969, at the Queen's Theatre in London. The madcap antics of the play take place in the examination room in a private psychiatric clinic. The lights fade up on the philandering Dr. Prentice in the act of stripping a gullible secretary when he is surprised by the entrance of his wife. Before the final curtain comes down, Prentice is accused of molesting a page boy, raping a nurse, and murdering a patient—none of which have occurred.

Dr. Prentice was played by Stanley Baxter. Robert Chetwyn directed. The production was booed soundly on opening night. Reviewer John Russell Taylor dispatched to the *New York Times* a negative assessment, calling the show "a calculated exercise in bad taste. . . . It compares lamentably with his earlier work, *Loot*. . . . In *Loot*, Mr. Orton took the pants

off the police; here he tries to do the same for psychiatrists, ignoring the
fact that the popular theatre already holds them in low esteem."[15] Taylor
also reviewed the play for *Plays and Players*, where he didn't mince words:
"I think *What the Butler Saw* is a very bad play. . . . Without characterization of some sort it all ceases to be funny—or even outrageous."[16] *What
the Butler Saw* was presented on May 4, 1970, at off-Broadway's McAlpin
Rooftop Theatre. Critic Clive Barnes of the *New York Times* was enthused,
calling the late Joe Orton "one of the most promising talents of our time"
and describing the play as "a black comedy of manners—funny, outrageous and almost terrifying in its anarchistic acceptance of logic as a way
of life."[17] Staged by Joseph Hardy, the play ran for 224 performances and
was selected among the top ten in *The Best Plays of 1969–1970*.

What the Butler Saw was revived by several off-off-Broadway troupes:
T. Schreiber Studio (1975), Academy Arts Theatre Company (1977), West-
side Arts Theatre (1981), Bouwerie Lane Theatre (1996), and New Group
Theatre (2000). The Manhattan Theatre Club presented the play in 1989,
teaming again director John Tillinger and actor Joseph Maher, who scored
a palpable hit in 1986 with the Manhattan Theatre Club's much-praised
production of *Loot*. British TV's program *Theatre Night* aired the play in
1985, with Dinsdale Landen as Dr. Prentice.

A biography of Orton, *Prick Up Your Ears* by John Lahr, was published
in 1978 by Knopf. The same title was used for a 1987 film, scripted by
Alan Bennett, directed by Stephen Frears, starring Gary Oldman as Joe
Orton and Alfred Molina in the role of Kenneth Halliwell. A play about
Orton and Halliwell, *Cock-Ups* by Simon Moss, was presented in London
by the fringe company Bridge Lane in 1983, with Richard Walker (Orton)
and Edmund Kente (Halliwell). Also focused on that tragic relationship
is the drama *Nasty Little Secrets* by Lanie Robertson, produced by off-
Broadway's Primary Stages in 1988, and, revised, in 1998, with Matthew
Mabe (Orton) and Craig Fols (Halliwell). Another biodrama about the
duo's turbulent affair, Simon Bent's *Prick Up Your Ears*, premiered in
Richmond, a borough of London, on August 26, 2009, featuring Chris
New (Orton) and Matt Lucas (Halliwell).

"Orton's comedy teased the society with its own evil and tested what
it held sacred," writes John Lahr in *Prick Up Your Ears: The Biography of
Joe Orton*. "In farce, Orton could marry terror and elation in his highly
stylized theatrical idiom. Violating social and familiar pieties, farce's
pandemonium created the panic Orton wanted in laughter. In tragedy,
character is fate; in farce, where characterization is minimized and action emphasized, mischief is fate. Orton understood the kinship between
tragedy and farce. And he made the most of it in *Loot*. . . . In *Loot* Orton's
laughter found new strength by tilting against death, the English police,
and the idea of English justice. 'One *must* shake the audience out of its

expectations,' he said. 'They need not so much shocking, as *surprising* out of their rut.'"[18]

Acting Edition: Samuel French, Inc.; Grove Press.

Awards and Honors: *Loot* won in London the *Evening Standard* Drama Award for the best play of 1966. A 1986 production in New York garnered the Outer Critics Circle Award as best revival.

In Leicester, Orton's hometown, a pedestrian concourse next to the Curve Theatre is named Orton Square.

NOTES

1. *Plays and Players*, November 1966.
2. Otis L. Guernsey Jr., ed., *The Best Plays of 1966–1967* (New York: Dodd, Mead, 1967), 121.
3. *New York Times*, March 19, 1968.
4. *Daily News*, March 19, 1968.
5. *Women's Wear Daily*, March 19, 1968.
6. *New York Post*, March 19, 1968.
7. *New York Times*, March 31, 1968.
8. *New York Times*, October 27, 1969.
9. *New York Times*, November 9, 1969.
10. *New York World-Telegram*, October 13, 1965.
11. *New York Journal-American*, October 13, 1965.
12. *New York Times*, October 13, 1965.
13. *New York Post*, October 13, 1965.
14. *Daily News*, October 13, 1965.
15. *New York Times*, March 7, 1969.
16. *Plays and Players*, April 1969.
17. *New York Times*, May 5, 1970.
18. John Lahr, *Prick Up Your Ears: The Biography of Joe Orton* (New York: Knopf, 1978), 173, 186, 189.

Don't Drink the Water (1966)

Woody Allen (1935–)

Woody Allen's comedy of Cold War intrigue, *Don't Drink the Water*, takes place in the American embassy of an unnamed country behind the Iron Curtain.

The lights fade up on Father Drobney, a priest who speaks with a foreign accent and is probably molded after Cardinal József Mindszenty of Hungary. Father Drobney tells the audience that he found sanctuary in the embassy six years ago and has been practicing magic tricks to pass the time. He proceeds to introduce key embassy personnel, who will soon be engulfed in a web of farcical shenanigans: Ambassador James F. Magee, a hard-nosed and dignified man in his mid-fifties; his son, Axel Magee, an eager Yale graduate whose career in the foreign service has been marred by a series of disasters, including expulsion from Japan, the Soviet Union, and the entire African continent; and Kilroy, the ambassador's bright-eyed, efficient aide who nurtures career ambitions.

The ambassador is summoned back home for political consultations. His son asks to be left in charge—what can go wrong in two weeks? The ambassador expresses concern, for the Sultan of Bashir is due to arrive for critical discussions about an oil deal. Axel promises to see "that the embassy remains a credit" to his father's record, and the ambassador consents.

Soon Axel Magee faces his first crisis. Gunshots are heard outside the embassy. Magee runs and opens the door. In burst Walter and Marion Hollander and their daughter Susan. The Hollanders are a Jewish family from Newark, New Jersey, on vacation. Walter is a typical American tourist with a loud, short-sleeved shirt and a camera in hand. His wife carries a TWA bag. The parents are in their early fifties; their daughter is a beautiful twenty-one-year-old. Right now they are in a state of panic. They were taking pictures in a restricted area and the Communist police are after them.

Krojack, the menacing leader of the secret police, enters ahead of several of his men, carrying an automatic weapon. With a booming voice, he

accuses the Hollanders of taking pictures of missile sites and rocket in-
stallations. "They have seen too much," barks Krojack. "They must die."

Magee tries to calm Krojack by pointing out that "espionage goes on
between our countries every day." Krojack warns that the embassy will
be surrounded from that day on, and exits in a huff. Walter Hollander
complains to his wife, "If you had listened to me, we would've taken a
cabana in Atlantic Beach. . . . I needed this like a growth."

Kilroy reports that the secret police have searched the Hollanders' hotel
rooms and found a notebook with suspicious notations about supplies
and troop movements. Walter explains that he is a caterer and the list is
about the upcoming Levine wedding—how much roast beef, how much
grapefruit, etc.

Magee is struck by Susan's good looks and is disappointed to hear
that she's engaged to a lawyer named Donald, who is "so confident and
totally in command." Her parents are enamored with Donald, especially
as compared with her previous boyfriends—a manic-depressive jazz
musician, a draft dodger, and a defrocked priest. She has danced with
the New York City Ballet and worked in a Greenwich Village coffee
shop—no, not as a waitress but repairing motorcycles. Right now her
interest is painting.

Father Drobney performs his magic tricks for the Hollanders—a cane
turns into flowers, a light bulb flashes in their hands. But the priest
becomes frantic when a cage he's displaying turns up empty, and he
looks under the desk for his rabbit. The embassy chef enters holding a
live rabbit and asks, "How do you like it? Rare, medium, well done?"
In short order, Drobney goes for the chef, the chef collides with Walter, Marion ducks to avoid getting trampled, and the room turns into
bedlam.

The next bit of buffoonery occurs when Drobney comes down the stairs
struggling to get out of a straightjacket. Marion attempts to help him and
they get entangled and drop to the floor. At that moment who enters but
the Sultan of Bashir and his veiled wife. The sultan is a huge, imposing
desert chieftain in full robes with dark glasses and a beard.

Magee apologizes and barely manages to smooth the ruffled sultan.
Kilroy tries to arrange a spy trade, releasing the Hollanders in exchange
for the Communist arch-spy Adolph Lopert, known as the Grey Fox.
But word comes that Lopert has hung himself in his cell, so the deal is
cancelled.

Susan tells her parents that she's fallen in love with Axel Magee. Walter
is furious about her giving up her lawyer fiancé for "a loser, the worst
prospect she's ever had."

A noise is heard from outside, gradually increasing to riot proportions.
Shots are fired in another part of the house. They all hide—behind a sofa,

under a desk, in a closet. A ticking time bomb comes flying through the window and lands on the floor. Walter picks it up but when he realizes that it is a bomb, he tosses it to Magee in panic. Magee breathes a sigh of relief after disconnecting the bomb. The noise of the crowd subsides. Kilroy was hit with a brick outside, and Magee asks embassy aides to carry him to his room.

Susan finds the situation exciting. She and Magee begin to hatch escape plans. Dig a tunnel? Sneak out in the back of the laundry truck? They decide to throw a party in honor of the Sultan of Bashir and use the occasion for the Hollanders to dress as guests and then leave with the crowd. Once outside, the embassy limousine will whip them away to the railway station. When told of the plan, Marion is thrilled while Walter is doubtful, more so when he hears that halfway to Istanbul they'll leave the train, will be met by a man driving a wagon loaded with hay, and go with him dressed as peasants. They'll then be taken to the seashore where a submarine will pick them up. Walter comments dryly to Marion: "It won't be any worse an ordeal than your sister's wedding."

The last scene of the play is both humorous and suspenseful as Walter and Marion leave the embassy masquerading as the bearded sultan and his veiled wife. Susan, too, is allowed to leave the country, with diplomatic immunity, as the wife of Axel Magee. Father Drobney marries them. They'll all meet soon in Newark.

* * *

Initially called *Yankee Come Home*, *Don't Drink the Water* tried out on the road and came to Broadway's Morosco Theatre on November 17, 1966. Stanley Prager directed; Jo Mielziner designed the scenery and lighting. The lead actors were Lou Jacoby (Walter Hollander), Kay Medford (Marion Hollander), Anita Gillette (Susan Hollander), Anthony Roberts (Axel Magee), and Dick Libertini (Father Drobney). Biographer Marion Meade writes in *The Unruly Life of Woody Allen* that "as the opening had approached, Woody was filled with dread. Displeased with some of the actors, he had premonitions of disaster which were confirmed in Philadelphia during a pre-Broadway tryout when his efforts were critically mauled. . . . Woody would never take rejection well. Hoping the comedy would work in New York but fearful of the critics, he conveniently disappeared on opening night and wound up playing billiards at McGirr's pool hall on Eighth Avenue. In what would become a lifelong pattern, he fled from the painful prospect of seeing his work judged while insisting that he cared nothing for the world's opinion."[1]

Most of the critics were dissatisfied. "*Don't Drink the Water* comes down like a one-liner getting ready for a television laugh-track," sniffed Walter Kerr. "The gags must become more and more outrageous because there's nothing sturdy under them."[2] Richard Watts Jr. agreed: "Its humor appears to be pressing too insistently, too constantly, too bent on being funny at all cost, until the wit becomes mechanical and takes on a comic strip quality."[3] Norman Nadel called the play a "gross farce" and complained of "a massive accumulation of club and television-type comedy lines, spoken by several stock company types."[4]

Other reviewers put on a happy face. "*Don't Drink the Water* is a comedy held by spit and disguised matzoh balls," asserted Martin Gottfried. "Yet there is no denying its continuous good fun. Woody Allen's play is undeniably funny. Very funny and very often."[5] John Chapman chirped, "Allen's imagination is duffy, his sense of the ridiculous is keen and gags snap, crackle and pop."[6]

The cast was lauded by the entire cadre of critics. "With Lou Jacoby carrying the banner of American independence abroad, we are presented with some very funny lines and incidents," wrote Richard P. Cooke. "Kay Medford, who looks as though the weight of the world were balanced on her head, is present to contribute her scratchy-voiced, dead pan comedy, and there's none better anywhere."[7]

Don't Drink the Water ran for 598 performances. It was adapted to the screen in 1969, directed by Howard Norris, featuring Jackie Gleason and Estelle Parsons as the Hollanders, and bringing back Richard Libertini in the role of Father Drobney. Twenty-five years later, in 1994, Woody Allen himself directed *Don't Drink the Water* for ABC TV and starred as Walter Hollander alongside a supporting cast that included Julie Kavner (Marion Hollander), Michael J. Fox (Axel Magee), and Dom DeLuise (Father Drobney). "Reviewers noted," writes Marion Meade in her biography of Allen, "that he had made no effort to modernize hopelessly stale material, the characters were cartoons, and the depiction of Arab characters was grossly insensitive."[8]

* * *

Woody Allen (Allan Stewart Konigsberg) was born on December 1, 1935, in Brooklyn, New York. His mother was a bookkeeper and his father was a jewelry engraver. The family was Jewish, and Allen spoke Yiddish during his childhood and attended Hebrew school for eight years.

Allen broke into show business at the age of fifteen when he started writing jokes for a local newspaper, reportedly pumping out an estimated two thousand a day, earning $200 a week. At nineteen, Allen began writing scripts for television's *The Ed Sullivan Show*, *The Tonight Show*, and Sid Caesar's *Caesar's Hour*. He was soon making $1,500 a week. Also at an early age, Allen developed a passion for music; he is an accomplished clarinetist, appearing occasionally at various jazz festivals.

Allen studied communication and film at New York University, where he failed a course and was eventually expelled. He later briefly attended City College of New York.

In 1961, Allen launched a new career as a stand-up comedian, debuting in a Greenwich Village club, the Duplex. A short man—he is five feet, five inches tall—Allen developed a neurotic, nervous, and intellectual persona for his routine, a move that secured regular gigs for him in nightclubs and television. Allen was inspired by humorists S. J. Perelman, George S. Kaufman, and Robert Benchley, and in turn he brought significant innovation to the comedy monologue genre.

Allen's first contribution to Broadway was providing sketches for *From A to Z*, a musical revue that opened at the Plymouth Theatre on May 20, 1960, and ran for twenty-one showings. Among the actor-singers were Hermione Gingold and Alvin Epstein.

Following 1966's *Don't Drink the Water*, Allen penned the comedy *Play It Again, Sam*, a title borrowed from the motion picture *Casablanca*. It opened at the Broadhurst Theatre on February 12, 1969, under Joseph Hardy's direction. Allen himself appeared as Allan Felix, a timid, insecure movie critic who, abandoned by his spouse, daydreams of Humphrey Bogart heroics and beautiful girls in miniskirts. Tough-guy Bogey (played by Jerry Lacy) goads Felix to become brave enough to make a conquest, and he has an affair with Linda Christie (Diane Keaton), the wife of his best friend (Anthony Roberts). Complications ensue.

The critics' reception was mixed. John Chapman called Woody Allen "a combination of Milquetoast and [Walter] Mitty" and found the comedy "pleasantly daffy,"[9] while Martin Gottfried belittled "a series of night club monologues pretending to be a play."[10] *Play It Again, Sam* ran for 453 performances. Allen, Keaton, Roberts, and Lacy reprised their roles in a 1972 film version of the play, directed by Herbert Ross.

Allen's *The Floating Light Bulb* is a semi-autobiographical play, centering on the Polacks, a middle-class family in the Brooklyn of 1945. A stuttering teenage son, Paul, tries to perfect magic tricks, including a floating light bulb illusion. A talent agent arrives at the house, ostensibly to audition Paul, but he proves to be more interested in Paul's mother. The play opened at the Vivian Beaumont Theatre in New York on April 27, 1981, and ran for sixty-five performances.

As a screenwriter, director, and actor, Allen made an enormous contribution to the cinema. His early films were formless comedies, based on a thin plot, stringing together a sequence of sight gags and one-liners. These include *What's New, Pussycat?* (1965), in which a disturbed fashion editor goes to a psychiatrist for help with his romantic problems; *What's Up, Tiger Lily?* (1966), a James Bond spoof; and *Take the Money and Run* (1969), described by Leonard Maltin as the "life story of a compulsive thief. Nonstop parade of jokes; some work, some don't, but the ones that *do* are a riot!"[11]

Beginning with *Sleeper* (1973), Allen cast new girlfriend Diane Keaton in a series of movies that steadily grew in quality and substance: *Love and Death* (1975), depicting the misadventures of a coward in the Napoleonic wars; *Annie Hall* (1977), an autobiographical love story, winner of several Academy Awards, including Best Picture, Screenplay, Director, and Actress; *Interiors* (1978), a rare domestic drama by this specialist in comedy; and *Manhattan* (1979), a lighthearted yarn about a New York writer and his cerebral friends.

Mia Farrow, Allen's next flame, became his leading lady in *Midsummer Night's Sex Comedy* (1982); *Zelig* (1983); *Broadway Danny Rose* (1984); *The Purple Rose of Cairo* (1985); *Hannah and Her Sisters* (1986); *Radio Days* (1987); *September* (1987); *Another Woman* (1988), a departure from comedy to drama; *Crimes and Misdemeanors* (1989), the melding of two stories, one tragic, one humorous; *Alice* (1990); *Shadows and Fog* (1992); and *Husbands and Wives* (1992).

Allen and Mia Farrow parted ways, personally and professionally, when she discovered nude photographs that Allen had taken of her adopted daughter, Soon-Yi. Following a headlines scandal, Allen married Soon-Yi.

Allen inserted criminous elements in some of his pictures: *Manhattan Murder Mystery* (1993), a comic thriller about a married couple who suspect that their seemingly harmless neighbor has murdered his wife; *Bullets over Broadway* (1994), about a 1920s playwright who sells out when he's offered a chance to direct his own work on Broadway with a gangster's moll in a key role; *The Curse of the Jade Scorpion* (2001), in which an insurance investigator in 1940s New York and his female superior are mesmerized by a nightclub hypnotist; *Match Point* (2005), wherein a tennis instructor who marries into high society murders his pregnant, demanding lover, and gets away with it; and *Scoop* (2006), a comedy-fantasy-mystery spotlighting a reporter who returns from the dead and enlists a magician to trap a serial killer.

Altogether, Allen wrote, directed, and starred in forty features in about as many years. According to Box Office Mojo, Allen's films have grossed a total of more than $424 million, with an average of $12 million per film. Allen appeared as himself in many documentaries, including *Wild Man Blues*, *The Concert for New York City*, and *Stanley Kubrick: A Life in Pictures*. A 2002 cable-television documentary, *Woody Allen: A Life in Film*, directed by film critic Richard Schickel, interweaves interviews of Allen with clips of his films. In 2003, Keith Black wrote, directed, and starred in the film *Get the Script to Woody Allen*, the tale of a neurotic young man who is determined to get his manuscript to Allen. The 2010 British comedy

Manhattan features two directors from Manchester, England, who travel to New York in order to make a documentary about the writer/comedian/director.

Acting Edition: Samuel French, Inc.

Awards and Honors: Woody Allen received fourteen screenwriting Academy Award nominations, more than any other writer. Allen's motion picture *Annie Hall* won four Oscars in 1977, including Best Picture, Best Screenplay, and Best Director. *Hannah and Her Sisters* won three in 1986, including Best Screenplay. Allen won the 1978 O. Henry Award for his short story "The Kugelmass Episode," published in *The New Yorker* on May 2, 1977. Allen twice won the César Award for Best Foreign Film, the first in 1980 for *Manhattan* and the second in 1986 for *The Purple Rose of Cairo*. In 1986, Allen won the Golden Globe for Best Screenplay for *The Purple Rose of Cairo*, and in 2009 he won the same award for Best Motion Picture, Comedy, or Musical, for *Vicky Cristina Barcelona*. At the 1995 Venice Film Festival, Allen received a Career Golden Lion for lifetime achievement. The following year, he garnered a lifetime achievement award from the Directors Guild of America. In 2002, he received the *Palme des Palmes*, a special lifetime achievement award granted by the Cannes Festival, whose sole other recipient is Ingmar Bergman. In June 2007, Allen received an honorary doctorate from Pompeu Fabra University in Barcelona, Spain.

NOTES

1. Marion Meade, *The Unruly Life of Woody Allen* (New York: Scribner, 2000), 71.
2. *New York Times*, November 18, 1966.
3. *New York Post*, November 18, 1966.
4. *World Journal Tribune*, November 18, 1966.
5. *Women's Wear Daily*, November 18, 1966.
6. *Daily News*, November 18, 1966.
7. *Wall Street Journal*, November 21, 1966.
8. Marion Meade, *The Unruly Life of Woody Allen*, 288.
9. *Daily News*, February 13, 1969.
10. *Women's Wear Daily*, February 13, 1969.
11. *Leonard Maltin's 2011 Movie Guide* (New York: Penguin, 2010), 1358.

Seven Days in May (1966)

Kristin Sergel (United States)

Seven Days in May, a 1962 best-selling novel of political intrigue by Fletcher Knebel and Charles W. Bailey II, was tautly transformed to the cinema two years later by screenwriter Rod Serling and director John Frankenheimer. Kirk Douglas portrayed Colonel Martin Casey, director of the Joint Chiefs of Staff, who uncovers a military plot, hatched by General James Scott (Burt Lancaster), to overthrow the government of President Jordan Lyman (Fredric March) and seize the White House.

In 1966, Kristin Sergel artfully adapted the book to the stage, presenting the complex, sometimes sprawling, narrative in an intelligent, well-organized, and fast-moving fashion.

Colonel Casey, a calm and collected Marine, becomes increasingly concerned by curious tidbits of information and enigmatic events around him: a coded message sent by his boss, chairman of the Joint Chiefs, General Matthew Scott, to various commanders of the Army, Navy, and Air Force; a secret military base with 3,500 men that springs forth in a Texas desert; a crumpled note, written by General Scott and found by Casey in a trash can, indicating the movement of troops, seven days hence, to positions in Chicago, New York, and Los Angeles.

When Casey catches Scott lying about a clandestine meeting in the dead of night, he decides, apprehensively, to share his anxiety with President Lyman. The president has only a 29 percent approval rating—"the lowest popularity rating for any President since they started taking the thing." The reason? In the midst of the Cold War, Lyman signed a nuclear disarmament treaty with Moscow, and the American people don't believe that the Russians will play by the rules.

The president calls a conference with a handful of trusted men: Paul Girard, his appointments secretary; Raymond Clark, a senator from Georgia; Christopher Todd, secretary of the treasury; and Art Corwin, a Secret Service officer. They decide that Senator Clark will fly to El Paso and check the hidden base; Corwin is to follow General Scott's movements; Girard will travel to Gibraltar for a meeting with Admiral Farley Barnswell, the recipient of Scott's note; and Casey is ordered to interview the general's girlfriend, Millicent Segnin, in New York.

Tension mounts during the next few days as the assignments are obstructed. Senator Clark is held prisoner at the El Paso base, and Paul Girard, after telephoning to report that he was "flying home with the goodies," is killed when a trans-ocean jet crashes and explodes northwest of Madrid. However, at the eleventh hour, Clark manages to get back with firsthand information, and an embassy attaché arrives from Spain to deliver Girard's cigarette case, which was found in the plane wreckage, containing a written confession, signed by Admiral Barnswell, of a coup planned for Saturday. A face-to-face encounter between President Lyman and Scott results in the resignation of the rebellious general.

The volatile proceedings of *Seven Days in May* lighten up in a fadeout sequence during which Casey's wife, Marge, who does not believe that he ever met the president, is shocked when an official arrives with a direct message from the White House announcing that Casey has been promoted to the rank of brigadier general and appointed as a personal aide to the president. "Dear! My Heaven!" utters Marge breathlessly.

In addition to its print, screen, and stage replicas, *Seven Days in May* was made for cable television as *The Enemy Within* (1994).

* * *

Following her adaptation of *Seven Days in May*, Kristin Sergel wrote *Dino*, the story of a seventeen-year-old who has just finished a four-year term at reform school; *Father Knows Best*, a comedy about a father who is afraid that his daughter may elope with her boyfriend; *Gentlemen Prefer Blondes*, based on the book by Anita Loos, the misadventures of blonde Lorlei and brunette Dorothy on their trip to Europe; *Winnie the Pooh* and *Winnie the Pooh: The Musical,* from the stories by A. A. Milne—all published by The Dramatic Publishing Company.

Fletcher Knebel (1911–1993) and Charles Waldo Bailey II (1929–), both highly regarded Washington correspondents, teamed to pen two other books: *No High Ground* (1960), an account of the Hiroshima atomic bomb, and *Convention* (1964), a political-chicanery yarn.

On his own, Knebel wrote a number of best-selling suspense novels, including *Night of Camp David* (1965), *The Zinzin Road* (1966), *Vanished* (1968, adapted to television 1971), *Trespass* (1969), *Dark Horse* (1972), *The Bottom Line* (1974), *Dave Sulkin Cares!* (1978), *Crossing in Berlin* (1981), *Poker Game* (1983), and *Sabotage* (1985). In 1987, Knebel published the nonfiction *Before You Sue: How to Get Justice without Going to Court.*

Acting Edition: The Dramatic Publishing Company.

A Case for Mason (1967)

William McCleery (United States, 1911–2000)

The world's most renowned literary attorney, Perry Mason, is the hero of more than eighty novels, scores of radio programs, a half-dozen movies, and two television series. On stage, he defended a client only once, in *A Case for Mason*, dramatized by William McCleery in 1967.

The play springs from Erle Stanley Gardner's *The Case of the Fiery Fingers* (1951). In addition to Perry Mason, McCleery recruited the characters of Della Street, the lawyer's highly efficient, wisecracking secretary; LAPD's Lieutenant Arthur Tragg, an intelligent, fair-minded adversary; and Sergeant Holcomb, a tough, two-fisted cop.

A Case for Mason takes place in the study of Bryan Bain's house on the outskirts of a California city. Bain, a best-selling author of popular fiction, is having a difficult time writing a different kind of novel, one that focuses less on action and more on character.

Bain's young live-in assistant, Nellie Conway, is intense and supportive. His middle-aged housekeeper, Victoria Braxton, is devoted and exacting. But the household is not happy, for Bain's second wife, Elizabeth, is shrewishly domineering. Sensing that Nellie is interested in her husband, Elizabeth accuses the assistant of stealing family jewelry.

Bain asks Perry Mason to look into the matter. Secretary Della convinces Perry to take on the trivial case, so that he will get out of the office and keep away "from those ringing telephones" and "those clients with the life and death emergencies."

By the end of the first act, the insignificant assignment turns into a murder case. Mrs. Bain is found dead in her bed and the family physician, Dr. Keener, decrees that she was poisoned.

Lieutenant Tragg and Sergeant Holcomb believe that Nellie, in love with her employer, lethally drugged Mrs. Bain's milk. Perry Mason disagrees. To the chagrin of the law officers, Nellie turns out to be innocent. For a while it seems that the husband, Bryan, is the culprit, but Mason sets up a trap by secretly switching on the house intercom and eavesdropping

507

on an incriminating confession by the housekeeper, Victoria. When Mason confronts her, Victoria admits to poisoning both of Bain's wives. She insists that the two Mrs. Bains married Bryan for his name and fortune, then made his life miserable. Now that they are both gone, he will be free to write "his beautiful books."

A Case for Mason clones some key elements from *Speaking of Murder* (1956) by Audrey and William Roos. In both plays the malefactor is a housekeeper obsessively in love with her employer, who murdered his first wife, then targets the second for extinction.

Not entirely convincing, and less than stylish, *A Case for Mason* is nevertheless breezy and diverting, retaining the premise of a seemingly airtight case against an innocent party, the rescue legalities by Perry Mason, and the climactic unmasking of the real culprit.

* * *

Perry Mason made his debut in Erle Stanley Gardner's *The Case of the Velvet Claws* (1933). He utilized his legal prowess in eighty-two novels, all published by William Morrow and Company, New York, and many printed simultaneously in Toronto, followed by numerous foreign editions. A few Mason cases went to press after the author's death in 1970.

The Perry Mason books became enormous best sellers, making the author a champion among mystery writers. E. H. Mundell's *Erle Stanley Gardner: A Checklist* asserts that "It is probable that Gardner has been read by more people than any fiction writer who ever wrote."[1]

Chris Steinbrunner and Otto Penzler's *Encyclopedia of Mystery and Detection* states, "Internal evidence in the Mason series indicates that the lawyer was born in 1891. He is described as a big man, but he is not heavy. Although he says that he has no time for sports or exercise, he remains fit and performs well in situations involving physical danger. He has long legs, broad shoulders, and piercing eyes in a rugged face. His thick, wavy hair and excellent speaking voice make him attractive to many women."[2]

However, the public image of Perry Mason is that of burly Raymond Burr, who early in his film career was cast as a villain in the Marx Brothers' *Love Happy* (1950), Raymond Chandler's *The Blue Gardenia* (1953), and Alfred Hitchcock's *Rear Window* (1954), but then was chosen to play Perry Mason in the long-running CBS television program (1957–1966).

According to *The Perry Mason TV Show Book* by Brian Kelleher and Diana Merrill, "One of the secrets of the Mason show was that, unlike other television mysteries of the time, the scripts concentrated less on the actual murder and more on looking for the clues and solving the case. In most other similar shows, the execution of the murder was the focal point, and the sequence of putting the clues together was secondary."[3]

Kelleher and Merrill relate, "Like *Alfred Hitchcock Presents*, another popular series running at the time, each Mason show had a last-minute twist ending. However, unlike homicides presented on Hitchcock's thrillers, the real murderer was never revealed on *Perry Mason* until the very last moment. This was in part to sustain the element of surprise that was critically needed for the show, especially since the viewer knew that Mason's clients weren't going to get convicted."[4]

The New Adventures of Perry Mason, presented by CBS TV in 1973, failed to ignite interest and was off the air by February 1974. In 1985, and until his death in 1993, Raymond Burr reemerged as Perry Mason in occasional two-hour made-for-television movies.

Perry Mason's career was less illustrious on the big screen. In the 1930s he was featured in six Warner Brothers motion pictures, all failures. Debonair Warren William portrayed the crusading lawyer in four of them; he was succeeded by Ricardo Cortez and Donald Woods.

On radio, Mason defended innocent clients in a fifteen-minute CBS program that ran daily from 1943 to 1955. He was also the knight-in-shining-armor of a comic strip during 1950–1952.

* * *

Erle Stanley Gardner was born in 1889 in the small town of Malden, Massachusetts, to parents who were proud to be of Mayflower stock. The family moved to California for business reasons: the company for which Gardner's father worked had gold mining interests there. Gardner's free-wheeling spirit got him suspended from the Orville Union High School when he drew a professor's caricature in the school's paper and on the front of the school's building.

Gardner enrolled at Valparaiso University in Indiana to study law, but following a boxing encounter with a professor he left town hurriedly by train. From then on he studied the law in lawyers' offices and by reading legal cases for an average of fifty hours a week for three years. He passed his bar examination in 1911. During the next ten years he practiced law as a junior partner for several well-known defense attorneys. His clients were mainly penniless Mexicans and Chinese.

In 1925, in order to supplement his income, Gardner took a stab at writing. He chose a pen name, Charles M. Green, and sent stories to pulp magazines. "I started in collecting rejection slips on a wholesale basis. My stories were terrible," said Gardner years later. "Every time I got a rejection slip, in place of getting discouraged I got mad."[5] His breakthrough came in 1923 with a novelette, *The Shrieking Skeleton*, which he submitted to *Black Mask*, home of Carroll John Daly, Frederick Nebel, Dashiell Hammett, and other hard-boiled writers. *The Shrieking Skeleton* is the story of a renowned scientist, Doctor Potter, who is murdered by his Japanese butler,

Kumi, to avenge his sister, whom Potter had seduced. Alva Johnston relates in her study *The Case of Erle Stanley Gardner* that the manuscript was initially returned to Gardner with an attached note by circulating manager P. C. Cody: "This is the most puerile story I have ever read. The plot has whiskers like Spanish moss on a Southern live oak, and the characters talk like a dictionary." Gardner went back to his typewriter and "rewrote *The Shrieking Skeleton* until he had stone bruises on his finger tips. . . . In its final version, *The Shrieking Skeleton* was not only accepted by *Black Mask* but was made the leading story in the issue of December 15, 1923. Erle received a check for $140, a cent a word for 14,400 words, and he was the proudest man in Southern California."[6]

Gardner's first success came with the creation of a series detective, Speed Dash, a "human fly" who would climb a building to enter a room containing evidence and, blessed with a photographic mind, would memorize the room in a tenth of a second. Other early pulp heroes were Lester Leith, a confidence man who steals money from criminals; the lawyers Ken Corning and Peter Wennick; Ed Jenkins, the Phantom Crook; and Sidney Zoom and his police dog, Rip.

Gardner soon realized that his most valuable asset was his legal background. His initial Perry Mason novels, *Reasonable Doubt* (published under the title *The Case of the Velvet Claws*) and *Silent Verdict* (published as *The Case of the Sulky Girl*) were rejected by several publishers but eventually accepted by William Morrow and Company, the firm that subsequently published the first editions of all his books. Other popular sleuths created by Gardner are small-town district attorney Douglas Selby and, under the pseudonym A. A. Fair, the team of private eyes Bertha Cool and Donald Lam, in a series distinguished by bright, humorous dialogue.

In the 1960s, concerned about recent trends in American literature, Gardner told the *New York Times*, "I have always aimed my fiction at the masses who constitute the solid backbone of America. I have tried to keep faith with the American family. In a day when the prevailing mystery story trends are toward sex, sadism and seduction, I try to base my stories on speed, situation and suspense."[7]

Popular culture scholar Francis M. Nevins called Gardner "one of the great natural storytellers," a writer who left behind "over a quarter of a century of rich creative work which will be read and reprinted and reread as long as the art of storytelling is cherished."[8]

* * *

William McCleery was born in 1911 in Hastings, Nebraska. He entered the University of Nebraska when he was just fifteen years old. It is reported that his mother, a musician, financed his college education by playing the piano and the organ for a movie house in Hastings. At nineteen, McCleery was a cub reporter for the *Omaha World-Herald*. After graduation in 1931, he traveled to New York.

McCleery held editorial positions with the Associated Press, Hearst newspapers, *Life* magazine, *P.M.*, and *Ladies Home Journal*. As an editor, McCleery was affiliated with Princeton University in the years 1963–1997; he founded *University: A Princeton Quarterly*, edited the book *The Human Nature of a University* (1969), compiled *Conversations on the Character of Princeton* (1986), and penned *The Story of a Campaign for Princeton 1981–1986*.

McCleery served as a member of the board of directors of Princeton's McCarter Theatre, and he was theatre reviewer for the Princeton area's *Town Topics* during 1970–1998.

McCleery had two comedies produced on Broadway. *Hope for the Best* (Fulton Theatre, April 23, 1945—117 performances) starred Franchot Tone as a popular gossip columnist, Michael Jordan, who wishes to shift gears and write more meaningful material. He is aided by young, sympathetic Lucille Daily, played by Jane Wyatt, and they get attached in more ways than one. *Parlor Story* (Biltmore Theatre, March 4, 1947—twenty-three performances) is the story of a former newspaperman, Charles Burnett, portrayed by Walter Abel, who has accepted a professorship on the faculty of a Missouri university and strives to become its president. Burnett is foiled by the plotting of the paper's editor, who wants him back.

Other plays by McCleery include the university-town comedy *Good Housekeeping*; in 1949 it was previewed on the road with Helen Hayes and her eighteen-year-old daughter, Mary MacArthur, but had to be cancelled due to the sudden death of Mary from polio. *The Lady Chooses* premiered in 1954 at the Westport Country Playhouse in Westport, Connecticut, featuring Faye Emerson as an idealistic, somewhat naive woman who unwittingly gets entangled in shady political maneuvers. An adaptation of the 1958 Peter DeVries novel *A Mackeral Plaza*, the story of a widowed clergyman who plans to remarry, was a failed pre-Broadway tryout but is regularly performed by amateur theatrical groups. *Good Morning, Miss Dove*, based on the 1954 best-selling novel by Frances Gray Patton and given its first production by the Peterborough Players in Peterborough, New Hampshire, in 1962, focuses on a strict yet beloved New England schoolteacher. Patricia Clark, the attractive thirtysomething editor of a top New York magazine, must choose between true love and career ambitions in the 1975 comedy *Hardesty Park*. *Match Play*, set in a contemporary newspaper publisher's office, was produced posthumously at McCleery's alma mater, the University of Nebraska, Lincoln.

Acting Edition: Samuel French, Inc. (in manuscript form).

Awards and Honors: In 1944, Erle Stanley Gardner was awarded a Pocket Books Gertrude as a member of the Million-Copy Club. A few years later he received a larger Gold Gertrude as a member of the Five Million–Copy Club. In the mid-fifties he had passed the fifty million mark and was given a special scroll. Gardner's *Court of Last Resort* won the Mystery Writers of America Edgar Award for Best Fact Crime in 1953, and he received a Grand Master Award from Mystery Writers of America in 1962. He was made an honorary alumnus of Kansas City University in 1955 and granted an honorary LL.D. by McGeorge College of Law in Sacramento, California, in 1956.

In 2009, the U.S. Postal Service initiated a set of stamps honoring television icons, including Perry Mason.

NOTES

1. E. H. Mundell, *Erle Stanley Gardner: A Checklist* (Kent, OH: Kent State University Press, 1968), introduction, n.p.

2. Chris Steinbrunner and Otto Penzler, *Encyclopedia of Mystery and Detection* (New York: McGraw-Hill, 1976), 280.

3. Brian Kelleher and Diana Merrill, *The Perry Mason TV Show Book* (New York: St. Martin's Press, 1987), 16.

4. Brian Kelleher and Diana Merrill, *The Perry Mason TV Show Book*, 16.

5. Dorothy B. Hughes, *Erle Stanley Gardner: The Case of the Real Perry Mason* (New York: Morrow, 1978), 77.

6. Alva Johnston, *The Case of Erle Stanley Gardner* (New York: Morrow, 1947), 25–27.

7. Chris Steinbrunner and Otto Penzler, eds., *Encyclopedia of Mystery and Detection*, 165.

8. Chris Steinbrunner and Otto Penzler, *Encyclopedia of Mystery and Detection*, 166.

Fortune and Men's Eyes (1967)

John Herbert (Canada, 1926–2001)

Similar to American playwright Miguel Piñero, who was incarcerated as a youth and drew on the experience to write the tough-as-nails *Short Eyes*, Canadian John Herbert was imprisoned as a teenager and his six-month ordeal in Ontario's Guelph Reformatory inspired the gritty prison drama *Fortune and Men's Eyes*.

The action unfolds in a Canadian penal institute where the overwhelming majority of prisoners are in their late teens and early twenties. The setting is a dormitory. There are four beds and the focus of the play is on the cell's four occupants. The whole upstage wall is barred and a corridor is visible; guards and inmates can be seen entering and exiting. A doorway leads to a toilet and shower room.

The lights fade up on Queenie, sitting on his bed upstage; Mona, leaning against the wall of bars; and Rocky, stretched on his bed. The playwright provides vivid descriptions of the characters. Queenie is a large, heavy-bodied youth of nineteen with the strength of a wrestler but very soft white skin—a strange physical appearance that combines softness and hulking strength. His mouth has a pouting, self-indulgent look, but his eyes are hard, cold, and icy blue. He is "coarse, cruel, tough and voluptuously pretty."

Mona is an eighteen-year-old who seems suspended between the sexes. His appearance is androgynous. He is slender, narrow-shouldered, long-necked, long-legged, but never ungainly. His face is Madonna-like, straight-nosed, patrician-mouthed, and sad-eyed. His real name is Jan, but not surprisingly, his nickname is "Mona Lisa."

Rocky seems older and harder than most nineteen-year-olds. He takes pride in harboring neither soft nor gentle feelings. He is "one who lives like a cornered rat, vicious, dangerous and unpredictable." He is handsome in a lean, dark, razor-edge way.

Metal doors clang open and shut, and heavy boots march along the corridor off-stage. "It's the new arrivals," says Mona. Rocky laughs, "Look at the queen watchin' the fish! See anything you can catch, Rosie?"

A guard enters with a youth who is about seventeen. The guard tells the new arrival that this is his assigned dormitory. Smitty is a good-looking, clean-cut youth of clear intelligence. He has the look of a collegiate athlete. The face is strong and masculine, yet a clear sensitivity softens the sharp outlines.

The guard exits. The fellows introduce themselves. Smitty does not want to reveal the reason for his incarceration. He was sentenced for six months. No, he's not queer; he has a girlfriend. Queenie warns Smitty that he may become "public property." He further warns Smitty to avoid any missteps and tells him that the guards never help; as a matter of fact, some of them are sadistic. A while back they whisked Mona to the storeroom, where they tied him to "a little machine that fastens your hips and ankles" and "banged him across the ass with a leather belt fulla holes."

Enter the guard called "Holy Face." He is a rugged-faced middle-aged man with a rigid military bearing. "He presents an impressive exterior of uniformed law enforcement, but one senses behind the unsmiling features some nagging doubt or worry," notes the playwright. The guard announces that it is Queenie's turn to take the mobile library around. Queenie exits and is soon seen wheeling the library cart.

The guard ushers Mona out to sick-call. Rocky tells Smitty that his one and only homosexual affair "with a big shot millionaire" resulted in his imprisonment. For a while he was living high—had a weekly allowance, a swell apartment, lot of booze—but once, when he was driving the man's Cadillac convertible, "that fruit" sent "the bulls" after him and he was picked up for stealing the Caddy.

Rocky offers Smitty his protection. "Stick out with the Rock an' you'll be looked up at," he says. Smitty hesitates. Rocky grabs the boy's arm, twists it behind his back and pushes him toward the shower room.

When the curtain rises, two weeks have passed. Smitty and Mona are lying on their cots, each reading a book. Rocky enters from the shower room as Holy Face brings Queenie in. The guard is suspicious of Queenie's frequent visits to the hospital. Mona shows Holy Face his library pass card, and the guard leads him out.

Smitty rolls a cigarette for Rocky. Rocky torments Queenie, accusing him of being jealous of his relationship with Smitty. Smitty asks that they stop treating him like "a piece of goods on the bargain counter."

Another guard enters, reminds Queenie of his participation in the upcoming Christmas concert, and takes Rocky out to "the big office." Left by themselves, Queenie tells Smitty that "Rocky's nowhere near top dog in this joint." If Smitty will relinquish his attachment to Rocky, says Queenie, he will spread the news that Smitty is the boss in this block.

Later that day Rocky orders Smitty into the shower and is pummeled by him. Queenie, triumphantly, tells Mona that there's a new king on the block, a king who's got everything it takes to run his own show, but nevertheless needs him, Queenie, to be at his side.

Act II takes place on Christmas Eve. Queenie returns from his performance in heavy makeup, wearing a platinum-blond wig, spangled sequin dress, and long black gloves, with large rhinestone jewelry on his ears, neck, and wrists. He carries a large feather fan which he throws open and subsequently uses in a bump-and-grind act. Mona enters, wearing a makeshift costume from Portia's court scene in *The Merchant of Venice*.

In a secluded corner, Mona tells Smitty how he was attacked and robbed by a gang of guys one payday. A cop observed him being beaten and kicked, but instead of coming to his aid, asked to be part of the event—sexually. Charges were made against him, an assigned lawyer was no help, and the judge—"fat, white-haired"—looked down at him and sent him to jail for six months.

Smitty confides that he stole a car to get his mother out of town, away from his drunken, abusing "slob of a father." His father sent the police after him. He slugged a cop when they were arresting him.

As Smitty and Mona trade confidences, Mona recites a Shakespearean sonnet: "When in disgrace with fortune and men's eyes / I all alone beweep my outcast state . . ."—the words that gave the play its title. Rocky and Queenie watch Smitty and Mona with heads close together, and react violently. "I'll give the bitch a bluebird!" cries Queenie as he smashes his fist into Mona's cheek. Smitty leaps up and punches Queenie. He turns to face Rocky and Queenie uses the advantage to put a wrestling hold on Smitty, pinning his arms behind his back. Rocky shakes Mona as though he were a rag doll, throws him to the floor, and raises his foot to kick his face, but Smitty breaks from Queenie, hurling the heavy blond away, and kicks Rocky in the groin. Rocky screams, doubling over with pain. Smitty then goes after Queenie just as the guard comes in, gun drawn.

The guard orders Smitty, Rocky, and Queenie to raise their hands and line up against the wall. He then pulls Mona to his feet and pushes him toward the corridor, saying, "You little pansy! You know what you got last time this happened, don't you?" They disappear along the corridor, with Mona screaming, "No! Oh, no, no, no, no . . ." Rocky and Queenie begin to laugh in derision. Smitty turns to them viciously and announces: "Listen to me, this is my show from now on." He warns Rocky to accept his leadership or "I'm going to demolish your mug so bad that no fruit will ever look at you again, let alone a woman." Smitty takes a threatening step toward Rockie and Queenie, and both hastily retreat to the shower room.

Clutching the bars of the back wall, Smitty hears the echoes of Mona's screams. As if he himself is whipped by unseen strokes of a lash, he contorts in pain and stumbles blindly downstage. After a moment he rises slowly from the hunched position to full height. His face now seems to be carved of stone, his mouth narrow and cruel, his eyes corresponding slits of hatred. The young man who came to the dormitory timid, frightened, and utterly naive has obviously gone through a thorough transformation.

Smitty looks upstage in the direction of the guards and speaks in a hoarse, ugly whisper, "I'm going to pay you back." He lights a cigarette, looks coolly out to the audience, and with a twisted, menacing smile says, "I'll pay you all back."

The lights fade to black, and the final slam of a jail gate echoes through the theatre.

* * *

Written and revised from 1963 to 1966, early versions of *Fortune and Men's Eyes* were rejected by several theatre companies in Canada. A reading of the play at the Canadian Shakespeare Festival prompted the drama critic of the *Toronto Star*, Samuel Nathan Cohen, to send it to New York publicist David Rothenberg, who had just produced Megan Terry's acclaimed anti–Vietnam War play *Viet Rock*. Rothenberg optioned the play and passed it on to Dustin Hoffman, a member of the Actors Studio. Lee Strasberg, the head of the studio, believed that *Fortune and Men's Eyes* would open doors to a previously taboo subject. Hoffman played Rocky alongside Jon Voigt as Smitty in a 1966 Actors Studio workshop of the play.

Produced by Rothenberg, *Fortune and Men's Eyes* premiered at off-Broadway's Actors Playhouse on February 23, 1967, directed by Mitchell Nestor. The cast included Victor Arnold (Rocky), Robert Christian (Mona), Bill Moor (Queenie), Terry Kiser (Smitty), and Clifford Pellow (Guard).

The *New York Times'* Dan Sullivan found *Fortune and Men's Eyes* "a distressing play in more ways than one," and felt that the drama "should have something more to recommend it than a campy bit part [Queenie], lots of dirty words and an entirely commendable indignation about a very real social problem. But that's about all I could find in it."[1]

Despite the critical drubbing, *Fortune and Men's Eyes* ran for 328 performances, after which the play traveled to Chicago and San Francisco, and then moved to playwright John Herbert's hometown of Toronto, where it ran for fifteen weeks at the Central Library Theatre. Producer-director Charles Marowitz selected the play for the opening attraction of his experimental Open Space Theatre in London during the 1968–1969 season. Upon entering the lobby, the audience was greeted by thumbprint-taking wardens, clanging metal doors, and flashing lights—an attempt to create a sort of a nightmarish atmosphere.

Reviewer Robert Cushman wrote in *Plays and Players*, "The dramatic progression is conventional enough, centering as it does on Smitty, the newest inmate, who begins by wanting no part of it ("I'm not queer. I've got a girlfriend") and ends, having gone through the rounds of the dorm bully, the camp queen, and the sensitive underdog, on top of the heap and all set to begin his own reign of terror. . . . If you are not burdened with stringent preconceptions about the avant-garde which are bound to be disappointing, the evening is worth seeking out."[2]

The Open Space production ran for nine months and moved to West End's Comedy Theatre. Peter Roberts, another reviewer for *Plays and Players*, reported that "the audience no longer has its fingerprints taken on arrival at the theatre," but he remained skeptical about the merits of the play: "I'm afraid I'm unwilling to swallow Mr. Herbert's homosexual horse-pill until he can devise a less syrupy julep for it."[3]

In 1969, Sal Mineo produced and directed *Fortune and Men's Eyes* at the Coronet Theatre in Los Angeles, with Don Johnson in the role of Smitty, transferring the production to New York, where it played at off-Broadway's Stage 73 for 231 performances. Almost twenty years later, in 1987, another off-Broadway revival ran at the Actors Playhouse for thirty-three showings.

In France, the French-language production of *Fortune and Men's Eyes* at the Théâtre Athénée, 1971–1972, became a cause célèbre protesting government censorship of the stage. At the play's opening night, the audience included luminaries such as Jean-Paul Sartre, Jean Genet, Simone Signoret, Jeanne Moreau, and Melina Mercouri. Right-wing governments tried to close productions in Turkey, Argentina, and South Africa, where the play was mounted with a racially mixed cast.

Throughout the twentieth century, *Fortune and Men's Eyes* has been presented in more than sixty countries in many translations. To this day, the play continues to affect audiences in countries where prison reform and discrimination against homosexuals are still strong public issues. It inspired the formation of the Fortune Society, a New York City–based organization for ex-offenders, which works to heighten public awareness of the conditions facing inmates.

In 1970, *Fortune and Men's Eyes* was filmed in a former city prison in Quebec, Canada, directed by Harvey Hart, with Wendell Burton in the role of Smitty. MGM released the movie the following year.

* * *

John Herbert Brundage was born in Toronto, Canada, on October 13, 1926. His father, Claude, once a professional athlete, lost his money in the

Depression. Herbert grew up in poverty but, he later said, "in a house that was nevertheless filled with literature, from the ancient Greeks to Shakespeare and Stevenson."[4]

Herbert studied at Toronto's New Play Society School for Drama and the National Ballet School (1955–1960). Alongside his sister, Nana Brundage, an actress, he founded and ran three pioneering theatre companies in Toronto: Adventure Theatre (1960–1962), New Venture Players (1962–1964), and the Garret Theatre (1965–1971). In 1972, Herbert cofounded the Maverick Theatre in Toronto and served as its artistic director for twenty-five years until his death, at age seventy-four, on June 22, 2001.

In addition to *Fortune and Men's Eyes*, Herbert wrote sixteen more plays, but few were produced professionally and most were never published. His essays and articles appeared in the *Village Voice, Saturday Night, Canadian Drama,* and *Fortune Newsletter* (a prison reform monthly published by Fortune Society).

Acting Edition: Samuel French, Inc. (in manuscript form); Grove Press.

Awards and Honors: Winner of the 1975 Chalmers Award for Best Canadian Play. John Herbert was made a lifetime member of the Actors Studio, New York, in 1967. In 1968 he was appointed honorary member of the board of directors of The Fortune Society. A year later he received special honors from the Library of Congress of the United States. In 1971 he became a member of France's Société des Auteurs et Compositeurs Dramatiques.

NOTES

1. *New York Times*, February 24, 1967.
2. *Plays and Players*, September 1968.
3. *Plays and Players*, December 1969.
4. Quoted in John Herbert's obituary, *New York Times*, June 27, 2001.

The Man in the Glass Booth (1967)

Robert Shaw (England, 1927–1978)

The Man in the Glass Booth, a psychological thriller about guilt and redemption, is based on the case of Adolf Eichmann, a Nazi colonel referred to as "the architect of the Holocaust." After World War II, Eichmann fled to Argentina and lived there under a false identity. In 1960 he was captured by Israeli Mossad agents and abducted to Israel, where he was tried for war crimes and crimes against humanity. He was found guilty and executed by hanging in 1962 in Ramla, Israel.

The Man in the Glass Booth raises its curtain on a palatial penthouse in Manhattan, the residence of Arthur Goldman, a real estate tycoon. French windows open to a roof garden full of statues and artificial trees. The city's towers are seen in the background. Servants come up in a noiseless in-house elevator carrying priceless paintings, a butler pours Goldman his morning coffee, and a secretary enters with the New York dailies. It is November 20, 1964, Goldman's fifty-second birthday, and he plans to go to the opera that evening, escorting a duchess.

Goldman is charming, eccentric, and sure of himself, but he keeps waving a pistol about, perhaps awaiting some danger. Curiously, when the thing he fears comes, he tosses the pistol into a tropical fish tank.

A flower man arrives in the elevator, unloads artificial flowering plants, and leaves. He soon returns with two young men, guns in their hands. They are followed by a stout woman, Mrs. Rosen, who is obviously their leader. "You are Adolf Karl Dorff," says Mrs. Rosen, "a colonel in the Einsatzgruppen, the mobile killing unit of the SS." Goldman does not deny the accusation. The young men, Israeli agents, search the apartment and frisk Goldman. One of them hits him in the stomach and he spits out a capsule of poison. He offers them a million dollars "hard cash" and raises it to three, then seven, then eight million.

The second act takes place in a Tel Aviv cell. Outside a peephole stands a guard. Inside, it is hot. Goldman, dressed in prison clothes, sits on the bed. Mrs. Rosen faces him. "Why did you pretend to be Jewish? Who killed Arthur Goldman?" she asks. In a jocular mood he admits to being Adolf Karl Dorff and requests to be allowed to wear his SS uniform at the pending trial.

During a blackout, the cell changes into a courtroom. A guard leads Goldman to a bulletproof glass booth. The presiding judge, the prosecutor, and Mrs. Rosen are seated at scattered tables. Goldman seems carefree and high-spirited as witnesses relate the horrors of the concentration camps and the atrocities committed by the Nazis. At the conclusion of each testimony, Goldman claps sardonically. Insisting that he conduct his own defense, he switches on a microphone from within the booth and relates with glee how in the camps he personally sought out the Jews who were spirited and rebellious, the ones who "smelled of freedom," and shot them. He also declares his admiration for Hitler: his generals lost him the war; his subordinates were unworthy; Hess was mad, Goering reviled, Himmler rejected. But the Fuehrer was loved, says Goldman, loved to the end—"Sieg Heil! Sieg Heil!"

The verdict "guilty" seems inevitable until an old woman in the auditorium rises and says quietly, "This man is not Dorff." The judge allows the woman, Mrs. Lehman, to take the witness stand. She testifies that the man on trial was never a Nazi but is in fact a Jewish survivor of the concentration camps. She describes how toward the end of the war, Colonel Dorff was shooting people methodically in the neck, then throwing the twisted bodies into the snow. When Russian soldiers entered the camp on horseback, Mrs. Lehman reports, Dorff dropped his gun and fell to his knees. "We all ran and tore at Dorff," says Mrs. Lehman. "We tore him to pieces."

After a long silence, Mrs. Rosen enters the glass booth and undoes Goldman's cuffs. He comes out of the booth and embraces Mrs. Lehman. "Why did you do it?" asks a perplexed judge. He posed as a Nazi war criminal, explains Goldman, in order to present the enemy as he really was—evil and unrepentant. As a former concentration camp inmate, he seeks to tell the world about the Nazi horrors to make sure they are never forgotten, to ensure continuing vigilance against repetition. He is willing to sacrifice his own life to that end.

Goldman returns to the glass booth, snatches the door key, and locks himself inside. He takes off his Nazi uniform. The guards and the court officials surround the booth and examine it, not knowing how to get the man out. They attempt to dislodge him by tilting the booth, hoping to pry him loose from underneath, but their efforts fail. He can never be dislodged, says the playwright, he can only be remembered. The lights fade.

* * *

Adapted by Robert Shaw from his own novel and directed by Harold Pinter, *The Man in the Glass Booth* opened at West End's St. Martin's Theatre on July 27, 1967. The London reviewers next morning offered varied interpretations of Arthur Goldman's self-sacrifice and generally faulted the play for obscurity. Reviewer Thomas Quinn Curtiss wrote in a dispatch to the *New York Times* that Robert Shaw "delivered a fascinating if enigmatic play which benefits from the exacting direction of fellow playwright Harold Pinter, and from a masterly performance by Donald Pleasence in the central role."[1]

The American critic Walter Kerr attended the opening night of *The Man in the Glass Booth* on his way to the Chichester Festival and, he wrote, could not detach this "calculated grotesque" from his mind. He was fascinated by the character of the Jewish financier who is "imperious, coddling, oily, fearful, garrulous in a fake Brooklyn accent, cheerfully unreasonable. . . . He seems to have invited his own capture. . . . He admits his crimes, glorifies in them. 'I had a ball,' he gloats. . . . He is a perfect war criminal. . . . It so happens that I was more taken up with the play, and readier to forgive its intellectual uncertainties and occasional theatrical gaucheries than most of the London daily reviewers."[2]

John Russell Taylor, in *Plays and Players*, stated that he liked Robert Shaw's play "for precisely the qualities that most of the critics seemed to find against it, in varying degrees according to taste. I liked it because it does not let itself become a play about the Jewish problem, Nazi guilt, the ethics of genocide, sadism as a way of life, or any of the other abstract notions which seem to be hovering in the wings. To some extent it is a play about all these things and more. But the extent is strictly delimited by the author's determination to make it, first and foremost, a play about a person, and a very strange and mysterious person at that. . . . Anyone (well, more or less) can present a thesis of sorts. But to create a character as complex, surprising and, in spite of everything, as convincing as Goldman—that is something else again. . . . If to experience magic in the theatre you are willing to accept a little mystery, this would be very much what you have been looking for."[3]

The Man in the Glass Booth ran for 151 performances and failed to become a commercial success. When the play was exported to New York's Royale Theatre on September 26, 1968, the reception by the critics was mixed. Richard Watts Jr. found it "A fascinating play . . . a play of striking theatrical effectiveness . . . a work of notable dramatic originality."[4] Leonard Harris believed it to be "dramatically viable . . . excellent drama,"[5] and Leonard Probst concurred: "The play is absolutely fascinating. . . . *The Man in the Glass Booth* is an exciting play and it's been done brilliantly."[6] Walter Kerr pointed out "the fanciful flourishes of titillating melodrama: unidentified strangers in elevators, men stealthily opening forbidden safes, revolvers dropped into fish tanks. . . . The evening is visual, tactile, best represented everywhere by the grotesque but intensely physical quality of Mr. Pleasence's performance. . . . The evening is a show and the showmanship is brilliant."[7] Clive Barnes liked "a simple melodrama, engrossing at its own level, and a fantastically effective vehicle for the bravura acting of Donald Pleasence and the subtly virtuoso directing of Harold Pinter."[8]

Negative assessments came from John Chapman, "It came to be an undramatic bore to me last night,"[9] and Martin Gottfried, "The story is basically pulp fiction . . . a crudely written and badly boring gimmick play."[10]

The Man in the Glass Booth ran for 268 performances. Jack Warden replaced Donald Pleasence on March 31, 1969. The play was filmed in 1975, directed by Arthur Hiller and starring Maximilian Schell in an Academy-nominated performance as Arthur Goldman. Off-Broadway's Jean Cocteau Repertory revived *The Man in the Glass Booth* in 1998. Reviewer Wilborn Hampton wrote in the *New York Times*, "The play is no less harrowing today than it was three decades ago, and the admirable Cocteau revival is a taut staging that Eve Adamson, the director, gradually builds in intensity to its final explosion of malevolence, with the accused in the dock reveling in murders he committed. But the play's jarring conclusion shocks even further and raises doubts about pat answers concerning the Holocaust." Hampton applauded Harris Berlinsky for turning the role of Arthur Goldman into "a quiet tour de force. . . . From a deceptively mild, low-key beginning, Mr. Berlinsky quietly creates his monster, or at least the semblance of a monster, reaching a chilling climax in Goldman's final monologue from his glass booth of dock."[11]

* * *

Robert Archibald Shaw was born in Westhoughton, Lancashire, England, in 1927. As a boy, he was an accomplished athlete, competing in rugby, squash, and track events. The first play he saw was *Hamlet* in 1944 with Sir John Gielgud in the West End. He studied for the stage at the Royal Academy of Dramatic Art and, in 1948, embarked upon a career as an actor. He gained experience in regional theatres throughout England, notably with the company at Stratford-on-Avon. In 1951 he joined the Old Vic, where he played Cassio in *Othello* and Lysander in *A Midsummer Night's Dream*. In addition to several lauded performances in the West End, Shaw appeared on Broadway as Aston in Harold Pinter's *The Caretaker* (1961–1962) and as Möbius in Friedrich Duerrenmatt's *The Physicists* (1964–1965). He distinguished himself on the screen as a SPECTRE assassin in the James Bond film *From Russia with Love* (1963); a relentless German Panzer officer in *Battle of the Bulge* (1965); a young Henry VIII in *A Man for All Seasons* (1966), for which he was nominated for the Academy

Award as Best Supporting Actor; General George Armstrong Custer in *Custer of the West* (1967); the Spanish conqueror Francisco Pizarro in *The Royal Hunt of the Sun* (1969); Lord Randolph Churchill in *Young Winston* (1972); a ruthless mobster in *The Sting* (1973); a sadistic subway-hijacker in *The Taking of Pelham One Two Three* (1974); an obsessed shark-hunting fisherman in *Jaws* (1975); the Sheriff of Nottingham in *Robin and Marian* (1976); a treasure hunter in *The Deep* (1977); and an Israeli Mossad agent in *Black Sunday* (1977).

As a writer, Shaw published his first novel, *The Hiding Place*, in 1960, and followed it with the novels *The Sun Doctor* (1961), *The Flag* (1965), *The Man in the Glass Booth* (1967) upon which he based his play, and *A Card from Morocco* (1969). His second play, *Cato Street*, about the 1820 Cato Street conspiracy, was produced by the Young Vic in London in 1971, starring Vanessa Redgrave and Bob Hoskins.

Shaw married three times and had ten children. His second wife was the actress Mary Ure. A heavy drinker most of his life, Shaw died of a heart attack in Ireland in 1978 while filming *Avalanche Express*. His remains were cremated and his ashes scattered near his home in Ireland.

Acting Edition: Samuel French, Inc.

Awards and Honors: A top-ten selection in *The Best Plays of 1968–1969*. *The Man in the Glass Booth* was nominated for a Tony Award as Best Play in 1969.

NOTES

1. *New York Times*, July 29, 1967.
2. *New York Times*, August 27, 1967.
3. *Plays and Players*, October 1967.
4. *New York Post*, September 27, 1968.
5. *WCBS TV*, September 26, 1968.
6. *NBC4 TV*, September 26, 1968.
7. *New York Times*, October 6, 1968.
8. *New York Times*, September 27, 1968.
9. *Daily News*, September 27, 1968.
10. *Women's Wear Daily*, September 27, 1968.
11. *New York Times*, February 25, 1998.

The Real Inspector Hound (1968)

Tom Stoppard
(England, Czechoslovakia-born, 1937–)

Agatha Christie's *The Mousetrap* has been packing London's St. Martin's Theatre since 1952, the longest-running play in theatre history. Young playwright Tom Stoppard, fresh from his success of *Rosencrantz and Guildenstern Are Dead* (1966), embarked upon a farcical play-within-a-play, *The Real Inspector Hound*, throwing sharp darts not only at Christie's thriller but at the whole genre of parlor whodunits, which he believed to be formalistic and cliché-sodden. Simultaneously, Stoppard savagely lampoons theatre critics—his former profession being a reviewer for a Bristol daily.

The lights come up on the drawing room of Muldoon Manor, an isolated mansion surrounded by creeping fog. The body of a man lies face down on the floor in front of a large chaise longue. Two men take their seats in an acting area next to the front row of the auditorium. They are first-night theatre critics for rival tabloids. Moon is a young second-stringer who covers his incompetence with pretentious analysis and flowery metaphors, cites among his sources Kafka, Sartre, Shakespeare, Beckett, Pinero, Pirandello, Dante, and Dorothy L. Sayers, and has a secret desire to murder his superior, Higgs, while protecting his position against a third-stringer, Puckeridge. Birdboot is a pompous old-timer, who consistently writes raves to get them blown up for the lobby of the theatre, and, while boasting that he is "a family man" devoted to his "homely and good-natured wife, Myrtle," is habitually giving flattering notices to accommodating actresses in order to bed them. In fact, Birdboot has already had a liaison with the ingenue who plays Felicity Cunningham in this evening's play, and he is curious about the leading lady who portrays Lady Cynthia Muldoon, the mistress of the manor.

A middle-aged, sinister-looking charwoman, Mrs. Drudge, enters and heads straight for the radio, switching it on, a comment poking fun at the excess use of radio announcements in murder mysteries.

RADIO: We interrupt our program for a special police message: the search still goes on for the escaped madman who is on the run in Essex. County police, led by Inspector Hound, have received a report that the man has been seen in the desolate marshes around Muldoon Manor [Mrs. Drudge gasps]. The man is wearing a darkish suit with a lightish shirt. He is of medium height and build and youngish. [A man answering that description creeps in, without Mrs. Drudge noticing.]

The charwoman turns off the radio and begins to dust and polish, and by way of tidying the room inches her way toward the body. Her discovery is imminent as she slides the chaise longue over the corpse, hiding it completely.

The telephone rings. Mrs. Drudge snatches it and rattles off, with a Cockney accent, expository information: "Hello, the drawing room of Lady Muldoon's country residence one morning in early spring. . . . Lady Muldoon and her house guests are here cut off from the world, including Magnus the wheelchair-ridden half-brother of her ladyship's husband Lord Albert Muldoon who ten years ago went out for a walk on the cliffs and was never seen again."

She catches sight of the suspicious character. He senses her stare, freezes, and straightens up, introducing himself as Simon Gascoyne, "a friend of Lady Muldoon, the lady of the house, having made her acquaintance through a mutual friend, Felicity Cunningham, shortly after moving into this neighborhood just the other day."

A tennis ball bounces through the French windows, closely followed by Felicity, who is in her twenties. She wears a pretty tennis outfit and carries a racket (burlesquing the leisurely environment pictured in cozy English whodunits). Simon confesses to Felicity that upon their last rendezvous he got a little carried away, but he loves another. Felicity announces, "I'll kill you for this, Simon Gascoyne!" bursts into tears, and rushes out.

Lady Cynthia Muldoon enters from the garden. She is an attractive woman in her thirties, and she too carries a tennis racket. Simon seizes her and glues his lips to hers. Critic Birdboot sighs, "She's beautiful—a vision of eternal grace, a poem." The sound of a wheelchair approaching is heard. It arrives bearing Major Magnus, "the crippled half-brother of Lord Muldoon who turned up out of the blue from Canada the other day." Felicity returns. She and Simon shove the chaise longue toward a card table, once more revealing the corpse to the audience, though not to the players. Felicity, Simon, Cynthia, and Magnus play bridge.

The lights on the set black out, leaving only Moon and Birdboot visible. Birdboot shifts his sentiments away from Felicity and sings the praises of Cynthia while predicting the play's denouement: "It seems open and shut—Magnus is not what he pretends to be and he's got his next victim marked down."

The telephone on the set rings. The lights come up to reveal Cynthia, Felicity, and Magnus being served coffee by Mrs. Drudge. A mournful baying is heard in the distance, and Felicity tenses: "It sounds like the cry of a gigantic hound!" Inspector Hound enters. On his head he wears a miner's helmet with a flashing light. On his feet are swamp boots. He carries a foghorn. Taking off hat, boots, and foghorn, he says, "It takes more than a bit of weather to keep a policeman from his duty." The inspector relates that he is after an escaped lunatic, "a youngish, good-looking fellow in a smart suit, white shirt, hatless, well-spoken—someone who on the surface seems as sane as you or I."

Inspector Hound finds himself standing on top of the corpse. They all now see it for the first time. The inspector picks up the phone, which, predictably, doesn't work, because "The lines have been cut!" He sends everyone to search the house, and all depart speedily in different directions, leaving the stage momentarily empty. Simon strolls through the French windows. He notices the corpse, crosses, and turns it over. There is a shot. Simon falls dead.

The "dead" phone starts to ring. It keeps ringing and Moon loses patience. He picks up the receiver and barks, "Hello!" Surprised, he tells Birdboot, "It's for you." Moon gives him the phone and returns to his seat. Birdboot explodes into the phone, admonishing his wife Myrtle for calling him at work. The play now becomes Pirandellian, blurring the barrier between fantasy and reality, between theatre and audience, as the critics unwittingly become more and more enmeshed in what is happening at Muldoon Manor. Birdboot is mistaken for Simon and eagerly steps into the role, fulfilling his desire to be a handsome young lover. In a climactic turn of events, Birdboot recognizes the body on the floor as Higgs, the first-string critic, and accuses Moon of murdering his superior. There is a shot and Birdboot falls dead.

Moon ascends the stage to unravel Birdboot's death and takes on the role of Inspector Hound. Quick revelations follow, topped by Major Magnus getting up from his wheelchair, removing his moustache, and declaring that he is Cynthia's long-gone husband, Albert, who lost his memory and joined the force, rising by merit to the rank of inspector. He is the real Inspector Hound. (This revelation tips one of the twist endings of *The Mousetrap*.)

Magnus-Albert-Hound turns to face Moon, who is shocked to recognize Puckeridge, the third-string critic. Moon blames him for killing Higgs and Birdboot, and begins to run away. Magnus produces a pistol and fires. Moon whispers with a trace of admiration, "Puckeridge, you cunning bastard," and dies. The curtain comes down on the corpses of

Higgs, Birdboot, and Moon, the three unfortunate theatre critics. Puck-eridge will now become a first stringer.

* * *

Tom Stoppard wrote the play between 1961 and 1962. Initially named *The Stand-Ins* and later *The Critics*, *The Real Inspector Hound* was presented at the Criterion Theatre, London, on June 17, 1968. Robert Chetwyn directed. The two critics were played by Richard Briers (Moon) and Ronnie Barker (Birdboot). Three varied notices were dispatched to the *New York Times*. Reviewer Irving Wardle regretted that "what really forestalls any breakthrough between illusion and reality is the fact that the critics—with their talk of opera cloaks and their fruity Edwardian phrases—are as much creatures of fantasy as the inmates of Lady Muldoon's drawing room."[1] Clive Barnes gushed: "Stoppard's play is enormously funny and not least when he is parodying critics and their notices. . . . I laughed and I laughed and I laughed."[2] Walter Kerr found the play "too slight and too short to fill a whole evening . . . nothing more than an extended revue sketch."[3]

On February 1, 1972, the spoof was revived at the Phoenix Theatre, Leicester, under Ian McKellen's direction. That same year it crossed the Atlantic to off-Broadway's Theatre Four, opening on April 23 with a companion piece, Stoppard's *After Magritte*, a comedy in which an inept Scotland Yard inspector falsely accuses a family of dancers of complicity in a crime known as the Crippled Minstrel Caper. It ran for 465 performances and went on tour with Robert Vaughan as Inspector Hound.

Seven years later, in August 1979, *The Real Inspector Hound* was produced by off-Broadway's New York Stages, eliciting the comment "This is the kind of unbelievable nonsense that is fun to try to believe" in *The Villager*,[4] and "a hilarious parody on the whodunit" by *Show Business*.[5] Stoppard himself staged a London revival at the National Theatre in 1985.

Accompanied by Stoppard's playlet *The Fifteen-Minute Hamlet*, *The Real Inspector Hound* was presented by off-Broadway's Roundabout Theatre in August 1992. Most of the reviews were positive. "Irrepressible sense of fun," cheered Edwin Wilson.[6] "Done again, beautifully, hilariously, under Gloria Muzio's direction," applauded Jerry Tallmer. "Wheels within wheels, tricks within tricks, illusions within illusions, jest within jest, until the whole wonderful apparatus bites off its own tail and maybe yours too."[7] *Time* magazine approved "an exquisite mockery of the dreary mysteries that clog the British stage and the critics who tout them."[8]

The naysayers included Howard Kissel, who found the play "dated . . . more a collegiate prank than a one-act play,"[9] and John Simon, who wrote, "shows us Stoppard parading his medals as sophomore-class wit."[10] Jan Stuart scoffed, "It comes off as oddly low-energy spoofery."[11]

The Real Inspector Hound continues to be revived in both England and the United States, with productions in London in 1998, at off-Broadway's T. Schreiber Studio in 2008, and at both the Chichester Festival and Chicago's Signal Ensemble Theatre in 2010.

* * *

Born Tomas Straussler in Ziln, Czechoslovakia, Tom Stoppard's Jewish family fled their native land, moving to Singapore in 1939 when the Nazis invaded. Two years later, the Strausslers were forced to flee again, this time from the invading Japanese. Tom's father, Eugene, was captured and died in a prison camp. Tom's mother soon married a British army major, Kenneth Stoppard, and the family moved to England in 1946.

Stoppard attended boarding schools in Nottinghamshire and Yorkshire but left school early, "bored and alienated by everyone from Shakespeare to Dickens besides." He never went to a university. During the 1950s, he worked as a journalist for the *Western Daily Press* and the *Bristol Evening World*. His assignments included humorous pieces and theatre critiques. Mostly, he reviewed plays presented by the Bristol Old Vic Repertory. He claims that viewing a 1958 production of *Hamlet*, with Peter O'Toole in the title role, was a defining moment for him; that's when he decided to become a playwright.

Stoppard's first play, *Enter a Free Man*, about a dreaming, imaginative inventor who gradually succumbs to the mundane world around him, was aired in 1963 by British Independent Television and eventually staged, on March 28, 1968, at London's St. Martin's Theatre, starring Michael Hordern. Stoppard's breakthrough came with *Rosencrantz and Guildenstern Are Dead*, a whimsical retelling of *Hamlet* from the point-of-view of its fringe characters. Said Stoppard: "Rosencrantz and Guildenstern are two people who have been written into a scheme of things and there's nothing they can do about it except follow through and meet the fate that has been ordained for them, which is to die violently."[12] Initially performed at the Edinburgh Fringe Festival by a group of Oxford undergraduates, the play was presented by the National Theatre Company at London's Old Vic in 1967. With this production, Stoppard became the youngest playwright ever to have a play mounted by this prestigious group. *Rosencrantz and Guildenstern Are Dead* was also a hit in New York, where it received the Tony and Drama Critics Circle awards for best play of 1967–1968. "Very funny, very brilliant, very chilling," wrote Clive Barnes in the *New York Times*.[13] Stoppard scripted and directed a movie version in 1990, featuring Gary Oldman and Tim Roth in the title roles.[14]

The laudatory reception of *Rosencrantz and Guildenstern Are Dead* catapulted Stoppard to the high echelons of British theatre. *The Real Inspector Hound* followed. During the late 1960s and early 1970s, Stoppard penned several one-act plays and radio and television episodes. Notable is the playlet *After Magritte* (1970), a dip into absurdism, revolving around an argument between spouses with a detective and a policeman drawn into the action.

Stoppard's next full-length play was *Jumpers*, a drama set in an alternate reality in which British astronauts have landed on the moon and "radical liberals" have taken over the British government. The play meshes farcical elements, lengthy speeches, and heavy philosophical references about the bizarre murder of an acrobat. *Jumpers* premiered at the Old Vic Theatre on February 2, 1972, with Michael Hordern and Diana Rigg in the lead roles. Under Peter Wood's direction, the play came to the Kennedy Center in Washington, D.C., on February 18, 1974, and moved to Broadway's Billy Rose Theatre on April 22, featuring Brian Bedford and Jill Clayburgh, running for forty-eight performances. The Royal National Theatre revived *Jumpers* in 2003, and the production migrated to Broadway the following year, receiving a Tony Award nomination for Best Revival.

Travesties unfolds primarily in Zürich, Switzerland, during World War I. Author James Joyce, Dadaist founder Tristan Tzara, and Communist revolutionary Vladimir Lenin are the main characters in a comedy that connects real-life characters with a presentation of Oscar Wilde's *The Importance of Being Earnest*. *Travesties* was first produced at the Aldwych Theatre in London on June 10, 1974, directed by Peter Wood (Stoppard continued to work with Wood throughout the coming decades). A subsequent production opened at New York's Ethel Barrymore Theatre on October 30, 1975, won the Tony Award as Best Play, and ran for 156 performances. The Royal Shakespeare Company revived *Travesties* in 1993.

Night and Day, a satire about the British news media, merges forms of fiction and nonfiction as it unfolds in an imaginary African country called Kambawa. A tribal war in the country is covered by the press using linguistic manipulation and double meanings. The play premiered on November 8, 1978, at London's Phoenix Theatre, designed by Carl Toms and starring Diana Rigg. It ran for two years.

Somewhat autobiographical, *The Real Thing* spotlights a playwright in search of self and questions the place of art in society. The play opened successfully at the Strand Theatre in London on November 16, 1982, and made it to New York's Plymouth Theatre on January 5, 1984, where it ran for 566 performances and won Tony Awards for Best Play, Best Actor (Jeremy Irons), and Best Actress (Glenn Close).

The title character of *Hapgood* is a thirty-eight-year-old British female spymaster who romances a Russian double agent during the Cold War, along the way juggling duty and motherhood. The original production, directed by Peter Wood and designed by Carl Toms, opened at London's

Aldwych Theatre on March 8, 1988, to tepid reviews. A revised version was presented by the Center Theatre Group in Hollywood, California, on April 12, 1989, with Judy Davis as Hapgood.

Arcadia unfolds with two parallel story lines, one beginning in 1809 and one in 1989, both set in Sidley Park, an English country home. In 1809, Thomasina Coverly, a precocious teenager who exhibits surprisingly advanced theories about mathematics, falls in love with her tutor, Septimus Hodge, a friend of Lord Byron, an unseen but pivotal character in the play. In the modern segment, Hannah Jarvis, an author, researches the identity of an elusive hermit who lived in Sidley Park in the early 1800s and concludes that it was Septimus Hodge. Directed by Trevor Nunn, *Arcadia* premiered at the Royal National Theatre in London on April 13, 1993, and won the Laurence Olivier and *Evening Standard* Awards for Best Play. *Arcadia* opened at New York's Vivian Beaumont Theatre in March 1995, again directed by Nunn but with a completely different cast, and ran for 173 showings. It was nominated for a Tony Award as Best Play. A regional production of *Arcadia* was mounted by the Arena Stage in Washington, D.C., in 1996–1997. David Leveaux staged revivals of the play at the Duke of York's Theatre in London (2009) and Broadway's Barrymore Theatre (2011).

A memory play, *The Invention of Love*, portrays the life of homosexual poet A. E. Housman, surrounding him with many notable authors of his era, including Oscar Wilde, Frank Harris, and Jerome K. Jerome. Blending historical and fictional characters, the play was presented by the Royal National Theatre, London, on September 25, 1997, directed by Richard Eyre and starring John Wood. It ran nearly a year in London and won the *Evening Standard* Award for Best Play. A Broadway run at the Lyceum Theatre commenced on March 29, 2001, and lasted 108 performances. Richard Easton portrayed the older Housman and Robert Sean Leonard the younger. Both actors won Tony Awards for Best Actor and Best Featured Actor in a Play.

Stoppard's magnum opus is *The Coast of Utopia*, a mammoth drama divided into three parts—"Voyage," "Shipwreck," and "Salvage." The trilogy, with a total running time of nine hours, premiered at London's National Theatre on June 22, 2002, performing in repertory. Trevor Nunn directed. In 2006, Jack O'Brien staged the sequential plays at New York's Vivian Beaumont Theatre for a combined run of 124 performances. Set in pre-revolution Russia, the epic story features some seventy characters and covers a thirty-three-year time span, 1833 to 1866. The main characters are author Ivan Turgenev, literary critic Bakunin Vissarion, and revolutionary thinker Alexander Herzen. *The Coast of Utopia* won 2007's Tony Award for Best Play.

Rock 'n' Roll focuses on the emergence of the democratic movement behind the Iron Curtain, with an emphasis on the artistic dissent against the Communist Party. The action unfolds over several decades from 1968 to 1990, rotating between Prague, Czechoslovakia, and Cambridge, England, and culminates with a concert given by the Rolling Stones in Prague. *Rock 'n' Roll* was presented at London's Royal Court Theatre and ran from June 3 until July 15, 2006. The premiere of the play was attended by Václev Havel, the playwright and first president of the post-Communist Czech Republic, and Mick Jagger of the Rolling Stones.

Stoppard adapted for the British stage plays by Austrians Arthur Schnitzler (*Undiscovered Country*; *Dalliance*) and Johann Nestroy (*On the Razzle*), the Hungarian Ferenc Molnar (*Rough Crossing*), the Spanish Federico Garcia Lorca (*The House of Bernarda Alba*), the Italian Luigi Pirandello (*Henry IV*), and the Russian Anton Chekhov (*The Seagull*). In 1983, he wrote an English libretto of Prokofiev's opera *The Love of Three Oranges*. Ten years later, he penned an English narration for Lehar's operetta *The Merry Widow*.

The indefatigable Stoppard has also contributed extensively to film and television. He penned the screenplays of *The Human Factor* (1980), *Brazil* (1985), *Empire of the Sun* (1987), *The Russia House* (1990), *Billy Bathgate* (1991), *Shakespeare in Love* (1998)—for which he won an Academy Award—*Enigma* (2001), and *The Bourne Ultimatum* (2007). He teamed with Clive Exton on the half-hour teleplay *The Boundary*, aired live on the BBC series *The Eleventh Hour*, July 19, 1975. *The Boundary* was later converted to a one-act play, published by Samuel French, London, in 1991. The teleplay reveals the secrets of a murder at a lexicographer's library with a touch of comic absurdity. The body of a woman is buried under disorderly piles of paper. It is Brenda, wife of librarian Johnson and mistress of librarian Bunyans. Was she murdered by one of them? And why is a pane of glass in the French window broken? What is the connection between the white-flannelled cricketer outside and the hidden corpse inside?[15]

"As a playwright, Stoppard is both playful and thoughtful, both serious and absurd, and both faithful and irreverent," writes Mikhail Alexeeff in *Stoppard in an Hour*. "His legacy is one of innovation and impressive diversity. His inspiration often stems from established material, but his inventiveness sets him apart from his predecessors and contemporaries. In a popular culture that increasingly relies on remakes, retreads, and retooling, it is hard not to marvel at what Stoppard has consistently accomplished. Using a known story to draw an audience, Stoppard has made the tired fashionable, the arcane accessible, and the plodding fun."[16]

Acting Edition: Samuel French, Inc.

Awards and Honors: Tom Stoppard was appointed Commander of the Order of the British Empire (CBE) in 1978 and was knighted in 1997. The same year he was made an Officier de l'Ordre des Arts et des Lettres by the French government. He was recruited to the board of the National Theatre in 1989. He won the Academy Award for *Shakespeare in Love* (1998), and Best Play Tony Awards for *Rosencrantz and Guildenstern Are Dead* (1968), *Travesties* (1975), *The Real Thing* (1984), and *The Coast of Utopia* (2007).

NOTES

1. *New York Times*, June 19, 1968.
2. *New York Times*, July 8, 1968.
3. *New York Times*, July 14, 1968.
4. *The Villager*, August 30, 1979.
5. *Show Business*, September 6, 1979.
6. *Wall Street Journal*, August 14, 1992.
7. *New York Post*, August 14, 1992.
8. *Time*, August 24, 1992.
9. *Daily News*, August 14, 1992.
10. *New York Times*, August 31, 1992.
11. *New York Newsday*, August 14, 1992.
12. *New York Times*, March 24, 1968.
13. *New York Times*, October 17, 1967.
14. A 2009 motion picture, *Rosencrantz and Guildenstern Are Undead*, written and directed by Jordan Galland, is a horror-comedy about an off-Broadway production of *Hamlet* financed by a pale entrepreneur who turns out to be a vampire. "Funny title, not so funny movie," wrote reviewer Gary Goldstein in the *Los Angeles Times* of July 16, 2010. "An ambitious satire of Shakespeare, vampires, small theatre, Tom Stoppard, serial womanizing, cops and more that starts off feeling clever and original but turns silly and diffused as its convoluted story spins out."
15. The English playwright Clive Exton (1930–2007) exhibited an affinity for matters of crime on stage (dramatizing Agatha Christie's *Murder Is Easy* in 1993), the silver screen (*10 Rillington Place*, 1970, based on the sensational John Christie–Timothy Evans murder case in 1940s England; *Crazy House*, 1973, called *Night of the Laughing Dead* in the Unites States, a horror spoof; *The Awakening*, 1980, an Egyptian tomb saga adapted from Bram Stoker's novel, *The Jewel of the Seven Stars*), and television (contributing to such shows as *Dick Baron, Special Agent, The Ruth Rendell Mysteries,* and *Poirot,* the enormously successful series starring David Suchet in what many believe is the definitive portrayal of the Belgian detective).
16. Mikhail Alexeeff, *Stoppard in an Hour* (Hanover, NH: Hour Books, 2010), 37.

Conduct Unbecoming (1969)

Barry England (England, 1934–)

Time: late 1800s. Place: the anteroom of a British regimental officers' mess in India. Playwright Barry England, who served in the Far East for two years as a subaltern, creates a military environment steeped in tradition and honor. Or so it seems.

The play begins with the arrival of two second lieutenants for a three-month probationary period with the regiment. Edward Millington, son of a much-honored general, turns out to be a drunkard and womanizer. He also has no intention of passing muster. "There is a ship, the *Doric Castle*, which sails to England in almost exactly three months to the day from now. I intend to be on her," he flippantly relates to his mate, the earnest Arthur Drake, who hopes to make the regiment his lifelong career.

During an officers' ball, Millington feebly accosts the regiment's sweetheart, Marjorie Hasseltine, an attractive widow. But the lady accuses him of a much graver offense—an attempted rape and the slashing of her backside with a saber.

Millington is set to be tried by a kangaroo court-martial under the presidency of the adjutant, Captain Rupert Harper, who assigns Drake to be the defending officer. The adjutant tells Drake that it is necessary to go through the motions but adds that "it is very much a *fait accompli.*" Drake says that he will do his best to defend Millington.

Millington is cynical about the proceedings, but Drake insists that he will get a fair trial. It soon becomes evident that the playwright's accusation of "conduct unbecoming" is not targeted at the cad Millington, but at the regiment's society of seasoned, code-honored officers and gentlemen. To their chagrin, Drake manages to puncture holes in the evidence of a succession of witnesses, including the regiment's doctor, Maurice Pratti; the second-in-command, Major Lionel Roach; the mess major domo, Pradah Singh; and Mrs. Hasseltine herself.

Drake proves that the widow was attacked a second time, by someone other than Millington, more viciously, on the evening in question. Millington is exonerated but there remains the question of the attacker's identity. Suspicion shifts from one officer to another and the suspense mounts until the final curtain when it turns out that the culprit is Major Roach. The motive is somewhat incongruous and less than convincing: Roach has a split personality, assaulting local women during his "Hyde" periods.

In a reversal, Millington stays with the regiment, while Drake, disillusioned, decides to submit his resignation.

* * *

Conduct Unbecoming was very successful when it originated at the Theatre Royal in Bristol (May 20, 1969) and then transferred to the Queen's Theatre in London (July 10, 1969). Critic John Spurling admired a play "complete with questions of honor, dark psychological undertow, class distinction and a liberal spicing of melodrama." Spurling applauded the visual "feast of scarlet jackets, jodhpurs, boots and spurs," and hailed playwright England as "a born story teller" who "tells his racy story without hollow pretensions," but "in just the way he finds it needs to be told."[1]

However, upon the arrival of *Conduct Unbecoming* to New York's Ethel Barrymore Theatre on October 12, 1970, the reviewers were sharply divided.

John Chapman hailed the play: "The tardy Broadway drama season got off to a rousing start last evening with the production of an English import, *Conduct Unbecoming*. It's like Kipling, but not as sloppy . . . absorbing entertainment."[2] Clive Barnes stated, "Quite a wonderful example of its genre. It is a whodunit, a why-he-did-it and a where-it-was-done of quite unusual interest and quality."[3] John J. O'Connor applauded, "It can't miss. . . . Super, absolutely super."[4] And John Schubeck cheered, "*Conduct Unbecoming* is the kind of stage dynamite that makes going to a play worthwhile."[5]

Among those who found *Conduct Unbecoming* less becoming was Walter Kerr, who lamented, "Its trouble is that it doesn't know it's 100 years out of date. . . . There may even be a rule about stage thrillers: Not everything important can take place out on the lawn, to be reported third-hand; something of the mystery must take place in front of us."[6] Martin Gottfried sniffed, "The mystery is solved in a series of melodramatics so ludicrous that one can only wonder about the English audiences who made this play a success on the West End and about Roger Stevens, the American producer who imported it. . . . This is the most preposterous, trite, ancient and boring production—a replica of the properly obsolete—that I have ever seen or could (not) imagine seeing."[7] Leonard Harris did not mince words on WCBS TV: "If there is one saving grace to this British drama, and I don't know if there is, but if there is, it is the reassurance that bad English plays, even hits, can be every bit as bad as bad American plays. . . . *Conduct Unbecoming*, with its frothy overacting, is dismal and heavy amateurism—a closet full of spiffy uniforms brought out to dress up a play with the dimensions and brain of a pea."[8]

Undaunted by the savagery of the naysayers, Otis L. Guernsey Jr. selected *Conduct Unbecoming* as one of the ten best plays of 1970–1971: "A colorful tale of warped values among the British officer caste of an Indian regiment in Her Majesty Queen Victoria's Imperial Army in the late 1800s. . . . There are fibers of reality running through what is ostensibly a simple theatrical tale of suspense in a highly colorful setting."[9]

Staged effectively by Val May with a large ensemble of scarlet-clad lancers going through pomp-and-ceremony rituals, *Conduct Unbecoming* ran on Broadway for 144 performances. A 1975 British movie version, filmed in Islamabad, Pakistan, and directed by Michael Anderson, featured an all-star cast that included Richard Attenborough, Michael York, Trevor Howard, Christopher Plummer, Stacy Keach, and Susannah York.

* * *

Barry England was raised in a Roman Catholic home and studied at Downside School. Following a stint in the army, he enrolled at the Royal Academy of Dramatic Arts as a playwright. The first of his plays to be produced was *End of Conflict* (1961), a drama about British soldiers serving in the Far East. England's second play, *The Big Contract* (1963), dealt with business shenanigans.

England scored big with his 1968 novel, *Figures in a Landscape*, the story of two prisoners of war who escape in an unnamed totalitarian country. Critics hailed England's gritty prose and called the book "a brilliant achievement." The novel was adapted to the screen in 1970, directed by Joseph Losey, starring Robert Shaw and Malcolm McDowell.

During the 1950s and 1960s, England contributed episodes to the British television series *Armchair Theatre* and *Play of the Week*. German television presented his play *End of Conflict* in 1965.

Acting Edition: Samuel French, Inc.

Awards and Honors: A top-ten selection in *The Best Plays of 1970–1971*. Barry England's 1968 novel, *Figures in a Landscape*, was nominated for the Booker Prize.

NOTES

1. Otis L. Guernsey Jr., ed., *The Best Plays of 1969–1970* (New York: Dodd, Mead, 1970), 67.

2. *Daily News*, October 13, 1970.

3. *New York Times*, October 13, 1970.

4. *Wall Street Journal*, October 13, 1970.

5. WABC TV, October 12, 1970.

6. *Sunday Times*, October 25, 1970.

7. *Women's Wear Daily*, October 13, 1970.

8. WCBS TV, October 12, 1970.

9. Otis L. Guernsey Jr., *The Best Plays of 1970–1971*, 13.

Dracula, Baby (1970)

Book by Bruce Ronald, Lyrics by John Jakes, Music by Claire Strauch

Bram (Abraham) Stoker (1847–1912) was an Irish civil servant before moving to London as business manager for the great actor Sir Henry Irving. In the fiftieth year of his life, following a hefty dinner, Stoker had a nightmare about a vampire rising from his tomb, and thus the story of Dracula was born.[1]

Stoker selected the name of the vampire from historical sources dating back to the fifteenth century about a ferocious, blood-thirsty Romanian prince, Vlad III (1431–1476), called Dracul— "the devil." The novel *Dracula*, published in 1897, still stands as one of the most brooding and horrifying works in the English language.

A 1970 musical comedy, *Dracula, Baby*, loosely based on the Stoker novel, features Count Dracula, Professor Van Helsing, Dr. Seward, and madman Renfield singing and dancing in the plains of Transylvania, the pubs of London, and the catacombs of Carfax. The book by Bruce Ronald, the lyrics by John Jakes, and the music by Claire Strauch all zip along energetically.

The curtain rises on a foot-stomping chorus of Romanian peasants as they express a fear of the night. They soon scatter, but Dracula, emerging from a mound of earth, catches a fleeing girl, bites her arm, tastes her blood, and makes an unpleasant face. "These local girls. Pfui! Anemic!" he growls, and decides then and there to leave for England, "the land of opportunity."

The matrons of Dr. Seward's establishment survey "patients" in the audience and croon contently about their "little sanitarium, a safe little haven on the moors." But the cozy atmosphere changes as Renfield escapes from his cell, searching for flies and spiders to devour. The next morning, Dr. Seward's ward Lucy is found "pale, wan, listless." The head nurse greets an unexpected, caped visitor and confides to the audience, "This whole place is going batty." Says Dracula, "I wish you wouldn't use that word." The Nurse finds the count handsome and offers him a leg of mutton in the kitchen. "Alas, I am on a—liquid diet," he responds. When the nurse exits, Dracula sighs: "A woman like that could make me forget how much I hate Daylight Saving's Time."

Renfield bursts into the room and falls at Dracula's feet: "I'm here, master, I'm here. Did you bring me any sugar?" "No!" rasps the count. "Sugar in your blood is bad for my teeth." Renfield and Dracula launch into a duet in which they both agree that "It's Good to Be Bad."

In a nearby rural tavern, escapee Renfield shares a beer with monster Frank and werewolf Harry. Van Helsing enters on a bicycle and immediately proves to be a natural pratfall klutz. He learns of Lucy's worrisome condition and rushes off to save the day, bumping, alas, into a tree.

In Lucy's bedroom, the young lady croons a love song, trying to convince her prim and proper fiancé, Arthur, that it is time to hold and kiss her.

Van Helsing arrives, checks Lucy's throat, and concludes that she is "in the evil grasp of a vampire."

"Poppycock," declares Arthur, but the professor assures him that there are such things as vampires. They put Lucy to sleep with a strand of garlic around her neck. The Nurse enters, sniffs, and detaches the garlic from the dozing Lucy to make sure that Arthur is not deterred by the smell. Dracula appears and wakes Lucy. He takes her in his arms, bends toward her neck as if to bite, but something stops him. He kisses her fiercely instead. Van Helsing enters, introduces himself as "scourge of evil things that go bump in the night," and urges Dracula to repent, telling him that vampires can be saved if they perform a good deed. The head nurse sings to the count that a man can be saved by the love of a good woman.

Later, in the Carfax catacombs, Dracula orders the witch Sylvia to invite "some classy creatures" to his wedding ceremony with Lucy. But he is forlorn. He can't get the Nurse out of his head. "I don't even know her name," he sighs.

The nuptial guests—ghosts, ghouls, warlocks, goblins, werewolves, and mummies—enter from the back of the auditorium, come down aisles, and menace the audience. The monsters vocalize "Wonderful, wonderful, wonderful day! No more gloom will haunt us—hooray!" They perform a lively ballet but stop when they realize that someone is approaching.

The Nurse runs in: "Watch out, Dracula, baby! They're coming for you." Harry the Wolfman snarls, but Dracula says quietly: "No. We cannot fight them. They bring the garlic and the silver bullet. Go, my friends, go. I will meet them alone."

Slowly the creatures disperse. Van Helsing, Seward, and Arthur enter, armed with stakes, guns, and strings of garlic. A fierce struggle ensues, hidden behind Dracula's cape.

The Nurse steps in: "He's changed. He sent his friends away so no one would be hurt. He's done a good deed!" And so it comes to pass, in this musical pastiche, that Dracula is reformed. When the rays of dawn begin to glow, the Nurse produces big black Hollywood-style sunglasses. "Here. Try these!"[2]

* * *

John William Jakes was born in Chicago, Illinois, on March 31, 1932. He began his literary career by selling fantasy and western stories to pulp magazines in the early 1950s while a freshman at Northeastern University, where he was enrolled as an acting major. He decided to trade the stage for the typewriter when he sold a science fiction story for $25.

Jakes enrolled in the creative writing program at DePauw University, graduated in 1953, and the following year earned an MA in American literature from Ohio State University. After completing school, he spent his days writing copy for several advertising agencies and at night wrote short stories in the genres of mystery, western, and science fiction, utilizing several pen names.

He soon plunged into writing full time. In the late 1950s and early 1960s, Jakes penned a series of detective novels, published by Belmont as original paperbacks, featuring the diminutive sleuth Johnny Havoc. Under the pseudonym Alan Payne, Jakes published softcover and hardcover whodunits. As Jay Scotland he penned historical novels. In the fantasy field, he created the "Brak the Barbarian" series. He contributed several *Man from UNCLE* novellas for the *Man from UNCLE* magazine, and novelized the film *Conquest of the Planet of the Apes* (1972).

Mingling fictional characters with historical figures, Jakes became known as "the godfather of the historical novel" with his eight-volume *The Kent Family Chronicles* (1973–1980), all best sellers adapted into an enormously successful television miniseries; the Main and Hazard families in the Civil War trilogy, *North and South* (1982), *Love and War* (1984), and *Heaven and Hell* (1987), televised in 1985, 1986, and 1994, respectively; and the Crowns of Chicago, whose saga evolves throughout the twentieth century in *Homeland* (1993) and its sequel *American Dreams* (1998).

A scholarly study of Jakes's novels, *John Jakes: A Critical Companion*, by Dr. Mary Ellen Jones of Wittenberg University, was published by Greenwood Press in 1996.

A devotee of Charles Dickens, Jakes dramatized *A Christmas Carol* and *Great Expectations*, both in 1997. Along with Dickens, "the greatest novelist in the English language," Jakes admires Zola, Balzac, Dumas, and Tolstoy, as well as thriller writers Georges Simenon, Robert B. Parker, Patricia Cornwell, Ken Follet, Evan Hunter/Ed McBain, and John D. MacDonald. He called the latter "one of the most consistently and unjustly underrated novelists of the last half of the twentieth century."

Jakes has nurtured a soft spot for the theatre and is a member of the Theatre Guild. Following his first play, 1970's *Dracula, Baby*, in 1972 he wrote the book and lyrics for *Wind in the Willows*; the melodramas *A Spell of Evil, Violence, Stranger with Roses*; and an adaptation to the stage of the story "For I Am a Jealous People" by science-fiction author Lester del Rey. In 1973, Jakes penned the book and lyrics of *Gaslight Girl*, once again combining forces with Claire Strauch, the composer of *Dracula, Baby*, to blend melodrama's old-stock characters of the virtuous heroine, the handsome hero, and the moustached villain with modern musical theatre elements.

* * *

Born in Dublin, Ireland, Bram (Abraham) Stoker was a sickly child who grew up to become a sinewy, six-foot-two athlete. Stoker planned to follow in his father's footsteps as a civil servant, but at Trinity College the young man changed course when falling under the spell of Romantic poets Byron, Keats, and Shelley. He excelled in the debate society and joined the dramatic club. He also began reviewing theatrical productions in Dublin's *Evening Mail*—without pay.

A glowing account by Stoker of Henry Irving's *Hamlet* brought the two together, and in 1878 Stoker was engaged as the business manager of Irving's theatre in London, the Lyceum, a position he held for twenty-seven years, until the famed actor's death in 1905. Among the productions Stoker serviced were: Shakespeare's *Hamlet, The Merchant of Venice, Romeo and Juliet, Macbeth, Cymbeline,* and *Richard III,* as well as Boucicault's *The Corsican Brothers* (from Dumas), W. G. Wills's adaptation of Goethe's *Faust,* Conan Doyle's *Waterloo,* Cervantes' *Don Quixote,* Tennyson's *Becket,* Sardou's *Dante,* and *The Bells,* a conversion by Leopold Lewis from the French, in which Irving portrayed his signature role—an Alsatian village burgomaster, Mathias, who years ago bludgeoned to death a Jewish merchant for his gold and has ever since been haunted by the sound of the bells on his victim's sleigh.

Well liked and respected, Stoker developed cordial and friendly relationships with luminaries of literature and the arts on both sides of the Atlantic, including Oscar Wilde (with whom he remained friendly despite "stealing" and marrying Wilde's sweetheart, Florence Balcombe), Alfred Tennyson, Arthur Conan Doyle, George Bernard Shaw, Henry James, Franz Liszt, James Whistler, Walt Whitman, and Mark Twain.

Although heavily taxed with the myriad details of running a theatre company, controlling its budget, and preparing its tours, Stoker made time to write eighteen books. His nonfiction output is comprised of *Duties of Clerks of Petty Sessions in Ireland* (1879), *A Glimpse of America* (1886), *Personal Reminiscences of Henry Irving* (1906), *Snowbound, the Record of a Theatrical Touring Party* (1908), and *Famous Impostors* (1910), in which he theorizes that Queen Elizabeth I died as a baby and court officials secretly substituted her with an infant boy. *Under the Sunset* (1881) is a volume of fairytales. "Not gruesome like the Grimm Brothers or fanciful like Hans Christian Anderson," asserts Barbara Belford in the biography *Bram Stoker*, "the tales are almost biblical, permeated with allegories of good and evil and an atmosphere of dreamlike unease."[3]

Stoker's first novel is *The Snake's Pass* (1891), a yarn of contraband and buried treasure. *The Shoulder of Shasta* (1895) recounts a mismatched summer romance between a delicate San Francisco girl and a grizzly mountain man, while *Miss Betty* (1898) connects an heiress with a dashing highwayman. *The Mystery of the Sea* (1902) is centered on letters written in cipher, and the *Jewel of Seven Stars* (1903) on an ancient Egyptian curse (filmed as *Blood from the Mummy's Tomb*, 1972, and *The Awakening*, 1980). Filled with demonic women are *The Lady of the Shroud* (1909) and *The Lair of the White Worm* (1911, filmed in 1989). A discarded chapter from *Dracula* was published posthumously as the title short story in the collection *Dracula's Guest* (1914, filmed in 1936 as *Dracula's Daughter*).

Acting Edition: The Dramatic Publishing Company.

Awards and Honors: John Jakes holds honorary degrees from five universities, including Ohio State. In 1995, Jakes was the recipient of a dual Celebrity and Citizen's Award from the White House Conference on Libraries and Information. That same year he received the National Cowboy Hall of Fame's Western Heritage Library Award for his short story "Manitow and Ironhand." In 1996, Jakes was inducted into the South Carolina Academy of Authors, and in 1997, he received the Professional Achievement Award of the Ohio State University Alumni Association. In 1998, the South Carolina Humanities Association awarded him its highest honor, for career achievement and support of the humanities, and in 2002 he received the Cooper Medal at the University of South Carolina.

The Bram Stoker Award is presented annually by the Horror Writers Association for superior achievement in twelve different categories of the genre. The award was first given in 1988.

There are at least fourteen vampire organizations and clubs throughout the world—from New Orleans, Louisiana, in the United States, to Chippenham, Wiltshire, in England, to Istanbul in Turkey. The Bram Stoker Society is located in County Dublin, Ireland, while the Miss Lucy Westenra Society of the Undead dwells in Jackson, Tennessee.

NOTES

1. Reportedly, Mary Shelley and Robert Louis Stevenson also dreamed, respectively, of *Frankenstein* and *Dr. Jekyll and Mr. Hyde* before committing their masterpieces to paper. There is little doubt that Stoker was well versed about the

literary vampires who preceded his Dracula—Lord Ruthven in John Polidori's *The Vampyre* (1819), Sir Francis in *Varney the Vampyre, or The Feast of Blood* (1847) by James Malcolm Rymer, and the lesbian vampires in Sheridan Le Fanu's *Carmilla* (1872).

2. Other song-and-dance adaptations inspired by Bram Stoker include *Dracula: The Musical*—book, lyrics and music by Rick Abbot, a topsy-turvy melodious endeavor in which Dr. Sam Seward, Professor Hezekiah Van Helsing, and "peculiar patient" Boris Renfield sing and dance frantically as they overcome the king of vampires; *The Dracula Spectacular*—Book and lyrics by John Gardiner, music by Andrew Parr, where sanatorium patients, village idiots, quicksand zombies, and the brides of Dracula partake in a whirlwind extravaganza; *Dracula Is Undead and Well and Living in Purfleet* (aka *Dracula or Out for the Count*)—by Charles McKeown, (the vampire "is flanked by an incompetent chorus of blonde Draculettes dressed in black lingerie"); *Dracula: A Musical Nightmare*—book and lyrics by Douglas Johnson, music by John Aschenbrenner ("The Bat," "Nosferatu," and "Renfield's Lament" are among the songs presented by a shoddy English touring company in cabaret style); *Dracula*—by Pip Simmons (in its 1976 London run, the fly-eating Renfield sang a song while hanging upside down, bound hand and foot in a straightjacket); *The Vampire and the Dentist*—book, lyrics and music by Weldon Irvine (Count de Cologne fixes his teeth with designs to bite into dental nurse Evelyn; this does not sit well with vampire Cristina); *Dracula*—book by Ian Mune, music by Stephen McCurdy (slanted to expose greedy villagers ready to exploit the wealthy count, thus deserving their retribution at the final curtain); *Dracula*—book by David Axelrod and Ronny Graham, lyrics by Axelrod, music by Sam Pottle (the count wins the hearts of Lucy and Mina by crooning sweetly "Come to me, come to me"); *I'm Sorry, the Bridge Is Out, You'll Have to Spend the Night*—by Sheldon Allman and Bob Pickett (mad scientist Dr. Frankenstein, his Monster creation, his hunchbacked assistant Igor, the ancient bandaged Mummy, Count Dracula, Renfield, and a clique of dancing Draculettes are gathered during a stormy night for some madcap shenanigans involving a pair of innocents—John and Mary—whose car broke down just outside the gate of an isolated castle); *Dracula*—book and lyrics by Christopher Hampton, music by Frank Wildhorn (composer of *Jekyll and Hyde*); and *Dragula*—by Keith Myers (a campy musical about a cross-dressing vampire who is on the prowl in gay London).

3. Barbara Belford, *Bram Stoker* (New York: Knopf, 1996), 139.

Sleuth (1970)

Anthony Shaffer (England, 1926–2001)

"For the enjoyment of future audiences it would be greatly appreciated if you would not disclose the plot of this play," stated a notice in the program of *Sleuth* when the play opened at the Music Box, New York, on November 12, 1970. The fun-and-games deceptions of Anthony Shaffer's thriller began when members of the audience took their seats and commenced to leaf through a playbill with a fictionalized cast list (in order of appearance) as well as biographical sketches of nonexisting actors.

The skullduggery of *Sleuth* takes place within the Wiltshire country manor of Andrew Wyke, a successful detective-story writer whose series hero, St. John Lord Merridew—"a classical scholar with a taste for good pipes and bad puns, but with a nose for smelling out evil"—is known to people all over the civilized world. The plush living room, with its engraved woodwork, wide windows, and circular staircase, is filled with books, records, liquor, bric-a-brac, and adorned by a variety of games, puzzles, and toys. In the corner there is a full-size "Laughing Sailor."

When the curtain rises, Andrew—tall, middle-aged, gone slightly to seed—is seated at his typewriter, absorbed in the denouement of his latest novel, *The Body on the Tennis Court*: "He carried the body out to the center of the tennis court, walking on his points along the white tape, which divided the service boxes. From there he threw it five feet into the court, towards the base line, where it was found, and then, with a neatly executed fouette, faced about and returned the way he had come, thus leaving no traces."

The doorbell rings. Andrew ushers in Milo Tindle—a young, slim, dark-haired neighbor. Following a few polite tidbits over drinks, Andrew suddenly says, "I understand you want to marry my wife." Milo is taken aback, but Andrew insists that he bears no grudge and is perfectly willing to grant Marguerite—"intolerably tiresome, vain, spendthrift, self-indulgent and generally bloody crafty"—a divorce, and plans to enhance his relationship with his Finnish mistress, Tea—"a Karelian goddess" whose "golden hair smells of pine, and her cobalt eyes are the secret forest pools of Finlandia."

Milo admits that his travel agency is financially insecure. Andrew proposes a scheme to the advantage of both: Milo will rob the estate of 135,000 pounds worth of jewelry, and sell it on the black market; Andrew will collect the insurance money. This will enable each to lavish his lady in royal style.

Andrew convinces Milo that the plan is foolproof. Milo dons a clown disguise and breaks in through an upstairs window, and both men shatter a safe with an explosive device, then ransack the home—overturning furniture, emptying drawers, scattering papers, smashing china figurines. Andrew suggests that Milo strike him cold so when the police come he'll be able to show them a real bump. Suddenly, Andrew produces a revolver from a desk drawer, points it at Milo, and reveals that the real reason for concocting the fake burglary was to create circumstances that will lead to Milo's death. He is perfectly entitled to tackle a man wearing a mask burglarizing his house in the middle of the night. The law will sympathize with him. Property has always been more highly regarded in England than people.

Milo pleads for his life but Andrew mocks the "little man" for believing that he would give up his wife and jewels. Andrew forces Milo to mount the stairs at gunpoint, to put on the clown's mask, and lifts the pistol to his head, pulling the trigger. Milo falls backward down the stairs and Andrew says, smiling, "Game and set, I think."

The second act begins two days later. Inspector Doppler of the Wiltshire County Constabulary arrives on the scene, investigating the disappearance of Milo. The inspector corners Andrew into relating the elaborate burglary plot but the author insists that he shot Milo with a blank cartridge. He fainted dead away, which was most gratifying, says Andrew. After a few minutes, Tindle recovered his senses and went off home. However, Doppler cases the premises and Andrew is dumbfounded when the inspector finds dry bloodstains at the bottom of the staircase. "I did not kill him! He left here alive," cries Andrew, but Doppler pronounces him under arrest for murder. Andrew, horrified, scuffles with Doppler, when the inspector removes a disguise and reveals that he is actually Milo.

Milo turns the table on Andrew still further. He tells Andrew that while he planted fake blood the previous day while the author was away, Tea came by. He raped her and strangled her—on the living room rug. About an hour ago he phoned the police and asked them to meet him here at ten o'clock tonight—it'll be a real policeman this time, Detective Sergeant Tarrant. He told Tarrant that Andrew, obsessed with game playing and murder considered as a fine art, fulfilled his life's ambition and committed an actual real-life murder, hiding the body somewhere where it couldn't be traced to him and left clues linking him with the crime, strewn about the house, certain that the pedestrian and simple-minded police wouldn't recognize them for what they were.

Milo then feeds Andrew hints to help him locate the incriminating evidence before the police arrive. Frantically, Andrew deciphers Milo's cryptic clues and manages to find Tea's bracelet in a fish tank, her shoe in the base of the plinth, and a stocking attached to the pendulum of the grandfather clock. It turns out, however, that the voice of Detective Sergeant Tarrant at the door is another impersonation by Milo, who then tells the shocked Andrew that Tea is alive and that she had enthusiastically agreed to help him fake her murder.

Andrew is shattered. Milo taunts him, deriding Milo's attachment to the English detective story. It is a dead world, sneers Milo, a world of coldness and class hatred, and two-dimensional characters; it's a world where only the amateurs ever win, and where to be a foreigner is to be automatically a figure of fun. In short, declares Milo, detective stories are the normal re-creation of a snobbish, outdated, life-hating, ignoble mind.

While Milo goes to collect Marguerite's fur coat, Andrew retrieves his gun. When Milo returns, Andrew announces that he will shoot him as a burglar—this time with real bullets. Milo laughs and says that he told the police about Andrew's mock crime and that if the writer were to shoot him now, the police would not believe the burglary story.

"That's all very ingenious, Milo, but I don't believe one word you're saying," grins Andrew, and shoots him. As Milo slumps to the floor, the sound of an approaching vehicle is heard and a flashing police car light shines through the window. The doorbell rings. Painfully Milo lifts his head, chuckles "Game, set and match!" and dies.

Andrew staggers helplessly, accidentally presses a button, and The Sailor laughs loudly as the curtain falls.

* * *

Following a pre-London preview at the Theatre Royal in Brighton, *Sleuth* was presented at West End's St. Martin's Theatre on February 12, 1970, garnering rave reviews and playing its cat-and-mouse games for 2,359 performances. The original cast—Anthony Quayle as Andrew Wyke and Keith Baxter as Milo Tindle—under the direction of Clifford Williams, with set design by Carl Toms, traveled to New York's Music Box on November 12, 1970, anchoring there for 1,222 showings. "One of the best melodramas I have ever seen. Maybe it is the best. Certainly it is the best since *Angel Street*," proclaimed John Chapman.[1] "A super show— the best of its genre since *Dial "M" for Murder*, and much cleverer," cheered Clive Barnes.[2] "So replete with skillful suspense and inventive tricks that it is fine fun for those of us who are fictional crime addicts," applauded Richard Watts Jr.[3] However, Martin Gottfried blasted *Sleuth* as "a dumb play, and not because its an old-fashioned mystery. . . . It's dumb because it claims to be cleverer (and isn't) and spends all its time setting up rules for games to play (rules it won't follow for games it can't play)."[4]

Sleuth scored a profit of $1,700,000 on its $150,000 investment.

* * *

Anthony Shaffer, who in *Sleuth* both reveres and mocks parlor-room murder mysteries, penned three genre novels in collaboration with his twin brother, playwright Peter Shaffer: *The Woman in the Wardrobe* (1951) and *How Doth the Little Crocodile?* (1952) under the joint pseudonym Peter Anthony, and *Withered Murder* (1955), bylined with their full names—all featuring a private detective named Mr. Verity, "an immense man just tall enough to carry his breadth majestically."

Shaffer confides that the inspiration for the complex *Sleuth* was Agatha Christie, "who he was surprised to discover is the most widely published author in the world."[5] In *Sleuth*, Anthony pays sly, tongue-in-cheek homage to Dame Christie, Anthony Berkeley, John Dickson Carr, R. Austin Freeman, Arthur B. Reeve, and S. S. Van Dine, as masters of the golden age, and to such hallmark devices as the ice dagger, the poison that leaves no trace, the monogrammed cigarette stabbed in the ashtray, charred violet notepaper in the hearth, Dusenberg tire marks in the driveway, the clutching hand from behind the panel, sinister Orientals, and twin brothers from Australia.

James Kline, in *Masterplots II*, suggests that while Shaffer "is lambasting the genre for being sterile, overly intellectual, and bloodless, *Sleuth* is also lauding the genre for its playful plot twists, elaborate deceptions, and unabashed ability to entertain."[6] Kline theorizes that "Andrew Wyke is the personification of the genre itself. He is quick-witted, theatrical, and obsessed with elaborate plot schemes. . . . Milo, young, vigorous and handsome, the son of an Italian immigrant, is a threat to Andrew. . . . Milo represents the world of flesh and blood reality. His world is in direct conflict with Andrew's universe of intellectual games, contrivances, and manipulation. Yet both worlds are potent ones. . . . In the end, it is Milo's world of facts, of real police detectives and real death that destroys Andrew's world of charades and betrayal. Or so it seems. For the main, overriding theme of *Sleuth* is the beguiling fascination this artificial world of games has on the world of fact. The audience is held spellbound by the play's string of deceits, fake murders, disguises, and manipulative acts. *Sleuth* therefore proves that Andrew's world is hardly dead."[7]

Stanley Richards included *Sleuth* in his anthology, *Best Mystery and Suspense Plays of the Modern Theatre*: "Here indeed was a playwright of major resources whose ingenious plotting was complemented by an impressive hand at creating singular characters and honing dialogue to its wittiest, most chillingly effective, 'where laughter and the scent of horror are intriguingly harnessed together.' . . . Perhaps the advent of Anthony Shaffer at this crucial moment in theatre history will come as a restorative balm to the stage thriller, a dramatic form that has intrigued, captivated, and entertained playgoers for more than a century."[8]

Sleuth became an overnight classic, spawning productions abroad, on the road, and in stock. During its robust Broadway run, Paul Rogers, Patrick Macnee, and George Rose, respectively, took over the role of Andrew Wyke, while Donal Donnelly, Brian Murray, and Jordan Christopher substituted for Milo Tindle. A touring company starring George Rose and David Haviland toured ninety-six American cities during 1972–1973. Michael Allinson and Donal Donnelly portrayed Wyke and Tindle in Toronto in 1971; Pierre Fresnay and Henri Garcin undertook the roles in Paris for the 1970–1971 season; simultaneously, two members of a visiting professional Turkish troupe from Istanbul, *Sleuth*ed it in England. During the 1970s and beyond, *Sleuth* played successfully at the Ahmanson Theatre, Los Angeles; American Conservatory Theatre, San Francisco; Manitoba Theatre Center, Winnipeg; A Contemporary Theatre, Seattle; Barter Theatre, Abingdon, Virginia; Stage West, Springfield, Massachusetts; Meadow Brook Theatre, Rochester, Michigan; Syracuse Stage, Syracuse, New York; Theatre by the Sea, Portsmouth, New Hampshire; Old Globe Theatre, San Diego, California; Theatre Calgary, Alberta; and the Glass Center Theatre, Corning, New York.

Gerald M. Berkowitz, in *Contemporary Dramatists*, points out: "*Sleuth* was an immense worldwide success that quickly bred dozens of other thrillers of the new (whodunwhat) genre, notable among them Ira Levin's *Deathwatch* and Richard Harris's *The Business of Murder*. The Agatha Christie–type whodunit, with corpses who didn't get up again and a murderer who was Someone-In-This-Room, seemed hopelessly old-fashioned when compared to plays in which the audience had to figure out what was really happening before moving on to the question of who was guilty."[9]

Shaffer adapted *Sleuth* to the screen in 1972. Under the direction of Joseph L. Mankiewicz, Laurence Olivier and Michael Caine exhibited tour-de-force performances as the two deadly antagonists. Both actors were nominated for a Best Actor Oscar, but lost to Marlon Brando in *The Godfather*. Director Mankiewicz lost to *Cabaret*'s Bob Fosse.

Michael Caine switched roles and played Andrew Wyke to Jude Law's Milo Tindle in a pale 2007 remake of *Sleuth*, scripted by Harold Pinter and directed by Kenneth Branagh.

* * *

Anthony Joshua Shaffer was born to a Jewish family in Liverpool, England, in 1926. His twin brother was renowned playwright Peter Shaffer. In the 1940s, Anthony worked in coal mines in Kent and Yorkshire. In 1950, he graduated with a law degree from Trinity College, Cambridge University, and began practicing as a barrister the following year. Concluding that the money was inadequate, Shaffer switched to advertising copywriting but by the end of the 1960s he changed course again, this time to playwriting.

Shaffer's first produced play, 1963's *The Savage Parade*, unfolds in a wine cellar in Tel Aviv, where a former high-ranking Nazi, hunted down in South America and brought to Israel in 1962, is interrogated by Haganah "judges" to determine whether he is "guilty in the first degree, or as an accomplice, of the death of six million Jews, gassed, burned, beaten, starved, shot, frozen, entombed, or otherwise put to death." In this initial effort, Shaffer established his knack for surprising plot maneuvers.

Sleuth is Shaffer's flagship play. His other stage ventures continued to display prankish and fiendish manipulations of the audience, constantly shifting, twisting, and shunning the obvious. *Murderer* (1975) is a send-off triggered by famous real-life assassinations. The play begins with a sequence during which painter Norman Bartholomew dismembers the corpse of his model, tossing arms, legs, and torso into a stove. Director Clifford Williams and designer Carl Toms of *Sleuth* contributed their sleight-of-hand expertise.

The Case of the Oily Levantine (1979), which became *Whodunnit* in its 1982 New York incarnation, is a spoof set in an English country manor in which a group of strangers gather for a leisurely weekend until one of them, a dastardly blackmailer, is stabbed to death with a sword.

Shaffer is the author of several television dramas, notably an adaptation of Wilkie Collins's 1868 classic, *The Moonstone* (BBC, 1992). He has also written a number of screenplays, including *Forbush and Penguins* (1972), an adventure shot in the Antarctic; the harrowing *The Wicker Man* (1973), novelized by Shaffer and Robin Hardy in 1978; Alfred Hitchcock's thriller *Frenzy* (1974); *Absolution* (1979), a boys' school melodrama starring Richard Burton, novelized by Shaffer in 1981; and three Agatha Christie conversions—*Death on the Nile* (1978), *Evil under the Sun* (1982), and *Appointment with Death* (1988), all featuring Peter Ustinov as Belgian detective Hercule Poirot.

Acting Edition: Samuel French, Inc. *Sleuth* is also included in Stanley Richards, ed., *Best Mystery and Suspense Plays of the Modern Theatre* (New York: Dodd, Mead, 1971).

Awards and Honors: A top-ten selection in *The Best Plays of 1970–1971* ("The best made, the most entertaining, the most effective use of the medium, and certainly not without meaningful overtones emanating from its suspense-story form. . . . Under the symbolical games-playing of his script there's a much larger situation implied: a distinguished but crumbling old order being hastened to its grave by the importunities of a brash new breed"[10]); The Antoinette Perry (Tony) Award, 1970–1971—Best Play; Outer Circle Award—Anthony Quayle as Andrew Wyke and Keith Baxter as Milo Tindle; Drama Desk Award—Anthony Quayle; Mystery Writers of America Edgar Allan Poe Awards—Best Play, 1971, and Best Motion Picture Screenplay, 1973.

NOTES

1. *Daily News*, November 13, 1970.
2. *New York Times*, November 13, 1970.
3. *New York Post*, November 13, 1970.
4. *Women's Wear Daily*, November 13, 1970.
5. Chris Steinbrunner and Otto Penzler, eds., *Encyclopedia of Mystery and Detection* (New York: McGraw-Hill, 1976), 10.
6. Frank N. Magill, ed., *Masterplots II, Drama Series* (Pasadena, CA: Salem Press, 1990), 1480.
7. Frank N. Magill, ed., *Masterplots II, Drama* Series, 1480.
8. Stanley Richards, ed., *Best Mystery and Suspense Plays* (New York: Dodd, Mead, 1971), 195, 197.
9. D. L. Kirkpatrick, ed., *Contemporary Dramatists*, 4th ed. (Chicago: St. James Press, 1988), 474.
10. Otis L. Guernsey Jr., ed., *The Best Plays of 1970–1971* (New York: Dodd, Mead, New York, 1971), 12, 13.

Child's Play (1970)

Robert Marasco (United States, 1936–1998)

What evil lurks within the walls of the St. Charles School for Boys?

Father Griffin expresses his concern at the growing number of kids getting hurt between classes, on the stairs, in the gym. An accident in the chemistry lab, a brawl in the dormitory seem to indicate that some of the students have become malevolent, trying to physically hurt one another. Instructor Paul Reese joins the conversation, relating that during a ball game, the kid Freddy was attacked by his teammates from all sides; they were beating him, clawing him, tearing at his face.

The violence escalates into frenzied sadism. The eyes of one student are gouged out, and another is found, half naked, hanging from the chapel's crucifix.

The pupils of St. Charles provide the vicious acts of *Child's Play*, but the central characters are three lay teachers: Joseph Dobbs (played on Broadway by Pat Hingle) is the affable, fatherly pedagogue who pampers the boys; Jerome Malley (Fritz Weaver) is a strict, harsh taskmaster of Greek and Latin; and Paul Reese (Ken Howard) is the young history tutor and athletic coach who finds himself torn between the two rivals.

Dobbs convinces the headmaster, Father Mozian (Michael McGuire), that Malley is the cause of the turbulence. Malley is fired and ends his life by throwing himself out a window. The school closes. The faculty members leave.

Dobbs insists on staying behind. After thirty years of teaching there, he has nowhere else to go. Dobbs remains, only to be surrounded by the menacing boys who are slowly closing in on him.

The final curtain falls without ever spelling out the mystical secrets of St. Charles School.

* * *

When *A Child's Play* opened at New York's Royale Theatre on February 17, 1970, most of the critics rejoiced: "A wonderfully powerful melodrama

. . . one stroke after another of genuine Grand Guignol horror," wrote Clive Barnes;[1] "It's a constantly engrossing play that Robert Marasco has fashioned . . . high-voltage theatre, and oh, so welcome," cheered Douglas Watt.[2] Richard Watts Jr. licked his chops: "The sense of menace lies almost entirely in the atmosphere, dark, baleful and ominous, and the eerie feeling of some brooding, mysterious evil let loose in St. Charles School seems more sinister than the traditional skullduggery of mystery plots."[3] Edwin Newman nodded: "*Child's Play* is a fairly rare bird in the theatre—a good, solid melodrama."[4]

Conversely, Joseph H. Mazo believed that "Marasco's structure is contrived and awkward, the play much too long for however flawed it is,"[5] and John O'Connor complained that while "Melodrama demands the airtight structure of a fine Swiss watch, Mr. Marasco's has more holes than an ordinary Swiss cheese."[6]

Child's Play ran for 342 performances. Director Joseph Hardy and designer Jo Mielziner crossed the Atlantic to stage a London production, but their dark, brooding approach met with critical and public resistance. "Melodrama shouldn't lack pace or guts," said reviewer Peter Ansorge, who also threw darts at Laurence Harvey, as the stern Jerome Malley ("remotely credible") and at Rupert Davies, as the apparently sympathetic Joseph Dobbs ("keeps a jolly countenance throughout, obviously hoping that there is nothing nastier in this play than there was in *The Browning Version*.")[7]

Stanley Richards included *Child's Play* in his *Best Mystery and Suspense Plays* of *the Modern Theatre*. "Just as the 1969–1970 season seemed to be at its lowest ebb," writes Richards, "*Child's Play*, an unheralded suspense drama by an unknown author, Robert Marasco, was brought to the stage of the Royale Theatre by producer David Merrick (customarily associated with gilt-edged theatrical packages and planetary marquee names) and it turned out to be the 'Sleeper' of the year. Mr. Marasco's evocation of the sinister in a Roman Catholic prep school promptly was extolled as a melodramatic triumph, a play of dark and deepening mystery and Gothic horror."[8]

Mr. Merrick subsequently produced a lackluster movie version of *Child's Play* (1972), directed by Sidney Lumet, starring James Mason, Robert Preston, and Beau Bridges.

* * *

Robert Marasco's contribution to the horror genre continued with his haunted house novel, *Burnt Offerings* (1973). It was filmed in 1976 by Dan Curtis, of *Dark Shadows* fame, featuring Karen Black, Oliver Reed, and Burgess Meredith, with a cameo appearance by Bette Davis.

Marasco also wrote the novel *Parlor Games* (1979), a psychosexual drama of siblings' possessiveness and dark secrets, as well as several unproduced screenplays.

Acting Edition: Samuel French, Inc. *Child's Play* is also included in Stanley Richards, ed., *Best Mystery and Suspense Plays of the Modern Theatre* (New York: Dodd, Mead, 1971).

Awards and Honors: Antoinette Perry (Tony) Awards, 1969–1970—Best Actor, Fritz Weaver; Best Supporting Actor, Ken Howard; Best Director, Joseph Hardy; Best Scene and Lighting Designer, Jo Mielziner. Outer Circle award, 1969–1970—Best Play. A top-ten selection in *The Best Plays of 1969–1970* ("It had the nightmarish quality of the not-quite-explained, the subliminal awareness of hidden evil.")[9]

NOTES

1. *New York Times*, February 18, 1970.
2. *Daily News*, February 18, 1970.
3. *New York Post*, February 18, 1970.
4. NBC4 TV, February 17, 1970.
5. *Women's Wear Daily*, February 18, 1970.
6. *Wall Street Journal*, February 19, 1970.
7. *Plays and Players*, October 1970.
8. Stanley Richards, ed., *Best Mystery and Suspense Plays of the Modern Theatre* (New York: Dodd, Mead, 1971), 347.
9. Otis L. Guernsey Jr., ed., *The Best Plays of 1969–1970* (New York: Dodd, Mead, 1970), 12.

The White House
Murder Case (1970)

Jules Feiffer (United States, 1929–)

The White House Murder Case, a biting dark comedy by famed cartoonist Jules Feiffer, takes place several presidential elections hence and alternates between two locales: the Oval Office in the White House and a battleground. Otis L. Guernsey Jr., editor of *The Best Plays of 1969–1970*, writes: "In Feiffer's fun-house-mirror view, soldiers on the battlefield are slowly coming apart from the effects of their own nerve gas, and much the same sort of thing is happening at commander-in-chief level, where the nerve gasses of power and militarism are destroying their creators." [1]

The curtain rises on a battlefield. There is the sound of bombardment, then the rattle of machine-gun fire. Colonel Dawn and Lieutenant Cutler crawl forward to see what is holding the advance. General Pratt strides in, stares down at them, and demands to know "what are American troops doing on their knees in front of a bunch of goddamned Brazilians?" Cutler leaps to his feet and salutes. A bullet cuts him. Bleeding badly, he whispers, "C-B-9-7." Colonel Dawn explains that the wounded lieutenant recommends that they activate CB97, a nerve gas, against the "Chicos."

The lights fade up on President Hale's office in the White House. Through the window there is a view of the Capitol. Five conference chairs are gathered around the president's desk. Evelyn Hale, the First Lady, is rapidly shuffling through her husband's papers as Professor Sweeney, the resident scientific expert, enters and warns her that the documents are classified. He tries to embrace her, but she rebuffs him. Enters Stiles, the postmaster general, and it is immediately clear that he is hostile to the First Lady. She coldly exits, and other secretaries arrive for a cabinet meeting with the president.

Parson, the secretary of defense, brings in his charts and tells everyone that to counter fierce enemy resistance, nerve gas CB97 was released, but a sudden shift of wind wiped out a whole battalion of Americans. General Pratt is summoned. The gas has half-paralyzed him, and he wobbles in using a cane. His face is covered with sores and he wears dark glasses.

He speaks through the amplification of a throat microphone. Barring the wind shift, Pratt says, CB97 would have "paid off." Enemy losses were twenty-five times heavier than among U.S. troops, he reports.

President Hale expresses his concern about the accident, since it is six weeks before an election. The cabinet members wonder what story the American public will swallow. Pratt suggests: a guerrilla patrol could have gotten behind our lines to unleash the gas. All endorse the fib enthusiastically.

President Hale sends his advisers to cook up the story and arrange for its release. He then calls his wife for an opinion. He tells her that an enemy shell hit one of the storage tanks, unleashing a deadly gas, but prior to an election he does not want to release such news. Evelyn Hale says crisply, "I think I want a divorce." She chides her husband for being dishonest with her and with the rest of the country. She will not be a co-conspirator. She wants the truth to be told.

On the battlefield, Lieutenant Cutler and Captain Weems are marching along their way, obviously in pain. The gas is having peculiar effects. Weems can't turn his head and has lost the power to blink. Cutler finds that his fingers are stiff and he can no longer feel any pain. Soon Cutler and Weems watch their hands break away from their bodies, followed by other organs disintegrating.

The lights go out in the Oval Office. A sound of scuffling is heard, followed by a pained gasp. The lights fade up to reveal Evelyn Hale lying prostrate and bleeding across the president's desk. In her chest, embedded like a stake, is a picket sign bearing the message "Make Love, Not War."

The play now begins to resemble a traditional whodunit. The president, along with Sweeney, Cole, Stiles, Parson, and Pratt sit around the desk and discuss the fatal assault on the First Lady. The president declares, "She was the best part of me, the moral center." He is determined to find the killer. The murder weapon is brought in, its point stained with blood. Attorney General Cole reports that examination disclosed two sets of fingerprints on the picket sign, his own and those of President Hale. However, both thumbs are pointing inward and downward—an awkward grip for impaling someone by a right-handed man, and both he and the president are right-handed.

Cole theorizes that whoever stabbed the First Lady had only his country's interest at heart and decided, possibly misguided, possibly half-mad, to protect the present administration which Mrs. Hale tried unceasingly to divide. Cole recommends that in the interest of national security, the investigation be dropped. The others consent, but President Hale is determined to pursue the inquiry. He questions the men as to their whereabouts at the crucial time. Cole says that he was in the anteroom, making a list of trustworthy news reporters. General Pratt states that he was in his office alone but points out that he is blind and half-paralyzed. Stiles declares that he was at his post office; Sweeney admits to making a phone call about CB97; Parson maintains that he wandered down the hall. In the best tradition of Agatha Christie, the president concludes that the alibis are worthless; any one of them could have committed the crime.

Parson pleads with them all to stop going at each other and instead use the incident to their advantage. They can rally the country by announcing that "the First Lady was assassinated by a suicide squad of Brazilian terrorists." The secretaries discard the idea, but come up with another: an accidental food poisoning while the First Lady was visiting Chicago.

The president insists on pressing his investigation and asks how the "Make Love, Not War" placard on the murder weapon could have been smuggled into the White House without anyone noticing. At eighteen by twenty-four inches it is too large to fit into a briefcase, and it is not creased. The president concludes that only Secretary of Defense Parson could have done it, hiding it among his Brazilian war charts.

The president's deduction turns out to be wrong and gives way to a twist ending. Postmaster General Stiles asks for a few minutes alone with the president, and while the others wait in the anteroom, he tells Hale that Parson didn't kill Evelyn. The placard wasn't carried in by Parson; it was mailed in and lay in the mailroom, ready to be used by the murderer. No one noticed anything unusual when the murderer picked it up, for he, Stiles, the postmaster general, killed the First Lady—by mistake. In the dark, instead of stabbing the president, he plunged the picket into the First Lady, who was at the desk.

The President is dumbfounded: "But why? We're friends!" Stiles explains that the latest polls made it clear that the party is through unless it had a fresh candidate, someone not connected to past blunders. As far as the public was concerned, the assassin belonged to the opposition party, someone with strong radical convictions. That would produce a sympathy vote that would sweep the vice president into office.

The party has been his life for forty years, says Stiles, and he refused to sit by while President Hale destroyed it. He has written a confession of murder which he believes is certain to bring down the Hale administration. However, he will withhold the confession if the president makes him secretary of defense. The president bargains with Stiles, offering him other posts, which Stiles refuses. Finally, they strike an agreement on the offer of secretary of state.

The president calls the others in and they all agree to announce that "the First Lady flew quietly to Chicago last night for a short vacation and there has been taken seriously ill. The doctors suspect food poisoning."

Lights fade up on an empty battlefield, the same lights as in the Oval Office—equalizing the notion of murder on a mass or personal scale. Clouds of gas form over the stage. The lights turn green. Curtain.

* * *

Directed by Alan Arkin, *The White House Murder Case* opened at off-Broadway's Circle in the Square on February 18, 1970. The cast included Peter Bonerz in the role of President Hale; Cynthia Harris as his wife, Evelyn; and Paul Benedict as Postmaster General Stiles. Critic Clive Barnes wrote in the *New York Times*, "Jules Feiffer is a very funny, very savage man. . . . In *The White House Murder Case* Mr. Feiffer takes a man-size swipe at our modern society. He thinks—if I understand him right—that we are becoming dehumanized by violence." Barnes hails a performance "dazzlingly directed by Alan Arkin and acted by a cast that must be a cartoonist's dream," but believes that "the idea of the play is a great deal more gripping than the play itself. . . . There is a load of sick fun in the play but it never accounts up. . . . Mr. Feiffer never brings his bird home to roost and to breed in the imagination. He is flippant where he should be flip, sloppy where he should be surgical."[2]

The White House Murder Case ran for 119 performances.

* * *

Jules Ralph Feiffer was born in New York City in 1929. He was small for his age. Bad at sports, he developed an appetite for comic strips. "I ate them, I breathed them, I thought about them day and night," writes Feiffer in his autobiography, *Backing into Forward*.[3] He worshipped writer-artists Will Eisner (*Spirit*), Milton Caniff (*Terry and the Pirates*), Alex Raymond (*Flash Gordon*), and Al Capp (*Li'l Abner*). With his pocket money he purchased the dime-priced *Action*, *Detective*, *All American*, *Daredevil*, and *The Claw*. As a teenager, he was also inspired by serial radio programs, notably *Suspense*, *Jack Armstrong*, *Don Winslow*, and *The Adventures of Sam Spade*, a show that got him to read Dashiell Hammett. He soon began to peruse other hard-boiled writers, including Ernest Hemingway, Raymond Chandler, Jack London, and James T. Farrell. "Hemingway's way with words, or rather his way of eliminating words, made sense to a cartoonist's imagination," confides Feiffer.[4] His screen heroes were Warner Brother's tough guys James Cagney, Edward G. Robinson, Humphrey Bogart, George Raft, Paul Muni, and most especially John Garfield. Expanding his horizons, he became aware of the plays of Arthur Miller, Clifford Odets, Maxwell Anderson, Sidney Kingsley, and Elmer Rice.

At sixteen, Feiffer gained his first bona fide experience as a cartoonist when he was hired to assist Will Eisner. He studied at the Arts Student League and Pratt Institute and served in the army during 1951–1953. In the mid-1950s he became a contributing cartoonist for the *Village Voice* and later a regular contributor to the *London Observer, Sunday Telegraph, Playboy*, and the *New Republic*. Beginning in April 1959, Feiffer's cartoons were syndicated nationally. He gradually gained international fame as a humorist and social commentator.

Along the way, Feiffer crossed paths, socially or professionally, sometimes both, with Alan Arkin, the farcical director of *Little Murders* and *The White House Murder Case*; the comedy team of Mike Nichols and Elaine May; noted theatre critics Kenneth Tynan and Robert Brustein; *Playboy* publisher Hugh Hefner and *Paris Review* publisher George Plimpton; playwrights Lillian Hellman, Herb Gardner, Arthur Kopit, Jack Gelber, and Jack Richardson; renowned cartoonist Al Hirschfeld; actresses Marlene Dietrich and Lauren Bacall; authors Truman Capote and Gore Vidal; film director Robert Altman and actor Dustin Hoffman; and presidential candidate Eugene McCarthy.

Feiffer's first play is the one-act *Crawling Arnold*, which was rejected by the Second City troupe of Chicago but was performed in Spoleto, Italy, and in London in 1961. It is the story of a man in his thirties who crawls on all fours, insists on a lemon peel in his martini, is forever misplacing his coloring book, and believes that he has discovered the forgotten value of being naughty. Arnold is hitting it off with a pretty social worker. When the alert sounds for an air-raid drill, Arnold joins Miss Sympathy on the floor and mischievously makes sure to break the all-clear mechanism.

In addition to *The White House Murder Case*, Feiffer's offerings on Broadway include the segment *Passionella* in the three-part musical *The Apple Tree*, a satire on career ambitions. It is about a chimney sweeper who achieves her goal of becoming a movie star (Shubert Theatre, October 18, 1966—463 performances). He also wrote the full-length *Little Murders*, a quirky comedy unfolding in a metropolitan locale going through chaos and violence. The middle-class Newquist family is divided by domestic strife, but when father, mother, daughter, and fiancé find themselves surrounded by thugs and bullets come flying through the windows, the Newquists unite and decide to fight back (Broadhurst Theatre, April 25, 1967—seven performances; an off-Broadway revival at Circle in the Square, January 5, 1969—400 showings).

Feiffer penned the segment *Dick and Jane* for the notorious avant-garde revue *Oh! Calcutta!*, created in 1969 by British drama critic Kenneth Tynan, consisting of various sketches and sex-related topics.[5] The revue ran in New York for more than 1,600 performances and in London for over 2,400 showings. A 1976 Broadway revival ran for thirteen years, with a total of 5,959 performances. A motion picture version was released in 1972.

Feiffer's *The Unexpurgated Memoirs of Bernard Mergendeiler* is a two-character one-act in which a boy and a girl exchange views about sex. Once

Bernard and Naomi conclude that sex is dirty, it releases their inhibitions. The playlet was joined by other short comedies and produced, under the title *Collision Course*, in 1967 in Los Angeles, and the following year at New York's Café Au Go Go, running for eighty performances.

Made up of brief sketches, vignettes, and monologues, all bitingly funny, is *Feiffer's People*, first produced in Edinburgh, Scotland, in 1968, and three years later in Los Angeles, California. *Knock-Knock*, a comedy about a pair of old Jewish bachelor recluses, opened at Broadway's Biltmore Theatre on February 24, 1976, was nominated for a Tony Award as Best Play, and ran for 152 performances. *Hold Me!*, blending a series of sketches, skits, and vignettes unified by the theme of urban confusion and angst, premiered at off-Broadway's American Place Theatre in 1977. *Grown Ups*, in which an affluent, dysfunctional family spirals into emotional chaos, opened at Broadway's Lyceum Theatre on December 10, 1981, was nominated for a Drama Desk Award, ran for eighty-three performances, and was adapted to television three years later.

The one-act *The Dicks* takes place in the lobby of a seedy old hotel in Florida. Ed, a veteran house detective, is unhappy with his new partner, who objects to peeping through keyholes or taking candid photographs of guests in their rooms and doesn't know the difference between dames and broads. The playlet was shown at the Ninth Annual off-off-Broadway Original Short Play Festival in 1984. *Eliot Loves* goes back to Chicago of the mid-1980s and focuses on a bachelor who is both enamored and terrified of a new girlfriend who is everything he ever wanted in a woman: intelligent, beautiful, warm, independent. The play was first produced by the Seattle Repertory Theatre in 1990.

Set in Brooklyn during the 1950s, *A Bad Friend* unfolds in the house of Shelly and Naomi Wallach, a middle-aged couple fervently opposed to McCarthyism, anti-Semitism, and exploitation of the working class. Their independent-minded teenage daughter, Rose, squirms under the weight of her parents' didactic principles and becomes increasingly rebellious. *A Bad Friend* premiered at off-Broadway's Mitzi E. Newhouse Theatre in 2003.

Feiffer has also written for the movies. In 1961, he won an Academy Award for *Munro*, a short animated cartoon about a boy who didn't fit into the army. Ten years later he was nominated by the Writers Guild of America for Best Comedy Written Directly for the Screen for *Carnal Knowledge*. Directed by Mike Nichols, the film traces the emotional and sexual confusion of two men from their Amherst College days in the 1950s through the Kennedy '60s. Less successful was *Popeye* (1980), scripted by Feiffer for director Robert Altman. The Sailor Man (played by Robin Williams) falls in love with Olive Oyl, adopts Swee'Pea, and clashes with enemy Bluto. *I Want to Go Home* (1989), directed by Alain

Resnais (famed for *Hiroshima mon amour*), is the story of a girl from Ohio who travels to Paris to absorb culture, which she finds lacking in the home of her cartoonist father.

Books published by Feiffer include *Sick Sick Sick* (1958) and *Passionella and Other Stories* (1959), two collections of strips from his work at the Village Voice, and *The Great Comic Book Heroes* (1977). Feiffer's memoir, *Backing into Forward*, was published by Doubleday in 2010.

Acting Edition: Samuel French, Inc.

Awards and Honors: A top-ten selection in *The Best Plays of 1969–1970*. ("Feiffer's skill with both drawing and writing pens in newspaper cartoons is one of the treasures of modern literature, and the actors and director of *The White House Murder Case* were on their mettle to reproduce the ironic visions of Feiffer's play-script.")[6] *The White House Murder Case* won Obie and Outer Circle Critics Awards, as did Feiffer's *Little Murders* a year earlier. The musical *The Apple Tree*, to which Feiffer contributed the segment *Passionella*, was a top-ten selection in *The Best Plays of 1966–1967*.

In 1961, Jules Feiffer was the recipient of a George Polk Award for his cartoons, and that year won an Oscar for his animated short *Munro*. The Pulitzer Prize for editorial cartooning went to Feiffer in 1986. In 1995, he was elected to the American Academy of Arts and Letters. In 2004, he was inducted into the Comic Book Hall of Fame, and that same year he received the National Cartoonists Society's Milton Caniff Lifetime Achievement Award. In 2006, Feiffer garnered the Creativity Foundation's laureate. Feiffer is also the recipient of a Lifetime Achievement Award from the Writers Guild of America.

NOTES

1. Otis L. Guernsey Jr., ed., *The Best Plays of 1969–1970* (New York: Dodd, Mead, 1970), 27.

2. *New York Times*, February 19, 1970.

3. Jules Feiffer, *Backing into Forward* (New York: Doubleday, 2010), 2.

4. Jules Feiffer, *Backing into Forward*, 77.

5. Among the contributors to *Oh! Calcutta!* were Samuel Becket, John Lennon, Sam Shepard, and Leonard Melfi. Most of the segments featured the cast naked (including Bill Macy).

6. Otis L. Guernsey Jr., *The Best Plays of 1969–1970*, 27.

Inquest (1970)

Donald Freed (United States, 1933–)

One of the most enduring controversies of the Cold War era is the trial and execution of married couple Julius and Ethel Rosenberg as Soviet spies. At the time, the Manhattan Project was the name given to the top-secret effort of Allied scientists to develop an atomic bomb. The Rosenbergs were accused and found guilty of delivering notes and charts of a crucial high-explosive-lens mold to Russian agents.

Playwright Donald Freed was inspired by Walter and Miriam Schneir's 1965 book *Invitation to an Inquest*, when penning *The United States vs. Julius and Ethel Rosenberg*, a docudrama about the "Atom Spy Ring." The play had its world premiere at the Cleveland Play House, the oldest resident professional theatre in the country, in 1969. It ran for nine weeks to full houses, but when the play (now called *Inquest*) came to New York the following year, director and cast were replaced.

When the audience entered the lobby of the Music Box Theatre, they were greeted with a sign: "There will be no curtain calls." Under Alan Schneider's direction, there was no curtain, and no intermission. The play began with frozen images on an upstage screen, including a picture of Hiroshima's victims and portraits of Senator Joe McCarthy and the FBI's J. Edgar Hoover, as well as a statement: "Every word you will hear or see on this stage is a documented quotation or reconstruction from events." Throughout the play, faces, occurrences, and newspaper headlines from the late 1940s and early 1950s were projected on a background composed of eighteen panels.

The action progresses on two platforms—one representing a courthouse, the other the interior of Julius and Ethel Rosenberg's home. While the case against the Rosenbergs is in progress, flashbacks revert back to incidents in the couple's personal life. The audience is the jury; dialogue is directed to them.

The sympathy of the playwright is clearly with the defendants. Irving H. Saypol, the United States Attorney for the Southern District of New York, and his prosecutor assistant, Roy Cohn, are bullies. Presiding Judge

Irving R. Kaufman is supercilious. The State's witnesses, David Green-glass and Harry Gold, come across as moustached villains.

On the other hand, Julius and Ethel Rosenberg (shrewdly cast by sympathetic actors George Grizzard and Anne Jackson) and their defense attorney Emanuel Bloch (portrayed by likable James Whitmore) are presented in positive, humane terms. Domestic sequences picture the Rosenbergs as a couple of lower-middle-class Jews from New York's Lower East Side. We see them as loving parents to two sons, we see Julius playing chess, Ethel singing operatic arias. Both are bewildered by their fate.

"The charge is conspiracy to commit espionage," declares Judge Kaufman. In his opening remarks, Prosecutor Saypol assures the jury that the evidence will show that the loyalty and the allegiance of the Rosenbergs was not to the United States but to Communism, both national and international, and that they stole, through Ethel's brother David Greenglass, who was stationed in Los Alamos, "the one weapon that might well hold the key to the survival of the nation"—the atomic bomb.

Emanuel Bloch pleads with the jury not to be influenced by the prevalent hysteria of the times and asks for "a fair shake in the American way."

Act I is largely devoted to the testimonies of David Greenglass and Harry Gold, who had previously pleaded guilty to their own roles in the case before becoming the chief witnesses for the prosecution. Greenglass, Ethel Rosenberg's brother, testifies that his brother-in-law, Julius, asked him to write up anything he knew about the atomic bomb. Julius told him that the Russians would pay for his schooling, and showed him a console table hollowed out to fit paraphernalia for photographic purposes. He gave Julius a sketch of a lens mold. Jello box sides served as a code of identity among the parties of the ring. He held up one piece of a Jello box and Harry Gold exhibited a matching piece when they first met.

In his cross-examination, defense attorney Bloch elicits from Greenglass that he was a business partner of Julius Rosenberg and they often quarreled.

Ruth Greenglass, David's wife, testifies that Julius Rosenberg confided to her that sharing the atomic bomb information with the Russians, an ally at the time, would likely prevent one nation from using the bomb as a threat against another. Rosenberg asked for physical descriptions of the project at Los Alamos, said Ruth, as well as the number of people employed there, including scientists.

Harry Gold, already convicted of espionage and serving a sentence of thirty years in a federal penitentiary, testifies that he served as liaison between a Russian spy, Anatoli Yakovley, and David Greenglass, contacting the latter in Albuquerque, New Mexico, introducing himself with a matching piece of cardboard.

In the second act, Emanuel Bloch calls Julius Rosenberg to the stand. The accused, New York born and thirty-three years old, denies any involvement with espionage, asserts that he is "heartily in favor of our Constitution and Bill of Rights," and maintains that he does not owe allegiance to any other country. When Prosecutor Saypol queries whether Julius or his wife Ethel have been members of the Communist Party, Rosenberg refuses to answer on the grounds that it might incriminate him.

Ethel Rosenberg, on the stand, also denies any espionage activities and insists, "Neither of us is guilty."

In his closing statement, Emanuel Bloch emphasizes that the entire case against the Rosenbergs lacks any kind of meaningful physical or documentary evidence, but relies on oral testimony by a shady David Greenglass and his "dolled up, arrogant" wife.

Irving Saypol points out that the case is one of the most important ever submitted to a jury in the United States, and declares that "the F.B.I. is never duped."

The foreman of the jury appears from the audience, mounts the stage, and announces that Julius and Ethel Rosenberg are "guilty as charged." Judge Kaufman sentences the Rosenbergs "to the punishment of death."

The last scene of the play takes place on death row at Sing Sing prison. Images of Jean-Paul Sartre, Albert Einstein, and the pope appear on the screen, asking for clemency, while Dwight D. Eisenhower states that he will not intervene in the matter.

The final moments are described in harrowing detail. The Rosenbergs, their heads shorn, are offered their last meal. Other prisoners stand frozen. Guards arrange the execution area. Enter a matron, a marshal, an electrician, and two doctors. A rabbi intones, "The Lord is my shepherd, I shall not want" and continues with the reading of the psalm as Julius Rosenberg is led in, pauses for a moment to give the rabbi his spectacles, and is strapped to the electric chair by two guards. The cathode is adjusted, the helmet lowered on the head to make contact with the shaven spot. Three electric charges dim the lights. The doctor approaches, opens Julius's shirt, listens, and pronounces him dead. The body is placed on a gurney and is wheeled out. Ethel Rosenberg enters, along with a prison matron, and the same ritual of death is repeated. The rabbi intones the Hebrew lament for the dead.

Emanuel Bloch addresses the audience with a mournful comment that his biggest mistake was "underestimating the capacity for cynicism and evil in high places."

The tantalizing question remains: were the Rosenbergs guilty or not guilty of espionage? Were they traitors, or the victims of a shameful episode in American history, fed by Cold War tensions, anti-Communist hysteria, and a touch of anti-Semitism?

* * *

The New York critics greeted *Inquest* with mostly negative assessments. Douglas Watt called *Inquest* "a disturbing document, as it was meant to be," but "nevertheless, I found it often tiresome theatre," a drama that "falls inescapably into the category of a propaganda play, thus demeaning its subject."[1] Richard Watts believed that "Mr. Freed is stacking the cards to advance his point," thus "does no service to the disputed memory of the Rosenbergs. It could make many suspect they were guilty."[2] Martin Gottfried sniffed: "The script is so choppy, its editing so abrupt, there is such emphasis on minor matters and such skimming on major ones, the transitions are so sudden and elementary matters are so ignored that you simply can't keep the story straight."[3]

Clive Barnes, however, called *Inquest* "one of the most gripping courtroom dramas of my experience,"[4] and the television reviewers were positive: Edwin Newman of NBC TV4 thought that the play was "slow to start, but finally chilling and disturbing."[5] John Bartholomew Tucker of WABC TV7 stated, "It's probably the most shattering thing I've seen all year on Broadway."[6]

Inquest ran for twenty-eight performances.

Perhaps by coincidence, almost simultaneously with the incubation and performances of *Inquest*, another docudrama about the Rosenbergs, Alain Decaux's *Les Rosenberg ne doivent pas mourir* (*The Rosenbergs Shall Not Die*), was produced in Paris during the 1968–1969 season. The play argued the innocence of the executed Americans.

Four decades later, in 2007, the case of Julius and Ethel Rosenberg was revisited in *The Brother*. The title refers to Ethel's brother David Greenglass, a collaborator of the Rosenbergs who informed on them and got off with only ten years in prison. Playwright Sam Roberts utilized information from now-declassified files. *The Brother* premiered at Chicago's Theatre Building.

In 1965, Walter and Miriam Schneir published the 500-page *Invitation to an Inquest*, in which they claimed that Julius and Ethel Rosenberg were "punished for a crime that never occurred." The book further accused the U.S. government of orchestrating a political frame-up of the Rosenbergs. In the mid-1990s, upon the release of intercepted Soviet wartime cables, the Schneirs changed their conclusions, now believing that the couple had lied and that Julius had indeed stolen military and industrial secrets. This shift is documented in Walter Schneir's *Final Verdict*, a slim book published by Melville House in 2010 (Walter Schneir died in 2009; Miriam Schneir completed the book).

* * *

Born in Chicago to a middle-class Jewish family and raised by a stepfather who was a successful merchant of military gear, Donald Freed has had multiple careers as playwright, novelist, screenwriter, and actor. In the 1950s and 1960s, he appeared in various television programs, including *Medic, Official Detective, Target, Men in Space,* and *Checkmate.*

In the 1970s, Freed worked as an investigative reporter for the Citizens Research and Investigation Committee. His findings led to writing numerous articles on the assassinations of John F. Kennedy, Robert Kennedy, and Martin Luther King Jr., and the events surrounding the Watergate scandal. His subsequent books were politically engaged and often dealt with true crime incidents. Among them were *Agony in New Haven: The Trial of Bobby Seale, Ericka Huggins, and the Black Panther Party* (1973); *Death in Washington: The Murder of Orlando Letelier* (1980), implicating the CIA in the murder of the Chilean diplomat; and *Killing Time* (1996), co-written with Raymond P. Briggs, an inquiry into the O. J. Simpson double-murder case of Nicole Brown Simpson and Ronald Goldman.

In 1978, the infamous Jim Jones engaged Freed to help in the matter of alleged plots by intelligence agencies against the Peoples Temple of Jonestown, Guyana. Freed concluded that there was a "massive conspiracy" against the Temple. On November 18, 1978, more than nine hundred Temple members committed mass suicide in Jonestown.

Freed also wrote several screenplays based on real-life events. *Executive Action* (1973), cowritten with Dalton Trumbo and Mark Lane and starring Burt Lancaster and Robert Ryan, portrays the assassination of John F. Kennedy as a conspiracy. *Secret Honor* (1984), written with Arnold M. Stone and directed by Robert Altman, features Philip Baker Hall as President Richard M. Nixon in a fictional account that follows his disgraceful exit from the White House. *Of Love and Shadows* (1994), adapted by Freed from a novel by Isabel Allende, tells the story of a magazine editor living under the yoke of the Pinochet dictatorship in Chile.

Among the many plays penned by Freed, notable are *American Iliad,* in which Richard Nixon, dying, looks back at his life. His reminiscences include glimpses of John F. Kennedy, J. Edgar Hoover, and Marilyn Monroe; *Alfred and Victoria,* an interpretation of the sensational scandal in which Vicki Morgan, the notorious mistress of Alfred Bloomingdale, sued the scion of the department store family for palimony; *Circe and Bravo,* set in the president's lodge at Camp David; *The Quartered Man,* the story of the last day in the life of a spy, George C. O'Connor, in Central America.

In *Veteran's Day,* three veterans—shell-shocked, injured, decorated— meet just before a ceremony to honor them. *Child of Luck* is a cynical view of American politics, depicting a scandalous political campaign for the presidency. *Hamlet (in Rehearsal)* pries into the Shakespearean masterpiece in the form of a play within a play. *The Death of Ivan Ilych* is based on the novella by Leo Tolstoy. Writer James Joyce and his wife Nora go through a vaudevillian give-and-take in *Is He Still Dead?* as they attempt to flee Nazi-occupied France in 1940. *Patient #1*, set in a futuristic secret psychiatric unit hidden in the Florida Everglades, focuses on a confrontation between a psychoanalyst and former President George W. Bush. *The White Crow: Eichmann in Jerusalem* pits an interrogator against the Nazi butcher Adolph Eichmann, who escaped to Argentina, was unearthed by the Israeli Mossad in 1960, and was finally brought to Israel for trial.

Freed was described by radical historian Studs Turkel as "the most political and pertinent of all U.S. playwrights."

Freed's novels are also topical. *Spymaster* (1980) narrates the saga of a Yale graduate who goes through the shady world of espionage in many fronts until he finally becomes the director of Central Intelligence. *The China Card* (2003) is a novel of international intrigue set against the backdrops of Washington, Moscow, and Peking. *Every Third House* (2005) incorporates fictional court transcripts, prison letters, and FBI memorandums into the life story of an imaginary Black Panther leader.

Freed served as artist in residence at the Workshop Theatre, University of Leeds, England (2006–2008) and as playwright in residence at York Theatre Royal (2007–2008), where he established a working relationship with Harold Pinter. He has also been playwright in residence at Dennison University, Ohio, and has taught creative writing at the University of Southern California for twenty-two years.

Acting Edition: Samuel French, Inc. (in manuscript form).

Awards and Honors: Donald Freed was the recipient of three Rockefeller Foundation Awards; two Louis B. Meyer Awards; The Unicorn Prize; The Gold Medal Award; The Berlin Critics Award; NEA award for Distinguished Writing; Hollywood Critics Award; PEN Literary Prize for Best Drama 2006—*The Devil's Advocate*, a play set on Christmas Eve during the 1989 U.S. invasion of Panama.

NOTES

1. *Daily News*, April 24, 1970.
2. *New York Post*, April 24, 1970.
3. *Women's Wear Daily*, April 24, 1970.
4. *New York Times*, April 24, 1970.
5. NBC TV4, April 23, 1970.
6. WABC TV7, April 23, 1970.

Count Dracula (1971)

Ted Tiller (United States, 1913–1988)

Count Dracula by Ted Tiller, first presented at Stage West in West Spring-field, Massachusetts, on December 10, 1971, takes place in the living quarters of Dr. Seward's Asylum for the Insane, north of London. Like the popular, often-revived 1927 stage version of *Dracula* by Hamilton Deane and John L. Balderston, this play is set in "the first half of the Twentieth Century," and the final scene transpires at the Carfax crypt. But in the more recent Tiller rendition, the vampire hunters discover the coffin's whereabouts not by tracking madman Renfield, but by chasing Mina in a car.

The list of dramatis personae in *Count Dracula* is similar to that of Deane-Balderston, but Tiller changed Van Helsing's name to "Heinrich," made Mina Murray a ward of Dr. Seward instead of his daughter, and added a broadly comic character, the doctor's niece, Sybil Seward. She is presented as a fluttering, talkative spinster with a yen for sherry and an eye for the continental count.

Surprisingly, Dracula reveals himself to be knowledgeable about English literature, and inquires of Renfield whether he has read *Oliver Twist*, comparing himself to Fagin as he instructs his surrogate to steal Van Helsing's crucifixes. The unholy relationship between the count and Renfield ends violently with the murder of the latter; his corpse is found dangling across a balcony rail, his bloody face upside down toward the audience.

In the Tiller adaptation, the vampire "admits" to Van Helsing that he is the infamous Count Voivode Dracula of the fifteenth century, and vows, "Long after you are forgotten dust, I shall still walk the earth and rule the night."

The proceedings are peppered with such props and special effects as a lit cigarette appearing from nowhere to be puffed by the count; two sets of white plastic fangs, one for Dracula, the other for Mina; three bats constructed of malleable wire, covered with dull black cloth, which fly over the audience; a high-backed mahogany chair rigged to swivel on its own, creating the effect of an invisible count sitting in it; and a box of sand fastened to receive the tip end of a wooden stake as it is supposedly driven into the count's heart (the stake is placed between Dracula's left arm and chest). A flash pot, a green spotlight, a fog machine, and silent electric fans are also utilized for various thrilling effects. Magically, Dracula vanishes in full view of the spectators.

Enhancing the mechanical wizardry is an usher stationed at the rear of the auditorium who lets loose a blood-curdling scream when Count Dracula bares his fangs and bends over Mina's throat. The usher pierced the eardrums of the viewers at Stage West and her colleagues did the same at the Cleveland Playhouse, Ohio, in 1974; at the Dallas Theatre Center, Texas, in 1975; at the Equity Library Theatre in New York City in 1977; and at the Museum Theatre in Richmond, Virginia, in 1981.

* * *

Ted Tiller was born in 1913 in Washington, D.C., and began his career as a radio broadcaster. He made his Broadway debut as an actor in the 1944 production of *Sing Out, Sweet Land!* His subsequent Broadway credits include *No, No, Nanette*, *The Great White Hope*, and *Witness for the Prosecution*.

Tiller frequently appeared in off-Broadway productions and with many summer-stock companies, including the Valley Players in Holyoke, Massachusetts, where he spent eleven seasons. He was also a TV scriptwriter and actor for such shows as *Omnibus*, *Home Show*, and the children's series *Mr. I. Imagination*.

In addition to *Count Dracula*, Tiller wrote the comedy-melodrama *Tight Spot* (1977), in which a best-selling novelist is nutty enough to buy an old lighthouse intending to make it her summer home, and finds herself, her estranged film-star husband, and his latest flame trapped on the top floor during the off season.

Acting Edition: Samuel French, Inc.

The Trial of the Catonsville Nine (1971)

Daniel Berrigan (United States, 1921–) and Saul Levitt (United States, 1913–1977)

Daniel Berrigan was born in Virginia, Minnesota, and grew up in Syracuse, New York. He began his Jesuit training in 1939 and after thirteen years of study entered the priesthood. He was active in community work in African American and Puerto Rican neighborhoods of New York City, and with his brother Philip (1923–2002) became passionately involved in civil rights and antiwar activities. In 1968, at the height of the Vietnam War protests, the brothers were joined by seven additional Catholic activists as they entered the draft board in Catonsville, Maryland, took 378 recruitment files, brought them to the parking lot, and set them on fire with homemade napalm.

The seven men and two women involved were arrested, tried, convicted, and sentenced to prison terms ranging from two to three-and-a-half years. After all appeals failed, the Berrigan brothers went underground. In 1970 Daniel was captured in Rhode Island by federal agents and was sent to serve his term in federal prison in Danbury, Connecticut.

Daniel Berrigan wrote the play *The Trial of the Catonsville Nine* in free verse. Saul Levitt adapted it into prose dialogue, basing his version on the transcripts of the trial, as he did with his 1959 courtroom drama *The Andersonville Trial*.

The time: Monday, October 7, 1968. The place: United States District Court for the District of Maryland. The curtain rises on Father Daniel Berrigan standing at a pulpit-like reading desk with the other eight defendants silhouetted behind him. Berrigan addresses the audience, reminding them of "that little business of pouring blood on draft records" (the defendants behind him pantomime the burning of the draft files).

Marshals enter carrying an American flag. Prosecution and defense attorneys follow and cross to their desks. Jury members take their seats in the jury box. The judge explains to the jury that this is an action of the United States against the nine defendants for seizing and burning records of the local draft board at Catonsville, Maryland. The defendants plead not guilty. Marshals bring in trash burners and boxes of charred ash—the evidence.

A prosecution witness, Mrs. Boyle, a matronly office clerk, describes how the intruders entered the draft board offices, went straight to the cabinets, emptied the drawers of 1-A classification files into a trash burner, and took them outside to be incinerated. David Darst, one of the defendants, testifies that the records were burned using "a very crude form of napalm—two parts gasoline, one part soap flakes."

One by one the defendants are called to the stand. They identify themselves as priests, nuns, divinity students, and ghetto teachers. They worked for the betterment of human conditions in Uganda, Guatemala, Yucatan, Mexico, the Dominican Republic, and in skid row areas of Chicago and New Orleans. They felt it was their duty to deal with the immorality of the Vietnam War. They joined vigils and demonstrations in Washington, D.C., and made a decision to protest the war by pouring their own blood on draft files, "in order to illustrate our horror over blood being shed in Vietnam," and destroying records "which are potential death certificates."

"There is a higher law we are commanded to obey," testifies the accused George Mische. "It takes precedence over human laws." Mary Moylan, one of two women among the accused, declares that as a nurse, her duty is "to preserve life. . . . To pour napalm on pieces of paper is certainly preferable to using it on human beings." The other female defendant, Marjorie Melville, agrees, insisting that there are moments when opposition needs to turn into action.

Philip Berrigan states that the defendants do not believe that they have committed a crime. They violated the law, but their motive was to illustrate genocide in Vietnam and corruption at home. His brother, Daniel, testifies that in 1968 he received an invitation from the government of North Vietnam to bring home three captive American airmen and witnessed the horrors of war firsthand.

With great passion Father Berrigan exclaims, "The time is past when good people can remain silent. . . . How many indeed must die before our voices are heard?"

In his summation, the prosecutor contends that the case is simply a matter of taking government property, throwing flammable material on it, and burning it beyond recognition. If people are entitled to be acquitted by virtue of their sincerity or conviction, then, according to the same logic, should not the people who commit other crimes also be entitled to acquittal?

The defense attorney for the Catonsville Nine maintains that this is a unique case, sharing the historic meaning of other great contests of law— such as the trials of Socrates and Jesus. As to the burnt records, this is

MT. LEBANON PUBLIC LIBRARY

not a question of driver's licenses "or licenses to operate a brewery," but records that directly affect life and death on a mass scale—life and death to young men.

The judge instructs the jury to decide the case not on the basis of conscience but solely on the basis of facts presented in court by both sides. The voice of the foreman of the jury is heard on a recorded tape as he announces the verdict: "Guilty."

* * *

Directed by Gordon Davidson and presented without an intermission, *The Trial of the Catonsville Nine* was first produced by the Center Theatre Group of Los Angeles at the Mark Taper Forum, then brought to New York by off-Broadway's Phoenix Theatre on February 7, 1971. Key roles were played by Ed Flanders (Daniel Berrigan), Michael Kane (Philip Berrigan), and William Schallert (Judge). Sam Waterston, Richard Jordan, and Nancy Malone enacted three of the defendants. "The play grew on you like a fine painting of an historical event," wrote Otis L. Guernsey Jr. in *The Best Plays of 1970–1971*. "It had scant physical action but increasing sympathy for everyone caught in this moral and legal cobweb. . . . Staged in a church which huddles near the travertine ostentation of the Lincoln Center complex, here was a piece of highly effective theater for our time, as relevant as a body count."[1] *The Trial of the Catonsville Nine* ran for 130 performances and moved to Broadway's Lyceum Theatre on June 2 for twenty-nine additional showings. The transfer triggered some cast changes, with the better-known Biff McGuire, James Woods, Michael Moriarty, and Josef Sommer taking over some of the parts.

The Trial of the Catonsville Nine came back to the Mark Taper Forum in Los Angeles on June 17, 1971, for fifty-four performances. John Stix staged the play for Baltimore's Center Stage, opening on October 31, 1971, featuring Ward Costello, John Newton, Roger DeKoven, and Earle Hyman, running for twenty-three showings. On February 3, 1972, *The Trial* commenced at the Studio Arena Theatre in Buffalo, New York, for twenty-four performances.

Also in 1972, Gregory Peck produced an eighty-five-minute film version of the play. He recruited Gordon Davidson to direct and several members of the original production to reprise their roles. That same year, *Der Prozeb gegen die neun von Catonsville* was broadcast on German television. In 1975, the play was televised in what was then Yugoslavia.

More than three decades later, with wars in Iraq and Afghanistan, *The Trial of the Catonsville Nine* was still deemed relevant. In 2009, the play was reincarnated by the University of Maryland at the Clarice Smith Center for the Performing Arts, and by the Actors' Gang Theatre, helmed by Tim Robbins, in Culver City, California. Reviewer Charlotte Stoudt of the

Los Angeles Times opined that "the Actors' Gang presents a lucid, impassioned revival of this free-verse courtroom drama," but added: "Despite the *Law and Order*–style sound cues used to button each scene, *Cantonsville* isn't exactly riveting courtroom theatre. While one is humbled by the Nine's moral rigor, the play is more sermon than debate."[2]

Later in 2009, the Actors' Gang traveled with *The Trial of the Catonsville Nine* to the Brisbane Festival in Brisbane, Queensland, Australia. On that occasion, Father Daniel Berrigan joined the cast.

Acting Edition: Samuel French, Inc.

Awards and Honors: A top-ten selection in *The Best Plays of 1970–1971*. Father Daniel Berrigan won the Lamont Poetry Award in 1957 and was nominated for a National Book Award in 1969. Saul Levitt's drama *The Andersonville Trial* was a top-ten selection in *The Best Plays of 1959–1960*.

NOTES

1. Otis L. Guernsey Jr., ed., *The Best Plays of 1970–1971* (New York: Dodd, Mead, 1971), 25–26.

2. *Los Angeles Times*, February 19, 2009.

Suddenly at Home (1971)

Francis Durbridge (England, 1912–1998)

Glenn Howard, a traveling salesman, and his wife Maggie share an elegant flat in a quiet London mews. The furniture includes two sofas, side tables, and an ornate cabinet. There are expensive pictures on the walls.

The curtain rises on Maggie Howard, somewhat coarse in speech and manner, and her younger sister, Helen Tenby, an intelligent-looking woman in her late twenties who runs a successful art gallery. The two women are dressed for an evening out—dinner and a show. Ruth Bechler, the household maid, a pretty girl from Munich, enters to say good-bye and leaves for the weekend.

The front doorbell rings. It is Sam Blaine, a former beau of Maggie's and a writer of thrillers. Maggie goes to her room to touch up her makeup, and Sam whispers to Helen that her sister is a junkie; he makes a gesture as if injecting his arm with a hypodermic. Helen exclaims, "I don't believe a word of it," but Sam responds, "Why do you think she's taken to wearing long sleeves all of a sudden?"

Another visitor arrives: Sheila Wallis, an attractive actress friend. Sheila says that she cannot join the theatre party because her father had an accident and she has to drive down to Eastbourne. Sheila asks Sam if he has found her diamond earring, the one she probably dropped at his place the week before. No, says Sam as he escorts Sheila out, she must have lost it somewhere else.

Enter Glenn Howard, Maggie's husband, carrying a Samsonite suitcase. He is described as one who oozes "an easy charm." Glenn has returned from a business trip to Paris. We learn that his salary is meager but the Howards live comfortably on Maggie's money.

The two sisters leave for the theatre. The doorbell rings and Sheila Wallis reenters. Glenn takes her in his arms. They remain together for a moment, then Glenn fishes a small package from his valise, obviously a drug, and hands it to her. They go over a plan that involves diamond earrings, a pair of white gloves, dark glasses, a car key, and a map.

The hatched scheme becomes clear in the next scene, when Glenn makes sure that Maggie has willed her fortune to him and suddenly attacks her, jamming a cushion over her face. A violent struggle ensues; Maggie's legs can be seen flaying in the air until her resistance subsides.

Glenn puts on a pair of white cotton gloves, takes a diamond ring from his pocket, and places it in Maggie's handbag. He pulls a sheet off the sofa, spreads it on the floor, and takes hold of his wife's body as the lights fade out.

Reminiscent of James M. Cain's classic *Double Indemnity*, but with a gender change, Sheila impersonates Maggie, wearing her dress, gloves, and sunglasses, takes Maggie's car to Keggleston Way, in the vicinity of Sam Blaine's home, drives the car slowly into a ditch and walks back to Coniston Lane, where she finds a telephone booth, tells the operator that she's Mrs. Glenn Howard and asks to be connected to her home number, reversing the charges. Glenn accepts the call, thus establishing that presumably Maggie is still alive.

Detective Inspector Norman Appleton informs Glenn that his wife has been murdered. Her body was found in a pond on Melston Heath. Glenn makes sure that the police know that Sam Blaine's home is located near the pond, that Blaine was a former lover of his dead wife, and that Blaine borrowed $4,000 from her.

In a twist, the maid, Ruth Bechler, is revealed as Glenn Howard's true love. Together they concocted Maggie's murder and used Sheila as a cog in the scheme. Now Sheila's services are not needed anymore. She has become a threat and has to go. As she is a junkie, an overdose of heroin will do it.

The play's climax is violent: Sheila realizes that she has been duped by Glenn and strikes at him. He grabs hold of her and attempts to force her across the room toward the bedroom. Sheila struggles frantically. In an attempt to free herself, she savagely bites Glenn's wrist. He viciously hits her across the face, knocking her unconscious. Ruth puts on white gloves and injects Sheila with a hypodermic. They drag her to the bedroom.

The doorbell rings. Inspector Appleton, Helen, and Sam enter. Glenn makes a case against Sam, when Sheila appears in the doorway of the bedroom, looking desperately ill. She shakily produces a gun from her coat pocket and fires twice at Glenn, who slumps forward, staggers a few feet, and collapses. Helen takes the gun out of Sheila's hand, and Ruth moves slowly toward Glenn's body as the curtain falls.

* * *

Suddenly at Home was first produced at the Theatre Royal in Windsor, England, on June 8, 1971. The play was subsequently performed at the Fortune Theatre, London, where it opened on September 30 and ran for more than seven hundred performances. Gerald Harper portrayed the villainous Glenn Howard. His ill-fated wife, Maggie, was enacted by Penelope Keith, and lovers Sheila and Ruth by Veronica Strong and Rula Lenska, respectively. Richard Berry directed.

* * *

Francis Henry Durbridge was born in Hull, Yorkshire, England, but lived most of his life in London. He was educated at a small private school in the Midlands and at Birmingham University, where he studied economics and English literature.

Durbridge worked briefly as a stockbroker's clerk before dedicating himself to full-time writing. Called by *Encyclopedia Mysteriosa* "the king of the British broadcast mystery,"[1] Durbridge penned more than thirty radio plays between 1938 and 1968, featuring novelist-detective Paul Temple, arguably the most famous of all the BBC radio sleuths. Assisted by his journalist wife Steve, Temple solved crimes in the milieu of the upper middle class. Simultaneously, beginning in 1938 and for the next four decades, Durbridge published thirty-some novels, many highlighting the cases of Paul Temple, some focusing on another series hero, Tim Frazer, an undercover man who gets involved in international intrigue.

The indefatigable author contributed to British television a dozen or so serials, all notable for suspenseful cliff-hangers, and if that was not enough, added to his name four film scripts[2] and eight stage thrillers.

The Durbridge plays include *The Gentle Hook* (1974), which begins with a career woman killing a man in self-defense, but soon more blood is spilled. In *Murder with Love* (1976), a much-hated womanizer is presumably bludgeoned to death by an irate husband, only to reappear alive and well in a tantalizing climactic twist. *House Guest* (1976) is the story of a kidnapping, while *Deadly Nightcap* (1983) depicts a greedy husband who plots to kill his wife and make it look like suicide.

In *Touch of Danger* (1987), the mistaken identity of a man who has been found dead in Munich triggers a series of events involving the CID, the CIA, and a terrorist organization. *The Small Hours* (1991) begins with the hijacking of an aircraft and develops into a complex adventure of relentless pursuit and attempted murder. In *Sweet Revenge* (1993), a famous conductor who is a notorious Don Juan is fed a controversial tranquilizer that causes a fatal heart attack. The police find it impossible to identify the culprit—there are too many angry husbands with a motive!

"Durbridge has no special message, no mission to examine the springs of violence or the motivation which leads a man to murder," says Melvyn Barnes in *Twentieth Century Crime and Mystery Writers*, "and seemingly no purpose other than to present to his audience one piece of craftsmanship after another. Nevertheless . . . Durbridge's ability as a skillful weaver of webs and a typically British exponent of the guessing-game has maintained his position as one of the most consistently entertaining crime writers."[3]

Acting Edition: Samuel French, Inc.

NOTES

1. William L. DeAndrea, *Encylopedia Mysteriosa* (New York: Prentice Hall, 1994), 104.

2. Francis Durbridge's films are *Send for Paul Temple*, featuring Anthony Hulme (1946), *Calling Paul Temple*, with John Bentley (1948), *Paul Temple's Triumph*, with Bentley (1950), and *Paul Temple Returns*, with Bentley (1952).

3. John M. Reilly, ed., *Twentieth Century Crime and Mystery Writers* (New York: St. Martin's Press, 1980), 523.

Something's Afoot (1972)

Book, Music, and Lyrics by James McDonald (United States), David Vos (United States), and Robert Gerlach (United States) Additional Music by Ed Linderman (United States)

Something's Afoot, a musical burlesque in the whodunit genre, borrows from Agatha Christie's *And Then There Were None* for its plot shenanigans and farcical darts.

The time is late spring, 1935. The action unfolds at the country estate of Lord Dudley Rancour, located on an island in the middle of a lake, somewhere in England. The entrance hall of Rancour's Retreat is distinctive, with many doors enabling split-second entrances and exits. Seven guests are invited for a weekend of merriment, all stock characters—Hope Langdon, the ingenue; Geoffrey, the juvenile; Dr. Grayburn, the family doctor; Nigel Rancour, the black sheep nephew; Lady Grace Manley-Prowe, the grande dame; Colonel Gillweather, the old army man; and Miss Tweed, an elderly amateur detective. The household servants include Letie, the saucy maid; Flint, the gruff caretaker; and Clive, the stiff butler. The host, replicating U. N. Owen of *And Then There Were None*, does not show up.

One by one the guests arrive, crooning hopes of "a marvelous, invigorating, glorious and stimulating . . . totally exasperating weekend!" Butler Clive announces that a severe electrical storm is rapidly approaching and that the rising water level of the lake has made the bridge to the mainland impassable.

The step on which Clive stands then blows up, leaving him dead. The ladies, of course, faint. Upon recovery, they join the men in singing, "Something's afoot . . . Something very scary . . . And the butler didn't do it!"

To the furious accompaniment of thunder and lightning, the marooned company, who in one way or another turn out to be intimately related, begin dropping off by fiendishly concocted devices: Dr. Grayburn is asphyxiated by gas emitted from the telephone; Lady Manley-Prowe is electrocuted upon touching the light switch; nephew Nigel is hit on the head and knocked to the floor by a sconce attached to the staircase post; a poisonous blowgun dart pierces Colonel Gilleweather's neck; Lettie, the maid, is sucked into an antique four-foot-tall Ming vase and gets eaten by a serpent; caretaker Flint explodes in the kitchen while lighting his pipe.

Miss Tweed whispers to Geoffrey and Hope that she has deciphered the killer's identity. She owes her deduction skills to books, she says, whodunits by Agatha Christie, Arthur Conan Doyle, Mary Robert Rinehart, Wilkie Collins, and Erle Stanley Gardner. And to *The Hound of the Baskervilles*, Dr. Watson, Roger Ackroyd, *The Thirteenth Guest*, *Baldpate* with its keys, *The After House*, *The Bat*, Shakespeare's *Richard 3* and *2*. But just as Tweed triumphantly announces, "The murderer is . . ." a spear rapidly tightens her muffler until she is strangled.

The only two survivors now suspect one another. However, a gramophone record reveals that the host, Dudley Rancour, rigged the lethal gadgets for various vengeful motives and has taken his own life as well. Hope and Geoffrey toast "The new day we've waited for." As sunshine pours in and birds are heard chirping, the young lovers succumb to drugged wine. And then there were none.

* * *

Something's Afoot began its route to Broadway at the Alliance Theatre in Atlanta, Georgia (1972); tried out at the Goodspeed Opera House, East Haddam, Connecticut (1973); warmed up at the American Theatre, Washington, D.C. (1973); was molded into shape by the American Conservatory Theatre, San Francisco (1974); and previewed at the Huntington Hartford Theatre in Los Angeles (1975). Directed and choreographed by Tony Tanner, with scenery designed by Richard Seger, the pastiche opened at the Lyceum Theatre on May 27, 1976. A program note pleaded: "For the enjoyment of future audiences it would be greatly appreciated if you would not disclose the ending of this play."

The critics abided by the request but otherwise were decidedly split. Clive Barnes avowed, "The music is terrible, the lyrics clumsy . . . camp taken to lengths that are almost as distasteful as they are ridiculous,"[1] while Christopher Sharp proclaimed, "What makes this show work so well is the liquid blend of words and music by Robert Gerlach and David Vos."[2] Douglas Watt found *Something's Afoot* "a campy musical murder mystery whose booby-trapped set upstages book, songs, and players,"[3] but Martin Gottfried believed that "the show is engaging and funny, refreshing in the originality of its idea and the modesty of its size."[4] T. E. Kalen complimented Tessie O'Shea for her portrayal of Miss Tweed "like a Margaret Rutherford come marvelously back to life";[5] however, television's Leonard Probst scoffed at the British actress, "who shakes, shimmies and congratulates herself."[6]

Something's Afoot ran in New York for sixty-one performances. It subsequently ran for 232 showings at London's Ambassadors Theatre and continued to spoof the genre at the Dallas Theatre Center (1977), the Cleveland Playhouse (1979), the Alaska Repertory Theatre (1980), and the Virginia Museum Theatre (1981). Since then, the musical has been produced by many community theatres and college drama departments.

In 1984, *Something's Afoot* was televised on *Showtime*, starring Jean Stapleton as Miss Tweed.

James McDonald, David Vos, Robert Gerlach, and Ed Linderman, writers of the book, music, and lyrics of *Something's Afoot*, have also collaborated on *Ladies First*, a 1984 comedy in which Jackie Kennedy invites Eleanor, Bess, Mamie, Pat, and Lady Bird to the White House and finds herself the brunt of much criticism.

Acting Edition: Samuel French, Inc. (including notes on special effects).

NOTES

1. *New York Times*, May 28, 1976.
2. *Women's Wear Daily*, May 28, 1976.
3. *Daily News*, May 28, 1976.
4. *New York Post*, May 28, 1976.
5. *Time Magazine*, June 7, 1976.
6. WNBC TV4, New York, May 28, 1976.

Night Watch (1972)

Lucille Fletcher (United States, 1912–2000)

The author of the classic radio play *Sorry, Wrong Number* created yet
another deadly encounter between a greedy, menacing husband and a
wealthy, distraught wife.

Night Watch, Lucille Fletcher's Broadway debut, unfolds in a plush
East Side town house in Manhattan. On an early winter morning, Elaine
Wheeler rouses the household with a blood-curdling scream. Hysteri-
cally, she relates to her husband John that she has just seen through a
window, in the gutted tenement across the street, "a—dead man. . . . He
was sitting there with his eyes wide open. Dead. Dead. Dead. . . . He was
bleeding. . . . His mouth. There was this trickle of blood like a dark snake
in the moonlight."

John, a Wall Street broker, calls the police. Officer Vanelli, who used to
be a guard in the Brooklyn Art Museum, is excited about the original Pi-
casso and Modigliani hanging on the walls but belittles Elaine's dramatic
story, as does brusque Lieutenant Walker, who informs her that a search
of the premises yielded neither blood nor any other sign of violence.

Elaine is in a fragile emotional condition since the death of her first husband, Carl, in a car accident, with a blonde girl "laying on the seat beside
him . . . her skirt up above her thighs." Elaine's state of mind deteriorates
further when she realizes that John has fallen in love with her sultry, red-
headed friend, Blanche Cooke, a nurse who is staying with them temporarily. Elaine's nerves are also put to the test by some eccentric characters
swirling around her—the German maid, Helga, a snoop who demands
money for a trip back home; the gay "neighborhood Peeping Tom," Curtis Appleby, who pops in and out to solicit a story for his *Kips Bay Tattler*;
a local deli owner, Sam Hoke, who resembles the corpse she saw; and a
psychiatrist, Dr. Tracy Lake, "who didn't even look professional." Have
they all joined forces to drive her mad?

When later that evening Elaine claims to have seen "a—woman . . . in that—other window, dead, like a limp rag doll," we wonder if this is a hallucination, or a cog in a diabolical conspiracy?

Lieutenant Walker searches the building, finds nothing, and scoffs at Elaine, requesting that she stop stirring up trouble and cease ringing his phone all day and all night.

Elaine also seems to be shattered by such items as a sailboat pin, little white flowers, a blonde wig, and the numbers 1-4-1-2-7 scrawled on a matchbook. John plans to send her to a Swiss sanitarium, away from "that evil old monstrosity" across the road. But at the end, the chain-smoking, troubled young heiress, tormented by the infidelities of two husbands, turns the tables 180 degrees—not unlike the topsy-turvy denouement of *Catch Me If You Can* (1965)—by coaxing John and Blanche to the tenement, shooting them both, and phoning Lieutenant Walker with the announcement that there are two bodies in the building across the street. She continues to babble that as soon as she discovered that her husband and her friend had betrayed her, she bought the building and secretly put a chair by the window. She then began to improvise on all sorts of silly little things so that everyone will think that she was crazy.

Elaine appeals to Lieutenant Walker to search the building. Otherwise, she says, the two bodies will forever be boarded with rats. Walker, gruffly, refuses to do so. "That's exactly what I always thought you'd say," mutters Elaine. She hangs up and smiles, "from the very beginning."

* * *

Night Watch, directed by Fred Coe, opened at New York's Morosco Theatre on February 28, 1972, to mostly favorable reviews. "Miss Fletcher knows exactly what she is doing, goes about her business with gratifying swiftness and comes up with a finish worthy of one of Roald Dahl's little nifties," wrote Douglas Watt.[1] "Miss Fletcher knows her way around in the field of deceptive skullduggery, and her new play, aided by an excellent cast of tricksters, headed by Joan Hackett, fulfills all the requirements for an evening of satisfying menace and mystification," chirped Richard Watts.[2] "This is the kind of play that makes you think of Hitchcock, and even its ingenuity—and it is ingenious—is that of a master poker player, rather than a detective writer," approved Clive Barnes.[3]

The naysayers were savage. "Every surprise is a cliché. . . . Most of its scenes and characters are unnecessary," sniffed Martin Gottfried.[4] "*Night Watch* is merely a lazy mystery. . . . Happens to be a flop, even on its own terms," frowned Leonard Harris.[5]

Night Watch ran for 121 performances, becoming a popular fixture with summer-stock companies and little theatres.[6]

The play was revived by Manhattan's Equity Library Theatre on December 4, 1986. A tepid movie version was made in England in 1973, directed by Brian G, Hutton, with Elizabeth Taylor and Laurence Harvey as the hostile couple.

* * *

Violet Lucille Fletcher was born in Brooklyn, New York, in 1912 to a father who was a marine draftsman. She attended Vassar College, where she received a degree in 1933, and she got her first job as a receptionist-typist at CBS Music Clearance, earning $15 a week. She soon began writing publicity items for CBS and articles for *Movie Mirror* and the *New Yorker*.

After a five-year courtship, Fletcher married composer Bernard Herrmann and together they worked on several projects. Herrmann wrote the score for his wife's television presentation of *The Hitch-Hiker*, and Fletcher penned the libretto for his operatic adaptation of *Wuthering Heights*. The couple was divorced in 1948.[7] The following year, Fletcher married writer Douglas Wallop, author of *The Year the Yankees Lost the Pennant*, on which the musical *Damn Yankees* was based.

Fletcher's career leaped forward when she wrote a half-dozen suspenseful radio plays, of which the better known are *The Hitch-Hiker* (1941), created for Orson Welles, a shuddery tale about a Brooklynite embarking on a cross-country drive, and *Sorry, Wrong Number* (1944), with Agnes Moorhead portraying a neurotic woman who overhears a murder plan on the telephone. Barbara Stanwyck played the role in a 1948 movie version, expanded by Fletcher; Shelley Winters in a 1954 live television broadcast of *Climax!*; Loni Anderson in a 1989 cable TV rendition. Both *The Hitch-Hiker* and *Sorry, Wrong Number* have been adapted to the stage by Fletcher, and published as companion pieces by Dramatists Play Service.

In the 1950s and 1960s Fletcher contributed episodes to the television series *Lights Out*, *Granada Workshop*, and *The Twilight Zone*.

Fletcher's novels of psychological terror are *Blindfold* (1960), *. . . and Presumed Dead* (1963), *The Strange Blue Yawl* (1964), *The Girl in Cabin B54* (1968), *Eighty Dollars to Stamford* (1975), and *Mirror Image* (1988). "The typical suspense novel of Lucille Fletcher is less concerned with the solution of a mystery than with the anticipation and fear which the protagonist and the reader experience," writes Kathleen Gregory Klein in *St. James Guide to Crime and Mystery Writers*. "Fear of the unknown, followed by relief of the tension, concluded with a destroying revelation which provides a distinctive twist to the plot."[8]

Acting Edition: Dramatists Play Service.

Awards and Honors: Mystery Writers of America Edgar Allan Poe Award, 1960—Best Radio Drama: *Sorry, Wrong Number* (Suspense/CBS).

NOTES

1. *Daily News*, February 29, 1972.
2. *New York Post*, February 29, 1972.
3. *New York Times*, February 29, 1972.
4. *Women's Wear Daily*, March 1, 1972.
5. WCBS TV2, February 28, 1972.
6. *Night Watch* proved its lasting potency when I staged it twice—during the summer of 1985 at the New London Barn Playhouse, New London, New Hampshire ("A good thriller will use you, abuse you, and pick your pocket," wrote Al Keith in *Upbeat*, June 25, 1985. "*Night Watch* succeeded admirably in doing all those things and more."), and in August 1986 at the Elmira College Summer Theatre, Elmira, New York ("There's an interesting mystery to solve, and a trick ending to savor," stated Danielle Farnbaugh in the *Star Gazette*, August 9, 1986).
7. Bernard Herrmann (1911–1975) composed his recognized intense music for Orson Welles's *Citizen Kane* and *The Magnificent Ambersons*; William Dieterle's *The Devil and Daniel Webster* (1941), for which he garnered his one Oscar; François Truffault's *The Bride Wore Black*; the science fiction *The Day the Earth Stood Still*, *Journey to the Centre of the Earth*, and *Fahrenheit 451*; the suspenseful *Hangover Square*, *Five Fingers*, *On Dangerous Ground*, *Cape Fear*, and *Obsession*; the period adventures *The 7th Voyage of Sinbad*, *The Three Worlds of Gulliver*, *Mysterious Island*, and *Jason and the Argonauts*; and the dramas *Anna and the King of Siam*, *The Egyptian*, *The Snows of Kilimanjaro*, and *Taxi Driver*. Herrmann will mostly be remembered for his association with Alfred Hitchcock, with whom he had a stormy but fruitful relationship, providing the music for *The Wrong Man*, *The Man Who Knew Too Much*, *Vertigo*, *North by Northwest*, *Psycho*, *The Birds*, and *Marnie*. For television, Herrmann wrote the theme music for the first season of *The Twilight Zone* and incidental music for episodes in *Alfred Hitchcock Presents*, *The Alfred Hitchcock Hour*, *Perry Mason*, *Gunsmoke*, *Rawhide*, and *The Virginian*.
8. Jay P. Pederson, ed., *St. James Guide to Crime and Mystery Writers*, 4th ed. (Detroit, MI: St. James Press, 1996), 364.

Fiddlers Three (1972)

Agatha Christie (England, 1890–1976)

Agatha Christie was eighty years old when she wrote her last play, a comedy-thriller initially called *Fiddlers Five*. Following a brief, problematic tour during the summer of 1971, the Queen of Crime rewrote the play, merged two of the characters, and changed the title to *Fiddlers Three*.

The plot concerns several collaborators who attempt to conceal the body of a dead tycoon in order to get their hands on a hundred-thousand-pound inheritance. What begins as a lark turns ugly when they realize that the cadaver was the victim of murder and that no doubt they will become the main suspects.

Fiddlers Three, directed by Allan Davis, opened at the Yvonne Arnaud Theatre in Guilford, Surrey, on August 1, 1972. Christie attended the premiere as guest of honor. On August 4, the *Surrey Advertiser* reported, "*Fiddlers Three*, alas, fails to live up to the author's standards. A plot of mystifying complexity and total implausibility finds its development and resolution through coincidences which would be accepted in farce, but rob the more sober medium of credibility."[1]

Fiddlers Three toured for a few weeks but never made it to the West End. It was a sad epitaph for Christie, author of such masterful plays as *Ten Little Indians*, *Witness for the Prosecution*, and *The Mousetrap*. She nonetheless remains the best-selling novelist of all time.

NOTE

1. Charles Osborne, *The Life and Crimes of Agatha Christie* (London: Collins, 1982), 227.

Lady Audley's Secret (1972)

Douglas Seale (England, 1913–1999)

Lady Audley's Secret, a pioneering novel of detection by Mary Elizabeth Braddon, was one of the most popular books of the nineteenth century and since its publication in 1862 has never been out of print. The three-volume first edition of *Lady Audley's Secret* is one of the great rarities of Victorian fiction.

"Murder, bigamy, adultery: These were the special ingredients that made the sensation novel so delectable to the Victorian palate," writes Susan Balee in her introduction to a 2005 publication of the book. "Indeed, it was these elements that gave the genre its 'sensational' reputation in the 1860s. Readers who devoured *Lady Audrey's Secret* were thrilled and frightened by its inversion of the ideal Victorian heroine. Lady Audley *looks* like the angel-in-the-house ideal of Victorian womanhood—she is blonde, fragile, childlike—but her behavior is distinctly villainous. . . . Part detective story, part domestic drama, *Lady Audley's Secret* became a runaway best seller of its era and beyond."[1]

The novel spawned many stage adaptations and several silent and talkie motion pictures. A 1972 musical version of *Lady Audley's Secret*, with book by Douglas Seale, lyrics by John Kunz, and music by George Goehring, sets the action in 1890s England. The curtain rises on the Lime Tree Walk leading to Audley Court. The villagers are in the midst of a folk dance. Phoebe, maid to Lady Audley, and butler Luke Marks, her betrothed, are among the dancers. Luke tries to steal a kiss but Phoebe resists. Luke declares that he'll break her high spirits when they are wed.

Lady Audley, young and beautiful, comes running in, closely followed by her husband, Sir Michael, seventy years of age and somewhat out of breath. Lady Audley has planned a series of festivities for Sir Michael's birthday. "What a happy old man you make me," he says, and contentedly sings "The English Country Life."

Sir Michael's daughter, Alicia, arrives dressed in a riding habit. She is looking for Sir Michael's nephew, Robert Audley, and is annoyed that

Robert is so late. Sir Michael decries Alicia's sour spirit, which reminds him of his first wife, Alicia's mother.

Phoebe breaks through the fourth wall and relates directly to the audience how much happier Lady Audley is in her marriage to Sir Michael than in her previous life as "the daughter of a ne'er-do-well and impoverished sea-faring man." She remembers sharing an attic room with Lady Audley, when they told each other their "closest secrets." Phoebe vows that Lady Audley's secret is safe with her.

Captain Robert Audley enters with a flourish—a handsome young man dressed in military uniform. He is accompanied by his friend George Talboys, who is wearing the clothes of deep mourning. George recently returned from Bombay and found out that his beloved wife, Helen, had passed away. George sings "That Lady in Eng-a-land," wherein he tells of the wife he left behind to be able to provide for her. The letters and telegrams he sent her from India were not answered, and he was shocked to read about her passing in a newspaper announcement: "Died in London, May 2nd, 1860—Helen, wife of George Talboys, R.I.P." George vows to find Helen's grave and raise a monument.

Alicia appears and greets Robert, who is curious about his stepmother. "A perfect wax doll, as regards complexion," says Alicia acidly. "Fair as the day when in good temper, but black as night if she can't rule everybody as she likes." Alicia shows them her watch, which contains a miniature painting of Lady Audley. Robert is impressed by the "gentle, innocent-looking face," but George is startled to see the image of his "dead" wife. He stalks away.

Alicia is upset that Robert has not asked her a particular question that she hoped he would. Lady Audley walks in and is taken by Robert's good looks. Robert, too, seems to be affected by "the prettiest little creature I ever saw." Alicia maneuvers Robert away. Left by herself, Lady Audley is about to swoon, her heart pounds, her temples throb, and she can scarcely catch her breath. The gallant captain has left his mark. Sir Michael, though good and kind, is elderly.

Lady Audley congratulates herself for the cunning device she used to convince her first husband, George, of her premature demise. Suddenly, someone touches her shoulder. She turns and recognizes George with a shriek. "You are a traitress, madam," he says, and threatens to expose her. She complains that she thought herself deserted when he went off to India and states ominously that she will use the power of her position to silence him. But George insists that "a prison's roof will cover the head" of this "bigamous wretch."

Lady Audley whispers an aside, "Die! Die! That is the only way of escape." She pretends to feel faint and asks George to bring her some water from the well. As he does, she creeps up, strikes him with an iron handle, and pushes him down the well. She does not realize that the butler Luke has witnessed the deed from behind a tree. Exalted, she sings "Dead Men Tell No Tales." (The playwright suggests that as the number progresses, the piano accompanist can get gradually carried away with his own exuberant playing, much to the annoyance of Lady Audley. At the conclusion of the song she can give him a disgusted look, take a pistol, and fire a shot at him as the curtain falls. The accompanist wears a bloody bandage on his head during the second act.)

Act II unfolds twelve months later in the conservatory of Audley Court. The butler and maid dance as they clean the room. Sir Michael enters with Alicia. He asks her to be patient with Robert, who has been distracted by the mysterious disappearance of his friend. Alicia sings "An Old Maid," expressing her concern for a lonely future, and Sir Michael agrees to speak to his nephew and hurry things along.

Alicia questions Lady Audley's sincerity, and Sir Michael rebukes her for speaking about his wife in such a manner. Lady Audley joins them, and Alicia suggests that cousin Robert, instead of moping in the library, call in the constabulary to search for his missing friend. Lady Audley does not think it is necessary to bother the police; after all, they know very little about George Talboys, who left without as much as a "thank you." Alicia runs off and Sir Michael pursues her, trying to give solace.

Luke, drunk, enters and threatens to blackmail Lady Audley: he tells her that he witnessed her pushing George down the well. She agrees to meet him after dark, bringing 100 pounds. He kisses her roughly, hints that there'll be more than money to give him tonight, and exits laughing.

Robert enters and announces that after twelve weary months of searching, he has found "the vital clue, the missing link in the chain." He shows Lady Audley a letter she wrote to George and accuses her of bigamy and, he suspects, murder. She snatches the letter and reminds him that exposing her will tarnish the Audley name forever. Robert demands that she leave the country or he will go to the authorities. Tomorrow he will accompany her to London and see her off on a boat train for Paris. Robert stalks out and Lady Audley decides to stick to her motto, "Death or victory."

Alicia enters in tears, followed by Sir Michael. She's upset because Robert has postponed their marriage and because she's seen the attraction between him and Lady Audley. Lady Audley decides to use Alicia's misplaced concern to her advantage. She tells them in the song "La De Da Da" that Robert swore his love to her, and she requests that Sir Michael send "the base fellow" away.

Robert enters and announces that he is embarking on a trip for a few days. He asks that Lady Audley come with him to London. Sir Michael is aghast. He accuses Robert of "carnality and lust" and demands that he leave immediately. They argue until Sir Michael is overcome and, clutching his heart, has to be carried off. Robert concludes that his uncle's outburst must be the result of Lady Audley's instigation. He leaves with a vow "to show her to the world in her true colors."

Robert takes a room at the nearby Castle Inn, where he encounters Luke at the bar. The inebriated butler mumbles about Lady Audley and her great secret. Late at night, Lady Audley sets the inn ablaze with a hurricane lamp, clearly hoping to rid herself of the two men who threaten her security.

The last scene takes place on Lime Tree Walk. Moonlight falls on the old well. Robert reveals himself to Lady Audley, who is shaken to find him alive. No, says Robert, he was not asleep when her wicked hands set fire to the inn, and he is going to avenge the murder of his friend. Lady Audley produces a stiletto from her stockings, but Robert wrenches the weapon from her hand. Phoebe enters, leading Luke, who is near death. Luke manages to point at the well, whispers, "She pushed him down that well . . . but George Talboys is . . . " and falls on the ground dead. At that moment, George Talboys appears. Though his motives were base, Luke saved him!

Lady Audley is petrified. She begins to stutter incoherently, and Phoebe reveals that, in truth, Lady Audley is mad. Her mother had been taken off to an insane asylum, and Lady Audley's blood is tainted with the same malady. Phoebe promised her lady never to tell this story to anyone. Lady Audley utters, "Let the grave, the cold grave, close over Lady Audley and her secret" and falls dead. All surround her body and croon "Forgive Her, Forgive Her." The curtain descends on a tableau of sympathy.

* * *

Lady Audley's Secret opened at off-Broadway's Eastside Playhouse on October 3, 1972, and ran for eight performances. The Shaw Festival of Niagara-on-the-Falls, Ontario, Canada, presented the musical in 1978, and the Dallas Theatre Center, Texas, produced it during the 1983–1984 season.

An introductory note in the published text of the play states: "In adapting the novel for the musical stage the authors have attempted to enter into the spirit of the period, and have drawn upon its musical and dramatic conventions in an effort to recapture the flavor, attitudes, and platitudes of Victorian England. Visually the play should have an undisguised air of theatricality. Gestures are grand, voices throb, the scenery is undeniably painted, the fire is an obvious but thrilling 'effect,' the piano player thrusts himself into the action underscoring every emotional exchange. In short, the audience must never forget that it is participating in an act of make believe."[2]

* * *

Lady Audley's Secret seems to be the only play on record written by Douglas Seale. A London-born actor/producer/director, Seale enjoyed a sixty-five-year transatlantic career on stage, screen, and television. He studied at the Royal Academy of Dramatic Art and got his first West End role in 1934 at the age of twenty-one. Following World War II, when he served in the Royal Signals, Seale joined the Shakespeare Memorial Theatre Company for two seasons at Stratford-on-Avon. A Shakespearean specialist, he directed *Caesar and Cleopatra* at the Birmingham Repertory Theatre; *King John* at Stratford, Ontario; *Henry V* at Stratford, Connecticut; and *King Lear* for the Main Shakespeare Festival in San Francisco. Seale also staged Henrik Ibsen's *A Doll's House*, John Osborne's *Look Back in Anger* in Cleveland, and Terence Rattigan's *The Winslow Boy* in New York.

In later years Seale focused on performing. He made his Broadway debut at age sixty with *Emperor Henry IV* in 1973, followed by *Frankenstein*, *The Dresser*, and *The Madwoman of Chaillot*. He earned a Tony Award nomination in 1983 as Selsdon Mowbray, the alcoholic actor, in Michael Frayn's comedy *Noises Off*. One of his last stage roles was the aging vaudevillian Billy Rice in the 1996 revival of Osborne's *Look Back in Anger*.

Beginning in 1937 and for the next sixty years Seale appeared in many television shows, including *The Lucie Arnaz Show*, *Amazing Stories*, *The Wizard*, *Cheers*, *Rags to Riches*, *Hunter*, *Family Ties*, and *The Golden Girls*. In the movies, Seale appeared as Count Arco in *Amadeus* (1984) and as Santa Claus in *Ernest Saves Christmas* (1988). He also provided the voice of Krebbs in the animated *Rescuers Down Under* (1990) and the voice of the sultan in *Aladdin* (1992).

Seale was married three times. His third wife was stage actress and three-time Tony Award nominee Louise Troy, who died of breast cancer in 1994. Five years later, Seale passed away at Manhattan's St. Vincent Hospital at age eighty-five.

* * *

Mary Elizabeth Braddon was born in Soho, London, in 1835. She was brought up by her mother, Fanny, who in 1840 separated from her solicitor husband upon discovering that he had been having an affair. Fanny was an avid reader, and under her influence, young Mary became acquainted with the novels of Dickens, Thackeray, and Bulwer-Lytton.

Tall, good-looking, and gifted with a fine speaking voice, Braddon decided upon the then-despised career of actress. Under the pseudonym "Mary Seyton," she performed with several companies, touring provincial towns in England and Scotland.

In 1860, Braddon left the stage and returned to London to pursue a writing career. She became the toast of the town with her first two novels, *Lady Audley's Secret* (1862) and *Aurora Floyd* (1863), both serialized in magazines belonging to publisher John Maxwell (1824–1895). Shortly after meeting Maxwell, Braddon set up a home with him, despite the fact that he was married and the father of six children. His wife was confined to a Dublin asylum. When she died in 1874, Braddon and Maxwell married and had six children of their own.

While raising twelve children, Braddon managed to write three novels per year, producing altogether more than eighty works, many with criminous plots. Allen J. Hubin's *The Bibliography of Crime Fiction, 1749–1975* lists 104 novels (some published under separate titles in England and the United States) and five short-story collections by Braddon. *Victorian Detective Fiction*, a catalogue collected by Dorothy Glover and Graham Greene, includes Braddon's *Henry Dunbar: The Story of an Outcast* (1864), in which the sleuth is Mr. Carter, a private detective; the detective of *Charlotte's Inheritance* (1868) is a lawyer, Vale Hawkehurst; and the detective of *Publicans and Sinners* (1873) is a surgeon, Lucius Davoren. Another surgeon, George Gerrard, solves the case of *The Cloven Foot* (1879); *Thou Art the Man* (1894) features an early female detective, Coralie Urquhart, a lady's companion; a professional investigator, Mr. Faunce of the CID Bow Street, is the hero of *Rough Justice* (1898) and *His Darling Sin* (1899); Sergeant Jo Peters is on *The Trail of the Serpent* (1890).

In 1866, Braddon founded *Belgravia Magazine*, which featured sensational novels, travel accounts, poems, and biographical sketches, all accompanied by lavish illustrations. She also edited *Temple Bar Magazine* and the Christmas annual *The Mistletoe Bough*, as well as contributing essays and poems to the periodicals *Punch* and *The World*. She died of a cerebral hemorrhage in 1915 in Richmond-upon-Thames, Surrey, England, and was interred in Richmond Cemetery. A bronze wall memorial plaque in Richmond Parish Church, which just calls her "Miss Braddon," was unveiled that year.

* * *

The first stage adaptation of *Lady Audley's Secret* was penned by William E. Suter (1811–1882), a prolific melodramatist who wrote such titles as *The Child Stealers*, *The Pirates of Savannah*, and *Outlaw of the Adriatic*. Suter's version premiered at the Queen's Theatre, London, on February 21, 1863, with Marion Jackson as Lady Audley. A great emphasis was placed on humorous elements, rendered by Bibbles (a butler) and Bubbles (a footman). A week later, a more faithful adaptation, by George Roberts, was produced at the St. James's Theatre, London, by manageress

Louisa Herbert, who also starred in the title role. A third Victorian version, darker and more violent, was provided by Colin Henry Hazlewood (1823–1875), author of more than a hundred plays. It debuted at the Royal Victoria Theatre, London, on May 25, 1863, with Maria Daly as Lady Audley. American actresses who exploited their art and temperament as Lady Audley at the turn of the twentieth century included D. P. Bowers, Mrs. McCauley, and Rachel Johnson.

The C. H. Hazlewood adaptation was revived, for sixteen performances, at Theatre Royal, Stratford East, on June 12, 1950, featuring Margaret Wolfit. An anonymous version opened at London's Princess Theatre on November 15, 1949, with Pat Nye, and ran for thirty-nine showings.

In 1965, Caryl Jenner's production at London's Arts Theatre, featuring Ursula Jones as Lady Audley, garnered praise in the monthly *Plays and Players* for the play's "well-oiled swift-moving plot," but reviewer Frank Cox objected to "too much sense of tongue-in-cheek panache hovering near the surface in the team of skilled performers." Cox advocated "a little less of the invitation to jeer and more awareness of the not-so-hidden quality of this particular piece."[3]

Brian J. Burton (1922–), author of the period melodramas *The Murder of Maria Marten, Sweeney Todd the Barber,* and *East Lynne or Lady Isabel's Shame,* dramatized Braddon's novel under the title *Lady Audley's Secret, or Death in Lime Tree Walk.* It opened at the Little Theatre in Leicester, England, on February 9, 1966, with Darien Thomas as the story's femme fatale. The text is punctured with thirty-nine musical cues to accent frequent shifts of mood. Burton recommends that his play be acted "very earnestly in the 'grand manner' with plenty of attack and projection with just an edge of overplaying."[4]

Constance Cox (1912–1998), who in 1952 adapted Oscar Wilde's short story *Lord Arthur Savile's Crime* into a three-act play, in 1976 went in the opposite direction and condensed the sprawling novel of *Lady Audley's Secret* to a one-act playlet, with all the action unfolding in the garden of Audley Court. At the climax of this mini version, Lady Audley draws a dagger from her belt and attacks Robert. After losing the encounter, she stabs herself to death.

Lady Audley's Secret was filmed as a silent feature in 1912, 1915 (titled *Secrets of Society,* starring Theda Bara), and 1920; adapted to television in England in 2000 with Neve McIntosh; broadcast that year in the United States on PBS's *Mystery!* series; and aired by UK's BBC Radio 4 in 2009.

Acting Edition: Music Theatre International.

Awards and Honors: Douglas Seale received the 1970 Joseph Jefferson Award for Best Director of a Play for George Bernard Shaw's *Heartbreak House* at the Goodman Theatre in Chicago, Illinois. In 1999, the London newspaper *Daily Telegraph* named *Lady Audley's Secret* one of the world's

100 best novels. A number of streets in Richmond, England, are named after characters created by Mary Elizabeth Braddon.

NOTES

1. Mary Elizabeth Braddon, *Lady Audley's Secret* (New York: Barnes & Noble, 2005), ix.

2. Douglas Seale, *Lady Audley's Secret* (New York: Music Theatre International, 1974), unpaginated.

3. *Plays and Players*, February 1965.

4. Brian J. Burton, *Lady Audley's Secret, or Death in Lime Tree Walk* (Birmingham, England: C. Combridge, 1966), 77.

Dracula (1973)

Crane Johnson (United States)

"*Dracula*, Dramatic Version Freely Adapted by Crane Johnson from the Novel by Bram Stoker" premiered at off-Broadway's Royal Playhouse, New York City, in August 1973 and ran the entire theatre season, until June 1974. The action unfolds in "the study of Dr. Seward in his English manor house" and replicates the outline of the popular Deane-Balderston adaptation, but Johnson takes liberties with plot maneuvers and the cast of characters.

In Johnson's *Dracula*, Dr. Seward and Lucy are lovers planning to get married. Mrs. Emily Harker, Lucy's aunt, is a house guest aiding in the preparation of the nuptial festivities. Professor Van Helsing, summoned by Steward to look into his fiancée's deteriorating health, is a whip-carrying, cigar-smoking woman.[1]

Count Dracula appears here only briefly, while the role of the asylum inmate Renfield has been enlarged, with more entrances, lines, and "moments" than any other character. One of the most fascinating scenes depicts a face-to-face encounter between Renfield and Van Helsing during which the professor asserts, "We metaphysicians are interested in being, of life both here and beyond; life on all manifest levels; of the transference of life." The madman squeals, "Oh yes, the transference. I know. I know. I know. There is life in everything. There is life in a fly and that life can be transferred. And there is life in a spider and that life can be transferred. And life in a sparrow . . . I catch a fly and swallow it. That life—the life of the fly becomes part of me, part of my life, and the spider I swallow becomes part of me, part of my life, and the sparrow I swallow becomes part of me, part of my life, and I am no longer merely Renfield, but *am* the fly, the spider, and the sparrow."

In order to protect Lucy, Van Helsing surrounds her with wild roses, mountain ash, garlic, and crucifixes. But inadvertently, the maid Abigail removes "the mess" of vampire antidotes, thus clearing the path for

Count Dracula to enter stealthily, approach the sleeping Lucy, and put his teeth to her throat as the lights fade.

In the next scene we learn that Lucy has died. Mournfully, Van Helsing concludes that she is the beautiful young lady who has been luring children playing out on Hampstead Heath, causing them to disappear and die—with two pinpricks on their throats. On the heels of an intense search for Lucy, they find her hidden in a coffin. Van Helsing reports to Seward that she drove a stake through Lucy's heart and then cut off her head: "Now your Lucy is at peace. . . . Her soul is free." However, the insatiable Count immediately shifts his attention to Mina Harker.

An investigation reveals that Dracula's Carfax home is a clone of Seward's abode—the two houses were built a hundred years ago on an estate owned by twin brothers. "Is it not possible there was made an underground passage between the two?" Van Helsing wonders. Presto: they swing a bookcase aside, discover an opening, and Seward exits through it with a wooden stake and a long knife.

Critic Howard Thompson of the *New York Times* praised Johnson's "modest production" and its four rotating casts: "Their unified dignity, the quaint, rustling Victorian garb and, above all, those lines make it eerily worthwhile. Leave the gore to all those flicks."[2]

Acting Edition: Dramatists Play Service.

NOTES

1. A note inserted into the acting edition of the play informs us, "During the run of the New York City production of *Dracula*, the part of Professor Van Helsing was portrayed by three different actresses. The first was a tall Black woman who was quite heavy. She wore colorful satin gowns, with lots of ostrich feathers and jewels. Actress number two was an English lady in her sixties, barely over five feet tall, and she played the role as if in an Agatha Christie mystery. The third was a young model who displayed beautiful gowns. All three were most successful and convincing in playing the role of Professor Van Helsing." Crane Johnson, *Dracula* (New York: Dramatists Play Service, 1975), 4.

2. *New York Times*, January 17, 1974.

Equus (1973)

Peter Shaffer (England, 1926–)

Why did a seventeen-year-old stable boy drive a steel spike into the eyes of six horses entrusted to his care? In a quest to decipher the motive for this bizarre crime, psychiatrist Martin Dysart attempts to journey into Alan Strang's mind by piecing together the circumstances that led to the act of violence. Peter Shaffer loosely based his psychological thriller on a real-life event. But, in a program note, the playwright asserts, "Every person and incident in *Equus* is my own invention, save the crime itself; and even that I modified to accord with what I feel to be acceptable theatrical proportion."[1]

Equus unfolds in a fenced-in square of wood resembling a railed boxing ring. The actors sit on scattered benches throughout the evening, stepping into the arena for their scenes. Some members of the audience are seated on raised tiers surrounding the set. Overhead hangs a battery of exposed spotlights. Downstage, to the left and right, stand two ladders on which are suspended horse masks made of alternating bands of silver wire and leather, to be donned by six actors emulating horses, wearing track suits of chestnut velvet, strutted hooves on their feet, and long gloves on their hands.

The published version of the script specifies that the horsemen should avoid the literal pantomime of the animal: "The actors should never crouch on all fours, or even bend forward. They must always stand upright, as if the body of the horse extended visibly behind them. Animal effect must be created entirely mimetically, through the use of legs, knees, neck, face, and the turn of the head which can move the mask above it through all the gestures of equine wariness and pride."[2]

The main action of the play takes place in the Rokeby Psychiatric Hospital in Southern England. The proceedings are divided into two acts comprised of thirty-five kaleidoscopic sequences, indicating a change of time or locale or mood.

Dysart's initial meetings with the disturbed Alan are confrontational. The boy mockingly sings commercial jingles and avoids any direct answers. Doggedly and methodically, Dysart breaks Alan's resistance and wins his confidence. Under the influence of a "truth drug" and hypnotism, the teen goes through a series of agonizing recollections.

Dysart learns of Alan's troubled childhood with a frigid, fanatically religious mother and an authoritarian, self-righteous father. Oppressed, the stable groom has formed a close relationship with his horses, riding them clandestinely at night, immersed in a brew of love, ecstasy, sexual desires, and godlike worship. His favorite equus ("horse" in Latin) is Nugget, "gentle as a baby, but terribly fast . . . mightiest of horses."

In a climactic scene, pictured through a flashback, Alan is coaxed to the stable at night by the attractive Jill Mason, but his attempt to make love falters. "I couldn't . . . see her," he tells Dysart, "only Him. Every time I kissed her—He was in the way."

Alan confides that when touching Jill, he longed for the horse Nugget. Exasperated, he snatches an invisible pick and, his face distorted, possessed, orders the girl out. She darts away from the barn. The six horses surround Alan, their hooves stamping angrily, accusing him of betrayal. Alan looks at them in terror and cries, "Eyes—white eyes—never close—eyes like flames—no more, no more, Equus." He moves slowly toward Nugget with the pick concealed behind his back. He stabs out Nugget's eyes, dashes at the other horses and blinds them, too.

A great screaming begins to permeate the theatre. The whole arena is filled with cannoning, blinded horses—and the lad dodging among them, avoiding their slashing hooves. Finally they plunge off into darkness and out of sight. Alan is left in convulsions on the floor.

Dysart scoops the boy into his arms and carries him over to a bench, soothing him, promising him that his dilemma is all over now, that he will have no more nightmares.

However, the psychiatrist laments that while untangling Alan's mental disturbance, exorcising his demons and delivering him to a safe, painless world, a high price will be paid—the loss of thrilling passion, entombment in mundane existence, the kind of sphere that he himself is saddled with: an unhappy marriage and a shrunken, pallid, and provincial way of life.

* * *

Equus was first presented on July 26, 1973, by England's National Theatre at the Old Vic, running for sixty performances in repertory. Alec McCowen played the psychiatrist, with Peter Firth as the adolescent offender. Firth joined director John Dexter and designer John Napier in a New York premiere at the Plymouth Theatre on October 24, 1974, for a whopping run of 1,209 performances. Anthony Hopkins played Dysart, supported by Frances Sternhagen and Michael Higgins as Alan's parents, Roberta Maxwell as Jill Mason, and Everett McGill as Horseman Nugget.

The critics were ecstatic. "Peter Shaffer's taut and rather flashy little thriller is gripping theatre," said Douglas Watt.[3] "By combining so skillfully the primal elements of theatre, by saying so much on one hand and leaving so much to our imaginations on the other, *Equus* becomes one of the most powerful and provocative theatrical experiences of our time," lauded Edwin Wilson.[4] "*Equus* proves, quite brilliantly, that there is nothing wrong with Broadway that a little ritual savagery can't help," wrote Howard Kissel.[5] "It is a kind of highbrow suspense story, a psychic and mythic thriller, but also an essay in character and motive. . . . It has a most refreshing and mind-opening intellectualism," claimed Clive Barnes.[6] "Simply a devastating experience . . . breathtaking," applauded Martin Gottfried.[7] "It is a devilishly masterful work of craftsmanship . . . As pure theatre, *Equus* is not to be missed," hailed Jack Kroll.[8]

During the long run on Broadway, Anthony Perkins, Richard Burton, Douglas Campbell, and Alec McCowen portrayed Martin Dysart; Thomas Hulce, Jacob Milligan, Keith McDermott, Ralph Seymour, and Michael Snyder enacted the role of Alan Strang.

Throughout the 1970s, *Equus* was presented at Studio Arena Theatre, Buffalo, New York; Queen Elizabeth Theatre, Vancouver; Manitoba Theater Center, Winnipeg; American Conservatory Theatre, San Francisco, California; Seattle Center Playhouse, Seattle, Washington; Theatre Calgary, Alberta; South Coast Repertory Theatre, Costa Mesa, California; Dallas Theatre Center, Dallas, Texas; Huntington Hartford Theatre, Los Angeles, California; Trinity Square Repertory Company, Providence, Rhode Island; John F. Kennedy Center, Eisenhower Theatre, Washington, D.C.; the Cleveland Playhouse, Cleveland, Ohio; Old Globe Theatre, San Diego, California; and National Arts Center Theatre Company, Ottawa, Ontario.

Equus has been resuscitated by Massachusetts' Berkshire Theatre Festival in 2005, with Walter Slezak as psychologist Martin Dysart and Randy Harrison as Alan Strang, and two years later at London's Gielgud Theatre, featuring Richard Griffiths, winner of the 2006 Tony and Olivier Awards for Best Actor in *The History Boys*, and Daniel Radcliffe, a nineteen-year-old actor made famous by the *Harry Potter* films. The West End production, directed by Thea Sharrock, was transferred to Broadway's Broadhurst Theatre in September 2008 for a limited engagement of twenty-two weeks. In the summer of 2009, the Chandler Studio Theatre of North Hollywood, California, revived *Equus* "with exceptional results," according to reviewer David C. Nichols in the *Los Angeles Times*.[9] *Equus* rode again at the John Drew Theatre in East Hampton, New York, during

June of 2010, with the marquee attraction of Alec Baldwin as Dr. Martin Dysart and Sam Underwood as Alan Strang.

Equus was adapted to the cinema in 1977. Sidney Lumet directed Richard Burton and Peter Firth in the lead roles. "Peter Shaffer's shattering play makes bumpy screen adaptation, its vivid theatricality lost on film," bemoaned critic Leonard Maltin.[10]

* * *

Peter Levin Shaffer was born to a Jewish family in Liverpool, England, in 1926. He is the twin brother of playwright Anthony (*Sleuth*) Shaffer, with whom he wrote three detective novels: *The Woman in the Wardrobe* (1951), *How Doth the Little Crocodile?* (1952), and *Withered Murder* (1955). The two siblings studied at Trinity College of Cambridge University and worked as conscripts in coal mines from 1944 to 1947.

Peter came to New York City in 1951 and worked as a salesman at Lord & Taylor's' department store, as a cashier at Grand Central Station, and as an assistant at the New York Public Library. In 1954 he returned to London, supported himself as a clerk for a music publisher and a literary critic for the weekly *Truth*, and launched his show business career penning *The Salt Land* (1955), a drama set in modern Israel, and *Balance of Terror* (1957), an espionage thriller, both broadcast on British television.

His first stage play, 1958's *Five Finger Exercise*, a tantalizing study of a dysfunctional middle-class family, was a smash hit, artistically and commercially, in London and New York, winning prizes on both shores of the Atlantic, including the New York Drama Critics Circle Award as Best Foreign Play. *Five Finger Exercise* was filmed in 1962 and televised as a BBC Play of the Month in 1970.

Additional successes by Peter Shaffer included the double bill *The Private Ear* and *The Public Eye*, amusing one-act plays sharing the theme of the eternal triangle (London, 1962; New York, 1963). The latter, about a suspicious accountant who engages an unorthodox private detective to spy on his wife, was adapted to the screen by Shaffer in 1972. *The Merry Roosters Panto*, aka *It's about Cinderella*, a variation on the traditional fairytale with music and songs, was written for Joan Littlewood's Theatre Workshop in 1963. *The Royal Hunt of the Sun*, a spectacular pageant concerning the sixteenth-century conquest of Peru, premiered at the Chichester Festival in 1964; it became the first work by a contemporary playwright to be done by the National Theatre at the Old Vic under the direction of Laurence Olivier. New Yorkers flocked to see the epic at the ANTA Theatre, beginning October 26, 1965, for 261 performances. At the climax, Spanish adventurer Francisco Pizarro allows his bloodthirsty men to strangle Atahuallpa, the God/King of the Incas, in the futile hope of conquering death. The play was filmed in 1969.

White Lies, a one-act about fortune-telling, and *Black Comedy*, a farce in which much of the action is supposed to take place in the dark with myriad mistaken identities, were introduced as companion pieces in Chichester, England, in 1965, and taken to Broadway's Ethel Barrymore Theatre two years later for 337 performances. In tandem with a new production of *Black Comedy* at the Lyric Theatre, London, in 1968, the first playlet was entirely revamped and retitled *The White Liars*. As such, the double bill was revived by New York's Roundabout Theatre Company in 1993, running thirty-eight performances.

The protagonist of *The Battle of Shrivings* (London's Lyric Theatre, 1970) is an elderly philosopher who pits his wits against a famous anti-liberal poet.

Amadeus, the celebrated drama of artistic envy that debuted at England's National Theatre on November 2, 1979, was imported to Broadway's Broadhurst Theatre on December 17, 1981, for 1,181 performances. The action unfolds from the point of view of Antonio Salieri, the First Royal Kapelmeister, who is overshadowed by the brash, uncouth Wolfgang Amadeus Mozart. Realizing that he is "sucked to oblivion," Salieri spreads the rumor that he was the one who murdered Mozart, hoping that his name shall thusly never be forgotten. However, the gossipmongers squash the story. *Amadeus* won the Tony Award for Best Play, as did director Peter Hall, designer John Bury, and thespian Ian McKellen as Salieri. *Amadeus* was adapted to the screen in 1984, garnering eight Oscars, including Best Picture, Best Actor (F. Murray Abraham), Best Director (Milos Forman), and Best Screenplay (Peter Shaffer).

Yonadab (London, 1985) was inspired by the Old Testament story of King David's sons, Amnon and Absalom; it is a lurid epic about incestuous rape, murder, and court intrigue. *Lettice & Lovage* was conceived by Shaffer as a vehicle for Maggie Smith in the role of a tour guide fired for romantically embellishing dull historical facts. The play opened in London in 1987, ran for three years, and came to New York's Ethel Barrymore Theatre in 1990, remaining for 284 performances.

"His plays traverse the centuries and the globe," wrote Benedict Nightingale in the *New York Times*, "raising questions that have perplexed minds from Job to Samuel Becket."[11]

For the silver screen, Shaffer scripted *Lord of the Flies* with Peter Brook (1963), an allegorical drama depicting a group of boys, marooned on an island after a plane crash, who become savage, and *The Pad (and How to Use It)* (1966), a comedy about a timid young man who is utterly nervous around the fair sex.

In 1982, *The Collected Plays of Peter Shaffer* was published by Harmony, New York, and Dennis A. Klein's bibliography, *Peter and Anthony Shaffer: A Reference Guide*, was published by G. K. Hall, Boston.

Acting Edition: Samuel French, Inc.

Awards and Honors: The Antoinette Perry (Tony) Award, 1974–1975—Best Play; John Dexter, Best Director. Drama Critics Circle Award—Best Play. Outer Critics Circle Award—Outstanding Production; Anthony Hopkins, Distinguished Performance; Peter Firth, Notable Performance by a Young Player. Drama Desk Award—Outstanding Foreign Play; John Dexter, Director; Anthony Hopkins, Actor. Los Angeles Drama Critics Circle, 1976—actor Brian Bedford; Fifteenth Annual Elliot Norton Award, Boston—actor Stephen Largay; a top-ten selection in *The Best Plays of 1974–1975* ("*Equus* is a drama of almost classic power").[12] Other Peter Shaffer plays picked by the theatrical annual are *Five Finger Exercise*, 1959–1960; *The Royal Hunt of the Sun*, 1965–1966; *Black Comedy*, 1966–1967; and *Amadeus*, 1980–1981. Peter Shaffer is the recipient of the *Evening Standard* Award, 1958 and 1980, and the Annual William Inge Award for lifetime achievement in the American theatre, 1991–1992. He became Commander, Order of the British Empire, in 1987, and was knighted by Queen Elizabeth II in 2001.

NOTES

1. Peter Shaffer, *Equus* (London: Samuel French, Inc., 1974), not paginated.
2. Peter Shaffer, *Equus*, not paginated.
3. *Daily News*, October 25, 1974.
4. *Wall Street Journal*, October 28, 1974.
5. *Women's Wear Daily*, October 18, 1974.
6. *New York Times*, October 25, 1974.
7. *New York Post*, October 25, 1974.
8. *Newsweek*, November 4, 1974.
9. *Los Angeles Times*, July 10, 2009.
10. Leonard Maltin, ed., *Movie & Video Guide, 1999 Edition* (New York: Signet, 1999), 405. The film producer of *Equus*, Elliott Kastner (1930–2010), had an affinity for suspenseful material. He produced motion pictures such as *Harper* (1966), from a novel by Ross Macdonald; four films based on Alistair MacLean novels: *Where Eagles Dare* (1968), *When Eight Bells Toll* (1971), *Fear Is the Key* (1972), *Breakheart Pass* (1975); and three movie adaptations featuring Raymond Chandler's private eye, Philip Marlowe: *The Long Goodbye* (1973), *Farewell, My Lovely* (1975), and *The Big Sleep* (1978).
11. *New York Times*, December 22, 1985.
12. Otis L. Guernsey Jr., ed., *The Best Plays of 1974–1975* (New York: Dodd, Mead, 1975), 13.

Short Eyes (1974)

Miguel Piñero (United States, Puerto-Rico born, 1946–1988)

Miguel Piñero wrote and developed his play *Short Eyes* in 1971 while incarcerated at Sing Sing penitentiary in southeast New York State. He was born in Puerto Rico on December 19, 1946, and came to New York City with his parents at age four. A short time later, his father disappeared, and mother and five children were forced into the street. Miguel's education consisted of one year at Junior High School 22 and brief attendances at four other schools. He stole food for his family to eat. At eleven, he was arrested for theft; at thirteen he joined a street gang, "The Dragons," and began shoplifting and hustling. He and his friends were caught robbing a jewelry store, and he was sentenced to three years on Riker's Island, where he was introduced to hard drugs. Paroled after a year, he went from one criminal activity to another. At twenty-four, Piñero was again caught and sentenced to five years in prison for the armed robbery of an apartment house.

At Sing Sing, Piñero became interested in the prison's drama workshop and wrote sketches about behind-the-bars life that were performed at shows in the prison. Not unlike Frenchman Jean Genet and Germany's Ernst Toller, he penned the full-length *Short Eyes* in his cell. Upon his parole in 1973, he joined New York City's Theatre of the Riverside Church as a playwright-in-residence, and became a member of The Family, an acting troupe of ex-convicts and ex-addicts who mounted plays under the direction of Marvin Felix Camillo.

The actress Colleen Dewhurst attended a performance of *Short Eyes* at the Riverside Church, where it opened on January 3, 1974, for a three-week run. She contacted producer Joseph Papp, who on February 28 took the play to his Anspacher Theatre for fifty-four showings and then transferred it to the Vivian Beaumont Theatre at Lincoln Center, where it opened on May 23, 1974, and ran for 102 performances.

The action of *Short Eyes* unfolds in the dayroom of the notorious House of Detention in New York City. The inmates are predominantly young black and Hispanic men awaiting trial. It is a large area, barren, furnished only with a few tables and several chairs. A gate leads to a shower room and slop sink. Upstage right is a TV set on a stand; upstage center are a toilet and drinking fountain. Above is a catwalk.

The dayroom is empty. It is early morning. An authoritative voice can be heard calling the roll. The men enter. Each ethnic group takes possession of its own table—the Puerto Ricans in one corner, African Americans in another, whites in a third. One of the Puerto Ricans, Julio Mercado, is a "pretty boy" of twenty-one. Called "Cupcakes," he is sexually desired by many of the convicts, and his entrance is greeted with stripper music. William "El Raheem" Johnson, a militant Muslim and a leader among the blacks, asks the guard, Mr. Nett, for a doctor's appointment. Omar, a black boxer in his mid-twenties, is something of a loner and flops in a corner. Cupcakes, John "Ice" Wicker, a tough black youth, and Juan Otero, a likable Puerto Rican, share cigarettes and begin a game of cards. Paco Pasqual, a Puerto Rican drug addict, suggests that the loser put his shirt over his hips and do a hula dance. Cupcakes refuses; he wants no part of this sort of game.

Charlie "Longshoe" Murphy, a tough Irishman, infuriates El Raheem by uttering a slur against Allah. They begin to wrestle. Nett comes in to break up the skirmish but is advised by the others to leave the combatants alone and let them get the fury out of their systems in a fair fight. Longshoe and Raheem accompany their blows with racial slurs. Finally, Longshoe is knocked clean across the room, and Nett pulls them apart. They leave for the showers.

A white newcomer, Clark Davis, enters the dayroom and is immediately taken under Longshoe's wing. This is Davis's first time behind bars. Longshoe points at the whites' table and explains the organization of prison life: "Black go on the front of the line, we stay in the back. . . . It's okay to rap with the blacks, but don't get too close with any of them. Ricans too. . . . We're the minority here, so be cool." Longshoe advises Davis that "if a spic pulls a razor blade on you and you don't have a mop wringer in your hands—run." Longshoe further warns Davis that as a good-looking kid, he better stay away from "bandidos" and not take gifts from anyone.

The guard Nett opens the gate and enters with Davis's belongings. He calls the newcomer "white trash" and "a sick fucking degenerate," relating that his eight-year-old daughter was molested by "one of those bastards, stinking sons of bitches," and warning "baby rapist" Davis to stay out of his sight or he's "gonna break your face up so bad that your own mother won't know you."

Called by his cell mates "Short Eyes," the prison slang for a child molester, Davis is considered the most despicable kind of criminal and finds himself ostracized. When he and Juan Otero are left by themselves in the dayroom to sweep up, Davis confides that he doesn't know whether or not he committed the crime. He remembers seeing a little girl that morning, then spent a month at Bellevue Hospital not recalling anything about her. Davis says that he needs someone to talk to. He has a wife and a kid whom he loves dearly. If he fights the case in court, they'll end up getting hurt. If he doesn't, society will never forgive him.

Davis keeps pouring his story into Otero's ear. When he was fifteen or sixteen he exposed himself to a little girl, a friend of his sister's who had come over to his house to watch cartoons on television. The incident happened when his sister left the room. The eight-year-old was Hispanic, with pale skin, very pretty. He told her he was a vampire and she laughed. When he moved close to her, she stopped laughing, stared at him, and backed away. Later, he had a full sexual experience with a little Puerto Rican girl from next door, the daughter of the new janitor, who enjoyed and asked to repeat the encounter. They did, three times a week, and soon thereafter he became "a pro, a professional degenerate," meeting little girls on the roof or in their basements. "I know what's right," agonizes Davis, "and I know what I'm doing is wrong, yet I can't stop myself."

Otero warns Davis that if he remains on the prison floor it will be like committing involuntary suicide. Soon some of the others drift back into the dayroom. Whatever the racial difference among them, they are all in agreement that Clark Davis is a pariah. Omar calls him a "freak." Cupcakes addresses him as "Sicky." Ice declares him a "faggot," and Longshoe pushes the "creep" around. Otero attempts to intervene on Davis's behalf, but soon the fellows begin hitting and kicking him anyway. The guard watches for a moment, closes the gate, and leaves. Omar, Longshoe, and Paco pick Davis up and put his head in the toilet bowl. They use him as a ramrod, making three runs at the toilet. Davis screams, the toilet is flushed, and the lights fade.

Half an hour later, Davis is taken away by police investigators for positive identification in a lineup. The others are busy with various diversions: Otero and Ice are playing chess; Longshoe is reading; Omar is fiddling with the TV set. In the shower area Cupcakes is drying his hair, when Paco sneaks up behind him and kisses him on the neck. Cupcakes, angry, suggests that instead of hitting on him, Paco should target the gringo who "does it with little girls."

A guard, Mr. Brown, lets Clark Davis back into the dayroom and closes the gate. Nett announces sick call. The men line up, and soon Davis and Otero are left alone. Davis confides that he intends to seek psychiatric help. Otero responds with some doubt and Davis, on the verge of tears, bemoans his treatment by a threatening mob, a hostile judge, and insulting medical checkups by "cranky" nurses who strapped him to his bed.

The men return and draw Otero into a conference of what to do about Davis. "He affects the whole floor," says Ice. "Anybody that has to rape little girls is a faggot," announces Paco. "He's a Whitey, a Devil," barks El Raheem.

Otero states, "You're letting this place destroy you," and Ice concedes, "This place makes animals out of us." But soon the men drag Davis toward the back of the dayroom. He calls for help. Mr. Nett appears at the gate, notices what's happening, and turns to go. Davis screams at Nett that he cannot just walk away, that he'll tell the captain, that he'll bring charges against him. Nett looks down the corridor to make sure no one is there, and says, "Kill him—it's self-defense."

Paco pulls out a homemade knife and gives the weapon to El Raheem. Omar and Longshoe grab Davis and hold him. El Raheem brings the blade to Davis's throat but he cannot bring himself to follow through. Longshoe takes the knife and furiously cuts Davis's throat. Everyone is silent for a moment. Nett then closes the gate and exits.

Several insults are thrown back and forth, and Longshoe, with knife in hand, attacks Ice. Paco throws a chair to Ice as a defense against the threatening knife. Longshoe and Ice circle one another. Cupcakes says, "Oh, my God, is this really us?" and the lights fade to blackout.

A short epilogue follows in which Captain Allard grills the inmates. They claim that while Davis committed suicide in the shower, they were watching *The Dating Game* on TV and didn't notice anything. Mr. Nett confirms the men's statements. The captain corners Nett and tells him he is aware that at the time in question, the television was not functioning. As a matter of fact, a repair order signed by the guard is in his file. Since the inmates told lies, and as Nett corroborated their story, he must be lying, too. However, Allard decides that for the good of the department he will suppress the damaging evidence, and tears up the repair order. Mr. Nett is to apply for sick leave and get out of sight for a while.

* * *

The New York critics greeted *Short Eyes* with unanimous acclaim. "Mr. Piñero writes very well indeed. His dialogue sizzles with truth," stated Clive Barnes.[1] "Foul-mouthed, shocking but strangely exhilarating prison melodrama," asserted Douglas Watt.[2] "The play is written, directed and performed most effectively," nodded Martin Gottfried.[3] "Marvin Felix Camillo has staged it admirably, and David Mitchell's setting is realistic and effective," lauded Richard Watts.[4] John Beaufort appreciated "a company which plays the hard-hitting text not only for its shock effect but for some of its deeper implications."[5] Jack Kroll found *Short Eyes* "an astonishing work, full of electrifying exuberance and instinctive theatricality."[6] Leonard Probst called it "a beautifully ugly play."[7]

Short Eyes was a success in Europe and catapulted Miguel Piñero to literary fame. Scripted by him and directed by Robert M. Young, the play was transferred to the screen in 1977. Piñero played the part of Gogo, a prisoner not appearing in the original. Bruce Davison portrayed Clark Davis. Tito Goya, Joseph Carberry, and Robert Maroff were recruited to reprise their stage roles of Cupcakes, Longshoe, and Nett. Curtis Mayfield composed the sound track.

Piñero continued to establish himself as an actor. He starred as God in a 1975 Philadelphia production of Bruce Jay Friedman's *Steambath* and landed supporting roles in the movies *The Jericho Mile* (1978), *Times Square* (1980), *Fort Apache, the Bronx* (1981), *Breathless* (1983), *Deal of the Century* (1983), and *Alphabet City* (1984). His television appearances included roles in *Baretta*, *Kojak*, and *Miami Vice*.

Short Eyes remains Piñero's major contribution as a playwright, though he continued to graphically provide glimpses of contemporary urban society in a series of one-act plays, mixing black, Latino, and Caucasian characters—both straight and gay—in matters of crime and violence, all using a language riddled with profanity and racial slurs. *Sideshow* (1974) features black and Puerto Rican prostitutes, pimps, hustlers, and drug addicts involved in a series of violent acts: young boys are raped, women are beaten, and a street fight ends with a stabbing death. *Paper Toilet* (1979) is a raunchy comedy unfolding in a public toilet in a Manhattan subway station where horny men, street-punk adolescents, and foul-mouthed cops cross paths. Raw and sizzling, six playlets by Piñero are collected in *Outrageous*, a 1986 softcover volume published by Arte Público Press, University of Houston, Houston, Texas.

In the 1970s, Piñero cofounded the still-thriving Nuyorican Poets Café, a haven for declaiming poetry about Puerto Rican life in New York, and edited an anthology called *Nuyorican Poetry*.

Addicted to narcotics and transgressive sex, Piñero died in 1988, at the age of forty-two, of cirrhosis of the liver. His ashes were scattered around the Lower East Side of Manhattan. The *New York Times* obituary said: "His themes revolved around life on the mean streets he knew best, populated by drug addicts and con men, pimps and prostitutes. Drugs and crime were a persistent theme as well in Mr. Piñero's own life."[8]

In 2001, Piñero's short, fiery life was captured in the R-rated motion picture *Piñero*, written and directed by Cuban-born Leon Ichaso, starring Benjamin Bratt in the title role. Rita Moreno plays Piñero's mother, and Mandy Patinkin portrays producer Joseph Papp, who moved Piñero's *Short Eyes* from Riverside Church to Broadway. Reporter Dan Shewey, in the *New York Times*, relates that director Ichaso first got the idea for a movie about Piñero in 1993, when he was shooting *Sugar Hill*, a film about a Harlem heroin dealer. "At dinner," writes Shewey, "cast and crew members would trade stories about Piñero, who was nothing if not a memorable character. Everybody you meet who knew Piñero got pleasantly ripped off or hustled or enchanted or taught a lesson about the street."[9]

In April 2010, the Downtown Urban Theatre Festival of New York City presented the one-act *Piñero Resurrected* by Michele Cuomo and Ian Gonzales Phillips, in which Piñero is lying in a hospital bed during the final hours of his life and suddenly finds himself transported back to the Lower East Side of his youth.

Acting Edition: Hill & Wang.

Awards and Honors: *Short Eyes* won the Obie Award and the New York Drama Critics Circle Award for best American play in 1974; it was a top-ten selection in *The Best Plays of 1973–1974*.

NOTES

1. *New York Times*, March 14, 1974.
2. *Daily News*, May 27, 1974.
3. *Women's Wear Daily*, March 14, 1974.
4. *New York Post*, March 14, 1974.
5. *Christian Science Monitor*, March 22, 1974.
6. *Newsweek*, April 9, 1974.
7. NBC TV, May 23, 1974.
8. *New York Times*, June 18, 1988.
9. *New York Times*, December 2, 2001.

Sherlock's Last Case (1974)

Charles Marowitz (United States, 1934–)

In press interviews, playwright Charles Marowitz claimed that he has never read the Conan Doyle stories but was inspired by the Basil Rathbone–Nigel Bruce films of the 1930s and 1940s. Marowitz penned a ninety-minute one-act play, *Sherlock's Last Case*, within fourteen days—to fill a blank slot for London's Open Space, a fringe theatrical company for which he was the artistic director.

The thriller opened on July 24, 1974, billed as the brainchild of writer Matthew Lang, staged by Charles Marowitz. Critic M. A. M. of *Stage & Television Today* chided director Marowitz for "insufficient pruning."[1] Other reviewers were mystified, intrigued, or repulsed by a Sherlock Holmes (played by Julian Glover) who is "arrogant, vain, avaricious and lecherous,"[2] and a "dogged, spluttering" Dr. Watson (Peter Bayliss).[3] *Sherlock's Last Case* ran for thirty-four performances.

In "A Background Note" attached to the published version of *Sherlock's Last Case*, Marowitz relates that the hastily assembled work had been performed by repertory theatres in Liverpool, Pitlochry, and Peterborough. When an American producer, George W. George, optioned *Sherlock's Last Case* for production in the United States, Marowitz admitted the true identity of the author and consented to expand the play into "a proper, full-length work."[4]

A two-act rendition of *Sherlock's Last Case* was slotted by the Los Angeles Actors' Theatre for the summer of 1984. "Despite a rocky start during which we replaced the lead three times and lost the original director in the second week, causing me to step in," confides Marowitz, "it finally got on and received a sympathetic press response and a somewhat rhapsodic public reception."[5] The cast included David Fox-Brenton (Sherlock Holmes), Dakin Matthews (Dr. Watson), Toni Lamond (Mrs. Hudson), and Peter Bromilow (Inspector Lestrade).

Sherlock's Last Case continued its American run at the Illinois Theatre Center, Park Forest, Illinois (March 1986), and the Kennedy Center's

Eisenhower Theatre, Washington, D.C. (July 1987), reaching Broadway's Nederlander Theatre on August 20, 1987, under the direction of A. J. Antoon, with Frank Langella (Holmes), Donal Donnelly (Watson), and Pat McNamara (Lestrade).

Among the many Holmes-Watson plays concocted throughout the years, *Sherlock's Last Case*, unfolding in 1897's Victorian England, is singular due to the shocking conclusion of act I. Lured to a dark cellar by Liza Moriarty, daughter of the infamous Napoleon of Crime, Sherlock Holmes—and the audience—is astounded by the revelation that the Moriarty angle is but a ruse ("Moriarty's daughter" was actually an out-of-work actress), and it is his ever-devoted sidekick, Dr. Watson, who has entrapped Holmes, cleverly clamping down his arms and legs in a dentist's chair and proceeding to mix deadly chemicals. "You arrogant, supercilious, egocentric, narcissistic, smug and self-congratulatory bastard," rasps Watson. "How you enjoy lording it over your bumbly, slow-witted, treacle-minded aide-de-camp. Your selfless, fawning, ever-faithful Boswell for whose benefit you paraded your brilliance and your ingenuity."

Watson sprays the bound detective with an acid-filled canister, muttering with relish, "Dust we are, to dust we return. Elementary, is it not, Holmes?" Holmes tries to wriggle out of the bonds' grasp, but after a few minutes is completely still. Content that there are no signs of life, Watson gathers his belongings, does a little dance and exits. The lights fade on the motionless body of Sherlock Holmes.

Act II takes place eighteen months later at 221B Baker Street and begins with happy news for Dr. Watson. Mrs. Hudson brings in the morning mail and it includes an invitation by Her Majesty the Queen "to accept a knighthood in the next birthday honours."

We learn that following Sherlock Holmes's sensational disappearance a year and a half ago, several imposters have attempted to convince Dr. Watson that they are his roommate and companion. When Inspector Lestrade wishes to present yet another claimant, Watson, annoyed, reminds him of "that fellow whose make-shift plastic surgery began to wilt in the gas-light." The latest candidate certainly looks like Holmes but from the moment he comes wheeling in, pumping Watson's hand, he speaks brightly and gaily—unlike Holmes. However, when the newcomer removes a small leather pouch from its old hiding-place, takes out a pinch of drugs, and shoves it into the bowl of his pipe, Watson steps back aghast—"Holmes, it really is you!"

Holmes explains that by a simple yoga exercise he managed to suspend respiration and deaden the pulse. His pipe saved him: "Thanks to a fortuitous wad of bally-packed tobacco, there was an air-block between the stem and the bowl." That gave Holmes forty-five seconds of oxygen to escape the deadly vapour. The toxic matter expanded the chair's leather clamps, enabling the agile detective to wriggle out and escape.

Before the final curtain falls, a remorseful Dr. Watson and a forgiving Sherlock Holmes are reconciled.

* * *

On the eve of the show's opening in New York, Frank Langella told Louise Sweeney of the *Christian Science Monitor* that "Charles Marowitz has written a very unique, 'what if' Holmes. He's not a traditional Holmes. . . . He's certainly more vain, more egocentric, far more mean. He's a snob. He's narcissistic and quite disdainful."[6] In an interview with the *New York Post*'s Stephen M. Silverman, Langella added that in this play Holmes is "so opinionated and prejudiced against everybody: women, Scots, Jews, servants. He's so singular in his approach to life, I certainly wouldn't want to have him to dinner."[7]

The New York reviewers were sharply divided. Frank Rich angrily denounced "writer Charles Marowitz and accomplices" for having "so completely diminished Victorian England's most beloved detective. . . . *Sherlock's Last Case* is resolutely unable to muster the characters, narrative suspense, wit or even the fogbound atmosphere of its prototype."[8] Ron Cohen complained that "Marowitz's story smacks more of heavy contrivance than dexterity, and the two major characters come across as peculiarly unlikable."[9] Joel Siegel scowled, "It's the writer and the director who've sucked the blood out of this Holmes."[10]

On the other hand, Howard Kissel found the play "full of surprises" and congratulated its "inventive theatricality."[11] Clive Barnes welcomed "a most entertaining night out, with Langella as your urbane master of revels."[12] Edwin Wilson warmly endorsed the "high camp" approach of author Marowitz and actor Langella, who "turn the Victorian sleuth into a figure of artifice and exaggeration, but do so with considerable skill and panache."[13]

Sherlock's Last Case ran 124 performances.[14] Out-of-town productions were undertaken by Trinity Repertory Company, Providence, Rhode Island (1988); Body Politic Theatre, Chicago, Illinois (1988); Bathhouse Theatre, Seattle, Washington (1991); the Duluth Playhouse, Duluth, Minnesota (1991); California Theatre Center, Santa Clara Valley (1996); Alley Theatre, Houston, Texas (1998); University of Miami, Florida (2003); the Center Theatre, Sautee-Nacoochee, Georgia (2003); University of Wisconsin, Stevens Point, Wisconsin (2004); Colony Theatre, Burbank, California (2005); and Actors Co-op, Hollywood, California (2009).

* * *

Born in 1934, New Yorker Charles Marowitz spent more than twenty years in London, where he became an influential playwright, critic, director, and producer. His West End credits include the mounting of Joe Orton's *Loot*, Sam Shepard's *Tooth of Crime*, and John Herbert's *Fortune and Men's Eyes*.

In California, Marowitz was a theatre critic for the *Los Angeles Herald Examiner*, artistic director of the Santa Monica Stage Company, and co-founder, in 1990, of the Malibu Stage Company, a tenure that lasted more than ten years. Marowitz has reshaped a dozen Shakespearean plays, including *Hamlet, Macbeth*, and *The Merchant of Venice*, and adapted works by Molière, Becque, Rostand, Feydeau, Ibsen, and Strindberg.

By Marowitz's own admission, his play *Clever Dick* (1986) "poaches shamelessly from territory staked out by Agatha Christie and other writers of her ilk." The farcical proceedings, unrolling in "an old country manor in rural England," center on the strychnine poisoning—twice—of a cantankerous old colonel and the shifting of suspicion from one weekend guest to another. There is an attempt to distinguish between the suspects who belong to the working class and others who are of the aristocracy, though they all seem to share a common denominator—sexual perversity.

In *Wilde West* (1988), Marowitz posits an imaginary meeting between Oscar Wilde and Jesse James in a Colorado saloon. *Stage Fright* (1998) pictures a deadly clash between two renowned actors and their nemesis, a sour drama critic. Marowitz himself directed the play for his Malibu Theatre, opening on June 16, 2000, featuring Nan Martin, Alan Mandell, and Jeremy Lawrence.

Sherlock's Last Case and *Clever Dick*, accompanied by a third Marowitz play, *Ah, Sweet Mystery of Life*, a rueful comedy of love and divorce, are assembled in *Potboilers*, published by Marion Boyars of London in 1986. Also brought out by Boyars is *The Marowitz Shakespeare* (1978) and *Sex Wars: Free Adaptations of Ibsen and Strindberg* (1982). Applause Books of New York published Marowitz's *Directing the Action* (1991), *Recycling Shakespeare* (1991), *Alarums and Excursions: Our Theatres in the Nineties* (1996), *The Other Way: An Alternative Approach to Acting and Directing* (1999), *Roar of the Canon: Kott and Marowitz on Shakespeare* (2001), and *The Other Chekhov: A Biography of the Actor-Director Michael Chekhov* (2004).

Acting Edition: Dramatists Play Service.

NOTES

1. *Stage & Television Today*, August 1, 1974.
2. *Times* of London, July 25, 1974.
3. *International Herald Tribune*, July 27, 1974.
4. Charles Marowitz, *Sherlock's Last Case* (Dramatists Play Service, New York, 1984), 6.

5. Marowitz, *Sherlock's Last Case*, 7.

6. *Christian Science Monitor*, August 18, 1987.

7. *New York Post*, August 20, 1987.

8. *New York Times*, August 21, 1987.

9. *Women's Wear Daily*, August 21, 1987.

10. WABC TV7, August 20, 1987.

11. *Daily News*, August 21, 1987.

12. *New York Post*, August 21, 1987.

13. *Wall Street Journal*, August 25, 1987.

14. In a sarcastic, bitter article appearing the following year in *Theatre Week* (May 23–29, 1988), Marowitz recounts his experiences bringing *Sherlock's Last Case* to New York. He laments the fact that he was not engaged to direct his own play ("My suspicion was that, being secretly wedded to his own power-drive, Frank Langella did not like the idea of so much power being vested in one person"); on the fourth day of rehearsals he found it "difficult to repress my squirms. I see laughs being obscured, comic business falling by the wayside, language turned fuzzy, and small attention paid to the delineation of characters"; the first run-through of the play was "grotesque" and the second "only marginally better." In desperation, "I ring Frank. I tell him in no uncertain terms that the show is doomed."

Frankenstein (1974)

Tim Kelly (United States, 1931–1998)

Perhaps the most prolific (albeit unknown) American playwright, Tim Kelly borrowed from Mary Shelley's original novel and some of its screen versions while adding wrinkles of his own, adapting *Frankenstein* in 1974 into a two-act play that unfolds entirely in a château on the shores of Lake Geneva, Switzerland.

Kelly's *Frankenstein* begins as a whodunit. Ernst Hessler, a Swiss police commandant, is investigating the murder of a child, William Franken-stein, the young brother of scientist Victor Frankenstein. Exacting, well disciplined, and a dedicated professional, Hessler pays a visit to the Fran-kenstein abode and cross-examines Frau Frankenstein, her son Victor, and housekeeper Sophie. The inspector relates that William's body was found near an encampment of Gypsies. A Gypsy girl named Justine was caught trying to sell William's cross. Justine claims that a man gave it to her, "a man large and stitched together like a rag doll," but she remains the main suspect.[1]

Later that night Victor reveals to his friend and fellow scientist Henry Clerval that he has discovered the cause of generating life and has dedi-cated himself to the wondrous creation of a human being. He has stealth-ily entered the city morgue and charity hospitals stealing human parts and created a live Creature. He has no doubt that his creation, "stitched together like a rag doll," had murdered little William. "There is blood on my hands for having created him," laments Victor.

Dumbfounded, Henry expresses his disbelief when the gigantic Crea-ture enters via the open French windows, takes a step toward his creator, and slowly appeals, "Frankenstein, help me."

In the second scene, Henry Clerval learns that the Creature has the power of locomotion and complete mastery of speech, reasoning, and deduction. In this Kelly adaptation, Henry's role is more substantial than in other stage versions, and he becomes a disciple of Victor Frankenstein, joining and abetting subsequent experimentations.

Elizabeth, Victor's fiancée, arrives to happily exhibit her wedding veil. As she and Victor exchange pleasantries, they are not aware that behind the laboratory's door, the Creature is eavesdropping. Later that evening, the Creature demands from Victor a companion to share his "wretched loneliness . . . one of another sex, as hideous as myself." The first act curtain falls on Victor and Henry caught up in the fever of a new adventure. They get shovels and at the dark of night leave for the church graveyard.

When the lights fade up on act II, machinery hums behind the laboratory door. It is obvious that Victor is experimenting with the Creature's bride-to-be. Henry walks in, carrying a bundle wrapped in paper, and we catch a glimpse of a severed human hand. Henry tells Victor that he got the hand at the city morgue, and Victor studies it with the aid of a magnifying glass.

Frau Frankenstein's voice echoes from the hallway. Henry takes the hand into the laboratory. Victor's mother complains that he has been moving farther and farther away from her and from Elizabeth. Henry returns, wearing a white smock, and whispers to Victor that the hand he brought won't do—"it bruises too easily." Victor locks the laboratory's door and he and Henry hurriedly depart for what he tells his mother is a "shopping trip."

Left alone, Frau Frankenstein opens a rusty box and rummages through it until she finds a ring of old keys. She unlocks the laboratory's door, screams, and stumbles back into the study, disoriented, horrified. The Creature looms up in the doorway and says, "Do not fear me. Do not scream." Mother backs away, breathing in tiny intakes, clutches her heart, then falls down with a spasm of pain. The Creature drops to his knees and says sorrowfully, "I meant you no harm." He cradles Mother's dead body in his arms.

It is raining outside when Inspector Hessler grills housekeeper Sophie. She is the one who found Frau Frankenstein sprawled out on the floor of the study. Sophie tells Hessler that Master Victor and his friend Herr Clerval have been bringing in all sorts of machinery—wires, rods, and electric bulbs. The master refuses to take care of himself and eats almost nothing. "It's been a bitter season for Victor Frankenstein," says the inspector. "His brother murdered, his mother taken so suddenly."

Enter Elizabeth, wearing black with a mourning veil, and Victor, with a black armband on. Henry follows them into the room. The inspector offers his sympathy and adds that the Gypsy girl, Justine, whose hanging is scheduled within a week, has asked to see Victor Frankenstein. Henry is concerned but Victor agrees to meet her. Elizabeth, emotionally drained, leaves the room as Hessler returns with Justine—young, pretty, forceful. The Gypsy girl pleads with Victor to believe in her innocence. She did not kill young Williams, she says. A man, "a terrible man, with great stitches across his face," gave her the incriminating cross, turned, and ran into the woods. But Victor claims that he sees murder in Justine's eyes, and the inspector drags her off. Neither Victor nor Henry intervenes to save Justine from the gallows.

However, belated pangs of conscience cause Victor to stop the creation of the monster's bride and destroy the electrical gadgets. In his wrath, the Creature throttles Henry by the neck and smashes his fist into the scientist's back. Henry crumples to the floor in a dying gasp. The Creature threatens Victor, "I shall be with you on your wedding night."

And the Creature is true to his word. The last scene unfolds on the eve of Victor and Elizabeth's wedding. The happy, albeit apprehensive couple returns home after the ceremony. Inspector Hessler surrounds their château with a dozen guards carrying shotguns "that would bring down a charging rhinoceros."

While Victor goes into the laboratory to destroy files and electrical paraphernalia, the Creature comes down from the attic, where he has been hiding all this time, and accosts Elizabeth. "You must die and Frankenstein must suffer," he says and grabs her by the throat. However, unlike the original Shelley novel and other stage adaptations of the work, this Tim Kelly version ends up happily. In the nick of time, Victor enters from the laboratory with a revolver in hand and empties it on the Creature. Clutching his side, the Creature stumbles his way through the French windows and into the garden. While Victor pours a glass of water for Elizabeth, from offstage we hear distant sounds of gunfire.

Inspector Hessler returns to report that the Creature, mortally wounded by the fusillade, ran into the lake; his men will drag the lake for the body. Elizabeth is relieved, "It's ended, Victor. Forever." Victor Frankenstein looks toward the lake and thoughtfully mutters, "I wonder," as the curtain descends.

Under the title *The Rage of Frankenstein*, the play was presented by off-Broadway's Carter Theatre on October 31, 1979. Ted Bank wrote in *Show Business*, "Playwright Tim Kelly has given us an unusually articulate and intelligent monster who speaks at length about his feelings and desires."[2] In addition to *Frankenstein / The Rage of Frankenstein*, Kelly also penned *Bride of Frankenstein Goes Malibu* (1976), *The Frankensteins Are Back in Town* (1980), and *Frankenstein Slept Here* (1984).

* * *

It is reported that the phenomenal Tim Kelly (1931–1998) wrote well over three hundred plays after his first stage endeavor, *Widow's Walk*, "a mystery thriller in three acts," was published in 1963. Specializing mostly in melodramas, Kelly dramatized works by Charles Dickens, Wilkie Collins, J. Sheridan LeFanu, Edgar Allan Poe, H. G. Wells, and Edgar Wallace, and recycled for the theatre the characters of Sweeney Todd, the Hunchback of Notre Dame, Varney the Vampire, Dracula, the Werewolf, and the Zombie—interweaving horrific elements with sly humor.

Kelly re-created the world's foremost consulting detective in the one-act *The Last of Sherlock Holmes* (1970), *Sherlock Holmes Meets the Phantom* (1975), and *Beast of the Baskervilles* (1984); in the full-length *The Hound of the Baskervilles* (1976), *Sherlock Holmes* (1977), and *The Adventure of the Speckled Band* (1981); and in the musical *Sherlock Holmes and the Giant Rat of Sumatra* (1987). Named after the famous sleuth, Shirley Holmes, a young coed, is the heroine of Kelly's *If Sherlock Holmes Were a Woman* (1969). Kelly's *The Adventure of the Clouded Crystal* (1982) deals with a stormy relationship between Sir Arthur Conan Doyle and the magician Harry Houdini.

For younger audiences, Kelly spotlighted Alice in Wonderland, Cinderella, Robin Hood, Tom Sawyer, the Three Musketeers, the Wizard of Oz—and Zorro.

Few of Kelly's plays made it to the New York scene, but many have been presented by colleges and little theatres. Kelly was the recipient of several university awards, and in 1991 beat more than three hundred entries to win the Elmira College Original Playwriting Contest with his blood-and-thunder drama *Crimes at the Old Brewery*. The play, depicting the squalor of Manhattan's Five Points during the 1850s, premiered, under my direction, at the college's Emerson Theatre on March 7, 1991. Helen Hayes attended.

Acting Edition: Samuel French, Inc.

NOTES

1. A production note by playwright Kelly states, "The Creature of Mary Shelley is not the monster of the film versions. He was tall, yes, but beyond that normal in most physical respects. The true horror lies in the fact that he is 'artificially created' from bits and pieces of dead men. That point is hammered in the play. . . . Keeping this in mind, his makeup should reveal many stitches. Corners of the mouth, neck, eyes, forehead, as well as the wrist."

2. *Show Business*, November 29, 1979.

The Picture of Dorian Gray (1975)

John Osborne (England, 1929–1994)

In 1889, during dinner at a London restaurant, the American publisher Joseph M. Stoddart cajoled Arthur Conan Doyle and Oscar Wilde to come up with an unusual yarn for his *Lippincott's Monthly Magazine*. Doyle offered Stoddart his second Sherlock Holmes novel, *The Sign of Four*, and Wilde created *The Picture of Dorian Gray*.

The Picture of Dorian Gray, Wilde's longest prose narrative, appeared as the lead story in *Lippincott's* of June 20, 1890. Wilde revised the novel, adding several chapters, for a book publication by Ward, Lock, and Company in April 1891.[1]

The Picture of Dorian Gray has since been adapted to the stage, screen, and television many times. Famed British playwright John Osborne, the vexed young man of *Look Back in Anger*, dramatized the novel in 1972, calling it "A Moral Entertainment." In his introduction to the published edition, Osborne wrote: "The fact remains that *The Picture of Dorian Gray* is not only a remarkable achievement of its time, given all its faults, but the germinal story is an inspired one like, say, that of Jekyll and Hyde. . . . It is a variation on the Mephistophelian bargain with the devil. . . . One of the things that has struck me about the original book is the feeling of willful courage and despair, the two qualities only too clearly embodied in the spirit of Wilde himself."[2]

Osborne believed that the role of Dorian Gray should be played by a woman ("As many people know, this was one of the parts cherished by Garbo") and that the set should be "an all-purpose hole-in-the-ground world."[3] The curtain rises on Basil Hallward's studio. Basil, a well-known artist, is painting in front of an upright easel. His friend since Oxford, Lord Henry Wotton, is sitting on a Persian divan, chain-smoking. Lord Henry expresses an interest in the subject of Basil's portrait, a vivid re-creation of young, handsome Dorian Gray, whom the artist met at a society house party. Basil explains that he was attracted to Dorian's "simple and beautiful nature" and offered to paint him. The portrait is almost completed.

Enter Dorian Gray. Upon observing his portrait, the aristocratic dandy sighs: "This picture will always remain young. It will never be older than, than this particular day in June. If only it were the other way around." Dorian adds that he would give his soul to keep his youth.

Wide-eyed Dorian and cynical, man-about-town Lord Henry establish an immediate rapport and go out together—the beginning of a bond between a Faustian young man and his tempter. Basil is left alone. Crestfallen, he sinks down onto his sofa, a look of pain crossing his face.

In the second scene, Lord Henry Wotton and his snobbish family lounge around chatting and gossiping. They are concerned about Dartmoor, Lord Henry's brother, who intends to marry an American girl of dubious heritage. "It is rather fashionable to marry Americans just now," laments Lord Henry. "American girls are as clever at concealing their parents as English women are at concealing their past."

As they converse, we learn that years ago Dorian Gray's mother, Lady Margaret Devereau, "an extraordinary beautiful girl," ran away with "a penniless young nobody," who was later killed in a duel. It was rumored that Lord Kelso, Lady Margaret's father, paid a Belgian brute to insult his son-in-law in public, "to pit him afterwards like a pigeon." Lord Kelso brought his daughter back home, but she never spoke to him and died before the year was out. She left a son, Dorian, who upon Lord Kelso's death inherited the family fortune.

Dorian arrives and at an opportune moment corners Lord Henry with the news that he has fallen in love with an actress, Sybil Vane, whom he had seen in a small East Side theatre playing Juliet. She does not know him by name—she calls him Prince Charming—but he has gone to see her backstage night after night. He plans to marry Sybil, buy her contract from the "hideous Jew" who has signed her for three years, and take her from this cheap troupe to a West Side theatre where she belongs. "She hasn't merely got art, a consummate art-instinct in her," gushes Dorian, "but she has personality. And a unique one." Skeptical, Sir Henry agrees to meet Dorian the next day for a performance of *Romeo and Juliet*.

In a small dressing room, Sybil Vane is putting on the costume of Juliet and relates to her mother and her younger brother James that she's enamored with the gentleman caller who has been attending her show nightly and has been sending her exquisite bouquets. Mrs. Vane is at first apprehensive. She urges her daughter to attach herself to Mr. Isaacs, the theatre's manager, who has advanced her fifty pounds to pay off their debts. But soon Mrs. Vane becomes attracted to the notion that Sybil will marry into the aristocracy. James, who is a sailor off to Australia, remains concerned. "If he ever does you any wrong," he tells Sybil, "I shall kill him."

Following a performance of *Romeo and Juliet*, Dorian Gray, Lord Henry, and Basil Hallward enter Sybil's dressing room. Desultory applause and a chorus of hisses can be heard from the stage. Dorian is upset: "Last night I thought she was a great artist. This evening she's merely commonplace and mediocre." Lord Henry shrugs: "What does it matter if she played Juliet like a wooden doll? . . . She's beautiful. What more can you want?"

Dorian asks the two men to leave. Sybil bursts in elated. She explains that before meeting Dorian, she had considered acting her only reality. Now, she says, Dorian's love has taught her what reality actually is, and she can no longer act. Dorian coldly states that Sybil, who used to stir his imagination, now doesn't stir even his curiosity. In fact, he declares, she produces no effect on him at all. "You are shallow and stupid," says Dorian. "I'll never see you again, I'll never think of you, I'll even forget your name." She throws herself, sobbing, at his feet but he stalks away.

At his studio, Dorian notices a slight change in the appearance of his portrait. There is a new, faint line of cruelty about the mouth. He covers the picture with a gilt Spanish leather screen.

Lord Henry arrives to inform Dorian that Sybil Vane has committed suicide. She was found dead on her dressing-room floor. According to the morning papers, she must have swallowed something by mistake, a liquid they use in theatres for painting scenery. She was seventeen. Dorian blames himself, asserting that he murdered Sybil as if he "had cut her throat with a knife." But Lord Henry assures him that if he had married the girl, "the whole thing would have been an absolute failure." Dorian's demeanor changes and cheerfully he agrees to accompany Sir Henry to the opera that night.

Basil Hallward comes to comfort Dorian and is astonished at Dorian's callous attitude toward Sybil's death. Basil wants to exhibit his picture in Paris but Dorian firmly objects, even forbidding the artist to lift the screen and look at it. "There is something fateful about the portrait," he whispers. "It has a life of its own." Basil departs, perplexed.

Left by himself, Dorian picks up the portrait, ascends several steps, and places it in a dark attic. He spreads a heavy coverlet over the picture, pulls down the window curtains, and exits, locking the door behind him.

During the first two acts the action progresses leisurely and realistically. In the third act, the pace is accelerated and some supernatural elements puncture the proceedings. The curtain opens on Dorian's semi-dark rooms, where floating about are ghostly apparitions of Sybil, her brother James, Basil, and Lord Henry, recognizable but grotesque, groaning, shrieking, giggling. The figures are twenty-year travesties of what they were. In contrast, Dorian Gray enters, beautifully dressed in evening clothes, looking as young and handsome as ever.

Dorian addresses the ghostly figures and orders them to leave. All abide except Basil, who is transformed into his human self, dressed for travel. He tells Dorian that he does not believe the constant rumors of his vile, depraved behavior. "Sin is a thing that writes itself across a man's face," says Basil. "It can't be concealed. . . . If a wretched man has a vice, it shows itself in the lines of his mouth, the droop of his eyelids, the moulding of his hands even." Dorian's pure, bright face, asserts Basil, proves his innocence.

Dorian invites Basil to see his portrait in the attic. He tears away the screen. Basil screams and falls to his knees. "Kneel with me, Dorian. Kneel," he says in anguish. We see the silhouettes of the two men kneeling. Then Dorian flashes a knife. Basil moans and falls. Dorian exits the attic, locks the door, and descends. He notices Basil's bag and coat and shoves them into a cupboard. He puts on his fur coat and hat and goes out, shutting the street door gently behind him. He rings the bell. His valet, Francis, appears, half-dressed and drowsy. Dorian explains that he had forgotten his latchkey, asks for the time and is let in, thus establishing an alibi.

The wheels of the plot now churn rapidly. In order to destroy all evidence, Dorian threatens a young chemist, Alan Campbell, to publicly expose a devastating secret unless he utilizes his expertise to destroy Basil Hallward's corpse and turn it into "a handful of ashes that I may scatter in the air."

An older James Vane, Sybil's brother, returns from Australia intent on avenging his sister's betrayer. He stalks Dorian and in a dark alley attacks him, clutching his throat with bare sinewy hands. In the nick of time, Dorian points at his young face. Sybil committed suicide eighteen years ago, and he seems to be no more than twenty years old. Convinced now that Dorian could not have known his sister, James loosens his grip and reels back. "My God!" he exclaims, "I would have murdered you!"

Dorian decides to destroy the picture that has recorded his litany of crimes. He goes up to the attic and, using the knife with which he had murdered Basil, he frantically stabs the canvas into fragments. The light flickers out, and a horrible, agonized cry is heard.

After a while, the door opens and footman Francis leads in two uniformed constables. They flash their lamps. Horrified, they see the scattered remains of the portrait and the body of a shriveled, wrinkled man in evening dress, a knife in his hand. It is the old carcass of Dorian Gray.

* * *

The manuscript of John Osborne's *The Picture of Dorian Gray* was reviewed glowingly by critic Romilly Cavan in the monthly *Plays and Players*: "The Osborne version is itself compact of style and wit, and surely quite a lot of the splendidly ornate pronouncements are all his own work, the very occasional anachronistic word serving to add zest to the paradox rather than to decrease the flavour of the *mot*."[4]

Osborne's adaptation was first performed at the Greenwich Theatre, London, on February 13, 1975. Clive Donner directed a cast headed by Michael Kitchen (Dorian Gray), Anton Rodgers (Lord Henry Wotton), John McEnery (Basil Hallward), and Angharad Rees (Sybil Vane). In his lukewarm review, playwright-critic Frank Marcus wrote in the *Sunday Telegraph* that he found it "a respectful rendering of the original, amounting in theatrical terms to no more than a hollow piece of Grand Guignol. . . . The director, Clive Donner, used all available resources of light and sound to create ghostly and lurid climaxes. . . . By and large, the words stuck obstinately to the printed page. The result was not particularly entertaining."[5]

The Picture of Dorian Gray ran for thirty-two performances. Osborne converted his play to a hundred-minute television version that was produced by *BBC Play of the Month* on September 19, 1976, starring Peter Firth (Dorian), John Gielgud (Lord Henry), Jeremy Brett (Basil Hallward), and Judi Bowker (Sybil). Following the TV presentation, literary critic Martin Amis wrote in *New Statesman* that "faced with the challenge of telescoping *Dorian Gray*, Osborne hit upon a novel and ingenious procedure: he took a bit from the beginning and he took a bit from the end. We stay close to Wilde, in *Digest* form, until the suicide of Sybil Vane, with Dorian being sullen, callous, lordly; we then move on, if you please, to the murder of Basil—with Dorian a cackling blackguard. What then could have happened to the lad? Well, two decades of rarefied debauchery, if you know your Wilde, but only an indeterminate bout of profligacy, if you trust your Osborne. . . . The heart of the story—which is the story of Dorian's corruption—is the section Osborne omits."[6]

* * *

The dark, supernatural elements of *The Picture of Dorian Gray* attracted filmmakers from the early days of the cinema. Silent pictures based on the novel were made in 1910, 1913, 1915, 1916, 1917, and 1918. Most notable is MGM's 1945 version, scripted and directed by Albert Lewin, starring Hurd Hatfield as Dorian Gray, George Sanders as Lord Henry Wotton, and Angela Lansbury as Sybil Vane. *Dorian*, aka *Pact with the Devil* (2001), is a modernization derived from the Wilde story, depicting a New York model (played by Ethan Erickson) selling his soul to his manager-devil (Malcolm McDowell). Played by Stuart Townsend, Dorian Gray is one of the Victorian hero/villains gathered in the 2003 adventure movie *The League of Extraordinary Gentlemen*.

London audiences saw a stage adaptation of the novel, by G. Constant Lounsbery, at the Vaudeville Theatre, on August 28, 1913, directed by and starring Lou-Tellegen, running for thirty-six performances. Disappointed New Yorkers went to the Broadway productions of *The Picture of Dorian*

Gray in May 1928, adapted by David Thorne (Biltmore Theatre, sixteen performances); in July 1936, adapted by Jeron Criswell (Comedy Theatre, sixteen performances); and in August 1936, adapted by Cecil Clarke (Comedy Theatre, thirty-two performances), all panned by the critics. A similar fate befell the off-Broadway offerings at the Bleecker Street Playhouse in August 1956, of an adaptation by Justin Foster presented arena-style and called by the *New York Times* "superficial and amorphous,"[7] and at the Showboat Theatre in August 1963, of a version adapted and directed by Andy Milligan. According to the *Times*, "Nothing that Wilde might have done in this extravagant search for experience could have been as horrifying as what the company associated with *The Picture of Dorian Gray* did to his memory last night."[8]

"A working script for the stage from the novel by Oscar Wilde," concocted by Jim Dine, was published by London's P. Petersburg in 1968. That same year, a one-man show of *Dorian*, penned and performed by John Stuart Anderson at London's New Arts Theatre, was lambasted by playwright David Hare, who asserted that "Anderson isn't capable of feeling each character anew when he's just whipped away from the last."[9] Anderson revamped his adaptation into an ensemble play, to be performed by a cadre of eight actors. Years later, in 1982, the revised version was distributed by Contemporary Drama Service of Downers Grove, Illinois. Also in 1982, a musical version by collaborators Jack Sharkey and Dave Reiser was published by Samuel French, Inc. Additional musicalizations of *The Picture of Dorian Gray* were created by the Hungarian Matyas Varkonyi (1990); the Americans Lowell Liebermann (1996), Allan Reiser and Don Price (1996), and Richard Gleaves (1997); and the Canadian team of Ted Dykstra and Steven Mayoff (2002).

One of the more successful dramatizations of *The Picture of Dorian Gray* was presented by off-Broadway's Irish Repertory Theatre in 2001. Realizing that the tale is too well-known to hold any shock value, adapter-director Joe O'Bryne decided, as reported by the *New York Times*, to "rediscover Wilde's wit and language. The Lord Henry character gets most of the Wilde-icisms, many of them still ringing with relevance."[10]

The Wilde story inspired a dance-drama conceived by Robert Hill for the American Ballet Theatre, premiering at Manhattan's City Center in 2003, and a rock opera written and produced by Barry Gordon, showcased at off-Broadway's Barrow Group Theatre in 2005. A Czech musical inspired by the novel debuted in Prague a year later.

In addition, 2008 was ripe with Dorian Gray appearances: an Australian dramatization by playwrights Greg Eldridge and Liam Suckling; a dance adaptation of the story by choreographer Matthew Bourne, which made its debut at the Edinburgh International Festival; a Grand Guignol–style production by Canadian Ian Case, staged for Halloween at Craigdarroch

Castle in Victoria, British Columbia; and a version with book, music, and lyrics by Randy Bowser, premiering at Pentacle Theatre in Salem, Oregon. In 2009, *The Picture of Dorian Gray* was adapted by Linnie Reedman, with music by Joe Evans, for a run at London's Leicester Square Theatre. It played to full houses. Glory Bowen adapted and directed a new two-hour version for off-Broadway's 440 Studios from June 5 to June 21, 2010.

* * *

John James Osborne was born in London in 1929. His father was a commercial artist and advertising copywriter, and his mother was a Cockney barmaid. He was educated at Belmont College in Devon, but was expelled for hitting the headmaster. In 1948, Osborne joined a touring company as an understudy and assistant stage manager. In the early 1950s, he appeared in several London productions, including *Don Juan* by Ronald Duncan and *The Good Woman of Setzuan* by Bertolt Brecht.

Osborne dabbled in playwriting with *The Devil Inside* (1950), a melodrama about a poetic Welsh youth, and *Personal Enemy* (1955), which he cowrote with Anthony Creighton, a play influenced by the McCarthy trials and the House Un-American Activities Committee. Osborne's first West End play, *Look Back in Anger*, which opened on May 8, 1956, at the Royal Court Theatre, was not only a smash hit but also the torchbearer of a wide variety of socially conscious dramas. Tony Richardson directed and Kenneth Haigh starred as Jimmy Porter, a fierce working-class rebel. Two years later, the play came to New York, where it ran for a year and was nominated for a Tony Award as Best Play. Richardson directed a 1959 movie version that featured Richard Burton.

During a span of three decades, Osborne penned more than twenty plays. Among those heralded as master works is *The Entertainer* (1957; filmed 1960), in which Laurence Olivier gave a tour de force performance as Archie Rice, a third-rate music-hall comedian. By introducing a family of run-down vaudevillians, Osborne presented the ills and decline of contemporary England. *Epitaph for George Dillon* (1957), cowritten with Anthony Creighton, is the story of a young, mediocre actor-dramatist haunted by his own doubts as a man and as an artist. The pageantry *Luther* (1961; filmed 1973) is highlighted by an intellectual duel between the rebellious monk, leader of the Protestant Reformation, and the pope's legate. The lead character of *Inadmissible Evidence* (1964; filmed 1968) is a middle-aged lawyer, Bill Maitland, who disintegrates both professionally and personally. *A Patriot for Me* (1965), based on fact, takes place in Warsaw, Prague, Dresden, and Vienna from 1890 to 1913 and relates the case of Alfred Redl, an Austro-Hungarian colonel, who was a homosexual blackmailed into spying for Russia. When Redl was found out, he shot himself. The centerpiece of the play is a magnificent baroque Viennese ballroom dance that is slowly revealed to be a drag ball.

Osborne adapted for the London stage Henrik Ibsen's *Hedda Gabler* (1972; televised 1981), the study of a bored upper-class woman. Still unperformed is *A Place Calling Itself Rome* (published 1973), based on William Shakespeare's *Coriolanus*, the bloody story of Rome's one-time hero who is expelled by the senate and returns as the head of an army seeking revenge. For the cinema, Osborne scripted Henry Fielding's novel *Tom Jones* (1963), a young man's rowdy adventure in eighteenth-century England. The film won an Academy Award for Best Picture. Osborne and director Tony Richardson also received awards.

In 1971, Osborne won kudos in the role of menacing Cyril Kinnear in the movie *Get Carter*. His follow-up appearances included *Tomorrow Never Comes* (1978) and *Flash Gordon* (1980).

Osborne was married five times. Among his wives were the actresses Mary Ure and Jill Bennett, the novelist Penelope Gilliatt, and drama critic Helen Dawson. He published two volumes of autobiography: *A Better Class of Person* (1981; televised 1985) and *Almost a Gentleman* (1991). His various newspaper and magazine writings were collected under the title *Damn You, England* in 1995.

Osborne died from complications of diabetes and alcoholism at the age of sixty-five.

* * *

Oscar Fingal O'Flahertie Wills Wilde (1854–1900) was born in Dublin, Ireland, into an Anglo-Irish family. He studied classics at Dublin's Trinity College, was an outstanding student, and received a scholarship to Magdalen College, Oxford, where he continued his education from 1874 to 1878. Decorative arts were his main interest. While at college, his long hair, mode of dress, and general demeanor were considered that of an "effeminate dandy."

After graduating from Oxford, Wilde returned to Dublin. He courted Florence Balcombe but she became engaged to Bram Stoker, author of *Dracula*. Wilde spent the next several years in Paris, went on a lecture tour in the United States, and settled in London, where he contributed articles and art reviews to the *Dramatic View* and *Pall Mall Gazette*. In 1885, he married Constance Lloyd, daughter of a wealthy Queen's Counsel, and they had two sons. In the early 1890s, Wilde's novel *The Picture of Dorian Gray*, two collections of fairytales, and the volume *Lord Arthur Savile's Crime and Other Stories* established his literary reputation. On stage, he had a series of popular comedies.

However, Wilde's widely known homosexual encounters, notably with the young Lord Alfred Douglas, led in 1895 to three successive *cause célèbre* trials, at the conclusion of which he was convicted of "gross inde-cency" and sentenced to two years' hard labor. Upon his release, Wilde spent his last three years, penniless, in Paris. He died of cerebral meningi-tis on November 30, 1900. His tomb in Pére Lachais was designed by the sculptor Sir Jacob Epstein.

Accounts of the real-life trials of Oscar Wilde were published by H. Montgomery Hyde in 1975, by Jonathan Goodman in 1995, and by Merlin Holland in 2003. Among others, biographies of Wilde include *The Life and Confessions of Oscar Wilde* (1914) by Frank Harris, *Oscar Wilde* (1987) by Richard Ellmann, and *The Stranger Wilde* (1994) by Gary Schmidgall. Peter Ackroyd penned *The Last Testament of Oscar Wilde* (1983), a fictional diary presumably written by Wilde when in exile in Paris after serving time in prison. In *The Wilde West* (1991), Walter Satterthwait conjures up Wilde's lecture tour in the United States as background for a tense mystery, in which the visiting author finds himself a suspect in the murder of prosti-tutes. The tour also serves Louis Edwards for a steamy adventure novel titled *Oscar Wilde Discovers America* (2003).

In a twist, Wilde becomes a clever sleuth in Gyles Brandreth's lively de-tective stories *Oscar Wilde and the Candlelight Murders* (2007), *Oscar Wilde and the Ring of Death* (2008, aka *Oscar Wilde and a Death of No Importance*), *Oscar Wilde and the Dead Man's Smile* (2009), and *Oscar Wile and the Nest of Vipers* (2010). While a student at Oxford, Brandreth wrote and pro-duced the play *The Trials of Oscar Wilde* (1974). Other plays about Wilde include *Oscar Wilde* (1936) by Leslie and Sewell Stokes, *The Importance of Being Oscar* (1961, arranged and acted by Michael MacLiammoir), *Dear Oscar* (1972, a musical with book and lyrics by Caryl Gabrielle Young), *Wildflowers* (1976) by Richard Howard, *Wilde West* (1988) by Charles Ma-rowitz, *Stephen and Mr. Wilde* (1993) by Jim Bartley, *Gross Indecency* (1997) by Moises Kaufman, *The Judas Kiss* (1998) by David Hare, *Goodbye Oscar* (1999) by Romulus Linney, *Aspects of Oscar* (2001) by Barry Day, *A Man of No Importance* (2002) by Terrence McNally, and Brian Bedford's one-man show, *Ever Yours, Oscar* (2009), featuring Wilde's correspondence.

Two excellent motion pictures about Wilde's traumatic life in the straight-laced Victorian era were made in England in 1960: *Oscar Wilde*, with Robert Morley, and *The Trials of Oscar Wilde*, starring Peter Finch. A third biographical movie, *Wilde* (1998), featured Stephen Fry in the title role.

A naughty pastiche by Graham Greene, *The Return of A. J. Raffles* (1975), spotlights Oscar Wilde's lover, Lord Alfred Douglas, as he solicits the help of gentleman-burglar Raffles to penetrate the safe of his father—an act of revenge for stopping his allowance after the affair with Wilde be-came known.

An odd couple of the Victorian era, Sherlock Holmes and Oscar Wilde met on two occasions. In the play *The Incredible Murder of Cardinal Tosca*

(1980), by Alden Nowlan and Walter Learning, good Dr. Watson learns from his roommate that his latest case revolved around a packet of compromising letters penned by Wilde. In Russell A. Brown's novel, *Sherlock Holmes and the Mysterious Friend of Oscar Wilde* (1988), Wilde, described as "a giant moth," arrives in 221B Baker Street to ask for the aid of the Great Detective in a case of blackmail in high society.

Acting Edition: Faber and Faber.

Awards and Honors: John Osborne was nominated for a Best Play Tony Award for *Look Back in Anger* (1958), *Epitaph for George Dillon* (1959), and *Inadmissible Evidence* (1966), and won a Best Play Tony for *Luther* (1964). Osborne received an Oscar for his screenplay of *Tom Jones* (1963) and a Lifetime Achievement Award from the Writer's Guild of Great Britain.

In 2000–2001, the New York Public Library for the Performing Arts marked the centennial of the death of Oscar Wilde with a series of public programs that included lectures, readings of Wilde's works, and motion pictures based on his plays.

NOTES

1. In the summer of 2009, a Boston antiquarian, Peter L. Stern, offered a rare first edition of *The Picture of Dorian Gray*, in dust jacket and a custom quarter-morocco slipcase, for $100,000.

2. John Osborne, *The Picture of Dorian Gray* (London: Faber and Faber, 1973), 12, 13.

3. John Osborne, *The Picture of Dorian* Gray, 14.

4. *Plays and Players*, January 1974.

5. *Sunday Telegraph*, February 16, 1975.

6. *New Statesman*, September 24, 1976.

7. *New York Times*, August 18, 1956.

8. *New York Times*, August 29, 1963.

9. *Plays and Players*, September 1968.

10. *New York Times*, March 23, 2001.

Murderer (1975)

Anthony Shaffer (England, 1926–2001)

One round of a teasing murder game was not enough for Anthony Shaffer. The author of *Sleuth* (1970) concocted yet another manipulative, macabre thriller—*Murderer*. While *Sleuth* lampoons the traditional detective story, *Murderer*'s satirical slings stem from famous real-life culprits of the past.

As the house lights fade, the protagonist, Norman Bartholomew, a handsome, smooth artist of about thirty-five, confides over the sound system his crystallized passion to become an assassin—not a casual killer in a barroom brawl or a senseless slayer in a squalid domestic squabble, but a great classical murderer, a man who understands the true nature of the art of murder. He wants to stand with Heath and Haig, and Christie and Crippen, and the other supremely notorious killers.

For the first thirty minutes of the play, silent action reveals Norman at his studio. He drugs the drink of his model-girlfriend, Millie Sykes, then places a scarf round the girl's throat and pulls it tight. Once she is dead, he strips the body of its clothes, removes a number of teeth with a pair of pliers, carries the corpse up the stairs to a bathroom, and tips it into the tub. He then descends to the cellar, returns with a half-dozen sacks, and begins to systematically dismember the dead woman with a knife, a hatchet, a handsaw, and an electric drill. He munches cheerfully on a sandwich as he dispatches bloody sacks into the stove. He turns on the television where the classic *M* flashes, with Peter Lorre as the Dusseldorf child murderer. He scrubs the bathroom floor and sterilizes the instruments of death, when suddenly the doorbell rings and a voice is heard, "Open up! Police!"

It is Sergeant Stenning, in uniform. A Peeping Tom neighbor, Mrs. Ramage, called the station and reported that she saw through the window the strangulation of a woman—"she thought it might be your wife"—and the carving of her body into pieces. Stenning says that it all sounds far-fetched, but explains that he has to check. Norman admits that "it's no secret in the village that my wife and I don't particularly get on."

Casing the place, Stenning stops near the stove and sniffs. His face wrinkled in disgust, he throws open the door, peers inside, recoils instantly, grabs a pair of fire tongs, and drags out a head. Astounded, the sergeant—and the audience—realize that it is a dummy. Norman giggles, extracts one of the limbs from the stove, and waves it under Stenning's nose. He relates that the dummy is made of expanded polystyrene, stiffened with wire and filled with stage blood—what film stuntmen refer to as Kensington Gore. Norman explains that he was play-acting the case of Buck Ruxton, the Parsee doctor who in 1935 murdered his wife and spent the whole night carefully draining her of blood, cutting her up in the bath, and making neat little bundles for disposal. It's a thrill hobby, babbles Norman. So far he has impersonated Frederick Henry Seddon, the Tollington Park killer who disposed of his tenant with arsenic; George Chapman, who poisoned three of his so-called wives with strychnine; and Henry Wainwright, the Whitechapel Road murderer. He likes to pay homage to the notorious murderers of the past, says Norman.

Stenning, the voice of pedestrian reality, admonishes Norman and tells him that at various times, in various places, he has seen the agony of murdered people and there was nothing compelling about it in any way. Before leaving, the sergeant sternly warns Norman to stop playing this kind of a dangerous game.

Norman relates to Millie, who has fallen asleep in the sauna, that he deliberately left the curtains open to taunt nosy Mrs. Ramage into calling the police. It's a safe bet now that the next time Mrs. Ramage reports sinister doings at chez Bartholomew, the sergeant will just think it's one of his games. With that assurance in mind, Norman confides to Millie a scheme to dispose of his wife, Elizabeth, a gynecological surgeon, who will never agree to a divorce. He is devising the most cunning murder plan ever devised in this country—it will be the perfect crime.

Elizabeth arrives—charming, vivacious, attractive, and on the right side of forty. While his wife bathes, Norman contemplates imitating the biblical Jael story, in which the Israelite beauty smote a nail unto the temple of Sissera. On second thought, he intends to throw an electric heater into the water. In another change of plans, inspired by the Crippen case, he disappears into the cellar and begins to dig a grave with a pickax.

After a while, Elizabeth calls, "Norman, your bride is waiting in her bath for her brandy." Norman is struck by a new thought: he will replicate the method of George Joseph Smith, the Brides in the Bath Murderer, who crept up behind them and slid their heads under the water and held them there. Cat-like, Norman approaches the densely steaming bathroom, pounces and thrusts the capped head under the foamy water. The legs thrash wildly, the hands claw the air, and then after an appreciable struggle, comes the cessation of all movement. Norman is elated, executing a whirling dance of triumph; "I've done it. . . . I've actually done it. Leopold and Loeb . . . Haigh and Kurten . . . Mahon and Ruxton . . . Landru and Rouse . . . and now Bartholemew! Norman Cresswell Bartholomew, the Dorchester Bath Tub Murderer!"

Laughing gaily, Norman contemplates how to dispose of the cadaver. The remote moorland grave? The weighted corpse in the canal? The unclaimed trunk at Victoria Station? The packing case sent to foreign parts? The corpse in the blazing car? The wrong body in the churchyard?

The bathroom door abruptly opens, and out of the steamy darkness walks Elizabeth, wearing a housecoat. Norman staggers back. She snaps on the bathroom light and we see Millie's body propped up in the sauna. Norman is aghast. Elizabeth tells him that sloshed with the bathroom steam and bubbles, he mistakenly drowned his mistress.

In another corkscrew twist, breathtakingly bamboozling Norman—and the audience—Millie springs up in the bath, very much alive. She and Elizabeth reveal to Norman that they joined forces "to show you what it felt like to do a real murder."

The two women believed that Norman's cure was that of homopathology, the science of treating a disease with a small dose of itself. His disease, say Elizabeth and Millie, was an addiction to murder fantasies, coupled with an ineradicable curiosity about what it would feel like to actually commit a murder himself. So they reckoned that the only thing to do was to let him find out. They show Norman a snorkel concealed under the soap dish, with which they fooled him into believing that Millie was drowned. Adding salt to Norman's wounded pride, Elizabeth and Millie solicited the aid of Sergeant Stenning in the execution of their charade.

When Millie and Stenning leave, the tables turn again. Elizabeth stretches on the sofa, arms extended in welcome, and Norman begins to caress her neck, saying, "What should Mrs. Ramage report this time, do you think? That I tickled you to death? (Elizabeth laughs.) Or hugged you to death? Or gnawed you to death? (Elizabeth laughs uproariously.) Or vacuumed you to death with the Hoover, or pressed you to death with the waffle iron? Or froze you to death amongst the iced bubblegum lollies? (Elizabeth laughs uncontrollably.) Or frizzled you up with the hairdryer? Or made you walk the plank into the goldfish pond in the garden?" The lights dim with Norman's hands around his wife's throat and her laughter becoming something else—an amorous chuckle—a kiss—or is it a fight for air?

* * *

Murderer was first presented in London's Garrick Theatre on March 12, 1975, navigated by the *Sleuth* team—director Clifford Williams and designer Carl Toms. Robert Stephens portrayed Norman Bartholemew.

This original version, though received well by the press and running successfully, lacked some of the mesmerizing ingredients of the playwright's 1987 revisions.

The new version includes an introductory monologue in which Norman describes his insatiable passion to commit a foolproof murder and join the wax effigies in Madame Tussaud's Chamber of Horror. Also added are some fiendish pendulum twists: here Norman actually drowns Millie in the steamy bathtub, mistaking her for Elizabeth; the mutual loathing between Norman and his wife is darker, deeper; in a more brutal climax, Norman places Elizabeth's head in the gas oven, but she manages to stab him fatally with the spit, then slashes him across the chest with her surgical scalpel.

"Norman," she tells the dying man, "listen to me . . . It's worth listening to, because you see you've finally made a convert . . ."

Acting Edition: 1979 version—Marion Boyars Publishers, London. 1989 revised version—Samuel French, Inc.

Sherlock Holmes and the
Curse of the Sign of the Four (1975)

Dennis Rosa (United States)

Sherlock Holmes and the Curse of the Sign of the Four, or The Mark of the Timber Toe is the title of a 1975 adaptation by Dennis Rosa, a playwright-director, who followed the structure of the Conan Doyle novel but, like William Gillette in *Sherlock Holmes*, inserted Professor Moriarty, Holmes's nemesis in other cases, into the proceedings.[1]

Rosa describes the Baker Street apartment as "a good size room, with a feeling of warmth about it." The room is filled "with all sorts of strange things, which represent Holmes's varied interests." A small table is covered with vials and chemicals—"this is Holmes' drug table." The curtain rises on the detective lighting a flame under one of the vials.

"Which is it today, morphine or cocaine?" asks Watson. "It is cocaine, a seven percent solution," answers Holmes as he gracefully injects a syringe into his arm. Watson warns the Great Detective that his drug habit is a pathological and morbid process that involves tissue changes and may leave him with a permanent weakness. Relaxing into his lounge, Holmes explains the need to stretch his brain "to its utmost capacities," most especially these days when he is immersed in a life-or-death battle of wits with Professor Moriarty, "the Napoleon of Crime."[2]

A young, dainty lady arrives, requesting an urgent appointment. Watson keeps staring at Mary Morstan, taken in by her beauty, as she tells them of the disappearance, nearly three years ago, of her father, an army officer who was in charge of the convicts' barracks in the Andaman Islands. A parchment was found among Captain Morstan's belongings with a strange cryptogram containing the plan of a large building and the attestation, "The Sign of the Four." This morning Mary received a letter inviting her to No. 3 Upper Norwood at seven o'clock.

Mary and Watson are wrapped in each other's gaze, while Holmes, in a burst of energy, places his hat on his head and happily exclaims, "The game's afoot!"

At Pondicherry Lodge, a luxuriously furnished abode, Thaddeus Sholto recounts "the remarkable chain of circumstances" through which his father, Major John Sholto of the Royal Indian Army, came into possession of the Agra treasure and smuggled it to England. The body of Thaddeus's brother, Bartholomew, is discovered in a closet, a poisoned dart in his neck, a note in his hand: "The Sign of the Four."

Holmes scrutinizes a circular, muddy footprint stamped in the mold of the window sill, and exclaims,"It is the impression of a wooden stump—the mark of the Timber Toe!" The outline of a diminutive foot belongs no doubt to an accomplice—"naked feet, great agility, small poisoned darts; an aborigine of the Andaman Islands."

The detective mocks Inspector Lestrade[3] by declaring that he would rather have the help of the mongrel Toby, with his amazing power of scent, "than that of the whole of the detective force of London."

Holmes's impersonation of an old sailor fools even Watson, and Mary says in admiration, "Oh, Mr. Holmes, you would have made an actor, and a rare one!" Pacing up and down the wharves with Toby, the "sailor" tracks Jonathan Small and his "savage" sidekick to the steamer *Aurora*. A police craft gives chase. Holmes asks Lestrade to turn the searchlight on the *Aurora* and leaps over the side, into the Thames.

Up to this point, the Rosa adaptation adheres faithfully to the events in the original novel. But in the last scene Rosa goes his own merry way.

Back in Baker Street, peg-legged Jonathan Small insists that he is innocent of Bartholomew Sholto's murder—"It was that hell-bound Tonga . . . I don't know what got into him . . . He always obeyed me in the past."

Holmes nods: "I believe you, Mr. Small."

He crosses to Thaddeus Sholto and declares, "This man is not Thaddeus Sholto. . . . This gentleman is none other than the master criminal of our time, Professor James Moriarty. . . . I fear that the real Thaddeus Sholto is dead. Killed by Moriarty, who then disguised himself as the man."

Moriarty aims his cane at Holmes and fires it as a gun, but misses. The pair struggle violently for the gun-cane. Small rips off his wooden leg and swings it at Moriarty, knocking the weapon from the blackguard's hand, forcing him to the floor. When Lestrade leads Moriarty to the door, the Napoleon of Crime says, "Inspector, there is not a cell or prison wall which could hold this mind when it is set on the thought of escape." He bows to Holmes, "Till we meet again."

The Rosa rendition now returns to reflect the spirit of the original source by having Watson propose to Mary and leaving Holmes alone by the fireplace, puffing on his pipe, as the lights fade slowly to black.

* * *

Rosa directed the premiere of *The Curse of the Sign of the Four* for the Alliance Theatre Company, Atlanta, Georgia, in April 1975. Phillip Pleasants appeared as Sherlock Holmes, supported by Mitchell Edmonds (Dr. Watson), Ed Holmes (Inspector Lestrade), Mimi Bensinger (Mary Morstan) and Philip Pira (Thaddeus Sholto). Subsequent productions were presented at the Dallas Theatre Center, Dallas, Texas (1976); Alaska Repertory Theatre, Anchorage, Alaska (1978); and the Cleveland Playhouse, Cleveland, Ohio (1981). In 2003, *The Curse* was offered by the Dorset Theatre Festival, Dorset, Vermont, and Broadway Onstage, Eastpointe, Minnesota.

* * *

A native of San Francisco, Dennis Rosa began his theatrical career on the West Coast as a performer and director. After completing work at the Pasadena Playhouse, he left California for New York. Rosa appeared off-Broadway and in summer stock, and he enacted the role of Prince Henry III in Broadway's *Becket*, alongside Laurence Olivier and Anthony Quinn. Rosa first encountered the Great Detective in 1972 when he directed his own adaptation of William Gillette's *Sherlock Holmes* for the Loretto-Hilton Repertory Company in St. Louis; the Cleveland Playhouse; and, in 1974, at the Trinity Square Theatre, Providence, Rhode Island. In 1977, Rosa staged a stylish, highly successful production of *Dracula*, starring Frank Langella in the title role (Martin Beck Theatre, New York, October 20, 1977—925 performances).

* * *

Arthur Conan Doyle was born on May 22, 1859, in Edinburgh, Scotland. He was educated at Stonyhurst College, where he pursued his interest in poetry, and at Edinburgh University, where he studied medicine. Among his instructors was Professor Rutherford, who "with his Assyrian beard, his prodigious voice, his enormous chest and his singular manner"[4] became the prototype for Doyle's fictitious character, Professor Challenger. His teacher Doctor John Bell—"thin, wiry, dark, with a high-nosed acute face, penetrating grey eyes, angular shoulders," whose "strong point was diagnosis, not only of disease, but of occupation and character"[5]—was Conan Doyle's inspiration for the creation of Sherlock Holmes.

Doyle moved to London and began to practice medicine, but he soon learned that "shillings might be earned in other ways than by filling phials" and wrote an adventure story called *The Mystery of Sassassa Valley*. To his pleasant surprise, it was accepted by the *Chambers Journal*. In 1880, he went as a ship surgeon on the whaler *Hope* to the Arctic seas and on the steamer *Mayumba* to Africa. The voyages were later utilized as backgrounds for his adventure novels.

Influenced by Mayne Reid, Jules Verne, Robert Louis Stevenson, and Henry James, Dr. Conan Doyle continued to moonlight writing stories for several journals. Attracted to the intricate criminous plots of Emile Gaboriau and the analytical detective stories of Edgar Allan Poe, Doyle wrote *A Study in Scarlet*, the first Sherlock Holmes vehicle (in an early draft, the sleuth was named Sherringford Holmes). Doyle sold the rights to *A Study in Scarlet* for twenty-five pounds, and the novel was featured in *Beeton's Xmas Annual* of 1887. "I never at any time received another penny for it," writes Doyle.[6]

Little did he know at the time that his consulting detective would become one of the most famous characters in English literature.

Conan Doyle penned a second Sherlock Holmes novel, *The Sign of Four* (1890), and a series of Holmes episodes for the *Strand Magazine*, but he believed that his true calling was writing historical novels. Alas, *Micah Clark* (1889), *The White Company* (1891), *The Refugees* (1893), *Uncle Bernac* (1896), and *Sir Nigel* (1906) are all but forgotten today. Conan Doyle attempted to liberate himself from his Frankenstein monster and devised the demise of Holmes in *The Final Problem* (1893), where the detective and his archenemy, Professor Moriarty, plunge to their doom at the Reichenbach Falls. However, public outcry forced Doyle to resurrect his hero in the novel *The Hound of the Baskervilles* (1902) and ensuing stories. Throughout his career, Doyle wrote fifty-six tales and four novels (the fourth was *The Valley of Fear*, 1915) featuring Holmes and his chronicler, Dr. John H. Watson.

During the Boer War, Conan Doyle served as a physician to a field hospital in South Africa. He recounted his experience in the highly regarded *The Great Boer War*. In 1902, he was knighted. A dip into politics was unsuccessful when in 1902 his run for a seat in Edinburgh was narrowly defeated.

As a playwright, Conan Doyle had a spotty West End record. In 1893, he collaborated with J. M. Barrie on a musical, *Jane Annie; or, the Good Conduct Prize*, and it lasted fifty performances. Later that year, his drama *Foreign Policy* closed after six performances. A one-act, *The Story of Waterloo*, became a successful vehicle for Henry Irving and kept performing annually from 1894 to 1917. *Brigadier Gerard* (1906), which Doyle based on his Napoleonic stories, had the popular Lewis Waller in the title role and ran 114 performances. Later that year, in New York, matinee idol Kyrle Bellew appeared as the brigadier, but the show struggled for sixteen showings. Several more plays followed, notably *The Fires of Fate* (1909), in which a dying man travels to Africa for a last fling; *The House of Temperley* (1909), a prizefighting melodrama highlighted by a bare-knuckles bout; and *The Speckled Band* (1910), a Sherlock Holmes adventure.

Stepping into the shoes of Sherlock Holmes, Conan Doyle cajoled Scotland Yard to reinvestigate the cases of George Edalji, a mixed-race student convicted for mutilating horses, and Oscar Slater, a German Jew jailed for the murder of an elderly woman. Upon the renewed probe, both Edalji and Slater were exonerated.

Conan Doyle was married twice. When his son Kingsley was mortally wounded during World War I, Doyle converted to spiritualism. He zealously advocated and pursued communication with the departed for the rest of his life. Conan Doyle died on July 7, 1930, of angina pectoris.

"The Sherlock Holmes stories will be read as long as humanity keeps its love for puzzles," wrote mystery writer Julian Symons. " . . . And Conan Doyle's behavior as a man was throughout his life almost wholly admirable. The indignation he felt at official cruelty or neglect, and his struggles to obtain justice for men personally uncongenial to him, show him as a man of an integrity rare in his own or any time."[7]

* * *

Sherlock Holmes was introduced in Arthur Conan Doyle's novel, *A Study in Scarlet*, published in *Beeton's Christmas Annual*, 1887, and by Lippincott in book form a year later.

The world's foremost consulting detective first appeared on stage in a musical satire, *Under the Clock*, cited as the earliest British revue. The dialogue was written by Charles H. E. Brookfield (who played Holmes) and Seymour Hicks (who played Watson). Edward Jones composed the music. *Under the Clock* was part of a triple bill produced at London's Royal Court Theatre on November 25, 1893.

Messrs. Brookfield and Hicks impersonated Holmes and Watson as a front for throwing acid darts at some eminent colleagues in the acting profession, their main target being Sir Herbert Beerbohm Tree. *The Theatre* monthly lashed back: "It is announced that every care has been taken to avoid hurting anyone's feelings in the course of the satire. But if this be the author's view, their feelings must be as hard to hurt as a rhinoceros. . . . As often as not it is vitriol that is used. . . . Taunts like these, levelled at Mr. Tree and others, are as cheap as they certainly are nasty. . . . People who want fun instead of a malicious chuckle, will find *Under the Clock* not exactly to their taste." The reviewer acknowledged "the personal success" of Seymour Hicks's clever mimicry, but opined that "imitations make up a very thin meal, and the curious jumble which, without rhyme or reason, mixes up Sherlock Holmes and his groveling adorer Dr. Watson, Emile Zola, the Lord Mayor, and the notable stage characters of the year, affords little more than a meager laugh here and there."[8]

Under the Clock enraged London for seventy-eight performances and moved to the Lyric Theatre for one more matinee on January 25, 1894. Photographs of the era depict Brookfield's Holmes in black tights, a short striped cape over his shoulders, a stubby beard, a thick moustache, and rumpled hair. Seymour's Watson sports a monocle on his right eye; a black high collar around the neck; a pirate's cap on his head; eyebrows that are darkened toward the center, arched to touch the nose; and lips uplifted, highlighted in the middle.[9]

The next Holmes appearance on stage occurred in *Sherlock Holmes*, an obscure five-act drama by the obscure Charles Rogers, premiering on May 28, 1894, at Theatre Royal, Glasgow, Scotland, with John Webb as the Great Detective and St. John Hamund as his Boswell. A Mrs. Watson and Billy, Holmes's errand boy, were among the dramatis personae. The venture ran for six performances.

Then, in 1899, came an important and lasting adaptation of Conan Doyle stories to the stage, made by the American actor-director-playwright William Gillette. Since then the floodgates have opened. During the twentieth century and beyond, scores of plays featuring the Great Detective have been written by various hands and produced on world stages.

Acting Edition: Dramatists Play Service.

NOTES

1. Archvillain Professor Moriarty appeared only briefly in the Holmes chronicles (notably in the short story *The Final Problem*), but "he looms large among the major figures of the Canon." Mathew E. Bunson, *Encyclopedia Sherlockiana* (New York: Barnes & Noble, 1994), 168.

2. Rosa borrows from the Doyle novel an alternative scene for those who find the cocaine sequence "unsuitable for their audience," in which Holmes goes through a lengthy deductive theory of the origins of Watson's newly acquired watch.

3. The Scotland Yard inspector who allies himself with Holmes in the original novel of *The Sign of Four* is Athelney Jones. Rosa appropriated for his adaptation the canon's better-known policeman, G. Lestrade, who appeared frequently in the published cases.

4. Arthur Conan Doyle, *Memories and Adventures*, 2nd ed. (London: John Murray, 1930), 32.

5. Arthur Conan Doyle, *Memories and Adventures*, 32.

6. Arthur Conan Doyle, *Memories and Adventures*, 91.

7. Julian Symons, *Portrait of an Artist: Conan Doyle* (London: Whizzard Press, 1979), 123.

8. *The Theatre* (London) 23 (1984).

9. Charles Hallam Elton Brookfield (1857–1913) and Edward Seymour Hicks (1871–1949) nurtured similar intense careers in the London theatre. Both were actors, dramatists, librettists, and directors. Brookfield made his first appearance on the stage in June 1879 and remained active for decades in a wide range of roles. His Shakespearean characters included Antonio in *The Merchant of Venice*, Montano in *Othello*, and Slender in *The Merry Wives of Windsor*. He had leading parts in

plays by notable British playwrights, past and present—T. W. Robertson, Edward Bulwer Lytton, Dion Boucicault, Robert Louis Stevenson, George R. Sims, Louis N. Parker, and Oscar Wilde. Some of Brookfield's most heralded portrayals were Louis XI in *The Ballad Monger*, Voltaire in *The Pompadour*, and Tony Lumpkin in *She Stoops to Conquer*. In *Wealth: An Original Play of Modern English Life* by Henry Arthur Jones (1889), Brookfield enacted John Ruddock, an oily young man who attempts to win the hand of a Yorkshire heiress but is rebuffed when the lass sees through his "villainous nature."

Seymour Hicks first walked on stage at the age of sixteen. He learned his craft by appearing in such melodramas as *The Two Orphans* and *The Ticket-of-Leave Man* and climbed up the ladder in plays by Britons J. M. Barrie and Frances Hodgson Burnett, Frenchmen Sacha Guitry and Louis Verneuil, and Americans Clyde Fitch and George M. Cohan. Among Hicks's prominent roles were the Mad Hatter in *Alice in Wonderland*, Captain Hook in *Peter Pan*, and Scrooge in *A Christmas Carol*, a character he re-created in a 1935 movie version. Hicks portrayed Bunny, Lord Peter Wimsey's stoic valet, in the motion picture *Haunted Honeymoon* (1940), based on Dorothy L. Sayers' play and novel *Busman's Honeymoon*.

During his sixty-two years in the theatre, Hicks appeared in nearly a hundred plays, not only in England but also in the United States, Australia, Canada, and South Africa. Hicks penned sixty-four plays—dramas, comedies, and musicals. His adaptations for the stage included the novels *Uncle Silas* by J. Sheridan Le Fanu (1893) and *The Dictator* by Richard Harding Davis (1910). Collaboration with playwrights Cosmo Hamilton, P. G. Wodehouse, and Ian Hay yielded long-running hits. In 1953, Hicks was knighted for his contributions to the theatre.

Murder among Friends (1975)

Bob Barry (United States, 1930–)

Developing a measure of cynicism about behind-the-scenes show business, theatrical agent Bob Barry concocted a frothy comedy-thriller, *Murder among Friends*, revolving around a Broadway matinee idol and his rich wife as they scheme to kill one another.

"Come to Mama," whispers Angela Forrester to talent scout Ted Cotton as they snuggle under the furry fireplace rugs, planning the murder of her husband, Palmer. A twist at the end of scene 1 has Palmer murmur to Ted, "Come to Papa," and the two men kiss, sealing the doom of the unsuspecting wife.

It seems that Ted has been plotting with each of the spouses to hire an unemployed actor, Larry, who will pose as a hit man, fake a burglary during an intimate New Year's Eve party, and shoot one of the Forresters. A tantalizing question surfaces: where has Ted placed his loyalty, and who is targeted to die—husband or wife? The play's wheels-within-wheels keep churning. When Larry tears into the room wearing a stocking over his face, waving a revolver, and chloroforming everyone in sight, it is Ted who is shot, tumbling down the stairs, bleeding, dying.

The next corkscrew turn reveals that it was actually Palmer who killed Ted, and that he now intends to finish off both Angie and Larry. However, the intended victims manage to trap Palmer into a recorded confession and save themselves by switching revolvers. The lingering duel between Angie and Palmer ends with a victory by the female of the species.

* * *

Murder among Friends opened at Broadway's Biltmore Theatre on December 28, 1975, to a mostly hostile reception. "A craftless play, choppily directed . . . soggy lines . . . in short, a mess," snapped Martin Gottfried.[1] "The trouble lies in the fact that Barry, in attempting a farce about murder, has given us nobody to root for," complained Douglas Watt.[2] "All the wise-cracks and throwaway lines hit the stomach like the proverbial

Chinese dinner—you're satisfied for the first hour, until the hunger pains begin again," winced Barbara Ettorre.[3]

On the other hand, Clive Barnes supported a play that "aims at nothing more than an evening's entertainment, and for most of the time is pretty much on target."[4] Kevin Sanders complimented "a slick, sophisticated show with an offbeat comedy style that is modern, irreverent, and very funny."[5]

Jack Cassidy, as Palmer Forrester, was singled out by all the critics. "Cassidy is absolutely perfect. He hits the role of the obnoxious, egotistical actor as easily as a token fits into a subway turnstile," announced Leonard Probst, who alas, found Janet Leigh, in her first Broadway appearance, "out of place out of Hollywood."[6]

Murder among Friends lasted only seventeen performances. This minor yet clever farcical thriller does not take itself too seriously and pitches tongue-in-cheek darts at the misanthropic practitioners of the New York theatre. It deserves renewed scrutiny by little theatres and summer-stock companies.

Acting Edition: Samuel French, Inc.

NOTES

1. *New York Post*, December 29, 1975.
2. *Daily News*, December 29, 1975.
3. *Women's Wear Daily*, December 29, 1975.
4. *New York Times*, December 29, 1975.
5. WABC TV, December 28, 1975.
6. NBC TV, December 29, 1975.

The Return of A. J. Raffles (1975)

Graham Greene (England, 1904–1991)

Graham Greene concocted another "entertainment" with *The Return of A. J. Raffles*, subtitled *An Edwardian Comedy in Three Acts*, based somewhat loosely on E. W. Hornung's characters in *The Amateur Cracksman*.

It seems that Raffles' chronicler, Harry "Bunny" Manders, falsified history by eulogizing his mentor's heroic death on the battlefield of Spion Kop during the Boer War. Being a fugitive from justice, the cricketer-cracksman exchanged papers with a comrade-in-arms who had his face blown off. Now Raffles has returned from South Africa incognito to resume, with relative safety, his clandestine activities. Bunny is ecstatic to welcome back a—literally, according to the naughty Greene—bosom friend.

The scene is set in Raffles' chambers in the prestigious Albany, Piccadilly, during the summer of 1900. Lord Alfred Douglas, infamous for his relationship with Oscar Wilde, flirts with the bisexual Bunny. Raffles, who "never looked twice at a woman," arrives unexpectedly in the guise of his nemesis, Inspector Mackenzie. He later admits to Bunny "there have been times when I have felt a little jealous, and this was one of those occasions. Finding you with Lord Alfred . . . I felt a little insecure, Bunny."

Lord Alfred suggests that they relieve his father, the Marquis of Queensbury, of the large amount of money he keeps in a bedroom safe, hidden behind the painting of a dog in a basket by Landseer. During a weekend of baccarat, says the lord, every guest will have brought cash to pay his losses. There will be thousands of pounds in the house that night. Lord Alfred wants to send his share of the booty to Oscar Wilde, who is exiled in Paris following his imprisonment and is "miserably poor."

Lord Alfred seeks revenge on his father—whom he describes variably as "abominable," "detestable," "disreputable," "moronic," "odious," "disgusting," "avaricious," "infernal," "obnoxious," "beastly," "monstrous," and "mean as hell"—for stopping his allowance after discovering his affair with Wilde.

Raffles is torn. He explains to Lord Alfred that he's had two passions in his life, cricket and burglary. He has begun to wonder whether it's possible to keep practicing them both. Burglary or cricket. What a choice! The burglar wins over the cricketer—"I'll need a list of all the house guests and the rooms they occupy, Lord Alfred."

The second act unfolds in the Marquis of Queensberry's bedroom at his Herefordshire country house. Raffles, disguised as a waiter, cases the place. Bunny climbs in through a balcony and urges Raffles to move fast. The gentleman-burglar admonishes him, commenting that one must never burgle in a hurry; it's bad for the nerves. Leisurely, Raffles opens the safe with one of his skeleton keys. They find a gold box on the dressing table, empty its contents of letters (which Bunny shoves into his pockets) and fill it with sovereigns.

Suddenly footsteps are heard. As Raffles and Bunny scramble to hide in the balcony, a lady of great beauty and poise enters, followed by a young maid. The maid, Mary, helps her mistress, Alice, to disrobe, since the lady intends to bathe in preparation for a secret rendezvous.

It is obvious to the two Peeping Toms that Mary desires Alice. Raffles whispers that occasionally he was attracted by a female object himself. In the absence of a good chef, he contends, women serve to warm the soup. The lady goes to her bath, the maid exits, and Bunny climbs down the balcony with the loot. Raffles remains to secure "all that lovely money lying around the baccarat table."

A soft knock on the door, a voice muttering coyly, "Alice, it's Bertie," and the bearded figure of the Prince of Wales enters. Unperturbed, the heir to the throne introduces himself to Raffles as "Mr. Portland," and there develops between him—smoking a cigar—and "Waiter Jones"—puffing on a Sullivan—a lovely repartee. The prince is genuinely touched by Raffles' firsthand account of the Boer War. Inspector Mackenzie appears in the doorway—dressed in atrocious tweeds, much given to loud nose-blowing into a large bandana—to announce that the German embassy is "out to get certain letters addressed to a lady staying here."

INSPECTOR: They were dangerous, sir?
PRINCE: They were worse, Inspector. They were badly written.

The inspector recognizes A. J. Raffles and claps a pair of handcuffs around his wrists. The gentleman-burglar strikes a bargain—freedom for the recovery of the embarrassing letters.

The third act, back at the Albany, is focused on a clash between Raffles and a German spy, Captain von Blixen. The playwright's satirical darts are aimed at the world of espionage (when von Blixen fails in his mission to usurp the incriminating letters, he says: "I insist on being shot as an officer and a gentleman"). At the end, the Prince of Wales approaches Raffles with a request: "Promise me that, in the future, England will know only Raffles the cricketer, and not Raffles the amateur cracksman." The world's foremost gentleman-burglar hesitates momentarily before saying, "Very well, I promise, sir."

* * *

Richard Kelly, in the biography *Graham Greene*, lauds *The Return of A. J. Raffles*: "Filled with witty dialogue, disguises, and dry humor, this quaint play takes some liberties with historical fact but captures the atmosphere and character of the turn of the century. . . . The central consciousness of the play reflects the freedom, fantasy, and energy of youth. Bertie acknowledges the fragile innocence of the period when he remarks to Raffles that they both belong to a unique moment in history."[1]

The Return of A. J. Raffles was presented by London's Royal Shakespeare Company in 1975. The play received lukewarm reviews but Graham Greene brushed them off, claiming that he enjoyed the rehearsal process: "The fate of the play is not important—the fun of testing the spoken word, of cutting and altering and transferring, of working with a group, of escaping solitude is everything."[2]

The Return of A. J. Raffles is a graceful, albeit mischievous, pastiche and a lovely yarn to boot. E. W. Hornung and Oscar Wilde must have seen it from their heavenly front-row seats, guffawing throughout, smoking a Sullivan, and holding hands.[3]

Acting Edition: The Bodley Head, Simon & Schuster. *The Return of A. J. Raffles* is also included in *The Collected Plays of Graham Greene* (New York: Penguin, 1985).

NOTES

1. Richard Kelly, *Graham Greene* (New York: Frederick Ungar, 1984), 177.
2. Graham Greene, *Ways of Escape* (Toronto: Lester & Orpen Dennys, 1980), 204.
3. A. J. Raffles appeared originally in E. W. Hornung's short story collections *The Amateur Cracksman* (1899), *The Black Mask* (1901), and *A Thief in the Night* (1905), and in the novel *Mr. Justice Raffles* (1909). Barry Perowne continued the exploits of the gentleman-burglar in a series of eight novels and short stories

published during 1933–1940. On stage, Raffles was the hero of *Raffles, the Amateur Cracksman* (1903) by E. W. Hornung and Eugene Presbrey, and *The Burglar and the Lady* (1905), an unauthorized play by Langdon McCormick that pits the gentle-man-burglar against detective Sherlock Holmes. Both plays and their production history are covered in Amnon Kabatchnik, *Blood on the Stage, 1900–1925* (Lanham, MD: Scarecrow Press, 2008).

Appendix A

Deadly Poison

Poison has claimed victims on the stage since Medea sent a robe smeared with a lethal concoction to her husband's lover, Creusa, who died painfully engulfed in flames (*Medea*, 431 BC, by Euripides). Heracles mortally wounds the centaur Nessus with a poisonous dart for having attempted to ravish his wife, the beautiful Deianira (*Trachiniae*, aka *Maidens of Trachis*, 413 BC, by Sophocles). Ironically, the mythological Greek hero suffers a horrible death after donning a garment dipped in poisoned blood, dispatched to him by Deianira, who was jealous of a liaison between her husband and the princess Ione (*Hercules on Oeta*, first century AD, by Seneca). Hamlet was killed by a poisoned rapier in the bloody denouement of Shakespeare's 1601–1602 masterpiece. Various venoms were served and swallowed in seventeenth-century Jacobean horror tragedies and nineteenth-century blood-and-thunder melodramas.

Setting aside the blowpipe darts in several dramatizations of Arthur Conan Doyle's *The Sign of Four* (1901, 1903) and the snakebites in Doyle's *The Speckled Band* (dramatized in 1910), *The Case of Lady Camber* (1915) is the first bona fide "poison play" of the twentieth century. In the end, it turns out that the lethal talin was not the cause of Lady Camber's demise. Yet the lingering suspicion that a jealous nurse poisoned her is the chief ingredient of suspense in the drama.

The 1920s and 1930s are considered the golden age of detective literature. Characters sip poison in the works of Agatha Christie, Dorothy L. Sayers, Georgette Heyer, Ellery Queen, and John Dickson Carr, and Anthony Berkeley's *The Poisoned Chocolate Case* (1929) led the pack. Simultaneously, poisoned concoctions became the hallmark of stage thrillers. A venomous mechanism that "strikes like a rattlesnake" is the instrument of death in *In the Next Room* (1923), dramatized by Eleanor Robson and Harriet Ford from the 1912 novel *The Mystery of the Boule Cabinet* by Burton E. Stevenson. Tondeleyo, a bored, greedy West African woman of mixed race, attempts to poison her English husband in Leon Gordon's *White*

Cargo (1923) but is forced to swallow the lethal "quinine" herself. A poisoned drink is served to an alcoholic, drug-taking, and abusive husband in *The Fake* (1924) by Frederick Lonsdale. Darts dipped in curare and shot from a blowgun are fatal in *The Call of the Banshee*, aka *The Banshee* (1927) by W. D. Hepenstall and Ralph Culliman. Playwright Roland Pertwee used prussic acid in *Interference* (1927), cyanide of potassium in *To Kill a Cat* (1939), and crystals of strychnine in *Pink String and Sealing Wax* (1944) as deadly catalysts. In A. E. W. Mason's *The House of the Arrow* (1928), a wealthy French widow is murdered at home by an arrow tipped in poison. In Mason's *No Other Tiger* (1928), a money-hungry dancer exchanges her friend's medicine with poisonous disinfectant to kill her, because she wants to keep an envelope stuffed with 40,000 pounds, which the friend had given her for safekeeping. In Somerset Maugham's *The Sacred Flame* (1928), a mother feeds a lethal overdose of pills to her helpless paralytic son to end his suffering. A murderous doctor prescribes a moneyed widow an overdose of veronal in *Alibi* (1928), a dramatization by Michael Morton of Agatha Christie's 1926 novel *The Murder of Roger Ackroyd*.

In Emlyn Williams's *Murder Has Been Arranged* (1930), a smiling villain, dressed as Caesar Borgia, poisons his uncle's drink during a costume party and inherits two million pounds. One of the many victims in Owen Davis's *The Ninth Guest* (1930) swallows prussic acid. *Dishonored Lady* (1930), cowritten by Edward Sheldon and Margaret Ayer Barnes, is a fictional Americanization of the notorious Madeleine Smith case in 1857 in Glasgow, Scotland. A society butterfly inserts pellets of strychnine into the coffee of her show business lover to clear the way for marrying a titled, wealthy suitor. In *How to Be Healthy Though Married* (1930) by F. Tennyson Jesse and H. M. Harwood, a fickle Frenchwoman attempts to dispose of her elderly husband with doses of arsenic, only to discover that her cowardly lover supplied her with harmless bicarbonate of soda. When the in-debt bank clerk of Jeffrey Dell's *Payment Deferred* (1931) decides to murder a visiting nephew for pocket money, he mixes his drink with cyanide.

Clytemnestra used an ax to murder Agamemnon in Aeschylus's *The Oresteia* (458 BC), but her modern incarnation, Christine Mannon in Eugene O'Neill's *Mourning Becomes Electra* (1931), gets rid of her husband Ezra with a vial of deadly poison. In Patrick Hamilton's *John Brown's Body* (1931), a renowned scientist has an affair with an underage girl, kills her brother during a fierce struggle, and decides to end his life "the Socrates way" by swallowing the contents of a little green bottle. His toothpaste mixed with potassium cyanide, a hoodlum comes to a sorry end in *Whistling in the Dark* (1932) by Laurence Gross and Edward Childs Carpenter. In John Van Druten's *Diversion* (1932), a jealous lover strangles a fickle actress and pleads with his father, a physician, for poison to commit suicide.

A dastardly blackmailer is shot and poisoned simultaneously in Arnold Ridley's *Recipe for Murder* (1932). In *The Locked Room* (1933) by Herbert Ashton Jr., the coroner finds small traces of arsenic in the stomach of a dead man, but it turns out that the victim was also shot in the heart and stabbed in the back!

The innocent wife of a brutal, alcoholic businessman is suspected of feeding him an overdose of sleeping potion in *Without Witness* (1933) by Anthony Armstrong and Harold Simpson. *Crime on the Hill* (1933), by Jack de Leon and Jack Celestin, is a prussic acid case. Bernard J. McOwen's *The Scorpion* (1933) portrays a femme fatale who is poisoned by a jealous native woman in the barracks of El Garah, a British outpost in the Sudan. The household maid is sent to her maker by a pinch of poison, while a pet bird is fed a toxic grape, in *Invitation to a Murder* (1934) by Rufus King. *The Eldest* (1935) by Carlton Miles and Eugenie Courtright focuses on a woman who is sentenced to life imprisonment for poisoning her husband, but is wrongfully acquitted in a new trial. The artist Geoffrey Carroll, the blackguard of Martin Vale's *The Two Mrs. Carrolls* (1935), attempted to poison his first wife and having fallen in love with a younger, more attractive neighbor, is now mixing the medicine for the sickly second Mrs. Carroll with poisonous tablets. Another dastardly husband is Bruce Lovell in *Love from a Stranger* (1936), adapted by Frank Vosper from Agatha Christie's short story "Philomel Cottage." Lovell's young bride Cecily discovers to her horror that she has married a serial killer, and saves her life by telling him that she had sprinkled arsenic in his coffee.

The title character of Barré Lyndon's *The Amazing Dr. Clitterhouse* (1936) empties a vial of heroin tablets into the drink of a blackmailer. Eva Raydon, the heroine of Marie Belloc Lowndes' *What Really Happened* (1936), almost pays with her life for the poisoning—via fourteen grains of arsenic—of her husband by another woman. In Lowndes' *Her Last Adventure* (1936), a murderer, when arrested, attempts to commit suicide with a concealed dose of strychnine. In *Blind Man's Buff* (1936) by Ernst Toller, an innocent man is accused of murdering his wife when the postmortem reveals the effect of cyanide. A disturbed, vengeful student pricks a classmate with a syringe filled with allopine and morphine, paralyzing him, in *Trunk Crime*, aka *The Last Straw* (1937) by Edward Percy and Reginald Denham. In James Reach's *The Case of the Squealing Cat* (1937), a tyrannical old millionaire is poisoned before he can alter his will. A parrot at the German consulate in New York dies after ingesting a poisonous grape in *Margin for Error* (1939) by Clare Boothe (Luce), and the Consul himself soon follows suit after drinking a glass of drugged whiskey.

Two endearing sisters from Brooklyn spike their elderberry wine with a pinch of arsenic when serving lonely men in the macabre comedy *Arsenic and Old Lace* (1941) by Joseph Kesselring. In James Reach's

Mr. Snoop Is Murdered (1941), a chain-smoking radio gossip columnist, while on the air, suddenly keels over—poisoned by a cigarette doped up with arsenic. Meek Harry Quincy schemes to get rid of his domineering siblings by having one of them poisoned and the other convicted of the crime, in *Uncle Harry* (1942) by Thomas Job. In *Murder without Crime* (1942) by J. Lee Thompson, sorrowful Stephen, taunted mercilessly by his landlord Matthew, intends to commit suicide by spraying poison in Matthew's whiskey, but Matthew, ever suspicious, switches glasses. In order to facilitate the escape of the Duke of Latteraine from prison, the rescuers dispatch the duke's incapacitated servant with a poisoned jug of wine, in *The Duke of Darkness* (1942) by Patrick Hamilton. A young wife spikes the eggnog of her wealthy elderly spouse with liquefied heads of sulfur matches in *Dark Hammock* (1944) by Reginald Denham and Mary Orr. An antique dealer tries to get rid of a nasty blackmailer with a poisonous dart shot from a blowpipe in Edward Percy's *The Shop at Sly Corner* (1945). Before Mary Hayley Bell's *Duet for Two Hands* (1945) even raises its curtain, a prominent surgeon has prescribed lethal tablets for his lover, an actress, who is pregnant with his child and makes demands upon him.

Caligula, the Roman emperor, forces a vial of poison into the throat of a rebellious patrician in Albert Camus's *Caligula* (1945). In Arnold Ridley's *Murder Happens* (1945), the proprietor of a seaside hotel, henpecked by a sickly but abusive wife, pours poison into her medicine bottle. *Portrait in Black* (1946), by Ivan Goff and Ben Roberts, depicts the wife of an invalid shipping tycoon teaming up with her lover, the family doctor, to dispose of her spouse via a lethal hypodermic. A youthful lover takes poison and stabs the queen in the double-death climax of *The Eagle Has Two Heads* (1946) by Jean Cocteau. The title characters of Jean Genet's *The Maids* (1947), the sisters Lemercier, insert ten pills of phenobarbital in their hated mistress's tea. In Aldous Huxley's *The Giaconda Smile* (1948), a woman in love with the husband of her "best friend," poisons the wife, only to learn that the husband is in love with another, younger woman—and marries her. In *The Hawk and the Handsaw* (1948), author Michael Innes nixes Hamlet's suspicion that his uncle Claudius poisoned his father, the king of Denmark. Postmortem reveals that the title character of *The Late Edwina Black* (1949), by William Dinner and William Morum, died of a lethal dose of arsenic. In *The Four of Hearts Mystery* (1949), adapted by William Rand from Ellery Queen's 1931 novel, the double murder of a newlywed couple takes place—off-stage—in an airplane after morphine is planted in vintage wine bottles. An artist is condemned to prison for providing her sadistic brother with a lethal dose of tablets, but the sleuth of Charlotte Hastings' *Bonaventure* (1949), a nun, proves her innocence. With pangs of conscience for seducing the wife of his best friend and subsequently killing him, the protagonist of Ugo Betti's *Struggle till Dawn* (1949) takes a deadly dose of poison.

For monetary reasons, a doctor kills his wealthy patient with an overdose of insulin in *Remains to Be Seen* (1951) by Howard Lindsay and Russel Crouse. Socrates is condemned to death by poison in Maxwell Anderson's *Barefoot in Athens* (1951). In Friedrich Duerrenmatt's *The Marriage of Mr. Mississippi* (1952), a public prosecutor, mistakenly suspecting his wife of infidelity, poisons her coffee. Did Sir Francis Brittain, of Raymond Massey's *The Hanging Judge* (1952), spike a blackmailer's drink with cyanide, or was it a suicide committed with the purpose of incriminating the judge? Upon losing a fortune in cards, a young Italian woman, who is the title character in Ugo Betti's *The Fugitive* (1953), pours rat poison into the winner's wine. James Reach's *The Girl in the Rain* (1953) is found unconscious on the road and seems to be suffering from amnesia—but is her malady only a sham? Could she be the notorious murderess sought by the police for the poisoning of several wealthy husbands? In David Campton's *The Laboratory* (1954), an apothecary in Renaissance Italy is visited by a court official, his wife, and his mistress, each asking for poison to dispose of the others. In Philip Mackie's *The Key of the Door* (1958), someone laced the medicine bottle of a much-hated actress with an overdose of sleeping pills. In Michael Gilbert's sardonically titled *A Clean Kill* (1959), the "other woman," a chemist, does away with the wife of her beloved by tainting whiskey with grains of chlorazolidene, a newly invented cleaning fluid. In Robert Brome's *The Unsuspected* (1962), the title character is a playwright who serves a lethal overdose of sleeping pills to everyone who impedes his quest for fame and fortune. In Michael Gilbert's *The Shot in Question* (1963), the medical examiner finds morphine residue in the victim's body. But who injected her with the fatal dose?

In Peter Barnes's *The Time of the Barracudas* (1963), a man poisons his wife for insurance money and later marries a widow who has killed several previous husbands for the same reason. The moustached villain of Brian J. Burton's melodrama *The Murder of Maria Marten, or The Red Barn* (1964) substitutes medicine with rat poison to kill his illegitimate child. Philip Mackie dramatized the George Simenon novel *Maigret and the Lady* (1965), in which Inspector Jules Maigret investigates the poisoning of a maid. In Hugh Wheeler's 1966 adaptation of Shirley Jackson's *We Have Always Lived in the Castle*, a disturbed young girl decimates a family by sprinkling sugar mixed with arsenic on their blackberries. One of the leading characters in Joe Orton's black comedy *Loot* (1966) is a nurse who, within seven years, poisoned seven husbands and is now anxious for one more conquest. In William McCleery's *A Case for Mason* (1967), the devoted housekeeper of a best-selling author poisons his two domineering wives so that he will be free to write "his beautiful books."

A venomous blowgun dart pierces the neck of an army colonel and the young lovers succumb to drugged wine in the musical spoof *Something's Afoot* (1973). A dotty old lady chokes to death on a slice of poisonous cake in Leslie Darbon's 1977 dramatization of Agatha Christie's 1950 novel *A Murder Is Announced*. Sherlock Holmes fails to save the life of a client who is murdered by a blowpipe's poison dart, in Paul Giovanni's *The Crucifer of Blood* (1978).

In *My Cousin Rachel* (1980), adapted by Diana Morgan from Daphne du Maurier's 1951 novel, suspense is achieved through lingering doubt: is the charming young wife gradually poisoning the elderly master of the house? Shirley Holmes, the heroine of Tim Kelly's *If Sherlock Holmes Were a Woman* (1982), attempts to solve the case of a dorm housemother found prostrated, seemingly dead, in her armchair. Was the victim's tea brewed with cyanide? Was the saccharine tinged with arsenic? Or was the instrument of death a poisonous blowdart? Xanax, a popular brand of Alprazolam, an anti-anxiety medication, is utilized for murder in *Over My Dead Body* (1984) by Michael Sutton and Anthony Fingleton, suggested by the 1968 novel *The Murder League* by Robert L. Fish. A simpleminded maid is murdered by a poisoned lozenge in Hugh Leonard's *The Mask of Moriarty* (1985) while a cantankerous colonel is dispatched by strychnine in Charles Marowitz's *Clever Dick* (1986). In Rupert Holmes's spoof *Accomplice* (1990), a determined wife pours a vial of nicotine into her husband's whiskey and soda, sprinkles salt all over the dip of salmon mousse to fatally affect his blood pressure, and stabs him with a poisonous syringe—but miraculously the poor man survives. In Simon Brett's *Murder in Play* (1993), the lovesick stage manager of a community theatre drops poisonous tablets into a backstage decanter of sherry, disposing of the leading lady and snagging her husband. The victim of Francis Durbridge's *Sweet Revenge* (1993), a notorious womanizer, is fed Zarabell Four, a controversial tranquilizer known to have potentially lethal side effects. In Robert Sheppard's spoof, *Agatha Christie's Greatest Case* (1997), the famous author investigates the murder of an English lord by rat poison. A doctor is accused of poisoning his wife in Jeffrey Archer's courtroom drama *The Accused* (2000).

Cyanide potassium, hyoscine, coniine, poisonous herbs, and overdoses of strong medicine are among the homicidal means introduced, respectively, in Agatha Christie's *Black Coffee* (1931), *Akhnaton* (1937), *Ten Little Indians* (1943), *Appointment with Death* (1945), *Verdict* (1958), *Go Back to Murder* (1960), *The Patient* (1962), and *Fiddlers Three* (1971).

Appendix B
Twentieth-Century Courtroom Dramas

1. Plays that unfold in a courtroom—civil, religious, military—or contain a pivotal courtroom scene:

Mrs. Dane's Defense (1900) by Henry Arthur Jones
The Living Corpse (1900) by Leo Tolstoy
Danton (1900) by Romain Rolland
Old Sleuth (1902) by Hal Reid
Resurrection (1903) by Henri Bataille and Michael Morton, adapted from
    Leo Tolstoy's 1899 novel
The Silver Box (1906) by John Galsworthy
Madame X (1908) by Alexandre Bisson
Justice (1910) by John Galsworthy
The Confession (1911) by James Halleck Reid
The Boss (1911) by Edward Sheldon
The Mystery of the Yellow Room (1912) by Gaston Leroux
The Adored One, aka *The Legend of Leonora* (1913) by J. M. Barrie
On Trial (1914) by Elmer Rice
The Ware Case (1915) by George Pleydell
The Man on the Box (1915) by Grace Livingston Furniss
Young America (1915) by Fred Ballard
Lightnin' (1918) by Winchell Smith and Frank Bacon
For the Defense (1919) by Elmer Rice
Daddy Dumplins (1920) by Rufus King and George Barr McCutcheon
In The Night Watch (1921) by Michael Morton
Saint Joan (1923) by George Bernard Shaw
The Adding Machine (1923) by Elmer Rice
The Mongrel (1924) by Elmer Rice, adapted from the German of Herman
    Bahr
Beggar on Horseback (1924) by George S. Kaufman and Marc Connelly
The Trial of Jesus (1925) by John Masefield

A Holy Terror (1925) by Winchell Smith and George Abbotts

An American Tragedy (1926) by Patrick Kearney, based on the novel by Theodore Dreiser

Caponsacchi (1926) by Arthur Goodrich, based on the poem *The Ring and the Book* by Robert Browning

Chicago (1926) by Maureen Watkins

The Pearl of Great Price (1926) by Robert McLaughlin

The Trial of Mary Dugan (1927) by Bayard Veiller

The Bellamy Trial (1928) by Frances Noyes Hart and Frank E. Carstarph

Machinal (1928) by Sophie Treadwell

A Free Soul (1928) by Willard Mack

No Other Tiger (1928) by A. E. W. Mason

The Trial of You (1928) by Vere Bennett

Potiphar's Wife (1928) by Edgar C. Middleton

Scarlet Pages (1929) by Samuel Shipman and John B. Hymer

The Silent Witness (1930) by Jack de Leon and Jack Celestin

Draw the Fires! (1930) by Ernst Toller

That's the Woman (1930) by Bayard Veiller

Cynara (1930) by H. M. Harwood and R. Gore Browne

Room 349 (1930) by Mark Linder

Precedent (1931) by I. J. Golden

Landslide (1932) by Ugo Betti

Nine Pine Street (1933) by John Colton and Carlton Miles

We, the People (1933) by Elmer Rice

Judgment Day (1934) by Elmer Rice

Legal Murder (1934) by Dennis Donoghue

They Shall Not Die (1934) by John Wexley

Libel! (1934) by Edward Wooll

Murder Trial (1934) by Sidney Bax

Night of January 16th (1935) by Ayn Rand

The Unguarded Hour (1935) by Bernard Merivale

Old Bailey (1935) by Campbell Dixon

For the Defence (1935) by John Hastings Turner

What Really Happened (1936) by Marie Belloc Lowndes

The Missing Witness (1936) by James Reach

Law and Order (1936) by Frederick Burtwell

Laughter in Court (1936) by Hugh Mills

Murder on Account (1936) by Hayden Talbot and Kathlyn Hayden

Blind Man's Buff (1936) by Ernst Toller and Denis Johnston

Young Madame Conti (1936) by Hubert Griffith and Benn W. Levy

Oscar Wilde (1936) by Leslie Stokes and Sewell Stokes

The Devil and Daniel Webster (1939) by Stephen Vincent Benet

Johnny Belinda (1940) by Elmer Harris

Native Son (1941) by Paul Green and Richard Wright

The Good Woman of Setzuan (1943) by Bertolt Brecht

Pick-up Girl (1944) by Elsa Shelley

Signature (1945) by Elizabeth McFadden

Angel (1945) by Mary Hayley Bell

Christopher Blake (1946) by Moss Hart

The Story of Mary Surratt (1947) by John Parick

The Trial (1947) by André Gide and Jean Louis Barrault, based on the novel by Franz Kafka

Blind Goddess (1947) by Patrick Hastings

The Exception and the Rule (1947) by Bertolt Brecht

The Caucasian Chalk Circle (1948) by Bertolt Brecht

Anne of the Thousand Days (1948) by Maxwell Anderson

The Vigil (1948) by Laszlo (Ladislaus) Fodor

Lost in the Stars (1949), book and lyrics by Maxwell Anderson, music by Kurt Weill, based on the novel *Cry, the Beloved Country* by Alan Paton

A Pin to See the Peepshow (1951) by F. Tennyson Jesse and Harold Marsh Harwood, adapted from Jesse's novel

Barefoot in Athens (1951) by Maxwell Anderson

Billy Budd (1951) by Louis O. Coxe and Robert Chapman, adapted from the novella by Herman Melville

The Trial of Mr. Pickwick (1952) by Stanley Young, based on Charles Dickens's *The Pickwick Papers*

Witness for the Prosecution (1953) by Agatha Christie

The Crucible (1953) by Arthur Miller

The Caine Mutiny Court-Martial (1953), dramatized by Herman Wouk from his Pulitzer Prize–winning novel

Carrington V.C. (1953) by Dorothy Christie and Campbell Christie

Can-Can (1953), book by Abe Burrows, music and lyrics by Cole Porter

His and Hers (1954) by Fay Kanin and Michael Kanin

Inherit the Wind (1955) by Jerome Lawrence and Robert E. Lee

The Lark (1955) by Jean Anouilh

Man on Trial (1955) by Diego Fabbri

The Remarkable Incident at Carson Corners (c. 1955) by Reginald Rose and Kristin Sergel

Time Limit! (1956) by Henry Denker and Ralph Berkey

The Ponder Heart (1956) by Joseph Fields, adapted from the story by Eudora Welty

Compulsion (1957), dramatized by Meyer Levin from his novel

The Defenders (1957), dramatized by Reginald Rose from his television show

Brothers in Law (1957) by Ted Willis and Henry Cecil

The Blacks (1958) by Jean Genet

The Resistible Rise of Arturo Ui (1958) by Bertolt Brecht

The Man Who Never Died (1958) by Barrie Stavis

You, the Jury (1958) by James Reach

The Trial of Dimitri Karamazov (1958) by Norman Rose, extracted from *The Brothers Karamazov* by Fyodor Mikhailovich Dostoevsky

The Legend of Lizzie (1959) by Reginald Lawrence

Anatomy of a Murder (1959) by Elihu Winer, adapted from the novel by Robert Traver

Rashomon (1959) by Fay Kanin and Michael Kanin, based on the stories by Ryunosake Akutagawa

Becket (1959) by Jean Anouilh

The Andersonville Trial (1959) by Saul Levitt

The Trial of Cob and Leach (1959) by Christopher Logue

One Way Pendulum (1959) by N. F. Simpson

Lock Up Your Daughters (1959), book by Bernard Miles, lyrics by Lionel Bart, music by Laurie Johnson, based on the novel *Rape upon Rape* by Henry Fielding

Between Two Thieves (1960) by Warner Le Roy, adapted from the Italian of Diego Fabbri

The Deadly Game (1960) by James Yaffe, adapted from the novel *Traps* by Friedrich Duerrenmatt

A Man for All Seasons (1960) by Robert Bolt

Settled out of Court (1960) by William Saroyan and Henry Cecil, based on the novel by Cecil

Daughter of Silence (1961), dramatized by Morris L. West from his novel

We're All Guilty (1962) by James Reach

Sequel to a Verdict (1962) by Philip Dunning

The General's Dog (1962) by Heinar Kipphardt

The Advocate (1963) by Robert Noah

License to Murder (1963) by Elaine Morgan

A Case of Libel (1963) by Henry Denker, adapted from the book *My Life in Court* by Louis Nizer

A Darker Flower (1963) by Tim Kelly

Blues for Mr. Charlie (1964) by James Baldwin

Inadmissible Evidence (1964) by John Osborne

Hostile Witness (1964) by Jack Roffey

Hamp (1964) by John Wilson

The Investigation (1965) by Peter Weiss

Alibi for a Judge (1965) by Felicity Douglas, Henry Cecil, and Basil Dawson, adapted from the book by Cecil

The People vs. Ranchman (1966) by Megan Terry

Justice Is a Woman (1966) by Jack Roffey and Ronald Kinnoch

The Man in the Glass Booth (1967) by Robert Shaw

For the Defense (1967) by James Reach

The Rimers of Eldritch (1967) by Lanford Wilson

According to the Evidence (1967) by Felicity Douglas, Henry Cecil, and Basil Dawson, adapted from the book by Cecil

The Trial of Lee Harvey Oswald (1967) by Amram Ducovny and Leon Friedman

Ivory Tower (1969) by Jerome Weidman and James Yaffe

The Lyons Mail (1969), adapted by George Rowell from *The Courier of Lyons* (1854) by Charles Reade

Conduct Unbecoming (1969) by Barry England

A Woman Named Anne (1969), adapted by Henry Cecil from his novel

Inquest, aka *The U.S. vs. Julius and Ethel Rosenberg* (1970) by Donald Freed

The Trial (1970) by Steven Berkoff, based on the novel by Franz Kafka

A Voyage round My Father (1970) by John Mortimer

Scratch (1971) by Archibald MacLeish, suggested by Stephen Vincent Benet's short story, "The Devil and Daniel Webster"

The Trial of the Cantonsville Nine (1971) by Daniel Berrigan

The Trials of Oscar Wilde (1974) by Gyles Brandreth

The Runner Stumbles (1976) by Milan Stitt

Cause Célèbre (1977) by Terence Ratigan

The Biko Inquest (1978) by Norman Fenton and Jon Blair

Breaker Morant (1978) by Kenneth G. Ross

Nuts (1980) by Tom Topor

Salt Lake City Skyline (1980) by Thomas Babe

The New Trial (1982) by Peter Weiss

Execution of Justice (1984) by Emily Mann

The Mystery of Edwin Drood (1985), book, lyrics, and music by Rupert Holmes, based on the unfinished novel by Charles Dickens

Never the Sinner (1985) by John Logan

To Kill a Mockingbird (1987) by Christopher Sergel, adapted from the novel by Harper Lee

A Few Good Men (1989) by Aaron Sorkin

2 (1990) by Romulus Linney

Green Fingers (1990) by Michael Wilcox

Slaughter on Second Street (1991) by David Kent

The Anastasia Trials in the Court of Women (1992) by Carolyn Gage

Hauptmann (1992) by John Logan

The Trial of Dr. Jekyll (1993) by William L. Slout

Ragtime (1997) by E. L. Doctorow

Gross Indecency (1997) by Moises Kaufman

Mock Trial (1997) by Romulus Linney

Aftermath of a Murder (1997) by George Singer

Juris Prudence (1997) by Jason Milligan

The Trial of One Shortsighted Black Woman vs. Mammy Louise and Safreeta Mae (1998) by Marcia L. Leslie

Parade (1998), book by Alfred Uhry, lyrics and music by Jason Robert Brown

Everybody's Ruby (1999) by Thulani Davis

* * *

The Accused (2000) by Jeffrey Archer

Judgment at Nuremberg (2001) by Abby Mann

Direct from Death Row the Scottsboro Boys (2005) by Mark Stein

The People vs. Mona (2007) by Patricia Miller and Jim Wann

The Last Days of Judas Iscariot (2007) by Stephen Adly Guirgis

The Lifeblood (2008) by Glyn Maxwell

Prisoner of the Crown (2008) by Richard F. Stockton

Thurgood (2008) by George Stevens Jr.

The Deep Throat Sex Scandal (2010) by David Bertolino

2. A trial looms in the background of the proceedings:

The Red Robe (1900) by Eugene Brieux

The Witness for the Defense (1911) by A. E. W. Mason

The Attorney for the Defense (1924) by Eugene G. Hafer

The Letter (1927) by W. Somerset Maugham

Coquette (1927) by George Abbott and Ann Preston Bridgers

The Front Page (1928) by Ben Hecht and Charles MacArthur

Gods of the Lightning (1928) by Maxwell Anderson

Midnight (1930) by Claire Sifton and Paul Sifton

The Children's Hour (1934) by Lillian Hellman

Winterset (1935) by Maxwell Anderson

The Winslow Boy (1946) by Terence Rattigan

The Gioconda Smile (1948) by Aldous Huxley

Requiem for a Nun (1951) by William Faulkner

The Dock Brief (1957) by John Mortimer

A Shot in the Dark (1961), adapted by Harry Kurnitz from *L'Idiote* by Marcel Achard

Lizzie! (1993) by Owen Haskell

* * *

For All Time (2008) by K. J. Sanchez

When We Go upon the Sea (2010) by Lee Blessing

3. Interrogations:

Enemies (1906) by Maxim Gorky
The Witch (1910), adapted by John Masefield from the Norwegian of H.
    Wiers-Jenssen
Hoppla! Such Is Life! (1927) by Ernst Toller
Men without Shadows (1946) by Jean-Paul Sartre
Montserrat (1949), adapted by Lillian Hellman from a drama by Em-
    manuel Robles
The Queen and the Rebels (1949) by Ugo Betti
Darkness at Noon (1951) by Sidney Kingsley
The Prisoner (1954) by Bridget Boland
The Lark (1955), adapted by Lillian Hellman from Jean Anouilh's *L'Alouette*
The Devils (1961) by John Whiting, adapted from the novel *The Devils of
    Loudun* by Aldous Huxley
The Savage Parade (1963) by Anthony Shaffer
In the Matter of J. Robert Oppenheimer (1964) by Heinar Kipphardt
The Trial (1972) by Anthony Booth
Are You Now or Have You Ever Been (1972) by Eric Bentley
The Recantation of Galileo Galilei (1973) by Eric Bentley
From the Memoirs of Pontius Pilate (1976) by Eric Bentley
Time to Kill (1979) by Leslie Darbon

* * *

New Jerusalem (2008) by David Ives
The White Crow: Eichmann in Jerusalem (2009) by Donald Freed
Conviction (2010) by Oren Neeman

4. In the jury room:

Resurrection (1903) by Michael Morton, adapted from the novel by Leo
    Tolstoy
The Woman on the Jury (1923) by Bernard K. Burns
The Jury of Her Peers (1925) by Edward Harry Peple
Ladies of the Jury (1929) by Fred Ballard
Good Men and True (1935) by Brian Marlow and Frank Merlin
Jury's Evidence (1936) by Jack de Leon and Jack Celestin
Ladies and Gentlemen (1939) by Ben Hecht and Charles MacArthur
Hanging Judge (1952) by Raymond Massey
Twelve Angry Men (teleplay aired on CBS's *Studio One* in 1954; play ver-
    sion published by Samuel French in 1955; Broadway debut, 2004) by
    Reginald Rose

Jury Room (1961) by C. B. Gilford
Judge and Jury (1994) by Mark Dunn

* * *

Prisoner of the Crown (2008) by Richard F. Stockton

5. Lawyers and judges off court:

At Bay (1913) by George Scarborough
The Last Resort (1914) by George Scarborough
Counsellor-at-Law (1931) by Elmer Rice
The Judge (1938) by Jill Craigie and Jeffrey Dell
See My Lawyer (1939) by Richard Maibaum and Harry Clork
Corruption in the Palace of Justice (1945) by Ugo Betti
The Magnificent Yankee (1946) by Emmet Lavery
The Cocktail Party (1949) by T. S. Eliot
The Deep Blue Sea (1952) by Terence Rattigan
Hanging Judge (1952) by Raymond Massey
Brothers in Law (1957) by Ted Willis and Henry Cecil
The Bargain (1961) by Michael Gilbert
Time of Hope (1963) by Arthur and Violet Ketels, adapted from the novel
   by C. P. Snow
After the Fall (1964) by Arthur Miller
East Lynne (1965) by Brian J. Burton, adapted from the novel by Mrs.
   Henry Wood
Alibi for a Judge (1965) by Felicity Douglas and Henry Cecil, from the
   book by Cecil
The Judge (1967) by John Mortimer
A Case for Mason (1967) by William McCleary, based on characters cre-
   ated by Erle Stanley Gardner
Jeremy Troy (1969) by Jack Sharkey
A Voyage round My Father (1971) by John Mortimer
Clarence Darrow (1974) by David W. Rintels, adapted from the book
   Clarence Darrow for the Defense by Irving Stone
First Monday in October (1978) by Jerome Lawrence and Robert E. Lee
Guilty Conscience (1980) by Richard Levinson and William Link
The Perfect Murder (1989) by Mike Johnson

Appendix C
Twentieth-Century Death-Row Plays

Throughout the twentieth century, there were quite a few plays that climaxed on death row in European and American prisons. The vaults of Newgate, the scaffoldings of the Tower of London, the batteries of the Bastille, and the cells of Sing Sing were captured on the stage with nerve-wracking effect.

Among the dramas that boasted last-minute hanging, garroting, or electrocution are the following: *Danton's Death* (written, 1835; first produced, 1902) by George Büchner; *The Campden Wonder* (1907) by John Masefield; *Man and the Masses* (1924) by Ernst Toller; *An American Tragedy* (1926) by Patrick Kearney, based on Theodore Dreiser's 1925 novel; *Spellbound* (1927) by Frank Vosper; *Machinal* (1928) by Sophie Treadwell; *Gods of the Lightning* (1928) by Maxwell Anderson; *The Criminal Code* (1929) by Martin Flavin; *The Last Mile* (1930) by John Wexley; *Smoky Cell* (1930) by Edgar Wallace; *Children of Darkness* (1930) by Edwin Justus Mayer; *Draw the Fires!* (1930) by Ernst Toller; *Midnight* (1930) by Claire Sifton and Paul Sifton; *Elizabeth the Queen* (1930) by Maxwell Anderson; *Two Seconds* (1931) by Elliott Lester; *Mary of Scotland* (1933) by Maxwell Anderson; *End and Beginning* (1933) by John Masefield; *They Shall Not Die* (1934) by John Wexley; *The Postman Always Rings Twice* (1936) by James M. Cain, dramatized from his 1934 novel; *Leave Her to Heaven* (1940) by John Van Druten; *Native Son* (1941) by Paul Green and Richard Wright; *Uncle Harry* (1942) by Thomas Job; *Antigone* (1943) by Jean Anouilh; *Joan of Lorraine* (1946) by Maxwell Anderson; *The Trial* (1947) by André Gide and Jean-Louis Barrault, based on Franz Kafka's 1925 novel; *Anne of the Thousand Days* (1948) by Maxwell Anderson; *Lost in the Stars* (1949) by Maxwell Anderson and Kurt Weill, based on the 1948 novel *Cry, the Beloved Country* by Alan Paton; *Deathwatch* (1949) by Jean Genet; *Song at the Scaffold* (1949) by Emmet Lavery, from the 1933 novel by Baroness Gertrud von le Fort; *Darkness at Noon* (1951) by Sidney Kingsley, from the 1940 novel by Arthur Koestler; *Requiem for a Nun* (1951) by William Faulkner; *Billy Budd* (1951) by Louise O. Coxe and Robert Chapman, from the 1886–1891 novel by Herman Melville; *A Pin to See the Peepshow* (1951) by F. Tennyson Jesse and Harold Marsh Harwood, adapted from Jesse's 1934 novel; *Murder Story* (1954) by Ludovic Kennedy; *The Quare Fellow* (1954) by Brendan Behan; *Compulsion* (1957) by Meyer Levin, dramatized from his 1956 novel; *The Man Who Never Died* (1958) by Barrie Stavis; *Channa Senesh* (1958) by Aharon Megged; *Frankenstein* (1959) by David Campton; *A Man for All Seasons* (1960) by Robert Bolt; *Gallows Humor* (1961) by Jack Richardson; *The Devils* (1961) by John Whiting; *The Advocate* (1963) by Robert Noah; *The Murder of Maria Marten, or The Red Barn* (1964) by Brian J. Burton; *The People vs. Ranchman* (1967) by Megan Terry; *Inquest* (1970) by Donald Freed; *The Runner Stumbles* (1976) by Milan Stitt; *From the Memoirs of Pontius Pilate* (1976) by Eric Bentley; *Breaker Morant* (1978) by Kenneth G. Ross; *Hauptmann* (1992) by John Logan.

Last-minute reprieves occur in *If I Were King* (1901) by Justin Huntly McCarthy; *The Cardinal* (1902) by Louis N. Parker; *A Working Girl's Wrongs* (1903) by Hal Reid; *The Woman in the Case* (1905) by Clyde Fitch; *How Hearts Are Broken* (1905) by Langdon McCormick; *For a Human Life* (1906) by Hal Reid; *The Confession* (1911) by James Halleck Reid; *Silence* (1924) by Max Marcin; *Beggar on Horseback* (1924) by George S. Kaufman and Marc Connelly; *The Threepenny Opera* (1928) by Bertold Brecht and Kurt Weill; *Fast Life* (1928) by Samuel Shipman and John B. Hymer; *The Front Page* (1928) by Ben Hecht and Charles MacArthur; *Midnight* (1930) by Claire Sifton and Paul Sifton; *Precedent* (1931) by I. J. Golden; *Riddle Me This!* (1932) by Daniel N. Rubin; *Chalked Out* (1937) by Warden Lewis E. Lawes and Jonathan Finn; *The Gioconda Smile* (1948) by Aldous Huxley; *Dial "M" for Murder* (1952) by Frederick Knott; *Hanging Judge* (1952) by Raymond Massey; *The Prisoner* (1964) by Bridget Boland; *Amazing Grace* (1995) by Michael Cristofer; *Parade* (1998), book by Alfred Uhry, music and lyrics by Jason Robert Brown.

* * *

Dead Man Walking (2000), opera, libretto by Terrence McNally, music by Jake Heggie; *Direct from Death Row the Scottsboro Boys* (2007) by Mark Stein; *Terre Haute* (2007) by Edmund White; *The Exonerated* (2008) by Jessica Blank and Erik Jensen; *When I Come to Die* (2011) by Nathan Louis Jackson.

Appendix D

Children in Peril

Children have come to a sorry end on stage ever since a vengeful Medea presented her philandering husband Jason with the bodies of their infants in Euripides' *Medea* (431 BC) and the king's assassins stabbed Banquo's children in Shakespeare's *Macbeth* (c. 1605).

Children have faced the Grim Reaper in many modern dramas. A grisly infanticide play, highlighted by a harrowing scene of a mother prodding her son to smother his newborn child, is *The Power of Darkness* (1886) by Leo Tolstoy. In the climax of *At the Telephone*, a 1902 Grand Guignol playlet by André de Lorde, a countryside businessman, on a visit to Paris, hears on the telephone the tortured screams of his six-year-old child as the little one and his mother are being strangled by a gang of tramps. An innocent mother is accused of killing her child in *How Hearts Are Broken* (1905) by Langdon McCormick. The villains of Hal Reid's *Lured from Home* (1905) kidnap little Helen Lindsay and plan to hurl her into a freshly dug excavation; the blackguards of Reid's *A Child Shall Lead Them* (1907) tie young Rita Lyle to a red-hot stove and place a powder keg next to her; both girls are saved in the nick of time. A little girl is locked in an airtight bank vault in the climax of Paul Armstrong's *Alias Jimmy Valentine* (1910). *The Child* (1913), by Elizabeth McFadden, depicts a childless Midwestern couple who kidnap a baby.

A mother strangles her illegitimate baby in John Galsworthy's *Windows* (1922), while another mother smothers her baby with a pillow in Eugene O'Neill's *Desire under the Elms* (1924). A murderous monk stabs a little boy to death as part of a blood-libel against the Jews of Prague in H. Leivick's *The Golem* (1925). *Post Road* (1934) by Wilbur Daniel Steele is centered on the kidnapping of an infant for ransom. Lillian de la Torre's *Remember Constance Kent* (1949) spotlights the English murderess who in 1860 cut the throat of her four-year-old half-brother with a razor. A six-month-old baby is suffocated in his cradle (off-stage) by the nanny in *Requiem for a Nun* (1951) by William Faulkner. In Maxwell Anderson's *Bad Seed* (1954), little Rhoda Penmark drowns classmate Claude in the pond, jealous that he won the penmanship medal she desired.

Inspired by a real-life homicide in Victorian England, Brian J. Burton's melodrama *The Murder of Maria Marten, or The Red Barn* (1964) spotlights a dastardly villain who substitutes medicine with rat poison to kill his illegitimate child. Edward Bond's controversial *Saved* (1965) depicts a baby stoned to death by a gang of Cockney toughs (on-stage). A group of spoiled, malevolent teenagers kidnap a ten-year-old girl and plan to eliminate her via an overdose of sleeping pills in *The Playroom* (1965) by Mary Drayton. The disturbed kid sister of *We Have Always Lived in the Castle* (adapted by Hugh Wheeler in 1966 from the 1962 novel by Shirley Jackson) drops an African American orphan, Jonas, to the bottom of a dumbwaiter shaft as an eerie "sacrifice." Three children in an attic play vicious games of predator and prey, accuser and accused, killer and victim in Jose Triana's *The Criminals* (1970). The heroine of Charlotte Hasting's *The Enquiry* (1972) is sent to prison for killing her brain-dead child, a crime actually committed by her husband. One of the lingering questions in Ira Levin's *Veronica's Room* (1973) is: Why did fifteen-year-old Veronica kill her kid sister Cissie? A black Philadelphia teenager senselessly shoots to death a twelve-year-old girl in *Zooman and the Sign* (1980) by Charles Fuller. A jealous brother pricks a baby with a poisonous arrow in *The Adventure of the Sussex Vampire* (1988) by Peter Buckley, based on a short story by Arthur Conan Doyle. A little girl is kidnapped for ransom and murdered in the dark netherland of Chicago in *Earth and Sky* (1991) by Douglas Post. In Steven Dietz's *Dracula* (1995), the count hands over a bag containing a tiny, crying baby to a pair of vixens who then proceed to plunge their teeth into the bag.

* * *

A baby girl is devoured by a caveman at the fade-out of one of the vignettes in *Apparition* (2005) by Anne Washburn. In *Coram Boy* (2007), adapted by Helen Edmundson from Jamila Gavin's novel, a nefarious "Coram man" buries babies alive in eighteenth-century England. The focal point of Chad Bekim's *'Nami* (2007) is the abduction of a little girl who was a survivor of the Indian Ocean tsunami. The title character of Howard Barker's short, poetic *Gary the Thief* (2010) is a ferocious working-class hoodlum who kills a baby and goes to prison.

Index

Note: Bold page ranges refer to the entry for that particular title in the book.

About the Author

Amnon Kabatchnik holds a BS degree in theatre and journalism from Boston University, where he won the Rodgers & Hammerstein Award, and an MFA from the Yale School of Drama. He has been a member of the director's unit with the Actors Studio in New York and has been appointed professor of theatre at the State University of New York at Binghamton, Stanford University, Ohio State University, Florida State University, and Elmira College.

Off-Broadway, Kabatchnik has directed, among other plays, the American premiere of Anton Chekhov's *A Country Scandal (Platonov)*; *Evenings with Chekhov*; *Vincent*, a drama about Van Gogh; and revivals of Maxwell Anderson's *Winterset*, John Willard's *The Cat and the Canary*, and Reginald Denham's *Ladies in Retirement*. At the Phoenix Theatre, he served as assistant to Tyrone Guthrie on Friedrich Schiller's *Mary Stuart* and Karl Capek's *The Makropolous Secret*, and to Tony Richardson on Eugène Ionesco's *The Chairs* and *The Lesson*. Kabatchnik's work in New York earned him the Lola D'Annunzio Honorary Citation for Outstanding Contribution to the Off-Broadway Theatre.

Kabatchnik has directed numerous dramas, comedies, thrillers, and musicals for national road companies, resident theatres, and summer stock. Crime-tinged plays he has staged include *Arsenic and Old Lace*, *Angel Street*, *The Mousetrap*, *Ten Little Indians*, *Dracula*, *Sleuth*, *Wait until Dark*, *Dial "M" for Murder*, and *A Shot in the Dark*. He has also directed productions in Israel and Canada.

Kabatchnik has written a weekly column of book reviews for the *Tallahassee Democrat*, the *Corning Leader*, the *Star-Gazette* of Elmira, N.Y., and the *Chemung Valley Reporter*. He has also contributed articles and reviews to *The Armchair Detective*, *Mystery News*, *Clues*, and other journals in the field of suspense.

He is the author of *Blood on the Stage: Milestone Plays of Crime, Mystery, and Detection: An Annotated Repertoire, 1900–1925* (2008), *Sherlock Holmes on the Stage: A Chronological Encyclopedia of Plays Featuring the Great Detective* (2008), and *Blood on the Stage: Milestone Plays of Crime, Mystery, and Detection: An Annotated Repertoire, 1925–1950* (2009), all published by Scarecrow Press.

Breinigsville, PA USA
03 April 2011
258996BV00002B/2/P

9 780810 877832

MT. LEBANON PUBLIC LIBRARY